THE BUDDHIST COSMOS:

A Comprehensive Survey of the Early Buddhist Worldview; according to Theravāda and Sarvāstivāda sources

By Punnadhammo Mahāthero

cakkavāḷaṃ atisambādhaṃ, brahmaloko atinīcako

"The circle of the world is too narrow, the world of Brahmā is too low."

Vimānavatthu Aṭṭhakathā 15, (I.B. Horner translation)

ISBN: 9781791731946
Imprint: Independently published

Website - www.arrowriver.ca

Contact the author - arfh@xplornet.com

Cover Illustration by Abhassaro Samenera

TABLE OF CONTENTS

0 INTRODUCTION

PART ONE—COSMIC SPACE

PART TWO—COSMIC TIME

PART THREE—THE WORLD OF BEINGS

PREFACE

The purpose of this book is to present a comprehensive description of the universe and its inhabitants as they were understood by the Buddhists of ancient India. This is the context within which the teachings of the Buddha were situated.

The material in this book should be of interest to both Buddhists and to students of myth and folklore. For the modern Buddhist, especially in the Western countries outside the historical range of the religion, the material in this book will hopefully fill a gap in her knowledge. The understanding of this background should make the experience of reading the suttas richer and more meaningful. This is the imaginative space in which all Buddhists lived until very recently, and even if it is no longer held literally in all details, this cosmology and mythology is still very much a living tradition in Buddhist countries today. The teaching of the Buddha is a many-faceted jewel, and each facet has its function. The brilliant analytic clarity of the Abhidhamma teachings challenges and engages the intellect, but do little to stir the heart. The vision presented in this book is one of a fascinating multi-faceted universe informed by the deepest teachings of the Dhamma.

Those who approach this book with an interest in the mythological systems of the world will also hopefully find something new. Ancient and medieval India was a fertile source of myth and legend coloured by profound philosophical speculation. The Theravāda Buddhist version of this mythos is perhaps the least known and studied outside the historic lands of its influence. Hopefully this book will serve as a step toward remedying that oversight. This cosmological system deserves to be closely studied not only because of its historic importance but because of its own intrinsic beauty. This is a detailed, complex and many layered cosmology quite different from anything conceived in the West.

ACKNOWLEDGEMENTS

(All names in alphabetic order)

I would like to take this opportunity to thank all those who read and critiqued parts of this book:

Brian Carniello, Oli Cosgrove, Aaron Gasparetto, Anthea Kyle, Bhikkhu Nyanatusita, Joanne Panton, Manfred Wierich and.

Also those who helped with advice on specific points, Jeffrey Armstrong, Dr. Bryan Levman and Dr. Suwanda Sugunasiri.

Special appreciation is given to Bhikkhu Nyanatusita, editor in chief of the Buddhist Publication Society, who helped to make the final form of this book presentable.

Mostly I would like to thank with great gratitude all my teachers along the path, too numerous to name all but especially Ajahn Amaro, Kema Ānanda, Ajahn Jayasaro, Ajahn Pasanno, Ajahn Sucitto and Ajahn Viradhammo.

0:5 CONTENTS OF THIS BOOK

The first section of the book deals with a description of the physical nature of the cosmos. The reader who is only familiar with the historical development of cosmology in the European context will find the Indian Buddhist version brand new. This is neither a geocentric nor a heliocentric model, but rather a Sineru-centric one. The fundamental image is the truly immense Mount Sineru[1] at the centre of the world-system around which everything else is arrayed. Beyond this single world-system there are an infinite number of other worlds, arrayed in horizontal and vertical hierarchies. This model has both a strangeness and a familiarity for modern readers. It is based on completely alien ideas, and therefore differs in almost every detail from the modern scientific model; and yet we can identify with its general principles. The ancient Indian model and the modern scientific one resemble each other much more than either one resembles the Aristotelian-medieval one in at least two important ways. First, the universe is conceived of as being either infinite or at least extremely vast and composed of a very great number of worlds. Second, the domain of human habitation is not at the centre of things but is confined to a periphery.

The next topic taken up will be the cosmological history of the universe: the origin, development and ending of the world-system. A basic idea to notice here is that in Buddhism there is no first moment of creation and no creator. We can trace from the texts the story of how this world-system originated, how it was populated and how it will come to its final destruction. But there were worlds before this one and there will be worlds after it as well. The cosmos as a whole has generally been seen by Buddhists as without a first beginning and without a final ending.[2] No matter how far back you go in time, there will always be a yesterday and no matter how far you look into the future, there will always be a tomorrow. The scale of time involved even for the lifespan of a single world is immense when compared to the pre-modern European linear eschatological view and once more we find a greater resonance with modern ideas.

The third topic, which will take up the bulk of this book, is a survey of the various kinds of beings which inhabit the cosmos. Traditionally the very diverse array of beings is divided into five *gati* or "destinations of rebirth" (DN 33). From lowest to highest, these are:

The ***niraya*** beings which live in great misery, in a world of fire and cruelty,

The **peta** beings which exist as wretched shades,

The **animals**,

The **humans**, and

The **devas**, beings of splendid subtle forms who enjoy long lives of bliss (in this fivefold scheme this category is taken to include the brahmās as well).

We shall see that this simple scheme is inadequate for anything more than the roughest outline. In practice, there are great variations within each category and there are numerous individual beings and in fact whole classes of beings which are difficult or even impossible to pigeon hole within one of the five *gati*. This was already apparent in ancient times, and later schools of Buddhism expanded this scheme to include a sixth *gati* for the **asuras**, ferocious beings endlessly at war with the devas.

A more useful and inclusive method of analysis is provided by the Abhidhamma, which divides all reality into four planes (*bhūmī*): the sensual-desire plane (*kāmābhūmi*), the plane of form (*rūpabhūmi*), the plane of the formless (*arupabhūmi*) and the supramundane (*lokuttara*, lit. "beyond the world.") The last is *nibbāna*, the unconditioned, and is not a part of the cosmos at all. The first three apply to levels of consciousness as well as realms of existence.

---

1 Mt Sineru is taller than the distance from the Earth to the Moon by modern reckoning.

2 This despite the Buddha's injunction that the question is unanswerable. See MN 63.

Kāmabhūmi is the realm of sense desire. The psyche of beings in this realm is dominated by the five physical senses and their motivation is normally to acquire pleasant sense experiences and avoid unpleasant ones. This is the most diverse and populous of the realms and includes beings in *niraya*, animals, petas, asuras, yakkhas, humans and all the various levels of devas below the brahmā world.

Rūpabhūmi is the realm of form. This is the abode of the various levels of brahmā beings. These beings have transcended sensuality; they have no gender and they take no coarse food, instead "feeding on bliss." There are altogether sixteen levels within this realm including the Suddhāvāsa, the "Pure Abodes" where those who have reached the third stage of awakening are reborn.

Arūpabhūmi is the formless realm. This is the realm of beings that have no physical bodies but are pure mind. It cannot therefore be located in space, spatial location being a physical property. There are four levels within this realm.[3]

The range of beings can also be sub-divided into four *bhūmi* by sub-dividing the sense desire realm into the *apāyabhūmi* ("unfortunate ground") and the *kāmasugatibhūmi* ("fortunate sensual ground.") The former constitutes *niraya*, the animal realm, the petas and the asuras. The latter is the sphere of humans and devas.[4]

The entire range of beings is often presented in late sources as a list of 31 realms.[5] See the table at the end of this section. There are also other ways, more or less inclusive, in that the various realms are categorized; the seven stations of consciousness (AN 7:44 & DN 33) and the nine abodes of beings (AN 9:24 and DN 33) for example. These simply divide the pie into different slices.

A quite different way of distinguishing beings is by their manner of birth. Buddhist theory recognizes four (DN 33) of those:

saṃsedajā yoni—Moisture born. Beings like maggots which are born in rotten food or other filth.

aṇḍajā yoni—Egg born. Beings that are born from eggs, like birds and snakes.

jalābujā yoni—Womb born. Beings that are born from the womb of their mother, as are mammals, including humans.

opapātikā yoni—Spontaneously born. These beings simply appear fully formed in their place of rebirth. This is the way devas, as well as beings in *niraya*, are born.

The terminology may be slightly confusing to some readers; in premodern western biology flies and other insects were thought to be "spontaneously born" but this mode is what the Buddhist literature would call "moisture born."

[3] See Bodhi, CMA p. 27 f.

[4] Bodhi, CMA p. 189 f.

[5] A preferred scheme of many modern summaries. The source appears to be the *Abhidhammatthasaṅgaha*, see CMA p. 189 f.

TABLE ONE—THE THREE PLANES AND THE THIRTY-ONE REALMS OF REBIRTH

WORLD	REALM	TRANSLATION	NOTES	LIFE-SPAN
ARŪPABHŪMI (formless world)	nevasaññānāsañña-bhūmi	plane of neither perception nor non- perception	Mind-only or "four khandha" realms. Equivalent to the formless jhānas.	84 KMK
	ākiñcaññabhūmi	plane of nothingness		60 KMK
	viññāṇañcabhūmi	plane of infinite consciousness		40 KMK
	ākāsānañcabhūmi	plane of infinite space		20 KMKR
RŪPABHŪMI (plane of form or "the fine-material world")	akaniṭṭha	peerless	Suddhāvāsa (Pure Abodes) Place of rebirth for anāgāmi (non-returners)	16 KMK
	sudassi	clear-sighted		8 KMK
	sudassa	beautiful		4 KMK
	atappa	untroubled		2 KMK
	aviha	not falling away		1 KMK
	asaññasatta	unconscious	body only, no mind	500 MK
	vehapphala	very fruitful	fourth jhāna	500 MK
	subhakiṇṇa	refulgent glory	third jhāna	64 MK
	appamāṇasubha	unbounded glory		32 MK
	parittasubha	limited glory		16 MK
	ābhassara	streaming radiance	second jhāna	8 MK
	appamāṇābha	unbounded radiance		4 MK
	parittābha	limited radiance		2 MK
	mahā brahmā	great brahma	first jhāna	1K
	brahmāpurohita	ministers of brahma		½ K
	brahmāpārisajja	retinue of brahma		1/3 K
KĀMABHŪMI (plane of sense-desire)	paranimmita-vasavatti	wielding power over the creation of others	devas	16 KCY
	nimmānarati	delighting in creation		8 KCY
	tusita	contented		4 KCY
	yāma	restrained		2 KCY
	tāvatiṃsa	the thirty-three		1 KCY
	cātummahārājika	the four great kings		500 CY
	manussa	human	*you are here*	not fixed
	asura	titans	duggati (states of misery)	
	peta	ghosts		
	tiracchāna	animals		
	niraya	hell		

(1 CY = 360 Celestial Days. 1 CD in the lowest heaven = 50 human years, length doubles with each level)
MK = Mahākappa, KMK = 1000 Mahākappa , CY = Celestial Year, KCY = 1000 Celestial Years

0:6 HISTORICAL CONTEXT

The cosmology presented in this book represents a snapshot, albeit a somewhat blurry one because the subject refuses to sit still. The ancient Indian cosmology was always a work in progress. The picture of the universe presented here has deep roots in Vedic and even pre-Vedic times, and afterwards continued to flourish and become elaborated in later Theravāda works and even more so in Mahāyāna and Vajrayāna Buddhism. The focus in this book is on the system as it was presented in the Pali canon and commentaries. This represents, more or less, the way the universe was perceived by Buddhists living in the first millennium after the Buddha.

I have tried to stay strictly within that chronological limit. Looking backwards, I have occasionally taken notice of the pre-Buddhist roots of the myth, particularly in the section on Tāvatiṃsa. However, this has not been done in any systematic way and my knowledge of the Vedas and other pre-Buddhist texts is inadequate to treat this issue as it deserves. The working out of the historical development of the Buddhist cosmology and mythology is a vast topic that would reward further exploration; only the barest hints will be found here. Looking forward beyond the age of its initial formulation, the Buddhist cosmology continued to evolve. The focus of this book is, as stated, on the canonical and commentarial texts, but I found it impossible to entirely ignore later works such as the 14th century Thai *Three Worlds According to King Ruang* and the Burmese sources as collected in the modern *The Great Chronicles of Buddhas*. Likewise, the Pali sub-commentaries, which belong to a later period, have been used where they clarify or expand on a topic of interest. One non-Theravāda source proved indispensable, particularly in the sections on cosmic space and cosmic time; that is the Sarvāstivāda work the *Abhidharmakośabhasya.* The Mahāyāna developments have been completely ignored. These areas, too, merit further study.

Some readers may be especially interested in determining how much is from the canon, and what was added by the commentaries. This should become clear if one pays attention to the references. In summary, the greater part of the structure of the cosmology presented here is found in the canonical texts. This includes the basic map of the world-system; Mt Sineru and the four island-continents.[6] The various realms of beings and their inhabitants are almost all found in the canon: the *nerayika*, the devas and brahmās, the nagās and *supaṇṇas* and yakkhas were all spoken of by the Buddha. What was added by the commentaries? A great mass of detail; most of the narratives which add colour and depth to the picture are from the commentaries, although a few quite detailed accounts can be found in the suttas themselves. The commentaries have also provided a greater orderliness to the mass of sometimes confusing and even contradictory details in the suttas, and sometimes this has been done by taking liberties with the plain meaning of the original text.

[6] Although the seven circular mountain ranges are a commentarial addition.

0:7 THE LANGUAGE

I have left many Pali words untranslated, which may be appreciated by some readers and deplored by others. My reasoning, to paraphrase something another translator once said, "It is better to not understand a word than to misunderstand it." So, in this book, I have resisted the easy temptation of calling the lowest realm "hell" and consistently referred to it as *niraya*. Likewise, I have not referred to "gods" living in various "heavens" but to *devas* living in various *saggas*. This is important because using names borrowed from other doctrinal systems based on completely different principles inevitably carries a baggage of false connotations. My hope is that reading this work the reader can place herself in the imaginative space of ancient India unbiased by concepts picked up elsewhere. The burden on the reader has, I hope, been lessened by the footnotes and by inclusion of a glossary. The entries in the glossary are intended not as full definitions, which can be found in the text itself, but as very simple and minimal reminders.

I have also made the decision to anglicize the plurals of Pali terms used in the text, hence *devas* rather than the strictly correct *devā*. This is mostly for ease of comprehension but also avoids the complication of Pali being an inflected language which English is not.

The quoted passages are my own translations unless credited otherwise in the notes. Any translation is inherently an approximation and the chief problem facing the translator is deciding between literalness and clarity. I have mostly tried to take a middle path between the two. Most of the longer narrative passages are condensed, leaving out many details that are not germane to the point trying to be made. However, whenever a passage is expressing something important about the nature of a kind of being or a realm of existence, I have leaned on the side of literalness in the hope of giving the reader a close approximation of the original rather than imposing my own ideas. I have been fairly liberal in including the original Pali phrases in brackets whenever other interpretations than my own are possible, or where I supposed that a reader with some knowledge of Pali might be curious about the original wording. Feel free to ignore these if they are of no interest to you.

0:8 BUDDHIST TEACHINGS

This book is not intended as a general survey of Buddhist teachings. Some of the general concepts of Buddhism which have a bearing on the cosmology are briefly explained in the necessary places. For those readers without a background in Buddhism, what follows is a very cursory outline of some of the principal ideas.

The Four Noble Truths

The Buddha's first discourse outlined the scheme of his teaching in the Four Noble Truths. These are the Truth of Suffering, the Truth of the Origin of Suffering, the Truth of the Cessation of Suffering and the Truth of the Path Leading to the Cessation of Suffering. The first Truth, that of suffering (*dukkha*) is, in an important sense, the theme of this book. It is the nature of this conditioned world and everything in it to be imperfect, unsatisfactory and incomplete. The second truth states that the origin of this suffering is found in craving (*taṇhā).* When craving is eradicated, the person can realize the unconditioned state which is the cessation of suffering. As a guide to accomplishing this, the aspirant must follow the Noble Eightfold Path laid out in the fourth truth; Right View, Right Thought, Right Speech, Right Action, Right Livelihood, Right Effort, Right Mindfulness and Right Concentration.

The Conditioned and the Unconditioned

This world is described as "conditioned" (*saṅkhata*). This means that no phenomena or entity within it is self-contained but is derivation of other phenomena and processes. All things, and all beings, arise and pass away according to causes and conditions. This is one aspect of *dukkha* ("suffering"). This is the nature of things in all realms of existence from the lowest to the highest. Nowhere is there any stability or permanence. Beings are born into this or that state of existence, live for shorter or longer lifespans, die and are reborn somewhere according to their *kamma* (lit. "actions", Skt. *karma*). This process of continual wandering is *saṃsāra.* The goal of Buddhism is to stop this process, to end the futile wandering through conditioned existence and to realize the "unconditioned" (*asaṅkhata*), which is *nibbāna* (Skt. *nirvāṇa*). When this is fully realized the person is an *arahant* or accomplished one for whom the process of rebirth and manifestation ceases.

Kamma and Rebirth

Beings existing in *saṃsāra* perform actions with body, speech and mind. This is *kamma* (Skt. *karma*) and such actions always have a later effect (*vipāka).* If the actions are skilful (*kusala*) they lead to pleasant results, if they are unskilful (*akusala*) they lead to painful results. Note that this terminology is preferred to the use of "good" and "evil" because kamma is not a divine judgement, but a natural law. At the moment of death, when the body ceases to provide a substrate for consciousness, the next moment of consciousness will arise in a new body determined by the kamma made by that individual.[7] This may be in any of the realms of being and may be either upward or downward depending on that person's kamma. This process of repeated rebirth is both beginningless and endless unless that person achieves full awakening and makes an end of it. There is no ultimate purpose served within the process of rebirth itself, and seeing into the futility of *saṃsāra* is an important aspect of waking up.

Not-Self

One of the most characteristic teachings of Buddhism is the *anattā* ("not-self") doctrine. It rejects the idea, so

[7] This assumes that the person is not an arahant and avoids the complex question of an intermediate state.

prominent in ancient India, of an abiding, unchanging, eternal self (*attā*, Skt. ātman) in beings which transmigrates from life to life. While Buddhism does teach that the process of conditioned existence continues in a new form after death, it denies any substantial entity which persists and moves on. Consciousness is not a thing but a process. The idea of *anattā* is related to the conditionality of all things; nothing can exist as a substantial entity because everything only exists as a reflection of other things. This teaching is quintessentially Buddhist and is found in all schools but is never found outside Buddhism.

Stages of Awakening

The Theravāda school has a scheme of the path to full awakening[8] occurring in four distinct stages. The first glimpse of *nibbāna* means that a person has reached the stage of *sotāpanna* ("stream-enterer,") which is essentially a purification of the view. A *sotāpanna* can never be reborn into the lower realms and will only be reborn seven more times at most, always in the human realm or higher. One who has attained the second stage is a *sakadāgāmī* ("once-returner") who can be reborn only once more in the human realm although he or she may be reborn several times in higher realms before attaining final *nibbāna*. One who has reached the third stage, where sensuality is completely transcended, is *anāgāmī* ("non-returner") and will never be reborn in the plane of sense desire again but can only be reborn in the *suddhāvāsa* ("Pure Abodes,") a special realm within the *rūpabhūmi*. One who has purified the mind from all the defilements and fully attained *nibbāna* is an *arahant* and is freed forevermore from the round of death and rebirth.

The Jhānas

The *jhānas* (Skt. *dhyāna*) are meditative attainments where a person's mind is elevated out of the plane of sense-desire (*kāmāvacara*) into the plane of form (*rūpāvācara*) or the formless (ārūpāvācara). These will be discussed more fully in the chapter on Brahmā beings because the mind of the human meditator is, when in jhāna, functionally equivalent to the level of consciousness innate in Brahmās. Jhāna is distinct from the stages of awakening discussed above in that they do not permanently eradicate the defilements and are not considered a final liberation, although they do assist in that process.

The Theravāda School

The Theravāda (lit. "School of the Elders") is that branch of Buddhism which is predominant in Sri Lanka and South-East Asia. It is the oldest extant school and has the most valid claim to be a faithful representation of the original Buddhism. The Theravāda has been very conservative in doctrine and has not departed far from the Buddha's original teachings. Doctrinally, the most prominent difference between Theravāda and the Mahāyāna schools is the Bodhisatta ideal. In Theravāda, the goal of the path is to become an arahant and make an end of further becoming. In the Mahāyāna this is considered a narrow goal and the practitioner is expected to make a bodhisattva vow to relinquish the attainment of final nibbāna and continue being reborn into saṃsāra for the benefit of all beings. In Theravāda, a Bodhisatta is someone who is on the path to Buddhahood, attainment of which is a very rare development,[9] and the aspiration to take this long and arduous path is only undertaken out of great compassion.

---

[8] In this book, I have used "awakening" instead of "enlightenment" which, although now standard, is not really equivalent to anything in the Pali.

[9] In the section on Buddhas, we shall see how extremely rare it is.

0:9 PALI PRONUNCIATION GUIDE

Pali originated as an oral language and does not have an alphabet of its own. In Thailand the scriptures are written in Siamese script, in Sri Lanka in Sinhalese script, and so on In the West, Pali is written in Roman script with the addition of diacritical marks.

For those unfamiliar with Pali names and terms, the pronunciation can be daunting at first. But it is really easier than it looks. Pali is completely consistent in its spellings and a given letter will always sound the same. The additional markings (diacriticals) are made necessary because the Indian alphabets have more letters than the Roman. The following is meant as an introduction.

Vowels:

a is always like the a in *father*, never like the a in *cat*.

e is like the English long a, as in *make*.

i is pronounced as in *machine*.

o is pronounced as in *vote*.

u is pronounced like the English oo sound, as in *moon*.

A macron over a vowel, such as ā or ū, does not change the intrinsic sound, but indicates that the sound is to be held longer.

Consonants:

Mostly as in English. Exceptions to note:

c is pronounced like the English ch as in *chop*.

v is pronounced like a soft English w, as in *week*.

ñ is pronounced as in *canyon*.

ṃ is the pure nasal sound, close to the English ng as in *song*.

A dot under other consonants indicates that it is a "retroflex" sound, meaning that the tip of the tongue is held back against the hard palate. This refinement can be safely ignored for a first approximation at sounding out the words.

h following another consonant, e.g. kh, th, bh etc. is not to be read as a separate letter but indicates that the preceding consonant is "aspirated" meaning that it is pronounced with a breath of air making it softer.

Doubled consonants are always pronounced separately and distinctly, as the t's in the English phrase *hot tar*.

0:10 ABOUT THE SOURCES USED IN THIS BOOK

This book is based for the most part on primary sources; particularly the Pali canon and commentaries.

The Pali Canon

The collection of texts known as the Pali Canon represents the most complete version of early Buddhist teachings still extant. They are divided into three *piṭakas* ("baskets"): the Sutta Piṭaka which is the record of the Buddha's discourses, the Vinaya Piṭaka which contains the rules and legal procedures for the bhikkhus and bhikkhunīs (monks and nuns) and the Abhidhamma Piṭaka which is a collection of technical and psychological teachings written in dry and precise language. The sources for this book are mostly found in the Sutta Piṭaka but the other two *piṭakas* have been cited where needed. The Sutta Piṭaka is divided into five *nikāyas*: the Dīgha, Majjhima, Saṃyutta, Aṅguttara and Khuddaka Nikāya. The first four of these are sometimes referred to as the "principal nikāyas." The Khuddaka Nikāya is a miscellany of mostly short books, some of which are certainly late additions.

Some of the principal texts of the *sutta piṭaka* which have especial interest in the study of Buddhist cosmology are:

Dīgha Nikāya 26 & 27, the Aggañña and Cakkavatti-Sīhanāda suttas which deal with cosmic time; origins, evolution and destruction.

Dīgha Nikāya 20, the Mahāsamaya Sutta recounts a visit of many devas and brahmās to the Buddha and includes a long list of their names. DN 32 is similar.

Dīgha Nikāya 18 recounts a visit of a brahmā being to the deva world.

Aṅguttara Nikāya 7:66 which deals with the end of the world-system

Aṅguttara Nikāya 3: 81 which is the best canonical description of the multiple world-systems

The Saṃyutta Nikāya has several sections dealing with specific types of beings; Devas (SN 1), Brahmās (6), Yakkhas (10), Nāgas (29), Supaṇṇas (30) and Gandhabbas (31)

The Majjhima Nikāya includes a few suttas with narrative portions relating to various aspects of the cosmological background. For example, MN 50 is a very interesting encounter between Māra and Moggallāna and MN 37 one between Moggallāna and Sakka.

This list is very incomplete but should be sufficient to demonstrate that the basic framework of the cosmology is found in the canon itself, even if many details are added by the commentaries.

The Commentaries—*Aṭṭhakathā*

The commentaries (*aṭṭhakathā*) are adjuncts to the canonical texts which serve to explain and expand on the original material. In part, they consist of word definitions which are often extremely useful for translating doubtful passages. More importantly for our purposes, the commentaries contain a wealth of stories full of fascinating detail. The commentaries to the first four nikāyas (Dīgha, Majjhima, Aṅguttara and Saṃyutta) are the work of Buddhaghosa,[10]

[10] This is not a complete list of his works. For details of Buddhaghosa's life and works, see the introduction to *The Path of Pu-*

a great scholar of the early fifth century A.D. Buddhaghosa, a North Indian, worked in Sri Lanka. There he found old commentaries (now lost) written in the Sinhalese language although based on Pali sources which were no longer extant. These he translated into Pali, collated and edited. We have no way of knowing how much of the commentaries we have are true reflections of the lost old commentaries from immediately after the Buddha's time, and how much represent Buddhaghosa's editorial license. Buddhaghosa appears to have been a careful and conservative scholar and it is doubtful therefore that he invented much of this material. All we can say for certain is that the commentaries became the orthodox position of Theravāda in later times, and that they incorporate much older material.

Buddhaghosa also produced a masterful summary of the teachings in the *Visuddhimagga*, a work principally dealing with meditation but which includes significant cosmological details and is often cited in this book.

Four texts of the Khuddaka Nikāya are of particular interest for the themes of this book; the Jātakas, the Dhammapada, the Vimānavatthu and the Petavatthu. The canonical parts of these four books are entirely in verse to which the commentaries have appended stories. The Jātaka and Dhammapada commentaries were among those composed by Buddhaghosa, those of the Vimānavatthu and the Petavatthu were produced by another great scholar, Dhammapāla, who lived some time after Buddhaghosa, probably in the seventh century A.D. The canonical verses of these four books are sometimes very cryptic and the stories are skilfully woven around them. The Jātakas are stories of the Buddha's previous births. The Dhammapada stories cover many topics and are used to illustrate various points of Dhamma raised by the verses. The Vimānavatthu stories are all about the deva realms, mostly descriptions of the pleasures of Tāvatiṃsa. The Petavatthu stories concern beings in the Peta realm (ghosts). Although these stories were composed quite late, they incorporate much older material. In the case of the Jātakas, some of the stories show signs of being Buddhist reworks of very old pre-Buddhist tales.

The Subcommentaries—*Ṭīkā*

Dhammapāla is also credited with composing a set of subcommentaries to Buddhaghosa's commentaries, known as the *ṭīkā*. I have not cited the *ṭīkā* very often in this book, because they represent late texts which stretch the already broad chronological framework of the cosmological view presented. In some cases they provide invaluable clarification to obscure passages in the primary text or the commentary, and in a very few instances long passages from the *ṭīkā* have been judged worth reproducing because of their intrinsic interest and the wealth of detail they provide.

The Abhidharmakośa

I have not been able to avoid using one source outside the Pali texts and that is the *Abhidharmakośa,* this Sanskrit text was composed by Vasubandhu, who lived in the fourth century C.E., and was therefore roughly contemporary with Buddhaghosa. It consists of two parts, first a text entirely in verse, the *Abhidharmakośakārikā*, and then a little later Vasubandhu's own prose commentary on the verses, the *Abhidharmakośabhāṣya*. Vasubandhu represents a transitional figure in Buddhism. The *Abhidharmakośa* is generally considered a text of the Sarvāstivāda School, one of the original eighteen schools of original Buddhism and doctrinally not far from the Theravāda. However, already in the prose commentary there are other influences present, particularly of the Sautrāntika School. Later in his life Vasubandhu converted to Mahāyāna and together with his brother Asaṅga founded the Yogācāra School. It is the prose commentary that I have mostly used here.[11]

It was not really possible to omit using this text even though it is somewhat outside the purview of the Theravāda. Vasubandhu presented a more systematically developed cosmological framework in the *Abhidharmakośa* than anything found in the Pali sources and can often help clarify the picture. The *Abhidharmakośa* does, however, sometimes

rification, Ñāṇamoli's translation of the *Visuddhimagga*.

11 See the extensive introduction to Poussin and Pruden's translation for further information about the provenance of this text.

diverge from the Theravāda system and these differences are indicated where necessary in the relevant places of this book. I have used exclusively the translation by Louis De La Valleé Poussin and Leo M. Pruden.

Important Secondary Sources

Two reference works were invaluable for the composition of this book.

The Dictionary of Pali Proper Names, G.P. Malalasekera, originally published by the Pali Text Society in 1938. This is an astonishing piece of scholarship, listing almost every proper name in the canon and commentaries together with sometimes lengthy synopses of the relevant sources together with references. It includes persons and places as well as notes on some of the classes of beings such as nāgas, supaṇṇas, the various kinds of devas etc. This is all the more impressive because it was composed before the invention of computers.

The Pali texts themselves were from the digitized canon produced by the **Vipassana Research Institute**: http://www.tipitaka.org. They were accessed via the **Digital Pali Reader** of Yuttadhammo Bhikkhu.

OVERVIEW

The textual basis of this book represents the nearly one thousand year span between the the time of the Buddha and that of Buddhaghosa and Vasubandhu with a little added clarification from the time of Dhammapāla.. The picture presented here is the view of the universe and its inhabitants held by Buddhists of that period. This picture remained substantially unchanged until the impact of modern science. In most of the Buddhist world this was not until the nineteenth century. It is hoped the reader will be able to suspend the use of hindsight and immerse himself in the perceptual world of those times.

0:11 ABBREVIATIONS

The following abbreviations are used in the notes. Numbering indicates the chapter and sutta and follows the Burmese recension. Where this differs from the numbers used in the most commonly accessible English translations, the numbers in the translation are given in brackets as (Eng. x, y). Numbers in references to the commentaries follow the chapter numbers in the main text, not in the commentary itself.

References to the *Abhidharmakośa* always include chapter and section number as well as page reference to the Asian Humanities Press edition of Poussin and Pruden's translation.

§	this mark indicates an internal reference to another section of this book.
-a	after another abbreviation; indicates the *Aṭṭhakātha* or commentary.
AENV	*The All-Embracing Net of Views*, (Brahmajāla Commentary) tr. Bhikkhu Bodhi
AK	*Abhidharmakośa*. English translation by Poussin and Pruden.
AN	Aṅguttara Nikāya; English translation: NDB
Ap	Apadāna
Abhidh-s	*Abhidhammattha Saṅgaha*; English translation: CMA
BPS	Buddhist Publication Society
Bv	Buddhavaṃsa
CDB	*Connected Discourses of the Buddha*, tr. Bhikkhu Bodhi
Ch	Chapter
CMA	A *Comprehensive Manual of Abhidhamma*, tr. Bhikkhu Bodhi.
Cv	Cūḷavagga (Vinaya)
Dhp	Dhammapada
Dhs	Dhammasaṅgaṇī (Abhidhamma)
DN	Dīgha Nikāya, sutta number; English translation: LDB.
DN-a	Dīgha Commentary; the *Sumangalavilāsanī*
DPPN	*Dictionary of Pali Proper Names*
eng	English; in footnotes refers to the English translation.
GGB	*The Great Chronicle of Buddhas*

It	Itivuttaka
Jāt	Jātaka Commentary, story number, English translation, PTS edition, E.B. Cowell, editor.
Khp	Khuddakapāṭha
Kv	Kathāvatthu
LDB	*Long Discourses of the Buddha*, tr. Maurice Walshe.
Mil	*Milindapañha*, English translation: I.B. Horner, PTS.
MLDB	*Middle Length Discourses of the Buddha*, tr. Bhikkhu Bodhi.
MN	Majjhima Nikāya; English translation: MLDB.
MN-a	Majjhima Commentary; the *Papañcasūdanī*
Mv	Mahāvagga
Nidd	Niddesa
-nid	Nidānakathā; following another abbreviation refers to the introductory section of a text.
NDB	*Numerical Discourses of the Buddha*, tr. Bhikkhu Bodhi
Pāc	Pācittiya (section of Vinaya Suttavibhaṅga)
Pār	Pārājika (section of Vinaya Suttavibhaṅga)
PED	Pali Text Society's Pali-English Dictionary
Pp	Puggalapaññatti
PTS	Pali Text Society
Pv	Petavatthu
Sd	Saṅghādisesa (section of SV)
Skt	Sanskrit
SN	Saṃyutta Nikāya; English translation: CDB
SN-a	Saṃyutta Commentary; the *Sāratthappakāsinī*
Sn	Suttanipāta
Sn-a	Suttanipāta commentary; the *Paramatthajotikā*
Vin-a	*Samantapāsādikā*, the Vinaya Commentary

-ṭ	after another abbreviation; indicates the *Ṭīkā* or sub-commentary.
Th	Theragāthā
Thī	Therīgāthā
Ud	Udāna
Ud-a	Udāna Commentary
Vibh	Vibhaṅga (Abhidhamma)
Vibh-a	Vibhaṅga Commentary, the *Atthasālinī*
Vin	Vinaya
Vism	*Visuddhimagga*
Vism-mhṭ	*Visuddhimagga* Commentary; the *Paramatthamañjūsā*
Vv	Vimānavatthu

PART ONE – COSMIC SPACE

1:1 THE BUDDHIST COSMOS

The primary realities in Buddhism are *saṃsāra* and *nibbāna.*[12] *Saṃsāra* consists of conditioned (*saṅkhata*) phenomena and *nibbāna* is the unconditioned (*asaṅkhata*). Of *nibbāna* this book will have comparatively little to say.[13] The entire cosmos, from top to bottom, encompassing all its fascinating and terrifying variety, is *saṃsāra*. It is the arena of all manifestation, action (*kamma*) and result of action (*vipāka*). It is dependently arisen, contingent, imperfect, and all forms within it are impermanent and subject to change and dissolution. Every realm, every being, every formation (*saṅkhāra*) is marked by the three characteristics of imperfection (*dukkha*), impermanence (*anicca*) and emptiness of any self-essence (*anattā*). *Saṃsāra* is suffering and change and it is all, in the last analysis, void.

The noun *saṃsāra* is derived from the verb *saṃsarati*, "to move about continuously, to come again and again."[14] This is the essence of the idea of *saṃsāra*, that all the beings in the cosmos are continually engaged in endless transformation and movement. There is no real satisfaction to be found anywhere within it, all this "faring on" is ultimately pointless. The goal of Buddhism is not found anywhere within these fantastically multiplied struggles and changes, but in making an end of it all and finding the ultimate peace and quiescence of *nibbāna*.

Saṃsāra is the cosmos; it encompasses the entirety of conditioned existence from the lowest to the highest realms of being. An important theme to grasp, and one often spoken about by the Buddha, is the incomprehensible vastness of *saṃsāra*:

> Bhikkhus, the beginning of this *saṃsāra* cannot be known. Suppose a man were to gather all the grass, sticks and branches in this continent of Jambudīpa and, having cut them into four inch pieces and placed them in a single heap, were to put them aside one by one, counting "This is my mother, this is my mother's mother, this is her mother …" That man would exhaust his pile of sticks before he reached the beginning of this *saṃsāra*. Why is this? It is because the beginning of this *saṃsāra* is not to be known. The first point of beings, wandering and passing from existence to existence (*saṃsarati*), obstructed by ignorance and bound by craving, is unknowable. For such a long time, bhikkhus, have you endured suffering, pain and misery, filling up the cemeteries (SN 15:1).

> For such a long time have you wandered and passed from existence to existence that the streams of blood flowing from having your head cut off is greater than the volume of water in the four great oceans. In this long time, bhikkhus, you have existed as cows, oxen, goats, sheep, chickens or pigs and had your head cut off. In this long time, you have existed as robbers and thieves and being taken, had your head cut off. (SN 15:13).

> The beginning of this *saṃsāra* is not to known. It is not easy to find a being who in this great long time has not previously been your mother, your father, your brother, your sister, your son or your daughter. For such a

12 Sanskrit = *nirvāṇa.*

13 For an excellent survey of the teachings about nibbāna see *The Island* by Ajahn Pasanno and Ajahn Amaro.

14 PED s.v. *saṃsarati.*

> long time, bhikkhus, have you endured suffering, pain and misery, filling up the cemeteries. Enough! Develop weariness (*nibbindati*) with all formations. Enough! Become dispassionate towards them. Enough! Become liberated from them. (SN 15:14 f.)

These quotations demonstrate that the problem of *saṃsāra* is not just a personal one. It is intrinsic to the nature of the cosmos. While the solution to suffering is personal (*ajjhatta*—"internal"), suffering itself is universal (*bahiddha*—"external"). We could say, without exaggeration, that all of manifest reality is a kind of dysfunction. The study of the cosmos is in essence a study of the First Noble Truth, the truth of *dukkha* or suffering. The Buddha enjoined us to comprehend the truth of *dukkha* (SN 56:11) and this means understanding *saṃsāra*. In this book we will be examining this reality in terms of the way the ancient Buddhists of India understood it. We need to begin by setting the stage, so to speak, and describing the physical arena in which the great cosmic drama of *saṃsāra* is played out.

1:2 THE FOUR GREAT ELEMENTS

Before we begin considering the details of the material universe, it may be useful to consider at least briefly the underlying physics on which it is based, according to the ancient Buddhist texts. The basic building blocks of matter are the four great elements (*mahābhutā*). These are earth (*paṭhavī*), water (āpo), air, or more correctly wind (*vāyo*), and fire (*tejo*). To these are sometimes added space (ākāsa[15]) and consciousness (*viññāṇa*) to make a list of six elements (DN 3).

The system of four or five elements (with space) is not unique to Buddhism and in fact predates it by many centuries. For example, the Taittirīyaka Upanishad states:

> From that Self (*Brahman*) sprang ether (ākāsa, that through which we hear); from ether air (that through which we hear and feel); from air fire (that through which we hear, feel, and see); from fire water (that through which we hear, feel, see, and taste); from water earth (that through which we hear, feel, see, taste, and smell). From earth herbs, from herbs food, from food seed, from seed man. Man thus consists of the essence of food.[16]

The system of Ayurvedic medicine is based on the idea of balancing the four elements.[17] The four elements are also found in the western tradition: their discovery is traditionally accredited to Empedocles.[18] Returning to the four elements as understood by Buddhism, earth (*paṭhavi*) has the quality of extension, hardness or the taking up of space, water (āpo) is viscosity or cohesion, wind (*vāyo*) is motion and fire (*tejo*) is heat and energy.[19]

The four elements may be divided into those that are internal (*ajjhattika*), parts of the human body and external (*bāhira*), belonging to the outer world. The internal elements are cited as suitable objects for meditation in, for example, the *Mahāsatipaṭṭhāna Sutta* (DN 22). Thus earth element is taken to be bones, skin, muscles, organs and so forth; water to be bodily fluids such as blood, pus, phlegm and urine; wind to be the breath as well as "upward going winds, downward going winds and winds in the belly" and fire is bodily heat and the energy of digestion.

The *Mahāhatthipadopama Sutta* (MN 28) deals with the external elements, emphasizing their impermanent and changeable nature by discussing what happens in the world when the elements are disturbed or destroyed.

> There is an occasion, friends, when the external water element is agitated (*pakuppati* lit. "angry"). At that time there will be the complete disappearance of the earth element.[20]
>
> There is an occasion, friends, when the external water element is agitated and villages, market towns, cities, provinces and whole countries are carried away. There is (another) occasion when the waters of the great ocean sink by a hundred yojanas, by two hundred yojanas, (and so forth until) the water in the great ocean is not sufficient even to wet one's finger tip.
>
> There is an occasion, friends, when the external fire element is agitated and villages, market towns, cities, provinces and whole countries are burned up. It is only when the fire reaches green grass, a road, stone, water

15 We will consider the nature of space in the section on the formless realms (§3:7,3).

16 Taittirīyaka Upanishad 2:1. Translated by Max Müller 1879:54.

17 *The Ayurvedic Institute*, s.v. "Doshas, Their Elements and Attributes", https://www.ayurveda.com/resources/articles/doshas-their-elements-and-attributes, accessed Mar 12, 2018.

18 Empedocles proved the existence of air as a physical substance by immersing a bucket upside down in water. *Internet Encyclopedia of Philosophy*, s.v. "Empedocles (c. 492—432 B.C.E.)", https://www.iep.utm.edu/empedocl/#SH3, accessed Mar 12, 2018.

19 Bodhi CMA p. 237 f., VM XI & SN-a 14:30.

20 This refers to the destruction of the world-system by a rainfall of caustic water at the end of a cycle. See § 2.8

> or a fair and open meadow that it is extinguished for want of fuel. There is (another) occasion when they seek (in vain) to make fire even with cock's feathers and dried scraps of hide.[21]
>
> There is an occasion, friends, when the external air element is agitated and villages, market towns, cities, provinces and whole countries are blown away. There is (another) occasion in the last month of the hot season when they seek to make wind by means of palm leaves and fans. At that time the wind is insufficient even to stir the grass on a thatched roof. (MN 28)

Whereas there were teachers in India like Pakudha Kaccāyana who taught that the four elements were among those things to be considered stable and permanent "like pillars" (DN 2), the Buddha always emphasized their changeable and impermanent nature. Further, they were not to regarded as the self or belonging to the self (SN 4:177). In short, the four elements upon which all material reality is based are themselves subject to the laws of conditioned existence; they are imperfect, impermanent, changeable and void of real self-substance.

All four elements are present in every instance of actual matter. One who has attained mastery of mind might focus on an object like a block of wood and perceive it as earth, water, air or fire because all these are present in the wood (AN 6:41). Similarly, among the listed psychic powers possible to one who has gained such mastery are walking on water as if it were earth or passing through solid objects as if they were water (DN 2). These ideas imply something beyond a materialist or naïve realist position. In the dependently arisen universe nothing can be considered a discrete, solid, self-sufficient entity.

The four element physics continued to be elaborated in the Abhidhamma and commentaries. Along side the essential four elements which are present in every real material instance there is an additional list of 24 secondary attributes of matter.[22] The majority of these are applicable only in the special case of the bodies of living beings. One important secondary element is that of space (ākāsa) which we will consider in the context of the formless realms (§3:7,3). In a later development only fully worked out in the sub-commentaries this became a kind of atomic theory. Clusters of the four great elements together with at least four of the secondary elements (colour, smell, taste and nutriment) form the smallest unit of matter, a *rūpa kalāpa*.[23] These represent the fundamental units of physical reality. The *rūpa kalāpa* are material instances of the Abhidhamma concept of a *dhamma*; the momentary "point-instant"[24] of existence.

Especially when considering these later developments, the names of the elements should not be considered as representing the ordinary substances of earth and water etc. but as mnemonic devices only. The elements in the Buddhist system are more like qualities or potentials of matter than discrete physical constituents. Thus, earth element is not strictly speaking some *thing* which possess the quality of hardness, it is hardness itself. The Abhidhammic concept of discrete dhammas does not allow for any duality of substance and quality.[25] In the later texts it is said that all four are present equally in all instances of physical matter and the differences observed in different substances are determined by the varying intensities of the four elemental qualities.[26]

Beside their importance as the fundamental constituents of physical reality, the four elements have at least two implications for the cosmology presented in these pages. Four of the five elements are said to be stacked vertically in the world-system. The earth rests on water which rests on air (wind) which rests on space.[27] And when that world-system comes to an end it will be destroyed either by fire, water or air (§ 2.7–2.8).

---

21 The commentary says they are only able to produce a small amount of heat even with such trifles, not like formerly. The idea seems to be that such things should burn easily, but now do not.

22 For a full list of these see CMA p.236.

23 Karunadasa, 2015, p. 215 f.

24 To use a phrase coined by the Russian Buddhist scholar Theodore Stcherbatsky.

25 Karunadasa, 2015, p 171-2.

26 Karunadasa, 2015, p. 177.

27 See Figure Two—*Cakkavāḷa* Cross-Section.

1:3 CAKKAVĀḶA—THE WORLD-SYSTEM

The basic unit of the Buddhist cosmos is the *cakkavāḷa* which may be translated as a "world-system." This is the functional, but not the structural, equivalent of a solar system in modern terms. The *cakkavāḷa* is like a solar system in that it is a grouping of "worlds" or "realms" that includes one sun and in which various kinds of beings live. Furthermore, as we shall see, it is a unit of cosmic space but not the entirety. There are countless other *cakkavāḷas* spread out through space, just as there are solar systems in modern scientific cosmology. However, we cannot push this analogy too far. The other *cakkavāḷas* are not associated at all with the stars, nor is the sun the central feature. The *cakkavāḷa* is grouped around the great central mountain, Sineru.[28]

The term *cakkavāḷa* is almost unknown in the canon,[29] and the concept is only fully developed in the commentarial literature. The canonical texts use *lokadhātu* (lit. "world-element") or just *loka* ("world") to refer to the world-system. The contents of *loka* are defined in the *Aṅguttara Nikāya* as:

> As far as the sun and moon revolve, shining in all directions, this is the world (*loka*). There is the moon, the sun, Sineru king of mountains, (the four island-continents of) Jambudīpa, Aparagoyāna, Uttarakuru, and Pubbavideha, the great ocean, (the six "sensual heavens" of) the Four Great Kings, the Cātumahārājika, Tāvatiṃsa, Yāma, Tusita, Nimmānarati, and Paranimmitavasavatti, and the Brahmaloka.[30]

The commentators no doubt introduced the term *cakkavāḷa* for the sake of precision. The word *loka* is extremely variable in its exact signification, even when modified as *lokadhātu* which may refer to one world-system or to some multiple of world-systems. The element *loka* may also be used to refer to a particular realm within a *cakkavāḷa* such as the *devaloka* or the *brahmaloka*. The commentary is often obliged to exactly specify what is meant by *loka* in any given context, for example:

> There are three (meanings of) *loka*; *okāsaloko* "the world of space", *sattaloko* "the world of beings" and *saṅkhāraloko* "the world of formations." The world of beings is meant here. (DN-a 2)

The *Pali Text Society's Pali-English Dictionary* (PED) devotes a page and a half to sorting out the various nuances of meaning of *loka*. It is not surprising that the compilers of the commentaries felt the need for a more precise term to refer to this very specific grouping of objects.

The word *cakkavāḷa* (Sanskrit *cakravāṭa, cakravāḍa, cakkavāla)* implies an enclosed circular space. The first element, *cakka*, is the word for a "wheel" and the second, *vāḷa* from Sanskrit *vāṭa* means "an enclosure or enclosed space."[31]

The fullest description of the *cakkavāḷa* is given in the *Visuddhimagga*:

> The diameter of a *cakkavāḷa* is 1,204,450 *yojana*. The circumference is 3,610,035 *yojana*. The whole rests on a layer of earth 240,000 *yojana* thick. This rests on a layer of water 480,000 *yojana* thick and this on a layer of vapor (*nabhamugga*) 960,000 *yojana* thick.
>
> The *cakkavāḷa* contains the following:

---

28 K. N. Jayatilleke (2009: p. 65–76) explores this analogy in his essay "The Buddhist Conception of the Universe".

29 There is only one use of the word *cakkavāḷa* in the four principal nikāyas, in a stanza placed at the end of the Mahāparinibbāna Sutta (DN 16) which the commentary says was added by the Sinhalese elders. It is also found in the Buddhavaṃsa and the Apadāna of the *Khuddaka Nikāya*, both of which are certainly late additions.

30 AN 3: 81 (eng. 3:80)—The original refers to one thousand such world-systems and has been changed here from the plural to the singular.

31 See Turner, *Comparative Dictionary of Indo-Aryan Languages* and Monier-Williams, *Sanskrit-English Dictionary*.

Sineru, the greatest of mountains which is 84,000 *yojana* high and descends into the sea a further 84,000 *yojana*.

Around Sineru there are seven circular ranges of mountains, each of which is one half the height of the preceding one. These are named, from the innermost to the outermost, Yugandhara, Īsadhara, Karavīka, Sudassana, Nemindhara, Vinataka and Assakaṇṇa. These ranges are adorned with many gems. Here abide the great kings (*mahārājā*) and many devas and yakkhas.

(Lying in the ocean around the outermost ring of mountains there are the four island-continents:) Jambudīpa which is 10,000 *yojana* across, Aparagoyāna and Pubbavideha which are each 7,000 *yojana* in size and Uttarakuru which 8,000 *yojana* across. Each of the island-continents is surrounded by five hundred small islands.

The moon is forty-nine *yojana* across and the sun is fifty. The realm of the Tāvatiṃsa devas (on the peak of Sineru) is 10,000 *yojana* in size. Likewise the realm of the Asuras (under the sea, at the base of Sineru). The *niraya* of Avīci (below Jambudīpa) is also 10,000 *yojana* across. Encircling the whole is a ring of mountains plunging 82,000 *yojana* into the sea and rising a like distance into the sky.

(In various places there are these great trees) each stand 100 *yojana* tall altogether, with a trunk 15 *yojana* around and 50 *yojana* high and with foliage extending 100 *yojana* around (and upwards to the same height). On the southern continent Jambudīpa there stands the Jambu tree, on Aparagoyāna the Kadamba tree, on Uttarakuru the Kapparukkha, on Pubbavideha the Sirīsa tree, in the realm of the asuras there stands the Cittapāṭali tree, in the place of the *supaṇṇas* (on the slopes of Sineru) there is the Simbali tree and in the realm of the Tāvatiṃsa devas there stands the Pāricchattaka tree.

The Himavā mountains (roughly speaking, the "Himalayas" located on Jambudīpa) are 500 *yojana* high, 3000 *yojana* in length and width and contains 84,000 peaks.

The number of *cakkavāḷas* is endless and in between are the Lokantaranirayas (the dark hell realms existing between worlds).[32]

All of these elements will be described in due course.

Taken together, these two passages from the Aṅguttara Commentary and the *Visuddhimagga* provide the most complete map of the *cakkavāḷa* we can find in the Pali sources. To complete the picture we need to turn to the *Abhidharmakośa* which supplies some of the missing measurements. There we are told that Sineru and the seven surrounding mountain rings are each as wide as they are tall, thus Sineru is 80,000 *yojana* across the base where it emerges from the sea, Yugandhara is 40,000 and so on. The mountain rings are separated by circular seas. The one between Sineru and Yugandhara is 80,000 *yojana* wide and each successive ring is half as wide as the preceding one. The celestial *saggas* (deva realms or "heavens") above the earth are each twice as high as the preceding one, thus the Yama world, the first of the six *saggas* is 80,000 *yojana* above the Tāvatiṃsa world at the peak of Sineru or 160,000 *yojana* above "sea-level' and the highest *sagga*, the Paranimmitavasavatti world, is 1,280,000 *yojana* above sea-level. If we include the lowest Brahmā world in the definition of the *cakkavāḷa*, as the Aṅguttara Commentary does, then it must be 2,560,000 *yojana* above the earth.[33]

32 Vism 7.40f. The original is partly in verse. This translation rearranges some of the elements and omits some poetic flourishes. Phrases in square brackets have been added for clarification. Oddly, a few of the proper names have been spelled differently here than elsewhere, and in a manner closer to the Sanskrit versions. This translation replaces them with the standard Pali forms. An almost identical passage is also found at Sn-a 3:7.

33 For measurements taken from the *Abhidharmakośa* see AK 3:5, p. 451 f.

FIGURE ONE—THE *CAKKAVĀḶA* TO SCALE

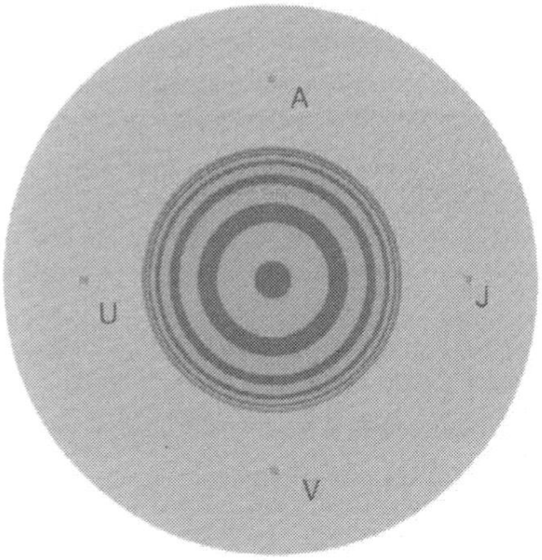

The central circle represent Mt Sineru, the dark circles are the mountain ranges. The blue areas are seas.

The four island-continents are indicated by the capital letters of their names.

For an idea of the scale, consider that the distance from the earth to the moon in modern reckoning would be somewhat less than the width of the Yugandhara range, the first circle out from Sineru.

This diagram is shown according to the ancient Indian convention, with East at the top.

FIGURE TWO—*CAKKAVĀḶA* CROSS-SECTION

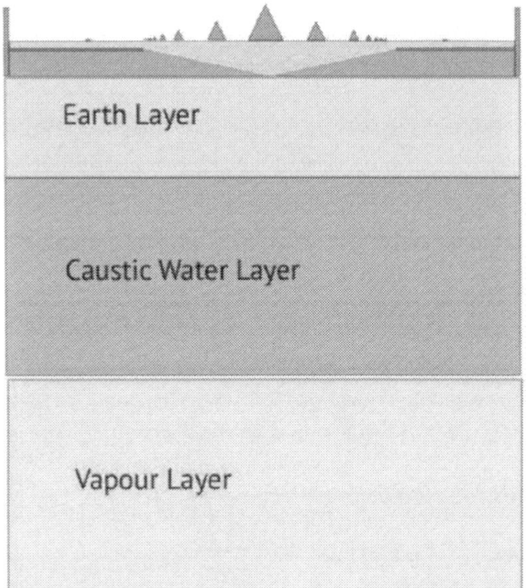

Drawn to scale.

FIGURE THREE—
VERTICAL MAP OF THE CELESTIAL DEVA REALMS

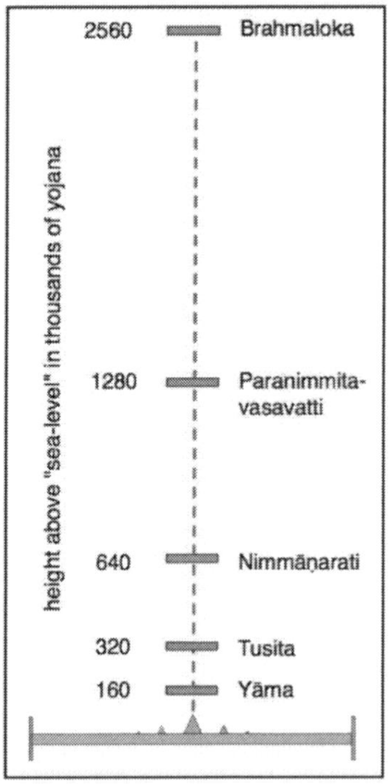

To summarize the picture of the *cakkavāḷa*: the world-system is dominated by the central mass of Sineru which is surrounded by seven rings of mountains separated by broad seas. In the outermost ocean belt are found four large island-continents and two thousand smaller islands. The southern island-continent, Jambudīpa, is where the familiar kind of humans live. The whole is surrounded by a ring of mountains which mark the boundary of the *cakkavāḷa*. Below the surface, the earth is supported by a layer of water which is supported by a layer of vapour. Above, in space, are the various *saggas*, each twice as far away as the preceding one.

The first thing to note about this map is the enormous scale of the world-system as conceived by the ancient Indians. If we take the *yojana* as being approximately twelve kilometres,[34] then Sineru is 960,000 km high and the entire *cakkavāḷa* is 14,453,400 km in diameter. By way of comparison, in modern reckoning the diameter of the earth is 12,756 km and the distance from the earth to the moon is 384,400 km or less than half the height of Sineru. The island-continent of Jambudīpa, which corresponds to the then known world of human habitation, has a width about three times the modern reckoning of the earth's circumference and a glance at diagram one will demonstrate that, physically, Jambudīpa is a very insignificant part of the whole.

The second feature which strikes us about this cosmos is the elegant symmetry and harmony of the whole. Horizontally, the system radiates out from the central mass of Sineru in rings of water alternating with rocky mountains, each successive ring one-half the size of its predecessor. Above, each *sagga* is twice as distant as the preceding one. The number seven is important; there are seven rings of mountains and seven intervening circular seas. Above the ground level of human habitation, there are seven *saggas* if we include the Brahmaloka. This number seven is a potent symbol and is prominent in many mystical systems around the world. There are seven days of the week,

[34] See the the appendix on units of measurement.

seven (astrological) planets,[35] seven chakras, seven musical notes and so forth. In the cosmological system we are considering here, we see the creative force of an unfolding cosmos emerging from the immense central mass of Sineru like resonant frequencies, and this applies both horizontally and vertically.

TABLE TWO—PRINCIPAL FEATURES OF THE CAKKAVĀḶA

TYPE	NAME	SIZE (in *yojana*)	NOTES
Central Mountain	Sineru	84,000	Tāvatiṃsa is situated on the peak
Mountain Range, Circular	Yugandhara	42,000	1st ring range, associated with sun and moon
Mountain Range, Circular	Īsadhara	21,000	2nd ring range
Mountain Range, Circular	Karavīka	10,500	3rd ring range
Mountain Range, Circular	Sudassana	5,250	4th ring range
Mountain Range, Circular	Nemindhara	2,625	5th ring range
Mountain Range, Circular	Vinataka	1,312.5	6th ring range
Mountain Range, Circular	Assakaṇṇa	656.25	7th ring range
Island-Continent	Jambudīpa	10,000	southern continent; the known world
Island-Continent	Aparagoyā	7,000	eastern continent
Island-Continent	Uttarakuru	8,000	northern continent; an earthly paradise
Island-Continent	Pubbavideha	7,000	western continent
Outer Ocean	Mahāsamudda	312,318.75 (width)	
Outer Wall	Cakkavāḷapabbata	82,000 (height)	sheer cliff walls limiting the whole

35 In the western reckoning at least. In India they add Rāhu, the eclipse planet.

1:4 SINERU

The *cakkavāḷa* is dominated by the huge central mass of Mount Sineru. This is the great axis of the world around which all else is arrayed symmetrically. Sineru towers 84,000 *yojana* into space and plunges an additional 84,000 *yojana* into the depth of the sea and is 84,000 *yojana* across at sea-level.[36] To grasp the immensity of Sineru, consider that by modern reckoning the distance from the earth to the moon would work out to 32,000 *yojana*.[37] Sineru is listed as one of the things which are "mighty and unique" (*mahanto so ekoyeva*).[38] It is called "The King of Mountains" (*pabbatarājā*).[39]

The name *Meru* or *Sumeru* for this mountain, which is well known from Sanskrit sources, is almost never found in the oldest strata of Pali texts. One verse passage in the Suttanipāta refers to the devas as *merumuddhavāsin* ("dwellers on Meru's summit") (Sn 3:11), and in another verse from the Dīgha Nikāya, Sineru is referred to as *Mahāneru* (DN 32). These variant names are also found in the commentaries and in some of the later books of the *KhuddakaNikāya*, usually as a poetic trope in verse passages.[40] Even in the commentaries, the name *Sineru* is by far the most common and will be used exclusively here.

The shape of Sineru is that of a steep, truncated four-sided pyramid. The northern face is made of gold, the eastern of silver, the southern of jewels (identified as sapphires in the sub-commentary) and the western is of crystal. Each face emits rays which, extending to the world's edge, determine the colour of the seas and the sky in that direction. Hence, to the south of Sineru, where we live, the seas and the sky are mostly blue, the colour of sapphires.[41] Sineru is described as being "beautiful to see" (Jāt 541).

On the summit of Sineru is a flat plateau on which stands the city of the Tāvatiṃsa devas. This city is said to be 10,000 *yojana* across (Sn-a 3: 7 & Vism 7.44). It is not clear whether this city is coterminous with the plateau or if there are open terraces outside the city walls.[42] If we make the assumption that the city covers the entire plateau, which would mean that it is also 10,000 *yojana*, then we can easily calculate the slope of Sineru, which works out to 58.05 degrees; which is quite steep.[43] This accords well with the image of the asuras attacking Tāvatiṃsa "swarming up the slope like ants ascending an anthill" (MN-a 37).

---

[36] AN 7:66. The *Abhidharmakośa* gives the height as 80,000 *yojana* and the underwater depth at 24,000 yojanas, AK 3:5. p 453.

[37] Taking the *yojana* at 12 km and the earth-moon distance as 384,401 km.

[38] MN-a 115. The others are the Buddha, the ocean, the sky, Sakka, Māra and Brahmā.

[39] For instance at MN 129, SN 22:99, AN 3:81 (Eng. 3:80), AN 5:196 among many other places.

[40] *Meru* is found for example at Thī 6:6, Jāt 506 and 537 as well as extensively in the Apadāna and Buddhavaṃsa. *Sumeru* is found only in one verse which is found at Thī 6:6 and in the parallel section of the Therīapadāna.
Neru is found in the phrase *nerurājāvalaṅkato* ("adorned like the king of Neru") at MN-a 53 and SN-a 35:196. It is fairly common in the verse sections of the Jātakas, but should not be confused with the golden mountain Neru in the Himavā (Jāt 379).
Mahāneru is used at Th 20:1 and Jāt 370.

[41] DN-a 32 and DN-ṭ 32. See also SN-a 15:3.

[42] There are mentionings of *sinerussa ālinde* at SN-a 11:1, which could be interpreted as terraces outside the walls but the context makes clear that these are "lines of defence" some of which are located well down the slopes of Sineru.

[43] See diagram 3. Note that if the plateau is larger than the city, then the slope would be even steeper.

FIGURE FOUR—SLOPE OF MT. SINERU

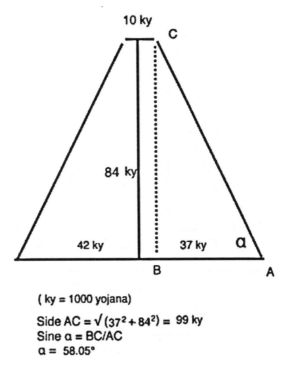

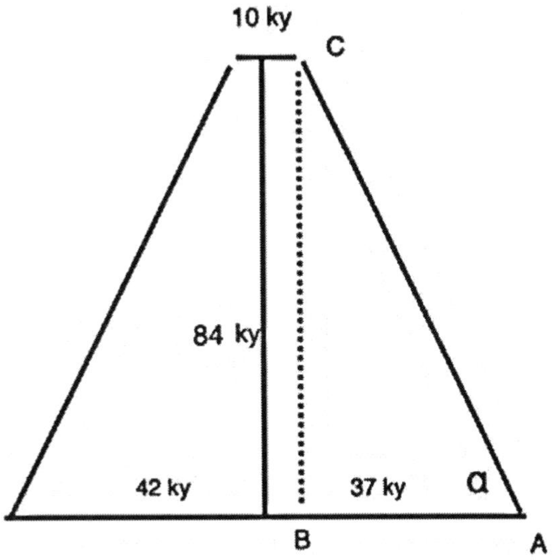

(ky = 1000 yojana)

Side AC = $\sqrt{(37^2 + 84^2)}$ = 99 ky

Sine α = BC/AC

α = 58.05°

The slope of Sineru derived by trigonometry. ky = 1000 *yojana*.

The shape and dimensions of that portion of Sineru lying beneath the sea cannot be described with certainty. The most likely assumption is that the mountain side continues to slope in the same way down to the sea-bed. This would make the width of Sineru at the bottom about 150,000 *yojana*. This assumption is supported by the statement that the sea floor slopes gradually from the foot of Sineru. It is here, at the underwater base of the mountain, that the dwellings of the asuras are located.[44] Another possibility, which can be seen in some old drawings, is that Sineru is lozenge shaped, that is to say, it tapers below the water at a reverse angle, resting on the sea-bed on a 10,000 *yojana* base. Although this seems absurd, it would accord with the concept of the asura realm as a mirror of Tāvatiṃsa, which will be discussed in Part Three (§ 3:3,23).

The slopes of Sineru are wooded, at least in part. It is on the lower slopes that the grove of Ṣimbali trees grows which is the home of the *supaṇṇas*.[45] Where Sineru slopes into the ocean there are sandy beaches where in ancient times holy men lived who were troubled from time to time by the passing of the asura armies (SN 11:10). The sands there are variously described as being silver (SN-a 11:10) or golden (Jāt 542, Eng. 546) and when something is very difficult to accomplish it is said to be "like fetching sand from the foot of Sineru."[46]

Looking beyond the Pali texts, we find a different and somewhat more elaborate picture of Sineru in the *Abhidharmakośa*. That text informs us that there are four terraces jutting out from the face of Sineru, the first at an elevation 10,000 *yojana* above sea-level and the others are spaced at 10.000 *yojana* intervals above that. These terraces are each said to have their inhabitants. On the first dwell a race of *yakṣas* (Pali = *yakkhas*) known as "Pitcher in their

---

[44] Ud-a 5:5. For the asuras see § 3:3,23.

[45] Jāt 31. The *supaṇṇas* are gigantic birds, see § 3:2,5.

[46] DN-a 1, MN-a 44, SN-a 14:15, SN-a 35:99, Jāt 542.

Hand" (*karotapānaya*), on the second the "Wearers of Crowns", on the third the "Always Intoxicated" (*sadāmatta*), and the fourth is the home of the Four Great Kings and the lesser Cātumahārājika devas (AK 3:5, p.462). This last habitation agrees with the Pali texts which also place the Cātumahārājika realm half-way up Sineru (Vibh-a 18:6).

The great importance of Sineru as the dominant physical feature of the *cakkavāḷa* is evidenced by its frequent use in similes, some of a proverbial nature.

> The Buddha asked, "What do you think is greater, bhikkhus? Sineru the king of mountains or a pile of seven pebbles the size of mung beans?" The bhikkhus replied, "Sineru king of mountains is greater, bhante, in comparison the pile of pebbles is of no significance." "Even so, bhikkhus, is the suffering remaining to a noble disciple who has attained to vision … compared to the suffering which has been eliminated by him. (SN 13:10)

An enormous quantity is called a *sinerumatto* ("as big as Sineru.") (MN-a 56) It is said that one cannot repay the gift of Dhamma even with a pile of costly goods as great as Sineru (MN-a 142). When something is impossible it is said to be like "trying to shatter Sineru with one's fist" or "climbing Mt Sineru" (DN-a 1). When something is truly wonderful or marvellous, often referring to a discourse of the Buddha, it is said to be "like lifting up Sineru, (DN-a 1) or like "Sineru flying into the sky," (Jāt 509) or like "turning Sineru around" (Jāt 532). When some pious individual wishes to express that his own virtue or understanding cannot be compared to that of the Buddha he might say, "It is like comparing Sineru to a mustard seed."[47] When a spiritual quality, such as faith, is firmly established it is said to be "as unshakeable as Sineru."[48] Some of these similes involve evocative images. We are told that Kumārakassapa's Dhamma discourse is like "like a thousand oil-lamps on the peak of Sineru" (MN-a 43). The Buddha Vipassī only gave a dhamma talk once every seven years, but when he did it was a momentous occasion. It was said to be like "bringing down the Milky-Way (the ākāsagaṅga, lit. "Sky-Ganges") or like using Sineru as a pestle to churn the great ocean."[49]

Among those outside of the Buddhist tradition, Sineru together with the "great earth" (*mahāpaṭhavī*) and the sea were considered eternal and not subject to change (MN-a 22 & SN-a 22:96). Certainly this view seems a natural, if naive, assumption; Sineru being the solid centre of this world, is the ever present background for all the changing drama of the lives of devas and humans. But the Buddha taught that even mighty Sineru is subject to change and dissolution. "This earth and Sineru, king of mountains, will be burned up and consumed" (AN 7:66). For an audience who lived in a world centred on the great Sineru, this was a powerful statement about impermanence indeed.

The Buddha, having himself transcended saṃsāric becoming, makes the ephemeral nature of all conditioned reality evident. There would be no better way to do this than to use Sineru, the symbol of unmoving solidity. When the Buddha ascended to Tāvatiṃsa heaven to teach Abhidhamma to the devas there, he did so by taking just two steps; he first placed his right foot on Yugandhara (the first and highest of the great circular ranges) and then placed his left foot on the peak of Sineru. These mountains "bent down like twigs" to receive his level tread (DN-a 30). Not only the Buddha, but some of his great disciples were able to work this kind of miraculous transformation. When Moggallāna made his own ascent to Tāvatiṃsa to consult with the Buddha about his return to earth, he did so by passing through the solid core of Sineru in such a way that he was visible to the people on earth the whole time. When the Buddha asked him what he would do if asked to perform a great supernormal feat, Moggallāna said he would put Sineru between his teeth and crush it like a bean, or else he would stroll about using the great earth as a sun-shade and Sineru as the stick (Dhp-a 14:2).

[47] DN-a 4, MN-a 22, MN-a 95, Dhp-a 1:8.

[48] DN-a 27, MN-a 47, MN-a 108 etc.

[49] SN-a 16:11 & AN-a 1: 191: ākāsagaṅgaṃ otārento viya *sineruṃ matthaṃ katvā sāgaraṃ nimmathento.*

1:5 THE SEVEN RANGES

Surrounding Sineru there are seven circular ranges of mountains, separated by seven circular belts of ocean. These are, from the inner ring surrounding Sineru, to the outermost:
Yugandhara—"Yoke-bearing". 42,000 *yojana* high

Īsadhara—"Lord-bearing"—21,000 *yojana* high

Karavīka—"The Cuckoo"—10,500 *yojana* high

Sudassana—"Beautiful"—5,250 *yojana* high

Nemindhara—"Rim-bearing"—2,625 *yojana* high

Vinataka—"Crooked"—1,312.5 *yojana* high

Assakaṇṇa.—"Many Cornered"—656.25 *yojana* high.[50]

Other than the simple statement of their respective heights, we are told little more about these ranges. They are called "the seven great peaks" (*satta mahāselā*) and "gigantic mountains" (*girī brahā*). They are said to be adorned with various jewels[51] and to be the dwelling place of great kings (*mahārājā*), devas and yakkhas.[52] As they rise gradually from Assakaṇṇa to Yugandhara, they are compared to a set of stairs (Jāt 541).

The only one of the seven which is given a little more individual description is the first and highest, Yugandhara. It is associated with the sun and moon which are sometimes described as "rising from Yugandhara," (DN-a 20, Dhp-a 2:3) as these heavenly bodies revolve around Sineru at the height of Yugandhara. In the Javanahaṃsa Jātaka the Bodhisatta was born as a golden goose (*haṃsa*) of supernormal speed and power.

> The two younger brothers of the Bodhisatta resolved to run a race with the sun. The Bodhisatta warned them, "the sun is swift, you cannot race it, you will be destroyed." But they, not heeding his words and not knowing their own strength, flew up to the level of the sun and sat upon Yugandhara. To save them, the Bodhisatta also flew up to Yugandhara and sat beside them. When the disk of the sun appeared, the geese flew after it. (Jāt 476)

There is also a great yakkha chief named Yugandhara, so-called because he dwells on that mountain (DN-a 32).

---

50 The list of names is found in verses at Vism 7.42, Sn-a 3:7 and Jāt 541. In the commentarial explanation of the verses we are told that each range is half the size of the preceding one. The translations of the names are literal. The *Abhidharmakośa* uses the same names, in their Sanskrit forms, in a slightly different order. See AK 3:5, p. 452.

51 The *Abhidharmakośa* says they are made of gold. AK 3:5. p. 453.

52 All this from Vism-mhṭ 7 and an almost identical passage at Sn-a 3:7. Are the *mahārājā* meant to be the *cātumahārājā*, the "Four Great Kings?" Probably, as Vibh-a 18:6 identifies their dwelling as half-way up the slope of Sineru, and this agrees with the *Abhidharmakośa*.

1:6 THE CIRCULAR SEAS

The spaces between the seven circular ranges of mountains are filled by seven circular seas, called *sīdantaramahāsamudda* ("great intermediate oceans") or just *sīdantara*. The one between Sineru and Yugandhara is as wide as Sineru is high, and each successive ocean is half as wide as the preceding one, diminishing in the same ratio as the heights of the mountains (Vism-mhṭ 7). These seas have some remarkable properties. The water in them is so "subtle" (*sukhu*) that nothing can float on their surface, "not even a peacock's feather." This is the reason for their name, *sīdantara*, the element *sīd-* derives from the verb *sīdati* "to sink" (Jāt 541).

One passage tells us that the waters of the sīdantaras are completely still, without waves or motion of any kind (Nidd 1: 14). But this is contradicted by a simile which occurs elsewhere which refers to a great sound as of many beings rejoicing. When the Bodhisatta renounced the home life the rejoicing of a multitude of devas was said to be like "the roaring of the sea inside Yugandhara" (Ap-nid). In another place, the sound of a great royal festival is compared to the sound made when "the wind off of Yugandhara strikes the middle of the sea" (Jāt 539).

There is also one mention of a *Nadī Sīdā* ("Sinking River") flowing between golden mountains deep in the Himavā. It has the same subtle nature as the Sīdantara Seas, so that "not even a peacock's feather" can float on the surface.[53] Given that the seven mountain ranges and their intermediate oceans are a late addition to the cosmology this river may be the original form of the idea.

The *Abhidharmakośa* lists eight qualities of the intermediate seas; their waters are cold, clear, light, tasty, sweet, not fetid and harmless to the throat and stomach (AK 3:5. p. 454). Given the special qualities of the water as given in both the Pali texts and the *Abhidharmakośa*, we can infer that these waters do not communicate in any way with the salt waters of the outer ocean.

The seven seas of Sīdantara are home to two tribes of mighty nāgas, the Kambala and the Assatara, who live in houses made of earth and stone and are so powerful that they cannot be caught by even the greatest of the *supaṇṇas*.[54]

---

[53] Jāt 541. Thanks to Bhante Nyanatusita for pointing this out.

[54] SN-a 30:1. For nāgas and *supaṇṇas*, great serpents and birds always at enmity, see § 3:2,5.

1:7 GREAT OUTER OCEAN

The great circular belt of ocean which lies between Assakaṇṇa and the mountains at the world's edge is referred to as the Mahāsamudda ("The Great Ocean.") In a few places reference is made to "the four Great Oceans." This is explained as meaning the four sections of the ocean which lie under the four faces of Sineru and get their colour from the rays emitted by that mountain.[55] The width of this oceanic belt can be determined by calculation; taking the given radius of the *cakkavāḷa* and subtracting the measure of the various mountains and intermediate oceans we arrive at a width of 312,318.75 *yojana*.[56] The size, depth and capacity of the great ocean are so vast it becomes a symbol of that which is immeasurable, like the mind of the *Tathāgata* (MN 72). It was widely believed by ignorant people that the ocean contains a bottomless abyss, but the Buddha denies this (SN 36:4). The ocean is home to innumerable living beings, ranging from great sea-monsters down to extremely minute creatures (SN 56:36 & AN 1:322, Eng. 1:333).

The asura Pahārāda once told the Buddha that the asuras take delight in the great ocean (*mahāsamudda*)because of its eight wonderful qualities (AN 8:19, AN 8:20, Ud 5:5). This passage is problematic in that sometimes it seems to be referring to the *sīdantara* at the base of Sineru, and at others to the world encircling great ocean. To begin with, the commentary explains what is meant by the asuras "taking delight in the great ocean":

> Their realm is on the lower portion of Sineru (*sinerussa heṭṭhābhāge*). They go in and out from there, and having created pavilions at the foot of Sineru (*sinerupāde*) there they delight in play. (Ud-a 5:5)

Leaving aside for the moment the problem of the precise location of the asura realm,[57] the obvious interpretation of this passage is that the asuras are enjoying the beaches of golden sand at the place where Sineru rises out of the first sīdantara. That this is not their actual home but a sort of holiday resort is indicated by two different words being used to describe their realm, and this place of sport—*sinerussa heṭṭhābhāge* and *sinerupāde* As pleasant as this beach-front property may be, swimming would not be among its attractions; recall that nothing can float in the waters of the *sīdantara*!

Turning to the eight "wonderful and marvellous qualities" (*acchariyā abbhutā dhammā*) of the great ocean:

1. The floor of the great ocean slopes gradually without any sudden precipice. The commentary explains this as meaning that from "the region of its shore" (*tīradesato*) where it has a depth of one *aṅgula* (a finger, or an inch) to its greatest depth at the "root of Sineru" (*sinerupādamūle*) where it reaches a depth of 84,000 *yojana*, there is only a gradual incline without any sudden dropping off.
2. The great ocean is of a stable nature (*ṭhitadhammo*) and does not overflow its limits. Does this mean that it has no tides?[58]
3. The great ocean does not tolerate a corpse, but quickly washes it onto dry land. The *Milindapañhā* says that this is because the ocean is the abode of great beings (*mahābhūtā*) (Mil 5:1,5, Eng. v.2, p.59).
4. The great rivers, such as the Gaṅgā ("Ganges"), Yamunā, Aciravatī and Sarabhū, which flow into the great ocean lose there their former names and become known as just "the great ocean."
5. Although all the rivers of the world flow into the Great Ocean, and rains shower down from the sky, there is never seen to be either a deficiency or an excess in its waters. From the commentary:

---

55 SN 15:3 & AN 3:81, eng. 3:80. The explanation is from the Saṃyutta commentary.

56 This makes the assumption that the width of the world bounding mountains is not included in the total diameter of the cakkavāḷa. This assumption agrees with the calculation done in the *Abhidharmakośa* which arrives at an ocean width of 322,000 yojanas derived from slightly different heights and widths for the mountain ranges.

57 This will be dealt with in § 3:3,23.

58 Ireland (1990: 75) translates "does not exceed the limits of the tide-line" but this is reading too much into the text.

The nature of the great ocean is such that it is never possible to say either "the rain devas are idle, let us put out traps and catch fish and turtles" or "there is so much rain that there is no place left to lie down." From the beginning of the kappa such rain as has fallen remains lapping at the edge of Sineru (*sinerumekhala*—lit. "the girdle of Sineru") and the level neither rises nor falls by so much as a finger-breadth. (Ud-a 5:5)

6. The great ocean is of a single flavour, the flavour of salt.
7. The great ocean contains many and various precious things, such as pearls, jewels, lapis-lazuli (*veḷuriya*—or perhaps, "beryl"), shells, stones, coral, silver, gold, rubies and cat's eye jewels (*masāragalla*). The commentary lists many sub-categories of these. In the commentary we hear of the *cakkavatti* ("wheel-turning monarch") diving into the sea with his retinue to harvest these precious jewels.[59]
8. The great ocean is the abode of mighty beings (*mahābhutā*) such as the *timi, timiṅgalo* (kinds of giant fish or sea-monsters), *asuras, nāgās* and *gandhabbas*.[60]

59 DN-a 17. For details see § 3:1,10.

60 These beings will all be described in Part Three. It is unclear why *gandhabbas* are here to be thought of as living in the ocean.

1:8 A TEXTUAL ISSUE

Given the geography we have described so far, that of Sineru surrounded by alternate belts of sea and mountain with a separate great outer ocean, it is hard to reconcile some discrepancies in the list of the ocean's marvellous qualities. That the great rivers of India flow into it, and that it is salty would indicate that the outer ocean is meant. But the introductory passage references the delight of the asuras, who live on the lower slopes of Sineru, and the commentarial passages frequently reference that mountain in explaining the marvellous qualities of the ocean. As well, we are told that the great ocean does not overflow its bounds, implying that it has no tides.

We can only make sense of this if we conclude that the seven ranges and the seven seas were late additions to the cosmological scheme, unknown at the time of the Buddha. The seven mountain ranges are named in only a very few places, all in the commentaries.[61] The same may be said of the seven *sīdantara*.[62] There is no real contradiction in the qualities of the great ocean because the canonical texts assumed a single great ocean extending from the base of Sineru to the world's edge.

This simpler version of the *cakkavāḷa* is also implied in a passage from the *Aṅguttara Commentary*:

> Just as in a great lake there may be a water-lily, a lotus bud with four leaves (*paṇṇa*, perhaps "petals"): the lotus bud is like Mount Sineru and the four leaves are like the four island-continents and the encircling waters take up the rest of the space. This is well known to great beings with psychic powers that travel through the air and see Mount Sineru and the rest in this way. (AN-a 1: 322)

There are several places in the commentaries where a long compound noun is used to represent the whole world by listing the most significant things in it. The contents of this list varies from place to place and it is significant to note which items are listed and which are not:

sineru-yugandhara-uttarakuru-himavanta-ādi (Uda 1:1, Vism-mhṭ 7)

"Sineru, Yugandharas, Uttarakuru, Himavā, etcetera."

himavanta-sineru-cakkavāḷa-mahāsamudda-candima-sūriyā (DN-a 1)

"Himavā, Sineru, cakkavāḷa, the great ocean, the sun and the moon."

pathavī-himavanta-sineru-cakkavāḷa-mahāsamudda-candima-sūriyā (MN-a 49)

"The Earth, Himavā, Sineru, Cakkavāḷa, the Great Ocean, the sun and the moon."

sineru-cakkavāḷa-himavanta-paribhaṇḍapabbate (SN-a 47:13)

"Sineru, Cakkavāḷa, Himavā, the Bounding Mountains."

Mount Sineru, as the central feature of the cosmology, is always included. Other elements which occur often are the Earth, Yugandhara and the Himavā. Other than Yugandhara, the seven ranges are never mentioned. The inclusion of the Himavā, which is a large mountain range on the island-continent of Jambudīpa, is noteworthy. Although it is the most massive feature on Jambudīpa, at a "mere" 500 *yojana* height (Sn-a 3:7) it is not to be compared with Sineru and

[61] Sn-a 3:7, Jāt 541, Dhs-a 2, Vism 7.42.

[62] SN-a 30:1, AN-a 4:42, Jāt 541 and Nidd 1: 14. The Niddesa is classed as canonical, but is certainly a late text.

even the lowest of the seven ranges; Assakaṇṇa, tops it at 656.25 *yojana*. It is odd that this feature would be considered important enough to include, but not the ranges beyond Yugandhara unless these were more recent flourishes on a simpler cosmology known at the time when these more or less proverbial phrases were coined.

Kloetzli (1983: 45f.) tentatively advances the hypothesis that the seven mountain ranges of the Buddhist *cakkavāḷa* correspond to the spheres of the seven planets in Hellenistic cosmology. This hypothesis is intriguing, but not entirely convincing. The differences between the two models are greater than any similarities, and no connection between the planets and the mountains are found in the Pali sources, except that the sun and moon rise from behind Yugandhara. However, it is within the realm of possibility that the Hellenistic system had some minor influence on this late flourish to the Buddhist *cakkavāḷa*.

1:9 CAKKAVĀḶAPABBATA—THE WORLD'S EDGE

The outer limit of the *cakkavāḷa* is defined by one final ring of mountains which encloses the whole system. This is the *cakkavāḷapabbata*, the "world-system mountain," also in a few places referred to as the *cakkavāḷasiluccaya*, "the world-system rock" (Sn-a 3:7) or the *cakkavāḷamukhavaṭṭi* (Dhp-a 3:7) ("world-system edge"). The height of this mountain ring is usually given as 82,000 *yojana*, thus being somewhat lower than Sineru (Vism 7.43 and Sn-a 3:7). However, this figure is somewhat problematic. The *Visuddhimagga* passage already cited which describes the physical structure of the *cakkavāḷa* says:

dve asīti sahassāni, ajjhogāḷho mahaṇṇave,

accuggato tāvadeva, cakkavāḷasiluccayo,

parikkhipitvā taṃ sabbaṃ.

Two and eighty thousand, plunging into the great sea,

Rising up the same, the world-system rock,

Surrounds the whole.[63]

The most straightforward interpretation of this would be that the mountains rise 82,000 *yojana* into the sky and plunge 82,000 *yojana* into the sea. However, the moon rise is said to be seen coming from the eastern *cakkakavāḷapabbata*, (DN-a 32) Implying a summit close to the height of Yugandhara, it may be that the *Visuddhimagga* passage means that the total height of the mountains is 82,000 *yojana*, with 41,000 rising above the ground. In any case, they must be higher than the level of the sun and moon, whose rays cannot penetrate into the outer void which is in many places said to be immersed in impenetrable darkness.[64] To add to the confusion, the *Abhidharmakośa* gives their height of the world-encircling mountains at 312–½ *yojana* (AK 3:5. p. 454). This low estimate obviously contradicts the idea that the sun and moon do not shine outside the world-system and seems to be derived from a perfunctory following of the scheme that each range of mountains is one half the height of the preceding one.

There is no detailed description of the *cakkavāḷapabbata* in the Pali sources, but we may infer that it rises from the sea as a steep cliff; the suffering beings in the *lokanatara niraya* ("inter-world hell") outside the wall of the world are said to cling to it "like bats."[65] The whole *cakkavāḷa* is compared to a wheel, with the *cakkavāḷapabbata* as the rim (DN-a 14). The *Abhidharmakośa* tells us that they are made of iron (AK 3:5. p452).

63 Vism 7.42. The same passage is found at Sn-a 3:7. These are the only places in the Pali texts that the height of these mountains is given.

64 See for example SN 56:46 and MN-a 123.

65 DN-a 14. For the *lokanatara niraya* see § 3:3,20.

1:10 MAHĀDĪPA—THE ISLAND-CONTINENTS

Within the great outer ocean there lie four island-continents (*mahādīpa*) each of which is surrounded by five hundred lesser islands (Vism 7.44). Even the four great islands are tiny compared to the scale of the *cakkavāḷa*. These islands are the abode of human beings. These island-continents cannot be equated with the continents of modern scientific geography. They are so remote that they cannot be reached by ordinary means, although beings with psychic power can visit them (Mil 2–3:7,9, Eng. v1, p117).

The southern continent, *Jambudīpa*, is the one upon which we live and upon which all human history as we know it has played out. It is shaped like a cart (*sakaṭasaṇṭhāno*), which is usually taken to mean a blunt nosed triangle with the narrow end facing south (KdpA 6 and Vism-mhṭ 7). This would roughly agree with the shape of the Indian sub-continent, which would have constituted the known world at the Buddha's time. It has been suggested that the term *sakaṭa* was a reference to the constellation Rohiṇī, roughly equivalent to Taurus; a triangular formation of stars with the apex being Aldebaran.[66] Jambudīpa is ten thousand *yojana* across at its greatest width (Vism 7.44).

The eastern continent, *Aparagoyanā*, is seven thousand *yojana* across and it shaped like a mirror (*ādāsasaṇṭhāno*), that is to say, round. The northern continent, *Uttarakuru*, is eight thousand *yojana* wide and is shaped like a chair (*pīṭhasaṇṭhāno*) which is generally taken to mean it is square like the seat of a chair. The western continent, *Pubbavideha*, it is half-moon shaped (*addhacandasaṇṭhāno*) and is seven thousand *yojana* wide (Khp-a 6 and Vism-mhṭ 7.1).

Jambudīpa is the only continent for which we have any information pertaining to its internal geography. It is, as we have seen, roughly triangular in shape and ten thousand *yojana* in extent (*parimāṇo*). It is not specified whether this refers to the north-south axis or to the northern base of the triangle; perhaps both measures are equal. Of these ten thousand *yojana*, three thousand comprise the habitat of humanity, three thousand are covered by the Himavā ("snowy") mountain mass and four thousand are covered by ocean (Ud-a 5:5). The area of human habitation we can take as being roughly equivalent to the Indian subcontinent of modern geography. The Himavā is a rough equivalent of the Himalayas and is the abode of yakkhas, nāgas, and wild animals as well as serving as a refuge for religious seekers. The six thousand *yojana* covered by sea presents something of a puzzle. The Pali, *padeso udakena ajjhotthaṭo samuddoti saṅkhaṃ gato*, can be read as meaning "this land is reckoned as having been submerged by the sea." A likely interpretation is that this refers to a large area which was flooded in some previous epoch[67]

It is said that in this Jambudīpa there are pleasant meadows, forests and lotus ponds but that these are few, whereas steep slopes, raging rivers, grounds full of stakes and stumps and rough mountains are far more common (AN 1: 322, Eng. 333). There are many thousands of human cities in Jambudīpa. In the remote past there were eighty thousand cities, but this has "now" (i.e. at the time the texts were compiled) dwindled to sixty thousand and will continue to dwindle in this declining age until there are only twenty thousand left (Sn-a 1:3).

The portion of Jambudīpa inhabited by humans represents the lands of ancient India and as such belongs more to the study of geography than to cosmology or mythology. It should be noted in passing that the measure given, three thousand *yojana*, is about 36,000 km or at least ten times greater than the actual extent of the sub-continent, whether measured north-south or east-west. This discrepancy may be attributed in part to the ancient Indian tendency to inflate large numbers but might also represent an awareness that the inhabited world was larger than India. However, most of the foreign lands known to ancient India could only be reached by a sea voyage and were probably considered as being among the five hundred minor islands associated with Jambudīpa. These would have included *Laṅkādīpa* or *Tambapaṇṇidīpa* (Sri Lanka), *Suvaṇṇabhūmi* ("The Golden Land" or S.E. Asia), *Bāveru* (Babylon) and the lands of the *Yona* (Ionians, or Greeks).[68]

---

66   See PED s.v. "sakaṭa".

67   Perhaps a memory of widespread flooding at the end of the last glaciation? There is a flood myth recorded in Śatapatha Brāhmaṇa 8:1.

68   See DPPN for these names.

1:11 THE HIMAVĀ

The Himavā (or Himavant) lying to the north of the lands of the humans, is 3000 *yojana* in extent, 500 *yojana* high and consists of 84,000[69] separate mountain peaks (Vism 7.42). Although many features of the Himavā are named and even described in the texts, we cannot say how they all lie in relation to each other, making it impossible to construct a map. In the introduction to the Kuṇāla Jātaka the Buddha conveys some bhikkhus to a secluded spot in the Himavā and while flying through the air with them, points out some of the landmarks:

> The Teacher by his own power took them up into the air and brought them to the Himavā. Standing in the sky over the delightful land of the Himavā he showed them its various features;
>
> Kañcana ("Golden") Mountain, Rajata ("Silver") Mountain, Maṇi ("Jewel") Mountain Hiṅgulika Mountain, Añjana Mountain, Sānu ("Table") Mountain, Phalika ("Crystal") Mountain and various other mountains.
>
> Five great rivers and the seven lakes; Kaṇṇamuṇḍa, Rathakāra, Sīhapapāta, Chaddanta, Tiyaggaḷa, Anotatta and Kuṇāla.
>
> This great Himavā is five hundred *yojana* high and three thousand *yojana* in extent. In one delightful region he showed them, by his own power, prepared resting places (*kataniväsa* i.e. shelters for hermits). In one region he showed them the abode of lions, tigers, elephants and other animals. He showed them pleasant groves, trees bearing flowers and fruits, various flocks of birds, flowers of the land and of the water.
>
> To the east of the Himavā is a golden plain, to the west is a vermilion plain. (Jāt 536)
>
> The picture we have of the Himavā is of a wild and magical place, thickly forested and mountainous.
>
> The earth there bears many kinds of herbs and flowering vines. There are elephants, buffaloes, deer, yaks, antelopes, rhinoceros, horned oxen, lions, tigers, panthers, bears, wolves, otters, wild cats and hares roaming about with their young, as well as great boars, snakes and families of elephants living in herds. There are *issa*-deer, *sākha*-deer, *sarabha*-deer, *enī*-deer, *vāta*-deer and *pasada*-deer. There dwell non-human beings (*purisālu*), *kinnaras*, *yakkhas* and *rakkhasas*.
>
> There are upright trees bearing clusters of delightful flowers on top. Spreading out among these trees are osprey, partridge, eagle, peacock, cuckoo, *jīvañjīvaka* birds, *celāvakā* birds and *bhiṅkāra* birds, living in flocks, mad with joy.
>
> There are many hundreds of mineral substances covering and adorning the region; red arsenic, yellow orpiment, vermilion, gold and silver. Such is this delightful forest. (Jāt 536)

When King Vessantara was exiled from his kingdom and fled to the Himavā, he at first tried to dissuade his wife, the loyal Maddī, from following him. He called the Himavā a "terrible forest, filled with wild beasts." In reply Maddī sang the praises of the Himavā in verse:

> When you see the elephant, the tusker sixty years of age,

[69] The reader encountering these numbers should be aware that ancient Indian texts often use numbers like 500 or 84,000 simply to indicate "a great many" without any implied precision.

Roaming alone through the forest, you will not long for your kingdom.

When you see the elephant, the tusker sixty years of age,

Wandering morning and evening through the forest, you will not long for your kingdom.

When you see the herd of she-elephants, with their lord in front of his flock; and hear the tusker trumpeting, the elephant sixty years of age; hearing that roar, you will not long for your kingdom.

From both sides the forest spreads, and when you see your every desire, wild beasts everywhere, you will not long for your kingdom.

When you see the deer bearing five-pointed antlers that come in the evening, and when you see the dancing of the *kimpurisas,*[70] you will not long for your kingdom.

When you hear the roar of the flowing river, and the song of the *kimpurisas*, you will not long for your kingdom.

When you hear the shout of the screech howl living in a mountain cleft, you will not long for your kingdom.

Lion and tiger, rhinoceros and buffalo; when you hear the roaring of these beasts in the forest, you will not long for your kingdom.

When you see a peacock dancing on the mountaintop, surrounded by his peahens, you will not long for your kingdom.

When you see the peacock, egg-born, gaily colored, dancing before his peahens, you will not long for your kingdom.

When you see the peacock, blue necked, crested, dancing before his peahens, you will not long for your kingdom.

In the winter, when you see the flowers springing from the earth, wafting their fragrance, you will not long for your kingdom.

When in the winter months, you see the fat green beetles (*indagopaka*)[71] covering the ground, you will not long for your kingdom.

When in the winter, you see the flowers covering the earth;

the *kuṭaja, bimbajāla*, and *loddapaddhaka* (names of flowers), blowing forth their gorgeous scent, you will not long for your kingdom.

When in the months of winter, you see the forest flowering with buds and blossoms, you will not long for your kingdom. (Jāt 547)

---

70 A small woodland being like a tiny human being. See § 3:4,6.

71 *Indagopaka*. Red Velvet Mite, an arthropod of the family *Trombidiidae*. The Pāḷi name for these small creatures means "Indra's herdsman." These mites have a bright-red rounded body with a velvety appearance and are parasitic on spiders and insects. See Dhammika 2018:52.

The Himavā is a prominent location in the Jātaka tales, featuring as at least a secondary locale in 167 Jātakas, or almost a third of the total. In these stories, the Himavā is clearly distinguished from the realms of human habitation. In one story a farmer searching for his missing cattle "leaves the paths of men and enters the Himavā" (Jāt 516). In another story, when the nāga prince Bhūridatta is lost, his three brothers divide their search into the world of the devas, the world of men and the Himavā (Jāt 543). Although human beings do not normally live in the Himavā, there are exceptions; it is the favoured locale for the ascetic spiritual seekers known as *isi* ("rishis"). No less than ninety Jātakas mention a spiritual seeker who has renounced the world and went to the Himavā taking the *isipabbajjā* ("hermit's going-forth") to live in a leaf hut and practise meditation, eating the fruits and nuts of the forest. Sometimes these hermits return to the lands of men for the rainy season, (Jāt 312) or to procure "salt and vinegar" (Jāt 313). These excursions often result in interactions with kings or other persons which constitute the main plot of the story.

Besides the ordinary hermits, the Himavā is also the abode of paccekabuddhas, fully awakened beings who arise in the ages between Buddhas.[72] It is also sometimes a place of refuge for exiled kings and princes.[73] Besides these, ordinary humans sometimes enter the Himavā to hunt[74] or to gather wood.[75] In the Jātaka stories these individuals are most often depicted as being of a low moral character, acting as the villain of the tale.

Many of the Jātaka tales are stories about animals and many, if not most, of these occur in the Himavā; there are fifty three Jātakas featuring animal characters which take place in the Himavā; these most often involve elephants, monkeys, lions and various kinds of bird.[76] The Himavā as depicted in the Jātakas is also the abode of various non-human beings, particularly the *kinnara* or *kimpurisa*, a race of diminutive bird-like little people.[77] It is also the preferred site for the yakkhas to hold their assemblies (Jāt 347).

72 Jātakas 40, 378, 408, 424 and 496. For *paccekabuddhas*, see § 3:1,14.

73 Jātakas 6, 234, 461 and 547.

74 Jātakas 117, 159, 221, 222, 423 and 501.

75 Jātakas 72, 219, 455, 512.

76 For a discussion of animal stories in the Jātakas see § 3:2,2.

77 Jātakas 481, 485 and 504.

1:12 LAKE ANOTATTA

The most important single feature of the Himavā is surely Lake Anotatta. This is one of the seven great lakes, each of which is fifty *yojana* in length and breadth and has a circumference of one hundred and fifty *yojana* (MN-a 54 and Ud-a 5:5). These measurements imply a circular shape. It is the source of all the great rivers of Jambudīpa including the five major rivers which water the human portion: the Gaṅgā (Ganges), the Yamunā, the Aciravati, the Sarabhū and the Mahī. A detailed description of Lake Anotatta and its environs is found in the commentaries:

> Lake Anotatta is surrounded by five mountain peaks; Mt Sudassana, Mt Citta, Mt Kāḷa, Mt Gandhamādana and Mt Kelāsa. All of these mountains are three hundred *yojana* high, shaped like a crow's beak, curving inward and thus covering over (or "concealing") the lake. Mt Sudassana is made of gold, Mt Citta is made of the seven precious things,[78] Mt Kāḷa is made of antimony (*añjana*), Mt Gandhamādana is made of chalcedony (*masāragalla*) and Mt Kelasa is made of silver.
>
> There, through the power of devas and nāgas, it rains and rivers flow and all these waters enter Lake Anotatta. The sun and the moon, as they travel overhead either to the north or to the south cast their light in between the mountains, but they do not shine onto the Lake from directly overhead. Thus it came to be called "Anotatta" (*an-ava-tatta*, "not warmed" i.e. "cool").
>
> There are bathing places there, with delightful jeweled stairs leading to a flat stone floor. The water is pure, clear as crystal and free of fishes and turtles. These places have arisen for the enjoyment of beings solely through the power of their kamma. In these places, paccekabuddhas, disciples possessing psychic power and rishis bathe and devas and yakkhas play in the water. (MN-a 54 and Ud-a 5:5)

The text goes on to describe the four great rivers which issue from Lake Anotatta. These flow out through four "mouths" (*mukkha*); the Lion's Mouth, the Elephant's Mouth, the Horse's Mouth and the Bull's Mouth. In the country surrounding each mouth, the appropriate species of animal predominates. Each of these rivers flows outward from one of the four cardinal directions (although the text does not specify the place of each mouth), flows completely around Lake Anotatta three times in a clockwise direction without interfering with the other rivers, and then finds its way to the Great Ocean (ibid). An attempt to sketch this geography will quickly reveal that it is quite impossible if we assume these are ordinary rivers. However, the course of the Gaṅgā, the great river which enters the human portion of Jambudīpa, is described in some detail and this includes both an underground tunnel and a portion where it passes through the air. Although it is not stated, we must assume the other rivers also possess these "overpasses" and "underpasses."

> The river issuing from the southern mouth of Anotatta flows three times around the lake; this stretch of the river is called the Āvaṭṭagaṅgā ("Winding Ganges"). It then proceeds in a southerly direction for sixty yojana across the surface of an upright rock; there it is known as the Kaṇhagaṅgā ("Dark Ganges"). Having struck the surface of the rock, it then rises up into the air forming a torrent of water three gāvutas[79] across which flies through space for sixty yojana. This portion of the river is named the Ākāsagaṅgā ("Sky Ganges"). The Gaṅgā then lands upon the rock called Tiyaggaḷā ("Triple Bolt")[80] and there the force of the water, breaking

[78] I.e. gold, silver, pearls, rubies, lapis-lazuli, coral and diamond.

[79] There are four *gāvutas* in a *yojana*.

[80] As in a door-bolt, meaning an obstruction.

> the rock, has made a fifty yojana pond and that portion of the river is known as the Tiyaggaḷapokkharaṇī ("Triple Bolt Pond"). From the banks of the pond, the river then cleaves the rock and enters (a cleft in) the boulder for a distance of sixty yojana where it is called the Bahalagaṅgā ("Dense Ganges"). After which it breaks into the solid earth and flows through an underground tunnel for sixty yojana. This portion of the river is named the Umaṅgagaṅgā ("Subterranean Ganges"). Then it strikes the horizontal rock called Viñjha and splits into five branches, like the fingers from the palm of a hand. Thereafter it is reckoned as five rivers; the Gaṅgā, the Yamunā, the Aciravati, the Sarabhū and the Mahī.[81]

The five rivers are thus all forks of the Ganges. The Aciravati is the modern Rapti River, which drains into the Ghagara which in turn may be identified with the Sārabhū (Sanskrit *Sarayū*) and the Mahī is the modern Gandak.[82] The basin of the Ganges River system was the central area for the ancient civilization of Buddhist India and was the region in which the Buddha wandered throughout his life. It was called the *Majjhimadesa*, the "Middle Country." The inhabited portions of Jambudīpa outside the Majjhimadesa were called the Paccantajanapada, "The Border Countries." It is not surprising that the mythical geography of Jambudīpa focuses on this river system to the exclusion of, for instance, the Indus.

That section of the upper Gaṅgā which flies through the air, the Ākāsagaṅgā, is visible from lower Jambudīpa and nowadays it is known as "the Milky Way." This identification is assumed but not made explicit in the Pali texts but it was a common heritage of ancient India that the Ganges descended from the heavens, and the idea is found in the *Bhāgavata Purāṇa*,[83] for example.

We can see in all this the great importance of Lake Anotatta as the ultimate source of the waters which give life to human civilization. We have seen that the waters of this lake are cool, pure and free of contamination by fish or turtles. The lake itself is centrally located and secluded by the mountains which overhang it. Water from Lake Anotatta was highly sought after for its cleansing and healing properties. On the night of the Bodhisatta's conception, his mother dreamt that the Four Great Kings took her in her bed to the shore of Lake Anotatta where female devas bathed her in Anotatta water (DN-a 14). During the rainy season that the Buddha spent teaching the devas in Tāvatiṃsa, he would return to Jambudīpa every day for his meal. Part of this daily routine was to rinse his mouth with the water of Lake Anotatta (Dhp-a 14:2). Indeed, this is the place where all previous Buddhas have rinsed their mouths, (MN-a 26) as well as paccekabuddhas (SN-a 3:20) and sometimes arahants (Dhp-a 8:2) and *anāgāmīs* (MN-a 23). When the paccekabuddhas meet for their *uposatha* ceremonies, the hall is magically prepared for them in advance; a wind springs up which cleanses the floor with water blown from Lake Anotatta (Sn-a 1:3). When the Buddha's arahant disciple Anuruddha came down with indigestion, it was only a drink of Anotatta water which could cure him (Dhp-a 25:12). It is even said that the devas brought King Asoka sixteen jars full of Anotatta water every day (Vin-a-nid). So highly prized was this water that King Vessavaṇa, the Great King (*Cātumahārājika*) of the North, sends the yakkhinīs (female yakkhas) who are in thrall to him to fetch it, and he works them so hard at this task that they sometimes die of exhaustion (Dhp-a 1:4).

Of the mountains which surround Lake Anotatta, Mount Gandhamādana is the most celebrated.

> Mount Gandhamādana is made of chalcedony and is the colour of Green Gram.[84] It has an abundance of the ten scents (of trees); the scent of roots, scent of heartwood, scent of sapwood, scent of inner bark, scent of

[81] MN-a 54 and Ud-a 5:5. I have slightly rearranged the order of the text for easier comprehension.

[82] See DPPN.

[83] *Bhāgavata Purāṇa*, 23: 5.

[84] *Mugga*—PED has "kidney beans" but the context seems to demand a green colour, due to the lush vegetation. Green Gram or Mung Bean, *Vigna radiata*, is a commonly cultivated plant which produces small green edible beans. See Dhammika 2018:152.

outer bark, scent of the trunk, scent of sap, scent of flowers, scent of fruit and scent of leaves. It is covered with many kinds of herbs. On moonless nights it glows as brightly as burning charcoal. (Ud-a 5:5)

The name *Gandhamādana* means "Intoxicated by Scents," and it is by all accounts a most delightful place. It is the home of the *kinnara* folk, a small bird-like people, as well as yakkhas and devas (Jāt 485, 540). But the beings most characteristic of Mt Gandhamādana are the paccekabuddhas, those who achieve full awakening in the dark ages which lie between the arising of Buddhas. They have the same penetration of reality as a Buddha, but they do not establish a teaching which survives their death. Sometimes there are hundreds of them in the world at once, and they have their dwelling and place of assembly on Mt Gandhamādana.[85]

> Gandhamādana is located in the Himavā. It lies beyond seven mountains (or mountain ranges): Cūḷakāḷapabbata ("Little Black Mountain"), Mahākāḷapabbata ("Great Black Mountain"), Nāgapaliveṭhana ("Nāga Encircled"), Candagabbha ("Womb of the Moon"), Sūriyagabbha ("Womb of the Sun"), Suvaṇṇapassa ("Gold Flank") and Himavantapabbata ("Snowy Mountain"). There (i.e. on Mt Gandhamadāna) is a slope called Nandamūlaka ("Root of Joy") where paccekabuddhas may be found. There are three caves, Suvaṇṇaguhā ("Gold Cave"), Maṇiguhā ("Jewel Cave") and Rajataguhā ("Silver Cave").
>
> At the entrance to the Maṇiguhā there stands a tree called Mañjūsaka which is a *yojana* high and a *yojana* across. On any day during which paccekabuddhas come, this tree flowers with every flower found on the land or in the water. This tree stands over the meeting hall of the paccekabuddhas, called the Sabbaratanamāḷa ("Pavilion of All Jewels"). The hall is swept clean of rubbish by a sweeping wind, sand which is made of all the jewels is spread over the floor by a leveling wind, a sprinkling wind fetches Anotatta water and sprinkles it around the hall and a fragrance-working wind gathers flowers from the fragrant trees in the Himavā and places them in the hall. A grass wind gathers grass and places grass mats in the hall. Thus are the seating places of the paccekabuddhas always prepared and ready for the day that they come and assemble there. Whenever a new *paccekabuddha* arises in the world, he goes there and all the other paccekabuddhas assemble and ask him about his meditation object (*kammaṭṭhāna*). (Sn-a 1:3)

As we have said, it is impossible to construct a coherent map of upper Jambudīpa from the Pali texts; the inconsistencies in the geography are just too great. Trying to fix the location of Mt Gandhamādana, therefore Lake Anotatta, in relation to the lands of human beings illustrates this problem. The seven mountain ranges, which are mentioned only in the passage cited and a parallel passage in the Apadāna Commentary (Ap-a 1:1,2), would imply a very great distance for the lake and its surrounding mountains from human habitations.

However, in the Vessantara Jātaka when the king and his family go into exile in the Himavā they leave the human lands from his brother's kingdom of Ceta[86] for a fifteen *yojana* journey to the site selected for their hermitage; Mount Vaṅka. The route they took is described by mentioning important landmarks. The very first is Mount Gandhamādana, from there they proceeded due north to Mount Vipula, then to a river named Ketumatī, then onwards to a Mount Nāḷika and then the Mucalinda Lake, from which they followed a mountain stream to its source in a small lake under Mt Vaṅka. This passage implies that Mt Gandhamādana lies just to the north of the human lands, as it is cited as their first landmark in the journey.[87]

To add to the confusion, in the Dhammapada Commentary there is the story of the visit of the Buddha and five

---

85 See for instance, MN-a 26, SN-a 3:20 AN-a 1:192 among many other references.

86 Located in present day Nepal according to the DPPN.

87 Jāt 547. Another problem is the mention of Mt Vipula which is a known mountain located near Rājagaha, very much within the human zone. Is this perhaps intended to be another mountain with the same name?

hundred bhikkhus to the elder Revata, Sāriputta's brother, who was dwelling at the Khadiravana (Acacia Grove) in the Himavā (Dhp-a 7:9). This account of this journey says that there were two possible routes to take from Savatthī. One was a round-about journey of sixty *yojana* through lands inhabited by human beings, the other a direct path of thirty *yojana* but through country inhabited by non-human beings (*amanussa*, which usually implies malevolent yakkhas). As the Buddha knew that the elder Sīvali, who was possessed of very great merit, was part of the company, he opted for the direct but dangerous route. The route taken is specified in another passage (which does not mention the possibility of a longer one) as follows:

> On the first day they reached the Banyan Tree, (presumably the one under which the Buddha stayed for a week shortly after his awakening under the Bodhi tree). On the second day they reached Mt Paṇḍava near Rājagaha. On the third day they came to the Aciravati River (a known tributary of the Ganges). On the fourth day they reached the ocean (*varasagara*). It was only on the fifth day that they entered the Himavā. On the sixth day they came to the Chaddanta Forest. On the seventh day they reached Mt Gandhamādana. There they stayed for a week waited upon by the deva Nāgadatta and thereafter proceeded in one day to the Khadiravana and Revata's hermitage. (AN-a 1: 207)

There is much that is difficult to make sense of in this itinerary, especially if this route is meant to be the direct path mentioned in the first passage cited. It doesn't make sense that the company travelled all the way to the sea before striking north, unless the word *varasagara* ("Noble Ocean") means something else entirely. Also, since they did not even enter the Himavā until the fifth day of a thirty *yojana* journey, it seems this passage also implies that Mt Gandhamādana lies not very far north of the human lands; certainly there is no mention of crossing seven mountain ranges.

As we have seen, there is some evidence that the geography of the whole *cakkavāḷa* was still being worked out in the commentarial period. The seven mountain ranges of the *Suttanipāta Commentary* may be an intermediate stage in the process and represent an early version of the seven ranges around Sineru. The names do not match up, but the inclusion of ranges named "Womb of the Moon" and "Womb of the Sun" is reminiscent of the role of Yugandhara as the place where these heavenly bodies reside.

By way of comparison, the *Abhidharmakośa* has nine "Ant Mountains" lying between the human lands and the Himavā. They are so called either because of their shape, or because they are low in comparison to the mountains of Himavā proper. Beyond those lies Lake *Anavatapta* (the Sanskrit form of Anotatta) from which flows the four great rivers named as the *Gaṅgā* (Ganges), the *Sindhu* (Indus), the *Vakṣu* (Oxus) and the *Sītā* (Yarkand), and beyond that lies Mount Gandhamādana (AK 3:5. p 456, & n. 393, p 531).

1:13 THE GREAT LAKES

Most of the other great lakes of Himavā are little more than names in the texts. There are stories about petas living in magical dwellings by the shores of Lake Kaṇṇamuṇḍa (Pv-a 2:12) and Lake Rathakāra, (Pv-a 3:3) and the Buddha gave a talk to a group of bhikkhus by Lake Kuṇāla (Jāt 536, story of the present). Otherwise we know nothing about either their location or character, with the exception of Lake Chaddanta which is described in some detail:

> Lake Chaddanta is fifty *yojana* broad. In the middle of the lake, for a space of twelve *yojana* around, no pond-scum (*sevāla*) or weeds (*paṇaka*) grow and the still water is like a beautiful jewel in appearance. Surrounding this central area is a belt of pure white lotuses, a *yojana* across. Surrounding this is a belt of pure blue lotuses, a *yojana* across. Then alternate belts of red lotuses and white lotuses, each surrounding the previous belt and each a *yojana* across, for seven belts altogether. This is surrounded by a belt of lotuses of mixed colours, also a *yojana* wide. Then, in water as deep as an elephant's flank, there is a belt of fine red rice. Around this lays a belt of small bushes covered in delicate and very fragrant flowers of blue, yellow, red and white colours. Thus, there are ten belts, each a *yojana* across.
>
> Around that is a belt where various kinds of beans grow, "little king beans", "great king beans" and "green gram" (*khuddakarājamāsa-mahārājamāsa-mugga*). Then a belt with vines upon which grow different kinds of squash, cucumbers and pumpkins. Then a belt of sugar-cane, growing as big as palm trees. Then a belt of plantains as big as elephant's tusks, then a belt of Sal trees, then one of jack fruits as big as water pots, then one of sweet tamarinds and one of mango trees, then a great jungle thicket of many kinds of plants and around all these stands a grove of bamboo. (Jāt 514)

(The widths of the various outer belts are not specified, but as the total for the inner belts do not make up the requisite width of the lake, we must assume that some of the outer ones lie in shallow water. If they are also taken as being one *yojana* broad, then everything up to the mango trees lies within the lake).

> Around the bamboo grove there are seven mountains. From the outermost inwards these are; the Cūḷakāḷa Mountain ("Little Black"), Mahākāḷa Mountain ("Big Black"), Udaka Mountain ("Watery"), Candimapassa Mountain ("Moon Flank"), Sūriyapassa Mountain ("Sun Flank"), Maṇipassa Mountain ("Jewel Flank") and the Suvaṇṇapassa Mountain ("Gold Flank"). These last are seven *yojana* in height and surround Lake Chaddanta like the rim of a bowl. The innermost flank of these mountains is golden coloured and its radiance causes the lake to resemble the newly risen sun. The outer mountains are in turn six *yojana*, five *yojana*, and then four, three, two and one *yojana* in height.
>
> At the north-east corner of the lake, at a place hit by a moist (i.e. cool) breeze, there grows a great banyan tree. Its trunk is five *yojana* around and is seven *yojana* high. Four branches grow outward in the four cardinal directions and a fifth grows straight upward. Each of these is six *yojana* long, so the overall height of the tree is thirteen *yojana*, and the distance from the end of one side branch to the other is twelve *yojana*. The banyan tree has eight thousand descending shoots and stands there as beautiful as a bare jewel mountain (*muṇḍamaṇipabbato*). To the west of the lake, on the Suvaṇṇapassa Mountain, there is a golden cave twelve *yojana* in size. (ibid.)

The environs of the lake, with its lush vegetation rich in edible plants, are home to the herd of Chaddanta elephants, the mightiest of all elephant-kind. The name *Chaddanta* means "six-tusked." These elephants live in the golden cave during the rainy season (*vassāratta*) and in the shade of the great banyan in the summer (*gimha*), enjoying the cool breeze.[88]

[88] ibid. For details of the various tribes of elephants, see § 3:2,2.

1:14 THE GREAT TREES

Seven of the locales within the *cakkavāḷa* are graced with a great tree which last for the entire kappa (AN-a 1: 322, Eng. 1: 333). Each of these stands one hundred *yojana* high with a trunk fifteen *yojana* in girth and foliage extending for a hundred *yojana* around (Vism 7.43).

The great tree of **Jambudīpa** is the *Jamburukkha.* The name can refer also to a common tree, the black plum tree, *Syzygium cumini.*[89] It was, for example, under one such tree that the young Bodhisatta Siddhattha experienced jhāna while his father, King Suddhodāna performed the ploughing ceremony. The shadow of this tree stayed miraculously stationary to provide shade to the young prince throughout the afternoon (MN-a 36). The singular great Jamburukkha is sometimes called *Mahājamburukkha* to distinguish it from the lesser trees (e.g. SN-a 47:13 & Dhp-a 14:2). The island-continent of Jambudīpa takes its name from this great tree, which is its emblem (*saññāṇabhūtā*) (AN-a 1: 322).

The location of the Jamburukkha is deep in the Himavā, (AN-a 1:322) most probably on the upper reaches of the Gaṅgā which is the source of all the major rivers of lower Jambudīpa. This is implied in a passage describing the origin of *Jambu* gold, a special high-quality gold panned from rivers, renowned for its colour and lustre:

> *Jambu* gold is found in the Jambu River. Where the great Jambu tree, with its fifty *yojana* branches, grows there flow many rivers. Onto both banks of these rivers fall fruit from the Jambu tree. From these fruit there arise golden shoots. The water of the rivers carries these shoots down all the way to the sea and this is known as "Jambu gold" (*jambonada*).[90]

When the Buddha was staying with the fire ascetic followers of Uruvelakassapa, he displayed several miracles as a prelude to converting them. In one of these, he fetched in an instant a fruit from the Jambu tree "after which Jambudīpa takes its name." He offered it to Uruvelakassapa, saying that it had "superb colour, superb aroma, superb flavour," but the ascetic declined, not feeling worthy of such a gift.[91]

On the island-continent of **Uttarakuru**, which is a kind of earthly paradise,[92] the great tree is the *Kapparukkha.* It is not possible to identify this with any known species.[93] The name indicates that it lasts for an entire kappa, a characteristic it shares with all the great trees. There are many *kapparukkhas* growing all over Uttarakuru, perhaps meant to be scions of the original great *Kapparukkha.* These trees provide the necessities of life to the inhabitants of that land; clothes, ornaments and food-stuffs hang down from the branches (AN-ṭ 9, 21). This has led many modern translations to refer to them as "wish-fulfilling trees." Devas too are said to take clothes from *kapparukkhas* (Sn 3: 11). The fabulously wealthy Jotika who married a maiden of Uttarakuru had one of these on the grounds of his estate, from which he made gifts of fine clothes to the people of the town (Dhp-a 26:33). In Buddhist countries offerings made to the *saṅgha* are sometimes hung on a small model of a *kapparukkha.*

The great trees of the other two continents are no more than names to us. That of **Aparagoyana** is the *Kadamba* tree, identified by the DPPN with the species *Nauclea cordifolia*, and that of **Pubbavideha** is the *Sirīsa* tree, identified with the *Acacia sirisa* (AN-a 1: 322).

---

89 The jambu tree has often been misidentified as the "rose apple tree," *Eugenia jambos* or *Syzygium jambos* in PED, etc. But Wujastyk (2004) has convincingly made the case for *Syzygium cumini* which, unlike the rose apple tree, is indigenous to India.

90 AN-a 4:6 for the fine quality of Jambu gold, MN-a 120 for its origin.

91 Vin Mv 1. The story as related in GGB p. 411 includes a statement that the Jambu tree is located "at the tip of" Jambudīpa. I have been unable to trace this statement in the original sources.

92 But a qualified one, see § 3:1,3.

93 DPPN says it is "sometimes a fig". The *Kalpavṛkṣa (*the Sanskrit form of the name*)* is known in Vedic lore as the wish-fulfilling tree raised up by Vishnu at the churning of the ocean. See *Britannica Library*, s.v. "Churning of the ocean of milk," http://library.eb.com/levels/referencecenter/article/82582, accessed January 9, 2017.

The great tree of **Tāvatiṃsa**, the realm of the devas situated at the summit of Mt Sineru, is the *Pāricchattaka*. This tree is identified with the earthly species called in Pali *koviḷāra* which according to the DPPN is the *Bauhinia variegata*. This tree is remarkable for its lovely orchid like flowers, and indeed the flowers of the Pāricchattaka tree seem to be its most important feature. The origin of this tree is explained as being due to the powerful kamma of a man called Magha. In very ancient times he, together with his thirty-two companions, did meritorious deeds on earth. Because of these deeds, they were reborn as Sakka and the other devas of the Thirty-three. One of Magha's righteous acts was the planting of a *koviḷāra* tree and the placing of a stone slab underneath it. By the power of this kamma, the one hundred *yojana* high Pāricchattaka Tree appeared in Tāvatiṃsa, together with Sakka's throne, the *paṇḍukambalasilā*, a huge stone slab described as being under the shade of the great tree.[94]

The Pāricchattaka Tree blossoms once a year, however we can infer that by this is meant a celestial year or one hundred earthly years.[95] The various stages of the budding flowers is eagerly watched by the devas and each new development is an occasion for rejoicing (AN 7: 69). The arrival of the fully blown flowers marks the beginning of a festival. The flowers are very beautiful, as radiant as the newly risen sun and they are visible for fifty *yojana* away. Their heavenly scent carries one hundred *yojana*.

The flowers do not have to be cut, winds arrive which sever the stalks of the flowers and blow them toward the Sudhamma Hall, the assembly place of the devas. Other winds sweep away the old dried flowers and strew the fresh blossoms around the seating places.[96] The pollen from the flowers covers the bodies of the devas with a golden powder so that it is as if they were painted with lacquer. For four months the devas play in this blossom festival, striking one another with the flowers (AN-a 7, 69 & DN-a 19).

As stated above, the devas do not have to labour to harvest the flowers of the tree, but sometimes they climb into the tree and pluck them for fun, making garlands of them. A story is told of a named deva Subrahmā who went with one thousand *accharās* ("nymphs", a class of minor female devas) to the Pāricchattaka Tree. Five hundred of the *accharās* climbed into the tree to make garlands, having first used the power of their minds to make the tree's branches bow down to receive them. In the denouement of this episode, all of these female devas die and are reborn in *niraya* causing Subrahmā in his distress to seek out the Buddha (SN-a 2:17).

The blossoms of the Pāricchattaka Tree are important emblems of Tāvatiṃsa. In one story Sakka gives one to an earthly woman whom he had transported to Tāvatiṃsa, to serve as a sign that she had really been there (Jāt 531). In another story, the hermit Nārada, who could travel to Tāvatiṃsa by psychic power, was resting by Lake Anotatta using a Pāricchattaka blossom as a parasol when he was accosted by three *devīs* (female devas), the daughters of Sakka, who had come there to bathe. They said it was not appropriate for any human or *dānava* (in this context, meaning an asura) to possess these "noble immortal" (*amaravara*) flowers, which were only suitable for devas (Jāt 535). Of course, the flowers are not really immortal; this may be taken as a poetic trope. The fact that Nārada was able to use one as a sun-shade demonstrates that the Pāricchattaka flowers are very huge in human terms.[97]

The Pāricchattaka festival described above is one of the four occasions upon which the devas assemble. One of the others is to mark the end of the earthly rains retreat of the Buddha's *saṅgha*. At that time, the devas travel to the human realm and "with Pāricchattaka blossoms and divine sandalwood in hand" invisibly attend the *Pavāraṇā* ceremonies which mark the end of the rains. Sakka goes to the Piyangudīpa Mahāvihāra on a small island off the Sri Lankan coast, and the rest disperse to various other *vihāras* around the Buddhist world (DN-a 19).

The beauty and glory of the Pāricchattaka Tree in full blossom is such that it is used as a metaphor for the glory of

94 Dhp 2:7—for more on Magha and Sakka see § 3:5,16.

95 For celestial years in Tāvatiṃsa see AN 3:71, (eng. 3:70).

96 The winds are named in the Pali as the "cutting wind", the "sweeping wind", the "spreading wind" etc.

97 But so are the devas, see § 3:5,9.

the halo around the Buddha's head (MN-a 11). When the Buddha entered *parinibbāna* (i.e. died) the devas showered down Pāricchattaka blossoms onto his lifeless body.[98]

In the **asura** realm, the great tree is the *Cittapāṭalī* (SN 48:69). We shall examine the asura realm in detail later (§ 3:3,23), but for now it must suffice to say that their realm is in many ways a kind of distorted reflection of the Tāvatiṃsa deva realm, and that the asuras having been cast down the slopes of Sineru in primordial time have been forever after making war upon the devas to attempt and regain their lost kingdom. The Cittapāṭalī Tree must resemble the Pāricchattaka Tree at least superficially because after the asuras had been cast down they did not at first realize that they weren't in Tāvatiṃsa anymore; it was only when the Cittapāṭalī Tree blossomed that they knew, "We are not in the deva world. In the deva world, there are Pāricchattaka flowers. Old Sakka has made us drunk and cast us down into the great ocean."[99]

The Pāricchattaka and the Cittapāṭalī Trees always blossom at the same time but have recognizably different blossoms (Dhp-a 2:7). Whenever their tree goes into flower, the asuras are reminded of their great loss, become enraged and swarm up the slopes of Sineru to make war upon the devas (AN-a 9,39). The DPPN says that the Cittapāṭalī Tree is "the (pied) trumpet-flower,"[100] and most translators have followed suit. Following this translation, the most likely species would be a heavenly multi-coloured counterpart of the mundane trumpet flower tree, the *Stereospermum chelonoides*, a tree native to India.[101]

The ***supaṇṇas*** are gigantic birds which live half-way up the slopes of Sineru in a grove of *simbali* trees.[102] These trees are identified by DPPN as being *Bombax ceiba,* "silk-cotton" or "kapok" trees.[103] Their great tree is also of this kind (AN-a 1: 322).

Trees have a very important place in the Buddhist literature. The Buddha was born under a Sal tree (*Shorea robusta*), attained full awakening under a Bodhi tree (*Ficus religiosa*) and passed away under a pair of Sal trees.[104] The Bodhi tree, or a leaf taken from it, was declared by the Buddha to be a suitable object for homage (Jāt-a 479). It is not surprising that these seven important places, the four island-continents and the three realms associated with Mt Sineru, should each be graced with a huge central tree which lasts for an entire age of the world and serves as the characteristic emblem of that place.

[98] DN-a16. The sutta says these were *mandārava* blossoms, which the commentary equates with the Pāricchattaka flowers.

[99] Jāt 31. See also SN-a 11:1, Dhp 2:7 and MN-a 37.

[100] DPPN s.v. "citta 1".

[101] Dhammika 2018:127,

[102] The *supaṇṇas* are described in § 3:2,5.

[103] Dhammika 2018:185,

[104] See GGB.

1:15 CELESTIAL REALMS

The Tāvatiṃsa realm is the highest *sagga* (deva realm or "heaven") which is still in physical contact with the earth, being situated on the summit of Mt Sineru. There are four additional *saggas* which are located in the space above in "aerial abodes" (AK 3:5, p. 465). These are, in order from the lowest to the highest; the realms of *Yāma*, *Tusita*, *Nimmānarati* and *Paranimmitavasavatti*. These realms, although not located on the "earth" are considered an integral part of the *cakkavāḷa*. The Pali sources are silent about the actual distances of the various *saggas* above Sineru, but there is a scheme outlined in the *Abhidharmakośa* in which each succeeding *sagga* is twice as high above "sea-level" as the preceding one. Thus, as Mt Sineru is 80,000 *yojana* high according to the same source, the *sagga* of the Yāma devas is another 80,000 *yojana* above the mountain's summit, or 160,000 *yojana* above "sea-level". Going upward, Tusita is 320.000 *yojana* high, Nimmānarati 640,000 and the Paranimmitavasavatti *sagga* is 1,280,000 *yojana* above the ground (AK 3:5, p. 467).

The realm of the first level of brahmā beings is also included in the *cakkavāḷa*.[105] The *Abhidharmakośa* continues the doubling scheme through the sixteen realms of the brahmās (AK 3:5, p. 467). There is a problem with this in that some of these levels ought to be considered as inhabiting the same cosmological space.[106] In any case, we are here concerned only with the first level brahmās which are part of a single *cakkavāḷa* according to the *Visuddhimagga* scheme. The *Abhidharmakośa* places the three grades of these in three separate levels which would then be 2,560,000, 5,120,000, and 10,240,000 *yojana* above sea-level respectively. There is a Pali source which gives us the height above ground for the first level brahmās (which should be taken as including all three grades). This text states that if a heavy stone is dropped from this realm and if it travels downward at 48,000 *yojana* per day, then it would strike the earth in four months' time. This works out to 5,760,000 *yojana*.[107]

If we accept the length of the *yojana* as being approximately twelve kilometres, then we can make a comparison of the ancient Buddhist *cakkavāḷa* to the modern scientific model of the solar system. The average distance of the moon to the earth is about 384,400 km or 32,000 *yojana* and the distance from the orbit of the earth to the orbit of Mars, the next planet out, is roughly 75,000,000 km or 6,250,000 *yojana*. Thus, the *cakkavāḷa* is very large in comparison to the earth-moon system but small relative to the entire solar system.

These various realms located in space above the earth can all be considered as increasingly subtle and refined versions of Tāvatiṃsa. There is much less to be found about them in the Pali sources by way of detailed description, compared to the abundant information about Tāvatiṃsa. We are, however, told that each *sagga* has its own Nandana Grove.[108] The *Abhidharmakośa* states that they are all ten thousand *yojana* in size (AK 3:5. p. 468). These details would strongly support the concept of these worlds as being variations on a single theme. Tāvatiṃsa translated onto increasingly elevated planes of being. We shall return to this theme when we discuss the various deva realms in Part Three (§ 3:5,24).

---

[105] At least according to the *Visuddhimagga* passage under consideration. Below we will see that elsewhere the first level of Brahmā is described as encompassing and above many thousands of cakkavāḷas. For details of the brahmā beings, see § 3:6.

[106] See discussion in § 3:6,4.

[107] SN-a 6:3. Obviously this is based on an ancient and obsolete understanding of physics and does not take gravitational acceleration into account.

[108] Jāt-nid. For Nandana Grove, see the chapter on Tāvatiṃsa; § 3:5,10.

1:16 THE STARS AND PLANETS

In the West, beginning with the ancient Greeks and continuing through the Hellenistic and medieval periods right down to modern times, cosmological speculation has been informed by a desire to explain the apparent movement of the sun, moon, stars and planets. By contrast, for the cosmology found in the Pali sources the heavenly bodies are at most a very minor theme.[109] The primary concern of the Buddhist cosmological system is to describe the physical matrix of *saṃsāra* and to find a place for all the various classes of beings in their different planes and with their different modes of consciousness, rather than an attempt to explain the observable physical universe.

The only detailed description of the movements of the celestial bodies found in the Pali texts is from the commentary to the Aggañña Sutta (DN-a 27). This text describes the origin of this world-system and its inhabitants.[110] At the beginning this earth was just one mass of water covered in darkness and the sun and moon were not yet manifest (*na paññāyanti*). The first beings to arrive here descended from the Ābhassara Brahmā world (the level of the second jhāna brahmās) (§ 3:6,13) and being self-luminous had no need of sun or moon. However, after savoury foam appeared on the surface of the sea and some of these beings tasted it out of curiosity, they took on a coarser material form, fell to earth and, losing their radiance, began the long devolution into human beings as we know them today. It was at this point in the story that the sun, moon and stars appear. The commentary describes the process thus:[111]

> Taking the foam piece by piece they ate of it. Then the sun and moon manifested (*pātubhaviṃsu*).
>
> Which manifested first? Who lives there? How big are they? Which goes above? Which goes swiftly? On how many tracks do they travel? On how many places do they shine?
>
> Both (sun and moon) manifested together but the sun was perceived first. When the self-radiance (*sayampabhāya*) of the beings disappeared, there was darkness and they became afraid. They thought, "Oh, it would be good (*bhaddakaṃ vatassa*) if a light were to manifest!" Then the circle of the sun appeared giving the people courage (*sūrabhāvaṃ*). Thus it was called *suriyā* ("the sun", *sūra* means "courage") Thus by day there was light, but at night there was still darkness. So they thought, "Oh! It would be good if another light appeared!" Having expressed this wish, the circle of the moon arose. Thus it is called *canda* ("the moon", *canda* means "a wish")
>
> The interior of the moon is a jewelled palace (*vimāna*). On the outside it is covered with silver. Both inside and outside are cool. The interior of the sun is a golden palace; the outside is covered with crystal. Both inside and outside are hot.
>
> The moon is 49 *yojana* across and 147 *yojana* around. The sun is 50 *yojana* across and 150 *yojana* around.[112] The moon is below, the sun is above. Just so they are arranged. The sun is above the moon by 100 *yojana*.
>
> The moon goes up slowly and moves across swiftly. It travels among the constellations. The moon approaches the constellations as a cow approaches her calf, the constellations themselves however do not move from their place. The sun goes up swiftly and moves across slowly.

---

109 See Kloetzli 1983: 18.

110 We will consider this more fully in the section on Cosmic Time, § 2:4-5.

111 The following details are all from DN-a 27 unless noted otherwise.

112 As in the dimensions for the *cakkavāḷa*, we see once again that the Pali commentaries were naive about the value of pi.

There follows a rather difficult passage describing the motions of the sun and moon. Consider that any astronomical system, be it geocentric, heliocentric or in this case Sineru-centric, must account for both the annual and the diurnal apparent movements of the sun, the monthly and daily motions of the moon as well as its phases and also the changing of climate through the seasons of the year. In the ancient Buddhist system, the alternation of day and night is explained by the sun orbiting around Mt Sineru. At any time, three island-continents receive some sunlight. For example:

> How? When it is midday here (on Jambudīpa) the sun is setting over Pubbavideha, (it is rising over Aparagoyāna) and it is the middle of the night in Uttarakuru.

Beside this daily rhythm, there is an annual spiralling in and out. In the month of Āsāḷha, corresponding to the Gregorian June-July, the sun and moon orbit close in the vicinity of Mt Sineru. Thereafter their orbits gradually expand until in the month of *Phussa*, December-January, they are orbiting close to the *cakkavāḷa* wall. Then the orbits gradually draw inwards again.

The Indian year, like the Thai, is divided into three seasons: the hot season, the rainy season and the cool season. In the Buddhist astronomical system these are associated with the division of the sun's annual spiral orbit into three "paths" (*vīthi*); the path of the goat, the path of the elephant and the path of the ox.

> Goats do not like water, elephants are pleased by it and oxen like a pleasant balance of heat and cold. Therefore, at the time when the sun and moon travel the path of the goat not one drop of rain falls. When they go by the elephant path, then the clouds trickle as if broken. And when they travel along the ox path, then we enjoy an even balance of heat and cold.

The sub-commentary adds that the altitude of the sun and moon also varies as they travel these paths, which accounts for the change in temperature on the earth. When they are on the goat path, in the hot season (roughly corresponding to the northern hemisphere summer) the sun is lower and closer to the earth. In the rainy season (roughly the northern autumn) as they travel the elephant path they are at their highest point and in the "cool" season they are somewhere in the middle. The changing temperatures affect the mood of the sky devas who make rain. When the weather is too hot, they do not feel like leaving their *vimānas* (dwellings) to come out and play, so no rain is made. In the rainy season, they rejoice in the cool weather, (always considered a good thing in northern India) and make sport by producing rain. In the "cool" season they come out to play occasionally, as the mood suits them (DN-ṭ 27).

The phases of the moon are explained in a way that is not too different from the modern scientific explanation. As the sun orbits around Sineru at less velocity than the moon, the angle between them is constantly changing. The light of the sun being so much greater than that of the moon, it causes the moon to cast a shadow which obscures part of its face. Since the sun is also at a higher elevation, once a month it is directly over the moon and the shadow obscures the entire disk. Two weeks later, the two bodies are at their maximum separation, with the sun directly opposite the moon and casting no shadow, "Just as a house at noon casts no shadow."[113]

The markings on the face of the moon are explained in the Sasa Jātaka. The Bodhisatta had been born as a hare and had made a vow to give alms to any beggar who came his way. Sakka, king of the Tāvatiṃsa devas, came to earth in the form of a brahmin ascetic to test the little hare's resolve. When the hare found he had nothing to give he decided to throw himself into the brahmin's camp fire to give him a meal of roast hare:

> The hare thought, "If there are insects in my fur, they will die." So he shook himself three times to cast them off, then like a royal swan descending into a lotus pond he leapt into the flames. But the fire did not even warm the pores of his skin; it was just like jumping into a pile of snow. "Brahmin, this fire of yours is unable

[113] DN-a 27. This simile would only be literally true in the tropics.

even to warm me. How is this?" "Wise hare (*sasapaṇḍita*), I am not a brahmin. I am Sakka and I have come here to test you." "Sakka, if not only you but all those living in this world came to test my generosity, they would never see me unwilling to give." Thus the hare made his lion's roar.

At that, Sakka said, "Wise hare, your quality (*guṇa*) shall be known for an entire kappa." So saying, he crushed a mountain and using its essence (*rasa*) drew an image of a hare on the circle of the moon.[114]

As for the shapes of the sun and moon, whether they are flat disks or spheres, or something in between, we are given no definite information. They must have some depth, though, because they are the abodes of many devas (SN-a 2:10). The motive power which carries the sun and moon along is said to be a "circle of wind" (*vātamaṇḍala*) (DN-ṭ 27). Elsewhere, it is said to the power of kamma of those beings born as devas in the sun and moon (SN-ṭ 2:10). The two explanations are not incompatible and the *Abhidharmakośa* indeed states explicitly that the kamma of those beings generates the wind (AK 3:5. p. 460). Eclipses are caused by the gigantic asura Rāhu seizing the sun or moon in his hand (partial eclipse) or in his mouth (total eclipse). We will consider Rāhu and his actions more fully in the chapter on asuras.[115]

Of the other planets and their motions, we hear next to nothing. Mars (*aṅgāraka*) is mentioned in the context of eclipses; it is said that Rāhu can seize not only the sun or moon but also "Mars and so forth among the constellations" (DN-a 1). This is a significant commentarial gloss because it recognizes Mars as being something other than an ordinary star. The passage in the text refers to predicting eclipses of the constellations as being one among a long list of things a good bhikkhu will not practice for gain.[116] It seems that the commentators were aware that there can be no eclipse of constellations, and therefore substituted "Mars and so forth."[117]

Venus is called *osadhitāraka* ("the healing star"). The PED expresses doubt about this identification but there is good reason to accept it. The *osadhitāraka* is often mentioned in similes expressing brightness and the language used is "just as the *osadhitāraka* shines in the early morning" (E.g. SN 2:29). Venus, of course, always appears in the sky in the late evening or early morning. Furthermore, in a graded list of things which are bright, the *osadhitāraka* is cited just before the moon (MN 79) and Venus is the brightest object in the sky after the sun and moon. Venus, or *osadhitāraka*, is associated not only with brightness but also with purity of colour, as an example of pristine whiteness (MN 77). Venus is called "the healing star" either because herbalists gather their herbs (*osadhi*) under its light, (MN-a 79) or because the rays of that planet have in themselves a healing quality (It-a 1:3,7). Venus is also a symbol of constancy, because it never abandons its own path to wander on another.[118]

There is no discussion of the nature of the fixed stars in the Pali texts. The *Abhidharmakośa* says that the "houses of the stars" are inhabited, like the sun and the moon, by deities of the Cātumahārājika class (AK 3:5. p 462). In the Pali sources, the stars are mostly mentioned in the context of the calendar. Ancient India used a complex lunar-solar calendar which divided the solar year into twelve months depending on which constellation (*nakkhatta*) the sun was presently moving through. Being prominent star groups cited along the ecliptic, they inevitably agree more or less with the western signs of the zodiac. The lunar month was divided into twenty-seven or twenty-eight "lunar mansions" cited along the same ecliptic. The Buddhists shared this same calendric system, as is evidenced for example by the naming of the months in the Buddha's biography (E.g. DN-a 14).

The study of the stars for the purposes of astrological prediction is recognized in the Pali texts but is generally

---

114 Jāt 316. The image of a hare in the moon may not be obvious to those living in northern latitudes, but closer to the tropics the moon is seen at different angle and the markings do indeed resemble a long-eared hare.

115 SN 2:10. For asuras see § 3:3,23.

116 DN 1, in the section on virtue.

117 Strictly speaking, planets cannot be eclipsed either.

118 Bv-a 2. See also DPPN s.v. "*osadhī*".

frowned upon, being listed as one of the modes of wrong livelihood forbidden to bhikkhus.(DN 1). There are several references to astrology in the Jātakas.

Once upon a time, when Brahmadatta was king in Bārāṇasi, the Bodhisatta was born into a banker's family, and upon coming of age was made the treasurer and was called Cūḷaseṭṭhi ("Little Banker"). He was wise, and skilled in knowledge of all the signs. One day, while he was on his way to attend on the king, he saw a dead mouse lying in the street. Calculating the position of the constellations at that very instant, he said aloud, "If a young man with vision (*cakkhumant,* lit. "endowed with eyes") were to pick up this mouse, he could make a living and support a family." A man from a poor family overheard this and thought, "This fellow knows what he is speaking about." He picked up the mouse and sold it in the market as food for a cat, getting a single *kākaṇikā* (a coin of very low value) for it. (Jāt 4)

The remainder of the story goes on to describe how he turned this trifling coin into a large fortune by one shrewd trade after another. Another story describes a dishonest ascetic using vain astrological predictions for his own petty ends. In the denouement, a wise man recites a verse ridiculing dependence on the stars:

Studying the constellations,

the fool misses his opportunity (*attha*).

Opportunity is opportunity's own constellation.

What can the stars do?[119]

Taken all together, the astronomical system embedded in the Buddhist cosmology appears remarkably rudimentary, and even naive. It seems to us, with the benefit of many centuries of hindsight, that it would have been a simple matter to refute a Sineru-centric system by observations of the diurnal and annual movements of the sun and other bodies. This is especially odd because Indian culture as a whole was not backward in development of astronomical science. A little after the time when the commentaries were written, Aryabhata published an astronomical treatise featuring a geocentric model with a rotating spherical earth.[120] Nevertheless, the Sineru-centric model long retained its predominance in Buddhist thought. The fifteenth century Thai work, *The Three Worlds According to King Ruang*[121] retains the same system, with only small modifications to the solar movements. Indeed, the world-system with Sineru at the centre and the sun and moon rotating around it remained the preferred model of all Buddhists well into modern times.[122]

It seems clear, therefore, that explanation of observable natural cycles was not a priority for the Buddhist cosmological system. What is its purpose then? In modern discourse there is a tendency to explain the whole structure away as being no more than an externalized model of internal psychological states. But this does not fit the case very well either. We have seen again and again how much the great mass of Sineru dominates the model of the *cakkavāḷa*. Not only in its enormous size but in its central location around which everything else is arrayed. What internal human psychological component comes close to a parallel for Sineru? The psychological explanation is informed more by modern individualist bias than by ancient thought.

Whereas the Buddhist model of the *cakkavāḷa* falls short as an explanation of natural and psychological phenomena,

119 Jāt 49. *Attha* is a broad concept and could also be taken to mean "profit, interest, significance etc." See PED.

120 *Britannica Library*, s.v. "Aryabhata," http://library.eb.com/levels/referencecenter/article/9749, accessed January 4, 2017.

121 Translated by Reynolds and Reynolds, 1982.

122 See Lopez, 2010. chap.1.

it does provide a wonderful conceptual framework for the central idea of *saṃsāra* as the conditioned realm from which we ought to be seeking an escape. By presenting a model of reality which incorporates very large dimensions in both space and time, it confronts us with the insignificance of our own separate existence. Far from prioritizing narrowly personal psychological concerns, all the drama of human history is put in perspective by being played out on one half of one small island-continent, vastly overshadowed by the much more titanic drama of the deva-asura wars being fought on the slopes of Mt Sineru. But even these struggles are seen as remote trivialities by the inhabitants of the higher celestial realms. The dilemma of *saṃsāra* is far greater than just our personal neurosis.

It cannot be forgotten, though, that there is another important place in the cosmos besides Mt Sineru. Whereas Sineru represents the great weight and power of conditioned existence, there is one spot, and one only from which the possibility of transcending the whole fascinating and terrifying construction can arise; the *Bodhimaṇḍa*, the one small sacred spot in Jambudīpa upon which all the Buddhas achieve supreme awakening.

1:17 MULTIPLE WORLD-SYSTEMS

When the Buddha was asked whether the world (*loka,* here meaning "the universe") was infinite (*ananta* lit. "boundless") or finite (*antavant,* lit. "bounded") he refused to answer, saying that whether the world is infinite or not, there is still suffering to be overcome and this kind of question is not beneficial for realizing nibbāna. As if this was not emphatic enough, he went on to say that if one holds a view as to the infinitude or otherwise of the world, then the holy life cannot be lived (MN 63). Despite this very clear declaration of the Buddha, the commentaries were not hesitant to declare that the number of world-systems is infinite (*anantāni cakkavāḷāni*).[123] "Four things can be understood as infinite: space, the *cakkavāḷas*, beings and the knowledge of a Buddha" (Dhs-a 1). This became the prevalent view of the Buddhist tradition as a whole.

Everything we have discussed so far is contained within a single *cakkavāḷa*; a central Mt Sineru, surrounding ranges of ring mountains and seas, four continents, the sun and the moon, the wheel of fixed stars, and the bounding wall. This may be considered the basic unit of the universe, a single world-system. The *cakkavāḷas* however are infinite in number and extend in all directions along a plane. They are closely spaced, with the outer walls touching each other, "like three cart-wheels". The rows of worlds are staggered, so that three world-systems adjoin one other and enclose a roughly triangular space 8000 *yojana* across. These spaces are perpetually dark and cold as the rays of the suns cannot reach them; they form the abodes known as *lokantarika niraya,* the "inter-world hells" which are populated by suffering beings (DN-a 14). All these multiple worlds rest on the "world-supporting waters" (*lokasandhārakaudaka*), an infinite ocean of caustic liquid (ibid.) which is 480,000 *yojana* deep. This ocean in turn rests on a layer of "wind" (*māluta*) 960,000 *yojana* in depth (Vism 7. 41).

The innumerable worlds, stretching out across the universal plane, are organized into structures or clusters. These need to be considered from both a horizontal and, when the brahmā realms are included, a vertical perspective. A complete and coherent model for the horizontal groupings is only found in the commentaries and the *Visuddhimagga.* In this scheme, the groups are called "Buddha fields" (*buddhakhetta*), and there are three hierarchical levels of them.

A "field of birth" (*jātikhetta*), consists of 10,000 *cakkavāḷas*. The *Aṅgutttara Nikāya* states that it is impossible for two Buddhas to arise simultaneously in one world-system (*eka lokadhātu*). The commentary to this passage specifies that a "world-system" in this instance is meant to refer to a field of birth of 10,000 worlds (AN-a 1: 277 & MN-a 115). It is impossible that a Buddha could arise anywhere within these ten thousand worlds other than in the "middle country" (*majjhimadesa* i.e. Northern India) of this specific world-system in which we reside (DN-a 19). The entire field of birth trembles when a *Tathāgata* descends into his mother's womb, when he is born, when he attains to Buddhahood, when he turns the Wheel of the Dhamma, when he abandons the life principle and when he enters *parinibbāna* (i.e. dies) (DN-a 28). While the fully developed concept of Buddha fields is found only in the commentary, we can find the germ of the idea in the canon, as for instance in the passage from the *Saṃyutta* describing the Buddha's first sermon, "the turning of the wheel", when it states that ten thousand worlds (*dasasahassilokadhātu*) trembled and quaked (SN 56:11). The commentaries reference this unit of ten thousand worlds often, as for example when the devas of ten thousand world-systems assembled to watch the Buddha tame the yakkha Āḷavaka (SN-a 10:12). In the text of the *Mahāsamaya Sutta* it is stated that devas from ten world-systems (*lokadhātu*) assembled to see the Buddha, but the commentary to the text amends the number to 10,000 world-systems (*cakkavāḷa*) (DN-a 20).

The next level of organization is a "field of authority" (āṇākhetta). This consists of one trillion *cakkavāḷas* or 100,000,000 Fields of Birth.[124] This is the sphere over which the Buddha's authority extends, as manifested in the power of invoking his protection by chanting *parittas* (protective verses), which are said to provide release from fear

---

123 AN-a 3: 81. See also MN-a 26 and Sn-a 3:7.

124 DN-a 28, which gives the number as 100,000 *ko ṭis* of worlds. See appendix on units for definition of a *koti* as 10,000,000.

of yakkhas and bandits (DN-a 28, MN-a 115, SN-a 11:3). According to the sub-commentary, the trillion worlds of a field of authority expand and contract together.[125]

The highest level is the "field of scope" (*visayakhetta*). This is boundless, encompassing the entire universe. It represents the sphere within which the Buddha can apply his knowledge, because "whatever the *Tathāgata* wishes to know, that he does know" (DN-a 28, & Vism 13:31).

The *Aṅguttara Commentary* adds a note to the effect that there are never two Buddhas existing anywhere in the universe at the same time and argues from the absence in the canon of a single mention of Buddhas in another world-system. This is an odd and extreme position to take, and seems to obviate the need for a special "field of birth" altogether. In a note, Bhikkhu Bodhi speculates that this statement may have been inserted to counter Mahāyāna doctrines which multiplied the number of Buddhas to infinity.[126] The Theravāda by contrast has always emphasized the great rarity of Buddhahood, and in this passage Buddhaghosa takes that principle to its greatest possible conclusion.

The definition of a field of authority in terms of *paritta* chanting seems insufficient. If we take into account references to another term indicating one billion worlds, a *tisahassimahāsahassilokadhātu* ("thrice a thousand world's great thousand-fold world system", i.e. 1,000 cubed), we can gain a little more understanding. Although the numbers do not agree, these do seem to be parallel concepts. The *tisahassimahāsahassilokadhātu* is cited as the extent over which the Buddha can, if he wishes extend his radiance and the sound of his voice (DN-a 19). This vast range of the Buddha's authority is illustrated by comparisons. If Mt Sineru was the wick of an oil lamp and the great ocean was filled with oil, its radiance would extend only over a single *cakkavāḷa*, but the Buddha's radiance can extend over a full *tisahassimahāsahassilokadhātu*. Likewise, if the whole *cakkavāḷa* were a drum with a skin extended to the outer walls and Mt Sineru was used as the striker, its sound would be heard only within one *cakkavāḷa*, but the Buddha can make the sound of his voice heard over the whole of a *tisahassimahāsahassilokadhātu*. This latter is first done by pervading the billion worlds with his radiance, and when beings advert to that, they are able to hear his voice (AN-a 3: 81).

Pali numbers can be ambiguous and it is possible to read *tisahassimahāsahassilokadhātu* as meaning three times a thousand. Buddhaghosa, the editor of the commentaries, was well aware of this problem and makes it clear that the number is to be read as 1.000 to the third power. He goes so far as to cite an otherwise unknown elder, Gaṇakaputtatissa Thera.[127] This unit of a billion worlds, the "thrice a thousand world's great thousand-fold world system", became a significant one in later Buddhism, although the confusion persisted between three thousand and a thousand cubed of world-systems.[128]

The system of Buddha fields as presented here is only fully worked out in the *Visuddhimagga*. Another late text, the *Apadāna* of the *Khuddaka Nikāya*, has an entirely different conception of a *buddhakhetta*. There (Ap 1:1,1) it is described as a special and fantastic realm with all the gorgeous panoply of lapis-lazuli pillars, gardens, lotus ponds, banners and garlands which we always find in ancient Indian depictions of paradisiacal places. There, all the Buddhas of the past together with many thousands of paccekabuddhas and arahants meet and discuss Dhamma. This picture is, to the say the least, quite unorthodox by Theravāda standards[129] and actually seems a precursor of Mahāyāna ideas. The anonymous author of this long poem appears to have been aware of this and phrases the introductory passages in such a way as to make it clear that it is his own imagination he is describing; "There on a silvery ground, I built a palace, many storied, jewelled, raised high to the sky," and "All the Buddhas of the past, the leaders of the world, together with their Orders and disciples, I created in their natural beauty and appearance." The tone of this text is that of a devotional poem and cannot be read as a part of the orthodox cosmological system.[130]

125 MN-ṭ 115. For contraction and expansion of the universe see § 2:4 & 2:7.

126 AN-a 1: 277 and Bhikkhu Bodhi, NDB, note 155.

127 AN-a 3: 81. See also Bhikkhu Bodhi, NDB, note 514.

128 See Kloetzli 1983: 61 f.

129 Such awakened beings are thought to have entered nibbāna and are no longer manifest in any conceivable realm.

130 See Barua 1946. The quoted passages are Barua's translation.

1:18 VERTICAL GROUPINGS OF WORLDS

The picture is greatly complicated when we turn to the vertical structure of the cosmos and the relation of the lower worlds to those of the brahmā beings.

The terrestrial level of the *cakkavāḷa* includes two sensual deva realms, the Cātumahārājika realm half-way up Mt Sineru and the Tāvatiṃsa realm at its summit. Situated in the space above there are, as we have seen, four additional sensual deva realms associated with each *cakkavāḷa*. Far above these are the sixteen realms of the brahmā beings. We shall have much more to say about the brahmās and their various realms and levels in Part Three, Chapter Six. For our present purposes let it suffice to say that these realms can be simplified into four levels, each of which corresponds to the state of consciousness experienced in one of the four meditative states known as *jhānas*. The brahmā beings are beyond the sphere of sensuality (*kāmābhumi*), which includes humans and devas, and belong to a higher plane of being called the sphere of form (*rūpābhumi*).

Physically, various realms of the brahmā beings are located high above and quite separate from the *cakkavāḷas* below, with each successively higher level of brahmā world encompassing a larger range of multiple worlds below. The image is of a nested pyramidal hierarchy. This idea is clearly present in the suttas but the details of a coherent scheme are not found even in the commentaries, and are only implied in the *Visuddhimagga*.

Mahābrahmā, the ruler of the first level brahmās, is said in the *Mahāsamaya Sutta* (DN 20) to rule one thousand worlds. The commentary goes on to state that he can illuminate a thousand worlds with one finger, and ten thousand with all ten fingers. The intention of this commentarial note was likely intended to bring the range of his authority up to the unit of a ten-thousand fold world system, equivalent to a field of birth.

We also have a sutta passage which speaks of various levels of brahmā beings who "abide resolving upon and pervading" (*pharitvā adhimuccitvā viharati*) various multiples of a thousand worlds. There are brahmās who pervade one thousand worlds, two thousand worlds, three thousand, four thousand, five thousand, ten thousand and a hundred thousand worlds.[131] We have already cited the passage which mentions the *tisahassimahāsahassilokadhātu*, the "thrice a thousand great thousand-fold world-system." This is part of a tripartite scheme which begins with a "lesser thousand-fold world-system" (*cūḷanikā lokadhātu*) of one thousand worlds "each with its Mt Sineru, four continents … (up to a first level) brahmā world", one thousand of which are encompassed in a "middling thousand-fold world-system" (*majjhimikā lokadhātu*) which encompasses one thousand of the first level, or one million *cakkavāḷas*. One thousand of these make a *tisahassimahāsahassilokadhātu* (AN-a 3:81). These two models are not fully compatible either with each other or with that of the Buddha fields. Furthermore, there is an internal problem in the threefold scheme. This outline is given in reference to a story about a great disciple, Abhibhū, of a former Buddha, who once pervaded one thousand worlds with his voice while standing in the brahmā world. This would imply that the first level brahmā world encompasses or "pervades" one thousand *cakkavāḷas*. However, the same text lists the contents of the thousand worlds as each including its own brahmā realm.

Clearly no definitive system of nested multiple worlds related to the brahmā levels can be found in the suttas. The *Visuddhimagga* does systematize these levels, at least by implication. Reading the passage describing the destruction of the worlds at the end of a cycle[132] we find a scheme which associates the brahmā levels with the Buddha fields. The simplest way to decipher this scheme is as follows:

1. Each of the ten-thousand worlds of a field of birth includes its own first level brahmā realm.

[131] MN 120. Or should this be interpreted as 1000 to the 2nd power, 3rd power etc.? The Pali is *dvisahasso, tisahasso* etc . The commentary says there are five kinds of pervasion; pervasion by mind, by kasiṇa (mental image as used for meditation), with the divine eye, with light and with the body. MN-a 120.

[132] The cosmic cycles of creation and destruction will be discussed in § 2:4f.

2. The entire ten-thousand fold system lies under a single second jhāna level brahmā realm
3. One hundred thousand of these units, or one trillion worlds, lie under a single third jhāna level brahmā realm and constitutes a field of authority.
4. An infinite number of these lie under a single fourth jhāna level brahmā realm, which encompasses the field of scope, or in plain language, the entire universe (Vism 13:31).

FIGURE FIVE—*VISUDDHIMAGGA* MODEL OF MULTIPLE WORLDS

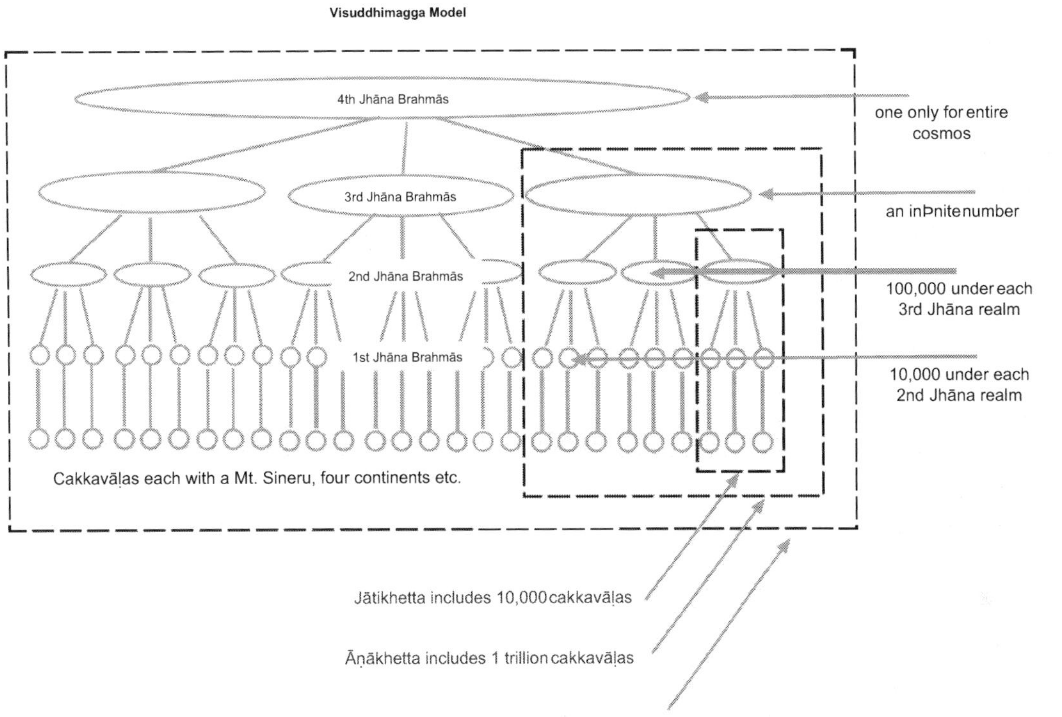

Showing the hierarchy of multiple worlds as they relate to the Buddha-Fields.

This map is admittedly conjectural, and the text may be interpreted in other ways, both in overall arrangement and in terms of numbers. We must move outside the Pali tradition and look to the *Abhidharmakośa* to find a fully explicated and coherent scheme of the multi-level nested cosmos, although here too there is some ambivalence between two alternate models. In the model which Vasubandhu prefers we have the following levels:

1. A *sāhasra cūḍika lokadhātu* ("small chiliocosm")[133] is a grouping of one thousand *cakkavāḷas* including a first jhāna level brahmā realm for each. There is one second jhāna level brahmā world extending over the whole thousand-fold system.
2. A *dvisāhasro madhyamo lokadhātuḥ* ("middle dichiliocosm") groups one thousand small chiliocosms, in other words it includes one million *cakkavāḷas* and one thousand second jhāna level brahmā realms. It includes one third jhāna level brahmā world extending over the whole.
3. A *trisāhasramahāsāhasro lokadhātuḥ* ("trichiliomegachiliocosm") groups one thousand middling chiliocosms. That is to say, it includes one trillion *cakkavāḷas*, one trillion first jhāna level brahmā realms (I.e. one cakkavāḷa for each 1st level brahmā realm), one billion second jhāna level brahmā realms and one

133 *Chiliocosm* is a term used by De La Vallée Poussin to refer to a "thousand-fold universe." He attributes its coining to Rémusat, see AK note 463 p. 538.

thousand third jhāna level brahmā realms. This trillion-fold world-system is surmounted by a single fourth jhāna level brahmā realm extending over the whole system.The universe as a whole contains an infinite number of such systems. (AK 3:5. p. 468 f).

Figure Six - Abhidharmakośa Preferred Model

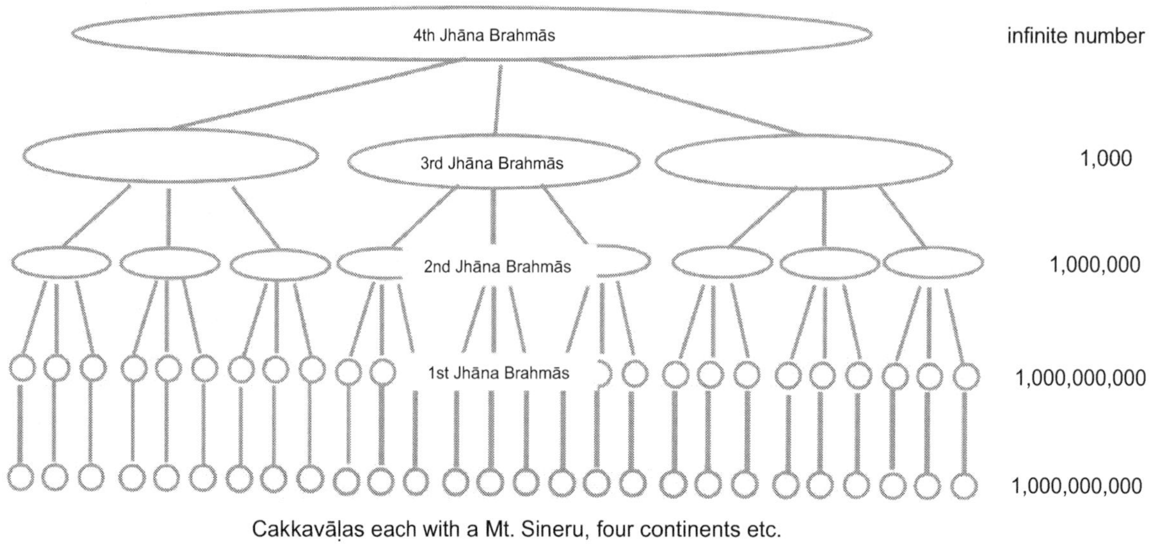

Abhidharmakoṣa Preferred Model of Multiple Worlds -
There are an infinite number of 4th level Brahmā realms.
Below each of these are 1000 3rd level Brahmā realms.
Below each of these are 1000 2nd level Brahmā realms.
Below each of these are 1000 1st level Brahmā realms.
Below each of these is one cakkavāḷa.

This scheme is assumed by Vasubandhu in his subsequent discussions. However, he does make mention of an alternate arrangement which he cites as "according to others", which implies that he takes it seriously enough to merit mentioning but that he does not endorse it. This is as follows:

1. One realm of first jhāna level brahmās extends over each thousand-fold world-system.
2. The realm of the second jhāna level brahmās extends over a middling system of one million worlds.
3. The realm of the third jhāna level brahmās extends over a great billion-fold world-system.
4. There is only one realm of fourth jhāna level brahmās which surmounts and extends over the infinity of space.

Figure Seven - Abhidharmakoša Alternate Model

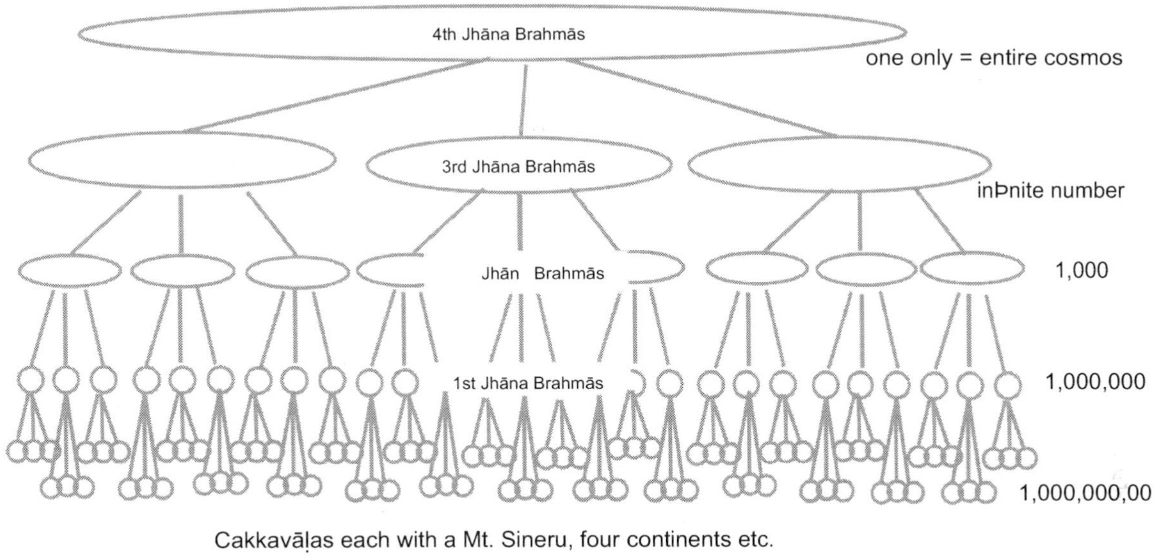

Abhidharmakoşa Alternate Model of Multiple Worlds -
There is only one 4th level Brahmā realm over the whole cosmos
Below this there are an infinite number of 3rd level Brahmā realms.
Below each of these are 1000 2nd level Brahmā realms.
Below each of these are 1000 1st level Brahmā realm.
Below each of these are one thousand cakkavāḷas.

It is neither necessary nor even possible to choose between these competing models of the cosmos. What they have in common is more important:

1. The universe is composed of an infinite number of worlds. At the "ground" level of the *cakkavāḷas* of the sense-desire sphere, these are essentially similar; centred on a Mt Sineru, having four island-continents which are the zone of human habitation and bounded by an outer wall. Above this are the sensual deva realms.
2. The higher realms of the *rūpabhūmi*, the realms of the brahmās, are organized hierarchically with each succeeding level presiding over some multiple (a thousand or ten thousand etc.) of the realms below (AK 3:5. p. 468).

The correspondence between this arrangement of realms and the mental states experienced in meditation is striking, and is perhaps the most important aspect of the whole cosmological scheme. The worlds of sense desire are the most complex and are multiplied endlessly, although all essentially the same. As we ascend through the realms and leave the world of sensuality behind, we find greater and greater simplicity approaching to unity at the top. This is most clearly expressed in the alternate *Abhidharmakośa* model which has just one realm of fourth jhāna for the entire universe. When we come to examine in detail the nature of the brahmā beings, this intriguing correspondence with meditative states will be explained further.

PART TWO - COSMIC TIME

2:1 NO BEGINNING

The Buddha said that a first beginning of *saṃsāra* cannot be discerned.[134] Strictly speaking, this is not a definite affirmation that the universe is beginningless. Indeed, whether the universe is eternal or not is one of the questions the Buddha categorically refused to answer. He discouraged such speculation on the grounds that it was useless for the project of awakening. Whether the world has a beginning or an end or both or neither has no effect on our situation in the here and now. The Buddha gave the simile of a man struck by a poisoned arrow who foolishly refused to have the arrow removed until all his questions about the arrow and the archer could be answered (MN 63).

This however, has done little to dissuade subsequent generations of Buddhists from thinking about the origins of the world. It is certainly the case that an assumption of a universe without a beginning is more in accord with the general principles of Buddhist philosophy than one which began at a single point in time. It is a cardinal idea of Buddhism that all phenomena are dependently arisen, that is to say, nothing arises without a prior cause. A singular moment of creation would be a very significant departure from this universal principle.[135] It is more logical to assume that for no matter how far back in time you go, there will always have been a prior moment.

The assumption of beginninglessness also harmonizes well with the general Indian tendency to see time as cyclical rather than linear, and this is also a central theme of the Buddhist view of cosmological time. It is important to bear in mind that when the texts speak about origins and endings, they are referring to a scope limited to a single world, or to speak more precisely, to a finite number of world-systems. There were worlds before this one and there will be others after it.

[134] SN 15:1. *anamataggoyaṃ, bhikkhave, saṃsāro.*

[135] To assume creation by divine fiat is not satisfactory either, because the divine creator must then be an uncaused entity.

2:2 THE KAPPA

The basic unit of cosmic time is a *kappa*. This word is somewhat variable in meaning[136] but is usually taken to mean a *mahākappa*, or great kappa, which is the time elapsed during an entire cycle of a world, from first origin to final dissolution. This is a very long time indeed, but the Buddha deliberately refrained from attempting to number it in terms of years. "It is not easy to reckon a kappa in terms of years, of hundreds of years, of thousands of years or of hundreds of thousands of years" (SN 15:5). Instead, the Buddha gave two similes to express the vastness of the time elapsed for a *mahākappa*.

> Suppose there were a great stone mountain, a *yojana* across, a *yojana* broad and a *yojana* high, without holes or fissures, one solid mass. And suppose that every hundred years a man would stroke it just once with a very fine piece of cloth. That rock would be worn away completely before the end of the kappa (ibid.).

> Suppose there were an iron-walled citadel, a *yojana* across, a *yojana* broad and with walls a *yojana* high. Suppose this citadel were filled with mustard seeds, very tightly packed. And suppose that a man were to come along every hundred years and remove just one mustard seed. That great heap of seeds would be exhausted before the end of the kappa.[137]

One reason that even the commentaries do not attempt to provide a number of years is that the concept of a year itself is problematic. A year is conventionally understood as the time elapsed for one full revolution of the sun around the ecliptic, but for part of the kappa, as we shall see, the "sun and moon are not evident." Also, the passage of time itself is different in the *saggas* (deva realms) with the "celestial year" varying according to the level.[138] These considerations would certainly make the length of a kappa "not easy to reckon in years."

In any case, the intention of the texts is to emphasize the extremely vast expanse of time involved in a kappa and the Buddha's purpose here is a practical one, related to the great project of liberation. He wanted to bring home to the listener the ultimate futility of *saṃsāric* existence:

> For so long have you endured suffering, pain and misery. For so long have you filled up the cemeteries. It is enough to be weary of all compounded things, to become dispassionate, to liberate oneself from them (SN 15:5).

---

136 For instance, in the commentary to the Mahāparinibbāna Sutta (DN-a 16) it is taken, in that context, to mean one full human life-span.

137 SN 15:6. Presumably it would be possible to calculate this to a fair degree of approximation.

138 This ranges from one day and night equal to one hundred human years in Tāvatiṃsa to sixteen hundred years in the Paranimmitavasavatti realm. A celestial year is 360 of such days. See § 5.

2:3 DIVISIONS OF A KAPPA

A *mahākappa* is divided into four phases, all of which are "not easy to reckon as so many years". These are therefore called the four *asaṅkheyya kappa* ("incalculable aeons"):[139]

kappa saṃvaṭṭa tiṭṭhati—the era in which it stands folded up, the empty universe between cycles.

kappa vivaṭṭati—the era, in which the universe unfolds, evolves or more literally "rolls out." The period during which a new universe comes into being.

kappa vivaṭṭa tiṭṭhati—the era, in which it stands unfolded. The evolving world as we know it, the period we are living in now.

kappa saṃvaṭṭati—the era, in which the universe folds in, devolves or more literally "rolls back." The great destruction at the end of a cycle.[140]

These represent an interminable cycle of new creation (albeit without a creator) followed by destruction and then a fresh creation; the whole process driven by natural law, principally the kamma of the beings inhabiting the worlds. The details of this great cosmic history are complex and often difficult to interpret. In what follows we will be relying principally on the Pali sources but cannot avoid frequent reference to the *Abhidharmakośa*, which has a very similar narrative but one in which those details which remain obscure or contradictory in the Pali sources are worked into a more coherent system. For example, the relative durations of the four *asaṅkheyya kappa*s are not specified in the Pali but the *Abhidharmakośa* informs us that they are of equal length (AK 3:6. p. 479). In should be noted that there are some potentially confusing differences in the terminology used by the Pali sources and the (Sanskrit) *Abhidharmakośa*. Unless otherwise noted, we will be using the Pali version of the terms, as found in the *Visuddhimagga*.

These cycles of creation and destruction affect many thousands of *cakkavāḷas* at once, and include some of the brahmā realms as well. We shall postpone the complex question of defining their precise limits until we have described the general picture of the cycles, but it should be borne in mind that in what follows we are not talking about a single *cakkavāḷa* only. The era in which a universe "remains folded up" (*vivaṭṭo tiṭṭhati*) is a long period during which that section of the cosmos is completely void. "The upper space and the lower space together are just one great darkness" (Vism 13: 42). "There is only space where the world once was" (AK 3:6. p. 477).

[139] There is the possibility of some confusion about the use of the various terms referring to divisions of time. See appendix on "Units of Measurement" for clarification.

[140] AN 4: 156. The list of the kappas there begins with *kappa saṃvaṭṭati*, the era of destruction. Note that the definitions of *saṃvatta* and *vivvaṭṭa* given in the PED are confusing and seem to be reversed.

TABLE THREE – DIVISIONS OF A KAPPA

DIVISIONS OF A MAHĀKAPPA				
Description	Aeon of world contraction; destruction by fire, water or air	Empty aeon	Aeon of world expansion; all the realms reformed and repopulated	Aeon of world existence; the aeon we are living in
Pali name from Vism	saṃvaṭṭati	saṃvaṭṭatiṭṭhati	vivaṭṭati	vivaṭṭa tiṭṭhati
Skt. name from AK	saṃvartakalpa	(not given)	vivartakalpa	(not named)
Sub-div. according to Abhidharmakośa	19 antarakappa to empty the world-system of beings, 1 for it to be destroyed	20 antarakappa of empty space	1 antarakappa to create the world 19 to fill it with beings (from higher Brahmā realms)	Human life-spans grow and shrink; 1 a.k. of shrinking from an "infinite" lifespanto 10 yrs. 18 a.k. of successive growth and shrinking from 10 yrs. to 80,000 and back again 1 a.k. of growth from 10yrs to 80,000

2:4 THE UNFOLDING KAPPA

The first thing to arise in the new cycle, at the outset of the *kappa vivaṭṭati*, is a great cloud which begins to rain upon the empty spaces of the former world-systems. At first the rain is gentle but it gradually builds up into a tremendous downpour which first dissolves all the "burnt places" (*daḍḍhaṭṭhāna*) of the previous worlds[141] and then gradually begins to fill up the empty space, until the water rises to the level of the brahmā world. It then begins to gradually subside and the various realms, empty as yet of living beings, appear one after the other from the top down. During this phase, the water is held in place by tremendous winds which blow all around the mass of water and underneath it, acting as a container (Vism 13: 42–43).

The *Abhidharmakośa* does not mention the great cloud, the rains or the mass of water, but attributes the creation of the new universe solely to a great wind which it explicitly states is caused by the past kamma of beings from the old universe (AK 3:6. p.477). The appearance of the abodes, including the palaces of the various orders of brahmā and deva, precedes the arrival of sentient beings. This is in accord with the general nature of these realms, where a *vimāna* (heavenly mansion) may appear in the deva world before the appearance there of its owner, made by the force of the kamma performed by a person while he is still alive in the human realm, and it stands there empty awaiting his rebirth.[142] The sentient beings of the old universe had all been reborn upwards into higher brahmā realms beyond the scope of destruction and they now begin to be reborn downwards into the new abodes, beginning again with the highest realms.[143] Human beings originate from beings being reborn from the Ābhassara or second jhāna level realm (Vism 13: 44 & DN 27).

The process by which these Ābhassara beings devolve into human beings as we know them now is explained in detail in the *Aggañña Sutta*.[144] These beings in their previous state in the brahmā realm were "mind-made, feeding on rapture, self-radiant, moving through the air and glorious."[145] These are standard epithets for beings in the brahmā worlds. "Feeding on rapture" (*pīti*) refers to the jhāna factor of joy which is a characteristic of second jhāna. Brahmā beings do not need to take any physical nourishment. As these beings lifespans came to an end and they passed away from the Ābhassara realm they were reborn into the vicinity of the earth. At first, and for "a very long time", they retained the characteristics of a brahma, as listed above, as well as being "spontaneously born" (*opapātikā*), meaning that when "born" they just flashed into existence fully formed; there being no gender distinctions and no sexual reproduction among brahmā beings. Although they were at this stage virtually indistinguishable from the Ābhassara beings they had been, the commentary makes clear that they should be classed as part of the human realm (*manussaloka*). This makes understandable what happens next.

At that time the earth was still submerged in the primordial water and was covered by great darkness, as the sun and moon were not yet manifest. The verb in the Pali is *paññāyati* which means "to be known, to be evident." This implies that the sun and moon were existent but not visible.[146] As the primordial water continued to subside, there formed on its surface a covering called *rasapathav*i ("tasty earth"). This is compared to the skin that forms on boiled milk as it cools down and is said to have been "endowed with colour, smell and taste." Its colour is compared to butter

---

141 There is somewhat of a contradiction here in that, as we shall see, the previous cycle of destruction is said to have left no residue, not even so much as an atom.

142 Dhp-a 16, 9. Perhaps not empty, as his retinue may also precede him.

143 See for example DN 1 which speaks of a mahābrahmā being born into an empty mansion at the beginning of a cycle.

144 DN 27. A detailed interpretation of this sutta relating it to modern science can be found in "Dhamma Aboard Evolution" by Dr. Suwanda Sugunasiri.

145 DN 27—*manomayā pītibhakkhā sayampabhā antalikkhacarā subhaṭṭhāyino.*

146 Sugunasiri's note 11.2 relates this to the state of the early earth according to modern science which was covered by a dense dark atmosphere.

or ghee, or to the golden flowers of the *Kanikāra* tree, the scent was like the subtle aromas found in the deva worlds and the taste as sweet as wild honey.[147] Some of the beings, those of a greedy nature (*lolajātika*)[148] wondered what this stuff could be and taking some of it up on the tip of their fingers, tasted it.

This was the critical moment in the primordial descent of these brahmā-like beings into devolved humans. It also makes clear that even before partaking of the nutritious essence, they could no longer be fully classed as brahmā beings. Brahmās are beyond the realm of sense-desire and in fact do not possess the senses of smell or taste.[149] Taking up some of the *rasapathavi* to taste is a complete departure from brahmā nature, and even their initial curiosity about it can be seen as an impulse more human than brahmic. The obvious symbolic interpretation of this passage is to see it as the entrapment of the elevated primordial mind into coarse materiality by the lure of sensuality. There is a striking parallel here to the account in Genesis where the fall of mankind is also through the agency of taste. Other readings are possible. Gombrich sees the entire *Aggañña* account as a satirical critique of brahmanical religion.[150] Sugunasiri finds another striking parallel for the descent of the Ābhassara beings with modern scientific theory. In this reading, the *rasapathavi* is the primordial soup of amino acids energized by photons from space; one somewhat creative breakdown of the word Ābhassara yields "hither-come-shining-arrow", which sounds like a poetic description of a high energy photon.[151]

Returning to our account, after the initial plunge into the sense realm of taste and smell was made, more and more of the beings began breaking off great chunks of the *rasapathavi* and eating them, thus further entangling themselves in the world of coarse sensuality. The result was that their bodies became coarser and their self-luminance disappeared. They were now plunged into darkness. It was at this point that the sun and moon appeared.[152] With the sun and moon, there began the reckoning of time by days, fortnights, months and years. This marks the end of the *kappa vivaṭṭati* and the beginning of the established world of the kappa *vivaṭṭa tiṭṭhati*. We might say that with the appearance of the heavenly bodies in their regular orbits, we have entered into ordinary historical time.

147 Some of these comparisons are taken from the commentary.
148 Lit. "born greedy". The commentary says they were those beings who had been of a greedy nature in the previous universe.
149 See § 3:6,2.
150 Gombrich, 2006: 86–87.
151 Sugunasiri, "Dhamma Aboard Evolution", p. 49.
152 We have already described this episode in § 1:16.

2:5 DEVOLUTION OF HUMANS

With the appearance of the sun and the moon the era of unfolding is finished and the universe stands completed as an abode of beings and as a theatre for the ongoing drama of *saṃsāra*. From here on the texts which deal with cosmological time focus on this human realm. The Aggañña Sutta (DN 27) is still the principal source for the next stages of human evolution, or more accurately, devolution.

At the outset of this unfolded aeon, the beings on earth are no longer quite so brahmā-like. They have fallen to earth and lost their radiance. But they are still glorious and long-lived relative to modern humans, and they are not yet divided into genders. As time goes on, beings lapse into greater and greater immorality and become coarser and shorter lived. There is a parallel evolution in their food source. The golden, sweetly delicious *rasapathavi* devolves in stages to the rice of today which requires hard labour to sow, harvest, thresh and cook.

The devolution process may be divided into seven stages and the process itself is represented by the types of nourishment available. At the beginning of a period of world expansion, beings descend from the Ābhassara Brahmā world, the earth is dark and unformed, and sun and moon "are not evident." The beings live in the air, "self-radiant, feeding on bliss."

At this point, the second stage occurs, and a nutritious foam, *rasapaṭhavī*, forms on the surface of the sea. Craving arises in the Brahmā beings and they take it up on the tips of their fingers to taste. They thereby enter the*kāmabhūmi* ("plane of sense-desire") and fall to earth.

As a result of the fall to earth, in the third stage, the beings' bodies coarsen; some become beautiful, some ugly. Arrogance and conceit arise in the beautiful and because of this, their source of food deteriorates, becoming *bhūmi-pappaṭaka* (a fungus?)

The exact meaning of *bhūmi-pappaṭaka* is problematic. Maurice Walshe translates it as "mushroom" and Rhys-Davids as "an outgrowth." Sugunasiri makes a suggestive comparison with the cognate Sinhala word *papaḍam* which refers to a thin and crunchy fried grain, sometimes called a "fritter" in English.[153]

The text tells us they were "like mushrooms" (*seyyathāpi nāma ahicchattako*) and the commentary says they grew in ponds of mud, which implies that the primordial waters were continuing to dry up. A literal translation ofthe passage describing the coarsening of the beings is as follows:

> As these beings continued to feed on the *rasapaṭhavī*, a coarseness descended into their bodies (*kharattañceva kāyasmiṃ okkami*), a discolouration (*vaṇṇavevaṇṇatā*) was perceived. Some beings were of a better colour (*vaṇṇavanto*) some beings of a bad colour. Then those beings with good colouring came to despise those with bad colouring, thinking "We are of a better colour, they are of a worse colour". Because of this pride of colour (*vaṇṇātimāna*) and this pride of birth (*mānātimānajātikā*) the *rasapaṭhavī* disappeared.

The phrasing of this passage lends some support to Gombrich's reading of the *Aggañña* as a critique of the brahmins' views on caste. The repeated use of the multivalent word *vaṇṇa* in various compounds is significant. I have translated it here as "colour" but it can also mean "complexion," "beauty" or even "caste." These ideas are all related in the ancient Indian context, because the caste system originated as a kind of apartheid imposed by the lighter skinned Aryans on the darker natives. The phrase "pride of birth" used near the end reinforces the idea that this passage represents a critique on the emergence of caste prejudice. Otherwise there would be no need for the phrase; after all, it makes little sense in the context of spontaneously born beings that have no ancestry![154]

---

153 Sugunasiri, *Dhamma Aboard Evolution*, note 14.1.

154 In passing we may note that more recent forms of colour prejudice would be anachronistic here. The "ideal" complexion was

In the fourth stage, the process continues with further coarsening, greater differentiation of appearance and more consequent arrogance among the good-looking. The *bhūmi-pappaṭaka* disappears and the food becomes creepers (*padālatā*). The creepers are said to resemble bamboo shoots. The commentary says they were sweet and describes them as *bhaddālatā*. *Bhadda* can mean either "lucky" or "an arrow." Perhaps these were something like arrow-root plants.

In the fifth stage, sexual differentiation arises with division into male and female. The building of houses begins to conceal acts of sexual intercourse between beings. Nourishment comes in the form of rice, quite different from the modern kind: it grows on unploughed land (*akaṭṭhapāko*), without husk or chaff. That which is taken for the morning meal is fully replenished by the evening. At that time cooking vessels also "arose" (*uppajjati*), which implies they were generated by the kamma of the beings rather than made in the ordinary fashion. Beings cooked their rice by placing it in one of these vessels and placing that on top of a special rock which spontaneously generated a flame.[155] They had no need of curries or spices because the rice took on whatever flavour they wished for (Vism 13:50).

The differentiation into genders is described as follows:

> So those beings enjoyed that unploughed rice, it stood as their food and their nourishment for a long time. So their bodies gradually became coarser. (Further) discolouration (*vaṇṇavevaṇṇatā*) was perceived. The females developed female organs and the males male organs. The women contemplated excessively on the men, and the men contemplated excessively on the women. Infatuation arose and lust arose in their bodies. Because of that lust, they practised sexual intercourse.
>
> So it came to pass that (other) beings saw them practising sexual intercourse and some threw dirt and some threw ashes and some threw cow dung at them, saying "Perish, unclean ones! Perish, unclean ones! How can one being do that to another?" (DN 27)

The *Aggañña Sutta* goes on to say that this is the origin of the custom prevalent in some places of throwing ashes at a newly wedded couple. "What was at one time considered unrighteous (*adhamma*) is now considered righteous (*dhamma*)." Those beings seen to be engaging in sexual intercourse were banned from entering villages or towns and so they began to construct huts for concealment.

The account in the *Visuddhimagga* is a little different, and relates the appearance of sexual differentiation directly to the eating of rice.

> From the eating of this coarse food, urine and faeces are formed in their bodies. To expel these substances, open wounds appear on their bodies. The males develop the male form, the females develop the female one. (Vism 13:51)

The development of sexuality is a critical transition in the devolution process. By becoming sexual those beings left behind the last vestiges of their primordial brahmā nature and can now be said to be fully human. It is interesting to see that this change was not a smooth one, and was for a time fiercely resisted by those not yet so "advanced" in the process. Sexuality and sexual desire are defining characteristics of the plane of sense-desire (*kāmabhūmi*) of humans and devas as contrasted with the form plane (*rūpabhūmi*) of the brahmā beings. These beings are now fully embodied in the coarse materiality of this level.

Some beings become lazy about the daily chore of gathering, and start storing rice for several days. The plants are

---

"golden" (*suvaṇṇavaṇṇa*) as is said of the Buddha's skin at MN 35. In the following sutta, white skin is listed among the ugly discolourations he experienced during his period of austerities.

155 This is the same method of cooking still used by the people of Uttarakuru. See § 3:1,3.

put under stress by this more intense harvesting and devolve into the modern type of rice which requires much work to plant and harvest. This leads to the institution of private property as each one seeks to work and protect his own field. It is significant that the storing of food stocks is seen as the sixth step in the decline from the state of nature. Storing up goods to enjoy later is said to be one of things an arahant will never do (AN 9:7). Human society as we know it begins now, with the institution of private property.

In the seventh and last stage, theft arises as some beings steal from others' fields, which leads to the institution of government to protect the innocent and punish the guilty. This is done by choosing one among them to be king, Mahāsammata "The Great Elect," who is the first among all human kings. There follows the institution of the four castes, and the *samaṇas* (ascetic wanderers) who are outside the caste system.

We will examine this stage of the process in more detail in Part Three, which deals with the human realm (§ 3:1,5). It is worth noting, however, the underlying political idea which this passage contains. Government and the caste system are not divinely ordained as the brahmins maintained, but are a socially agreed construct. This is a very early precursor of the "social contract" theory of politics elaborated by such thinkers as Locke and Hobbes. It can also be said that in this view government is not a positive good but a necessary evil, made so by the increasingly immoral nature of mankind.

2:6 THE FUTURE OF HUMANITY

The *Aggañña* account takes us up to a time that may be thought of as the early historical period, with modern humans living in towns and villages, farming and paying taxes to an organized government. Another sutta in the Dīgha Nikāya, the Cakkavatisīhanāda Sutta, (DN 26) carries the story from the distant past to the present to the far future when the Buddha Metteyya will arise in the world.

This begins with the rule of a *cakkavatti* ("Wheel-Turner", a universal monarch)[156] named Daḷhamemi. This king ruled the world righteously until the day he retired from the world in old age and handed authority over to his son. Six successive monarchs ruled in this manner, fulfilling all the duties of a *cakkavatti*. But the seventh in the line neglected one of those duties by failing to give wealth to the poor. As a result of this, some of the poor people took to robbery. When one was apprehended and brought before the king he pleaded that he only stole because he had no other means to live, so the king gave him some wealth to start a business.

Obviously, this was an ill-considered procedure and others took to robbery in order to get wealth from the king. To put a stop to it the king now went to the opposite extreme and had the next culprit executed. This caused the desperate people to take up arms and engage in armed robbery. Thus begins a long period of renewed decline in the human race. With each succeeding generation there ensued a decline in life-span, beauty (*vaṇṇa*) and morality. At the time of the righteous kings the human lifespan was 80,000 years and the process of decline may be summarized as follows:

TABLE FOUR—HUMAN DECLINE IN THE CAKKAVATISĪHANĀDA SUTTA

Because of ...	Lifespan declines to ...
violence	40,000 years
lying	20,000 years
speaking evil of another	10,000 years
adultery	5,000 years
harsh speech & idle chatter	2000–2500 years
covetousness & hatred	1000 years
wrong views	500 years
adhammarāga, visamalobha & *micchādhamma* (see below for explanations)	200–250 years
lack of respect for elders	100 years

Each stage represents one generation, for example the people who lived for 10,000 years had children who lived only 5,000 years and so forth.

The moral lapses of the generation whose children lived only 200 or 250 years are given somewhat vague names in the text of the sutta, but these are precisely defined in the commentary. *Adhammarāga* means literally "unrighteous desire" and is defined in the commentary as referring to incest. *Visamalobha* means "immoderate greed" and is defined by the commentary as being an excessive desire for material goods. *Micchādhamma* means something like "wrong

[156] For the concept of *cakkavatti*, see § 3:1,10.

ways" which is vague enough to refer to almost anything, but the commentary says it refers to homosexuality, "Men desire men and women desire women."[157]

This far into the sutta, we have presumably reached the present time, or at least the time of the Buddha. The span of human life as given in the Pali canon is one hundred years; a common formula is "one lives long who lives for a hundred years or a little more."[158] The sutta passes over the time of the Buddha Gotama in silence and moves on into a future of further decline. The nadir of human existence is reached when the lifespan will have declined to just ten years. This period is described in the text as follows:

> There will come a time when the lifespan of humans is just ten years. Amongst these people, girls will reach the age of marriage at five years old. Among the people with a lifespan of ten years the flavours of butter, ghee, oil, honey, treacle and salt will have disappeared. Among them, the *kudrūsaka* grain will be the chief food, just as rice and meat are today.
>
> Among the people with ten year lifespans, the ten ways of right conduct will have completely disappeared and the ten ways of wrong conduct will prevail. Among them, the word *kusala* ("moral", lit. "skillful") will not exist, so how could moral actions exist? Among the people with ten year lifespans, there will be no (respect for) mother or father or *samaṇas* or brahmins, nor for the elders of the clan. Now those who do show such respect are considered praiseworthy, in that time it will be considered praiseworthy to lack respect for mother and father etc.
>
> Among the people with ten year lifespans no account will be taken of mother, aunt, mother-in-law, teacher's wife or other such revered women. The entire world will go together in confusion, like goats or pigs or cocks or dogs or jackals. (The sub-commentary makes the meaning clear; they will take their own mothers and so forth "as if they were their wives").
>
> Among the people with ten year lifespans fierce animosity, anger and hatred will arise. They will have the minds of killers. Between mother and son, between father and son, between brother and sister, fierce animosity, anger and hatred will arise. Just as when a hunter sees his prey, they will have the minds of killers.
>
> And among those people there will come to be a seven day "sword time" (*sattha-antarakappa*).[159] They will perceive one another as if they were wild beasts. Sharp swords will appear in their hands (the commentary explains that anything they hold in their hands, even a blade of grass, will turn into a weapon). Taking the swords, and crying out, "There is a beast! There is a beast!" they will slay one another. (DN 26)

This is how the devolving process will end in our world, but the commentary goes on to explain that in some cycles it may unfold differently. There are three kinds of *antarakappa* ("intermediate period"), all of which result in a great destruction of living beings:

1. A *dubbhikkha* ("famine") *antarakappa* occurs when the chief defilement of the people is excessive greed (*lobha*). When the great famine is over, most of the people who have died are reborn as petas (hungry ghosts)

---

[157] DN-a 27. In a parallel passage from the *Aṅguttara* Sub-commentary (AN-ṭ 3:56) *micchādhamma* is defined as "Indulgence in some base of lust (*rāgassa vatthuṭṭhānaṃ*) other than that considered good by the world's standards", which obviously makes the actual definition dependent on social norms. See NDB, n.414, p.1645. There seems to be no direct reference to homosexuality anywhere in the Sutta Pitaka itself.

[158] *Yo ciraṃ jīvati, so vassasataṃ appaṃ vā bhiyyo*—DN 14, SN 15:20 etc. The span of life is given as one hundred also at *Visuddhimagga* Ch 8 and Abhidhamma Vibhaṅga Ch 18.

[159] *Antarakappa* = "intermediate period".

because of the power of their longing for food.

2. A *roga* ("disease") *antarakappa* occurs when the chief defilement is confusion (*moha*). After the great plague most of the beings are reborn in the deva realms, because their concern for each other's suffering, lead them to develop minds filled with loving-kindness (*mettā*).
3. A *sattha* ("sword") *antarakappa* occurs when hatred (*dosa*) prevails among the people. Most of the slain are reborn in *niraya* (the hell realms) because of the many acts of killing they have committed (DN-a 26).

According to the *Abhidharmakośa,* the two continents of Aparagoyanā and Pubbavideha do not suffer any of these extreme calamities, but when Jambudīpa is going through them, the people of the eastern and western continents do suffer from "wickedness, bad colour, weakness, hunger and thirst" (AK 3:6, p. 490). By inference we can conclude that Uttarakuru does not endure any special sufferings at all at these times.

However it unfolds, the *antarakappa* means that most of the human beings in the world are killed. It marks the end of the declining period of the cycle. There are, however, a few survivors who begin a new ascending period. In the case of a "sword time" as in our sutta, those who survive are the few who hide themselves in the forest to avoid the killing spree. When they emerge and find one another, they mutually agree to take on the precept of not killing. By taking on just this much morality their lifespan doubles to twenty years. In the next phase of the world's evolution the lifespan doubles in each generation as the people become more ethical in stages, until the peak of 80,000 years is again reached.

The world then will have reached its zenith in a kind of golden age, albeit one that might not appeal to us in all its particulars. The text describes it as follows:

> Among those people who will live for 80,000 years only three diseases will be known; desire (*icchā*), hunger (*anasana*), and old age (*jarā*). The island-continent of Jambudīpa will be powerful and wealthy. (The roof eaves of each house will overlap those of its neighbour)[160] in the villages, towns and royal cities. Jambudīpa will be so full it will seem to be without any gap,[161] just like a thicket of reeds or bamboo. The Bārāṇasī of today will be a royal capital city named Ketumatī, powerful and wealthy, with many people and provisions. In Jambudīpa there will be 84,000 cities with Ketumatī as the chief. (DN 26)

It will be at that time that both a *cakkavatti* ("wheel-turning") monarch named Saṅkha, and the future Buddha Metteyya[162] will arise, the last Buddha of this *mahākappa*.

This is as far as the account in the Cakkavatisīhanāda Sutta takes us, and there is no indication in the Pali sources that this cycle of decline and recovery is repeated. However, if we turn to the *Abhidharmakośa* we find that that text adds some further sub-divisions to the four major divisions of a *mahākappa*. Each of the major phases of the cycle is divided into twenty *antarakappa*[163] of equal length. In the unfolding aeon it takes one *antarakappa* for the world to be formed and nineteen for it to be filled with beings descending from the *Ābhāsvara* realm (Pali = Ābhassara). In the unfolded aeon we are considering here, the first *antarakappa* begins with the beings arrived from the Ābhāsvara plane who have a potential lifespan of "infinite" length. This really means their lifespan is longer than the *antarakappa*, but none of them live to see it. That is because during the rest of that first *antarakappa*, the lifespan of the humans declines as we have seen in the account of the *Aggañña Sutta*, down to a lower limit of ten years. This is followed by eighteen *antarakappas* where the lifespan rises up by stages to eighty thousand years and then declines again to ten years.

[160] This is the commentarial explanation of the odd phrase *kukkuṭasampātika*. lit. "cuckoo collision". Walshe renders it as "the cities will be but a cock's flight one from the next".

[161] *Avīci maññe phuṭo*. Avīci is the worst of the nirayas and one of its many agonies is the dense crowding. The commentary takes this meaning and interprets the phrase as meaning "as crowded as avīci." But this would be an unusual use of a name which almost never occurs in the canon. Avīci here may not be a name at all but a negation of *vīci*, "an interval".

[162] Sanskrit = Maitreya

[163] Note that this term is used differently in the Pali sources. See appendix on units.

The last *antarakappa* is one of increase only; the lifespan increases one last time to eighty thousand years before the *mahākappa* comes to an end.

FIGURE EIGHT
VARIATIONS OF HUMAN LIFESPANS DURING THE AEON OF EXISTENCE
According the *Abhidharmakośa* system

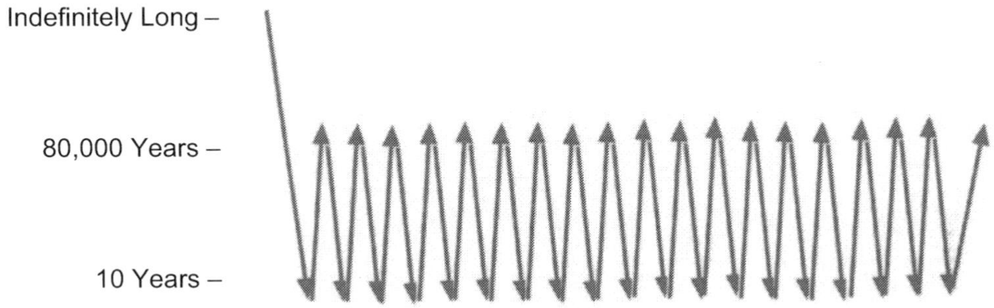

Although these refinements are not found in the primary Pali sources, a version of this basic structure was known and accepted by the Theravāda Buddhists of Burma, at least.[164] The modern work, *The Great Chronicle of Buddhas* by Mingun Sayadaw, citing the old Burmese chronicles as a source, states that each of the five Buddhas of our *mahākappa* arise in a different *antarakappa*, and always during the phase when lifespans are declining.[165] This is said to be because during a phase when lifespans are increasing it is difficult for beings to understand the truth of impermanence.

[164] The Thai cosmological treatise *The Three Worlds According to King Ruang* makes no mention of it.

[165] GGB p. 190 f and p. 205-206. For the Burmese Chronicles, see "Burmese literature", *Britannica Library*, http://library.eb.com/levels/referencecenter/article/18189, accessed January 4, 2017. and Bischoff, 1995.

2:7 THE DESTRUCTION OF THE KAPPA

At the end of a cycle the world may be destroyed by fire, by water or by wind. The destruction by fire is the most common type, and the kappa we are presently living in will end this way. The sources give the most attention to this type of ending and we shall follow their lead by first describing destruction by fire in some detail.[166]

The first sign that the world is coming to an end is the appearance of a great cloud, the *kappavināsakamahāmegho* ("aeon destruction great cloud") which extends over one trillion (*koṭisatasahassa*) *cakkavāḷas*.[167] There follows a great rain which delights the people who eagerly plant their crops, but when the rain stops it stops for good. There follows a drought that lasts for many hundreds of thousands of years.

One hundred thousand years before the final ending, some brahmā beings see the signs and warn the devas of the sense-desire sphere. Some of these in turn take on the role of "world-marshals" (*lokabyūha*) and descend to earth to warn those in the human realm (Vism-mhṭ 13).

> These sense-sphere devas, with top-knots loosed,[168] with hair disheveled, with sorrowful faces, wiping the tears away with their hands, wearing dyed cloth all awry,[169] travel about the human realm making this announcement:
>
> "In one hundred thousand years the end of the kappa (*kappuṭṭhāna*) will come. This world will perish. The great ocean will dry up and this great earth together with Mt Sineru will be burnt up and destroyed. The world will be destroyed as far as the *brahmaloka*. Develop loving-kindness, my dears, develop compassion, develop sympathetic joy, develop equanimity my dears. Honour your mother, honour your father and pay respect to the elders of your clan. Be wakeful, be not heedless."
>
> So they go about the paths of men, making this announcement. This is the great uproar at the end of a kappa.[170]

A hundred thousand years may seem like a long time ahead for such an announcement to raise much concern, but it should be recalled that, according to the *Abhidharmakośa* scheme, these humans living near the end of the final *antarakappa* will have lifespans measured in tens of thousands of years. The admonition to the people is to develop the four *brahmavihāras*, meditations that when perfected will ensure rebirth into the *brahmaloka*. This will be necessary, because all the abodes of the sense-desire sphere will soon be destroyed. There will be no place for these beings to be reborn except in the upper reaches of the *rūpaloka*.

The living beings all die out during the great drought. This great emptying begins from the bottom up and the nethermost *niraya*, Āvici, is the first to become empty.[171] No more beings are reborn there as those in the human realm develop minds full of *mettā* ("loving-kindness"), spurred on by a sense of urgency. Even the animals develop *mettā* toward their children and their siblings and take either human or deva birth (AN-a 7:66). The migration of beings is

---

[166] The principal Pali sources are AN 7: 66 the *Sattasūriya Sutta* or "Sutta of the Seven Suns" and Vism 13.28f. which inserts this cosmological history into the section on the psychic power of past life recall, in order to clarify the phrase "He recalls many kappas of the world folding in and many kappas of the world folding out. "

[167] Vism 13.32, this cloud is not mentioned in the Aṅguttara account.

[168] *Muttasirā*. Translation follows the suggestion of Vism-mhṭ 13.

[169] *Virūpavesadhārino*. Vism-mhṭ 13 attributes their unkempt appearance to the sorrow and fear engendered by the coming end of the world.

[170] Sn-a 2:4. See also Vism 13.34. AN-a 7:66 has a slightly different version, the devas there fly about in the sky and warn beings that "there is nothing permanent here, develop loving-kindness etc. "

[171] This was considered problematic and Buddhaghosa adds that "some say" that beings in Āvici do not die until near the end, with the arrival of the seventh sun.

gradually upward as the realms empty out and most are eventually reborn in the Ābhassara realm, the realm of the second jhāna brahmā beings which is the lowest realm that will remain after the flames consume everything below.

The sources are cognizant of the theoretical problems posed by this process. Buddhaghosa, in the *Visuddhimagga*, says, "There is no rebirth in the brahmā world without jhāna, so how do those, being obsessed with the scarcity of food, manage to be reborn there?" The answer is that by practising morality and developing *mettā* they can at least take rebirth in one of the sensual sphere *saggas*, and there attain jhāna before those worlds too are destroyed. Others are reborn upward simply on the strength of kamma made in previous lifetimes, because in the vast time scale of *saṃsāra* it is impossible that a being might be without some superior kamma (Vism 13: 33–35). After all, the beings living in all of these realms must be reborn somewhere: "There comes a time when this great earth burns up, but there is no ending of the suffering of those beings wandering on fettered by ignorance and craving" (SN 22:99).

The *Abhidharmakośa* too discusses this problem and also suggests that beings unable to attain jhāna are at first reborn in one of the sensual deva realms, and attain jhāna there. That text includes all the human inhabitants of the island-continent of Uttarakuru in this category, "because they are unable to leave the *kāmadhātu* (sensual desire sphere)." The *Abhidharmakośa* also suggests that some beings in *niraya* do not escape but are reborn into the *niraya* realm of some *cakkavāḷa* outside the range of destruction (AK 3:6. p.476). This view is also supported by the Pali sub-commentaries.[172] During this process of dying out, no beings are reborn into the lower levels of the *cakkavāḷa*, before the great fire begins there is no one left alive below the Ābhassara level. The *Abhidharmakośa* says this process takes nineteen *antarakappas* to complete, leaving one antarakappa for the process of physical destruction (AK 3:6. p.479).

After all the living beings have died and been reborn into the brahmā worlds the process of physical destruction of the multiple world-systems begins with the appearance in the sky of a second sun, the *kappavināsakasūriya* ("aeon destroying sun"). This sun rises when the original sun is setting and vice versa, so that the whole world is always in daylight. This sun is unlike the original sun in that it is not the abode of any devas but is a purely physical phenomenon. The sky is now completely clear of any clouds or mist, and the heat of the two suns dries up all the streams and lesser rivers of the world, excepting only the five great rivers: the Gaṅgā, the Yamunā, the Aciravatī, the Sarabhū, and the Mahī.

This is followed, after a long period of time, by the appearance of a third sun. Now when one sun is setting, one is at the zenith and the other is setting. The new sun, added to the others, dries up the five great rivers.

After another long period a fourth sun appears and now the great lakes of the Himavā dry up; Lake Anotattā, Sīhapapātā, Rathakārā, Kaṇṇamuṇḍā, Kuṇālā, Chaddantā, and Mandākiniyā.

The fifth sun gradually evaporates the waters of the great oceans until there remain only shallow pools, like "the hoof-prints made by cattle."

With the sixth sun, the great earth together with Sineru, king of mountains, begins to "smoke, smoulder and fume" (*dhūmāyanti saṃdhūmāyanti sampadhūmāyanti*). The whole world is filled up with the swirling of oily fumes (AN 7:66).

After yet another long period the seventh and final sun appears and now everything bursts into flame. Mount Sineru and the entire *cakkavāḷa* is consumed by fire and winds carry the flames upward burning all the *saggas* of the celestial devas and even the world of the first jhāna brahmās. The fire is so intense that it leaves no ash behind; everything is consumed, the fire does not go out until even the very smallest particles (*aṇumatta saṅkhāra*) are consumed.[173] We now have come back to the empty universe, "one great gloomy darkness."

The Pali texts are silent about how and from where the additional six suns arise. The *Abhidharmakośa* says that they arise because of the collective kamma of the beings who had inhabited the world, and can only do so after the

[172] DN-ṭ 1. See Bodhi, AENV p. 153.

[173] All these descriptions are taken from AN 7:66 and Vism 13.41.

world has been emptied of beings. The wind which fans the flames is a "wind of the *rūpadhātu*", i.e. the *brahmaloka* (AK 3:6. p.491). In one of Poussin's footnotes he cites the *Vibhāṣā* (a Sanskrit text) as mentioning four theories regarding the suns; that during the life of the world the extra suns remain hidden behind Yugandhara, that the original sun divides into seven, that the one sun simply takes on seven times greater force or that the extra suns exist in a hidden form until the kamma of beings causes them to manifest on the physical plane (AK p. 542, note 497). The third possibility, that a single sun increases in power, is not so different from the modern scientific view about how this solar system will end, with the sun becoming a huge red giant and consuming the inner planets.

The medieval Thai work *Traibhūmikathā*, "The Three Worlds", adds a colourful detail. According to that source, it is the oily bodies of the gigantic sea-monsters living in the Sīdantara oceans which, catching fire, provide the fuel for the great conflagration which burns up Mt Sineru and the other great mountain ranges.[174]

The Buddha spoke the *Sattasūriya Sutta* with a specific didactic purpose in mind; he wished to make clear to his listeners the impermanence of all phenomena. To his ancient Indian listeners, nothing in the world would have seemed so permanent and stable as Mount Sineru and the great ocean. And yet the time will come when even the great ocean, so inconceivably vast, would dry up so that there would not even be enough water left to wet a finger joint. And Sineru, the massive and mighty "king of mountains" would burn up so completely that not even ash would remain. Throughout the sutta there is the repeated refrain:

> Impermanent, oh bhikkhus, are all conditioned things. Unstable, insecure are all conditioned things. It is enough to become disenchanted with all formations, to become dispassionate towards them, to become liberated from them. (AN 7: 66)

174 Reynolds, *Three Worlds According to King Ruang*, p. 309-310.

2:8 DESTRUCTION BY WATER AND AIR

The canonical suttas mention only this destruction by fire. The commentaries add two other possible endings of a kappa; destruction by water and destruction by air (E.g. AN-a 4:156). The germ of this idea, however, is found in Majjhima Nikāya 28, the *Mahāhatthipadopama Sutta* ("The Greater Elephant's Footprint Sutta"). In a portion of that sutta the Buddha discusses the four elements and stressing their impermanent and unreliable nature he says that both the internal elements of one's body and the external elements of the world may become disturbed. He says there will come a time when the external water element becomes disturbed and the earth element will cease to exist. The commentary explicitly relates this to the āposaṃvaṭṭakāla, the kappa ending by water. The disturbance of the air element manifests in dead calms or ferocious destructive winds and the commentary connects the latter with the *vāyosaṃvaṭṭakāla*, the kappa ending by air (or wind). That the Buddha was not intending to refer to the world's end in this sutta is made clear in his description of the disturbance of the external fire element. He says that there comes a time when great fires burn up whole cities and towns and sweep across the countryside until they encounter open water, mountains or other obstacles. The commentary has to admit this does not refer to the *tejosaṃvaṭṭakāla*, the kappa ending by fire because that fire burns everything and leaves no ash.[175]

The destruction by water begins with the appearance of a great cloud that ends the kappa (*kappavināsaka-mahāmegha*). Rain begins to fall from this cloud, at first gently but gradually increasing to a tremendous deluge. This rain is not ordinary water but caustic water (*khārudaka*) which is highly corrosive. It will be recalled that this is the same kind of water on which the whole *cakkavāḷa* floats. As this corrosive water rains down upon the worlds it dissolves everything down to the finest particles of matter. The water is held in place as if in a vessel by powerful winds and reaches as high as the Ābhassara brahmā world (the realm of the second jhāna brahmā beings) which is also dissolved. The lowest realm escaping destruction this time is the Subhakiṇha world of the third jhāna brahmās. The waters only subside after everything in all these worlds has been totally destroyed.

The destruction by the wind element begins with a wind that ends the kappa (*kappavināsanatthaṃ vāta*) which begins gently at first, blowing around the fine dust. It gradually gains in strength and ferocity until it is lifting up gigantic boulders and hurling them around. In the last ferocious phase of the great wind the Sinerus of multiple world systems are flung through space smashing each other to bits. This time everything is destroyed up to and including the Subhakiṇha world and the realm of the fourth jhāna brahmās, is the only one to escape destruction (Vism 13: 56 f).

The three modes of world destruction follow a fixed pattern. There are seven *mahākappas* which end in fire, followed by one which ends in water. This pattern of eight *mahākappas* is repeated seven times and is then followed by a series of seven more destructions by fire, followed by one destruction through air. Thus, the whole cycle lasts sixty-four *mahākappas*, which not coincidentally, is the lifespan of a Subhakiṇha brahmā (Vism 13: 65).

[175] MN 28 and commentary. The text also mentions another disturbance of the fire element, a time will come when people will be unable to kindle a fire even with feathers and hide parings. The commentary, seemingly at loss to explain this odd statement, says that these will be the only fuels available and are inadequate to make any heat.

2:9 HORIZONTAL EXTENSION OF DESTRUCTION

We have seen that establishing a coherent system for the ordering of the multiple *cakkavāḷas* under their respective *brahmalokas* is somewhat problematic. The pattern which is most often cited in the later Pali sources is that of the three Buddha Fields; the Field of Birth consisting of 10,000 *cakkavāḷas*, the Field of Authority of 100,000 *koṭi* of worlds, that is to say, one trillion *cakkavāḷas* and the Field of Scope which is of infinite extent. The *Visuddhimagga* states that it is the Field of Authority of one trillion worlds which undergoes destruction at the end of each *mahākappa*.[176] However, this simple scheme does not dove-tail at all well with the alignment of the *cakkavāḷas* under the brahmā worlds. There is a hint of a more complex system. Immediately following the paragraph listing the three kinds of destruction and giving their upper limits in the first, second and third jhāna level *brahmalokas*, Buddhaghosa then says "In detail, it is always one of the three Buddha-fields that is destroyed. The Buddha-fields are three: the Field of Birth, the Field of Authority, and the Field of Scope" (Vism 13:31). It would work out more neatly with the rest of the cosmological scheme if it were to be understood that the ten thousand worlds of the Field of Birth were those destroyed by fire, that is all the worlds under a single Ābhassara (second jhāna) brahmā world, and the trillion world-systems of a Field of Authority under their single Subhkiṇha world were those destroyed by water leaving the infinity of worlds under the one and only Vehapphala to be destroyed once every sixty four kappas by wind. Admittedly though, this is forcing something onto the texts that is not explicitly there.[177]

Nor is the *Abhidharmakośa* any clearer about this point. In the section describing the division of the universe into "chiliocosms" it is stated that "the destruction and the creation of the universes lasts the same time." Poussin cites the commentary (*Vyākhyā*) as clarifying this to mean, "Rather, destruction and creation of the universes of one group take place at the same time" (AK 3:5. p.468–69 & n.464, p.539).

Thus, although there is some uncertainty in interpretation, but we can state the following as definite conclusions by way of summary:

1. The various destructions by fire, water and air all affect multiple world-systems. The horizontal scope is subject to different interpretations but the *Visuddhimagga* strongly favours the idea that all three of these cycle ending events destroy one trillion *cakkavāḷas*.
2. The vertical extent of the destructions is agreed among all sources. The destruction by fire burns everything up to and including the first jhāna *brahmaloka*. The destruction by water dissolves all of this plus the second jhāna or Ābhassara level. The destruction by wind pulverizes everything up to and including the third jhāna level *brahmaloka*, the Subhakiṇha world. In all cases nothing at all of the affected realms remains.
3. The Vehapphala or fourth jhāna level *brahmaloka* escapes all these destructions and serves as the last refuge into which beings may be reborn.

This last point raises an important doctrinal question; does this mean that the persistence of the Vehapphala realm somehow violates the Buddhist law of impermanence (*anicca*)? The *Visuddhimagga* does not address this question but the *Abhidharmakośa* provides an answer. According to that text, the Vehapphala level does not properly constitute a "sphere" but is composed of individual abodes of beings which arise and fall away with those beings (AK 3:6. p 495).

The *Visuddhimagga* and the *Abhidharmakośa* provide two quite different explanations for the causes of the specific destructions. According to the *Visuddhimagga* the universe is destroyed on account of the three unskilful roots

[176] This is explicitly stated at the outset of the section on world-cycles and Buddhaghosa frequently makes reference to the *koṭisatasahassacakkavāḷa* which suffer the various calamities together. This view is also supported by the sub-commentary at MN-ṭ 115.

[177] This scheme also presents its own conceptual problem; the destructions of all worlds would have to be in synch if at the end of 64 kappas all were destroyed together by wind.

(*akusalamūla*), the root defilements of desire (*rāga*), ill-will (*dosa*) and confusion (*mohā*). In a kappa which is to end by fire the defilement of greed is predominant among beings. In one ended by water, it is ill-will and when confusion predominates, the world will end by wind.[178] The *Abhidharmakośa* provides a quite different scheme which relates the cycles of destruction to the jhāna factors involved in the highest world destroyed. The highest world destroyed by fire is the first jhāna *brahmaloka* and the "vice" (i.e. the coarsest factor remaining) in first jhāna is *vitakka-vicāra* or thought formation "which burns the mind and is similar to fire." The destruction by water reaches up to the second jhāna level of the Ābhassara beings and the coarsest factor remaining in that jhāna is *pīti* ("rapture" or "joy") "which being associated with physical well-being renders the body soft and flabby; it is similar to water." The destruction by wind reaches up to the third jhāna world of the Subhakiṇha brahmās. The third jhāna has in and out breathing as its "vice", which is a form of wind.[179] (The physical breath is supposed to cease in fourth jhāna) (AK 6:3, p. 924). This explanation very neatly expresses a parallelism between the microcosm of the meditator moving through the jhānas and the macrocosm of worlds evolving and coming to periodic destruction.[180]

178 Vism 13.64. The text goes on to cite another view held by some which changes the causal factors to *dosa*—fire, *rāga*- water, *moha*—wind.

179 AK 3:6. p 494. For a summary description of the jhānas and jhāna factors see the chapter on brahmās in § 3:6,8.

180 See Gethin 1997.

2:10 THE BUDDHAS IN COSMIC TIME

The Theravāda tradition has always emphasized the extreme rarity of Buddhahood. We have already looked at the rarity of a Buddha in cosmic space; there can only ever be one Buddha at a time in the ten thousand worlds of a Field of Birth, or in another interpretation, in the entire infinite cosmos. The Buddhas are equally rare in cosmic time. There are six kinds of *mahākappa* according to the number of Buddhas who appear during its duration. These are designated as follows in the Buddhavaṃsa Commentary:

Suññakappa—An "empty" aeon in which no Buddha arises.

Sārakappa—An aeon in which only one Buddha arises. *Sāra* means "pith or essence" and is used, for example, of heart-wood.

Maṇḍakappa—An aeon with two Buddhas. *Maṇḍa* means "cream of", as in the choicest part of anything, or literally the "cream" of milk.

Varakappa—An aeon with three Buddhas. *Vara* is "excellent or noble."

Sāramaṇḍakappa—An aeon with four Buddhas. Sāramaṇḍa combines *sāra* and *maṇḍa* meaning something like "the best of the best."

Bhaddakappa—An aeon during which five Buddhas arise. *Bhadda* means "auspicious or lucky" and this often translated as a "fortunate aeon." The kappa we are currently living in is a *bhaddakappa* (DN-a 14).

(Note that within a *mahākappa*, if there are to be more than one Buddha they arise in separate *anatarakappas*).

Of these, the *bhaddakappa* is by far the rarest. Most kappas are empty of Buddhas. To illustrate the rarity of a Buddha's appearance in the world, consider the history of the Buddhas before Gotama. Many kappas ago, the Buddha Gotama of our historical period was a brahmin named Sumedha and it was in that lifetime that he first made his aspiration (*abhinīhāra*) for Buddhahood before the Buddha Dīpaṅkara. That was during a *sāramaṇḍakappa*, and Dīpaṅkara was the last of four Buddhas. This was followed by an incalculable number (*asaṅkheyya*) of *suññakappas* devoid of Buddhas.[181] Then there was a kappa in which a single Buddha, Kondañña, arose. This was in turn followed by "many" more empty aeons before a *sāramaṇḍakappa* with four Buddhas. Then again many more empty aeons before a *varakappa* of three Buddhas.

After another unspecified series of empty kappas we come to a time one hundred thousand kappas before our own. From here on the sources provide us with a detailed history with specific numbers and names. We can summarize this in the following table:

[181] GGB p. 113 puts the number at 100,000 *kappas* plus four *asaṅkhyeyya*. It is not clear what an *asaṅkheyya* means in that context. The *Abhidharmakośa* does calculate the number, arriving at a figure of one quadrillion (10^15) kappas, see AK 3:6 p. 480.

TABLE FIVE—PREVIOUS BUDDHAS

Kappas Before Present	Kappa Type	Buddhas
100,000	sārakappa	Padumattara
99,999—3,605?	70,000 suññakappas ?	
3,604 ?	maṇḍakappa	Sumedha, Sujāta
3,603—1803	1800 suññakappas	
1802	varakappa	Piyadassi, Atthadasī Dhammadasī
1801–95	1706 suññakappas	
94	sārakappa	Siddhattha
93	one suññakappa	
92	maṇḍakappa	Tissa, Phussa
91	sārakappa	Vipassī
90—32	58 suññakappas[1]	
31	maṇḍakappa	Sikhī, Vessabhū
30—1	29 suññakappas	
present	bhaddhakappa	Kakusandha, Koṇāgamana, Kassapa, Gotama, Metteyya[2]

(Note that some of the numbers do not add up properly. The most glaring discrepancy is in the first long series of *suññakappas*; the text gives 30,000 but it would seem actually to be 96,394 if the rest of the figures are to add up. Elsewhere, minor adjustments have been made for consistency).

Analyzing these numbers it would seem that in one hundred thousand kappas there have been only eight during which Buddhas arose, and this following a series of empty aeons said to be "incalculable." Combining this with the idea that when a Buddha does arise, he is unique in at least ten thousand world-systems, we begin to appreciate the extreme rarity of this accomplishment. The chance of being born into any given world at a time when a Buddha's teachings are extant is very small.

PART THREE - BEINGS

CHAPTER ONE - THE HUMAN REALM

3:1:1 KĀMĀVACARA—THE PLANE OF SENSE DESIRE

All of reality may be divided into four levels or planes; the *kāmabhūmi* (" plane of sense desire"), the *rūpabhūmi* ("plane of form"), the *arūpabhūmi* ("formless plane") and the *lokuttara* ("supramundane") (Abhidh-s 1:3). The last, the supramundane, is not a plane of existence like the others; it is *nibbāna*, the unconditioned and unmanifested. It transcends ordinary existence and is not part of the cosmos. That cosmos, the abode of all the various kinds and levels of sentient beings, therefore, is divided into three planes only. The plane of sense desire is the most variegated and complex. It includes the lower realms of *niraya*, the *petaloka* and the animal realm. The asuras, too, can be considered among these unfortunate existences.[182] The plane of sense desire also includes a range of existences classified as fortunate, beginning with the human realm and including all the devas of the earth and sky and those of the six *saggas*. The plane of form is the realm of the brahmā beings, divided into sixteen levels. The most refined and subtlest plane, the formless plane, is the abode of the formless or mind-only beings.

All the beings of the plane of sense desire are characterized by mental processes informed by the five physical senses through which they relate to the outer world. The impulses that dominate their mental life and bodily actions are a desire to obtain pleasant sense experiences and to avoid unpleasant ones. Although sense-desire consciousness is the default level for beings born into this plane of existence, it is possible for them to experience mind-moments classified as belonging to higher planes, as for instance when a human meditator enters jhāna and experiences consciousness at the level of the plane of form. Nevertheless, the tyranny of sense-desire is the ordinary operating mode of beings living here, in the *kāmabhūmi*. We will examine all the various levels of being within this plane, but let us begin our tour of the cosmos close to home, with the human realm.

---

[182] Although they are difficult to fit into the standard lists. See § 3:3,23.

3:1:2 MANUSSALOKA—THE HUMAN REALM

The realm of human beings (*manussa*) is an appropriate place to begin with, not only because most of the readers of this book are presumably human beings, but because it may also be considered in an important sense as the centre of the cosmos. Below are the realms of suffering and above are the heavenly worlds of pleasure and bliss. Here, in the human realm, there is a balance of pleasure and pain. This means that full awakening is most readily attained here; there is (for at least some humans) neither so much pain that the being is overwhelmed into helplessness, nor so much pleasure that he or she is unable to discern a problem with *saṃsāric* existence. Furthermore, it is always in the human realm that Buddhas arise, the highest development of any kind within the entire cosmos. Although the lifespans of humans are very brief and their pleasures paltry compared to that of the deva worlds, still the wisest of the devas wish for a human rebirth and the chance it affords for spiritual liberation.[183]

We can easily take our human existence for granted, but understood in the context of the entire cosmos it is an exceedingly rare and fortunate position to be in. It is a general rule of the cosmos that the lower realms are greatly more populous than the higher ones. The Buddha said that if the number of human beings were represented by the dirt under his fingernail, the number of beings in *niraya* would be equivalent to all the dirt on the great earth (SN 56:97). If a being once falls into the lower realms, his chance of regaining a human state is compared to the chances of a blind turtle in the great ocean, who comes to the surface once every hundred years, of putting his head by chance through a yoke floating on the surface of the sea (SN 56:47 & MN 129).

There is a very great range of variation among human beings, and it is said that no two humans are ever exactly alike, even identical twins (AN-a 7:44). In the next sections, we shall consider some of the ways human beings vary from one another.

---

183 As did Sakka, king of the Tāvatiṃsa devas, at DN 21.

3:1:3 INHABITANTS OF THE FOUR ISLAND-CONTINENTS

Human beings (*manussa*) live on the land masses within the world-seas which lie between the central mountain rings and the edge of the *cakkavāḷa*. There are four main island-continents (*mahādīpa*), each with a grouping of smaller subsidiary islands. The different inhabitants of the four islands constitute the primary division of mankind.[184]

About the physical characteristics of the people who live on these island-continents, the Pali sources say little. We are told that the humans who live on each continent have faces shaped like the landmass on which they dwell; thus those of us living here on Jambudīpa have roughly triangular faces with broad foreheads and sharp chins, those living on Aparagoyāna have round faces, the folk of Uttarakuru have square faces and those of Pubbavideha have faces that resemble the semi-circle of a half moon (Vism-mhṭ 7).

Venturing beyond the Pali texts, we can glean a little more from the *Abhidharmakośa*, which gives the average height and life-span of each race. The inhabitants of Jambudīpa, our island-continent, vary between three and a half and four "elbows" in height. Taking an "elbow" to be about forty five centimetres that would mean a height ranging from about 157 cm. (5' 2") to 180 cm. (5' 11"). The people of Pubbavideha are twice that size, eight elbows or 3.6 metres in height. That size is doubled again in Aparagoyāna to 16 elbows or 7.2 metres, and doubled again in Uttarakuru, where humans are said to be 32 elbows or nearly 14.5 metres high (AK 3:5. p. 469). However, these gigantic sizes are not supported in the Pali sources. The layman Jotika was married to a woman of Uttarakuru who had been brought to Jambudīpa by the devas (Dhp-a 26:33). It is hard to conceive of such a marriage were the wife indeed eight times taller than the husband! No mention is made of her being a giantess.

In the Abhidhamma the span of human life is given as "unfixed". This is primarily a reference to the humans of Jambudīpa where the life-span of humans waxes and wanes with the phases of cosmological history from a maximum of 84,000 years to a minimum of just ten years.[185] According to the *Abhidharmakośa* the life-spans on the other continent-islands are fixed. People in Pubbavideha live for 250 years, those on Aparagoyāna for 500 years and those dwelling on Uttarakuru enjoy a life of 1000 years in length.[186]

Regarding the character of the beings on the different island-continents, we are told that the humans of Uttarakuru surpass those of Jambudīpa and even the devas of Tāvatiṃsa in three respects:

amama, apariggaha—Unselfishness, freedom from acquisitiveness.

niyatāyuka—They have a fixed life-span. This means they are not subject to untimely death. The commentary further informs us that the humans of Uttarakuru always live for one thousand years and upon death always go to a *devaloka*. Premature death is of course common for the humans of Jambudīpa and may occur among the lower devas by, for example, death in battle with the asuras.

visesaguṇa—The excellence of their qualities. The reading here is doubtful; the Sinhalese and Siamese recensions have *visesabhuno* which Bhikkhu Bodhi renders with "their living conditions are exceptional."[187]

On the other hand, the humans of Jambudīpa surpass those of Uttarakuru and the Tāvatiṃsa devas in the three qualities of;

sūra—Heroism.

satimant—Mindfulness. In the deva worlds there is only happiness and in *niraya* only misery and neither of these conditions is conducive to mindfulness; only among the humans of Jambudīpa is there a suitable mix of the two.

idhabrahmacariyavāsa—Here it is possible to live the holy life. As the commentary says, only in Jambudīpa do

---

[184] Khp-a 5. For the physical description of the islands, see § 1:10.

[185] See Bodhi, CMA p. 196 and DN 26 & 27 and Part Two of this book.

[186] AK 3:5. p.470. The thousand year life-span in Uttarakuru is also supported by the Pali at AN-a 9:21.

[187] AN 9:21. See Bhikkhu Bodhi's note on *visesabhuno*, NDB, note 1885.

Buddhas and paccekabuddhas arise, and only here is it possible to follow the eightfold path in fullness (AN-a 9:21).

The Pali sources tell us almost nothing about the mode of life in Aparagoyāna and Pubbavideha, except that we know the people of the latter do not build houses but sleep out of doors (Th-a 20:1). Two passages describe in some detail the life of the Uttarakuru folk, however these are not entirely consistent. A long passage in the sub-commentary portrays the Uttarakuru people as living in a state of primitive simplicity and purity:

> The distinctive nature of the inhabitants of Uttarakuru, and the power of their merit, will now be described. Here and there throughout their land accumulations of leaves, branches and twigs make up peaked dwellings in the delightful trees, and these are arranged in a way suitable for human habitation. They dwell wherever they like, in one tree or another. The tops of these trees are always in flower. There are also ponds filled with red and white lotuses and water-lilies and other such plants, all wafting forth delightful scents continuously.
>
> Their bodies are tall and free of blemishes, perfect in height and girth, unconquered by old age, free of wrinkles, grey hair and other such faults. Their strength and vigour is not diminished as long as life lasts. They live without exertion; there is no agriculture or trade and the search for nutriment is without suffering. They possess neither male nor female slaves; no one is made to labour. There is no danger from heat or cold or flies and mosquitoes, reptiles or snakes. Just as in the morning during the last month of summer there is even heat and cold, so there all the time there is even heat and cold. There no one suffers from injury or annoyance.
>
> Without farming or cooking they enjoy sweet fragrant rice; the grains are pure, without powder or husk. Thus eating, they suffer no leprosy, boils, skin disease, consumption, wasting sickness, asthma, epilepsy or aging and so forth. Indeed no disease arises there at all. There no one is hump-backed or dwarfish or blind or crippled, lame or halt. No one is defective or deformed in any way.
>
> The women there are not too tall, not too short, not too lean, not too fat, not too dark, and not too pale. Their bodies are very beautiful. They have long fingers with brown finger-nails, firm breasts, thin waists and faces like the full moon. They have large eyes, soft bodies, shapely thighs[188] and white teeth. They have deep navels, slender calves, long black hair and round bellies, neither too much nor too little (body) hair. Their female organs are warm, pretty and pleasant to the touch. They are delicate, kindly and pleasant in their speech and are adorned in various ways. The women always look as if they were sixteen years old, the men as if they were twenty-five. There, there is no attachment to wife or child. This is the nature of that place.
>
> Once each week women and men live together in sensual enjoyment. Afterward, with passions extinguished, they go their own ways. There it is not like here; there is no suffering caused by conception, pregnancy or child-birth. From its red mantle[189] the child emerges comfortably from the mother's womb like a golden statue, not smeared with phlegm and so forth. This is the nature of that place. The mother having given birth to a son or a daughter makes a place for them beside the road and without concern goes wherever she likes. There the baby lies and is seen by men and women passersby who offer it a finger. By the power of their kamma, the finger produces milk and it is this which the baby drinks. In this way they grow, and in a few days gain strength. Then the girls go among the women and the boys among the men.

[188] *Sahitorū*—the translation of this rare word is uncertain

[189] *rattakañcukato*—the placenta?

The wish-fulfilling trees[190] there provide clothes and ornaments. Cloth hangs down from the tree; variously coloured, fine and delicate to the touch. Ornaments, many and various, hang down from the trees; resplendent with shining rays, encircled with many jewels, fashioned in many ways such as "garland work", "creeper work" or "wall work."[191] They are made to adorn the head, the neck, the hands, the feet and the hips. These golden ornaments hang down from the wish-fulfilling tree. There various kinds of musical instruments hang down from the tree; lutes, drums, cymbals, conches, flutes and so forth.[192] There are also many fruits the size of water pots with sweet taste. Whoever eats them doesn't suffer from hunger or thirst for a week.

The river there has very pure water; its banks are beautiful and delightful, sandy and free of mud. The water is neither too cold nor too warm and is covered with water flowers whose fragrance is wafting about all the time. There, there are no thorny hedges, rough plants or creepers. There flourish only flowers and fruits free of thorns. Sandalwood and ironwood trees freely trickle forth syrup. Those wishing to bathe leave their clothes on the river bank, descend into the water and bathe. They go up or down stream or cross to the other side and take whatever clothes they find there. There is no idea of "This is mine, this is another's." There is on account of that no quarrelling or dissension.

Every seven days there is enjoyment of sexual intercourse, and from there they go away free of lust. Wherever they desire to sleep, there in the trees is found a bed. In death, these beings see neither sorrow nor joy. At that time, they put aside their adornments, and at the instant of death a bird carries the corpse away to another island. They have no cemeteries or charnel grounds. And after death they do not go to *niraya* or to the *petaloka* or to an animal birth. By the natural power of the five precepts, (see Vism 1:41) they always arise in the *devaloka*. They always live a full thousand years and by nature they keep all the precepts. (AN-ṭ 9:21)

The other source, the Āṭānāṭiya Sutta, Dīgha Nikāya Sutta 32, is a long poem full of mythological elements, many of them obscure. One section concerns Uttarakuru and it begins with a picture not unlike that of the previous text:

There is delightful Kuru, beautiful Mahāneru.[193]

There people live free of desire, free of grasping.

(Commentary) There is no sense of ownership of clothing, goods, food or drink. There is no taking of women as wives. "This is my wife" is not known.

(Subcommentary) When a son sees his mother, milk drips from her breast and by this sign he knows her.

(This last detail is presumably meant to prevent inadvertent acts of incest).

They do not sow seeds, nor pull the plough.

The people eat rice without farming or cooking.

The pure fragrant rice grains are without chaff or husk.

Cooked on magic stones (*tuṇḍikīra*), thus they enjoy their food.

190 *kapparukhesu* locative plural.

191 *mālākamma-latākamma-bhittikamma*—presumably styles of decoration.

192 This is abbreviated from a long list of musical instruments, most of which cannot be identified precisely.

193 Another name for Mount Sineru. The apparent placing of Uttarakuru in the vicinity of Sineru is perplexing.

(Commentary)—The pot is cooked over a fire without smoke or embers by means of the so-called "Jotika Stones"[194] (*jotikapāsāṇā*). Three of these stones are placed together and the pot is put on top. The stones produce heat to cook the rice.

The poem then changes tone completely when it introduces Vessavaṇa as king of Uttarakuru. This being is a great yakkha lord, and the Great King of the North. We will have more to say about him in the chapter on the Cātumahārājika Devas (§ 3:5,7).

Having made oxen pull carriages (*ekakhuraṃ*),[195] they travel about in all directions.

Having made beasts (*pasuṃ*) pull carriages they travel about in all directions.

(Commentary)—Thus mounted, Vessavaṇa's servant yakkhas travel about the land.

Using women as vehicles they travel about in all directions.

(Commentary)—Pregnant women are mostly used as vehicles. They sit on their backs to travel. They are truly made to endure this back-bending burden. Other women are yoked to carts.

Using men as vehicles they travel about in all directions.

(Commentary)—Having seized men, they yoke them to carts. They are unable to seize those of right view; it is mostly barbarian border folk (*paccantimamilakkhuvāsika*) that they take. Once one of these country folk lay down near a certain elder and slept. The elder asked, "Do you sleep a lot, layman?" "Yes, bhante, the slaves of Vessavaṇa are tired every night."

This commentarial explanation would imply two things. First, the slaves are taken from Jambudīpa which is where the "barbarians" live, and second, they are not taken by brute force but enslaved by magical means, thus possessing right view serves as a protection.

Using girls as vehicles they travel about in all directions.

Using boys as vehicles they travel about in all directions.

(Commentary)—The boys and girls are yoked to chariots.

Mounted in such vehicles they ride about in every direction on the errands of their king.

Elephants, horses, divine carriages (*dibbaṃ yānaṃ*), palaces and litters are prepared for the use of their glorious great king.

(Commentary)—These vehicles are equipped with noble seats and sleeping places. They arise through the magical power (ānubhāvasampanna) of the king.

[194] Jotika was a lay follower of the Buddha whose life was full of marvels. His wife was from Uttarakuru and she brought a set of these stones with her. See DPPN.

[195] *Ekakhuraṃ*—This is a very rare word and the translation is uncertain. A literal interpretation would be to take it as an adjective modifying "oxen" and meaning "single-hoofed", a reading supported by the only other incident of this word in Jāt 544, where the commentary glosses it with *abhinnakuro*. "unbroken hoof", but the context here implies some kind of vehicle. Maurice Walshe (LDB, p. 274) translates it as "single-seated", as good a guess as any.

There too are cities, well built in the air.

(Commentary)—Well created by the king, the cities come to be.

(names of cities ...)

Āṭānāṭā, Kusināṭā, Parakusināṭā,

Nāṭasuriyā, Parakusiṭanāṭā.

Kasivanto lies to the north.

Janoghamaparena,

Navanavatiya and Ambarāmbaravatiya.

A royal city is called Āḷakamandā.

But the royal city of their great king Kuvera is called *Visāṇā*.

From this Great King Kuvera took the name *Vessavaṇa*.

(Commentary)—He was once a brahmin named Kuvera, living before the Buddha. He owned seven sugar-cane fields and made much merit from their proceeds. Reborn as a *cātumahārājika deva*, he was later made king in Visāṇa and took that name.

The emissaries of the king are now made known;

Tatolā, Tattalā, Tatotalā,

Ojasi, Tejasi, Tatojasī, Sūro, Rājā, Ariṭṭho, and Nemi.

(Commentary)—There are also Sūrorājā and Ariṭṭhanemi. Each of these investigates and advises on various matters. They are known as the twelve *yakkharaṭṭhikā* ("yakkha officials") and they pass their reports on to the twelve *yakkhadovārikā* ("yakkha door-keepers") who pass them on to the Great King.[196]

Thus, one image of Uttarakuru is that of an earthly paradise where the people live in a state of primitive purity. Onto that is grafted another image, that of a realm where powerful yakkhas live in aerial cities and enslave human beings to use as draught animals. What are we to make of these two discordant elements? It may be that the human Uttarakuru folk are protected and guided in their innocence by the yakkhas, who only enslave "barbarians" from Jambudīpa.

On the other hand, to take a more critical view, we may have here muddled traces of two ancient and separate traditions. The idea of Uttarakuru is older than Buddhism. In his *Epic Mytholo*gy which draws on the Vedas and Puranas, Hopkins says this about Uttarakuru:

The Uttara Kurus are another class of Northern saints and seers, living beyond the gate barred by the head of

[196] It is interesting that the commentary adds two additional officials to make up the number twelve, which is then repeated in the number of door-keepers. Is this some echo of solar symbolism with the king as sun attended by the twelve houses of the zodiac?

the monster Mahisa, south of Nila and on the flank of Meru. They live ten thousand and ten hundred years and are buried by birds. They have heavenly felicity in food and freedom; their clothes are grown by trees; their women are not restrained. They associate with spirits born of water and fire and mountain, and where they live, Indra "rains wishes" and jealousy is unknown.[197]

[197] Hopkins 1915: 186.

3:1:4 GENDER

Human beings may be classified in different ways; by gender, caste and nationality for instance.

The inhabitants of the *kāmabhūmi,* the "sense desire realm" which includes humans, animals and devas, as well as the inhabitants of *niraya* and the petas, are as a rule divided into two genders, male and female. Human beings are no exception. The gender of the individual is determined by the possession of either the femininity or masculinity faculties (*itthindriyaṃ* or *purisindriyaṃ*).

> The femininity faculty has the female sex as its characteristic. Its function is to show that 'this is a female'. It is manifested as the reason for the mark, sign, work and ways of the female.
>
> The masculinity faculty has the male sex as its characteristic. Its function is to show that 'this is a male'. It is manifested as the reason for the mark, sign, work and ways of the male. (Vism 14:57–58)

The commentary to the Dhammasangaṇi of the Abhidhamma has a long passage discussing the femininity and masculinity faculties:

> It is on account of the femininity faculty that the female organ (*itthiliṅga*) and so on exist … The hands, feet, neck and breast of a woman are not formed like those of a man. In a woman, the lower body is smooth (*visado*), the upper body is shaped (*avisado*). The hands, feet and face are all small. The marks by which she may be known are as follows: the flesh of her breasts is rounded (*avisado*), on her face there grows no beard or whiskers. The way a woman binds her hair and wears her clothes is not like that of a man. Their behaviour is charming. When females are young girls they play with dolls (*cittadhītalikāya,* lit. "images of little daughters") and with little mortars and pestles. They make strings of clay beads.
>
> A woman's way of walking, standing, lying down, sitting, eating and chewing are graceful (*avisado*). If a man is seen going about like this he is said to be walking etc. like a woman.
>
> The state of womanhood (*itthattaṃ*) and the womanly nature (*itthibhāva*) both mean the same thing. Born of kamma, it originates at the time of conception (or "rebirth-linking" *paṭisandhi*). Just as a seed is the cause of the tree branches which rise to the sky, so the femininity faculty is the cause of the female organ and so forth. The femininity faculty is not perceivable by the eye or by the mind but the female organ and so forth is perceivable …
>
> The male organ and so forth should be considered the opposite of the female. A man's hands, feet, neck, breast and so forth are not shaped like those of woman. His upper body is smooth (*visado*), his lower body is lumpy (*avisado*). His hands and feet are large, his face is large. The flesh of his breast is smooth (*visado*) and he grows a beard and whiskers. The manner in which he binds his hair and wears his clothes is not like that of a woman. When a young boy, he plays with toy chariots and ploughs, he plays at digging channels in the sand. His way of behaviour is straight-forward (*visado*). If a woman is seen acting in this way, it is said she is acting like a man[198].

---

[198] Dhs-a 2. The translation is admittedly problematic. Much rests on the interpretation of the rare word *visado* and its opposite *avisado*. These words do not occur at all in the canon. When it occurs elsewhere in the commentaries *visado* either means "clean, pure" (as at Vism 4:43) and is paired with *parisuddha*, or "clear, distinct" (as at Vism-mhṭ 11 and MN-a 4) and may be paired with the synonym *vibhūta*. It might even mean "sharp, accurate" (as at Vism-mhṭ 20 where it is paired with *tikkha*). Visado and avisado occur several times in the passage translated here and it proved impossible to convey any kind of sense

The same passage goes on to discuss indeterminate or intermediate cases. The Vinaya texts record rare cases of a man changing into a woman or the reverse. "A certain bhikkhu went to sleep in the form of a man, having beard and whiskers and so forth, but all this disappeared in the night and he woke up in the form of a woman" (Vin Pār 1). There is also an incident of spontaneous sex-change recorded in the *Dhammapada Commentary*:

> At that time in the city of Soreyya, the son of the treasurer was going along in a carriage together with one of his good friends and a retinue of servants. They were riding to the reservoir with the intention of bathing. At the city gate they saw the elder bhikkhu Mahākaccāyana putting on his outer robe before entering the city for alms. Seeing the golden colour of the elder's body, this thought came into the mind of the treasurer's son, "Oh, that this elder could be my wife, or that my wife could have the golden colour of his body." When he entertained this thought, his male organ disappeared and there appeared in its place a female organ. Feeling ashamed he leapt from the carriage and ran off. His attendants did not know what had happened and could not find him. (Dhp-a 3:9)

In the continuation of the story, she lives as a woman for several years in another town, marries and has two children. Eventually, on encountering Mahākaccāyana again, she begs his forgiveness and is transformed back into a man. His former husband seems to have taken it well, in that he suggested they continue to live together but the treasurer's son has had enough of the home life and takes ordination as a bhikkhu under Mahākaccāyana. It was said of him that he was the father of two sons and the mother of two more, and that he loved the latter more until such time as he became an arahant and was beyond all partial affection (ibid.).

There is also mention of hermaphrodites (*ubhatobyañjanaka,* lit. "marked with both characteristics"). However, none of these cases violates the rule that an individual may only possess one of the two sexual faculties and not both. The hermaphrodites are said to be divided into those with predominantly male characteristics and those who are predominantly female.

The passage concludes with a discussion of the kamma leading to a male or female birth. Typically enough, it begins with the statement that of the two, the male birth is better (*uttama*) and the female birth lesser (*hīna*). But, interestingly, it is not the ethical quality of the kamma that determines gender, but the strength of it. Good (*kusala*, lit. "skilful") kamma strengthens both sex faculties and bad (*akusala*) kamma diminishes them. However, if the kamma is strong (*balava*) it favours a male birth, and weak (*dubbala*) kamma favours a female birth (Dhs-a 2).

This, at least, is the explanation given in the Abhidhamma. The commentary to the *Dhammapada* gives quite a different explanation:

> It is not possible that there is a woman who was not a man at some time in the past, nor a man who was not a woman. Men who commit transgressions with other men's wives, when they die suffer in *niraya* for many hundreds of thousands of years and when they return to the human state it is in the form of a woman for one hundred existences.
>
> Even the elder Ānanda during his wandering in *saṃsāra* was at one time born into a clan of blacksmiths and in that existence committed adultery with another man's wife. After suffering in *niraya*, by the residue of his kamma he was reborn fourteen times as some man's concubine (*pādaparicārikā itthī*), and only after seven more (female) rebirths was the seed of his actions exhausted.
>
> On the other hand, women who make merit with acts of generosity and putting aside the desire for a female

using a single pair of english words. In general, a woman's appearance and mannerisms are said to be *avisado* except that her lower body is *visado*. Conversely, a man's appearance and mannerisms are *visado* except that his lower body is *avisado*.

existence, establish the thought "by this act of merit may I obtain a male existence", after death will be reborn as men. Likewise, a woman who is a devoted wife (*patidevatā hutvā*, lit. "she is a *devatā* for her husband") and respects his authority obtains thereby a male existence.[199]

Some passages of the Saṃyutta Nikāya discuss women.[200] Some reflect the social reality of ancient India, as when a woman is called "the best of possessions,"[201] or when we are told that a woman may gain control over her husband through the possession of five powers (*bala*); beauty, wealth, relatives, sons and virtue, but that in spite of these a man can always gain control over his wife through the possession of the single power of authority (*issariya*) (SN 37:27 -28). When King Pasenadi of Kosala was displeased that his wife Queen Mallikā had given birth to a daughter, the Buddha told him that a woman may turn out better than a man; she may be wise and virtuous, become a dutiful wife and give birth to a son who becomes a hero (SN 3:16). There are said to be five kinds of suffering endured by women and not by men; while still young they are made to leave their own family to live with their husband's, menstruation, pregnancy, childbirth and being required to serve a man (SN 37:3). (It may be noted that two of these are social conventions and three are biological realities). Against all this, we hear the voice of the bhikkhunī Somā addressing Māra:

What does womanhood matter?

With a mind well restrained,

Insight unfolds and all things are clearly seen (SN 5:2).

Besides the hermaphrodites mentioned above, another class of sexually intermediate persons is mentioned in the Vinaya. These are the *paṇḍakas*. Five kinds of male paṇḍakas are listed:

āsittapaṇḍaka—"one who satisfies his passion by taking another's organ in his mouth and is thus sprinkled with the impure discharge." (āsitta = "to be sprinkled with")

usūyapaṇḍaka—"one who watches others taking their pleasure and satisfies his desire through the feeling of envy." (*usūya* = "envy, jealousy")

opakkamikapaṇḍaka—"One whose testicles (lit. "seeds') have been removed in some way" (i.e. a eunuch, *opakkamika* = "by some contrivance")

pakkhapaṇḍaka—"One who, through the power of his unskilful kamma, is a *paṇḍaka* during the dark half of the month, in the bright half of the month his passions are calmed." (*pakkha* = "part, section") According to the sub-commentary, "some say that the *pakkhapaṇḍaka* becomes a woman during the dark half of the month, and a man during the bright half.")

napuṃsakapaṇḍaka—"One who from the moment of rebirth is not fully formed (*abhāvako*)" (i.e. born a eunuch, *napuṃsaka* = "a not-male").

None of these *paṇḍakas* may be accepted for ordination as bhikkhus (Vin MVa 1:47).

There are also eleven kinds of defective females. This list is found twice in the Vinaya texts; once as a list of insults that a bhikkhu should not utter to a woman, (Vin Sd 3) and once as a list of persons who are ineligible for ordination as bhikkhunīs (Vin Cv 10:3). They are mostly women with some defect either in the genitals or in the menstrual cycle.

animitta—"she lacks the sign of the female, there is a defect in the key-hole" (*kuñcika*).

nimittamatta—"the sign of the female is seen to be incomplete."

alohita—"the flow of blood is dried up."

dhuvalohita—"blood is ever flowing, like running water."

---

199 Dhp-a 3:9. This is very probably the later of the two explanations.

200 See especially SN 37:1 f.—the *Mātugāmasaṃyutta*.

201 SN 1:77—*bhaṇḍānamuttamaṃ*.

dhuvacoḷa- "she is constantly wearing the (menstrual) rag, always making use of it."

paggharanta—"her urine is always flowing."

sikharaṇi—"the fleshy nail has gone outward" (*bahinikkhantāaṇimaṃsā*). This is difficult to decipher, perhaps it means an enlarged clitoris (*sikharaṇī* lit. means "mountain peak nail").

itthipaṇḍakā- a woman *paṇḍaka*, "without the sign".

vepurisikā—"she has a beard and whiskers; a woman like a man".

sambhinna—"the passages for faeces and urine are mixed up."

ubhatobyañjanā—"She has both female and male signs," a hermaphrodite.[202]

A NOTE ON GENDER STATUS

Although it is strictly speaking outside the scope of this book, it is really not possible to leave the topic of gender without addressing the issue of gender status in the Pali texts. This is a vast topic and I do not propose to treat it exhaustively here but do wish to make three salient points.

First, it must always be borne in mind that ancient India was a patriarchal society. This is clearly evident in, for example, the stories about the deva realms where among the pleasures enjoyed by male devas are huge retinues of female *accharās*, celestial dancing girls. It is naive and anachronistic to expect modern, western standards of gender equality to apply.

Second, there are only a very few passages found in the canon itself (as opposed to the commentaries) which a modern reader would consider misogynistic. Almost all of these occur in short suttas in the *Aṅguttāra Nikāya* and as they are not to be found in the parallel recensions of the Chinese Āgamas, may very well be late interpolations.[203]

Third, and this is of primary importance, the Buddha was unequivocal in stating that women do have the potential for full awakening (Vin Cv 10). From the Buddhist point of view, all else that may be said of men and women and their respective positions, merits and demerits is of trivial consequence.

[202] Definitions from Vin Sd 3.

[203] See the discussion in Bodhi 2012: 60f.

3:1:5 CASTE

One of the most basic ways of dividing and classifying humanity in ancient India was into the four castes or *vaṇṇa* (lit. "colours or complexions"). To modern westerners and, as we shall see, to the Buddha, this division seems like an arbitrary social convention. To most Indians at the time, however, it seemed as natural and as fundamental as gender or ethnicity.

When speaking about caste in the Buddha's time it is important not to be anachronistic and assume the existence of the later system, which became more rigid and more complex over the centuries.[204] There were four *vaṇṇas*. In the order preferred in the Buddhist texts they were; the *khattiya* (warrior-nobles), *brāhmana* (in English "brahmins"; priests), *vessa* (merchants and farmers) and *sudda* (labourers). The brahmins, however, preferred a different order which put them on top. To the brahmins, who represented religious orthodoxy, the division into *vaṇṇas* was a natural one, ordained at the creation of the world by the sacrifice of a primordial being as recounted in the *Ṛg Veda*:

When they divided Puruṣa how many portions did they make?

What do they call his mouth, his arms? What do they call his thighs and feet?

The Brahman was his mouth, of both his arms was the *Rājanya* (*khattiya*) made.

His thighs became the *Vaiśya*, from his feet the Śūdra was produced.

The Moon was gendered from his mind, and from his eye the Sun had birth;

Indra and Agni from his mouth were born, and Vāyu from his breath.

Forth from his navel came mid-air the sky was fashioned from his head,

Earth from his feet, and from his ear the regions. Thus they formed the worlds.

Seven fencing-sticks had he, thrice seven layers of fuel were prepared,

When the Gods, offering sacrifice, bound, as their victim, Puruṣa.[205]

In the Buddhist texts the brahmins are depicted as being very proud of their caste. A brahmin who became a bhikkhu recounts how he has been abused by his former friends:

The brahmins say this, "The brahmins are the senior caste (*seṭṭho vaṇṇo*), other castes are base (*hīnā*). The brahmins are white, other castes are dark. The brahmins are pure, not non-brahmins. The brahmins are the true sons of Brahmā, born from his mouth. They were created by Brahmā and are Brahmā's heirs. And you, who were of the highest caste, have gone over to the base caste, the shaven head ascetics, dark and menial, kinsmen of Brahmā's feet (DN 27).

The Buddha did not accept this view of the origin of the castes. First he ridicules it by asking how brahmins could have sprung from Brahmā's mouth when we see brahmin women giving birth and nursing their babies like any other women, (ibid.) then he proceeds to offer an alternative explanation which makes the division into castes a practical human institution instead of a primordial or divine dispensation. The *Aggañña Sutta* (DN 27) describes the origins of this world system and the devolution of human beings from Ābhassara Brahmās. After the humans

---

[204] See T. W. Rhys-Davids, 1903, chap. 4 and Eraly 2004: 94f.

[205] Rig Veda, hymn 40, tr. by R.T.H. Griffith. The Sanskrit forms of the caste designations are used; *vaiśya* = *vessa*, śūdra = *sudda*.

had reached something like our present state, various evils that had not been known before appeared among them; "stealing, reproaches, speaking falsely and beating with sticks" in the course of disputes over the allocation of the rice fields. So the people got together and decided to appoint one among them who was chosen as being "the most handsome (*abhirūpataro*), the most good-looking (*dassanīyataro*), the most pleasant natured (*pāsādikataro*) and the most powerful (*mahesakkhataro*) and appointed him as their leader. His duties would be "to make known those who ought to be made known, to banish those who ought to be banished, to admonish those who ought to be admonished and to seize those who ought to be seized."[206] In return, the community would provide him with a share of the rice and mangoes, he would not be required to do any other work and he would be held supreme among them (DN-a 27).

This individual was given the title *Mahāsammata*, "the Great Chosen One" because he was chosen by the people. He was also the first *khattiya*, so called because he was "lord of the fields" (*khettānaṃ adhipati*) in charge of their allocation. He was also given the title of *rāja* ("king") because "he delighted them with Dhamma" (*dhammena pare rañjeti*) (ibid.). In the time of King Mahāsammata, there were no harsh punishments such as beatings with sticks or amputation of the hands and feet; these were introduced later by rough (*kakkhaḷa*) kings.[207] King Mahāsammata reigned for an entire *asaṅkheyya kappa* (an "intermediate kappa" here probably meaning one twentieth of an unfolded kappa). This was a very long life-span even for that time when the ordinary human span was eighty thousand years (Jāt 422). He was the precursor of the Buddha in two ways. Mahāsammata was a previous rebirth of the Bodhisatta, (DN-a 27) as well as the founding ancestor of the lineage of kings from which the Sakyan rājas (and therefore Suddhodana and his son Siddhattha who became the Buddha) claimed descent (DN-a 20, Vin Mv 1:41).

We can see that in the Buddha's account the institution of a ruling caste of warrior-nobles originated as a practical measure to deal with the social problems which began with agriculture and private property. This is emphasized when the Buddha concludes his description by saying that:

> This was the ancient, original designation of the circle of *khattiyas* (*khattiyamaṇḍala*). Their birth was the same as that of other beings. They were like the others, not unlike them. It was according to nature (*dhammena*) not unnatural. (DN 27)

The origin of the other castes was explained in a similar naturalistic manner. The brahmins originated among those people whose reaction to the increase of evil doing was to withdraw from society:

> They thought, "Evil has arisen among beings. Now theft is known, reproaches are known, false speech is known, punishment and banishing are known." So they went to the forest and made there huts of leaves and meditated in them. With the embers and smoke of the hearth extinguished, with the mortar and pestle laid aside, they went into the villages, towns and cities to gather alms for their breakfast and supper and returned to their leaf huts to meditate. (ibid.)

Thus they were called *brāhmana* because they kept away (*bāheti*) from evil doing. They were also known as *jhāyaka*, "meditators". In their origins, then, the brahmins were very much like the *samaṇas* of the Buddha's time; alms mendicant, forest dwelling contemplatives. But in the course of time they departed from their true and original function. Some brahmins were unable to meditate and returned to the towns and villages, where they compiled and taught the Vedas. These were called *ajjhāyaka*, "non-meditators", and although this began as the lower designation, in time people came to esteem these *ajjhāyaka* more. "At one time for a man to recite mantras was considered a low thing, now to say that a person holds many mantras is considered the highest birth."[208]

---

206 DN 27 terms defined as according to the commentary.

207 Jāt 472. This text also says that banishment was not yet practiced although this contradicts the text of DN 27.

208 DN-a 27. Maurice Walshe (LDB footnote 848) points out that the true etymology of *ajjhāka* is probably *adhy-āyaka* meaning

Other persons, fond of sexual intercourse and engaging in various trades (*visukammante*) became known as the *vessa* caste. Cow herding and trade are especially mentioned as *vessa* occupations. Yet others took to low and cruel ways of life such as hunting and these became known as the *sudda* caste, those who "quickly descend into contemptible ways."[209] For all of these castes the Buddha repeats the refrain introduced at the end of the story of the Mahāsammata: "Their birth was the same as that of other beings. They were like the others, not unlike them. It was according to nature (*dhammena*) not unnatural." All of the four castes represented, in the Buddhist account, purely functional, occupational distinctions. The minimizing of the idea of caste as a fundamental, natural human distinction is also seen in the often repeated saying of the Buddha that "by birth one is not a Brahmin,"[210] redefining the term into an ethical one which can with justice be applied to a person of any *vaṇṇa*. Likewise, the universality of caste is challenged by noting that among the Yonas (i.e. "Ionians" or Greeks) there are only two castes; slave and free (MN 93).

Even within the strictly north Indian context, at least two significant groups were considered outside the four *vaṇṇa* caste system altogether. Some were below the formally defined castes, considered beneath even the *suddas*; mostly this was due to following occupations considered unclean, but it is likely these folk derived from tribes of non-Aryan origin.

> There are persons without hope. Here, a person is born into a lowly family (*nīca kula*), a *caṇḍāla* ("outcaste") family, or a family of bamboo workers, or a family of hunters, or a family of tanners, or a family of refuse-cleaners. Wretched (*dalidda*), having little to eat, having a hard life, winning his livelihood only with difficult toil; he is ugly (*dubaṇṇo*, lit. "of bad colour"), with unsightly features, dwarfish, sickly; blind or crippled, lame or broken bodied. He does not get food or drink, or clothing or vehicles, adornments or ointments, nor a good house, nor a lamp for light. If he hears that such and such a *khattiya* nobleman is to be anointed with the *khattiya's* sprinkling, it does not occur to him to ask, "When will I be anointed with the *khattiya's* sprinkling?" He is a person without hope.[211]

The other group are those who have left the caste system by leaving ordinary lay society; the *samaṇas* including especially the Buddhist bhikkhus. In the Buddhist *saṅgha* (monastic order) any distinction of caste was ignored:

> Just as when the great rivers, the Gaṅgā, the Yamunā, the Aciravatī, the Sarabhū and the Mahī, empty into the Great Ocean, they lose their former designations and become just Ocean; so too, when men of the four castes, *khattiya*, *brāhmaṇa*, *vessa* and *suddā*, go forth from the home life into homeless in the *Tathāgata's* dispensation, they abandon their former names and clans and are known just as *samaṇā sakyaputtiyā* ("ascetic sons of the Sakyan"). (AN 8: 19)

It should be emphasized that the Buddha's approach was always to downplay the importance of birth in determining the character of a person. A wise and virtuous person could arise from any of the four *vaṇṇas* or indeed from "*caṇḍālas* or *pukkusas*" ("outcastes and refuse collectors") (AN 3: 58). The Buddha is recorded as having ordained various

a reciter. Cf. *Critical Pali English Dictionary*, "*ajjhāyaka*, m. (from *ajjhāyati*, cf. sa. ādhyāyika, *adhyāyin*), one who studies (the Vedas), skilled in the Vedas, a brahmanical teacher. *ajjhāyati*, pr. 3 sg. (prob, denom, from *ajjhāya* [sa. *adhyāya*], cf. *sajjhāyati*), to study, learn by heart".

209 DN-a 27. No clear etymology is given for *sudda* in the text or commentary.

210 MN 98 for one example among many.

211 AN 3: 13. Some terms are translated following the interpretation of the commentary. Of note is the term translated "tanner" which is *rathakāra* in the Pali. A more straightforward translation would be "chariot-maker" but this seemingly did not seem "low" enough for the commentator. The emphasis on having no hope for a noble anointing ceremony supports the idea of a non-Aryan origin for these outcaste groups.

low-caste and outcaste individuals, among them Sunīta the refuse collector (Th 12:2) and Upāli the barber.[212] In the Buddhist view, caste is only "natural" in that birth into a higher or lower caste is determined by the kamma made by an individual in a previous existence (MN 129).

It is important to qualify these remarks, however, by noting that the Buddha did not attempt to effect a general social reform. He ignored caste distinctions within his own *saṅgha*, but he never sought to abolish them in the wider society. Indeed, we sometimes see the Buddha defending the primacy of the *khattiyas* over the brahmins. For example, when seeking to humble the overweening pride of the brahmins he notes that in a mixed marriage of a *khattiya* and a brahmin, the offspring would be accepted as well-born under existing caste rules by the brahmins but not by the khattiyas (DN 3).

[212] Vin Cv 7. He was ordained before several high caste Sakyan nobles so that he would always be senior to them.

3:1:6 HUMAN SPACE GEOGRAPHY OF JAMBUDĪPA

FIGURE NINE—MAP OF THE MAJJHIMADESA AT THE TIME OF THE BUDDHA

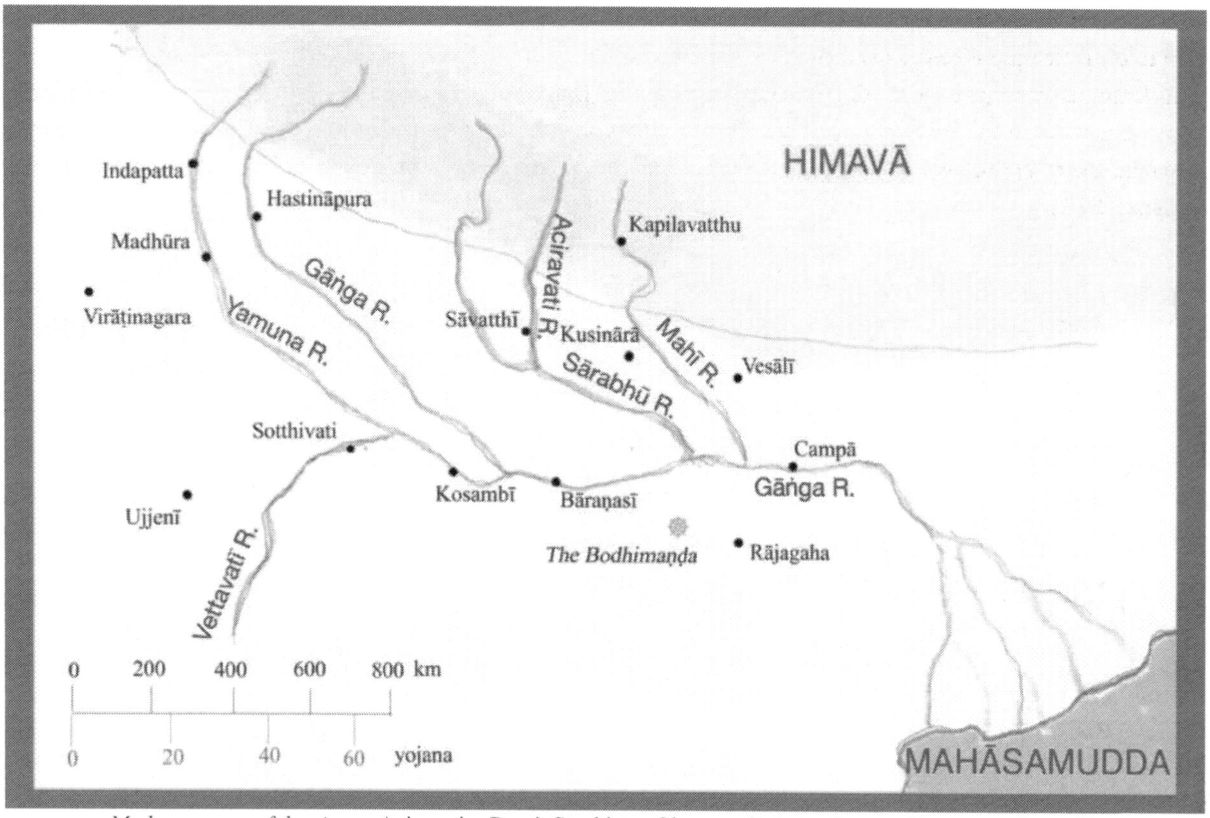

Modern names of the rivers: Aciravati = Rapti, Sārabhū = Ghagara, Gaṅgā = Ganges, Vettavatī = Betwa[213]

In Part One we looked at the geography of the northern half of Jambudīpa, the southern island-continent (§ 1:11 f.). The southern half, which is roughly speaking the equivalent of the Indian sub-continent, is the abode of familiar human existence. The zone of high civilization and culture was considered to be the Ganges valley; the *majjhimadesa* ("middle country"). The rest of the known world was considered the *paccantimā janapadā* ("border countries") and was thought of as relatively rough and barbarous. The *majjhimadesa* is the place where Buddhas, paccekabuddhas, *cakkavatis* and other great and noble beings are born (AN-a 1:170). It is considered relatively rare to be born in the middle country, more common but less fortunate to be born in the border countries where bhikkhus and bhikkhunīs seldom travel and the Dhamma is not heard (AN 8:29). The people of the border countries are characterized as *aviññātāra milakkha* ("ignorant barbarians").[214] The precise borders of the *majjhimadesa* are impossible to define, in part because they are defined with place names that are now obscure, and in part because it was an intentionally vague concept. The commentary says that for some purposes all of Jambudīpa can be considered as the *majjhimadesa* and only the other island-continents as *paccantimā janapadā*. As well, the same passage gives the district of Anurādhapura

[213] Sources used for map: Law 1932, DPPN; mapsofindia.com; Google Maps, & *Britannica Library*, s.v. "India," accessed January 4, 2017, http://library.eb.com/levels/referencecenter/article/111197#214184.toc.

[214] Ibid. *milakkha* is the Pali form of the Sanskrit *mleccha* which the PED says is an onomatopoeic imitation of the strange sounds heard in foreign languages. This is reminiscent of the Greek division of the world into civilized Hellenes and barbarians who made a noise like "bar-bar".

in Sri Lanka a kind of honorary middle-country status (AN-a 1:323).

The locale of the *majjhimadesa* has some legal status in the context of the Vinaya rules of the bhikkhus. Within the middle country a quorum of ten bhikkhus is required to perform an ordination, whereas outside those bounds only five are needed (Vin Mv 5). Some of the minor rules are also relaxed outside the bounds of the *majjhimadesa*; for example *pācittiya* 57 forbids bathing more than once a fortnight but this rule is suspended for all bhikkhus living outside the middle-country (ibid.). The most important spot in the *majjhimadesa*, and indeed in the whole ten thousand fold world-system, is the *Bodhimaṇḍa*, the site where all the Buddhas attain to full awakening. Located near the town of Gayā, it is the spot where Gotama sat under the Bodhi Tree on the night of his great awakening (Jāt 479).

There is a list of sixteen "great nations" (*mahājanapada*) existing in India in the Buddha's time, fourteen of which were within the bounds of the *majjhimadesa*. This list was not exclusively a Buddhist one, but a common Indian concept as versions existed in the Jain literature as well as the *Mahābharata*.[215] Moving roughly from east to west, the fourteen great nations of the middle-country are listed below[216] (Note that the capital or chief cities of these are indicated on the map above).

Aṅga—capital city: Campā. By the time of the Buddha, Aṅga was no longer an independent nation but was subject to Magadha. Its territory likely extended all the way to the coast. Aṅga had a prosperous mercantile economy.

Magadha—capital city: Rājagaha. Magadha was the most important and powerful kingdom in India at the time of the Buddha and for a long time afterward. Magadha became the nucleus around which future pan-Indian empires like the Mauryas and the Guptas coalesced. The kings which ruled during the Buddha's lifetime were Bimbisāra and his son and murderer, Ajātasattu. Bimbisāra was an early convert to Buddhism and the kingdom became an important centre of the new religion. The Magadhan language, traditionally considered to be the basis of Pali, was held to be the purest form of Aryan speech (Vin-a, Pār 1). Indeed, Magadhi was held to be the "root language" (*mūlabhāsa*) of all beings; (Vism 1.25) that language which a child would spontaneously speak if it heard no other. It is also the speech which is most commonly used in various non-human realms including *niraya*, the *devalokas* and among speaking animals like nāgas and *supaṇṇas* (Vibh-a 15).

Vajjī—capital city: Vesālī. This was a confederation of several tribal republics, the most important of which were the Licchavī. The Vajjī confederacy, too, fell to Magadha shortly after the passing of the Buddha. The Licchavī nobles were renowned for the beauty of their bodies and their adornments; the Buddha once remarked that those who have never seen the devas of Tāvatiṃsa should look upon the Licchavī to get an idea of what they must be like (DN 16). The Licchavī had a supernatural origin. The queen of Bārāṇasī had given birth to a shapeless lump of meat and the king, being ashamed, had it placed in a casket and put in the Ganges where it was recovered by an ascetic. The lump developed into two children, a boy and a girl. They had the odd characteristic that their abdomens were transparent so that the contents of their stomachs could be seen, hence the name Licchavī, from *līna-chavī* ("thin skin"). When grown, these two married each other and gave birth to sixteen pairs of twins which were the founders of the Vajjī clans (MN-a 12).

Kāsi—capital city: Bārāṇasī (modern Varānasi or Benares). At the time of the Buddha Kāsi was not an independent kingdom but had been absorbed by Kosala. The capital, Bārāṇasī, was a very ancient and important city. In ancient times it had been the political and cultural centre of all India. Many of the Jātaka stories begin with the words, "when Brahmadatta was king in Bārāṇasī," just as a European tale might begin with "once upon a time." The Buddha gave his first sermon, the *Dhammacakkappavattana Sutta*, (SN 56:11) at the deer park near Bārāṇasī, making this the site where the Buddhist religion began.

Mallā—capital city: Kusinārā. In previous times, Mallā had been a powerful kingdom with a fortified capital

[215] For the Buddhist version see AN 3: 71 (eng. 70) and AN 8: 42. See Law 1932, note 22 to ch.1.

[216] Unless otherwise indicated, the sources for this section are the DPPN and Law 1932.

named Kusāvatī. By the Buddha's time it had declined in importance and split into two tribal republics. Kusāvatī was now a small town called Kusinārā, so unimpressive that Ānanda derided it as being no more than a small backwoods settlement unsuitable for the Buddha's *parinibbāna*. Nevertheless, the Buddha chose it, recalling the former importance of the place. The Mallā, although a small nation, appear to have had some martial strength, in that they later put up a stiff resistance to Alexander.

Kosala—capital city: Sāvatthi. After Magadha, Kosala was the second most powerful kingdom at that time in India. Its king during the Buddha's lifetime was Pasenadi who was another early convert to the new faith. Sāvatthi was the site of the Jetavana monastery where the Buddha spent altogether nineteen rainy seasons. Sāvatthi was a city renowned for its wealth, and was said to be home to 57,000 families, (Vin-a Sd 13) so the total population must have been at least five or six times that. Both Kāsi and the Sākyan republic, birthplace of the Buddha, were vassals of Kosala.

Vaṃsa—capital city: Kosambī. Vaṃsa was a kingdom to the west of Kosala. Its capital, Kosambī, was a large city on the Yamuna River and became an important Buddhist centre. It was at one of the monasteries in Kosambī that there occurred a famous quarrel among the bhikkhus over a trivial point of *vinaya*, causing the Buddha to leave them and spend the rainy season in the forest attended by an elephant and a monkey.

Ceti—capital city: Sotthivati. There were two countries inhabited by the Ceti people; the older nation was located in the far north, in what is now Nepal but by the time of the Buddha a southern colony in the modern district of Bundelkhand had assumed a greater importance. The location of the capital, Sotthivati, is doubtful. It may have been more or less as shown on the map above, or it may have been located in the northern Ceti country. Little more is known about this nation.

Surasena—capital city: Madhūra. Surasena was a kingdom located on the upper Yamuna. In the Hindu epics it was the scene of one of Krishna's adventures and a Buddhist version of this tale is recorded in the Ghata Jātaka (Jāt 454). The capital, Madhūra, was evidently ill-favoured. A sutta in the Aṅguttara Nikāya lists five disadvantages of Madhūra: the ground is uneven, it is dusty, it has fierce dogs and bestial yakkhas and it is difficult to obtain almsfood there (AN 5: 220).

Pañcāla—capital city: Hastināpura. The nation of Pañcāla was divided into two small kingdoms, North and South Pāñcāla, separated by the Ganges. It was often at war with the Kurus to the north. Several cities are mentioned as Pāñcāla capitals at various times. Hastināpura seems to have been the most important. It was already a very ancient city in the Buddha's time and is an important locale in the Hindu epic, the *Mahābharata*.

Kuru—capital city: Indapatta. The Kuru people claimed a fantastic origin; their ancestors were people of Uttarakuru, the earthly paradise on the northern island-continent, brought to Jambudīpa by the *cakkavatti* Mandhāta (DN-a 15). Descended from this high lineage, they were renowned as being of "sound body and mind" (*kallasarīrā, kallacittā*) (MN-a 10). and no doubt because of their excellent capabilities, the Buddha spoke some of his most profound suttas there, including the Mahāsatipaṭṭhāna Sutta and the Mahānidāna Sutta (DN 22 & DN 15). There is also a Jātaka story attesting to their remarkably punctilious keeping of the precepts.[217] Besides the capital, Indapatta located very near modern Dehli, the other important town was Kammāssadhamma were the Buddha always delivered his teachings when visiting the Kuru country.

Macchā—capital city: Virāṭanagara. Little can be found about these people in the sources. They may been closely associated in some way with Sūrasena, because in one list of nations the two names are given combined in a compound, *macchasūrasena* (DN 18). The name means "fish", which is odd for a people living well inland. It is doubtful whether Macchā should be counted as part of the *majjhimadesa*.

The four remaining *mahājanapadas* are definitely outside the bounds of the middle-country are:

[217] Jāt 276, the Kurudhamma Jātaka.

Avanti—capital city: Ujjenī. Avanti was a powerful kingdom, rivalling Magadha and Kosala. Ujjenī was a very ancient city and a mercantile and cultural rival of Bārāṇāsī. Although several well known arahant bhikkhus, including Mahākaccāna, came from there, Buddhism does not appear to have prospered in Avanti during the Buddha's lifetime. It was at the request of Mahākaccāna that the Buddha relaxed several *vinaya* rules for those living outside the *majjhimadesa*; the request was made because ten bhikkhus could not be found to make a quorum for ordination. Later, however, Ujjenī became a very important Buddhist centre having close relations with Sri Lanka. The great grammarian Kaccāyana lived there and it can be said that the Pali language as we know it was formalized in Ujjenī.[218]

Assaka—capital city: Potana or Potali. Assaka was a kingdom in the south, centred on the Godavari River. It was home to the hermit Bāvārī who sent sixteen of his pupils to question the Buddha; their dialogues forming the *Pārāyanavagga* of the *Suttanipāta* (Sn 5).

Gandhāra—capital city: Takkasīlā. Gandhāra was a wealthy kingdom in the far north-west, in the modern Punjab. Around the time the Bodhisatta was born, Gandhāra fell to the Persian Empire, but it retained its cultural and mercantile links with India. Takkasīla was an important centre of learning and it is a common motif in the Jātakas that the young hero first studies under a famous master at Takkasīla before undertaking his adventures. The education was based on Vedic lore, but was broad enough to include the science and practical arts of the day. A common summary of the curriculum is given as "the three Vedas and the eighteen branches of knowledge."[219]

Kamboja—Another country of the far north-west was Kamboja. The people of this country were considered barbarous or *anariya* ("non-aryan"). As an example of their savage ways it is said that they killed and ate frogs, worms, grasshoppers, snakes and so forth (Jāt 543). Kamboja was located in what is now Afghanistan. The country was famed for the quality of its horses.

One additional nation which is very important for Buddhist history needs to be mentioned, although it is not included in the sixteen *mahājanapadas*:

Sākya—capital city: Kapillavatthu. Although the commentaries and the later tradition makes Siddhattha a prince, and his father the king, this is nowhere stated in the suttas and according to history the Sākyans were governed by an aristocratic republic. It was under some kind of vassalage to Kosala, and this may be why it isn't included among the *mahājanapadas*. Before the end of the Buddha's lifetime the Sākyan republic was invaded and its people massacred by King Viḍūḍabha who succeeded Pasenadi on the throne of Kosala. The Sākyans claimed a high lineage; they traced their origins to King Okākka, a direct descendent of the primordial king Mahāsammata.[220] There is another tradition which gives the Sākyans an even more illustrious ancestry. The Sanskrit form of Okākka's name is Ikṣvāku, and, according to the Valmiki Rāmāyaṇa, he was the grandson of the sun god Vivasvāna (an epithet of Sūrya).[221] That this connection was still present in the mind of the Sākyans of the Buddha's time is evidenced by his epithet, ādiccabandhu ("Kinsman of the Sun"). At any rate, this pride of birth led directly to the downfall of the Sākyan Republic. When King Pasenadi asked the Sākyans for a woman to be one of his wives, they felt that his caste status was beneath theirs

---

218 Malalasekera: 1994:179f.

219 *Aṭṭhārasannaṃ vijjaṭṭhānānaṃ*; e.g. Jāt 50. There are some variant lists of the 18 branches of knowledge. The list in the *Chāndogya Upaniṣad*, which is probably the oldest extant, is as follows: The Ṛgveda, Yajurveda Sāmaveda & Ātharveda (the four Vedas), the Itihāsa Purāṇa (the Bhārata), the "Vedān of the Vedas, Pitrya (grammar & the rules for the sacrifices for the ancestors), Rāśi (the science of numbers), Daiva, (the science of portents), Nidhi (the science of time), Vākovākya, (logic), Ekāyana, (ethics), Devavidyā, (etymology), Brahmavidyā, (pronunciation, ceremony & prosody), Bhūtavidyā, (the science of demons), Kṣatravidyā, (the science of weapons), Nakṣatravidyāṃ, (astronomy), Sarpavidyā (the science of serpents & poisons), and Devajanavidyā (the sciences of the genii, such as the making of perfumes, dancing, singing, playing, and other fine arts). The English translations are following Max Müller (1879:109).

220 The chronicle of the Mahāvihāra in Sri Lanka, the *Mahāvaṃsa*, gives the whole genealogy from Mahāsammata down to Siddhattha Gotama.

221 Valmiki Rāmāyaṇa. Ayodhya Kānda. Sarga 110.

and they avoided polluting one of their own by passing off a slave girl as a true born Sākyan. This was the mother of Viḍūḍabha, and when he learnt the truth he destroyed the Sākyan nation over the perceived insult.

FOREIGN COUNTRIES

Countries outside the Indian sub-continent are seldom mentioned in the Pali sources, and almost never in the oldest texts. When such places are mentioned, it is usually in the context of a sea-voyage. To the Indians of the Buddha's time, India plus the Himavā was Jambudīpa and any foreign countries they had any inkling of were thought of as being located on one or another of the five hundred minor islands which surrounded the great island-continent. Among those names which do appear we can list the following:

Yona—The Yona were a foreign, i.e. a non-aryan, people usually identified in modern sources with the Greeks; the word *yona* being taken as derived from *Ionian.*[222] This is certainly accurate for later sources but makes no sense in pre-Asokan India. The only reference to Yonas in the four *nikāyas*, i.e. in the oldest texts, which definitely predate the invasion of Alexander, is one passage in which the Buddha denies the universality of the caste system, citing the example of the "Yonas and the Kambojas" who had only two castes, master and slave (MN 93). This would certainly have been true of the Greeks, and the close association with the Kambojans would imply a location in or near Bactria but the Buddha lived more than two centuries before there were any Greeks in Bactria. It is possible that the ancient Indians knew of the existence of Greece. From the other side, Herodotus certainly knew something of India, although his History filled it with fantastic monsters. The Niddesa, a relatively late source, contains a long list of places men go to by sea in search of wealth which includes both *Yona* and *Paramayona* ("Beyond Yona.") (Nid 1:15) which would speak against an identification with Bactria. Yona may have originally meant simply "a foreigner" and later came to be specifically identified with the Greeks.

Bāveru—Bāveru was another kingdom to which Indian merchants sailed. A Jātaka tale tells of such a voyage and includes one fantastic detail, that the people of Bāveru had never seen a bird before encountering the merchants' tame crow (Jāt 339). Modern sources identify this kingdom with Babylon.[223]

Suvaṇṇabhūmi—"The Golden Land" is mentioned in several stories as a distant land reached by sea to which merchants would sail seeking riches. It must have been a difficult and dangerous passage. Of the six voyages which are described, five end in shipwreck[224] and one nearly comes to disaster through a prolonged period without any wind (Pv-a 4: 11). Suvaṇṇabhūmi referred to somewhere in South-East Asia, probably the Burmese coast.

Laṅkādīpa—Sri Lanka, the island of Ceylon, is, despite its great importance to the later history of Theravāda Buddhism, never mentioned in the suttas. One of the Jātaka stories refers to sailors shipwrecked there and encountering man-eating yakkhas (Jāt 196).

We hear nothing at all of places further afield, such as China, Persia or Arabia. To the Buddha's contemporaries, the known human world was basically the sub-continent, identified with Jambudīpa.

---

222 See for example DPPN entry "Yona".

223 Eg. Rhys-Davids, Malalasekera and Law.

224 Ud-a 1: 10, Pv 1:10, Jāt 360, Jāt 442, Jāt 539.

3:1:7 KINGSHIP

The older form of government in India was republican but by the Buddha's lifetime it was well along the way of an historical shift to monarchy. Most of northern India was already dominated by the two powerful monarchies of Magadha and Kosala. Gotama Buddha himself came from a republic, and there are decidedly republican elements in the original procedures of the *saṅgha*, as laid out in the *vinaya* texts. Nevertheless, there is an implicit assumption in the Pali texts that monarchy is the natural form of government.

The Buddhist tradition has had an ambivalent attitude toward kingship. We have already seen[225] that the Buddha denied a divine origin to monarchy, seeing it rather as a purely human pragmatic social construct. It was a necessary evil. In the *Mahādukkhakkhandha Sutta* (MN 13) the Buddha, in describing the perils in attachment to material possessions, lists among the disasters which may befall a property owner that "thieves or kings or nasty relatives" may seize it (MN 13). The Buddha once contemplated whether or not it was possible to rule as a king without committing evil kamma. Significantly, we are not told the answer to that question (SN 4:20).

Among the duties of a king which would entail incurring evil kamma were the waging of war and the dispensation of justice. Justice in ancient India was by all accounts swift and harsh. In the *Aṅguttara Nikāya* there is a long list of punishments which the king's men might inflict on a criminal. They might have him flogged with whips or canes, or beaten with clubs. They might cut off his hands, feet, ears or nose. Or they might subject him to various tortures. These are colourfully named and most were no doubt intended to be fatal:

Bilaṅgathālika—"The Porridge Pot." The top of his skull is opened up and a hot iron ball dropped in to cook his brains.

Saṅkhamuṇḍika—"The Conch-Shell Shave." They flay the skin off his face and head and pull it off by the hair and then polish the top of his skull by rubbing it with coarse gravel.

Rāhumukha—"Rāhu's Mouth." They force his mouth open with a stake and light a lamp inside it. **Jotimālika**—

"The Fire Garland." They wrap an oiled cloth all around his body and then set it on fire. **Hatthapajjotika**—"The

Radiant Hand." They wrap his hand in an oiled cloth and light it so that it burns like a lamp.

Erakavattika—"The Grass Cripple." They peel strips of skin from his neck downward and tie them around his ankles, so that he trips and falls on his own skin.

Cīrakavāsika—"The Bark Razor." They flay the skin off his upper body and let it hang down to his ankles, so that it looks as if he is wearing a bark dress.

Eṇeyyaka—"The Antelope." His wrists and ankles are bound with iron shackles and he is staked to the ground on all-fours. Then fires are lit all around him and kept burning until he is dead. After he dies, the iron posts are removed and his arm and leg bones driven into the ground. (*pour encourager les autres*?)

Baḷisamaṃsika—"The Meat-Hook." His body is beaten all over with a double-pronged hook until the skin, flesh and sinews come apart.

Kahāpaṇika—"The *Kahāpana*." (A *kahāpana* was a middling value coin). With a sharp knife, chunks of flesh the size of a *kahāpana* piece are cut out of his body.

---

225 § 2:5. See the Aggañña Sutta, DN 27.

Khārāpatacchika—"The Lye Rub." After being beaten, his body is covered in strong lye and rubbed with a brush until all the skin and flesh is removed down to the bones.

Palighaparivattika—"Around the Pole." He is made to lie down on his side and a stake is driven into his ear all the way through to the ground below. He is then seized by the feet and turned around and around.

Palālapīṭhaka—"The Straw Mattress." A skilled torturer cuts his skin, breaks his bones and then pulls up a mass of flesh by his hair and twists it into knot like a straw wick.

Or, less imaginatively, they might have him boiled in oil, devoured by dogs, impaled on a stake or simply cut off his head (AN-a 2:1). No one could accuse ancient Indian rulers of being "soft on crime!"

Despite all of this, some element of a cosmic or sacred quality adhered to kingship. Whether or not kings followed the path of Dhamma affected more than their personal kamma, indeed it had cosmic consequences:

> When kings (*rājā*) are righteous (*dhammika*), then the royal vassals (*rājāyutta*) are righteous. When the royal vassals are righteous, then the brahmins and householders are righteous. When they are righteous, then the people of the towns and countryside are righteous. When they are righteous, the moon and the sun turn about evenly (*samaṃ parivattanti*), and because of that, the constellations and stars turn about evenly. Because of that, the days and night turn about evenly. Because of that, the months and fortnights turn about evenly. Because of that, the seasons and years turn about evenly. Because of that, the winds blow evenly and in the proper order. Because of that, the devas do not become agitated. Not being agitated, the devas bestow proper rainfall. With proper rainfall, the crops ripen. With the ripening of the crops, human beings enjoy food and become long-lived, beautiful, strong and without sickness. (AN 4: 70)

Righteousness for a king is defined by the ten *rājadhammas*:

Dāna—Generosity. The foundation of all ten.

Sīla—Morality, defined as keeping the five precepts.

Pariccāga—Having a charitable nature, defined as freely giving gifts.

Ajjava—Uprightness.

Maddava—Mildness or Gentleness.

Tapa—Religious austerity, defined as keeping the *uposatha* vows, i.e. keeping the eight precepts on the days of the full and new moon .

Akkodha—Freedom from anger.

Avihiṃsā—Freedom from cruelty.

Khanti—Patience, forbearance.

Avirodhana—Absence of enmity, gentleness. (Jāt 534)

This was obviously an ideal seldom met with in reality. The only monarch contemporary with the Buddha whom he called a "righteous king" (*dhammarājā*) was Bimbisāra of Magadha (DN 2, DN 18). In the early period of the earth's history, at the time when human lifespans were of indefinite length, there was a long dynasty of 84,000 *dhammarājas* beginning with Makhādeva and ending with Nimi, who was taken up by Mātali, the charioteer of the devas, to visit Tāvatiṃsa. Each of these kings spent 84,000 years playing childish games, 84,000 years serving as viceroy, 84,000 years ruling righteously as a *dhammarājā*, after which they abdicated and spent the remaining 84,000 years of their lives as ascetics living in the forest (MN 83). These kings ruled at Mithilā, which was the capital of Videha (a member of the Vajjian Confederacy), which therefore enjoyed a period of more than 7,000,000 years of beneficent rule.[226] In later times, King Asoka became the exemplar of righteous rule for Buddhist monarchs.

---

226 The grandfather of Makhādeva was called Sāgaradeva (sāgara = "the sea") and there was a legend that he created the sea by digging it out. This was not meant to be taken seriously, but given as an example of idle speculation. See DN-a 1.

3:1:8 THE MAHĀPURISA

This story is told about events shortly after the Bodhisatta Gotama's birth:

> There was, at that time, an ascetic (*tāpasa*) named Asita[227] who was a confidant (*kulūpaka*) of King Suddhodana. He had mastery of the eight attainments (*aṭṭhasamāpattilābhī*, i.e. the jhānas of form and the formless). After eating his daily meal he would go to the deva realm of Tāvatiṃsa for the day's abiding. On one such occasion he happened to see all the devas ecstatically rejoicing:
>
> > Full of joy were the company of devas, delighted.
> >
> > Together with their lord, Sakka.
> >
> > Dressed all in the purest white, were the devas.
> >
> > Waving cloth (banners) and making great praise.
> >
> > This was seen by Asita during his day's abiding.
> >
> > Seeing the devas, with joyful hearts, exultant.
> >
> > Asita having paid his respects, spoke thus;
> >
> > "Why is the company of devas so exceedingly pleased?
> >
> > On account of what do you wave cloth with great delight?
> >
> > "Even when there was battle with the asuras,
> >
> > And victory for the devas.
> >
> > There was not such joy in the company of devas.
> >
> > What wonder have you seen that you wave those cloths so?
> >
> > "They are shouting, they are singing, they are crying out.
> >
> > They are waving their hands and dancing about.
> >
> > I ask you, dwellers on Meru's peak;
> >
> > Resolve quickly my curiosity."
> >
> > (The devas reply):
> >
> > "A Bodhisatta, a peerless gem,
> >
> > Has been born in the human world, for its happiness and well being,

227 In the Jātaka version his name is given as Kāḷadeva. Both names are references to a dark complexion.

In the Sākya country, in the village of Lumbinī.

It is because of this that we rejoice.

"He is supreme among all beings, the highest person.

He is the lord, the greatest of all mankind.

In the forest of the seers, he will set the wheel turning.

Like the lion, lord of beasts, uttering his mighty roar!"

Asita at once left the deva world and proceeded to King Suddhodana's house in Kapilavatthu. Having entered and taken a seat, he was greeted courteously and then said to the king, "A son has been born to you, Mahārājā, may I see him?" The king had his son brought forth, richly adorned, intending to have the baby offer homage to the seer. But the great person (*mahāpurisa*, i.e. the baby Gotama) turned his feet around and quick as lightning placed them on the matted hair of the ascetic's head; for there is no person in the world worthy of receiving a Bodhisatta*'s* homage. Asita rose from his seat to pay homage to the Bodhisatta, and seeing this wonder, his father the king also made *añjali* to the baby (i.e. saluted him with joined palms). Asita looked at the marks with which the Bodhisatta was endowed (*lakkhaṇasampattiṃ*) and asked himself, "Will he become a Buddha or not?" and determined that without a doubt, he would. Having seen the future, he smiled, knowing "This is a wonder-person!" (*acchariyapurisa*) Then Asita considered whether or not he would live to see the baby become a Buddha, and he determined that he would not. Before the Bodhisatta*'s* full awakening, he knew he would die and be reborn in the formless realm. "I shall not be able to see this wonder-person become a Buddha, alas, great is my loss!" and he wept.

The people there asked him, "Dear sir, why did you first smile and then cry out. Is our lord's son in any danger?" The ascetic replied, "He is in no danger, he will become a Buddha."

On the fifth day after the Bodhisatta*'s* birth, they bathed his head and held the ceremony of naming. The royal palace was anointed with the fourfold scents with parched corn as the fifth. Flowers were strewn about and milk-rice was prepared. One hundred and eight brahmins, who had mastered the three Vedas, were invited. These took their seats and were offered milk-rice with honey and shown every honour. (The king) asked "What will become of him?" Among the brahmins there were a group of eight beginning with Rāma who were versed in the signs. Seven of these held up two fingers and announced two possible destinies for the boy. "If he takes up the life of a householder, he will become a *cakkavatti*, a wheel-turning monarch. if goes forth (*pabbajamāna*) then he will become a Buddha." But the youngest of them all, a brahmin named Kondañña, seeing the marks with which the Bodhisatta was endowed, held up just one finger and said, "This one will not take a place among the householders, having drawn away the veil he will become a Buddha." And so, because he was destined for every success (*siddhi*) in the world they named him Siddhattha.[228]

The brahmin seers in this episode are versed in the skill known as *lokāyatamahāpurisalakkhaṇā,* (DN 3 & MN 91) the science of knowing the marks of a "great man" (*mahāpurisa*). This was part of the complete education of a

[228] Prose sections taken from Jāt-nid. Verse section from Sn 3:11. Kondañña later went on to become one of the five ascetics who followed the Bodhisatta and he was the first of the Buddha's disciples to attain stream-entry at the preaching of the Dhammacakkappavattana Sutta, SN 56:11.

brahmin, which was defined as having three branches: (1) knowledge of the Vedas, (2) grammar and (3) the science of the great man's marks (AN 3: 59, eng. 3:58).

Although *mahāpurisa* is occasionally used in reference to a great man in a generic sense, as one who is spiritually advanced,[229] it more often has a very specific sense and refers to an extraordinary human type who comes into the world only rarely. A *mahāpurisa* in this technical sense has two possible destinies open to him; if he remains in the householder's life he will become a *cakkavatti*, a universal "wheel-turning" monarch, but if he renounces the world he will become a Buddha. The male pronoun is used here advisedly, because a *mahāpurisa* is always a man (MN 115 & AN 1:279–80). (The reason for this will become clear when we examine the individual marks). The *mahāpurisa* can be seen as the ideal human type. He is always endowed with three qualities; wisdom, compassion and resolve (*paṇidhisamādāna*). The last quality means that whatever he sets his mind on accomplishing, that he achieves (DN-a 3). *Mahāpurisas* are only born in the *majjhimapadesa* and nowhere else (DN-a 2).

The lore concerning the bodily marks by which a *mahāpurisa* can be recognized is inserted into the Vedas by *suddhāvāsa brahmās*[230] when they know that one will soon be born. These inserted passages become known as the *buddhamantā*. After the passing away of the Buddha or the *cakkavatti*, these passages disappear from the Vedas (MN-a 91). While it is true that the precise listing of the thirty-two marks as given in the Pali texts is not found anywhere in the pre-Buddhist literature known to us, there is mention in the *Bhāgavata Purāṇa* of something very like them when King Parikṣit recognizes the seer Sukadeva Goswāmi by certain physical signs. This was done by the science called *samudrika*, an art required of kings.[231]

---

[229] SN 47:11—where a *mahāpurisa* is one who is said to have a liberated mind and to dwell in the four foundations of mindfulness.

[230] I.e. brahmas of the "Pure Abodes," who have reached the third stage of awakening. See Chapter 6, Section 16.

[231] *Bhāgavata Purāṇa* 1: 19; pointed out to me in a personal correspondence from Jeffrey Armstrong.

3:1:9 THE 32 MARKS OF AMAHĀPURISA

The body of a *mahāpurisa* has thirty-two marks (*mahāpurisalakkhaṇa*) by which he may be recognized. Each of these marks is derived from some specific kamma performed by the *mahāpurisa* in a previous existence, and each confers some special benefit. These marks are as follows:[232]

1. His foot has an even tread (*suppatiṭṭhitapāda*), so that whenever he takes a step, his entire foot touches the ground. This sounds like simple flat-footedness, ("others have a hollow in the middle of the foot where the upper part is raised up, but he does not.") but the commentary explains that it also means something more. If the Buddha were to step onto a low spot in the ground, the earth itself would rise up in that place "like a smith's bellows" so that his tread remained even. Likewise, when the Buddha ascended to Tāvatiṃsa to teach the Abhidhamma, he did so in two steps only. On his first step he placed his foot on the peak of the Yugandhara Range, which is forty-two thousand *yojana* high, the mountain receding so his step would be level. His second step took him to the summit of Mt Sineru in the same manner. Further, wherever he steps any stumps or sharp sticks, rocks or potsherds as well as filth like dung or spittle, goes away so that he steps onto smooth clean earth.

This mark derives from having in the past undertaken mighty deeds for a righteous purpose. In the Buddha's case, this kamma was made when he was born as a squirrel. During a mighty flood, his nest was washed away by the sea. For seven days he kept his young alive by baling the water out of the nest with his tail. The benefit conferred by the mark of a level tread is that the *mahāpurisa* cannot be impeded by any hostile force. In the case of a *cakkavatti* this refers to human foes, in the case of a Buddha, to both external adversaries and to internal defilements.

2. The soles of his feet are marked with a thousand-spoked wheel. This mark arises from the kamma of having provided beings in the past with protection and the necessities of life. The benefit is that the *mahāpurisa* will enjoy a large retinue; for a *cakkavatti* this means retainers and vassal kings, for a Buddha a large following of bhikkhus, bhikkhunīs and lay followers.

The wheels are described as "complete with hub, spokes and rim." This language mirrors the description of the wheel which appears in the sky to a *cakkavatti*, of which these wheels may be taken as miniature representations. However the commentary adds something else; inscribed within the rim are a series of tiny images. Thirty-five are listed: a spear, a "splendid calf",[233] a spiral,[234] a swastika (*sovattika*), a wreath, a set of fine garments, a pair of fish, a wicker chair, an elephant goad, a palace, an arched gateway, a royal parasol (*setacchatta*), a sword, a fan, a peacock's tail, a yak tail whisk,[235] a turban, a jewel, a feather (*patta*), a wreath of jasmine flowers, a blue water-lily, a red water-lily, a white water-lily, a lotus (*paduma*), a white lotus (*pundarīka*), a pitcher full of water, a full dish, the ocean, the world-system (*cakkavāla*), the Himavā mountains, Mt Sineru, the sun and the moon, the constellations, the four island-continents and the two thousand minor islands.[236]

These designs must be too small to see with the naked eye. The symbolism is mixed. Some of them, for instance the parasol and the whisk, are symbols of sovereignty; others are auspicious signs such as the spiral and the swastika. Yet others are marks of abundance like the full pitcher. The last few are obviously of cosmological import. A few are

---

232 Descriptions of the marks are taken from the commentary to the Mahāpadāna Sutta, DN-a 14. The references to the kamma and the results involved are from the commentary to the Lakkhaṇa Sutta, DN-a 30.

233 *Sirivaccho*—the translation is uncertain. The sub-commentary glosses with *siriaṅgā*, a "splendid limb" or perhaps a "mark of splendour" „ which does not help much.

234 This translation is conjectural. The Pali is *nandi*, which likely should be read as *nandhi* "a strap or thong". Sub-commentary glosses as *dakkhiṇ*āvatta "winding to the right".

235 *vāḷabījanī*—translation is according of the sub-commentary which glosses as *cāmarivālaṃ*..

236 GGB gives an expanded list of one hundred and eight images, each of which is said to occur in its own separate circle. The author cites a late Burmese source for this.

hard to understand, like the wicker chair and the pair of fish; no doubt they possessed some significance in ancient times which is now lost.

3, 4 & 5. He has long heels, long fingers and toes and an upright brahmā-like body (*brahmujugatta*). These marks derive from having renounced violence in previous lifetimes. The commentary specifies this a little more. One who creeps up on others to do them harm is reborn with deformed feet, one who habitually makes a fist to strike others is reborn with short or twisted fingers and one who goes about killing others is born with a dwarfish or bent body. The *mahāpurisa*, having refrained from these things, is born with a tall straight body and well-formed feet, fingers and toes. The benefit to the *mahāpurisa* in possessing these marks is that he will live a long life and no foe can ever kill him.

The long heels are described as being as long as the rest of the foot and coming to a round point. The *mahāpurisa's* long fingers and toes are described as being all of the same length and tapering like a candle-wick. His straight body resembles that of a brahmā in that it does not in the slightest incline forward, backward or to either side like the bodies of ordinary people. Instead, it is as straight and upright as a gate-post in a deva city.

6. His body has seven "protruberences" (*ussada*), the two hands, the two feet, the two shoulders and the back. *Ussada* is defined by the Pali English Dictionary as "protuberance, bump, swelling" and in this context means that those areas of a *mahāpurisa's* body are fleshy or muscular. The kamma resulting in this mark is the giving of fine and delicious food, and the receipt of same is the result.

The commentarial description says that while ordinary beings have little flesh in these places so that the veins and tendons of the hands and feet show through, and the bones of the back and shoulders are evident, this is not so for the *mahāpurisa*. He has sufficient flesh covering these places so that veins, tendons and bones are well concealed and his body resembles a golden statue.

7 & 8. He has soft and tender hands and feet, and his hands and feet are "net-like" (*jāla-hatthapāda*). The kamma which produces these marks is the practice of the four *saṅgahavatthu*, ("bases of kindness") which are generosity, kindly speech, good deeds and impartiality. The result is that the *mahāpurisa* is beloved by his followers.

The softness of a *mahāpurisa's* hands and feet is compared to ghee which has been strained one hundred times through cotton cloth, and they remain soft and tender throughout his life, even when he gets old. The "net-like" mark is compared to the hood of a snake or to a net window built by a skilled carpenter. The fingers and toes being, as we have seen, of equal length, stand a little apart from each other and are joined by a web of skin.

9 & 10. The *mahāpurisa* has highly placed ankles (*ussaṅkhapāda*). The ankles of other people are like nails binding the foot, restricting its motion. The ankles of the *mahāpurisa* are placed higher up on the leg, allowing the foot to move freely in all directions. When he walks, the upper body remains motionless, like a golden statue aboard a ship, and the soles of his feet are visible from all sides, not just from behind as in the case of other people.

He has upward turning body-hairs. The body-hair of a *mahāpurisa* curls and points upward, as if looking into his face.

He bears these marks because in previous lives he spoke Dhamma to the people for their welfare and happiness. The result of these marks is that, if he becomes a *cakkavatti*, he becomes the foremost of all householders but if he becomes a Buddha, he becomes the foremost of all beings whatsoever.

11. The *mahāpurisa* has legs like an antelope. The flesh is distributed evenly all around, not thicker in the back like in other people's legs. He acquires this mark because in past lives he quickly mastered some skill, art, craft or way of conduct. The result of this mark is that the *mahāpurisa* quickly acquires everything needful for the life of a supreme king or of a Buddha, as the case may be.

12. The skin of the *mahāpurisa* is of such a delicate fineness that no dust or dirt can adhere to it. His skin sheds all manner of impurity just like a lotus leaf sheds water. It may be asked, then, why the Buddha is described as

bathing? The answer is threefold; to cool or warm his limbs, to make merit for the donors and to set an example for his disciples. He acquired this mark by asking pertinent questions of wise ascetics or brahmins and the result of it is that the *mahāpurisa* enjoys great wisdom.

13. The *mahāpurisa* has a golden complexion. The colour of his skin resembles gold that has been polished with vermillion powder and rubbed with a panther's fang. (Why this curious instrument was used for polishing gold is not explained). He acquired the merit to obtain this mark by being free of anger even when subjected to abuse and by making many gifts of fine cloth in previous lives. The result is that whether he becomes a Buddha or a *cakkavatti*, he will receive fine rugs, cloth and other such goods.

14. The *mahāpurisa* has the mark called *kosohitavatthaguyho* which refers to some peculiarity of the genital organs. *Kosa* in its most general meaning stands for "any cavity or enclosure containing anything, viz. a storehouse or granary," but also more specifically, "the membraneous cover of the male sexual organ, the praeputium." The relevant definition of *ohita* is "hidden, put away." *Vattha* is "cloth, clothing" and *guyha* is "to be hidden, hidden in." The compound *vatthaguyha*, "that which is concealed by cloth", is a euphemism for the genitals. The PED renders the whole compound as "having the pudendum in a bag."[237]

The commentary makes clear what this means when it says that the *mahāpurisa's* male organ resembles that of a bull or similar animal, and that it has the appearance of the pericarp of a lotus (DN-a 14). In bulls and horses the penis when flaccid is entirely withdrawn within the prepuce, the outer skin which in a human male culminates in the foreskin, and it emerges only when erect.[238] That this mark did not impair normal functioning is evident in that the Buddha fathered a son, and indeed one of the characteristics of a *cakkavatti* is that he has one thousand sons, "all heroes" (DN 3).

The *kosohitavatthaguyho* mark is sometimes taken to mean that the Buddha's penis was somehow introverted or withdrawn entirely within his body. This is the assumption in some Mahāyāna texts, for instance. It appears to be based on an early mistake in rendering an Indian dialect into Sanskrit which resulted in *kośopagatavastiguyha*, "something hidden in the lower belly."[239] There is also a Mahāyāna sutra surviving only in Chinese which takes the "normal" state of the Buddha's genitals to be like a lotus, but from this emerges at will a penis with which he can manifest various miraculous transformations, including wrapping it seven times around Mount Sineru![240]

This mark is acquired by the *mahāpurisa* because in previous lives he united loved ones who had become separated, mother with child, sibling with sibling and so forth, to their great happiness. If he becomes a *cakkavatti*, the result of the *kosohitavatthaguyho* is that he will father one thousand heroic warrior sons. The text (DN-a 30) says that if he becomes a Buddha, the result is the same. Although it is not explicitly stated, even in the commentary, we have to assume that this is to be taken figuratively meaning that he will have many spiritually heroic disciples.

It is because they are physically incapable of bearing this mark that women cannot be Buddhas or *cakkavattis* (AN-a 1:279–280).

15 & 16. The *mahāpurisa* has limbs proportioned evenly like a banyan tree. This means that the span of his arms is equal to his height. Also, while standing he can touch both knees with the palms of his hands without stooping. These marks are acquired by the kamma of wisely judging those under his authority in previous lives, knowing clearly what each individual deserves. The result for a *cakkavatti* is that he shall be wealthy in gold and silver and his storehouses always full of grain. A Buddha shall be wealthy in spiritual goods; having a great measure of faith, learning, morality and so forth.

---

237 All definitions from the PED.

238 See Sendel..

239 Kieschnick & Shahar 2013: 235, note 8.

240 Dhammika 2010.

17, 18 & 19—The front part of the *mahāpurisa's* body is as well proportioned as that of a lion. This does not mean that the rest of his body resembles a lion, which is perfect only in the fore parts. "There is no master craftsmen or master of psychic power in the entire world that can create an image which resembles the perfection of the *mahāpurisa.*" Also, the upper part of the *mahāpurisa's* back is smooth, with no visible hollow between the shoulder-blades. The flesh there is as smooth as a golden shield. Lastly, the throat of the *mahāpurisa* is even all round (*samavaṭṭakkhandha*).[241] Other people's necks may be long or crooked like a bird's but not so the *mahāpurisa.* The flesh of his throat is even all round and when he speaks, it is like thunder arising from the clouds of the sky and there is no bulging of tendons or veins in the neck.

These marks are acquired by formerly having sought the welfare of the many folk (*bahujana*), both in material goods such as fields, sons, elephants and slaves and in spiritual goods such as faith, morality and learning. If he becomes a *cakkavatti*, then his wealth will never diminish or be lost. If he becomes a Buddha, then his spiritual virtues will never diminish.

20. He has a supremely developed sense of taste. With seventeen thousand nerves distributed throughout his body and ending in his mouth, when the *mahāpurisa* takes a morsel of food, the essence is conveyed throughout his body. This is how the Bodhisatta was able to survive on such lean fare as a single rice grain a day during his years of austerity. Other people do not have this power and most of the nutritive essence of their food is lost, which makes them subject to many diseases.

This mark is gained by having refrained in previous lifetimes from harming living beings with sticks and stones. The result is that the *mahāpurisa* will always have good digestion and suffer but little from disease.

21 & 22. The *mahāpurisa* has deep blue eyes (*abhinīlanetta*). Pali, like many ancient languages, does notclearly distinguish between black and blue, *nīla* representing both.[242] However, in this case the colour "blue" is clearly intended because the commentary says that the colour is like that of a flax flower. His eyes are also compared to a decorative window opening into a *vimāna* (deva palace). The *mahāpurisa* has eyelashes like those of a newly born red calf. Although the eyelashes are specially mentioned, this mark refers to the perfection of the entire eye, which is neither sunken like that of an elephant or protruding like that of a mouse, but perfectly placed, and resembles a well polished gem. The eyelashes themselves are soft, very fine and black (*nīla*).

These marks are acquired because the *mahāpurisa* in previous existences always looked at people directly, and with kindliness, never sidelong like a crab and never with a poisonous (*visāci*) glance. As a result of this mark, the *mahāpurisa* is looked upon with affection by all classes and kinds of beings.

23. His head resembles a royal turban (*uṇhīsasīsa*). The commentary gives two explanations of this mark, which are not mutually exclusive. The first is that the *mahāpurisa* has a band of flesh running across the forehead from ear to ear, which resembles the wrapping of a royal turban. Indeed the resemblance is not accidental, kings adopted the use of this turban in imitation of a *mahāpurisa's* forehead. The second explanation is that his head is perfectly round, not misshapen in any way like those of other people.

This mark is acquired by having previously been foremost in skilful behaviour; the keeping of precepts and fasts, honouring mother and father and in generosity. As a result of this mark, he enjoys the loyalty of his followers.

24 & 25. The *mahāpurisa* has just one body-hair growing from each pore (*ekekaloma*).[243] He also has a remarkable tuft of hair above the nose, between the eyebrows called *uṇṇā* (lit. "cotton wool"). When a strand of this hair is taken by the tip and stretched out, it is half as long as his arm. When released, it curls back into a clock-wise spiral with the

[241] *Ṣamavaṭṭakkhandha*—lit. "the mass is even around." It is not clear why this phrase should refer to the throat, but both the description in the sutta, and the commentarial explanation, make it clear that it does.

[242] However, *kaṇha* and also *kāḷa* mean "black" exclusively. There does not seem to be an exclusive word for "blue".

[243] The commentary to the *Mahāpadāna Sutta* fails to explain this term, I have followed the usual explanation, as found for example in the GGB p. 238. The verses in the *Lakkhaṇa Sutta* (DN 30) do include the phrase, "from no pore do two hairs grow".

tip pointing upward. It is pure white in colour and exceedingly soft and fine. The *uṇṇā* is said to be very beautiful and is compared to a silver star mounted on a golden plate, or a stream of milk being poured from a golden pitcher, or to the morning star.

These two marks were acquired by the kamma of always speaking the truth. The result is that the *mahāpurisa* will be obeyed by his followers.

26 & 27—The *mahāpurisa* has forty teeth, twenty in the lower jaw and twenty in the upper. These teeth are perfectly even, without irregularities of any kind, as if carved from a conch shell. Other people might have rotten teeth, or blackened teeth, but those of the *mahāpurisa* are always pure, shining white.

These marks were obtained because in previous lives the *mahāpurisa* never spoke slander but always sought to reconcile the differences between those who were at odds with one another. As a result of these marks, his followers will be harmoniously united, not divided one against another.

28 & 29. The tongue of the *mahāpurisa* is very long, broad and flexible. As this mark is not readily visible, when the Buddha wanted to demonstrate it to dispel the doubt of enquiring brahmins he first rolled his tongue into a tight tube resembling a pin. In this way he displayed it's flexibility. To demonstrate its length, he stuck the tip of it into each ear in turn. To demonstrate its broadness, he covered the whole of his forehead with it (eg. MN 91). Also, the *mahāpurisa* has a very clear brahmā-like voice. This is because his organs of speech are purified and not obstructed by phlegm and bile. His voice is compared to that of an Indian cuckoo (*karavīka*).[244]

These marks were gained by refraining from harsh speech in previous existences, and always uttering speech that was pleasant to hear, agreeable and useful to the many folk. As a result of having these marks, the *mahāpurisa's* speech is always listened to attentively.

30. The *mahāpurisa* has jaws like a lion. In the case of a lion, only the lower jaw is perfectly formed but in the case of a *mahāpurisa* both jaws are like this. They are compared to the half-moon. He bears this mark because inprevious time his speech was meaningful and connected to the Dhamma.

By the power of this mark, if he becomes a *cakkavatti* he cannot be overcome by any human foe. If he becomes a Buddha, he cannot be overcome by anything at all, whether it be human or non-human enemies or internal defilements.

31 & 32. The teeth of a *mahāpurisa* are even, and his canine teeth are very bright. The teeth of ordinary people have gaps between them into which bits of food get lodged while eating. This is not so in the case of a *mahāpurisa*. His teeth are evenly placed without crookedness or gaps, like a row of diamonds. Also his four canine teeth are exceedingly white, and are compared to the morning star.

He obtained this marks by having practices right livelihood and refraining from such wrong livelihoods as robbery or deceit. As a result of these marks, the *mahāpurisa's* followers will be pure.

In addition to these 32 marks of a great man, passing mention is occasionally made in the commentaries to eighty minor marks (*asīti anubyañja*).[245] However these are nowhere described in the commentaries or even the sub-commentaries and we have to go to medieval sources to find a list. The 12th century Buddha biography poem *Jinālaṅkāra* is cited by *The Great Chronicle of Buddhas* for the list printed there (GGB p. 243 f). We do not propose to examine these in detail but just to make a few general observations. The great majority of these minor marks are not as unusual as the major marks, but are simple statements of physical beauty; "neat and smooth fingernails and toenails," "well proportioned body," "glossy teeth," "body free of moles or freckles," etc. Only two would fall definitely into the category of the supernormal, and both of these are mentioned elsewhere in the commentaries. The *mahāpurisa* has the strength of "one thousand *crores* of Kalavaka elephants." In the *Saṃyutta Commentary* there is a description of the

[244] The *karavīka* bird (*Cuculus micropterus*) is said to have a particularly clear and melodious song.
[245] For example at DN-a 16, DN-a 30, MN-a 140, AN-a 3:64.

strength of different classes of elephant and the Buddha is there said to have the strength of ten Chaddanta elephants (the strongest kind, a magical breed of flying elephant). Each class of elephant has some multiple of the strength of the preceding class and doing the requisite math, this means that the Buddha had the strength of 100 billion men! (SN-a 12:22)

The other extraordinary sign included among the 80 minor marks is the *ketumāla* ("garland of rays") which emanates from the head of a *mahāpurisa*. This is always mentioned in reference to the glorious appearance of a Buddha and is usually included along with the 32 major and 80 minor marks.[246] This is to be distinguished from another remarkable feature of a Buddha's appearance, the presence of six coloured rays which emanate from his body, called the *buddharasmi*. These emanated for a distance of 80 *hattha* (cubits) from his body. Golden rays issued from his trunk in all directions. Rays "the colour of a peacock's neck" (*moragīvavaṇṇa*, copper-sulfate colour/peacock blue) issued upward from the hairs of his head. Rays "the colour of red coral" (*pavāḷa*) issued from his feet and spread out along the ground. White rays issued from his teeth, eyes and nails.

Crimson (*mañjeṭṭha*) coloured rays emanated from "that place where the red and yellow colours are mixed." Finally, brilliant (*pabhassara*) rays emanated everywhere (Ud-a 8:6). Obviously, some of this description is somewhat obscure. Later tradition settled on blue, yellow, red, white, orange and brilliant as a combination of the other five as the colours of the Buddha's rays, as can be seen in the Sri Lankan Buddhist flag.

One remaining oddity of the Buddha's physical appearance may be mentioned, if only to dismiss it. It has been held by some that the Buddha was three times the height of a normal man, and this can sometimes be seen rendered in old Sri Lankan art where a gigantic Buddha towers over his diminutive disciples. This is based on a single passage in the *Vinaya Commentary* (Vin-a Sd 6) which discusses units of measure and says that a *sugatavidatthi* (Buddha's span) is three times that of a middle sized man's. All the smaller units of measure in India (as in most places) were based on the dimensions of the human body. A *vidatthi* was a hand-span. If all the Buddha's dimensions were extrapolated from this, he would have been more than five metres tall. There are several passages in the suttas which indicate that while he may have been tall, he was not freakishly so; for instance when King Ajātasattu fails to recognize him among his disciples at a distance (DN 2). Why the Vinaya compilers inserted this odd measurement remains a mystery.[247]

246 For example, Ud-a 1: 10, Sn-a 1:11, Vv-a 83.

247 See the discussion in Thanissaro, 2007, Vol. 1, p. 559-60.

3:1:10 THE *CAKKAVATTI*—WORLD MONARCH

As we have seen, two possible careers are open to the *mahāpurisa*, depending on whether he follows the way of a householder or of a *samaṇa*. In either case, he reaches the extreme pinnacle of his chosen path. If he goes forth into homelessness as a *samaṇa*, he becomes a Buddha; but if he remains in the life of a householder, he reaches the highest possible worldly status, that of a *cakkavatti*, a "Wheel-Turner" or universal monarch.

The summary description of a *cakkavatti* is as follows:

> If he remains as a householder, he will become a *cakkavatti* king, a righteous (*dhammika*) *dhammarāja*, conqueror of the four quarters, establishing security in all the lands, endowed with the seven treasures: the wheel-treasure, the elephant-treasure, the horse-treasure, the jewel-treasure, the woman-treasure, the householder-treasure and the counsellor-treasure. He will have more than a thousand sons, heroes with manly bodies who defeat all hostile armies. He will conquer the whole earth bounded by the sea with Dhamma, without the use of stick or sword, and will rule it by Dhamma.[248]

The commentary expands on some of these terms (we shall examine the seven treasures in some detail below): He is called *dhammika* because he acts for the welfare of others, and *dhammarāja* because he acts for his own welfare. He is conqueror of the four quarters because he is the lord (*issara*) of the world with its four oceans, adorned with four continents. He is victorious over all enemies and all kings are his subjects. "He establishes security over all the lands" means that all his vassals are content in their duties and no rebellion against him is possible. His thousand plus sons are all fearless, with bodies like devas. If any enemy dared to stand against them, they would be able to crush them with their great strength. But the king (and presumably his sons) kill no living beings and keep the five precepts (DN-a 3). It seems that the *cakkavatti* has the potential of overwhelming force but never has to use it.

The *cakkavatti* moreover enjoys four special powers (*iddhi*). First, he is more beautiful than other humans. Second, he has a lifespan surpassing that of other men. Third, he enjoys excellent health, freedom from illness and good digestion. And fourth, he is greatly beloved by everyone in his realm, like a father is loved by his children. It is said that once a *cakkavatti* was driving through the park to take the air and people asked the charioteer whether he would drive slower so that they could enjoy the sight of their monarch longer (MN 129). All classes of people cherish not only the sight, but also the words of a *cakkavatti*. When addressing one of their assemblies, they are delighted and cannot hear enough of his speech. The commentary preserves brief summaries of these speeches. To the *khattiyas* (warrior-nobles) he says, "How, fathers (*tāta*, a respectful endearment), are the duties of a king fulfilled? By preserving the traditions." To the brahmins he says, "How, teachers (ācariya), are the mantras (i.e. the Vedas) recited and taught to your students? By your obtaining offerings and cloth and keeping the precepts." To the householders he says, "How is it, fathers, (*tātā*) that the royal authority rules not by the use of the rod, or fetters or oppression? By the king (*deva,* often used metaphorically for royalty) rightfully bestowing wealth, so that the crops may prosper." To the *samaṇas* he says, "How, venerable sirs (*bhante*) are the requisites of the going-forth obtained? By diligence in the duties of a *samaṇa*" (AN-a 4:130).

There is a striking parallelism between a Buddha and a *cakkavatti*, especially in regard to the symbolism of the wheel. Just as the Buddha is said to have turned the wheel of the Dhamma (*dhammacakka*) "which cannot be turned back by any *samaṇa* or brahmin or deva or māra or brahmā or anyone in the world," (SN 56:11) so too the *cakkavatti* is said to turn the wheel by the Dhamma (*dhammena cakkaṃ vatteti*) which cannot be turned back by any hostile human being (AN 5: 131). The commentary to this passage specifies that this is the āṇācakka, "the wheel of power," in

[248] This passage occurs several times in the Dīgha Nikāya, at DN 3, DN 14, DN 26, and DN 30.

distinction to the wheel of Dhamma turned by the Buddha. (We will examine the important theme of the *cakkavatti*'s wheel below). Both of these "wheel-turnings" represent moments of profound cosmic-historical significance, one on the worldly and one on the spiritual planes. The *cakkavatti* possesses five qualities by which he effects this turning. He knows what is proper (*atthaññu*), that is, he knows the role of a king. He knows the doctrine (*dhammaññu*), that is, he knows the traditional teachings. He knows the measure (*mattaññu*), that is, he knows the proper limits of punishment and force. He knows the time (*kālaññu*), that is, he knows when it is time to enjoy the bliss of kingship, when it is time to pass judgement and when it is time to tour his lands. And he knows the assemblies (*parisaññu*), that is, he knows that this is the assembly of the *khattiyas*, this of the brahmins, this of the *vessas*, this of the *suddas* and this of the *samaṇas*.[249] The same text goes on to ascribe a parallel set of five factors to the Buddha.

The happiness experienced by a *cakkavatti* is like a pebble compared to the Himavā Mountains when it is compared to the happiness experienced in the deva realm (MN 129). Nevertheless, the life of a *cakkavatti* is said to be the pinnacle of joy and pleasure possible for anyone in the human realm, because of the seven treasures and the four powers. It would take an individual of extraordinary character indeed to renounce this world dominion. When the young Siddhattha Gotama left home to begin his spiritual quest, as he stood at the town gate Māra tempted him with these words, "My dear, do not depart. Here, in seven days' time, the wheel-treasure will manifest for you and you will have the rulership of the four great island-continents and the two thousand lesser islands. Remain hear, my dear." But the Bodhisatta refused this blandishment, "having the *cakkavatti* kingship placed in his hand, he tossed it aside like a lump of spittle" (Jāt-nid 2).

We have seen that the idea of kingship is problematic for Buddhism. Although it has a purely mundane origin as a socio-political mechanism to keep order, and is in practice often an oppressive, violent and rapacious institution, nevertheless it is not entirely without a sacred component. The *cakkavatti* resolves this dilemma and represents the ideal perfection of kingship. The *cakkavatti* is truly a universal monarch, uniting the entire earth under one rule, including distant countries not ordinarily within the ken of the folk of the *majjhimadesa*. Furthermore he does this "by Dhamma" without the use of violence. As we shall see in the following sections, all the kings of the earth submit to his moral force without warfare. As well, he is not a looter of his subjects but a benefactor, bestowing security and wealth to all classes of people. We shall see below that one unusual source of revenue available to a *cakkavatti* is the vast store of precious gems and gold available on the floor of the ocean, which he harvests by the supernormal power of the wheel-treasure. In his personal life, too, he is exemplary. It is true that he enjoys an abundance of sense pleasure, like any Indian *mahārāja*, but he knows the limits and the proper times for that and never neglects his duties. Furthermore, he always keeps the precepts and the *uposatha* vows.

This ideal of the *cakkavatti*, ruling by Dhamma, was influential as a model for later kings in Buddhist Asia, even if only as a propagandistic trope.[250] Obviously, no king in historical times has managed a truly universal monarchy. However, King Asoka, who united all of the Indian sub-continent and attempted to rule according to principles of Dhamma, has been accorded status as a *dīpacakkavatti*, which is a lesser kind of *cakkavatti* who unites only the single island-continent of Jambudīpa (Vin-a Pār 2). Buddhist tradition predicts that there will be one final *cakkavatti* in this kappa, Saṅkha, who will rule at the same time as the appearance of the last Buddha in this kappa, Metteyya (DN 26).

---

249 AN 5: 131. The explanations of the terms are taken from the commentary.

250 See Tambiah, *World Conqueror and World Renouncer*, 1976, which looks at how the *cakkavatti* ideal influenced the Buddhist kings of South-East Asia.

3:1:11 CAKKARATANA—THE WHEEL TREASURE

One of the defining attributes of a *cakkavatti* is the possession of seven wonderful "treasures" (*ratana*). The first and most important of these is the *cakkaratana*, the "Wheel Treasure." This is a marvellous Wheel that appears in the sky and signifies a deserving king as a *cakkavatti*. It is integral to his career and is the defining symbol of his status. Its appearance in the sky over his palace marks the outset of his reign as a *cakkavatti*, and he peacefully conquers the world by following in its wake. Should he fail in his duties, the Wheel disappears and his power is at an end.

In the commentary to the *Mahāsudassana Sutta* (DN-a 17) there is a detailed description of the *cakkaratana* ("Wheel Treasure"). It is an *uposatha*-night and King Sudassana, having made much merit by extravagant alms-giving, has retired to an inner chamber and sits cross-legged, meditating on the virtue of his generosity when the Wheel appears:

> It manifests like a mass of sapphire, cleaving the surface of the eastern sea. Displaying a divine splendour it is thousand-spoked, complete with nave and rim, perfect in every way.
>
> The nave is made of sapphire. In the middle are tubes[251] made of finest silver which gleam like a row of pure teeth in a smiling mouth. The central opening is like the full moon. Both inside and outside are lined with plates of silver. These plates surround the tubes and in the place where they join, can be seen clear well-made inscriptions. The nave is perfect in every way.
>
> There are a thousand spokes made of the seven precious things.[252] They are radiant like the rays of the sun. At their ends are jeweled capitals,[253] where can be seen clear well-made inscriptions. The spokes are perfect in every way.
>
> The rim sparkles with rays like the rising sun. Like a smiling mouth, it is made of dark red smooth pure coral. But the joints are like the splendour of the evening sun, or like Jambu gold.[254] Around the circle at the places of junction can be seen clear well-made inscriptions. The rim is perfect in every way.
>
> On the back of the rim in between every ten spokes there is a coral pole with a hole cut into it, like a flute. When the wind moves through it, it makes a sound like very skillful music played by a five piece orchestra. The sound is lovely, delightful, pleasing and intoxicating. The coral stick has above it a white parasol. On both sides flow down wreaths of flowers. Two rows thus of flowers held by one hundred parasols[255] adorn the rim.
>
> On two of the pipes in the nave there are the faces of lions,[256] from which there comes a red woolen ball like the rising sun, the size of a palm tree trunk, glorious and resplendent with rays like the full moon. From these there hang down two strings of pearls, like a smiling face, like the sky-river.[257]

---

251 *Panāḷi*—usually refers to a water pipe. The exact meaning here is obscure. I am taking the word as plural which fits the context.

252 Gold, silver, pearls, rubies, lapis-lazuli, coral and diamond.

253 This is conjectural. The Pali has *ghaṭaka-maṇika*. These words can refer to different kinds of pots and *ghaṭaka* can also refer to a kind of architectural capital which goes on top of a pillar.

254 A special kind of very fine gold.

255 Another reading found in some versions has the flowers held up by spears, two spears per parasol, one on each side. This depends on whether one key word is *sata* "hundred" or *satti* "spear". See Karunaratne 1969.

256 *Sīhamukhā*—which might also be interpreted as "lion's mouths".

257 *Akāsagaṅgāga*—"the space Ganges", the Milky Way. This whole paragraph is very difficult to interpret, in particular the ar-

When the Wheel turns in the sky it seems like three wheels are turning there. Thus it is perfect in every way.

When the Wheel manifests, it is first seen by the people of the royal city:
As the people, after eating their supper, sit in their doorways or engage in friendly conversation in the streets and cross-roads and their children play at games, the *dhammacakka*[258] approaches through the air. It flies neither too high nor too low, but just at the level of the tree-tops. From the distance of twelve *yojana*, the sweet delightful sound reaches the ears of the people in the town. From the distance of one *yojana*, the shining, resplendent array of many colours reaches their eyes as the Wheel approaches the royal city.

When they hear the sound, they ask, "Where is this sound coming from? Who is making it?" As they consider this in their hearts, a brilliant light is seen approaching from the eastern direction. One person says to another, "It is a marvel! Formerly the moon was alone in the sky, now there are two full moons like a pair of royal swans travelling through the sky!" Another person says, "What are you saying? That is not a second moon, surely it is the sun, with its brilliant red and gold rays." Yet another says, "You are mad! How could the sun be chasing through the sky after the moon? Surely it is a *vimāna*,[259] brilliant and covered in many gems, produced by meritorious deeds." But someone else says, "Friends, you are talking nonsense. This is a very auspicious sign that a *cakkaratana* ("Wheel Treasure") should come to be!"

This friendly talk ceases as the Wheel moves away from the disc of the moon and approaches the city. Someone asks, "For whom has this Wheel arisen?" He is answered, "It can be no other, but our own Mahārāja ("Great King") who has fulfilled the duties of a Wheel-Turning Monarch (*cakkavatti*) for whom this wheel has come." So the crowd of people, now seeing and knowing, follow the Wheel as it makes a circuit of the city walls, clockwise seven times, as if to make clear its intention in coming for the king. The king's harem stands in the windows of the palace; overcome with happiness and wonder they honour the Wheel by throwing flowers.

The king is told about this wonder by his retinue, gets up from his meditation seat and goes out onto the audience balcony[260] to see it by himself.

The king thinks, "I have heard that that when a properly anointed *khattiya* king, after having rinsed his head and performed the *uposatha* kamma on the fifteenth day of the month, then sees this *cakkaratana* appearing at the upper storey of the palace, complete and perfect with a thousand spokes, with rim and nave, then this king is a *cakkavatti* ('Wheel Turner')."[261] The Wheel then moves up and down in the sky by one or two inches, in confirmation. The king takes a golden pitcher with a spout like an elephant's trunk and sprinkles water onto the Wheel saying, "Conquer, Sir Wheel!"[262] Thus has been done by all *cakkavattis* throughout the course of time.

An interesting question to raise at this point in the narrative is the size of the Wheel. This is nowhere clearly stated

rangement of the various elements. Later iconography often showed the Wheel being supported by two lions with strings of pearls or flowers coming from their mouths. See Karunaratne 1969.

258 *Dhammacakka* = "Dhamma Wheel". An unusual use of this term, which usually refers to the purely metaphorical Wheel turned by the Buddha by his teaching.

259 *Vimāna*—abode of a deva, a mansion endowed with the power of flight.

260 The "balcony" is called *sīhapañjara* ("lion's cage") in Pali. The subcommentary describes it as being on an upper floor of the palace and used when the king wants to address his subjects.

261 This passage from the sutta, DN 17.

262 *Bhavaṃ cakkaratanan-ti.*

and actually appears to be variable. On the one hand, the tubes that make up a small part of its structure are said to be as big as palm-tree trunks and the approaching Wheel is visible to the townsfolk from a *yojana* away. On the other hand, when it approaches the palace it hovers just outside the king's balcony and indicates its affirmation by moving up and down a couple of inches. This does not seem to support the idea of a massive size implied earlier.

As soon as these words are spoken, the *cakkaratana* rises into the sky and turns. The king mounts his carriage and it rises into the air to follow the Wheel. Then the king's attendants also rise up into the air, carrying the royal parasol, fly-whisk, cowrie shell and so forth, and so does his harem. Then the royal army, arrayed in various kinds of armour and mail, arrayed in various splendid and glorious ways, raising aloft banners and pennants, also rise up in the air. Finally the three officers, the viceroy (*uparāja*), the general (*senāpati*) and the overlord (*pabhu*) mount a vehicle and rise up to follow the king. The king's servants in the town go around beating a drum and announcing, "Our king has become a *cakkavatti*, everyone should adorn themselves according to their means and assemble." Then all the townsfolk pay homage in various ways to the Wheel, throwing flowers and so forth. They all rise up into the air to follow the king.

His retinue extends over the space of twelve *yojana*, and there is among them not one with a broken body or soiled garments; pure is the company of the *cakkavatti*.

The company of the *cakkavatti* travels through the air like wizards (*vijjādharapurisa*), as if they were going along a flat surface strewn with sapphires. The company travels along just above the tree-tops, neither too high nor too low, as they cross the country. Anyone who wishes to gather flowers or fruits from the trees can do so. The people standing on the ground are able to clearly observe them and to say, "There is the king, there is the viceroy, there the general." As the people travel along, they can assume any posture they like and can even work at their various arts and crafts, just as if they were on the ground.

Taking the company of the *cakkavatti* along with it, the *cakkaratana* goes around the left side of Mount Sineru, travels for seven thousand *yojana* across the great ocean and comes to the island-continent of Pubbavideha. And at whatever place the Wheel comes to rest, the king establishes a settlement, together with his four-fold army.[263] There in a space twelve *yojana* across, thirty-six *yojana* around, they make camp. There all necessities are easily obtained; there is shade and water on a piece of pleasant, smooth and level ground. Above stands the Wheel, as a sign.[264] Seeing this sign, the people descend and having bathed and taken some food, they build themselves dwellings wherever they like.

The foreign kings come to this settlement of the *cakkavatti*, but not to make battle against it. In the presence of the *cakkaratana*, there is no one who would venture to raise their weapons against its majestic power (ānubhāva). The kings having come there, one by one, offering their wealth and their sovereignty, pay homage to the *cakkavatti* by bowing down with their jeweled top-knots to the *cakkavatti's* feet and say, "Come great king! Welcome great king! We are yours, please admonish us." And the *cakkavatti* advises them in this way, "Do not kill living beings! Do not take that which is not given! Tell no lies! Take no intoxicating drink! Enjoy your food!"[265] How far do these kings follow this advice, considering that not everyone now follows the

---

[263] i.e. infantry, cavalry, chariots and elephants.

[264] *Akkhāhata*—lit. a "proclamation"

[265] These speeches taken from the sutta, DN 17. The king's advice to his vassals are the five precepts (slightly rephrased) plus one more phrase; *yathābhuttañca bhuñjathā*. As Maurice Walshe notes, "the meaning is doubtful." He translates the phrase as "be moderate in eating" and cites Warder's translation as "rule (collect taxes) in moderation." See Walshe, LDB note 472, p. 577. I take it to mean that the vassal kings are given permission to continue to enjoy the fruits of their rulership.

advice of the Buddha? They do follow it, because they are wise and learned.

After giving this admonishment to the kings of Pubbavideha, the *cakkavatti*'s people eat their breakfast, then again take to the air, following the Wheel across the eastern ocean. Then the Wheel plunges into the sea to a depth of a *yojana*. Wherever the Wheel strikes the waves, the water draws back like a cobra that has smelled poison; the waters of the sea fall away and become like walls of lapis-lazuli. In that instant, as if to display the fortune and merit of the *cakkavatti*, the floor of the sea is exposed, strewn with many kinds of jewels. The company of the king, seeing the jewels, takes up as many as they wish, filling their laps and so forth. When they have taken their fill, the Wheel turns around again and begins to ascend. The waters of the ocean are overpowered by the majesty of the *cakkaratana* and draw away from the circle of its rim.

Having conquered Pubbavideha, the *cakkavatti* turns south over the ocean, desirous of conquering Jambudīpa.

The Wheel-Turning King with his army and retinue repeat the performance on Jambudīpa, Aparagoyāna and Uttarakuru, each time establishing a camp, receiving the submission of the local monarchs and giving them the formal admonishment. After each continental conquest, the Wheel again plunges into the sea and the king's people take up the jewels lying strewn on the sea-bed.

Thus King Mahāsudassana established his sovereignty over the four quarters of the earth. In order to observe his domain, the king together with his company rises up high into the sky and looks over the four island-continents together with the five hundred minor islands, just like looking at four lotus flowers in a mountain lake. Then according to the wish of the king, the Wheel returns to the royal capital city. Thereafter it stands near the inner city, its radiance dispelling the darkness of night, so that no lamps or torches are needed there (DN-a 17).

Having obtained the sovereignty of the whole *cakkavāḷa* the *cakkavatti* is not idle. He examines the condition of the people and at the right time he sits in judgement. Those who ought to be admonished, he admonishes. Those who ought to be raised up, he raises up. Everywhere he puts everything into its proper place. (AN-a 1: 188)

3:1:12 THE SEVEN TREASURES

A *cakkavatti* is possessed of seven wonderful treasures (*ratana*). The first and most important of these is the Wheel-Treasure (*cakkaratana*), already described, which appears first and acts as the emblem of his authority.

The second to appear is the Elephant-Treasure (*hatthiratana*).

After the appearance of the Wheel-Treasure, the counsellors of the king prepare a suitable place for an auspicious elephant. They make a piece of ground level and clean and smear it with sandalwood paste and sweet fragrances. Below, it is strewn with various fragrant flowers, and above it they place a golden canopy, adorned with sparkling stars. It has a pleasing appearance like a deva's *vimāna.*

"The Divine Elephant Treasure (*deva hatthiratana*) will come here," they say.

As previously, the king, having made a great act of giving, takes the eight precepts and sits, contemplating his merit and by the power of that merit calls forth an elephant of the Chaddanta or of the Uposatha tribe,[266] who wishes to enjoy the king's honour and hospitality.

Very much like the rising sun are the Elephant Treasure's adorned, neck, feet and face. His body is of pure white. He rests on the seven supports: his four limbs, his trunk, tail and noble organ (*varaṅgaṃ*) all touch the ground.[267] His major and minor limbs are well formed. The tip of his trunk is like a beautiful open red lotus. Like a powerful yogi (*iddhimā yogī*) he is able to fly skillfully through the air. Anointed with red arsenic powder, the elder elephant comes from the Rajata Mountains to stand in that place. (If he comes from the Chaddanta tribe, it is the youngest that comes. If from the Uposatha tribe it is the eldest).

When the king has fulfilled all the duties of a *cakkavatti* monarch and speaks his thought, then the elephant comes. This Mahāsudassana did and the elephant came from his natural elephant habitat and stood there. When the Elephant Treasure makes its appearance, and is seen by the elephant keepers, they with great delight go quickly to announce it to the king. The king comes quickly and sees it with a delighted mind. He thinks, "It would be a good thing if this elephant can be tamed."

Thinking thus, he approaches the elephant which hangs down its ears like a tame calf, seeing that it is the king who approaches. The king desires to mount it, and his retinue, knowing his intention, brings the Elephant Treasure golden flags and ornaments and covers it with golden netting. The king makes the elephant sit, and he mounts it with a seven-jeweled ladder and wishes it to fly into the sky. Immediately upon the arising of this thought, the great elephant rises like a royal swan into the sapphire-blue sky.

From that place he does what is called a "circle tour". By the time the royal company has finished their morning meal the king has travelled on the elephant over the entire earth and returned to the royal capital. This is the great power of the *cakkavatti*'s Elephant Treasure. (DN-a 17)

The next to appear, the Horse-Treasure (*assaratana*), is acquired in an identical way. The counsellors prepare a place for it, the king does his royal duties and then the horse comes. It is mounted by the king and flies into the air to make a circuit of the earth. The Horse Treasure is described as follows:

---

266 Two tribes of powerful, magical elephants. See § 3:2,2.

267 The definition of the seven supports is from the sub-commentary. Maurice Walshe wrongly translates *sattappatiṭṭho iddhimā* as "of sevenfold strength". LDB p. 281.

> By the power of the king's merit a horse of the Sindh race appears. It is resplendent like a mass of clouds in the autumn, adorned with lightning flashes. Its feet and snout are red. Its pure, smooth and compact body resembles the radiant moon. Its head is black like a crow's neck or like a royal sapphire. Its head is adorned with black hair well arrayed like *muñja* grass delicately curled.
>
> Going through the sky, he is called Valāhako ("the cloud"), the royal horse who came and stood in that place. (ibid.)

After the horse, the Jewel-Treasure (*maṇiratana*) is the next to appear. This is a marvellous, self-luminous gem stone.

> After the appearance of the Horse-Treasure, there emerges the Jewel-Treasure. It is four *hattha*[268] across, about the size of a wagon-wheel. From both ends, which are like pinnacles, there are very pure strings of pearls. It is adorned with two gold lotuses and attended by a retinue of 84,000 gems. The Jewel-Treasure is splendid like the full moon with its attendant retinue of stars. It comes from Mount Vepulla.[269]
>
> The Jewel-Treasure is a beryl,[270] beautiful, well-formed, eight-sided, well-polished, pure, very clear, clean and perfect in all its parts. The lustre of this jewel radiates for a *yojana* in all directions. The king decided to investigate the quality of this jewel and fixing it atop his standard, went out in the darkness of night with his four-fold army. (DN 17)
>
> Wherever they went, the lustre of the jewel extended for a *yojana* round about. The light was like that of the rising sun, and the farmers started to plough the fields, the merchants opened their shops and the labourers began their work. "It is daytime," they thought. Thus did the Jewel-Treasure manifest for the king. (DN-a 17)

The next to appear is the Woman-Treasure, *itthiratana*, a marvellously beautiful woman who will become the *cakkavatti*'s chief queen. In the story of King Mahāsudassana, this queen was named Subhaddā.

> Then there appears to the king the Woman-Treasure. She is lovely, beautiful, amiable, excellent, fair complexioned; she is not too tall, not too short, not too thin, not too fat, not too dark and not too pale. She surpasses the beauty of human women, and approaches the beauty of a *devī*. Her skin is as soft to the touch as cotton wool or the fluff of the silk cotton tree. In the cold season, her limbs are warm to the touch, and in the hot season they are cool. Her body bears the scent of sandalwood, and her mouth smells like a lotus. The Woman-Treasure always rises in the morning before the king, and goes to bed at night after him. She is always obedient and pleasant in her speech and manner. The Woman-Treasure would never be unfaithful to the king even in thought, much less in body. (DN 17)

The commentary adds a few details. The Woman-Treasure always comes either from Uttarakuru, where women are extraordinarily beautiful, or from the royal family of Madda. In the explanation of the adjective *dassanīyā* ("beautiful") it says that whoever lays eyes upon her becomes "deranged" (*kiccavikkhepa*) (DN-a 17). Presumably, the *cakkavatti* is made of stronger stuff than most human males.

After the Woman-Treasure, the Householder-Treasure (*gahapatiratana*) appears to the king. He is a man who due to his excellent kamma is born into great wealth and the king appoints him as finance minister (*dhanarāsivaḍḍhako,*

---

268 A *hattha* is a fore-arm length, i.e. a cubit. Four *hattha* would be five feet or about a metre and a half.

269 DN-a 17. Vepulla is a mountain near Rājagaha.

270 *Veḷuriya* might also mean lapis-lazuli.

lit. "wealth-increaser"). With the power of the "divine eye" (*dibbacakkhu*), also derived from his kamma, the Householder-Treasure can see a buried treasure even a *yojana* below the surface of the earth (ibid.).

Then the Householder-Treasure appeared before the king. With the power of his divine eye, possessed as a result of his kamma, he could see where a treasure was buried, both owned and ownerless. He approached the king and said, "Remain at ease, deva,[271] I shall produce wealth for you." At one time the king decided to test the Householder-Treasure and boarding a boat with him took it to the middle of the Ganges River. There he said, "Householder, I would have some gold and coin." The householder replied, "Well then, great king, have the boat taken to the river bank." "It is right here, householder, that I would have gold and coin." So the Householder-Treasure put both hands into the water and pulled up a pot filled with gold and with coins. "Is that enough, great king, will that do, will that suffice?" "That is enough, that will do, that will suffice." (DN 17)

The final treasure to appear is the Counsellor-Treasure (*pariṇāyakaratana*).

Then the Counsellor-Treasure appeared before the king. He was a man learned, wise, clever and skillful.[272] He undertakes that which should be undertaken, he abandons that which should be abandoned and he maintains that which should be maintained. He approached the king and said, "Be at ease, great king, I shall advise you." (ibid.)

The Counsellor-Treasure was like the king's eldest son. By the king's merit and his own good kamma he knew the content of other people's minds. He could determine if anyone within twelve *yojana* intended the king's welfare or the king's harm. The king was well satisfied with him and appointed him adviser for all his affairs. (DN-a 17)

271 Here, *deva* is uses as a respectful mode of address.

272 *Paṇḍito viyatto medhāvī paṭibalo.*

3:1:13 INDIVIDUAL CAKKAVATTIS

Although it is the rule that only one *cakkavatti* can arise in a world-system at any given time, (AN 1: 278)both time and the number of world-systems in the cosmos are beyond counting. This means that in cosmological time and space there have been an infinitude of *cakkavattis*. The Buddha claimed that in his long wandering in *saṃsāra* he had himself been, among many other things, a *cakkavatti* hundreds of times.[273] Despite these vast numbers only a very few *cakkavattis* are mentioned by name in the texts.

One of the most extensively treated is **King Mahāsudassana, (**DN 17 & Jāt 95) one of the previous births of the Buddha, who may serve as an archetype for the career of all the *cakkavattis*.

We first hear of Mahāsudassana in the *Mahāparinibbāna Sutta*, (DN 16) the sutta which describes the end of the Buddha's life. The Buddha has chosen the little town of Kusinārā in the Malla country for the site of his decease. Ānanda protests, "Please, venerable sir, do not pass away in this small, barren remote town."[274] and goes on to name several large famous cities as more dignified sites for this event. The Buddha replies that he should not say this, in ancient times Kusinārā was the site of the great city of Kusāvatī, the capital of the *cakkavatti* Mahāsudassana. The following sutta[275] serves as an appendix to this passage and describes in detail the career of King Mahāsudassana. This begins with the king performing the *uposatha* fast and the subsequent appearance of the Wheel and his bloodless conquest of all four continents. There then follows the appearance of the other six treasures of a *cakkavatti*. All of these events occur in the same way for every *cakkavatti*.

Some particulars of King Mahāsudassana's reign are mentioned. He undertook extensive public works in the form of public bathing ponds and charitable distribution centres. These were all built with lavish magnificence; the bathing ponds were lined with tiles of gold, silver, beryl and crystal and had staircases leading into the water made of the same precious materials. The charitable centres also operated on a scale well beyond mere soup kitchens:

> King Mahāsudassana thought, "Suppose that on the banks of the bathing ponds I were to establish place of giving, such that those who want food can get it, those who want drink can get it, those who want clothing can get it, those who want vehicles can get them, those who want furniture can get it, and those who want women can get them and those who want gold or coins can get that.[276]

King Mahāsudassana's palace was built for him by Vessakamma, the architect of the devas. It was called the *Dhammapāsāda* ("Dhamma Palace") and was of great size and magnificence. The Dhammapāsāda measured a full *yojana* from east to west and a half *yojana* from north to south. The decorations and furnishings are described at great length and everything was made of gold, silver, beryl and crystal. Among the notable ornaments of the palace were two nets of tinkling bells, one of gold with silver bells and one of silver with golden bells. When the wind stirred these bells the sound they made was like that of a skilled five piece orchestra; this sound was "lovely, exciting, pleasant and intoxicating,"[277] and when it was heard the thirst of all the male and female drunkards[278] in the city of Kusāvatī was relieved.

The king's wealth was legendary and is described as being in sets of eighty-four thousand. He had eighty-four

---

273 AN 7:62. The same is stated for the legendary teacher Sunetta at AN 7: 66.

274 *Khuddakanagarake ujjaṅgalanagarake sākhānagarake*, translated by Maurice Walshe poetically as "this miserable little town of wattle-and-daub, right in the jungle in the back of beyond!" LDB, p. 266.

275 DN 17, the *Mahāsudassana Sutta*.

276 The commentary to this passage expands the mention of women to say that "those who want to be with women can get that." This implies that a kind of state brothel is meant.

277 *Vaggu ca rajanīyo ca khamanīyo ca madanīyo ca.*

278 *Dhuttā* and *soṇḍā.*

thousand cities and the same number of palaces, gabled halls (*kūṭāgāra*), couches, elephants, chariots, jewels, wives, civil servants (*gahapati*),[279] noble retainers (*khattiya*), and cows. As well, he had eighty-four thousand *koṭi*[280] of garments and made eighty-four thousand offerings of boiled rice morning and evening. The wealth of a *cakkavatti* is considered to be the summit of sensual enjoyment in the human realm, and yet compared to the pleasure enjoyed in the deva realm it is like a pebble compared to the Himalaya Mountains, and neither of these is even fit to be compared to the attainment of *nibbāna* (MN 129).

In the end, King Mahāsudassana was wise enough to see the emptiness of all this wealth and he spent the last period of his life living in celibacy and meditation. His last conversation with Queen Subaddhā (the Woman Treasure) is worth recounting:

> After many years, many hundreds of years, many thousands of years Queen Subaddhā said to herself, "It is long since I visited King Mahāsudassana. Suppose I were to go see him now?" She told the women of the harem to wash their heads and dress in their golden robes, "It is long since we visited King Mahāsudassana, we shall go to see him now." She had the Householder Treasure muster the fourfold army and when all was ready Queen Subaddhā accompanied by the women of the harem and the fourfold army went to see King Mahāsudassana.
>
> King Mahāsudassana heard their approach and wondered, "What is this great sound of many people?" He left his chamber to investigate and saw Queen Subaddhā leaning against the door-post. "Do not enter Queen, stay there."
>
> Then the king ordered one of his servants to fetch his golden couch and place it outside the palace, among the golden palm trees he had had erected there. There he lay himself down in the lion's posture[281] with one foot placed upon the other, with mindfulness and clear comprehension. Seeing him like this, Queen Subaddhā thought, "Very clear are the faculties of King Mahāsudassana, his complexion is very bright and pure. May this not be the time of his passing away!"
>
> She said to him then, "Deva,[282] of your eighty-four thousand cities, Kusavāti is the chief. Arouse desire for it, make an intention to live! Of your eighty-four thousand palaces, the Dhamma Palace is the chief. Arouse desire for it, make an intention to live!" And so she went through the whole inventory of his wealth.
>
> The king replied, "Devī, for a long time your words were dear and pleasing to me. but now at the end they are not so."
>
> "How then, Deva, should I speak to you?"
>
> "You should speak thus; "All things dear and pleasing will change, will be lost, will become otherwise. Do not, Deva, die filled with desire, to do so is suffering, to do so is blameworthy. Of your eighty-four thousand cities, Kusavāti is the chief. Abandon desire for it, do not arouse the intention to live … " (And so forth through the entire inventory of King Mahāsudassana's possessions).

279 Lit. "house-holders". I take them to be a kind of palace staff because their chief is said to be the *gahapatiratana*, the "Householder Treasure" who serves as a kind of finance minister.

280 A *koṭi* is a numerical value equal to ten million, so the king had eight hundred and forty billion garments! See appendix on units of measurement.

281 *Sīhaseyya*—this is the posture assumed by the Buddha at the time of his parinibbāna.

282 Here used as a common term of address to royalty.

> Queen Subaddhā cried out and wept, and then wiping away her tears she repeated this speech back to King Mahāsudassana.
>
> King Mahāsudassa died shortly afterward; just as a householder falls into drowsiness after enjoying a big meal, so did the approach of death feel to King Mahāsudassana. After death, he appeared in the *brahmaloka*.[283]

Mahāsudassana lived in a period when the human life-span was much longer than it is now. It is said that he spent eighty-four thousand years engaged in childish play, eighty-four thousand years as the viceroy (*oparajja*), for eighty-four thousand years he ruled as universal monarch and for another eighty-four thousand years he "lived the holy life" (*brahmacariyaṃ cari*) in the Dhamma Palace.[284]

Another *cakkavatti* whose story is told in some detail is **Daḷhanemi**.[285] He was the founder of a lineage of *cakkavattis*. When he had ruled for many thousands of years the Wheel slipped from its position in the sky. Daḷhanemi knowing this to be a sign that his lifespan was nearing its end, passed on his authority to his son, shaved his hair and beard and took up the life of a religious ascetic.

Shortly after this, the Wheel disappeared altogether. The new king consulted with one of his learned counsellors and was told not to grieve because,

> The Ariyan Dhamma Wheel is not an inheritance from your ancestors. Instead, you must perform the duties of a *cakkavatti*, and then it may come to pass that on a full moon night, when you have bathed your head and are performing the *uposatha* rite on the royal balcony, then the Ariyan Dhamma Wheel may appear to you, thousand-spoked, with hub and rim, complete in all its parts.
>
> The duties of a *cakkavatti* are then explained in some detail:
>
> Making the Dhamma your support, you should honour the Dhamma, respect the Dhamma, esteem the Dhamma, reverence the Dhamma. Honouring the Dhamma, you should take it as your emblem and your banner and acknowledge the Dhamma as your overlord.
>
> You should establish righteous (*dhammika*) protection, watch and ward, over your kinsfolk, your army, your nobles (*khattiya*) and dependents, over brahmins and householders, over city folk and country folk, *samaṇas* and brahmins, as well as the birds and beasts.
>
> Do not allow any unrighteousness (*adhammakāra*) to exist in your kingdom. To those that are in poverty, give wealth. And whatever *samaṇas* and brahmins may dwell in your kingdom who have gone beyond pride and negligence, who live with patience and forbearance, calmed, disciplined and cooled; these you should approach and consult with from time to time, asking them what is skillful, what is unskillful, what is blameless and what is blameworthy, what should be followed and what not, and what actions will lead in time to misery and suffering, and what actions will lead to well-being and happiness. And having heard them, you should thereafter avoid unskillful actions and perform skillful actions. These are the duties of a *cakkavatti*. (DN 26)

The new king followed this advice and performed the duties of a *cakkavatti*. As a result, the Wheel appeared to

[283] DN 17. This translation is somewhat abridged.

[284] Ibid. The numbers 84 (7x9) and 84,000 occurs not only here, but in many other contexts beginning with the Vedic religion and continuing in Buddhism, Jainism and later Hinduism. See Shah, undated.

[285] His story is told in DN 26.

him and he went to on to complete the career of a *cakkavatti* by a bloodless conquest of all four continents. In his turn, he also saw the Wheel slip from its place, handed over power to his own son and went forth into asceticism. This pattern was followed by a third, fourth, fifth and sixth succeeding king.[286] However, the seventh king in Daḷhanemi's line failed in the duty of providing wealth to the poor. As a result, not only did the Wheel not appear for him, but crime became prevalent in his realm as the poor sought wealth by other means. This began a whole cascade of evil developments; punishment, violence, falsehood and so forth and initiated the long cycle of cosmic decline during which human lifespans diminish. This is the cosmic-historical phase in which we are presently living.[287]

The same sutta which tells the story of King Daḷhanemi and his heirs also predicts the arising of a future *cakkavatti* named **Saṅkha**. He will rule during a future period of the cosmic cycle, when human life-spans have again risen to eighty thousand years. His capital city will be Ketumāti, on the site of Barānāsī (Benares) . He will rebuild the renowned one hundred storey palace of the ancient king Mahāpanāda.[288] During his reign the final Buddha of this kappa will also arise, who will be known as Metteyya. After ruling for some unspecified time, King Saṅkha will give up the palace of Mahāpanāda, dedicating its use to *samaṇas*, brahmins, wanderers, the poor and destitute. He will then shave his hair and beard and ordain as a bhikkhu under Buddha Metteyya (DN 26).

Two other *cakkavattis* are known to have lived at the same time as a Buddha. One unnamed *cakkavatti* lived during the time of Sujata Buddha, in a previous kappa. He is said to have given the four continents as a gift offering to the *saṅgha*.[289] During the time of Kondañña Buddha, during a previous kappa, the Bodhisatta who eventually took birth as Siddhattha Gotama was a *cakkavatti* named **Vijitāvī** who undertook to provide for one trillion bhikkhus.[290]

At one time Ānanda had taken birth as a *cakkavatti* by the name of **Kāliṅga**.

> One day King Kāliṅga surrounded by his retinue which stretched over thirty-six *yojana* mounted his elephant which resembled the peak of Mount Kelāsa, intending to visit his mother and father with grand pageantry. The king and his retinue ascended into the air and went on their way.
>
> However, when they reached the site of all the Buddhas' victories, the very navel of the earth, the *Mahābodhimaṇḍa*,[291] the elephant was unable to fly any further. The king urged him to go on, admonishing him again and again, but the elephant was unable to fly over that place.
>
> The *purohita* (chief brahmin) of the king descended to earth to investigate and ascertained that this place was indeed the Mahābodhimaṇḍa. He rose up in the air again and reported this to the king. "This is the place where all the Buddhas have utterly destroyed the defilements. No one can fly over this circle, not even Sakka himself. Descend to earth, sire, and pay homage."
>
> But the royal elephant, pierced again and again by the goad, had been unable to endure the pain and had died. The king did not know that his mount was dead and still sat on his back. The *purohita* told him, "Majesty,

286 Other than Daḷhanemi, none of these kings are named in the texts.

287 See § 2:5 & 2.6.

288 for Mahāpanāda see Jāt 489.

289 Jāt-nid 1. This offering was said to have been emulated by King Aśoka who gave the whole of Jambudipa (i.e. India) to the Saṅgha and redeemed it with four hundred thousand gold pieces. See Strong 2014:287.

290 Jāt-nid 1. Malalasekera states in the DPPN entry "*cakkavatti*" that *cakkavatis* always arise in dark kappas during which no Buddha appears. These two counter-examples prove that must be an error. "One trillion bhikkhus"—the text gives the number as *koṭi-satasahassa*, a hundred thousand *koṭi*. Admittedly *koṭi* as a numerical term is somewhat flexible but is usually taken to mean ten million.

291 *Mahābodhimaṇḍa*—"the great circle of awakening" is the spot near Bodhgaya where all the Buddhas sit and attain full awakening.

your elephant is dead. Mount another." By the power of the king's merit another elephant of the Uposatha breed appeared at that place in an instant. As soon as the king had dismounted the first elephant, its carcass fell to the earth.

King Kāliṅga was delighted by the Mahābodhimaṇḍa and he ordered that all the inhabitants of the world should pay homage to the Bodhi Tree with garlands of flowers for seven days. (Jāt 479)

There is one *cakkavatti* who enjoyed a particularly spectacular career, this was King **Mandhātu**.

Mandhātu was endowed with the seven treasures and the four powers and established a universal monarchy (*cakkavattirajjaṃ*). When he clenched his left fist and sprinkled it using his right hand, in an instant (lit. "in a finger-snap of time") there fell a rain of the seven precious things, knee deep; so wonderful a man was he. For eighty-four thousand years he engaged in childish play, for eighty-four thousand years he served as viceroy (*oparajja*) and for eighty-four thousand years he ruled as *cakkavatti*. The measure of his life-span was incalculable.[292]

One day the king was unable to satisfy some sensual desire and so became discontented. His councillors asked him why he was looking unhappy and he replied, "Considering the power of my merit, what is this kingdom? Is there another place more delightful?" They answered, "The *devaloka*, great king."

So having sprinkled the Wheel, King Mandhātu together with his retinue went to the realm of the Cātumahārājika Devas. The Four Great Kings came forth to greet him with garlands of deva flowers in their hands and surrounded by a great company of lesser devas. Having received him, they took him into their realm and gave him kingship over it. There, surrounded by his own retinue, he exercised kingship for a very long time.

But there too he was unable to satisfy his desire and he grew discontented. The Four Great Kings enquired as to why he looked unhappy and King Mandhātu asked, "Is there another deva realm more delightful than this one?" "There is, deva,[293] another *devaloka* of which we are the servants. The Tāvatiṃsa devaloka is more delightful than this." King Mandhātu having sprinkled the Wheel went forth with his retinue to the Tāvatiṃsa *devaloka*. There Sakka the *devarājā* came forth to greet him with garlands of deva flowers in his hand and surrounded by a great company of lesser devas. Sakka took him by the hand and said, "Come this way, great king."

While the king was walking along among the company of devas, his chief councillor[294] took the Wheel and together with the king's retinue descended to the paths of men and entered his own city. Sakka led Mandhātu into the realm of Tāvatiṃsa and divided the *devatās* into two companies, having severed his realm in two he gave one half to Mandhātu to rule. From that time, there were two kings ruling in the kingdom. As time went by, Sakka exhausted his thirty-six million year lifespan and died. Another Sakka came into existence there. This Sakka, too, lived out his lifespan and died. In this way, thirty six Sakkas died and yet Mandhātu in his human state continued to rule over the deva kingdom.

---

[292] *Asaṅkhyeyya*. This word is also used to indicate a fixed period of time, one of the four phases of a *mahākappa*. However in this case the noun *kappa* is absent so I am inclined to interpret it literally.

[293] *Deva* was a common form of address to a monarch; ironically used here by an actual deva addressing a human being.

[294] *Pariṇāyakaratana*—one of the seven treasures, not as Cowell translates "his eldest son", Cowell 1995, Vol. II, p. 217.

As time went on the measure of the king's sensual desires increased and the thought occurred to him, "What is half a kingdom to me? I shall kill Sakka and make myself the sole king." But he could not kill Sakka. Desire (*taṇhā*) was the root of his downfall. His life force began wasting away and his body was afflicted with old age. But a human body cannot be destroyed in a *devaloka*, so he fell to earth and landed in a park. The park keeper announced his arrival to the royal family and they came and prepared a couch for him in the park. There the king lay, exhausted.

They asked him, "Deva, do you have anything to tell us?" He replied, "You may announce this to the populace; the great king Mandhātu, ruler of the four continents and the two thousand islands, a *cakkavatti*, having ruled for a long time over the realm of the Four Great Kings, came to rule in the *devaloka* through the lives of thirty-six Sakkas, was unable to satisfy his desires and now his time is done." Having said this, he died and went according to his kamma. (Jāt 258)

Mandhātu has a double connection to Gotama Buddha. Not only was he a previous birth of the Buddha himself (ibid.) but he was also the Buddha's ancestor, and himself a direct descendent of Mahāsammata ("the great elect"), the first king chosen by the people in the dawn of time.[295]

One other detail is told of Mandhātu's reign. It seems that while he was ruling together with Sakka in Tāvatiṃsa, sitting beside him on the *paṇḍukambala* throne, Mandhātu began to think himself the equal of Sakka, and becoming accustomed to existence in the *davaloka* he grew forgetful of his human domains. In his absence the chief councillor ruled in his place as a viceroy, with Mandhātu's sandals placed on a golden slab as an emblem of authority. The Wheel in the meanwhile had fallen and became stuck fast in the earth. Many people from the other three island-continents had come to Jambudīpa during Mandhātu's reign, thinking, "It is in Jambudīpa that there arise Buddhas, paccekabuddhas, great disciples and *cakkavattis*. The noblest humans are born there, Jambudīpa is the best and most delightful land." Now, with the Wheel earth-bound they were unable to return home and they asked the viceroy to give them lands in Jambudīpa to live. This was the origin of the Kuru land settled by the people from Uttarakuru, Videha settled by those from Pubbavideha and Aparanta by those of Aparagoyāna.[296]

King Mandhātu is reckoned "foremost in the enjoyment of sensual pleasures," (AN 4: 15) because he enjoyed the sensual delights of both the human and deva worlds through a very long life (AN-a 4: 15). His career, and his final words, are emblematic of the truth that desire can never be satiated.

[295] Sn-a 2:13 gives the genealogy, see also DPPN under *Okkāka*. For Mahāsammata see DN 27.

[296] DN-a 15. DPPN identifies the countries as follows: Kuru was "district around Thānesar, with its capital Indapatta, near the modern Delhi", Videha was a "kingdom bordered on the Ganges, (across from) Magadha", and Aparanta "comprises the territory of Northern Gujarat, Kāthiāwar, Kachch and Sindh ".

3:1:14 PACCEKABUDDHAS

Before considering the highest manifestation of a *mahāpurisa*, a fully awakened Buddha, we need to put him into context by briefly examining the other classes of awakened beings.

There are three kinds of persons who have fully realized *nibbāna*, made an end of birth and death and fully transcended *saṃsāra*. These are the *arahant*, the *paccekabuddha* and the *sammāsambuddha* ("perfectly self-awakened one.")[297] All three are *arahant* ("perfected"). The first category, the *arahants per se*, are *sāvaka* ("disciples"), because they attain to full awakening during the dispensation of a Buddha and have his teachings as a guide. The other two are qualified as "self-awakened" (*-sam*)[298] because they attain to full awakening purely by their own efforts, without the benefit of a guide.

The appearance of a *sammāsambuddha*[299] in the world is a very rare event of profound cosmological importance. As we have seen, there may be only one such Buddha in a field of ten thousand world-systems at a time (§ 1:17) and many aeons may pass without any Buddha arising at all. During the periods when no Buddha teaching is extant, that is to say during the great majority of cosmic time, some individuals may become fully awakened by their own efforts but without undertaking teaching on a large scale or founding a movement which survives their death. These are the paccekabuddhas.

The word *pacceka* is defined by PED as "each one, single, by oneself, separate, various, several", and *paccekabuddha* is often translated as "solitary Buddha" or "silent Buddha." The definition of a *paccekabuddha* as given in the commentaries is, "A *paccekabuddha* is awakened by himself, but he does not awaken others. He penetrates the essence of the meaning (*attharasa*) but not the essence of reality (*dhammarasa*). They are not able to formulate the transcendent truths into words and teach them. Their realization is like a dream seen by a mute person" (Sn-a 1:3).

The *paccekabuddha* is portrayed as living the life of an ascetic (*samaṇa*), wearing the "yellow robe" and going for alms with a begging bowl.[300] They usually live in remote places, particularly on Mt Gandhamādana in the Himavā (§ 1:12). They travel to the habitations of ordinary humankind by flying through the air with their psychic powers (E.g. Dhp-a 10:11).

The image of a *paccekabuddha* as being "solitary" is mainly based on the *Khaggavisāṇa Sutta* of the *Sutta Nipāta*,[301] which praises in repeated stanzas the virtue of a solitary life with the refrain, "Wander lonely, like the rhinoceros." Although the text does not explicitly mention paccekabuddhas, the commentary interprets the entire sutta as being about them, with stories of individual paccekabuddhas attached to various stanzas. Elsewhere in the sources, the *paccekabuddha* is not always portrayed as being a lonely wanderer but is depicted as living in community with other paccekabuddhas. A common number is five hundred; at one time there were five hundred paccekabuddhas living in a cavern in Mt Isigili near Rājagaha (MN 116). Five hundred are often mentioned as dwelling on Mt Gandhamādana (Dhp-a 10:11). There is one very curious story about a woman, Padumavatī, who on account of the merit made by giving five hundred grains of rice and a lotus flower to a *paccekabuddha* had her wish granted and became the mother of five hundred sons, all of whom became paccekabuddhas when they reached adulthood. It is said that only one of these sons was born from her womb, in the natural way, and the rest were "moisture-born" (*saṃsedajā*).[302]

297 Pp 2, "What persons are at peace? The *paccekabuddha* and the tathāgata's arahant disciples. What person is at peace and pacifies others? The Buddha".

298 The *paccekabuddha* is sometimes referred to as *paccekasambuddha*. See for example DN 16 and MN 26.

299 Generally, when the word "Buddha" appears unmodified, it is referring to a *sammāsambuddha*.

300 See for example Dhp-a 1:7, 2:1, 10:11. See also Kloppenborg 1983 for a thorough discussion of *paccekabuddhas*.

301 Sn 1:3. See Kloppenborg 1983 for a discussion.

302 AN-a 1:237. *Saṃsedajā* usually refers to the mode of birth of such things as maggots which arise from decay. It is hard to imagine exactly what it might mean in this context.

It is also not quite accurate to call them "silent." They do live in community and take disciples. However, a *paccekabuddha* is unable to teach the profound aspects of the Dhamma he has seen and their students are given instruction only in the "minor duties", which would have included basic meditation instruction (Dhp-a 21:1).

3:1:15 THE SAMMĀSAMBUDDHA

The appearance of a Buddha in the world is an exceedingly rare event. As we have seen, (§ 2:10) there can only ever be one Buddha at a time in a field consisting of ten thousand *cakkavāḷas*. Furthermore, long ages may pass between Buddhas when the teachings are utterly forgotten. A Buddha is the supreme form of manifestation in the entire cosmos. When a Buddha-to-be is born, he declares his status immediately upon emerging from his mother's womb:

> It is the natural order of things (*dhammatā*) that immediately after being born he places his feet firmly and evenly upon the ground with his face to the north and takes seven steps under the shade of a white parasol.[303] Then he stands surveying the four directions and declares in a majestic voice,[304] "I am the highest (*aggo*) in the entire world, I am the eldest (*jeṭṭha*) in the entire world, I am supreme (*seṭṭha*) in the entire world. This is my final birth; there will be no more becoming for me." This is the natural order of things. (DN 14)

The Abhidhamma defines a *sammāsambuddha* thus:

> What person is a *sammāsambuddha*? Here a certain person who from among those things (*dhammā*) not heard before awakens to the truth by himself; he attains omniscience (*sabbaññuta*) and mastery of the powers (*balesu vasībhāvaṃ*). This person we call a *sammāsambuddha*" (Pp 1)

The doctrine of the Buddha's omniscience became very important to the tradition in the commentarial period. In the Jātakas, the attainment of omniscience is frequently cited as the goal of the Bodhisatta and becomes virtually the equivalent of Buddhahood.[305] However, judging by the evidence of the suttas, the Buddha does not seem to have claimed this for himself. In the Tevijjavacchagotta Sutta (MN 71) the ascetic Vacchagotta asks the Buddha if what he has heard from others is true, that:

> The *samaṇa* Gotama is all-knowing (*sabbaññū*) and all-seeing (*sabbadassāvī*), that he claims unbroken knowledge and vision thus: walking or standing, sleeping or waking, knowledge and vision are continually present.

The Buddha definitively rejects this claim, saying that those who speak thus are misrepresenting him. When Vacchagotta inquires as to what he might say to others if asked, so as to represent the Buddha's position correctly, the Buddha answers that he should cite the Three Knowledges of a Buddha (*tevijja*). That is, the knowledge of all his past lives "through many kappas of unfolding and infolding", the knowledge of the way beings rise and fall according to their kamma and the supreme knowledge of destruction of the root defilements (āsavā).

The position becomes more nuanced in the Kaṇṇakatthala Sutta (MN 90) in which King Pasenadi asks the Buddha if it is true that he asserted that it is not possible for anyone to be "all-knowing and all-seeing and to have unbroken knowledge and vision." The Buddha denied having said this and corrected the statement of his position; he had said that it was not possible for anyone to know all and see all at once (*sakideva*). While this statement falls short of an actual claim to omniscience, it certainly leaves the door open for what became the established doctrine in the Theravāda tradition: that of a kind of qualified omniscience. While the Buddha is capable of knowing all things, he only actually knows something if and when he adverts his mind to it; he does not know all things simultaneously.[306]

---

303 The white parasol, *setacchatta*, was an emblem of sovereignty. The commentary says it was held aloft by devas who were invisible to the onlookers.

304 Āsabhiṃ, lit. "bull-like".

305 See for example, Jāt 72, Jāt 132, Jāt 148, Jāt 547, etc.

306 Mil 4:1,2 (eng. v1, p142). See also the long passage from the *Visuddhimagga* commentary which Ñāṇamoli has translated as

This view is also supported by the Buddha's statement that, "whatever can be seen, heard, sensed or cognized … that I know" (AN 4: 24). In a note, Bhikkhu Bodhi comments that this way of phrasing would seem to limit the knowledge of the Buddha to that which can be known and this "would exclude much of the future, which is not predetermined."[307] Perhaps we should not investigate this matter too closely; the Buddha also said that trying to conceive the range of a Buddha's knowledge can only lead to either frustration or madness (AN 4: 77).

The other part of the definition of a *sammāsambuddha* mentions the "powers" (*bala*) of a Buddha. There are some variant lists but the standard one consists of ten powers,[308] and these also are mostly concerned with defining the supernormal knowledge of a Buddha. The ten powers are:

1. The knowledge of the possible and the impossible. There is a long list of these. It includes various aspects of right view, such as "it is not possible that a person possessed of right view should regard any compounded thing as permanent." The list also says that it is impossible that two Buddhas or *cakkavattis* can co-exist in the same world-system. It is further stated that it is impossible for a woman to become a Buddha, a *cakkavatti*, Māra, Brahmā or Sakka. Finally it is stated that is impossible that a skilful bodily action will lead to an unhappy result and the reverse.
2. The knowledge of the workings of kamma and its result.
3. The knowledge of the "ways leading everywhere" (*sabbatthagāmini paṭipada*). This refers to knowing which thoughts and actions lead to rebirth into a particular realm.
4. The knowledge of the various elements in the world. This is the knowledge of the aggregates, elements and bases which comprise the world.
5. The knowledge of the diversity in the disposition of beings.
6. The knowledge of the inferior or superior faculties and characters of other beings.
7. The knowledge of the various factors and aspects involved in the jhānas and other meditative states.
8. The recollection of all his previous existences going back many kappas.
9. The knowledge of the passing away and re-arising of beings. He sees various beings of good or bad character passing away from one existence and re-arising in another happy or miserable state.
10. The knowledge of the destruction of the root defilements (āsavā). This constitutes the complete purification of his being and is synonymous with the attainment of buddhahood.

Some of these powers may be shared by other awakened beings but are present in their fullness only in a *sammāsambuddha*. Taking the recollection of past lives as an example, those of other sects may recollect back 40 kappas at a maximum. Ordinary arahants may recollect back between 100 and 1000 kappas. One of the eighty great disciples can recall back 100,000 kappas. The two chief disciples can recall one *asaṅkheyya* and 100,000 kappas. A *paccekabuddha* can recall two *asaṅkheyya* and 100,000 kappas. But there is no limit to how far back a *sammāsambuddha* can recall.[309] A little later in the same text, this is represented metaphorically with the power of each person's knowledge of recollection compared to a source of light. The knowledge of a yogi from another sect is like the light of a glow worm. The light of an ordinary arahant is like that of a candle. That of a great disciple is like a torch, that of a chief disciple is like the morning star. But the knowledge of a *paccekabuddha* is like that of the moon and that of a *sammāsambuddha* is like the sun in all its glory adorned with one thousand rays (Vism 13: 19).

There is a profound archetypal aspect to the lives of the *sammāsambuddhas*. The career of every Buddha which appears in the world follows a stereotypical pattern. This is illustrated by the circumstances surrounding his conception

---

note 7 to chapter 7 of *The Path of Purification*.

307 Bhikkhu Bodhi, NDB, note 662.

308 AN 10:21 and MN 12 list the ten powers. AN 6: 64 has an abbreviated list of six and AN 5: 11 has a quite different list of five. The definitions are taken from the Abhidhamma Vibhaṅga 16,10.

309 Vism 13.16—an *asaṅkheyyā* in this context may mean a multiple of *mahākappas*, as in the *Abhidharmakośa* system.

and birth. The *Mahāpadāna Sutta* (DN 14) contains a passage which details the events in each Bodhisatta*'s* early life:

1. Every Bodhisatta descends into his mother's womb mindful and fully aware (*sata sampajāna*). This means that his conception is not like that of ordinary people who are overwhelmed by confusion and forget their previous existence. The Bodhisatta had spent his immediately prior existence as a deva in Tusita, and he has descended into the human realm voluntarily and consciously at the request of the other devas.
2. When the Bodhisatta descends into his mother's womb, a brilliant light illuminates the entire ten thousand-fold world-system, even including the *lokantarika nirayas*.[310]
3. The four Great Deva Kings (*cātumahārājika*) descend to the expectant mother's chamber and stand constant guard with drawn swords over the Bodhisatta and his mother.
4. After the Bodhisatta has entered her womb, his mother becomes completely virtuous and keeps the precepts flawlessly.
5. While the Bodhisatta is in her womb, no sensuous thoughts of sexual desire enter into the mind of his mother. Should any man attempt to approach her with desire, his feet become rooted to the spot, as if bound by divine chains.
6. Nevertheless the Bodhisatta*'s* mother fully enjoys the pleasures of the five senses in the form of music, food and costly garments and ornaments which, due to the great kamma of the Bodhisatta, stream in as gift offerings from all directions.
7. While she is bearing the Bodhisatta in her womb, his mother is free of all disease and distress. Furthermore, the fetus is fully visible to her. She sees him seated cross-legged within her womb in peaceful repose.
8. Seven days after the Bodhisatta*'s* birth, his mother dies. The commentary says this is because, having borne the Bodhisatta, her womb is now like a sacred chamber and must not be defiled by the entrance of any man's seed. And since she is still in the prime of her life and very beautiful, it would be impossible for her to guard her womb.
9. Whereas the period of gestation for most women is somewhat variable, for the Bodhisatta*'s* mother it is always precisely ten months.[311]
10. The Bodhisatta*'s* mother always gives birth while standing up.
11. When the Bodhisatta emerges from his mother's womb he is received on a golden net by *suddhāvāsa brahmās*.[312] He is then passed to the Four Great Kings who receive him on a cloth of cheetah hide (*ajinappaveṇī*[313]). He is only then handed over to the human attendants.
12. The newly born Bodhisatta therefore does not come into contact with the earth. He is laid out on a piece of pure white cloth and the Four Great Kings announce, "Rejoice, *devī*, a son of great power is born to you!"
13. The Bodhisatta emerges pure and clean from his mother's womb, undefiled by blood or mucus.
14. Two streams of water appear from the sky, one warm and one cool, and ceremonially bathe the Bodhisatta and his mother.
15. The Bodhisatta immediately after his birth takes seven steps and, standing under a white parasol, announces "I am the highest in the world, I am supreme in the world, I am the eldest in the world. This is my last birth, for me there will be no more becoming."
16. A great light fills the ten thousand-fold world-system as it did at the time of his conception.[314]

In the passage describing each of these wondrous events, the text concludes with the refrain *ayamettha dhammatā* which may be rendered, "this here is the natural order." The life of a Buddha follows a fixed pattern as an unfolding

---

310 The "inter-world hells". See § 3:3,20.

311 Ten lunar months is meant which would be closer to nine months in our calendar.

312 Devas of the "Pure Abodes" who are ānagami. See § 3:6,17.

313 Following PED definition. GGB has "black antelope hide".

314 DN 14 and commentary.

of natural law. Perhaps nothing illustrates the archetypical pattern of a Buddha's career so evocatively as an incident following his meal of milk-rice received from the girl Sujatā just prior to his awakening. When the Bodhisatta had finished his meal, he placed the golden cup into the stream of the Nerañjarā River where it came to rest with a clinking sound upon a pile of three other golden cups left there by the three previous Buddhas of this kappa. The sound wakened the ancient nāga king Mahākāla who exclaimed his surprise that another Buddha had come into the world.[315]

The great cosmic significance of the key events in the Buddha's life is shown by the manifestation of many signs and wonders. These occur when a Bodhisatta is conceived, born, awakened and when as a *sammāsambuddha* he preaches the first discourse and when he enters *parinibbāna* (i.e. dies). Besides the great light mentioned in the sutta, the commentaries embellish the list with many more. Musical instruments spontaneously begin playing by themselves. Everywhere those in bondage are freed as chains and prison walls burst asunder. The blind can see, the deaf hear and the crippled walk. Trees burst into fruit and flower, and even the fires of *niraya* go out temporarily.[316]

The single most important moment in all of cosmic history is not the awakening of a Buddha; rather, it is the moment when he successfully passes his teaching on and the first of his disciples has his "dhamma eye opened" (i.e. he attains *sotapātti*, the first of four stages of awakening). This moment is called the "Turning of the Wheel of Dhamma" (*dhammacakkaṃ pavattita*). For Gotama, the historical Buddha of our epoch, this occurred when, shortly after his own awakening under the Bodhi Tree, he spoke a discourse on the Four Noble Truths to his five former companions in austerity. One of them, Kondañña, declared, "That which is subject to arising, is subject to cessation." The content of this utterance is significant because it does not follow from the content of the Buddha's talk in any obvious or logical way. Kondañña had attained to the first stage of awakening and had an independent glimpse of ultimate truth. The Buddha declared "Kondañña knows!" and a great cry of rejoicing spread upward through the cosmos, beginning with the local *bhūmma* ("earth-bound") devas and spreading from them from realm to realm all the way to the brahmā worlds. "The Bhagava ("Blessed One") at the deer park of Isipatana in Bārāṇasi has turned the supreme Wheel of Dhamma; it cannot be turned back by any *samaṇa* or brahmin or *māra* or deva or brahmā whatsoever in the world!" (SN 56:11) At that moment the cosmic game of *saṃsāra* changed. There was now a way out, a door to the deathless had opened for all beings.

A *sammāsambuddha* is the ultimate state possible for a human being; he is the "best of bipeds (*dvipadaṃ seṭṭho*)" (SN 1:14). Indeed, having transcended *saṃsāric* becoming he is, in a sense, beyond the entire cosmos.

> Just as a lotus is born in the water, grows in the water but stands above the water undefiled by the water; so is the *Tathāgata* born in the world and grows up in the world, but has overcome the world and stands undefiled by the world. (SN 22:94)

Some schools of Buddhism were unwilling to allow the Buddha human status at all. One of the controversies in the Kathavātthu records a refutation of the view that the Buddha never really took human birth at all but remained in the Tusita *devaloka* and merely sent a mind-made body (*nimmitarūpa*) to the earth to teach the Dhamma.[317] This docetic approach is quite contrary to the spirit of the original texts. While the Pali texts exalt the state of Buddhahood, they never deny the human state from which it was achieved. In the Buddha's last days, he suffered from the ravages of age like any other mortal: "this body is like an old cart held together with straps."[318] A large part of the wonder of the Buddha's extraordinary accomplishment is that it was done here, in the ordinary human realm.

---

315 Ap-a-nid. See also GGB p. 303.

316 From the Buddhavaṃsa commentary, in GGB p. 227-28.

317 Kv 18: 1. In the Pali commentaries the Buddha did occasionally make use of a *nimitta* body for special purposes. See DN-a 20 and Dhp 14:2.

318 DN 16. Another of the Kathāvatthu dialogues refutes the view that the Buddha's excrement smelt like perfume. Kv 18: 4.

CHAPTER TWO – THE ANIMAL REALM

3:2:1 TIRACCHĀNA—THE ANIMAL REALM

In Buddhist cosmology, animals are considered a separate *gati* or destination of rebirth. The most common term in Pali for "animal" is *tiracchāna* which derives from *tiraccha* "across, obliquely" conveying the idea that animals go about on all fours with their spines horizontal to the ground (See PED). The word *tiracchāna* is sometimes used as an adjective meaning "debased or lowly" in such compounds as *tiracchānakatha* "idle chatter", lit. "animal talk" or *tiracchānavijjāya* "low knowledge" referring to such arts as astrology, palmistry etc (DN 1). In the Vinaya rule forbidding the killing of animals, (Vin Pāc 61) *tiracchāna* is defined as equivalent to *pāṇa* which means "breathing thing". The animal realm is often referred to collectively as the *tiracchānayoni*, "the animal womb."[319]

The *tiracchānayoni* is said to be the most diverse of the five *gati* (SN 22:100) (destinations of rebirth). In the commentary to the Vinaya rule cited above, when an example is needed for the very smallest and most inconsequential animal, bed-bug eggs (*maṅgulabījaka*) are mentioned (Vin-a Pāc 61). On the other end of the scale, the largest animals of all are certain giant sea-monsters which can be as big as one thousand *yojana* from head to tail (Jāt 537). A birth as an animal is considered one of the unfortunate ones, better than *niraya* but worse than becoming a peta (MN 97). The particular suffering of the animals is described as being subject to capture in nets and traps or to being forced to pull carts by use of a whip or a goad (AN-a 1: 418). Immoral behaviour in general leads to rebirth as an animal, (AN 10: 176) but certain actions are specifically cited, including the holding of false-views (*micchādiṭṭhi*),[320] cruelty, (AN 6:18) breaking precepts (AN 8: 40) and concealing offences (AN 2: 26). A person who sneaks around to commit misdeeds is said to be subject to rebirth as a creeping animal such as a snake, scorpion, centipede, mongoose, cat, mouse or owl (AN 10: 216).

The *Bālapaṇḍita Sutta* (MN 129) attributes birth in the animal world to greediness for flavours (*rasādo*) and to the doing of evil deeds (*pāpāni kammāni karitvā*). The text especially mentions brahmins who eagerly chase after offerings, being reborn as those animals who chase after the flavour of dung, cocks, pigs, dogs and jackals. The sutta goes on to elaborate on the suffering endured in the *tiracchānayoni*:

> There are, bhikkhus, living beings arisen among the animals (*tiracchānagatā pāṇā*) who live in darkness, grow old in darkness and die in darkness. These include moths, maggots and worms, among others. Those fools who are greedy for flavours and commit evil deeds here, when their time comes and the body breaks up after death arise in companionship with those beings that live in darkness.
>
> There are animals that live in water, grow old in water and die in water. These include fish, turtles and crocodiles … There are animals that live in filth, grow old in filth and die in filth. They live in rotten fish, stinking corpses, rotten food, cesspools and sewers. Those fools who are greedy for flavours and commit evil deeds here, when their time comes and the body breaks up after death arise in companionship with those beings that live in filth.
>
> I could speak in very many ways, bhikkhus, about the sufferings in the *tiracchānayoni*. It is not easy to find a parable to express it, so great is the suffering of the *tiracchānayoni*.

---

319 See for instance the list of the five *gati* in DN 33.

320 DN 12—"Wrong view leads to one of two destinies, either *niraya* or an animal birth.".

Suppose, bhikkhus, that a person was to throw a yoke with a single hole into the great ocean, and it was carried about in all directions by the winds. Suppose there were a blind tortoise that emerged from the ocean once every hundred years. What do you think, bhikkhus, would that tortoise put his neck through the hole in the yoke? – He might, bhante, after some very long period of time. – Sooner, bhikkhus, would that blind turtle put his neck through the yoke than would a fool escape back to the human realm once having fallen to a lower realm (*vinipāta*).

Why is that? Because there is no dhamma-faring there, no peace, no doing of good deeds or making of merit. There is only mutual devouring there; there the strong consume the weak.

If, bhikkhus, that fool after some long time regains the human state it is into a low family that he is born; a family of outcastes, hunters, bamboo gatherers, carters or refuse cleaners. Among such clans is he reborn. There he is poor; he finds little food with much difficulty. There clothing is hard to come by. He is of bad colour, ugly, deformed, sickly, blind or crippled or palsied. He gets no food, drink, clothing, vehicles, garlands, dwelling, bedding or lights. There he misconducts himself by body, speech and mind and at the break-up of the body he arises after death in a lower birth, even in *niraya*. Such is the nature of the total and utter fool. (MN 129)

Thus it is easy to fall into the animal realm, but difficult to escape it. The number of humans and devas who fall into the lower realms is greater than the number who take a better rebirth, (SN 56:97 f, Eng. 56:102 f.) and the number of animals who are reborn as humans or devas is small (SN 56:105, Eng. 56:123 f.). The number of beings in the animal realm is very great indeed. "The number of ants or termites in a single mound is beyond count" (MN-a 122). The number of beings in the seas, presumably all to be counted as animal, is greater than the total number of beings on land (AN 1:322, Eng. 1:333). Making escape difficult also is the possibility of repeated rebirth as an animal. We hear of several cases of beings being reborn five hundred times in sequence as an animal. A brahmin was reborn as a goat and killed five hundred times because he had committed animal sacrifices (Jāt 18). A greedy-minded bhikkhu who cheated an arahant out of his meal suffered multiple lower rebirths, including five hundred times as a dog who could never find enough food (Jāt 41). The only sure way to escape from an animal birth is to become a *sotāpanna*, one who has attained the first stage of awakening (SN 55:1).

Although an animal birth is in general one of great suffering, some animals, relatively few in number, enjoy a more pleasant existence. For example, a royal elephant that lives in the king's household and enjoys good food, lodging and adornment, (AN-a 4:232) or other elephants, dogs, horses and cattle that live among humans and are treated well (AN 10:177). This would include those animals we nowadays refer to as "pets". These cases are said to be the results of mixed kamma: when previously human they misconducted themselves by body, speech and mind but were generous and gave food and drink to ascetics and brahmins (ibid.). It should also be noted that powerful beings such as nāgas and *supaṇṇas* are counted as *tiracchāna*. When aspiring to rebirth as a deva, the nāga prince Bhūridatta scorned his present state as "a frog-eating animal existence" (Jāt 543).

In Buddhist cosmology, beings may be born in one of four ways: womb-born, as for example humans and other mammals, egg-born as in the case of birds, moisture-born, which is the way insects and worms were thought to arise and the spontaneous birth of devas and some other non-human beings, who simply appear fully formed at their new birth.[321] Animals can take any of the four kinds of birth (Vism 17:154). Maggots and other such small beings that live in filth are said to "moisture-born." Some of the higher nāgas and *supaṇṇas* are born spontaneously, fully formed, like the devas. The *Aṅguttara Commentary* mentions in passing that there are cases of animals giving birth to humans and

[321] See introduction.

vice-versa, but without giving examples (AN-a 1:275). We might cite Jātaka 523 in which a female deer eats some grass on which an ascetic has urinated, and by swallowing some of his semen gives birth to a human boy. Also, in the Bhūridatta Jātaka, a nāga female takes a human prince as her lover and gives birth to two children described as human, albeit with a somewhat "watery" nature. Later in the same story, one of these children, a girl, marries a nāga king and gives birth to nāga children (Jāt 543).

Animals take a wide variety of nutriment:

> Compared with the food of a crocodile, that of a peacock is subtle. Crocodiles eat even stones; they do not find them vile but digest them. Peacocks eat snakes, scorpions and such animals. But compared to the food of the peacock, the food of the hyena is subtle. They eat horns and bones abandoned even three years ago. Moistened with saliva, these become as soft and tender as tuber roots. Compared with the food of hyenas, the food of elephants is subtle. They eat the branches of various trees. Compared to the food of elephants, the food of buffalo, elk and deer is subtle. They eat even the sapless leaves of various trees Compared to these, the food of cattle is subtle, and they eat moist or dry grass. Compared to these, the food of hares is subtle. Compared to the food of hares, the food of birds is subtle. Compared to birds, the food of village rustics is subtle.[322]

Animal consciousness is called *ahetuka*, "rootless" (AN-a 4:21). This term from the Abhidhamma is defined as follows:

> The word *ahetuka* means without roots, and qualifies those types of consciousness that are devoid of the mental factors called *hetu*, roots. These types do not contain any of the three unwholesome roots—greed, hatred and delusion—nor do they contain the three bright roots—non-greed, non-hatred and non-delusion— which may be either wholesome or indeterminate. Since a root is a factor which helps to establish stability in a *citta* ("consciousness-moment"), those *cittas* which lack roots are weaker than those which possess them[323] …

This means in practice that an animal goes through life experiencing the results of previous kamma and has little ability or opportunity to make fresh kamma. This should be considered a matter of degrees. For example, considering the potential for negative kamma, while a higher animal like an elephant is capable of some degree of trickery and deceit, this is not to be compared to the tangled level of corruption of which a human being is capable (MN 51). Escape from this realm is generally possible only as a result of old kamma made in a higher birth coming to a delayed fruition. There are, however, exceptions to this rule. It is said that when "animals such as deer or birds hear a Dhamma talk, pay homage to the *saṅgha* or to a *cetiya* ("stupa", presumably by circumambulating it) they make skilful (*kusala*) kamma whether they know it or not … And when cows, dogs, biting flies or lions and tigers harass a bhikkhu or deprive him of life, they make unskilful (*akusala*) kamma, whether they know it or not" (AN-a 4:171). An example of a humble animal escaping to a better rebirth is the frog who listened to the Buddha's teaching:

> The Buddha was teaching Dhamma to the four-fold assembly by the banks of a pond near the city of Campa. At that moment, a frog emerged from the pond thinking, "This is what is called Dhamma." Settling down at the back of the crowd, he grasped the sign of Dhamma (*dhammasaññāya nimitta*) in the sound of the Buddha's voice. Just then a certain shepherd came to listen to the Dhamma. Without seeing the frog, he planted his staff on the ground to lean on, and crushed the body of the frog. With his mind gladdened by the

322 MN-a 9. The text goes on through the various classes of human society and then the various grades of devas.

323 Bhikkhu Bodhi, CMA, p. 40.

sign of Dhamma, the frog died and was reborn in Tāvatiṃsa as a deva in a twelve *yojana* golden *vimāna*, as if waking from a dream. Finding himself surrounded by a company of *accharās* (heavenly dancing girls) he wondered, "From whence did I come to this place?" Examining his previous life he asked himself, "By what kamma did I obtain this present state of enjoyment?" He saw no cause other than grasping the sign of Dhamma in the Buddha's voice. (Vv-a 51 & Vism 7.51)

Another story which illustrates the same principle concerns the five hundred bhikkhus who were Sāriputta's students and to whom he entrusted the Abhidhamma:

When the Buddha taught the devas in Tāvatiṃsa daily for an entire rainy season, each afternoon he would return to earth and pass on the synopsis of the teaching to Sāriputta. These became the seven books of the Abhidhamma and Sāriputta first taught these to a select group of five hundred bhikkhu disciples. They had all been small bats living in a cave at the time of Kassapa Buddha. As they hung from the ceiling of the cave, two bhikkhus were reciting the Abhidhamma aloud as they did walking meditation. The bats grasped a sign in the sound of the bhikkhus' voices. They did not understand the meaning, "these are the aggregates, these are the elements etc." but simply by grasping the sign after death they were reborn in a deva world. They remained enjoying the bliss of a deva existence for the entire period between Buddhas and were then reborn as householders in Sāvatthi during the time of Gotama Buddha. (Dhp-a 14:2)

Good kamma was also made by the elephant and the monkey who served the Buddha during one rainy season. The Buddha had been staying at the monastery near Kosambi but the bhikkhus there had proved to be quarrelsome so he left to dwell alone in the forest:

In that forest the Buddha spent the rains retreat happily, attended by an elephant named Pālileyyaka.[324] That elephant had left his herd and entered the jungle thicket seeking ease and comfort. "Here I live crowded by male elephants, female elephants, young elephants and baby elephants. They chew up all the grass and break all the branches and they foul the water I want to drink. When I come out of the water after bathing the female elephants come and rub their bodies against me. What if I were to go away and live alone?"

Entering the forest he saw the Buddha sitting at the root of a *sāl* tree.[325] The elephant approached the Buddha and paid homage to him. Taking a branch from the *sāl* tree he used it as a broom and swept the ground, and picking up the Buddha's water-pot with his trunk he fetched water fit for drinking. Then the elephant made a fire with a fire-drill and threw heated stones into a small rock pool, to provide the Buddha with hot water for bathing. After that he gathered various wild fruits for the Buddha to eat.[326]

When the Buddha went for his alms-round in the village the elephant carried his robes and bowl on his head, although the Buddha forbade him from entering the human village. When the Buddha had returned to his place in the forest and finished his meal, the elephant put away his robes and bowl and taking a branch stood fanning him. During the night the elephant, taking up a stout branch in his trunk, paced up and down through the forest until dawn. Thinking "I shall protect the teacher" he kept away danger from wild beasts. Ever after that forest was called the *Pālileyyakarakkhitavanasaṇḍo*, "The Protected by Pālileyyaka Jungle Thicket."

---

324 Spelled in DPPN as Pārileyya.

325 Śāl or *shala* tree, *Shorea robusta.* See Dhammika 2018:179.

326 Although the text does not specify, it can be assumed that the fruits were those kinds specifically allowed in the Vinaya as medicines, otherwise they would not be allowed for eating in the afternoon. see Vin Mv 6.

A certain monkey saw the elephant doing all these duties for the Buddha and he thought, "I shall do something too." One day he found a honey-comb on a branch and he brought it to the Buddha. The monkey wondered, "Will he eat it or will he not?" When the Buddha put aside the comb without eating it, the monkey investigated the reason why and discovered that there were larvae in the comb. These he carefully removed and gave the comb back to the Buddha, who now ate the honey.

The monkey was so happy that he began leaping and dancing among the tree branches. But one of the branches he grasped broke off and he fell to the ground and was impaled on a broken stump. With his mind purified by thoughts of the Teacher (*satthari pasanneneva cittena*) the monkey died and was reborn in a thirty *yojana* golden *vimāna* in Tāvatiṃsa attended by a thousand *accharās*, he there he was known as *Makkaṭadevaputto*, "Monkey Deva".

When the rains retreat ended, a party of bhikkhus led by Ānanda arrived to take the Buddha back. As they were leaving the forest, the elephant stood across the Buddha's path, not wishing to see him leave. The Buddha spoke to him, saying "Pālileyyaka, I am leaving now and I will not return. In this form of existence (*attabhāva*) you cannot practice jhāna (one-pointed meditative absorption) or *vipassāna* (meditative insight into reality), nor attain the paths and fruit. The abodes of humans are an obstacle and a danger for you, you must turn back." The elephant stood sobbing with his trunk in his mouth and as soon as he lost sight of the Buddha he died of a broken heart and was reborn in a thirty *yojana* golden *vimāna* in Tāvatiṃsa attended by a thousand *accharās*. There he was known as *Pālileyyakadevaputta* (Dhp-a 1:5).

When Siddhattha left home to seek Buddhahood, he rode his loyal horse Kanthaka as far as to the river Anomā. After his master left him, Kanthaka also died of a broken heart and was immediately reborn in Tāvatiṃsa (Vv-a 81).

An example of an animal making unskilful kamma is the dog who had previously been a haughty brahmin named Todeyya. He had treated the Buddha with contempt, addressing him with the familiar "*bho*" as a deliberate insult. As a result he was reborn as a dog in his own home, with his former son as his master. When the Buddha came by this house on his alms round, the dog barked at him and as result was reborn in Avīci *niraya* (DN-a 10).

Beings cannot gain spiritual awakening in the animal form. We have seen the Buddha explaining this to the elephant Pālileyyaka. In no story does an animal, even a nāga, gain the stage of *sotāpanna*. The state of *tiracchāna* is listed as one of the nine inopportune times for hearing the Dhamma (DN 33). Whenever we encounter animals performing spiritually positive actions, the end result is always a deva-realm rebirth. Of course, escape from the lower realms is itself a significant spiritual accomplishment and in their new state awakening now becomes a possibility. In Buddhism, there is no eternal damnation.

A Note on Plants: Plant life (*bhūtagāma*) is not considered sentient and cannot make kamma or experience the result of kamma. Vegetable life is called *ekindriya* ("one-facultied") meaning that it has life only but not consciousness (Vin Sd 7). Killing a plant is not a violation of the first precept. There is, however, a *vinaya* rule for bhikkhus which forbids taking plant life (Vin Pāc 11). The story explaining the rationale for this rule is somewhat ambiguous. It begins with a bhikkhu who was chopping down a tree and in the process injured a deva living in that tree. To be precise, while chopping, he accidentally severed the arm of the deva's son. There is more than a hint here that the deva is not only inhabiting the tree, but in some manner identified with it: chopping a branch is the equivalent of chopping off his arm. But the identification is not complete, the deva and his son are not killed with the tree but are able to move into a better tree given them by the Buddha.[327] Despite this story, the reason given for the rule in the end is that the lay people were scandalized to see bhikkhus cutting down trees, an action deemed inappropriate for *samaṇas*. In other

[327] From the sub-commentary. See Thanissaro, 2007, Vol. I, p. 324 f.

words, the rationale for the rule was not given as compassion for plant life, but preserving the good reputation of the *saṅgha*. The ambiguity in the story speaks to a prevalent animist view in Indian society which was not accepted in mainstream Buddhist theory.

3:2:2 ANIMALS IN THE *JĀTAKA* TALES

One hundred thousand kappas ago the ascetic Sumedha made an aspiration for Buddhahood in the presence of Dīpankara Buddha, and was duly recognized by him as a Bodhisatta, a being on the path to Buddhahood. The path of a Bodhisatta is long and arduous, encompassing many hundreds or thousands of life-times. Sumedha was eventually reborn as Siddhattha Gotama, the Buddha of our present age. The Jātakas are a collection of stories recounting episodes in some of the previous lives of Gotama Buddha during his long career as a Bodhisatta.[328]

The Jātaka collection in the Theravāda canon consists of five hundred and forty-seven separate stories. Of these, more than a third of the total feature animals as prominent characters. The Bodhisatta himself was some kind of animal in one hundred and seventeen stories. The following table summarizes the various animal births of the Bodhisatta:

TABLE SIX – ANIMAL BIRTHS OF THE BODHISATTA

ANIMAL	NUMBER OF BIRTHS	ANIMAL	NUMBER OF BIRTHS
HOOFED MAMMALS		**BIRDS**	
deer or stag	9	swan or goose	8
antelope	2	ruddy goose	2
horse	4	peacock	3
bull or ox	4	quail	5
buffalo	1	partridge	2
Sub-Total	**20**	crow	2
CARNIVORES		water-crow	1
dog	1	vulture	4
lion	10	dove or pigeon	6
jackal	2	cock or fowl	2
Sub-Total	**13**	Indian cuckoo	1
MIS'C MAMMALS		wood-pecker	2
monkey	11	hornbill	1
elephant	7	parrot	9
rat	2	bird, unspecified	4
hare	1	*supaṇṇa*	1
Sub-Total	**21**	Sub-Total Birds	**53**
Sub-Total All Mammals	**54**	**REPTILES AND FISH**	
		nāga	3
		monitor lizard	3
		fish	3
		frog	1
		Sub-Total Reptiles	**10**
		TOTAL ALL BIRTHS	**117**

(Note: the identification of species is sometimes problematic, especially for the various birds).

One of the eighteen kinds of birth that a Bodhisatta cannot take is an animal birth lesser than a quail (*tiracchānayoniyaṃ vaṭṭakato pacchimattabhāvo*), (Sn-a 1:3) a statement which implies a hierarchy among the animal species. Very often the Bodhisatta is represented as the king of a group of animals. Thus, in Jātaka 15 he is a deer

[328] See Jāt-nid 1 for the story of Sumedha. For a detailed description of the theory of bodhisattahood see GGB.

followed by a herd of deer, in Jātaka 140 he is a king of the crows (*kākarājā*), in Jātaka 20 he is a monkey king (*kapirājā*), in Jātaka 129 he is a rat-king (*mūsikarājā*) and so forth. Sometimes his animal followers are identified as previous births of his contemporary disciples, the *buddhaparisā* or "Buddha assembly" (e.g. Jāt 20). In other instances, the animal followers are identified as previous births of the Sakyan clan (Jāt 502).

Many other characters known from the suttas had previously taken animal births and featured in the Jātaka tales:

Devadatta, the Buddha's cousin who turned evil and tried to kill him three times, features in twenty-eight animal Jātakas, seven times as a jackal and three times as a crocodile, animals considered to have a low moral character.

Devadatta also took birth as a deer, lion, monkey (five times), elephant, quail, crow, hawk, cormorant, parrot, chameleon and snake. The animal forms of Devadatta consistently represent the villains in the stories.

Ānanda, another cousin of the Buddha who served as his loyal attendant for many years, appears in animal form in twenty-one Jātakas. He took birth in a wide range of animal forms: as a deer, bull, dog, jackal, monkey, otter, goose, vulture, pigeon, parrot, crab, nāga and tortoise. He usually played the role of a junior companion of the Bodhisatta.

Sāriputta, one of the Buddha's two chief disciples, the one renowned for his penetrating wisdom also appears as an animal in twenty-one Jātakas in a wide range of species, having been born as a deer, horse, lion, monkey, goose, crow, owl, osprey, *supaṇṇa*, snake, nāga and tortoise.

Moggallāna, the other chief disciple, who was renowned for his mastery of the psychic powers, appears as an animal in fifteen Jātakas in the form of a tiger, jackal, monkey, elephant, rat, goose and *supaṇṇa*. In three separate stories the two chief disciples are big cats and companions, Sāriputta always being a lion and Moggallāna a tiger.

Kokālika, the evil-minded bhikkhu who disparaged the chief disciples, was an animal in seven Jātakas, appearing as a donkey, jackal, crow, and crocodile. His animal character is always evil, foolish or both.

Uppalavaṇṇā, one of the two chief female disciples took an animal birth in five stories, appearing as a deer, mynah bird, monitor lizard and nāga.

The Buddha's former wife **Rāhulamātā** featured as an animal in four stories, as the Bodhisatta's mate. Likewise his son **Rāhula** appeared in three animal Jātakas but only once as the offspring of the Bodhisatta.[329]

Several other persons from the Buddha's time had taken one or two animal births in the Jātakas. Particularly interesting is the birth of **Māra** as a snake (Jāt 389) and the Jain founder, known to the Buddhist sources as **Nigantha Nātaputta**, as a crow (Jāt 339).

Of the animal species featured in the Jātakas, **monkeys** are the most common, appearing in thirty stories. There are three Pali words translated as "monkey": *kapi*, *makkaṭa* and *vānara*. The word *vānara* means "forest dweller" and likely represents a generic word for monkeys of any kind,[330] but the other two words seem to indicate separate species. In the stories, *kapi* monkeys and *makkaṭa* monkeys display very different characters. Whenever the Bodhisatta takes rebirth as a monkey, it is always as a *kapi* (or a *vānara*) and such monkeys are portrayed as having a clever or even a heroic character.

> At one time when the Buddha was travelling with a company of bhikkhus, they stopped by the banks of *Naḷakapāna* ("Drinking Reed") Pond. There the novices gathered reeds to be made into needle-cases for the bhikkhus, but they were found to be hollow throughout, without a single knot from root to tip, thus useless for that purpose. The bhikkhus asked the Buddha if there were any reason for the unusual reeds growing here. In answer, the Buddha told a story of the past.
>
> In bygone times, there had been a *dakarakkhasa* ("water ogre") living in this pond, who used to devour all who came to drink from it. At that time, the Bodhisatta had come to birth as a king of the monkeys (*kapirājā*).

[329] Jāt. 172 where he was a lion cub sired by the Bodhisatta

[330] *vānara* is sometimes used interchangeably with the other two terms within a single story, see Jāt 20, 268, 273

He was as big as a young deer and was the leader of a troop of eighty thousand monkeys (*vānara*) whom he protected from danger in their forest home.

When the troop came to the pond of the *dakarakkhasa*, the Bodhisatta saw that while there were foot-prints of animals leading into the water, there were none leading out, so he knew that a *rakkhasa* lived there and was eating the animals that came to drink. When the monkeys refrained from going down into the water, the *rakkhasa* came out in a horrible form and challenged the monkey-king. The Bodhisatta said to him that his entire troop of eighty-thousand monkeys would be able to drink from the pond without being eaten.

The Bodhisatta had a reed brought to him, and reflecting upon the *pāramis* (spiritual perfections) he blew into the reed and it became hollow throughout, without a single knot. Then the Bodhisatta determined (*adhiṭṭhāsi*), "May all the reeds around this lake become hollow." Now, through the greatness of a Bodhisatta's goodness, his determinations (*adhiṭṭhāna*)[331] always succeed. So, all the reeds around the pond became hollow through and through. The monkey-king and his entire troop of eighty-thousand monkeys each took one of the hollow reeds and sitting safely on the bank of the pond, drank their fill before returning unharmed to the forest.

The reeds of Naḷakapāna Pond have remained hollow ever since, and will remain hollow for the duration of a kappa. The hollowing of those reeds is one of the four Kappa-long Miracles (*kappaṭṭhiyapāṭihāriyāni*) which will endure until the end of this world-cycle.

At the conclusion of the story, the Buddha identified the characters. "At that time, Devadatta was the *dakarakkhasa*, the eight-thousand monkeys were my followers (*buddhaparisā*) and I myself was the monkey-king." (Jāt 20)

Makkaṭa monkeys are portrayed quite differently; they are mischievous, destructive and foolish. This fits the macaque or rhesus monkey. Macaque is a Portuguese word, but it may have been borrowed from a local dialect.[332]

Long ago, when Brahmadatta was King of Bārāṇasi, the Bodhisatta was born as a brahmin who renounced sense pleasures to live as a hermit by the banks of the Gaṅgā in the Himavā. One day while he was sitting in the doorway of his hut, a bold and wicked monkey (*makkaṭa*) came up and tried to put its penis in his ear. The Bodhisatta prevented him from doing this, and retained his equanimity.

Sometime later, it happened that a tortoise came up out of the Gaṅgā River and lay sleeping on the bank with its mouth open. The naughty monkey (*lola-vānara*) seeing this stuck its penis into the tortoise's mouth. Waking up, the tortoise snapped its jaws shut like someone closing the lid of a chest, which was very painful for the monkey.

Unable to bear the pain, the monkey wondered, "Who can free me from this suffering? Who can I go to for help? Only the ascetic can free me, it is proper that I go and see him." Carrying the tortoise in his hands, the monkey went to see the Bodhisatta who spoke to him in verse:

What, is that your alms-bowl?

You have quite a handful, brahmin.

---

331 *Adhiṭṭhāna* is one of the ten *pārami*, spiritual qualities which are to be perfected by a Bodhisatta as a prerequisite of Buddha-hood.

332 Dr. Bryan Levman, private correspondence.

Where did you go for alms?

What lay followers did you approach?

The monkey replied, also in verse:

I am a foolish monkey (*kapi*),

I have touched that which should not be touched.

If you would be so good as to free me,

I will go away to the mountains.

The Bodhisatta then addressed the tortoise:

Tortoises are of the Kassapa clan,

Monkeys (*makkaṭa*) are Koṇḍañña clansmen.

Kassapa, release Kondañña,

You are committing sexual misconduct.

The tortoise was pleased with the words of the Bodhisatta and released the monkey's penis. Being freed, the monkey bowed to the Bodhisatta and ran away without looking back.[333]

The conclusion of the story may seem obscure: the internal commentary to the Jātaka explains that by the caste rules, the Kassapa and Kondañña clans do not inter-marry and for them to have intimate relations is considered sexual misconduct. The monkey in the story is referred to in the prose section as a *makkaṭa*. That he refers to himself as a *kapi* may just be an attempt to appear more respectable in the eyes of the hermit. The tortoise and the monkey were identified as previous births of two chief ministers in the Kosalan government.

Jackals (Pali *siṅgāla*) also feature prominently in the Jātakas, appearing in twenty-two tales. The character of jackals is portrayed in the Jātakas as generally low, nasty, tricky and cunning. Jackals are called "the most ignoble of animal births" (*adhamo migajātānaṃ*) (Jāt 172).

At one time an ox carcass was dragged by some villagers and left under a castor-oil tree (*eraṇḍarukkha*). A jackal came along to feed on it, and a crow sat in the branches of the tree hoping to get some too. The deva of the tree spoke this verse:

Of beasts, the jackal is the lowest (*anto*),

The crow the least of birds,

The castor-oil the least of trees;

Here all three are met together![334]

---

[333] Jāt 273—this Jātaka is not translated into English in the PTS collection. For a translation, see Dhammika 2008. Dhammika also identifies *makkaṭa* with macaque.

[334] Jāt 295. The commentary glosses *anto* with *hīna*, "low, inferior, base, despicable" and *lāmako* "inferior, low, sinful".

When a jackal was caught defecating in a well, his excuse was "This is the law of jackals, passed down from our fore-fathers. Jackals defecate wherever we drink, so there is no cause for blame." HIs captor remarks, "If this is the law (*dhamma*) of jackals, what can their lawlessness (*adhamma*) be?" (Jāt 271)

Given the low and nasty character of jackals, it is not surprising that Devadatta took birth as one in seven Jātaka stories. A common motif parallels the way Devadatta attempted to imitate the Buddha and become a great teacher in his own right:

> At one time the Bodhisatta was a lion and Devadatta a jackal. The lion was returning home from the hunt one day when he came across the jackal. Unable to escape, the jackal lay down on his belly and said he wished to serve the lion. The lion accepted and took him to his dwelling place and there day by day the jackal grew fat on the scraps of the lion's kills.
>
> One day a feeling of pride arose in the jackal and he said to the lion, "I am ever a burden to you, my lord. You always bring back the meat which I eat. Today, you remain here and I shall go forth and kill an elephant." The lion told him, "Jackal, you are not of the kind which can kill elephants. Elephants are big and strong. You remain here and I will kill an elephant."
>
> Despite being forbidden by the lion, the jackal issued forth from the cave and three times cried the jackal's cry "*bukka! bukka! bukka*!" Looking about, he saw a black elephant in the plain below and thinking, "I shall leap on his head!" he jumped down from the cliff, but turning around in the air he landed at the elephant's feet. The elephant lifted up his forefoot and brought it down upon the jackal's head, smashing it to bits. The elephant went off trumpeting as the jackal lay on the ground groaning. The lion, seeing this, said, "Through pride was this jackal destroyed." (Jāt 335)

The greedy habits of jackals often get them in trouble, and on rare occasions, they can even learn a valuable lesson and change for the better:

> At one time the Bodhisatta came to birth as a jackal. Once, when searching for food he came across the carcass of an elephant. "What a great pile of food I have found!" He bit into the trunk, but it was like biting the handle of a plough. "There is nothing to eat here!" So he tried biting into the tusk but that was as hard as a stone pillar. He bit the ear next, but that was like the hard edge of a basket. Gnawing on the elephant's stomach was like trying to bite his way into a stone granary. Its feet were like mortars, its tail like the pestle.
>
> Everywhere he tried to bite into the elephant, he found nothing to eat until he found the anus, which was like biting into soft pastry. "Now I have found soft food in this carcass!" So beginning there, he ate his way into the elephant's belly. He devoured the kidneys, and growing thirsty, he drank the blood and when he became tired he stretched out in the elephant's stomach and fell asleep. "Here in this elephant carcass, I have abundant food and drink, and a pleasant home to rest in. Why should I go anywhere else?"
>
> But by and by the heat of the sun and the wind dried out the elephant's carcass and as the corpse withered, the jackal's doorway closed up leaving the inside in darkness. For the jackal, it became like a birth in the *lokantara niraya*.[335] The elephant's flesh withered and dried up, and all the blood was gone. The jackal grew frightened and dashed to and fro inside the elephant's belly like a ball of flour in a cooking pot, but he was unable to escape.

[335] The dark hell between world-systems, see § 3:3,20.

After the jackal had endured this torment for a few days, it began to rain. The carcass became moistened and swelled up back to its original size, and the anus opened up enough for a little light to shine through, looking like a star in the sky. "My life is saved!" The jackal backed up into the elephant's head then took a running leap through the anus as quick as he could. The hole was so tight it tore all the hair off the jackal's hide. At first, when he got out, he was so frightened that he just kept running. But when he stopped at last and saw the state of his hairless body, he exclaimed "This suffering of mine has no cause other than my own greed. From this day forward, I shall never be greedy again, nor shall I ever go inside an elephant carcass!"[336]

Crows (*kāka*) feature in twenty-two Jātakas. We have seen that crows are called "the lowest of the birds," being in many respects the avian equivalent of the jackals. Like the jackals, they are portrayed as tricky and thieving. There are several stories of crows attempting to steal food from human kitchens and coming to a bad end because of it.[337] The following story illustrates the trickiness of crows:

Certain merchants of Kāsi went to sea taking along a land-finding crow.[338] In the midst of the ocean, the ship was wrecked and the crow found his way to an island on which there dwelt a large flock of birds. The crow thought, "Here there is a large flock of birds. It would be excellent to eat their eggs and their young. I shall use trickery on them."

So he landed in the midst of them and stood on one foot with his mouth wide-open. "Who are you?" the birds asked, and the crow replied "I am Dhammiko" (i.e. "the righteous one") "Why do you stand on one foot?" "If I put my other foot down, the earth could not bear my weight." "Why do you stand with your mouth open?" "I eat no other food, but only the wind." The crow then spoke a stanza in praise of living righteously. The island birds decided the crow must be a holy bird (*bhaddako pakkhī*) "a twice-born one who stands on one foot speaking Dhamma."[339]

The birds said to the crow, "Sir, as you eat nothing but wind, would you look after our eggs and our young while we go for food?" The crow agreed, and as soon as the birds were gone the villain (*pāpo*) ate their eggs and their young ones until his belly was full. When the birds returned they found the crow standing on one foot with his mouth open as before. Seeing the loss of their eggs and their young, they raised a disturbance, but did not suspect the crow because they thought him a righteous bird who lived on air.

However, the king of the birds was the Bodhisatta and he reasoned that before this crow came they had not lost any eggs or young ones. So the next time the birds went feeding, he stayed behind and hid himself to watch the crow. The crow ate the eggs and the young birds as before. So when the birds came back, the bird-king called a meeting and told them what had happened and the entire flock fell upon the crow and striking him with beak and claw and wing they beat him to death.[340]

Sometimes the crows, even in the midst of their thievery, display something of a nobler character:

Once upon a time, when Brahmadatta was king of Bārāṇasi, the Bodhisatta was born as a king of the crows

336 Jāt 148. A similar story is told of a jackal birth of Moggallāna in Jāt490.

337 Jāt 42, 274, 275, 375 and 395.

338 *Disākāka* lit. "direction crow". These birds were released from the ship to find land, the sailors taking note of the direction in which they flew. See Vism 21.65.

339 "Twice-born," *dija* is a punning reference to both birds, who are born when the egg is laid and again when it is hatched, and to brahmins who are born the second time when initiated.

340 Jāt 384. A very similar story involving a jackal who preys on a colony of rats by pretending to a false piety is told in Jāt 128.

named Supatta ("Good Wing"). He had a queen named Suphassā ("Good Touch") and a general named Sumukha ("Good Beak", this was Sāriputta). He had eighty thousand followers and they all lived near to Bārāṇasi.

Queen Suphassā came to have a craving for human food from the royal kitchens and told her husband the king, "I have a desire to eat the food of the King of Bārāṇasi, my lord,[341] and if I don't get what I want, I shall surely die." King Supatta sat down to think and his general Sumukha approached him, "What troubles you, great king?" The king of the crows told him what the Queen wanted and Sumukha replied, "Do not think about it, great king. You stay here today, and I shall fetch the food."

So Sumukha gathered the crows together and they flew to Bārāṇasi. He posted companies here and there near the kitchen to keep watch and he himself, together with eight crow-warriors took up a position on the kitchen roof. He spoke to his soldiers, "When the king's servant comes out with the dishes of food, I will make him drop them. When he drops the dishes, my life is finished. Four of you gather up as much rice as you can, and four of you get the fish and meat. Take the food to Supatta and his wife. If he asks you where his general is, say that I am following shortly."

When the king's servant emerged from the kitchen bearing a platter of food, Sumukha flew down and landed on his chest, striking him with his talons. With his beak he struck at the man's nose while beating his face with his two wings. The king was watching from an upper storey of the palace and he cried out from a window, "Hey, you there, drop the food and catch that crow!" The man seized Sumukha to bring him before theking, and the other crows descended to pick up the food.

Sumukha the crow general was brought before the king of Bārāṇasi who spoke to him thus, "Crow, have you no shame? You have broken the nose of my serving man and spilt my food. Have you no regard for your own life, why do you do such things?" The crow answered, "Great King, our king lives near here. His queen developed a craving for human food and when I learned of this, I sacrificed my life to satisfy it. That is why I have done these deeds."

The king was pleased with the crow's character. "Although we give our human subjects great honours, we cannot win this kind of friendship. Even though we might give them a whole village, still they will not sacrifice their lives for us, as this crow does for his king." The king afterward showed great honour to the crows, sending them food of both kinds (i.e. rice and meat) and Supatta the king of crows taught Dhamma to the human king of Bārāṇasi and established him in the five precepts. It is said that the teachings of Supatta the crow lasted for seven hundred years. (Jāt 292)

A crow story of particular interest is the Bāveru Jātaka in which Nigaṇṭha Nāṭaputta appears as the crow. Nigaṇṭha Nāṭaputta was a rival teacher and an older contemporary of the Buddha's. He has been identified with the founder of the Jains, now more commonly known as Māhāvīra. There are several references to him in the suttas, generally unflattering.[342]

At one time the Bodhisatta came to birth as a peacock and Nigaṇṭha Nāṭaputta as a crow. Some merchants took the crow along as a land-finding crow and sailed across the sea to the land of Bāveru. Until that time,

341 *Deva*—a mode of address to kings.
342 See DPPN for "Nigaṇṭha Nāṭaputta".

the inhabitants of Bāveru had not seen a bird of any kind. On seeing the crow, they exclaimed, "Look at the beautiful colour of this bird, at the perfection of its throat its beak and its eyes like jewels!" They asked the merchants to give them the crow and the latter pretended to be reluctant to part with it, bargaining the price up to one hundred *kahāpaṇas* (a unit of money). "It is very useful to us, but as we wish to be your friends, we will sell it to you." The Bāveru people put the crow in a golden cage and fed it with various kinds of meat and fruits, taking very good care of it. So in a land where there were no other birds, a crow endowed with the ten bad qualities (*asaddhammā*) obtained the highest gain and glory.

After some time the merchants returned to Bāveru. They brought along a peacock they had caught and had trained to sing at the snap of a finger and to dance at a clap of the hands. The Bāveru people were amazed, "This king of birds is of great beauty and very learned. You must give him to us!" This time the price was settled at one thousand *kahāpanas*. They kept the peacock in a cage made of the seven precious things and fed him with meat and fruit as well as syrup made from honey and other sweet things. While the highest gains came to the peacock, the honour paid to the crow diminished, and no one wanted to look at it. When the crow could not get any more food at all, it uttered a cry, "*Kāka*", and flew away to live on a dung-heap. (Jāt 339)

Bāveru is identified by the DPPN with Babylon, which would have been sufficiently remote from the Ganges Valley so as to seem exotic enough not to have any birds. The ten *asaddhammā* with which the crow was said to be endowed are not specified. There is a list of seven *asaddhammā* at Dīgha Nikāya 33: these are moral qualities beginning with lack of shame but it seems that in the present context they are probably physical qualities like an unpleasant colour, unpleasant voice etc. In caste conscious India a dark complexion was always considered undesirable. For example, in Jātaka 451 a crow seeks to obtain the golden colour of a goose and asks the latter about his diet only to be told that the crow's ugliness is not the result of his food but of his kamma.

The **Lion**, (*sīha*), is considered the king of the beasts.[343] Lions feature in twenty Jātaka stories. The Bodhisatta was born as a lion ten times, Sāriputta three times, Rāhula (Siddhattha's son) twice, Rāhulamātā (Siddhattha's wife) once as was Devadatta. Generally the lion displays a nobility of nature, and this is several times contrasted to the baseness of jackals.[344] The lion's roar is singled out as a special attribute, which fills all other animals with fear.[345]

The lion's noble nature can sometimes seem like caste prejudice with its attendant emphasis on personal purity:

At one time the Bodhisatta came to birth as a lion. One day, after killing some animal and eating his fill, the lion went down to the lake to take a drink. Just then a fat boar also came down for a drink.The lion saw him and thought, "Some other day I shall eat this one. But now, if he sees me here he won't come back again." So he crept away to the side away from the lake. The boar, seeing this, thought, "It is because he is afraid of me that this lion sneaks away. It is fitting that I challenge him!" Raising his head, the boar challenged the lion to battle:

"I am a four-footed one, so are you! Come, my dear,[346] turn around, don't run away from fright!"

The lion replied, "Dear boar, today there shall be no battle between you and I. But come here in seven days and then we shall fight." The boar went to his kin-folk, and bristling up boasted, "I shall do battle with a lion!"

343 Jāt 32 where the lion is elected *catuppadā rāja*, "king of the four-footed". Elsewhere the lion is called *migarāja*, "king of beasts", see for ex. AN 4:33.

344 Jāt 143, 152, 172, 188, 335, and 397 are all variations of this motif.

345 See Jāt 152 where the sound of the lion's roaring frightens a jackal to death. See also SN 22:78 "The lion is the king of beasts, his roar terrifies all animals".

346 *Samma* no doubt meant as an ironic insult.

But his relatives were terrified, "Now you shall bring us all to destruction! Not knowing your own strength, you would fight a lion! When the lion comes, he will kill us all! You should not act so savagely!"

The boar asked them what he should do. They advised him to roll in a pile of dung each day for seven days and on the day of the battle to stand upwind of the lion. The lion being an animal of a cleanly nature, will smell his body and not wanting to go near him, concede him the victory. This the boar did, and when the lion smelled the boar covered in filth he said, "My dear boar, this is a pretty trick you have thought of. If you were not covered with filth, I would take your life. Now I don't want to bite your body, or even touch it with my foot. I give you the victory."

The boar returned to his kin and boasted "I have beaten the lion! Victory is mine!" But the boars were afraid that the lion would return and kill them all so they left that place never to return. (Jāt 153)

At other times the lion can demonstrate a constructive leadership role among the animals:

Once upon a time a hare was resting underneath a palm-tree and the thought occurred to him, "If the earth were to break up, where could I go?" Just then, a ripe fruit fell out of the tree onto a dry palm leaf, makinga loud noise. The hare thought, "The earth is breaking up!" and without looking back he sprang up and began running in fear for his life. Another hare saw him running along and asked what was the matter. Without looking back he answered, "The earth is breaking up!" So the other hare began running along behind him. One after another more hares joined the flight until a thousand hares were running along together.

A deer saw them running and joined in, then a boar, an elk, a buffalo, a rhinoceros, a tiger, a lion and an elephant all joined in the stampede. Each one asked "what is happening?" and on being told that the earth was breaking up, became afraid and began to run along. So by degrees the host of animals came to cover an entire *yojana*.

At that time the Bodhisatta had come to birth as a lion. When he saw the great host of animals running by he too asked what was happening and was told that the earth was breaking up. But the Bodhisatta thought, "The earth is in no way breaking up. It must have been some loud sound that one of them heard. If I don't make an effort, they will all come to destruction. I must save their lives!"

With the speed of a lion[347] he ran ahead of the animals to the foot of a mountain and standing there gave three loud roars. In fear of the lion, all the animals stopped and stood huddled together. The lion questioned them:

"Why are you running?"

"The earth is breaking up."

"Who saw it?"

"The elephants know all about it!"

But when he asked the elephants, they said they knew nothing about it, but that the lions knew. The lions said the tigers knew, the tigers said the rhinos knew, they said the oxen knew, the oxen said the buffaloes knew,

[347] According to the *Three Worlds According to King Ruang*, tr. Reynolds, p. 87, the lion is so swift that he can utter a roar.then leap a distance of three yojanas to stand and listen to his own roar as it follows after!

they said to ask the elk, the elk said to ask the boars, the boars said it was the deer who knew. The deer said, "We don't know, it is the hares who know all about it." When the Bodhisatta asked the hares, they said, "This one told us."

So the Bodhisatta turned to the hare and asked,

"Did you see the earth breaking up?"

"Yes, sir, I saw it."

"Where were you staying when you saw it?"

"Underneath a palm tree near the ocean. I was just thinking about the earth breaking up when I heard a terrible noise and started to run away."

The Bodhisatta thought that no doubt a ripe fruit had fallen onto a dried palm leaf, and that he ought to go there and find out all about it. So he turned to the host of animals and told them, "I am going with this hare to the place where he says the earth is breaking up. I shall find out all about it and return here. All of you just remain in this place until I return." So taking the hare on his back the lion ran to the shore of the ocean and seeing the ripe fruit lying on a palm leaf he knew that in fact the earth was not breaking up.

The lion returned to the herd of animals and told them all about it. "So do not be afraid." The animals were calmed and they dispersed from that place. If the Bodhisatta had not taken action, the whole host of them would have run all the way into the ocean and perished. (Jāt 322)

The introduction to this Jātaka says that the story is told to explain the origin of a proverbial saying. When something which at first seems important turns out to be meaningless, it is said to be "like the noise the hare heard."[348]

Elephants (*hatthī*) feature in eighteen Jātaka stories. The Bodhisatta came to birth as an elephant in seven of them; other persons from the Buddha's lifetime who had previously been elephants in Jātaka stories include Devadatta, Mahāmāyā (the Bodhisatta's mother), Moggallāna and Nanda. Elephants display a complex range of character traits in the Jātakas. Sometimes they are violent and unpredictable: "elephants kill even those who foster them," (Jāt 161) but more often they are brave and noble.

Long ago, an elephant walking through the forest pierced his foot with a thorn from an acacia branch. The wound swelled up with pus and became very painful. In his suffering he heard the sounds of wood being pounded and he thought, "There must be some carpenters working there. Perhaps they will help me."

The elephant entered a clearing and there found a camp of carpenters from the town cutting wood. He lay down and showed them his swollen foot. The men cut around the thorn with an awl and drew it out with a cord. They washed the wound with hot water and applied medicine to it, and soon it was healed completely.

The elephant thought, "These carpenters have saved my life. It is proper that I do them service." So from that day hence he lived with the carpenters and carried wood for them, fetched their tools and helped by holding one end of the measuring string. At meal-time each carpenter gave him one portion of food, so the elephant had five hundred portions in all.

[348] Jāt 322 story of the present.

Now, this elephant had a son, a fine young elephant white all over. When he grew old he went into the forest and fetched this young one and brought him to the carpenters. "Now I am old, so in payment for your nursing me to health, I give you this young one to serve you in my stead." And he went away back to his forest haunts.

The young elephant served the carpenters faithfully and did his work well. After work, he liked to bathe in the river. The carpenters' children would play with him, in the water and on the land. Now, well born (ājānīya) animals like elephants and horse never make dung in the water, but only on the land. But one day after a heavy rain, some of the young elephant's dung washed into the river and was carried down-stream. It went all the way to Bārāṇasī where it got stuck in a bush by the river-bank.

When the king's elephant trainer brought the royal elephants down to the river to bathe, they caught the scent of the dung of a well-born elephant and refused to enter the water. With their tails up in the air, they all ran away from there. The elephant trainer found the dung and told the king he would do well to secure such a noble animal for his own service.

So the king and his company set out by boat up the river until they reached the carpenter's camp. The carpenters for their part did honour to the king and were willing to surrender the elephant to him, but the elephant refused to go. "What is the matter, good elephant?" "You should pay the carpenters a fee to cover the expense of feeding me." So the king ordered that one hundred thousand *kahāpaṇa* (a unit of money) be placed by the elephant's trunk, and another by his tail and each of his four feet. But still the elephant would not go until each of the carpenters, together with their wives and children, were given cloth for new garments as well. Then, with a last look at the carpenters, the elephant went away with the royal company.

When the king reached Bārāṇasī he had the whole city richly decorated and led the elephant in a circumambulation around the city and thence into the elephant's stable. This too was richly adorned and equipped and the elephant was sprinkled all over. The king always treated the elephant like his own dear friend and he gave over half the kingdom to him. From the time of the coming of the elephant, the king came to rule over the whole of Jambudīpa.

It came to pass that the queen conceived, and while the baby was still in her womb, the old king died. No one told the elephant that the king had died, for fear of breaking his heart. But the king of Kosala, hearing of the death of the king of Bārāṇasī, decided to attack the city and seize it. He laid siege to it, but the city did not yield hoping for the birth of a royal prince.

When the queen gave birth to a boy, she brought it to be shown to the elephant. She entered the elephant stable surrounded by her royal councillors and laid the baby, wrapped in richly decorated cloth, before the feet of the elephant. "Lord (*sāmi*), your friend is dead, we did not tell you for fear of breaking your heart. This is your friend's son. The king of Kosala is making war upon him and he is being defeated. You must either kill the boy yourself, or win him back his kingdom!"

The elephant caressed the child with his trunk, then lifted him up to his head before handing him back to the queen, saying "I shall defeat the Kosalan king!" The royal councillors dressed the elephant and fitted him out with richly adorned armour. They opened the city-gates and he issued forth trumpeting. The enemy army scattered and ran away in great fear as the elephant smashed up their fortifications. He took the king of Kosala by the top-knot, carried him into the city and flung him down at the feet of the young prince. Some of the men of Bārāṇasī took up weapons to kill the Kosalan king, but the elephant stopped them. He admonished the Kosalan, "Do not be heedless because our king is young." and let him go. After that, all of Jambudīpa fell into the hands of the young king of Bārāṇasī and no enemy ever dared oppose him. (Jāt 156)

Some elephants have magical powers. We are told that elephant kind is divided into ten tribes. The *kāḷāvaka* ("black") or common elephant has the strength of ten men. Each of the nine successively higher tribes has the strength of ten elephants of the previous tribe. The names of these elephant tribes, in order, are: *gaṅgeyya* ("of the Ganges"), *paṇḍara* ("white"), *tamba* ("copper"), *piṅgala* ("tawny"), *gandhahatthi* ("fragrant elephant"), *maṅgala* ("auspicious"), *hemavata* ("Himalayan"), *uposatha* ("holy day"), *chaddanta* ("six-tusked"). This means that a *chaddanta* elephant has the strength of ten billion men.[349] The higher elephant tribes are sometimes attributed with the power of flight (Jāt 122).

In the Chaddanta Jātaka the Bodhisatta is reborn as a *chaddanta* or "six toothed" elephant and it includes this detailed description:

> In bygone times 80,000 mighty elephants (*hatthināgā*) travelled through the sky by their magical power (*iddhimanta*) and settled in the Himavā beside Lake Chaddanta. At that time, the Bodhisatta came to be born as the son of the elephant chief. He was white all over except for his face and his feet, which were red. When he came of age, he was 88 *hattha* high and one 120 *hattha* long.[350] His trunk was like a silver rope and was 58 *hattha* long; his tusks were 15 *hattha* around and 30 *hattha* long and they shone with rays of six colours. (Jāt 514)

The **Goose** (*haṃsa*) features in eleven Jātakas. The Bodhisatta, Ānanda, Moggallāna and Sāriputta were all recorded as having been born as geese. The bird called *haṃsa* in Pali is variously translated as goose, swan and duck but is most likely meant to be the bar-headed goose, *anser indicus*. This is a bird that has always been considered sacred in India because of its unusual beauty and because of its remarkably high altitude flights. The bar-headed goose migrants between Central and South Asia, flying over the high passes of the Himalayas.[351]

Just as the lion is reckoned as king of the beasts, the goose is the king of birds. His election to this position was however a contested one:

> At the beginning of the kappa (world-cycle), human beings assembled and chose among themselves one who was best-looking, endowed with good conduct and other suitable qualities and made him their king (*rāja*). The four-footed animals assembled and made a certain lion their king and in the great ocean the fish made the fish Ānanda their king. The birds assembled together on a flat rock in the Himavā and said among themselves, "The humans have elected a king, so have the four-footed animals and the fish. But we have no king, and it is not fitting that we continue in this lawless manner (*appatissavāso*). It is fitting that we choose a king, let us find someone with the suitable qualities and raise him to the state of kingship."
>
> They looked around and chose an owl. "This is the one we like." A proclamation was made three times and all the birds consented twice, but on the third proclamation a crow spoke up. "If this bird makes such a face while he is being consecrated as king, what would he look like if he were angry? If he made a face at us while he were angry, we would be broken and scattered like salt thrown into a hot pan. I do not like it, I do not want this bird made king."
>
> The crow flew up into the air crying, "I do not like it! I do not like it!", the owl chasing after him. The

[349] SN-a 12:22. The text goes on to say that the Buddha has the physical strength of ten chaddanta elephants!

[350] A *hattha* is a unit of measure similar to the old english "cubit" measuring about one-half a meter. This would make the elephant about 44 m high and 60 m long.

[351] http://news.nationalgeographic.com/news/2011/06/110610-highest-flying-birds-geese-himalaya-mountains-animals/

remaining birds chose a golden goose (*suvaṇṇahaṃsa*) for their king and went their separate ways.

(This story was told to explain the eternal animosity between owls and crows). (Jāt 270)

In a sequel, the newly elected king of the birds chooses a mate for his beloved daughter:

At the beginning of the kappa, men chose a king amongst themselves and the four-footed animals made a lion their king, the fish made Ānanda theirs and the birds elected a goose to be their king. Now, the goose king had a beautiful daughter and he gave her a boon, that she might choose a husband of her own liking.

So the king of the birds bade all the kinds of birds to assemble and they all came, geese and peacocks and many other kinds, and assembled on a big flat stone. The king called forth his daughter and said, "My dear, choose now a husband to your own liking." The young goose looked over the various birds and saw the peacock with his jewel-like neck and his decorated feathers. "This one shall be my husband."

The birds told the peacock that he was the choice of the king's daughter and he was overcome with joy. He cried out, "Before today, you have not seen my power!" and he spread out his wings and throwing aside all shame began to dance, exposing his body.

The goose-king saw this and said, "I will not give my daughter to one who is so shameless. He has neither self-respect nor does he care what others think." Instead, the king chose one of his own nephews to be his daughter's husband. The peacock was disgraced and flew away from there. (Jāt 32)

Geese are particularly admired for their power of very high and swift flight. Sometimes this is taken to a supernormal level:

Once, when Brahmadatta was king of Bārāṇasi the Bodhisatta came to birth as a very swift goose (*javanahaṃsa*) living on Cittakūṭa Mountain with a following of ninety thousand geese. He was a good friend of the human king.

It came to pass that two of the youngest geese in the flock decided to run a race with the sun. Despite being forbidden by the Bodhisatta, they left one morning before the sun had arisen and flew up to Mt Yugandhara and sat there waiting.[352] When he learnt where they had gone, the Bodhisatta said, "They cannot race with the sun, they will perish midway. I must save their lives."

So he too flew up to Mt Yugandhara. Just then the sun rose and the young geese flew after it, with the Bodhisatta following behind. It was still morning when the younger of the geese grew tired, he felt like the joints of his wings were on fire. "Brother, I cannot do it!" he cried out. The Bodhisatta replied, "Fear not, I will save you." He caught the young goose in his out-stretched wings, comforted him and took him back to Mt Cittakūṭa. After placing him among the other geese, the Bodhisatta flew off again to catch up with the sun. Close to noon, the elder of the young geese also grew exhausted and the Bodhisatta saved him too.

Just then the sun was at its zenith and the Bodhisatta said, "Today I will test the sun's power." With one swift motion he soared to the top of Mt Yugandhara again and then with another he caught up with the sun. Having reached the sun he flew sometimes in front of it, and sometimes behind it. Then the Bodhisatta considered, "There is no purpose (*attha*) in my racing with the sun; it is a pursuit born out of unwise reflection (*ayonisomanasikāra*). What does this matter to me? I should go to Bārāṇasi and teach the Dhamma to my

[352] Mt Yugandhara is first and highest of the ring mountains which encircle Mt Sineru. It is 42,000 yojanas high and at the level of the sun's passage through the sky.

friend the human king."

The Bodhisatta went to Bārāṇasi. There, the king gave him a golden stool to perch upon, anointed his wings with oil refined a hundred thousand times and gave him sweet corn to eat off a golden platter, and sweet water to drink from a crystal goblet. The goose told the human king about his race with the sun, and the king asked if he could show him. "Great king, it is not possible to see such swiftness, but I can show you something like it."

So the Bodhisatta arranged that four of the king's best archers would stand with their backs to a pillar in the courtyard facing the four directions. He himself perched atop the pillar with a bell fixed around his neck. "When I display my swiftness, you will not be able to see me but you will hear the bell." At the same instant the four archers fired each an arrow into the four directions. The goose caught all four arrows in flight and laid them on the ground by the feet of the archers.

"This, great king, is not by swiftest speed, nor even my middling speed but only an inferior and lesser speed."

"My dear, is there then anything at all faster than you?"

"Yes indeed. Faster than my swiftest speed, a hundred time faster, a thousand times, a hundred thousand times is the wasting away, the destruction and the breaking up of the life-principle (āyusaṅkhāra) of beings." Then he discoursed on the moment by moment cessation (*khaṇikanirodha*) of the physical and mental factors. On hearing this teaching, the king was overcome by the fear of death and fell to the earth unconscious. The crowd of onlookers were also filled with terror. They sprinkled water on the king's face and he regained consciousness. The Bodhisatta said to him, "Great King, fear not but always practice recollection of death, walk in the Dhamma, give gifts and make merit. Be vigilant, King!"[353]

We cannot leave the topic of animal stories in the Jātakas without looking at the Sabbadāṭha Jātaka in which a jackal leads an army of animals in a bid for world domination:

At one time, Brahmadatta was king in Bārāṇasī and the Bodhisatta was his *purohita* (chief brahmin adviser to the king). He had studied the Three Vedas and the Eighteen Sciences and was versed in a spell (*manta*) called the "earth conquering spell" (*pathavījayamantaṃ).* He was sitting on a rock one day practising this spell when he was overheard by a jackal lurking in his den. (The jackal was Devadatta). Now, this jackal had been a brahmin in his last life and had learnt that spell then, so he was able to master it even in his jackal existence. Having finished his repetition the brahmin said, "Surely I have mastered the spell now." The jackal left his hole and said, "Ho, brahmin, I have learnt the spell better than you!" and ran off as quick as he could go. The brahmin gave chase crying out: "Stop that jackal! He will do great harm!" But the jackal escaped.

He came across a female jackal and gave her body a little nip. "What is this, sir?" "Do you know me or not?" "Yes, I know you." And she accepted him. He used the earth conquering spell and brought several hundred jackals under his command, as well as elephants, horses, lions, tigers, boars and many other animals. He made himself their king, taking the name Sabbadaṭṭha ("All-Fang") and the she-jackal became his queen consort. He had two elephants stand side by side with a lion on top straddling both and he himself together

[353] Jāt 476. There is a mistranslation in the PTS edition by W.H.D. Rouse. He says this goose was conceived "without natural cause" which is a misunderstanding of the abhidhamma term *ahetuka* explained above. In this context it merely means he was born as an animal. Cowell, 1995, Vol. 4, p. 132.

with his queen sat on the lion's back. Great was his glory and becoming intoxicated by it he determined to take the city of Bārāṇasī. With his whole army of the four-footed he approached the city, and his host spread over twelve *yojana*.

The Bodhisatta spoke to the king, "Do not fear, my lord, this jackal is my responsibility and I know how to deal with him." Standing above the gate of the city he called out to the jackal, "Jackal, how do you think you can take this city?" "I shall make the lions roar and while the people are trembling with fear, we shall kill them all and take the city." "These noble lions, red in paw and with their royal manes, will never obey an old jackal like you." With stubborn pride the jackal replied, "I shall make this lion I am sitting on roar," and he gave it a sign by kicking it with his foot.

With his mouth near to the elephant's head, the lion roared ferociously three times. The elephants trembled in fright causing Sabbadaṭṭha to fall to the ground where the elephants trampled his head, crushing it to bits and killing him. The rest of the elephants also panicked and began attacking one another, and all the other animals as well, even down to the hares and cats. Only the lions managed to escape to the forest, the rest were all reduced to a heap of carcasses covering twelve *yojana* in front of the city.

The Bodhisatta had an announcement made throughout the city, to the beat of drums. "Whoever wishes to have fresh meat, take whatever you like." The people took as much meat as they could eat and they dried the rest to keep it. It was at this time that people first learnt the art of drying meat. (Jāt 241)

3:2:3 MAKARA - MONSTER FISH

The largest of all animal kind are the *makara* "sea monsters" or *mahāmaccha* "great fish." These are enormous fish that live in the ocean reaching lengths of many hundred *yojana*. The sources are somewhat inconsistent in describing them. The Mahāsutasoma Jātaka (Jāt 537) describes them as living on sea-weed (*sevāla*) but in most other places they are depicted as being ferociously carnivorous, even taking delight in the devouring of ocean-going ships (APa 1:49).

There are various lists of these great fish. These lists are not consistent with each other and it is not entirely clear whether these are meant to represent species or individuals:

A list of three: *timi, timiṅgala, timitimiṅgala*. The *timiṅgala* can devour the *timi* (as the name implies, *galo* means "devouring") and the *timitimiṅgala* can devour the other two (UDa 5:5).

A list of six—ānanda, timinanda, ajjhāroha—these three are all 500 *yojana* long: *timiṅgala, timirapiṅgala, mahātimirapiṅgala*—these three are all 1000 *yojana* long (Jāt 537).

A list of seven—*timi*—200 *yojana* long, *timiṅgala*- 300 *yojana* long, *timirapiṅgala*- 500 *yojana* long, ānanda, timinanda, ajjhāroha, mahātimi—these four are all 1000 *yojana* long (DN-a 15).

A list of eight—The same as above but adding the *timipiṅgala* which is 400 *yojana* long (SN-a 12:60).

One passage illustrates the fantastic size of these *makaras*:

> In the great ocean there is a fish called *Timi* that is 200 *yojana* long ... (the rest of the list of seven is given as above). Let us illustrate the size of the *Timirapiṅgala* (which is 500 *yojana* long). When it flaps its right fin, the water of the sea is agitated for 500 *yojana* around. Likewise, for its left fin, its tail and its head. But when it sports in the water, flapping both its fins and shaking its head and tail from side to side, then the water is stirred up for 700 or 800 *yojana* around that place like water boiling in a pot. Even water 300 *yojana* deep cannot cover its back. Thus it thinks, "They say the ocean is deep, but how can it be called deep when it cannot even cover my back?" (SN-a 12:60 & DN-a 15)

This description is given by the commentary as a simile to explain an exchange between the Buddha and his disciple Ānanda; when Ānanda says he understands dependent origination the Buddha says, "Say not so! This dependent origination is deep." The intention of the commentator is to say that it is not deep for the wise Ānanda, but is so for other beings.[354]

It was mentioned above that one of these *makara* was elected by the fish as their king. His reign did not end well:

> In bygone times there were six great fish in the ocean. Of these, Ānanda,[355] Timinanda, Ajjhāroha were all five hundred *yojana* long and Timiṅgala, Timirapiṅgala, Mahātimirapiṅgala were all one thousand *yojana* long. They all ate sea-weed (*pāsāṇasevāla*). Of these, Ānanda lived alone in one part of the ocean and many fish came to see him. One day the fish spoke among themselves, "The two-footed and the four-footed beings have all chosen kings for themselves, but we have no king. Let us make a king!" They were all of one mind and one wish and made Ānanda their king. From that day on, the fish would come morning and evening to pay their respects to him.

[354] This belies the plainer reading of the text which is that the Buddha is implying that Ānanda does not fully understand the depth of the teaching.

[355] Not to be confused with the Buddha's disciple of the same name.

One day Ānanda was feeding off sea-weed from the side of a mountain and without knowing it swallowed a fish. Having eaten this flesh, he felt his whole body thrilled. "What could this be, that is so sweet?" Spitting a piece from his mouth he saw that it was the flesh of a fish. "All this time I did not know these were good to eat!" Ānanda then thought about how to get more, "Every morning and evening the fish come to pay me their respects. If I make it obvious that I am eating them, not a single one will ever come again but they will all escape far away. I must wait until they are leaving and catch one or two of the stragglers from behind and then eat them."

And so he fed thereafter. The fish, seeing the decline in their numbers, wondered, "From where does this threat to our kinfolk arise?" One wise fish thought, "I do not like what this Ānanda is doing. I will investigate it." When the fish went the next time to pay their respects, the wise fish hid himself in Ānanda's ear. When Ānanda dismissed the fish, he ate the last one from the rear of the school. Having seen this for himself, the wise fish told the others and they became frightened and fled away.

Ānanda had by that time become so greedy for the flesh of fish that he took no other food. Soon he became weak with hunger. "Where could they have gone to?" While searching for the fish Ānanda came to a certain mountain. "The fish must be hiding near this mountain. I think they must have fled here and hidden themselves for fear of me. I shall encircle the mountain and search it out." So from his head to his tail he covered both sides of the mountain thinking, "If they live in here they will try and escape."

Coming around the mountain, Ānanda saw the end of his own tail and thought, "This fish has tried to cheat me by hiding here." Very angry, he bit off with a loud chomp a fifty *yojana* piece of his own tail, thinking it was the flesh of another fish. This was extremely painful. The smell of his blood went out into the water and brought a host of fish who began biting Ānanda from his tail to his head. Because of his great size, he was unable to turn around and he came to destruction there. The fish reduced his body to a mountainous heap of bones. (Jāt 537)

3:2:4 THE NĀGAS

The nāgas are powerful and magical serpents. They share many characteristics with their European and Chinese mythological cousins, the dragons. The nāgas are quick to anger, loyal allies, but dangerous enemies. Like dragons, they are often found guarding treasure-hoards, and among their weapons is often found a poisonous or fiery breath.

According to the *Pali-English Dictionary*, the word *nāga* is cognate with the old English word *snaca*, from which is derived the modern English *snake*. In the Pali, the word *nāga,* while not nearly as multivalent as *yakkha*,[356] does have some other uses that must be distinguished. It is very often used to refer to an elephant, especially a large impressive bull.[357] By extension, it is sometimes used as an honorific term for the Buddha or great arahants, especially Moggallāna and Sāriputta. It may also be used, mostly in verse passages, to refer to ordinary snakes, especially cobras. Finally there is a rather rare usage of *nāga* to refer to a species of tree, now known as ironwood.[358] Nevertheless, the problem of definition is much smaller than in the case of yakkhas; the class of beings known as nāgas is defined sharply enough to avoid confusion, the only doubtful cases being possible confusion with ordinary cobras.

The natural appearance of a nāga is that of a large, hooded serpent, resembling a giant cobra. However, they may also assume a human-like appearance at will. Many of the mythological beings in the Buddhist cosmology are capable of changing their form; we have several incidents in the sources of this power being used by yakkhas, devas and *supaṇṇas*. But the nāgas, it seems, are the greatest masters of shape-shifting, so that this power becomes almost a defining characteristic.

> A certain being, although he had made meritorious kamma sufficient for a heavenly rebirth, was also guilty of having incestuous relations, so when he passed away he was reborn as a water-dwelling frog-eating nāga. He was disgusted and troubled by his bodily form and conceived a wish to return to the human state. "I shall seek ordination among the sons of the Sakyan, (Buddhist monks) they are followers of true Dhamma and of good moral habit. Surely if I become one of them, I will quickly win a human birth."
>
> So, assuming the shape of a brahmin youth, the nāga approached the bhikkhus and was granted ordination. After some time, he was sharing a hut with a fellow bhikkhu and when the latter got up in the middle of the night to do some walking meditation outside, the nāga fell comfortably into a deep sleep and reverted to his natural snake-form. When the bhikkhu returned to the hut he saw snake's coils protruding from the window, and when he opened the door he saw the whole hut was filled from top to bottom with a giant snake. He cried out in alarm, and other bhikkhus came running to see what was the matter.
>
> Having ascertained that the first bhikkhu was in fact a nāga, they took the case to the Buddha. The Buddha said that nāgas were not able to develop the *dhammavinaya* ("doctrine-and-discipline") as bhikkhus. "You should instead keep the *uposatha* vows (eight precepts) on the nights of the new and full moon, and in that way you will quickly return to the human state." The nāga left with sadness and uttering cries of distress. (Vin. Mv 1:63)
>
> The Buddha then told the monks that a nāga will always revert to his natural form when falling asleep, or when

[356] See the chapter on yakkhas in § 3:4,2 for a discussion of the multiple uses of this word.

[357] Although *nāga* as elephant is usually quite distinct from *nāga* as serpent, there is the case of Sakka's magical elephant Erāvaṇa who is referred to among the nāgas in the Mahasamaya Sutta, DN 20.

[358] There is also an ethnic group of South India known as Nāgas, and while they have some mythological connection with the serpent-nāgas, this is not something we need concern ourselves with, as it does not come up in the Pali sources.

having sexual relations with another nāga.[359] He then decreed than no animal (*tiracchānagato*) should henceforth be ordained. And to this day, as part of the ordination ceremony every aspirant is asked "*Manusso 'sī?*" ("Are you human?") (Vin. Mv 1:63)

The shape-shifting ability of nāgas is not limited to the human form. In one story, a nāga changes into the form of a jewel ornament on an ascetic's robe, to escape from a hungry *supaṇṇa* (Jāt 154), and in another episode a nāga princess assumes the form of a frog as a disguise (Jāt 543). Perhaps most remarkable of all, a nāga once changed himself into a ship to rescue some shipwrecked sailors:

> During the time of Kassapa Buddha, a ship was wrecked at sea by a mighty storm. There were only two survivors, and clinging to a plank they came to be washed up on a small island. Now one of these men was a follower of the Buddha and a *sotāpanna* (stream-enterer). In his distress he took refuge in the Triple Gem (Buddha, Dhamma and Saṅgha). A king of the nāgas had been born on that island and he, sensing the man's goodness, came to their rescue. He transformed himself into a great ship with its masts of sapphire, its ropes of silver, the anchor and the oars of gold. A deva of the ocean (*samuddadevatā*) served as helmsman and stood on the deck crying out: "Anyone bound for Jambudīpa?" (Jāt 190)

Sometimes, however, a nāga may be afflicted with a great weariness (*kilamati*) on account of five things: his rebirth as a nāga, the shedding of his skin, sleepiness, mating with his own kind and fear of death. This weariness can prevent him from changing into a human form (Dhp-a 14:3).

Another magical aspect of the nāgas is the nature of their dwelling places. These are usually underwater: in lakes, ponds, rivers or the ocean. However, the water seems to serve more as a gateway to the nāga realm than as an actual abode. In the Bhūridatta Jātaka, the entrance to one nāga dwelling (*bhavana*) is said to be by way of a whirlpool in the Yamunā River, yet later in the same story some nāgas escape into that place by sinking through the earth (Jāt 543). When King Uggasena wished to visit the nāga world, the nāga king Campeyya by his magical power created (*attano ānubhāvena māpesi*) a golden road leading there, lined with golden towers adorned with lapis lazuli shields (Jāt 506). Furthermore, the descriptions of nāga realms, although usually entered via a river or a lake, do not sound at all submarine. There are verses spoken in praise of the beauty of the nāga world in a few Jātakas (e.g. Jāt 506 & 524) and they mention mango-groves, flocks of birds, even lakes and ponds.

On the other hand, there does seem to be something watery about nāgas. They are listed among the dwellers in the great ocean, (AN 8:19) and the commentary says that their palaces (*vimāna*) are on the crest of the ocean waves, (AN-a 8:19) which also high-lights the magical and illusory character of the whole nāga world. Their semi-aquatic nature is illustrated by the following episode from the Bhūridatta Jātaka:

> Prince Brahmadattakumāra had been exiled by his father, the king of Bārāṇasi, and was living in a hut near the place where the Yamunā empties into the great ocean.[360] It so happened that a nāga woman, whose husband had died, had taken to wandering in her melancholy on the shores of the sea near that place. She, missing the sensual pleasures of the married state, seduced the prince and made him her husband. After some time, they had two children, a boy and a girl.
>
> When some years had passed, messengers came from Bārāṇasi to inform the prince that his father was dead, and he had inherited the throne. He told his nāga wife: "Come with me, my dear, and you shall be chief queen among sixteen thousand women." She replied that that was impossible, "You are human, but I am nāga. We

[359] According to the commentary to this passage, he will also assume a snake's form at the time of rebirth, while shedding his skin and at the moment of death.

[360] In actual geography the Yamuna empties into the Ganges.

have a deadly poison, and are very quick to anger. If I become annoyed with one of your other wives over some trifling matter, I could scatter her to ash with just a single glance."

She could on no account be persuaded to come to Bārāṇasi, but she did relent in the matter of the children. She warned, however, that they were half-nāga and so had a delicate and watery nature (*udakabījakā sukhumālā*). "They would surely die from such a long journey exposed to the wind and the sun. You must make a large hollow vessel, like a boat, and fill it with water and they may travel along in that. Furthermore, you must have a pond dug near the palace in which the children can play. In that way they will be happy and healthy." (Jāt 543)

Despite this, the nāgas also have a connection to the fire element. One common motif that occurs in the stories is a battle of supernormal power between a bhikkhu and a nāga, usually occupying the "fire-hut" (*agyāgāra*) of the "matted-hair ascetics" (*jaṭila*). It may be that there was some connection with fire and serpent worshipping cults, and their conquest by Buddhism. The first mass-conversion to the new faith was the one thousand *jatiḷas* under the leadership of the three Kassapa brothers. To win over the *jatiḷas*, the Buddha performed a series of supernormal miracles beginning with the taming of a nāga living in their fire-room:

Having arrived at the hermitage of Kassapa of Uruvelā, the Buddha asked: "If it is not troublesome for you, may I spend the night in your fire-hut?" The ascetic answered that it was not troublesome for him, but that there was a fierce nāga living in that place, "he is fierce, powerful, poisonous, terrible" (*caṇḍettha iddhimā āsiviso ghoraviso*)! The Buddha assured Kassapa that he would not be harmed, and Kassapa entered that fire-room, where he sat cross-legged, with his body erect and mindfulness established.

The nāga, seeing the Buddha, was not happy, and emitted smoke. The Buddha emitted smoke in return. The Buddha thought to himself: "I shall conquer this nāga's heat with heat without destroying him." Growing angry, the nāga blazed forth fire. The Buddha, having entered into the fire-element (*tejodhātuṃ samāpajjitvā*), blazed forth fire. The *jaṭilas* surrounded the fire-hut and were dismayed to see it full of a mass of flames. "The Great *Samaṇa* is beautiful, but surely he will come to destruction!"

In the morning the Buddha put the nāga, now tamed, into his bowl and showed it to Kassapa: "Here, Kassapa, is your nāga. His fire is now exhausted." (Vin Mv 1: 12)

Very similar is the encounter of the bhikkhu Sāgato with a nāga in another *jaṭila* fire-hut (Vin Pac 51). In this case, the grateful villagers plied the monk with fermented liquor, and becoming intoxicated, he lay down in the Dhamma Hall with his feet pointing towards the Buddha. This was the occasion for the Buddha laying down the rule against strong drink.

Another incident which illustrates the theme of religious conversion is the encounter of Moggallāna with the nāga Ahicchatta:

Aggidatta was a brahmin who had gone forth as an ascetic and now led a large assembly. He taught that the mountains were their refuge, the forest was their refuge, and the trees were their refuge. Aggidatta instructed his followers that whenever a thought of sensual desire should arise, they should collect a jar full of sand and deposit it in a certain place. In time, this grew into a great mound, and a powerful *nāgarājā* ("nāga king") named Ahicchatta took up residence there. The ascetics worshipped him and paid him great honour.

> One day, Moggallāna came to the hermitage of Aggidatta and asked for a night's lodging. Aggidatta, fearful that Moggallāna would take away his followers, refused. The elder then said that he would spend the night on the sand-hill of the nāga. During the night, the ascetics saw flames blazing up in that place, and surely thought that the visiting bhikkhu was being destroyed by the nāga.
>
> In the morning Aggidatta said, "Well, let us see if that *samaṇa* is alive or dead!" But when they arrived at the sand-hill, Moggallāna was sitting peacefully on top with the nāga respectfully sheltering him from the sun with his spread-out hood. (Dhp-a 14: 6)

There is some intriguing symbolism here: an animist cult worshipping a serpent who lives on the heap of their collected defilements.

Somewhat different was the encounter of the novice Cūḷasumana and the nāga Pannago.[361]

> Cuḷasumana had been ordained as a novice while still a young boy. It is said that he attained to state of an arahant while getting his head shaved. One day, his teacher Anuruddha was suffering from a stomach ailment and when he told Cuḷasumana that it could be cured by a draught of the medicinal waters from Lake Anotatta, the novice offered to undertake the journey. Using his supernormal power, the boy flew the five hundred *yojana* to the lake through the air.
>
> At that time there lived a powerful *nāgarājā* ("nāga king") named Pannago in the lake. As Cūḷasumana was approaching, Pannago was sporting in the water, enjoying sensual delights with his retinue of dancing girls. Seeing the novice overhead, the nāgā grew angry: "Who is this shaveling ascetic who flies over my domain, scattering the dust of his feet on my head? No doubt he has come here for some water from Anotatta, but he shall not get it!" So saying, the nāga spread his hood over the fifty *yojana* of the lake, covering it up like a pot with a lid.
>
> The novice announced that he was here to get medicine-water for his teacher. The nāga refused to allow it: "To the east there is the River Ganges, go and get water from there. The water of Lake Anotatta you shall not get!"
>
> Cūḷasumana announced that he would show the power (ānubhāva) of the *Buddhasāsana* ("Buddhist religion"), win a victory, and take the water for his teacher. Hearing this, the devas of the sky came and paid homage to Cūḷasumana. The word of the coming battle spread through the cosmos, through four world-systems, and devas and brahmās from various realms came to witness and pay homage to Cūḷasumana. They were spread as thickly in the air around Lake Anotatta as grains of sand.
>
> Assuming the form of a brahmā god twelve *yojana* high, Cūḷasumana descended from the sky and trod with his foot on the hood of Pannago the nāga and the waters squirted forth from that place like a stream of urine (*muttamuttaṭṭhānato*). The assembly of devas saluted the victory, crying "Sadhu! Sadhu! Sadhu!" while Cūḷasumana collected a jar of water. The nāga was deeply humiliated in the presence of a multitude of devas. (Dhp-a 25: 12)

The most spectacular battle of all was the encounter of Moggallāna with the nāga Nandopananda. The Buddha, it seems, had surveyed the ten thousand fold world-system and the *nāgarājā* Nandopananda had come into the sphere of his vision as one who was in the grip of wrong view, but was ripe for conversion. He also saw that Moggallāna was the

[361] The name is spelled Pannaka in the DPPN.

only one among his disciples who could tame this powerful nāga. With this in mind, he proceeded with five hundred bhikkhus to visit Tāvatiṃsa *devaloka* on the peak of Mt Sineru, and as the company of the Buddha travelled through the air, they passed over the abode of Nandopananda:

> At that time, Nandopananda was reclining on his jeweled couch under a white parasol enjoying a banquet surrounded by three troops of dancing girls and his company of nāgas, surveying the array of fine food and drink that had been prepared. Then he saw the Buddha and his company of five hundred bhikkhus passing directly overhead on their way to Tāvatiṃsa.
>
> This evil thought arose in the mind of Nandopananda: "These little shaven headed ascetics are going in and out of Tāvatiṃsa directly over my dwelling. From now on they will no longer be scattering the dust of their feet on our heads!" He rose from his place and, having gone to the foot of Mt Sineru, Nandopananda changed his form (into that of a snake) and wrapped his coils around the mountain seven times. Rearing up, he spread his hood over Tāvatiṃsa so that it was entirely covered and hidden from sight.
>
> Then, in the Buddha's company, the elder Raṭṭhapala said, "Lord, from this place we could previously see Mt Sineru together with Tāvatiṃsa, and the Vejayanta Palace adorned with banners. What is the cause that we cannot see it now?" "Just now the *nāgarājā* Nandopananda has become angry and he has covered Tāvatiṃsa with his hood and plunged it into darkness." Rātthapala and all the bhikkhus in turn asked the Buddha for permission to tame the nāga, but he refused them all except for Moggallāna.
>
> Moggallāna assumed the form of a gigantic nāga and wrapped his coils fourteen times around Nandopananda, then rearing up his hood over the nāga king's hood, he crushed him down against Sineru. Nandopananda caused his body to emit smoke, but Moggallāna saying, "Not only you can make smoke, but I can too," also emitted smoke from his body. The nāga's smoke did not afflict the elder, but the elder's smoke afflicted the nāga. Nandopananda emitted fire, and so did Moggallāna. The nāga's fire did not afflict the elder, but the elder's fire afflicted the nāga.
>
> Nandopananda wondered who it was that crushed him against Sineru and afflicted him with fire and smoke: "Who are you?" "I am Moggallāna." "Then resume the form of a bhikkhu." Returning to his natural form, Moggallāna went into the nāga's right ear and came out of his left ear; he went into the nāga's left ear and came out of his right ear. He went in one nostril and came out the other. Then he went into Nandopananda's open mouth and walked to and fro inside his belly.
>
> The Buddha called out, "Moggallāna, beware, this is a nāga of great power!" Moggallāna replied, "Venerable sir, I have mastered the four bases of power (*iddhipādā*), developed them, made much of them, thoroughly practiced them. I could tame a hundred, a thousand, a hundred thousand nāgas like Nandopananda."
>
> Nandopananda thought, "I did not see him going in, but when he goes out I shall catch him with my fangs and chew him up." He said aloud, "Venerable sir, come out! Your walking to and fro inside my belly is annoying me!" The elder went and stood outside and seeing him there, Nandopananda issued a blast of wind from his nostrils. But Moggallāna quickly entered the fourth jhāna and the wind was unable to stir so much as a hair on his body. All the other bhikkhus, it seems, could have performed all the supernormal feats up to this, but no one else could have entered jhāna quick enough to save himself at the end. This is why the Buddha gave only Moggallāna permission to tame the nāga.

> Nandopananda thought, "My blast has been unable even to stir the hairs of his body. This is a powerful *samaṇa*!" Moggallāna now assumed the form of a *supaṇṇa* and demonstrating the *supaṇṇa*'s wind[362] he gave chase to the nāga. Nandopananda now assumed the form of a young man and falling to the elder's feet, asked him for refuge. Moggallāna said, "The teacher is here, take refuge from him." So he led the nāga, now tamed and bereft of his poison, to the Buddha. Nandopananda took refuge and the Buddha dismissed him saying, "Be happy, *nāgarāja*." (Vism 12:108f.)

Another significant repeating motif in the stories about nāgas is the contrast between sensuality and renunciation. The nāga realm is always portrayed in extravagant language as being a sensual paradise: the enticements are natural, artificial and erotic. The natural surroundings of a *nāgabhavana* (dwelling place of nāgas) are always described as idyllic: smooth, level ground, lush vegetation, fragrant with flowers especially lotuses, resounding with the cries of swans, (Jāt 543) mango groves that bear both fruit and blossom continually, (Jāt 524) and so forth. (Note once again, that this park-like environment is reached by going underwater). The palaces of the nāga kings dwell in are equally fantastic: they are commonly described as having a thousand pillars and the building material of choice islapis-lazuli (*veḷuriya*) although gold and silver are also commonly employed in the trim.[363]

Of course, no ancient Indian sensual paradise would be complete without hordes of lovely female attendants, and the dwellings of the nāga lords are no exception. The palace of the nāga king Bhūridatta is "full of splendid young maidens" (*pūrā kaññāhi jotare*) as is that of king Saṅkhapāla, whose women wear golden bracelets shaped like serpents and are described as "slim-waisted, lovelier than lotus blossoms" (*sabbattamajjhā padumuttarābhā*). These nāga females serve their lord and his guests with delicious and variegated food, by playing music for them and by more intimate attentions (*kāmakāra*, "making pleasure.") (Jāt 524) The nāga women have a magically seductive quality about them, a power that the *nāgarāja* Vimalā was shamelessly asked his daughter, Princess Irandhatī, to employ for his own ends, a request the text says was "improper" (*ananucchavikaṃ*):

> King Vimalā of the nāgas wished to recruit a champion in order to seize and kill the sage Vidhura, because his queen had declared a longing for the wise man's heart. He asked his daughter, the lovely princess Irandhatī to procure one for him. She, for her part, was not loathe to undertake the task, for she was by nature full of lustful desire (*kilesābhiratabhāva*). Irandhatī adorned herself with ornaments and a fine red gown, and went forth to a mountain peak in the Himavā. There she prepared a bed of fragrant flowers and performed a delightful dance, singing a song with her sweet voice:
>
> "What *gandhabba*, or *rakkhasa*, *kiṃpurisa* or man, what sage, will get to satisfy his every desire, acting as my husband the whole night long?" (Jāt 546, Eng. 545)

(This was how Puṇṇaka, the yakkha chief, whom we will meet later, got into so much trouble).

Another nāga maiden who acted immorally is mentioned in the Kharaputta Jātaka (Jāt 386). This was a female nāga who was married to a human king. At one time the king and his nāga wife were in the palace gardens, and while he was otherwise occupied she slipped away to the lotus pool. There she saw a male water snake, and reverting to her snake form had sex with it. This episode illustrates both the sensuality and the essentially animal nature of nāgas, despite their often appearing in human form.

Very often, these descriptions of lavish sensuality serve as a counterpoint for a great renunciation. In two Jātakas concerned with nāgas, no. 524 and no. 543, a *nāgarāja* determines to keep the fortnightly *uposatha* fast in order

---

362 *Supaṇṇas* are the enemies of nāgas and the wind made by their wings is one of their principal weapons.

363 Same two Jātakas.

to win a better rebirth. King Saṅkhapāla longed to be reborn human, and Bhūridatta aspired to rebirth as a deva of Tāvatiṃsa. It should be noted here, that although we meet many virtuous nāgas in the literature, they are never depicted as reaching or even aspiring to the state of *sotāpanna*. This is because, although a nāga birth may be a refined and pleasant one, it is still classed as within the animal realm, a "frog-eating existence" (*maṇḍūkabhakkha attabhāva*), as King Bhūridatta scornfully described it. Even the noblest of nāgas is not capable of transcending the sensual realm altogether. The motivation for Bhūridatta's asceticism was that while visiting Tāvatiṃsa with his father to attend a council, he developed a longing for the beautiful palaces of the gods, and for the heavenly nymphs (*devaccharā*), more beautiful even than the nāga maidens (Jāt 543).

Nevertheless, it were those nāga maidens that made it impossible for either king to keep his precepts while remaining at home, so in both stories, the king decides to practise the *uposatha* in the human realm, coiled up on an ant-hill in snake form. Both are there seized and abused by snake-charmers, but keep their vows by non-resistance.

> Unable to keep the purity of his *uposatha* precepts in the nāga palace, surrounded by lovely female attendants, Bhūridatta went up to the human world and coiled his snake-body up on top of an ant-hill near the banks of the Yamunā. "Whoever desires my hide, my flesh, my bones or my blood, let them take it!"
>
> In the course of time, an evil minded brahmin betrayed the *nāgarājā* to the snake-charmer Ālambāyana. When he saw that Ālambāyana was coming to seize him, Bhūridatta determined not to break his vows. "No matter if he cuts me up, cooks me or impales me on a stake, I shall not allow anger to arise." The snake-charmer smeared himself with magic ointment and uttered his protective mantras while the great nāga lay on his ant-hill unmoving. Then Ālambāyana seized Bhūridatta by the head and forcing open his mouth, spat into it a powerful drug which he had held in his own mouth for the purpose. Although he was outraged by this act of uncleanliness, Bhūridatta did not so much as open his eyes. The charmer then took the nāga by the tail and shook him violently, forcing him to vomit up his food. He then laid the serpent out on the ground and pummeled him with his hands as if kneading a pillow, crushing his bones in the process. Having subdued his victim, the charmer forced him into a basket; it was too small to hold his mighty coils, so Ālambāyana mercilessly drove them in with the heels of his feet. (ibid.)

A related theme is that of a human being, who visits the nāga world and at first enjoys sensual bliss; for instance, the nāga king Saṃkhapāla gave his guest, the nobleman Āḷara, the loan of three-hundreds of his wives (Jāt 524). But after a year of such pleasures, the human visitor grew disenchanted with sensuality and left to become an ascetic (Jāt 524 & 472). An interesting variation occurs in the Bhūridatta Jātaka. In contrast to the virtuous men in the other tales, this concerns an evil-minded brahmin.[364] He too stayed for only a year, but instead of transcending sensuality through wisdom, he had quite a different reaction:

> After staying a year in the nāga world, the brahmin, because of the paucity of his merit (*mandapuññatāya*) was no longer able to enjoy the sensual pleasures of that realm. The nāga world was like an empty hell-realm (*lokantaranirayo*) to him, the gaily decorated palace like a prison and the ornamented nāga maidens like female yakkhas. So he decided to feign a desire for renunciation in order to win King Bhūridatta's leave to return to the human realm (Jāt 543).

This demonstrates the magical and illusory quality of the nāga world and its wonders. Because the brahmin had made insufficient good kamma, he was unable to retain the perception of pleasure.

[364] The same individual who later betrays Bhūridatta to the snake-charmer for the price of a jewel. It should be noted that in general brahmins are not portrayed in a favourable light in the Jātakas.

Magical powers of transformation and illusion are among the defining features of nāga existence. These are well illustrated by the following description of the hapless Bhūridatta being forced to perform by the snake charmer:

> Setting his basket in the village square, the snake-charmer called out: "Anyone who wants to see a nāga dance, come!" When a crowd had assembled, he bade the *nāgarājā* to come forth. He ordered Bhūridatta to make himself become huge, to become small, to become round, to manifest a suit of armour, to show forth his hood, to make two hoods, three hoods, even up to one hundred hoods. He bade him appear great and noble or small and meek, to become invisible and to then become visible again. He ordered him to change colour from blue to yellow to crimson to white and to scarlet. He was made to breathe forth fire, water and smoke. Thus the nāga demonstrated his dancing powers (*attabhāve nimminitvā naccaṃ*). The people were amazed, and the snake-charmer made a thousand pieces of gold that day (ibid.).

We would be remiss to leave poor Bhūridatta in the hands of the cruel snake-charmer. The episode whereby he regains his liberty reveals some intriguing details of nāga-lore:

> When Bhūridatta did not return to the nāga world after his fast, his three brothers set out to look for him; one went to the deva world, one to the Himavā, and the eldest, Sudassana, went to the world of men. Sudassana assumed the guise of a matted-hair ascetic for the purpose. Out of her great love for Bhūridatta his half-sister Accimukhī wished to come along, and assumed the form of a little frog and hid herself in Sudassana's hair.
>
> They followed the trail of Bhūridatta and the charmer through many villages and towns, everywhere hearing tales of the wondrous snake who performed such amazing tricks. At last they came to Bārāṇasī, the royal capital, where a great crowd had assembled in the palace court-yard to see the great nāga perform for the pleasure of the king. When Bhūridatta emerged from his basket he surveyed the crowd. Now, nāgas will not dance if they see any *supaṇṇas*, because of fear, or any of their relatives (ñātake), because of shame.[365] Seeing Sudassana standing there, he went and laid his head on his brother's foot.
>
> The snake-charmer, misinterpreting the gesture, grew alarmed and thought that Bhūridatta had bitten the ascetic. Sudassana assured him that his snake was harmless, but claimed to have a frog with a powerful poison and challenged him to a wager as to which was mightier. The snake-charmer, under the eyes of the king and of the whole town, was unable to refuse the contest.
>
> At a word from Sudassana, Acimukkhī hopped from his hair into the palm of his hand and spat up three drops of poison before hopping back. Sudassana cried aloud with a mighty voice: "This land will be destroyed! This land will be destroyed! Alas, this land will be destroyed! There is no place I can drop this poison. Should I cast it on the earth, all the crops and plants would wither and die. Should I throw it into the air, no rain would fall for seven years. Were I to throw it into the water, the fish and turtles and all that live in the sea would utterly perish."
>
> Alarmed, the king asked how the poison could be neutralized and Sudassana gave directions that three pits were to be dug. The first was to be filled with various medicines, the second with cow-dung and the third with divine medicine (*dibbosadha*). When this was done, Sudassana threw the drops of poison into the first pit, which burst into flames which leapt to the second and then the third, consuming all their contents. The

[365] Cowell mistranslates ñātake as "actors" and this is followed in the DPPN. This makes no sense either according to the dictionary meaning, or the context.

> fumes from the last fire blew over the snake-charmer who was standing nearby and he was instantly afflicted with the white leprosy (*setakuṭṭhi*). In great fear, he cried aloud that the nāga was released from bondage. Hearing this, Bhūridatta emerged from the basket and assumed a form as glorious as a deva-king, adorned with wonderful ornaments (Jāt 543).

The Saṃyutta Nikāya has some information about the modes of birth of nāgas. Nāgas may take any of the four kinds of birth. Those born spontaneously are considered superior to the others, the moisture-born are considered next best, then the womb-born and the lowest class are the egg-born nāgas (SN 29:2). The order of these classes seems odd, since other moisture-born creatures are things like flies, born in filth. It may be because the egg-born nāgas are considered common snakes, or very much like them. We also learn that all nāgas give birth in mountain pools in the Himavā; there they teach their young to swim before letting them travel to the more dangerous ocean waters (SN 45:151). A being is born into a nāga existence because of making ambivalent kamma (*dvayakārī*) by body, speech or mind and by having a desire to be born there (SN 29:7 f.).

Two nāgas are especially associated with the incidents surrounding the Buddha's awakening. One of these is Mahākāḷa, who has a life-span equal to a full kappa.[366]

> Before his final supreme effort, the Bodhisatta partook of a meal of milk-rice offered by Sujātā in a golden cup. Having finished his meal, the Bodhisatta set the cup into the Nerañjarā River with the aspiration: "If I am to be victorious in my quest for Buddhahood, may this cup float upstream." It did so, riding swiftly against the current until it came to a whirlpool which led to the *nāgabhavana* of the great nāga lord Mahākāḷa. There it sank, coming to rest against the three golden cups left by the three previous Buddhas of this world-age.
>
> On hearing the metallic sound of the golden cups striking each other, the *nāgarāja* exclaimed in joy: "It seems just yesterday that a Buddha arose in the world, and already there is another!" (GGB v1, p. 303)

The other nāga important in the life of the Buddha is Mucalinda. After the Buddha's awakening, as he sat rapt in meditative bliss, a great rain-storm began and the nāga Mucalinda protected the Buddha by wrapping his coils around him and sheltering him with his out-spread hood (Ud. 2:1). This scene became a popular motif in Buddhist art.

When the Buddha cleansed the city of Vesālī of a plague by chanting the *Ratana Paritta*, he was given great honour by humans, devas and nāgas. For their part, the nāgas of the Ganges provided five hundred jewelled boats to carry the Buddha and his retinue back across the river. The Buddha created five hundred mind-made (*nimitta*) duplicates of himself so that each nāga's boat would be equally honoured. Before crossing the river to return to Magadha, the Buddha and his company of bhikkhus visited the nāga realm where they were offered a meal and the Buddha taught Dhamma to the assembly of nāgas.[367]

One very important and recurrent theme is the enmity of nāgas and *supaṇṇas*, but we will defer that for the discussion of *supaṇṇas* in the next section.

---

[366] The *Abhidharmakośa* makes brief mention of eight great nāgas who live for an antarakappa and sustain the Earth. There is nothing like this in the Pali sources. AK 3:5, p.472-3.

[367] Dhp-a 21:1. The Buddha also created many more nimitta Buddhas to visit the pavilions in the sky set up by the devas.

3:2:5 THE *SUPAṆṆAS*

A Note on Nomenclature: These beings, huge mythical birds, are perhaps better known to most readers as *garudas*. However, in the Pali sources they are almost always referred to as *supaṇṇas*, which etymologically means "well winged." *Garuda* is a Sanskrit word; the Pali version is *garuḷa*. This form does occur in the sources but infrequently and almost always in verse.[368] In these verse passages it is sometimes used poetically to refer to common birds.[369] In this book, we will follow the Pali sources and refer to them as *supaṇṇas*.

The *supaṇṇas* are very large indeed. A king of the *supaṇṇas* may have a wing-span of one hundred and fifty *yojana* (AN-a 3:81). We hear of one such *supaṇṇa* complaining that he cannot find enough empty space to spread his mighty wings: "They say that space is infinite. How can it be infinite when I cannot even get enough room to flap my wings and make a wind?" (DN-a 15) Together with their great size, the *supaṇṇas* are possessed of tremendous strength; they are able to uproot whole banyan trees (Jāt 412, 543). As well, they have the power to raise a great wind (*supaṇṇavāta*) with the flapping of their wings (Jāt 518). With this wind, they can cleave the ocean waters asunder and reveal the nāgas in their abode, (Jāt 412) or raise a storm which threatens to knock down houses and plunges an entire city into darkness (Jāt 360).

They also have other magical powers:

> A young *supaṇṇa* was in the habit of visiting the king of Bārāṇasī to play at dice. For this purpose, he would assume the form of a beautiful human youth. The queen's handmaidens were struck by the young man's good looks, and reported to the queen that a beautiful young man was playing dice with the king. Curious to see him, the queen adorned herself with all her finery and jewels and repaired to the gaming-room. When the *supaṇṇa* and the queen looked at each other, they were smitten with desire. Using his supernatural power (*attano ānubhāvena*), the *supaṇṇa* raised a storm and plunged the whole city into a profound darkness. He made off with the queen, unseen by anyone, and returned to his abode with her (Jāt 360).

The *supaṇṇas* make their dwellings mostly in groves of *simbali* trees (SN 48:70). These are identified by the PED as *Bombax ceiba*, known in English as Silk-cotton or Kapok trees. A large community of *supaṇṇas* is specifically mentioned as living in a *simbali* forest on the slopes of Mount Sineru (Jāt 31).

> At one time, when the devas were making war against the asuras, Sakka at the van of a mighty host drove his terrible chariot of victory, a hundred and fifty *yojana* in size, down the slopes of the mountain. When they came to the grove of *simbali* trees they cut through them like so many reeds and the trees tumbled into the ocean. At once there began a great wailing cry. Sakka asked his charioteer, Mātali, "What, friend, is that cry which wrings my heart with compassion?" (*atikāruññaravo*) "That, my lord, is the cry of the young of the *supaṇṇas*, stricken with the fear of death as their homes are thrown into the sea." On hearing this, Sakka ordered the host to turn around and withdraw, even if it meant forsaking victory that day (ibid.).

The principal food of *supaṇṇas* is nāgas, and it is in the context of the eternal enmity between these two mighty races that we most often encounter *supaṇṇas* in the literature.

> A *supaṇṇa*, seeking his food, beat his wings to create a wind which drove the ocean waters asunder and exposed the domain of the nāgas. The *supaṇṇa* seized a nāga-king by the head and flew away with him, back

[368] *Supaṇṇa* occurs 82 times in the Jātakas, *garuḷa* only 14. The latter form is almost unknown outside the Jātakas.

[369] See for example Jāt 210 where it refers to a small bird. The commentarial gloss explains that all birds may be called *garuḷa* as a form of respectful address.

to his home in the Himavā. On the way there, the nāga, in his struggle to get free, wrapped his tail around the branch of a great banyan tree. The *supaṇṇa*, not knowing the cause of the obstruction, made a mighty leap into the sky and the entire tree was torn away, roots and all.

Reaching his nest, the *supaṇṇa* tore open the nāga's belly with his beak, ate the fat, and let the rest of the body fall into the sea. It was only then that he noticed the banyan tree, still wrapped within the nāga's coils.

"That tree was of great comfort to a hermit who has his dwelling near it. I wonder if I have made bad kamma. I should go and ask him about it." So the *supaṇṇa* assumed the form of a young brahmin student and went to the hermit's abode. Feigning ignorance, he asked about the great hole in the earth, and was told it was made when a *supaṇṇa* tore up a banyan in his struggle with a great nāga. The hermit went on to explain that no bad kamma was made by the *supaṇṇa* or by the nāga in the act, because neither had intended to destroy the tree.

Delighted by this answer, the *supaṇṇa* revealed his identity and in his gratitude gave the hermit the gift of a powerful spell (*manta*), the *alampāyanamantaṃ* which was an offering beyond price (Jāt 543).

In the contest between the nāgas and *supaṇṇas*, the nāgas at one time had an advantage, which they later lost in a secret defense:

A nāga and a *supaṇṇa* were both separately the disciples of a naked ascetic. One day the *supaṇṇa* asked the hermit about the difficulties his people were having in catching their prey, with a great many *supaṇṇas* perishing in the attempt. "There must be some secret in this matter." The ascetic promised to find it out. When he next saw the nāga, he asked him about it, but the nāga kept his counsel and refused to reveal the secret defense. But at last, the wily ascetic managed to convince the nāga that he would keep his secret, and only wanted to satisfy his own curiosity.

Trusting in the hermit, the nāga explained, "We swallow heavy rocks, and when the *supaṇṇas* struggle to lift us out of the water, they are themselves dragged under and many of them perish this way. If the fools were to take us by the tail, instead of by the head, they could hold us upside down and force us to vomit up the stones. But they do not know this."

Alas! The hermit was not worthy of the trust the nāga bestowed upon him, and the secret was passed on to the *supaṇṇa*, and now the *supaṇṇas* always take their prey by the tail. (Jāt 518)

Occasionally, the *supaṇṇas* can rise above their hunger and make peace with the nāgas. This happened later in the above story: when the *supaṇṇa* had seized the nāga the latter begged for his life and called upon the *supaṇṇa*'s compassion. The latter relented, and let his fellow student go, but the secret of the nāgas' defence was lost forever.[370] Another such incident is related in the Vidhurapaṇḍita Jātaka, where Sakka, a human king, a nāga king and a *supaṇṇa* king were all the students of the sage Vidhura, and fast friends besides. When the four were contesting who had demonstrated the most virtue, the nāga claimed that even in the presence of the destroyer of his race, he felt no anger and the *supaṇṇa*'s boast was that even in the presence of his favourite food, he was able to overcome his hunger (Jāt 543).

Supaṇṇas are subject to all four modes of rebirth, as are the nāgas. Just as in the case of the nāgas, these form hierarchically arranged classes. Each kind of *supaṇṇa* will only catch and eat nāgas that are of the same, or a lower order.

[370] The incident with the banyan tree in Jātaka 543 is specifically mentioned in the text as having occurred before this secret was lost; hence the nāga was seized by the head, leaving his tail free to grapple with branches.

Thus, a spontaneously born *supaṇṇa* will eat any kind of nāga, but a moisture-born one will not eat a spontaneously born nāga; a womb-born *supaṇṇa* will eat only womb-born or egg-born nāgas and an egg-born one will eat only egg-born nāgas (SN 30:2).

While the *supaṇṇas* are not included among the retinues of one of the Four Great Kings, they are mentioned as forming one of the five lines of defence against the asuras (Jāt 31).

CHAPTER THREE—THE LOWER REALMS

3:3:1 PETAS—HUNGRY GHOSTS

The *petas* (Sanskrit: *preta*) are wretched beings tormented primarily by hunger and thirst. The word *peta* has been translated as "ghost", "hungry ghost," "the departed"[371] or "afflicted spirit".[372] A female peta is called a *petī*. The Sanskrit made a distinction between the *pitaraḥ*, honoured spirits of the ancestors, and the *preta*, tormented ghosts. These concepts are somewhat merged in the Pali *peta*.[373] The derivation of the word is according to the *Pali English Dictionary* to be *pa + ī,* lit. "gone before". It may also be related to the word for "father," *pitar*. Thus, *pettika* means "paternal" and *pitāmaha* means "ancestral" (lit. "grandfathers") (MN 82) One's ancestral domain is *pettika visaya*, which is often used figuratively to represent, for instance, the object of meditation as opposed to the world of the senses (SN 47:6). Compare this to *pettivisayaṃ* which means the state of existence of a peta.[374] The word *peta* may also simply indicate the dead, or even a physical corpse. Thus, the *Dīgha Commentary* states that "the dead (lit. 'those whose time is done') are called peta" (*petā nāma kālaṅkatā*), (DN-a 32) and a verse from the *Suttanipāta* refers to a body on the funeral pyre as "the peta, the departed one" (*petaṃ kālaṅkataṃ)* (Sn 3:8).

Taking all this into consideration, the translation of *peta* by "ghost" is not too far off the mark. Although the state of being a peta is considered a distinct realm of rebirth, one of the five *gati*, (DN 33) petas are associated with the ancestors, and with the dead. As we shall see, the descriptions of individual petas often portray their forms and their sufferings as closely related to the deeds of their previous existence as human beings. They are wretched, helpless shades of the flesh-and-blood beings that once walked upon the earth.

DESCRIPTION

Individual petas vary greatly in form, but some characteristics may be regarded as "normal" for this class of being, as they recur again and again in the descriptions. The typical peta is naked, ugly and stinking (Pv-a 1:6). He is emaciated by his long hunger, lean, with prominent ribs and veins (Pv-a 2:1). They are "hungry and thirsty, living off the gifts of others, very miserable, deprived of happiness" (Ud-a 2:8).

> Some are clothed in rags, others covered only by their hair
>
> The petas wander in search of food, going this way and that.
>
> Having roamed far, and finding nothing,
>
> Overcome by hunger, they stagger and fall swooning to the earth. (Pv 3:1)

The petas in one passage are said to be between sixty and eighty *hattha* in size.[375] This would make them gigantic in human terms, twenty-seven to thirty-six metres tall. This is hard to reconcile with most of the stories which make no reference to their size in their various encounters with human beings. The petas always sleep on their backs, because they have too little flesh and blood to support any other posture (DN-a 16). They are often called "miserable

---

371 H.S. Gehman.

372 Bhikkhu Bodhi.

373 PED entry "peta", see also Bhikkhu Bodhi trans of AN, NDB, note 2169

374 See SN 25:1 for one among very many instances.

375 DN-a 15. A *hattha* is the distance between the elbow and the end of the fingers, about sixteen inches.

denizens of Yama's world."[376] They are normally invisible and were seen, for instance, by Moggallāna only because he possessed the *dibbacakkhu* ("divine eye") psychic power (SN-a 19:1). However, they are on rare occasions seen by ordinary persons:

> The wealthy lay follower Soṇa Koṭikaṇṇa was travelling with a merchant caravan to Ujjeni. One night the caravan stopped to rest in a pleasant wood. Soṇa was troubled by the noisy group and moved his sleeping mat a little distance away, seeking more seclusion. In the morning, the caravan left early, forgetting Soṇa who awoke to find himself alone.
>
> He hurried down the road, hoping to catch up with them. Under a large banyan tree he encountered a very ugly fat man who was tearing off his own flesh and eating it. "Who are you?" asked Soṇa. "I am a peta." "Why do you do this?" "It is the result of my own past kamma. I was a dishonest merchant in the city of Bhārukaccha who cheated others out of their property. Furthermore, when I was approached by *samaṇas* and brahmins, I told them to go eat their own flesh. Because of these deeds, I have come to this suffering."
>
> Continuing down the road, a little further on Soṇa encountered two boy petas (*petadārake*) with black blood oozing from their mouths. Upon being asked, they told him that they had been boys in Bhārukaccha and their family lived by selling perfume. Their mother was going out to offer food to an arahant bhikkhu one day when they reviled her. "You are giving our property away to these *samaṇas*! May the food you give him turn to black blood in his mouth." For this deed, they were reborn in *niraya*, and passing from there with some residual kamma remaining they had come to this state of suffering.
>
> Having had these experiences, Soṇa developed a fear of the horrors of *saṃsāra* and asked the elder Mahākaccāna for the going-forth (*pabbāja*, the initial or novice ordination into the order of bhikkhus). (Ud-a 5:6)

Koliya, one of King Bimbisāra's ministers, also saw a peta:

> Once there lived a hunter who lived by killing deer in the forest. Whenever he returned to his home village he would give morsels of meat to the village children, and once, some flowers.
>
> When he died he was reborn as a peta with an ugly, deformed body. He was naked except for a garland of flowers upon his brow. He did not know food or drink but walked, as if dreaming, upon the surface of the Ganges River ever seeking his village and his kin.
>
> There he was seen by Koliya who was returning by boat from a royal mission. (Pv-a 3:1)

Very often, the particular suffering endured by a peta is directly related to their former misdeeds:

> Once there was a land-owner with a barren wife. Wishing for sons, he took a second wife. When she conceived, the first wife grew jealous and gave her a drug to induce a miscarriage. Two months into her pregnancy, the blood flowed forth and the baby was lost. The first wife was suspected of the crime, but when accused by her husband she swore a false oath: "If I am guilty of this deed, may I eat the flesh of my own sons."
>
> As a result, upon death she was reborn as a *petī* with an ugly form and a foul, putrid odour. She was naked and covered with flies. Every dawn she would bring forth five baby boys, and again at sunset five more. Her

---

[376] *duggato yamalokiko*—translation is Gehman's.

heart burning and smoking with hunger, she would each time devour them all but even this was never enough. Nor did she ever get anything to drink. (Pv-a 1: 6)

Polygamous marriages in ancient India were often the scene of bitter rivalries between co-wives. The following excerpt is another example. It also illustrates nicely the relationship between kamma and result. (In the original, the dialogue is in verse).

A land-owner of Sāvatthi had two wives, Mattā and Tissā. Tissā was faithful, calm and pleasant to her husband. Mattā was faithless and angry and barren besides. When Mattā gave birth to a son, Tissā became even more hostile to her rival and began to abuse her in various ways. After death, she became a wretched *petī* and appeared before Tissā.

"You are naked, ugly, covered in veins, emaciated with your ribs standing out. Who are you, standing there?"

"I am Mattā, you are Tissā. We were co-wives. On account of my evil kamma, I have gone to the world of the petas (*petaloka*).

"I was violent, abusive, jealous and miserly. Because I spoke harshly to you, I have gone to the world of the petas."

"This I know. But I would ask you something else, why are you covered in dirt?"

"Seeing you once, freshly bathed and adorned, seated in pleasant conversation with our husband, I grew angry and jealous. Taking a handful of dirt, I threw it over your head. As a result of that deed, I am covered in dirt."

"This I know. But I would ask you something else. Why are you covered with itchy scabs?"

"Once we were gathering herbs in the forest. You took medicinal plants, I took the *kapikacchu* plant.[377] Without your knowing it, I sprinkled some into your bed. As a result of that deed, I am covered in itchy scabs."

"This I know. But I would ask you something else. Why are you naked?"

"There was a social gathering of friends and family. Our husband invited you, but not me. So, without your knowledge I hid your clothes. As a result of that deed, I am naked." (Pv-a 2:3)

Another example:

Moggallāna once saw a peta buried up to his neck in a cesspit. The peta told his story. "I was a householder who supported a bhikkhu of bad character. This bhikkhu was greedy and selfish; he was attached to my household and jealous of other bhikkhus. Listening to his words, I too began to abuse the good bhikkhus. As a result of that, I am a peta in a cesspit."

Moggallāna asked him what became of the evil-minded bhikkhu. "I am standing on his head. My food is what others defecate; the bhikkhu lives upon what I expel." (Pv-a 4:8)

---

377 *Mucana prutitus* according to the PED.

Most descriptions of petas portray them in a more or less human form, albeit often frightful and ugly. In a few instances, they have animal characteristics. For instance, we are told of a snake-peta who had the head of a man and the body of a snake, (Dhp-a 5:12) and of a pig-peta with a man's head on a pig's body (Dhp-a 20: 6). In one case, we hear of an actual animal reborn as a peta:

> At one time, Moggallāna saw a crow-peta with a body twenty-five *yojana* in size enduring suffering on Gijjhakūṭa ("Vulture's Peak"). When asked by what kamma he had acquired this body, the peta explained that he had been a crow at the time of Kassapa Buddha and had stolen three mouthfuls from a food offering. As a result, he was reborn in Avīci *niraya* and passing from there with kamma remaining, took form as a crow-peta. (Dhp-a 5: 12)

In the stories the petas are generally too powerless to harm human beings, despite their horrifying appearance. It is said in one place, however, that they have a poisonous breath which can cause sickness (Jāt 510).

3:3:2 MOGGALLĀNAS VISIONS OF PETAS

Moggallāna was one of the Buddha's chief disciples, renowned for his psychic powers. He very frequently had visions of beings like petas and devas invisible to others. There is a collection of such anecdotes in the *Lakkhaṇasaṃyutta* of the Saṃyutta Nikāya (SN 19:1 f.). The twenty-one separate suttas each follow the same pattern. The Buddha, together with many bhikkhus, is dwelling upon Gijjhakūṭa, ("Vulture's Peak") a hill near Rājagaha. As Moggallāna, together with another bhikkhu named Lakkhaṇa, is walking down the hill in the morning to seek alms, Moggallāna smiles. Lakkhaṇa asks him the reason for this and Moggallāna tells him to wait, he will answer in the presence of the Buddha. Later, when they have returned and finished their meals, Moggallāna explains that he saw a peta, and describes it. The Buddha says that in the past, he too saw this peta and explains the kamma that led to its particular rebirth.

The first peta is described as a skeleton flying through the air pursued by various birds of prey that peck and stab at it, causing it to howl in anguish. The Buddha explains that this peta had once been a cattle-butcher in Rājagaha and after suffering in *niraya* for many hundreds of thousands of years; his remaining kamma had caused him to take this form (SN 19:1).

The twenty-one short repetitive suttas of the *Lakkhaṇasaṃyutta* follow this general pattern. The petas described fall into a few groups of similar cases:

Those pursued by birds—Besides the skeleton, there was a "lump" of flesh (*maṃsapesiṃ*) and a "piece" of flesh (*maṃsapiṇḍa*), a skinless man, a skinless woman, a foul-smelling and ugly woman and a headless trunk all described in the same way as flying through the air being tormented by crows, vultures and hawks. Most of these had been various kinds of butchers, but the headless trunk had been an executioner, the skinless woman had been an unfaithful wife and the ugly woman had been a fortune-teller (*ikkhaṇikā*). The commentary states that she served the yakkhas, literally "did a slave's work for the yakkhas" (*yakkhadāsikammaṃ karontī*). This probably means that she allowed herself to become possessed, allowing the yakkha to act and speak through her.[378]

One more case in this group falls outside the general pattern. This being is described as a *kumbhaṇḍa purisa*, a *kumbhaṇḍa*-man. A *kumbhaṇḍa* is a type of being to be described in a later chapter, (§ 3:4, 5) a kind of lesser deity or demon whose distinguishing characteristic is a pair of enormous testicles. When the peta in this sutta walks, he is obliged to throw his testicles over his shoulder, and when he sits, he uses them as a cushion. He too is seen by Moggallāna flying through the air, torn by fierce birds. He had been a corrupt magistrate. The commentary explains his peculiar kamma: because he did fraudulent dealings in secret, his private parts were now exposed and because he inflicted unjust punishments on others, these same private parts now became an unbearable burden for him (SN-a 19:10).

The commentary to these passages explains that the birds are not really birds but yakkha-birds, because the peta beings would be invisible to ordinary birds (SN-a 19:1). We will discuss the ambivalent word *yakkha* later,[379] but in this context it may be interpreted as "spirit-birds."

Those cut by their sharp hairs—There was a peta with body-hair[380] like swords which were moving up and down and striking him as he flew through the air, uttering cries of pain. Likewise there was one with body-hair like spears, another with hair like arrows and two with needle-hairs. The second needle-hair peta is described a little differently. In his case, the hairs penetrate various parts of his body and emerge elsewhere. "They enter his mouth and come out of his chest; they enter his chest and come out of his belly etc." Most of these had followed various cruel professions, such as hunter or torturer. The second needle-hair peta had been a slanderer (SN 19:5–9).

378 SN 19, suttas 1,2,3,4,13,14 & 16.

379 See § 3:4,2.

380 In Pali, there is a different word for head-hair and body-hair; *kesa* and *loma* respectively.

Corrupt Saṅgha—The first of these was a peta who had been a corrupt bhikkhu. He now flew through the air in the form of a bhikkhu with his robes and bowl constantly burning with fire. Likewise there was a corrupt bhikkhunī, a corrupt *sāmaṇera* (novice), a corrupt *sāmaṇerī* (novice nun) and a corrupt *sikkhamāna* (probationary nun), all with burning robes and bowl (SN 19:17–21).

Miscellaneous—A few of the petas don't fall into any of the above categories. There was a man who had committed adultery now reborn as a peta with his head submerged in a pit of dung (SN 19:11). There was another who had once put dung into the bhikkhus' bowls and now was submerged in dung and compelled to eat it with both hands (SN 19:12). And there was a woman flying through the air with her body black with soot which was constantly burning and cooking her as she uttered cries of pain. She had once thrown a brazier of hot coals over a rival (SN 19:15).

A close look at this text indicates that most of the lore which came to be associated with petas was a relatively late development within the Buddhist tradition. It is significant that nowhere in the *Lakkhaṇasaṃyutta* itself these beings are explicitly called *petas*. It is the commentary which makes this identification. For example, the being in the first sutta is simply called a "skeleton" (*aṭṭhikasaṅkhalika*) and the commentary to this passage says "the being called a skeleton should be considered as one reborn in the *petaloka* ("peta-realm") (SN-a 19:1). In general, most of the details about petas come from the commentaries. Although the name and concept of *peta* as a suffering ghost is found in the canon, references there are few and sketchy. Often, the canon uses the word *peta* simply to indicate the dead.[381]

There remains the odd detail of Moggallāna's smile. In the text of the *Lakkhaṇasaṃyutta* Moggallāna himself explains it this way:

> "While descending from the Gijjhakūṭā Mountain, I saw a skeleton going through the air pursued by crows, vultures and hawks who were attacking its ribs, pecking, tearing and biting as it uttered cries of pain. I thought, 'How wonderful it is, how marvelous it is (*acchariyaṃ ... abbhutaṃ*) that even such beings as this exist!'" (SN 19:1)

The commentary recognizes that this seems an incongruous response, although its solution will still seem unsatisfactory to many readers:

> "Having seen such a being, the elder should have been moved to compassion. Why then did he smile? ... He reflected, 'Not having seen the truth, persons obtain such a form. I am freed from such a becoming. This is a gain for me, a great gain for me!'"(SN-a 19:1)

This arahant's smile proved such a difficulty for the tradition that when the Abhidhamma came to analyze all the possible modes of consciousness into eighty-nine types, this consciousness could not be fit into the scheme without being admitted as a unique type all its own, the *hasituppādacitta*, "smile producing consciousness". It causes smiling in arahants about things "that are not sublime" (Vism 14:108 & AbhSan 1:10).

---

381 See for ex. DN 14, SN 2:25, Sn 4:6.

3:3:3 TRANSFERENCE OF MERIT

Traditionally, the petas have been seen as the recipients of transferred merit. In brief, the idea is that when a meritorious deed is done by a living person with the earnest wish "may this benefit my dead relatives" the merit is received by the petas who experience an alleviation of their suffering as a result. The transfer of merit remains an integral part of lay Buddhist practise to the present day.

The key text is the *Tirokuṭṭapetavatthu* ("The Petas Outside the Walls Sutta") of the *Petavatthu*[382] and its commentary. –

> Ninety-two kappas ago, in the time of the Buddha Phussa, there were three royal princes who gave great support to the Buddha and his *Saṅgha*. Many of the common folk also became lay followers, but there were others who were corrupt of heart. They hindered the offerings, taking and eating the food themselves, and even burning down the eating hall.
>
> For ninety-two kappas, these two groups of citizens continued in the round of rebirth. The faithful were reborn in one *sagga* (heaven) after another; the wicked went from *niraya* to *niraya* (hell). In the present kappa, at the time of the Buddha Kassapa, the wicked ones were born as petas. At that time, people having given, would dedicate the gift (*dānaṃ datvā uddisanti*) for the sake of their departed relatives (ñātakānaṃ petānaṃ atthāya). Then those petas would obtain good fortune (*sampatti* which implies deva-like pleasure).
>
> The petas of our story observed this, and approached the Buddha Kassapa to ask how they too might experience such happiness. He told them, "Now you cannot. But in time to come there will arise a Buddha named Gotama. One of his followers will be King Bimbisāra who was a kinsman (ñāti) of yours ninety-two kappas ago. He will make a gift to the Buddha and dedicate the gift to you, and you will receive it." When he said this, to the petas it seemed just like they would receive happiness the next day.
>
> In the time of the Buddha Gotama the three princes, together with a thousand of their men, were reborn in the Kingdom of Magadha. One of the princes' officials became King Bimbisāra of Magadha. All of these became early followers of the Buddha. Upon hearing the Buddha discourse on the Dhamma, King Bimbisāra attained to the fruit of *sotāpatti* (first stage of awakening). He then invited the Buddha and his bhikkhus to a meal-offering on the following day. When the petas heard this, they said to one another "Now the king will make an offering, and dedicate the gift to us." And they stood surrounding the palace full ofhope.
>
> But when the king made his offering the next day, he was thinking only about the Buddha, wondering where he was dwelling now. Therefore, he did not dedicate the gift to anyone. The petas, having not received a donation (*dānaṃ alabhantā*), were now without hope and throughout the night filled the palace with horrifying cries of distress. The king was filled with fear and the next day asked the Buddha about it.
>
> "Do not fear, great king, no harm will come to you. Those are former kinsmen of yours, arisen among the petas. For the time between Buddhas they have been wandering as they awaited your offering to a Buddha and the dedication of the gift to them. Yesterday, you made a gift without a dedication and, having lost hope, they uttered cries of distress."
>
> The king then asked, "Can they then receive a gift?" (*dinne te labheyyuṃ*) "Yes, they can." So Bimbisāra

[382] Pv 1:5. The canonical verses are also found at Khp 7.

invited the Buddha to come again the following day, and the Buddha consented in silence. The next day King Bimbisāra had a great offering (*mahādāna*) prepared. The petas stood outside the walls, thinking "Today we might get something." The Buddha caused them to become visible to the king.

As Bimbisāra offered water to the Buddha, he thought "May this be for my kin." At that moment there arose lotus ponds for the petas, in which they bathed and drank, relieving their pain, thirst and fatigue and they became golden coloured. When the king offered rice and other food to the Buddha, at that very moment there arose for the petas deva-like rice, curries and dainties. These they enjoyed, and became fat (*pīṇindriyā ahesuṃ*). The king gave cloth and dwelling places to the Buddha and the bhikkhus, and there arose for the petas deva-like garments, palaces, beds and bedding, everything decorated in many ways. The Buddha made all the good fortune of the petas visible to the king, who was delighted at the sight. (Pv-a 1:5)

This story is taken from the commentary and frames the canonical verses which are then spoken by the Buddha to the King:

Outside the walls they stand, and at the cross-roads.

They stand by the door-posts, having returned to their homes.

An abundance of drink and food, both hard and soft is served,

But no one remembers these beings, experiencing their own kamma.

They who are compassionate should give to their kinfolk,

Pure food and drink, delicious, timely and appropriate.

"May this be for my kinfolk, may my kinfolk be happy!"

And these, having come together, the assembled departed kin (ñātipetā)

Thoroughly rejoice (*anumodare*) at the abundant food and drink.

"Long live our kinsfolk, the cause of our receiving this.

They have made an offering (*pūjā*) for us. The givers will not go without reward (*phālā,* lit. 'fruit')."

There is no ploughing there, nor fields of cattle to be found.

There is no trading done there, nor buying or selling for gold.

They are supported by gifts, the petas, those whose time has gone (*kālagatā*).

Just as water which has rained in the hills, flows down into the valleys,

Just so, a gift given here, benefits the petas.

Just as the rivers fill the ocean

Just so, a gift given here, benefits the petas.

"They gave to me, they worked for me, my relatives, friends and companions."

Give offerings to the petas, remembering what was done in the past.

Neither crying, nor sorrow nor any lamentation

Is of use to the petas, our kinsfolk who stand there.

But the offerings given to the well-established *Saṅgha*,

Have long lasting benefits, it is their proper cause.

Thus the duty of kin (*ñātidhammo*) has been explained:

respectful devotion (*pūjā*) made for the petas.

Strength has been given to the bhikkhus,

in doing so you have made not a little merit (*puñña).* (Pv 1:5)

This sutta, or selected stanzas, are often chanted by Theravāda bhikkhus as an acknowledgement when offerings of food or other requisites are made by the lay people. Used in this way, it is called an *anumodana*, literally a "rejoicing."

The *Petavatthu* is a text consisting of verses, to which the commentary adds framing stories. Most of the verses and stories are about petas, their suffering and the kamma which brought it about. In about a third of the stories, the suffering of the peta is relieved when someone dedicates an offering to an arahant bhikkhu, or to the saṅgha, on their behalf.

At one time there lived a master weaver who was a devout follower of the Buddha. But his wife was otherwise, she was without faith, unhappy, full of wrong views and miserly. Once, when her husband was preparing an offering of food and cloth for the bhikkhus, she cursed him, saying: "Whatever food or drink you give to those *samaṇas*, followers of the Buddha, in the next world may it become dung, pus and blood. And whatever clothes you give them, may they become red-hot iron plates!"

When his time came, and the weaver died, he was reborn as a tree-deva of great power and splendour in the Viñjha Forest.[383] His stingy wife became a petī living not far from his abode. She was naked, ugly and overcome with hunger and thirst. She approached the tree-deva and begged him, "My lord, I have no clothes and I wander about extremely hungry and thirsty. Please give me clothes and food." The deva offered her some sublime deva food (*dibbaṃ uḷāraṃ annapānaṃ*), but as soon as she grasped it, it became dung and pus and blood. He gave her a cloak, but as soon as she put it on, it became a blazing sheet of iron. So with great suffering, and crying aloud, she wandered away.

A little later, a bhikkhu who had gotten separated from his travelling companions chanced upon the dwelling of the tree-deva. Seeing him, the deva assumed a human form, welcomed him and invited him into his abode. The deva offered the bhikkhu some ointment for his feet, paid his respects and took a seat. As it happened, just then the *petī* returned and again begged for clothing and food. When she was given these things, it happened just as before. The deva asked the bhikkhu if there were any way to free her from the peta realm.

383 For tree-devas, see § 3:5,3.

"There is. If one makes a gift to the Buddha, the Noble Saṅgha or even to one bhikkhu, and dedicates it to her, and if she rejoices in it (*anumodati*) then she will be freed from her suffering."

Upon hearing this, the deva offered food and drink to the bhikkhu and dedicated it to the *petī*. Instantly, she had a sufficiency of deva-food and became plump and satisfied. The deva then offered to the bhikkhu a set of deva-clothes (*dibbasāṭakayugaṃ*) for the Buddha, again dedicating the gift to the *petī*. She was at once attired in deva-clothes, richly decorated and adorned like an *accharā* (celestial nymph). (Pv-a 1:9)

As this story illustrates, it is useless to attempt to give anything directly to a peta. Only the dedication of a gift given to another is effective, and one given to the Buddha, the Saṅgha or an individual bhikkhu is especially potent in this regard. This has led some modern readers to a cynical view; H.S. Gehman in the introduction to his translation expresses the opinion that the emphasis on giving to the bhikkhus gives the impression that "there was a mercenary motive in compiling the tales."[384] However, the practice of benefitting the dead through gifts was not an entirely new doctrine of the Buddhists, but rather a beneficial joining of two pre-Buddhist ideas. First, it had long been considered meritorious in India to support religious seekers, "*samaṇas* and brahmins." Second, there was a widespread practice of making offerings to various spirits and deities, especially the departed ancestors. A form of this practise survived among some Buddhists. We learn from the Kathavatthu that certain schools defended direct offering to petas, a position opposed by the Theravāda (Kv 7:6). There is however a faint trace of the older trend in the Pali canon itself. A stanza of the *Petavatthu* attributed to the Buddha says:

With whatever kind of ceremony (*kiñcārammaṇaṃ*), the generous person makes a gift

To the *pubbapete* ("forefathers" or "bygone petas") to the *vatthudevatā* ("local deities")

And to the Four Great Kings, guardians of the world[385]

... With this they are honoured (*pūjitā*) and the giver does not go without reward (*phalā,* lit. "fruit"). (Pv 1:4)

The concept of "transferring merit" seems contrary to the general Buddhist theory of kamma, which is made by oneself alone. Consider Yama's injunction to the newcomer at the gates of *niraya*:

"These bad kammas were done by you alone, not by your mother, your father, your brother or sister, nor by your friends or your relatives, nor by the devas. By you were these deeds done, and it is you who will experience the results."[386]

The commentaries developed a theory by which this contradiction was resolved. For transference of merit to be effective three things must be present:

1. A gift is given to a "suitable field of merit." The word for "field" is *khetta,* the word used for a farmer's field, and the metaphor is deliberately agricultural. One sows the "seeds" (*bīja*) and harvests the "fruit" (*phala*). The practical meaning is that the recipient of the gift should be a worthy person, ideally the Buddha, in practise usually a bhikkhu. However, any righteous person will do. In one place Sakka says that in the past he gave alms for ten thousand years to ten thousand fire ascetics without result, but when a righteous person (*sīlavanta*) ate his alms-food he was reborn in the *brahmaloka*. In one story a man who sees a peta and wishes to help him, merely dedicates the merit when he pays his barber (Pv-a 3:1). Nevertheless, these are exceptions, and by far the usual practise is to make offerings of food, cloth

[384] Gethin, *Tales of the Departed*, Intro. p. xi in "Minor Anthologies IV", PTS.

[385] See chap. on Cātumahārājika Devas in § 3:5,6.

[386] MN 130. For Yama, see § 3:3,11.

or other requisites to a bhikkhu or to the *saṅgha* as a whole.

2. The donor must "dedicate" (*uddissati*) the offering for the benefit of the peta. If this is not done, the petas cannot benefit, as Bimbisāra found out. If the person to whom the offering is dedicated is not in the peta realm, the benefit goes to some other relative of the donor; and in the beginningless *saṃsāra* it is impossible that one does not have some kin in the peta realm.[387]

3. Finally, the peta himself must acknowledge the act by rejoicing (*anumodati*) in the sign of merit (*puññanimittaṃ*). This is the detail which makes the whole consistent with the theory of kamma. A mind moment of rejoicing in the good is itself an act of good kamma. In their helpless condition, this is usually the only meritorious act of which a peta is capable.[388]

A further restriction on this practise is that merit can only be transferred to petas (AN 10: 177). The Milindapañhā, a late source, restricts this further by speaking of four classes of peta:

1. **Vantāsikā**—those who feed on what has been vomited up
2. **Khuppipāsino**—those who are tormented by hunger and thirst
3. **Nijjhāmataṇhika**—those who are consumed by craving
4. **Paradattūpajīvino**—those who live on the gifts of others

The text goes on to say that only the last kind is able to receive transferred merit (Mil 5:3.4 Eng. v2 p123f.). There is no basis for this division in the canon, and in the few places where these or similar terms appear in the commentary it would be more straightforward to understand them as epithets applying to petas generally rather than as specific types.[389] It does indicate that the scholarly tradition represented by the Milindapañhā was becoming increasingly uncomfortable with the idea of transferring merit, no matter how popular it was among ordinary Buddhists.

387 For this last point see AN 10: 177.

388 Except where otherwise noted, these points are taken from Pv-a 1:1.

389 See Ud-a 2:8 and Sn-a 2:2.

3:3:4 THE PETALOKA AND OTHER REALMS

Unlike *niraya*, the *petaloka* does not have its own geographical location. Generally, they wander on this earth invisible to most humans. Nevertheless, we are told that there was a large *petaloka* outside Rājagaha, (MN-a 133 & SN-a 1:20) presumably the abode of the petas seen by Moggallāna. There are also said to be peta-cities of great size.[390] Usually, however, the petas seem to be solitary beings often haunting places familiar to them from their human existence as sorry shades of their former selves:

> Moggallāna came upon a peta while passing through a sugar-cane field. The peta was tormented by hunger and thirst but unable to partake of the abundant sugar-cane.
>
> > "I am destroyed, I am devoured. I try and try to take some food.
> >
> > I weep, but a poor fragment of myself (*chinnathāmo*, lit. "a cut self")
> >
> > Of what kamma is this the result?"
>
> Moggallāna explained that in his human life he had been walking along eating sugar-cane when a poor man came up behind him and begged for some. At first he ignored the man's pleas. After some time, without turning around, he contemptuously held a piece of sugar-cane out behind his back for the beggar to take. Moggallāna told him that now he could only take sugar-cane from behind his back. The peta did so and found he could now eat to his heart's content. (Pv-a 4:5)

The peta in the story seems quite confused by his situation, and may not even have been aware that he was a peta. The image of a peta as a "fragment" of a human life is also illustrated by a set of similes given by the Buddha for the five *gati* (destinations of rebirth). The human realm is described as like coming to rest under a tree with soft grass below and abundant shade above and the peta realm like a tree with bare rocky ground below and only patchy shade above. Only the simile for these two realms use the imagery of a tree, emphasizing the idea of the peta world as a poor shadow or "fragment" of the human one (MN 12).

Sometimes the *petaloka* takes on an otherworldly quality as a separate kind of reality, parallel to our own. The unwary can at times find themselves crossing over:

> Two hundred years after the Buddha, King Piṅgala of Suraṭṭha was returning with his army from a campaign in aid of the Moriyas. At mid-day they came upon a foul place (*paṅka*), a desert of the petas.
>
> But they saw a pleasant road. The king told his charioteer, "This road is delightful. It looks safe, peaceful and fortunate. Turn the chariot in here, by this way we shall return to Suraṭṭha." So the chariot went in, at the head of the fourfold army.
>
> Afraid, a man of Suraṭṭha spoke to the king:
>
> > "We have entered upon a wrong path. It is terrifying, horrible.
> >
> > Ahead, we can see the road, but behind us we cannot!
> >
> > "We have entered upon a wrong path. The servants of Yama are close by.

390 MN-a122. The peta-cities are two or three *gavutas* big, there are four *gavutas* in a *yojana*.

The wind blows with an inhuman smell and a cruel voice." (Pv-a 4:3)

The peta world can also be seen as transitional between *niraya* and the human realm. Very often in the stories a peta is said to have already spent some long period suffering in *niraya* and expired from there with some residual kamma remaining *(kammassa vipākāvasesena)* (E.g. Pv-a 1:2). We already have encountered a couple of examples of this. Less often, the peta is on his way to *niraya*. In a few stories, the peta tells his human visitor that in a fewmonths he will die and be reborn in *niraya*. Usually, this fate is averted by the human being making a transference of merit in due time.[391]

The petas are not all entirely wretched. There are said to be some petas of "great knowledge and power" (*petamahiddhikāna vijjamānattā*), (Ud 8:6) and it is sometimes difficult to distinguish between these and the *bhumma-devas* (earth-bound devas).[392] After receiving transference of merit, the petas are described as enjoying deva-like pleasure and are sometimes addressed as "*devatā*" thereafter (Pv-a 1:10 & Pv-a 2:1). The lower devas and the petas seem to share the same cosmological "space" and sometimes interact, as seen in the story of the weaver and his wife recounted above. Another story involves devas and petas dwelling together:

> Once, in Bārāṇasī there dwelt a brahmin family, man and wife together with two sons and a daughter. The children all became devout followers of the Buddha but the parents had no faith, and made no merit. It came to pass that in a terrible storm their old house collapsed and all five were killed. The mother and father became petas, and the children bhumma devas. These were seen by the arahant bhikkhu Saṃkicca and one of his disciples.
>
> The five were travelling together to attend an assembly of the yakkhas (*yakkhasamāgama*). The elder son led the procession, riding on a white elephant. The younger son travelled in a chariot drawn by four mules, and the daughter was borne in a litter. Her radiance illuminated the ten directions.
>
> Following in the back went the two petas on foot. They were black in colour, with coarse tangled hair. They carried heavy iron mallets and cursed each other with harsh words. Their skin was horribly wrinkled and they dripped pus and blood. They were very frightful in appearance. They would strike one another with their mallets and drink the blood and pus from the wounds, but this did not satisfy them and they were always hungry. (Pv-a 1: 11)

---

[391] See Pv-a 1:10, Pv-a 2:7 & Pv-a 4:3. In the last case, it seems his ultimate fate was not averted, but his sufferings as a peta were, in the interval, diminished.

[392] See Pv-a 2:9, where it is not at all clear whether the being is a peta or a deva.

3:3:5 VIMĀNAPETAS

There is another type of peta that is not entirely wretched. The *vimānapetas* are a special kind of peta who experience both pleasure and pain due to their mixed kamma. The name, also spelled *vemānikapeta*, indicates a peta who lives in a *vimāna*. This is the type of magical or celestial mansion, often capable of flying through the air, in which the devas live.[393]

Vimānapetas vary greatly in their circumstances, but most characteristic are those who spend part of their time enjoying deva-like bliss and another part enduring the suffering of a peta.

> In the days of the Buddha Kassapa there were five hundred married couples, devout lay followers, who joined together to do good works. The men built bridges, parks and so forth. They also built a *vihāra* (monastery). The women would travel as a group to make offerings there. On one such journey, while staying at a public hostel on the way home, one of the women was seduced by a rogue and spent the night with him.
>
> Her husband heard rumours of her misdeed and confronted her. She denied it, and pointing to a dog said, "If I have done such a wicked deed, when I am reborn may I be eaten by a crop-eared dog such as this!" The other women also lied to protect her, "If we know anything about this may we become her slaves in the next life."
>
> The adulteress was consumed by remorse for her deed and soon wasted away and died. She was reborn as a *vimānapetī* in a *vimāna* by Lake Kaṇṇamuṇḍa in the Himavā. As the other women died, one by one, they reappeared there also, as her slaves and experienced the suffering of slaves.
>
> (There follows a description in verse spoken by a prince who eventually found her there and became her lover):
>
> Here are stairways of gold upon golden sands,
>
> Everywhere sweet delightful scents.
>
> Sweetly blow the winds, resounding with the cries of heron and geese.
>
> This is not a human city,
>
> Your many palaces of gold and silver
>
> Gleam brightly in the four directions.
>
> You have five hundred slave girls,
>
> Richly adorned with sea-shell bracelets,
>
> You have golden couches with deer-skin coverlets.
>
> When you lie down on them, you enjoy great sensual happiness.
>
> Until midnight comes, then you rise and go outside.
>
> There you go to the pleasure grove adorned with lotus-ponds.

393 *Vimānas* will be described in § 3:5,12.

There you stand on the fresh grass, beautiful one!

There a crop-eared dog devours you, limb by limb.

When you are all eaten, made into a skeleton,

Then you fall into the pond, and your body is made whole again.

Then with all your major and minor limbs, charming and dear to my sight,

You put on your garments and return to my presence. (Pv-a 2:12)

She endured this nightly torment for five hundred and fifty years until the prince found her, and it was another hundred and fifty before he learned of it. He broke the spell by killing the dog with an arrow, a quite un-buddhist exception to the rule that one cannot directly help a peta (ibid.). A similar case is that of the deer-hunter who used to kill by day and night until persuaded by a righteous friend to take a vow to refrain at least at night from killing living beings. After death, as a *vimānapeta* he enjoyed extravagant deva-like bliss during the night, but each day was pursued and devoured by a pack of dogs (Pv-a 3:8). In one story, we encounter *vimānapetīs* who lived on islands in the sea, spending alternately seven days as beautiful devīs and seven as wretched *petīs*.[394]

Sometimes there is a mixture of pleasure and pain or loss without reference to any transformation at particular times.

> In the time of Kassapa Buddha there lived in Bārāṇasi a woman of great beauty who made a fine living as a prostitute. She was particularly known for her long luxurious hair. It came to pass that some rivals of hers put a drug in her bathing powder which caused all her hair to fall out. Ashamed of her appearance, she left the city and eked out a living making and selling liquor. Once, she stole the garments of some men who were lying drunk and unconscious. At another time, she gave some sweet-cakes to a bhikkhu and stood holding a parasol over him as he ate. At that time, she made the aspiration (*anumodana*), "May my hair be long, delicate, glossy, soft and with curling tips!"
>
> When her time came she died and because of her mixed kamma (*missakakamma*) she was reborn all alone in a golden *vimāna* in the middle of the ocean. Her hair was long and beautiful, just as she had wished, but because she had stolen the men's' clothes she was naked. For the entire time between two Buddhas, she was reborn again and again into the same golden *vimāna*, and she was always naked.
>
> In the time of Gotama Buddha it happened that a storm at sea drove a merchant ship bound for Suvaṇṇabhūmi up to her island and the *petī* and her *vimāna* appeared to the merchants aboard. They called out to her, "Come out, lady, show yourself." She replied, "I am naked. I am ashamed to come out covered only in my hair. I have made only a little merit."
>
> They offered to give her a cloak, but she explained that she could not use that which is given to her directly (*hatthena hatthe*, lit. "hand to hand"). "But there is one among you who is a devout lay follower of the Buddha. Give to him some clothes, and dedicate the offering to me." So the merchants bathed and anointed the Buddha's disciple and presented him with some clothes. Immediately, the *petī* received food and drink and was dressed in fresh, clean garments of the finest cloth. She emerged from her *vimāna* smiling.

394 Jāt 439. More will be said of these *vimānapetīs* of the sea in the chapter on *niraya*, see § 3:3,22.

> In further conversation, she told the merchants that a terrible fate awaited her. In four months more she would die and be reborn in *niraya*. Compassion arose in the mind of the lay disciple and he suggested that she make a gift to these sailors, keeping in mind the qualities of the Buddha, and thereby she would be released from *niraya*. To this she consented and gave the sailors deva-food, garments and jewels. She bade them upon their return to Sāvatthi to pay respects to the Buddha in her name. Then by her own psychic power (*attano iddhānubhāvena*) she caused their ship to reach their destination in a single day. (Pv-a 1: 10)

In some stories a *vimānapeta* is seen enjoying a pleasant deva-like existence in the present with only the imminent prospect of a fall into *niraya* distinguishing him from a true *bhumma deva*. This was the case of the peta encountered by the King of Suraṭṭha whom we encountered travelling down a peta road:

> The king and his party travelling down the peta road came upon a banyan tree, dark like a thunder-cloud. Approaching, the king descended from his elephant and there saw jars of water and loaves of bread. There they saw a person with the appearance of a richly ornamented deva.
>
> "Welcome, Mahārāja! It is good that you have come. Drink the water, eat the bread, conqueror."
>
> The king asked him, "Are you a deva or a *gandhabba* or perhaps Sakka?"
>
> "I am neither a *gandhabba* nor a deva nor Sakka, but a peta, come here from Suraṭṭha."
>
> The *vimānapeta* told his story. He had been a man of Suraṭṭha given to false views and miserliness. However, his daughter had made offerings to the bhikkhus on his behalf, and that was why he was enjoying his current blissful existence. Nevertheless, in six months he would die and be reborn in the terrible *niraya*, there to burn for hundreds of thousands of years. (Pv-a 4:3)

In this case, the story does not have a happy ending. It seems the daughter's merit-making bought him only a temporary respite. There is no mention of the peta escaping his miserable destiny.

SUMMARY

As we have seen, the petas vary greatly amongst themselves in terms of appearance and degree of suffering. In many cases their suffering is directly related to the kamma they made in their previous human lives. The peta world can also be considered as a transitional space, a kind of half-way house between the human world and *niraya*, inhabited by beings coming and going. They also represent the departed ancestors which are recipients of transferred merit. They are associated with the dead. One way to think about them is to regard the peta existence as a kind of imperfect or partial rebirth. Instead of moving on to a fully embodied new existence, they wander the earth as a suffering fragment of their human selves.

3:3:6 *NIRAYA* REALMS OF TORMENT

The worst possible plane of rebirth in the Buddhist Cosmology is *niraya*. This word is often translated as "hell" although some translators have chosen to call it "purgatory," probably to emphasize that no state of existence in Buddhism is permanent. The etymology given by the *Pali-English Dictionary* says that the word means "to go asunder, to go to destruction, to die." The explanation for the name given by the commentaries says that, "It is called *niraya* because it is without enjoyment (*niratiatthena*), without pleasure" (*nirassādaṭṭhena*—lit. without taste) (MN-a 12). Frequently in the suttas a stock phrase occurs which lists three epithets of *niraya*: *apāya*, *duggati* and *vinipāta*.[395] *Apāya* means a state of loss; the commentary says that it means that happiness is not to be found there. *Duggati* means an unfortunate or miserable rebirth and *vinipāta* means falling to a bad place. The first two epithets are also used to refer to the lower realms in general and may therefore also be applied to rebirth as a peta or an animal, and sometimes to the asuras as well.

Beings that, while existing in some other realm, create very negative kamma, are reborn in *niraya*. It is a place of great suffering, and the tortures experienced here are described in gruesome detail. Despite the superficial similarity, we must be careful not to confuse the Buddhist conception of *niraya* with the idea of Hell. They differ in at least two important respects. First, *niraya* is not a place of judgement, because in Buddhism there is no one to do the judging. The suffering there is a direct result of the kamma done by the sufferer himself and arises by a kind of natural law. (This is true despite the somewhat bureaucratic role of Yama, Lord of *niraya*, to be considered below). Second, the torment of *niraya* is not eternal. This is considered a type of rebirth with its own limited life-span, which although it may be very long, is nevertheless finite. When a sufferer's kamma is exhausted, he deceases from *niraya* and is reborn elsewhere.

[395] See for instance AN 1:43and MN 12.

3:3:7 KAMMA LEADING TO *NIRAYA*

Kamma (Sanskrit *karma*) in Buddhism means "action", or more technically, a volitional action originating in the mind which acts as the cause for an effect (*kammavipāka*) experienced later, and which may effect the post-mortem destination. Skilful (*kusala*) action leads to a favourable rebirth (*suggaṭi*) in the human, deva or brahmā realms. Unskilful (*akusala*) action leads to rebirth in the unfavourable or lower realms (*duggati*) of which *niraya* is the worst. Generally speaking, two kinds of kamma have the greatest effect on determining the destination of a being seeking rebirth: habitual kamma, such as the routine acts of killing done by a butcher or the single kamma occurring at the time of death when the mind dwells on some skilful or unskilful object.[396]

Various unskilful actions are specified as leading to a rebirth in *niraya*. Breaking the five precepts is the most obvious example,[397] but many other transgressions are mentioned. A bhikkhu may go to *niraya* if he praises the unworthy, disparages the worthy, is stingy or conceited in regard to lodgings or supporters and if he wastes the gifts of the faithful (AN 5: 237). The three fires of passion, anger and confusion (*rāga, dosa, moha*) lead there (AN 7:47). Miserliness (Jāt 450) and ingratitude (AN 4: 213) are also states of mind which lead one toward *niraya*. Reviling or abusing worthy beings such as arahants, or pure *samaṇas* and brahmins, is mentioned many times and is said to lead to a long period of suffering in *niraya*.[398] However, an evil deed done by a generally good person does not necessarily lead to *niraya*. As an analogy it is stated that a lump of salt placed into a small glass of water makes it salty, but does not affect the taste of the water if it is thrown into a large lake (AN 3:101, Eng. 3:100).

Especially wrong view (*micchādiṭṭhi*) is a cause for rebirth in *niraya*. "Bhikkhus, I see no single thing which compares to wrong view for causing a being to arise after death in *niraya*" (AN 1:304, Eng. 1:312). This is because the holding of wrong view can lead a person into committing grave moral transgressions based upon that view (It 3:3,1). An obvious example in the context of ancient India was animal sacrifice, which the Buddha very much opposed.[399] Not all wrong views can lead a person into the kinds of action which tend toward *niraya*. Three in particular are specified: *ahetukadiṭṭhi, akiriyadiṭṭhi, natthikadiṭṭhi*. Literally translated these are the no-cause view, the no-action view and the nothing-exists view i.e. nihilism. These three are all variants of the denial of kamma and *vipāka*, or the idea that there is no future result from deeds. It is easy to see how this view might tend to an immoral life. *Sakkāyadiṭṭhi*, or the "personality view" which postulates a real self (*atta*), while a hindrance to awakening, does not lead to *niraya* since the holder of this view would still accept the idea of action having a result and be morally restrained (AN-a 1:304).

There are five actions which have a certain result, determining that the transgressor will be reborn in *niraya* without fail. These are the killing of one's mother or father, the killing of an arahant, wounding a Buddha and creating a schism in the *saṅgha* (AN 5: 129). Conversely, the attainment of *sotāpatti*, "stream-entry", the first stage of awakening frees a being forever from the danger of taking rebirth in *niraya* or the other lower realms. Such a one is able to say "*khīṇanirayomhi*", "I have destroyed *niraya*" (AN 10. 92).

---

[396] The theory of kamma is complex and nuanced, and the presentation in the suttas is somewhat different from that in the abhidhamma. It is beyond the scope of this book to enter more deeply into this topic. Interested readers are referred to "Good, Evil and Beyond" by P.A. Payutto for a good short survey.

[397] AN 5: 145. The five precepts forbid killing, stealing, adultery, speaking falsehood and drinking liquor.

[398] Jāt 541, AN 4:3, AN 10:89 are among the very many examples.

[399] See Sn 2:7, SN 3:9 and AN 7:47 for examples.

3:3:8 LOCATION OF *NIRAYA*

Avīci, the Mahāniraya, (the "Great *niraya*"), is part of the *cakkavāḷa* (Sn-a 3:7) and is located beneath the earth. Most of the other *nirayas* are presumably located adjacent to it. (The various specific *nirayas* will be considered in a separate section below). The commentary to the *Visuddhimagga* states that Avīci is located below Jambudīpa, the southern continent upon which we live.[400] There are several incidents mentioned in the texts of especially heinous wrong-doers who fell through the earth directly to *niraya*. The most well-known is Devadatta, the Buddha's cousin who attempted to kill him three times and who caused a schism in the *Saṅgha*.

> When Moggallāna and Sāriputta had won most of his renegade disciples back to the Buddha, Devadatta, knowing that he had failed in his attempt to replace the Buddha, vomited hot blood and remained very ill for nine months. At the end of this time, he determined to approach the Buddha and make a contrite apology for all the evil he had done.
>
> Too weak to walk any distance, he had his remaining disciples carry him to Jetavana in a litter. The Buddha's disciples heard of this and informed the Blessed One who said, "It is not possible, bhikkhus, that Devadatta will see me again in this existence." The bhikkhus were puzzled by this, but it was a matter of natural law (*dhammatā*) that through creating a schism, Devadatta had made such weighty kamma that he would never again be able to see the Buddha, and that his next birth would be in *niraya*.
>
> On approaching the bank of the pond outside Jetavana Vihāra ("Jeta's Grove Monastery" where the Buddha was in residence), Devadatta asked to be let down to bathe. As soon as his feet touched the earth it opened up to swallow him. He sank gradually into the ground, up to his ankles, his knees, his waist, his chest, his neck. Just before his jaw bone disappeared, he uttered a stanza in praise of the Buddha, thereby making merit with his last utterance.
>
> He reappeared in the Mahāniraya with a hundred *yojana* body. The top of his head was buried in the red-hot iron ceiling, his feet in the red-hot iron floor. Stakes protruding from the walls pierced his body from every direction, passing right through him and leaving him standing there immobile. There he will remain among the flames of *niraya* enduring great suffering for the duration of the present kappa (world-age).
>
> But the Buddha predicted that after the passage of one hundred thousand kappas more, Devadatta will become a *Paccekabuddha* named Aṭṭhissaro, on account of the merit made by him at the end of his life.[401]

Nor was this the first time that Devadatta had fallen directly into *niraya*. There are many Jātaka stories in which the villain is said to be Devadatta in a previous birth. In a few of these, the earth opens up at the end of the story and the wrong-doer falls directly into Mahāniraya.[402] In the Sīlavanāga Jātak*a* (Jāt 72) the Bodhisatta is an elephant and Devadatta a forester. The forester is saved by the elephant but then cruelly mistreats him, sawing off his tusks at the root.

> The forester taking his prize went on his way. No sooner had he left the sight of the Bodhisatta when the great earth, two hundred and forty thousand *yojana* thick, able to bear Mt Sineru and the Yugandhara Mountains, able to bear smelly loathsome dung and urine, was, as it were, unable to bear his wickedness and tore open

---

[400] See *Path of Purification*, p. 202, note 15.

[401] Paraphrased from Dhp-a 1: 12 and see GGB p. 895.

[402] Jāt. 72, 222, 313 and 457.

a fissure. The flames of the great *niraya* Avīci issued forth and enfolded the ingrate like a blanket and he fell into the earth.

Including **Devadatta**, five persons during the Buddha's life-time were swallowed by the earth and fell directly into *niraya*. The others were:

Ciñcā, the female wanderer who falsely accused the Buddha of getting her pregnant.

Suppabuddha, the father of Devadatta and of Rāhulamātā (the Buddha's former wife). Suppabuddha got drunk and insulted the Buddha.

Nandamāṇavaka, whose crime was raping the arahant bhikkhunī Uppalavaṇṇā.

Nandaka the yakkha who struck Sāriputta a blow on the head also suffered this fate.[403]

The normal mode of arriving in *niraya*, however, is spontaneous rebirth (*opapātikā yoni*) which means that after death, a being simply appears fully formed with a body appropriate for the realm in question. Even in the rare cases of those who reach *niraya* by falling directly through the earth, it stated that the being does not go to *niraya* in their human body, but dies during the process and there is then spontaneously reborn (Ud-a 4:4).

[403] Mil 4:1, 1, eng. v1 p141.See Horner's notes 3-6 for references.

3:3:9 LIFE-SPAN IN *NIRAYA*

The span of time a being suffers in *niraya* is determined by its individual kamma. In most cases it is very long, many hundreds of thousands of years.[404] Causing a schism in the *saṅgha*, as Devadatta did, leads to a kappa spent in *niraya*, although the commentary qualifies this as meaning an *antarakappa,* (It-a 1:2,8) which is a subdivision of a full kappa (depending on context it might be anywhere from one fourth to one eightieth of a *mahākappa*). The most extreme example of a prolonged period of suffering in *niraya* is the case of Kokālika who repeatedly reviled Sāriputta and Moggallāna and refused to apologize or admit his fault. When he died, the Buddha declared that he had gone to Paduma Niraya, "The Red-Lotus Niraya", and would stay there for a very long time:

> The bhikkhus asked the Buddha how long was the span of life in the Paduma Niraya. The Buddha replied it was not easy to reckon the years, as so many thousands of years or so many hundreds of thousands of years. The bhikkhus asked if it were possible to give a simile to illustrate the length of time.
>
> The Buddha said it was possible. "Suppose, bhikkhus, there were a Kosalan cart-load (which is four times the measure of a Magadhan cart-load) full of sesame seeds. If a man were to remove one seed every hundred years, this would complete the period of one life-time in Abbuda Niraya. Twenty of these make the life-span in Nirabbuda Niraya. Twenty of these make the life-span in Ababa Niraya … (this continues for ten multiples of twenty altogether concluding with …) twenty lives in Puṇḍarīka Niraya equals one in Paduma Niraya. (AN 10: 89)

The commentary to this text, true to the ancient Indian love of manipulating huge numbers, if not to the Buddha's injunction, specifies this period as a number of years. It calculates the length of time of one *abbuda* by beginning with a *koṭi* (ten million) of years and multiplies that by further factors of ten million six additional times. Thus, one *koṭi* of *koṭis* equals one *pakoṭi*, one *koṭi* of *pakoṭis* equals one *koṭipakoṭi* etc. If this calculation is done in full and expressed in modern notation we would have a life-span in Paduma Niraya equal to more than 5.12 times 10 to the 53rd power years![405]

If the story of Kokālika represents the longest life-span in *niraya*, surely the case of Queen Mallikā, told in the *Dhammapada Commentary*, represents the shortest. Mallikā was the queen of King Pasenadi of Kosala. She was a devout follower of the Buddha and had made many meritorious offerings to the Saṅgha. She and the king were very much in love. Mallikā led a virtuous life with only one lapse:

> One day Queen Mallikā went into the bathing room to wash herself. Her favourite pet dog followed her in. As she was bending over to wash her calves, the dog began to have sexual relations with her. She enjoyed the sensation and stayed there, allowing the act to continue. Just then, King Pasenadi approached and looked into the window of the bathing room.
>
> When the queen emerged, the king confronted her. "Perish you vile woman! How could you do such a thing?" "What have I done, deva?" (kings were often so addressed) "You were having sex with a dog in there!" "No, I did not" "I saw it with my own eyes! I do not believe you, you vile woman." "Great King, whoever looks

---

[404] See SN 3:20 & SN 6:10 & SN 19:1 & SN 19:21.

[405] The *Suttanipāta* also has a version of the *Kokālika Sutta*. The conclusion of the verse portion states that "the wise have calculated the number of sesame seeds and count the length of one *paduma* as a *nahuta* (10,000) times five *koṭi* (10,000,000) plus 1200 *koṭi* more." This comes out to 5.12 hundred billions. This stanza does not follow naturally upon the preceding ones and may be a late addition. Sn 3: 10.

through that window sees two persons where there is one." "You are lying!" "Great King, if you want proof, you may go into the bathing room and I'll look through the window and tell you what I see."

Being of a foolish nature (*mūḷhadhātuko*) King Pasenadi believed her words and entered the bathing room. Mallikā peered through the window and said, "Foolish fellow! Why are you having sex with that she-goat?" "My dear, I have not!" "I do not believe you; I saw it with my own eyes." (Dhp-a 11:6)

In her mind, Mallikā could never forget that she had committed two grave offences, having sex with an animal and falsely accusing her husband of the same. When her time came to die, instead of recollecting her many meritorious deeds, she thought about this incident at the last moment and was subsequently reborn in Avīci *niraya*.

After her death, King Pasenadi went to see the Buddha to ask him where Mallikā had been reborn. The Buddha gave a talk on the Dhamma and made the king forget to ask his question. So Pasenadi returned on the following day and the same thing happened, and so on each day for one week. On the eighth day, Mallikā deceased from *niraya* and reappeared in the Tusita *devaloka* (one of the heavenly worlds). And the Buddha was able to tell Pasenadi where she was (ibid.).

3:3:10 NERAYIKASATTA AND NIRAYAPĀLA — THE BEINGS IN *NIRAYA*

The beings dwelling in *niraya* may be divided into *nerayikasatta* and *nirayapāla*. *Nerayikasattas* are the beings whose bad kamma has caused them to be reborn into that state of suffering. The *Nirayapālas* are their wardens and torturers. The bodily form of a *nerayikasatta* seems to be generally anthropomorphic since in the descriptions of the tortures we find references to familiar body parts like heads, arms and legs. However their form might be described as "deformed and loathsome" (*virūpā jegucchā*), (Jāt 541) and in one incident we hear of a being with a human body and a fish's head (MN 50). Despite the extreme tortures of burning, dismemberment, crushing and so forth experienced by these beings they cannot die until their kamma is exhausted (MN 129). The ordinary rules of nature do not apply in *niraya* because this is a realm generated by the evil kamma of its beings. It is, for instance, stated that the reason the fire of *niraya*, much hotter than any earthly fire, does not consume the *nerayikasattas* is because of the power of kamma (Mil 2–3:4,6 Eng. v1 p91f.). The *nerayikasattas* are cited as examples of beings who do not enjoy any meritorious kamma and who experience only painful sensations (AN 4:233).

The *nirayapālas*, lit. "*niraya* guards" are the beings who torture the *nerayikasattas* in various ways. There was a controversy in early Buddhism as whether these are actual beings, i.e. possessed of consciousness and subject to death and rebirth, or merely illusory projections generated by the kamma of the sufferers themselves (Kv 20:3). The Theravāda position is that they are actual beings. People who act as torturers in the human realm may be reborn as *nirayapālas* (AN-a 3:36). In another passage it is stated that teachers who led their disciples astray with false teachings can be reborn as *nirayapālas*, and their students as the *nerayikasattas* they torture.[406] The *nirayapālas* are occasionally referred to as *rakkhasās*, (Jāt 530) a rather loose designation in Pali usage derived from a class of Vedic demon. The *nirayapālas* are said to enjoy their work as they run about to and fro hacking at the *nerayikasattas* with various weapons. "They like nothing better than causing pain, for them it is like sport" (Jāt 530). Sometimes they feign compassion, for example one may ask a *nerayikasatta*, "Are you hungry, my dear?" (Using *mārisa,* an affectionate mode of address) and when answered in the affirmative, the *nirayapāla* forces a red-hot iron ball into the mouth of the victim (M 129).

[406] MN-a 11. The passage adds that the teachers might also be reborn as lions and the students as the beasts on which they prey.

3:3:11 YAMA

One being of great importance in the *niraya* realm is Yama, the King of *niraya* or Lord of Death. The figure of Yama has his roots in the Vedic period. In that mythology, Yama was the first human, and also the first man to die, so he became the King of the Dead. He had a twin sister named Yamī, and although there is a passage in the Ṛg Veda where he refuses her sexual advances because of the incest taboo, it is also assumed that they were the progenitors of the human race. The Buddhist Yama is not to be confused with the devas of the Yāma realm, the third *kāmavācara devaloka* (sensual heaven), although there may be an ancient link between the two in that the Vedas also describe a paradisiacal realm of the righteous dead ruled by Yama, and this is also the third level of heaven.[407]

The Buddhist Yama, as found in the canon and commentaries, is not a very well defined character. There is even some confusion as to how many Yamas there are. Most references to him use the singular and it is generally to be assumed that Yama is an individual. The *Mahāsamaya Sutta* (DN 20) mentions a long list of beings coming to see the Buddha among whom are "the two Yamas" (*duve yamā*). This is a text much influenced by pre-Buddhist sources and may reflect the Vedic idea of Yama having a twin. Another text speaks of four Yamas, one at each gate-way to the Mahāniraya.(AN-a 3:36).

Although he is called King Yama (*yamarājā*) in a couple of places, (MN 130 & AN 3:36) and the four unhappy states of rebirth are said to be his domain..[408] In the text where we have the only significant glimpse of Yama in action, he seems more to be acting as a door-keeper, admitting wrong-doers to *niraya*:

> When, after death, a wrong-doer reappears in *niraya*, the *nirayapālas* seize him by his arms and take him to King Yama. "This person, oh king (*deva*) has no respect for mother or father, for *samaṇas* or brahmins, or for the clan elders. Inflict punishment on him, oh king."
>
> Then Yama examines and questions the man in regard to the first divine messenger (*devadūta*). "Good sir (*ambho purisa*) have you never seen in the world of men the appearance of the first divine messenger?" "I have never seen it, venerable sir (*bhante*)."
>
> "My good sir, have you never then seen in the world of men a young tender infant lying in its own excrement and urine?" "I have seen this, venerable sir."
>
> "My good sir, you are a learned man, intelligent and old in years. Have you never thought that you too are subject to birth (i.e. rebirth), that you have not transcended birth, that you had better do good deeds with body, speech and mind?" "I was not able to, venerable sir, I was negligent."
>
> "My good sir, you have been negligent in not making good kamma with body speech and mind. Certainly, they will deal with you according to your negligence. These bad kammas (actions) were done by you alone, not by your mother, your father, your brother or sister, nor by your friends or your relatives, nor by the devas. By you were these deeds done, and it is you who will experience the results."
>
> (Then King Yama questions him in a similar way about the remaining divine messengers: an old person, a sick person, a criminal being tortured or flogged and a dead body. The man's replies are the same in each case and so is Yama's final admonishment).

---

[407] Wallis 1887: 65-66.

[408] Dhp 4:1—*yamalokañcāti catubbidhaṃ apāyalokañca.*

Then King Yama is silent and the man is taken by the *nirayapālas* to be tortured.[409]

The *Aṅguttara Commentary* tells us that not every being comes before Yama after death. Only those with little evil are questioned in this way, the great evil-doers go to *niraya* straight away, "just as a thief caught red-handed does not need an inquiry" (AN-a 3:36).

It seems from the passage above that King Yama is not at all eager to see the man condemned to the sufferings of *niraya* and is seeking to find some possibility of escape for him. It is significant that the man's own kamma is responsible for his doom, and that in the end Yama merely acquiesces in silence. There are other indications that Yama is not entirely happy with his role. It is said that he wishes for a human birth, and to have the chance to hear the Dhamma taught by a Buddha (AN 3:36). Yama is said to be a *vemānikapeta*, a type of being with mixed kamma who spends part of his time enjoying deva-like pleasure and part of it in peta-like suffering.[410] He is not to be considered an evil or demonic being; he is called a "righteous king" (*dhammiko rājā*) (AN-a 3:36). In the end, Yama comes across as a tragic figure.

There is an amusing anecdote in one of the Jātaka tales about a palace gate-keeper who wept when the evil king died, while the rest of the city rejoiced. When asked why he wept, he said that he was afraid that the king, who would regularly punch him on the head as he walked by, would strike Yama and be sent back to earth, being deemed too evil for *niraya* (Jāt 240).

Yama is also associated with death. A series of stanzas in the *Dhammapada* speak about the danger of facing death unprepared, and two of them mention Yama:

> You are a withered leaf, now the servants of Yama approach
>
> You stand at the mouth of death, with no provision for the journey. (Dhp 18, verse 235)
>
> Now he is brought to loss, he has come into the presence of Yama.
>
> There is no dwelling place between, you have no provision for the journey. (Dhp 18, verse 237)

Finally, there is one detail about Yama that seems somewhat out of line with the rest of what we know about him. Yama is said to possess one of the Four Great Weapons.[411] This is the *nayanāvudhaṃ*, "the eye-weapon", meaning that he can kill with his gaze. It is stated than when Yama is angry, with a single glance he can scatter and destroy many thousands of *kumbhaṇḍas* like sesame seeds on a hot pan (SN-a 10:12). Why he would destroy *kumbhaṇḍas* in particular, who do not seem otherwise to be associated with him, we are not told.[412]

---

409 MN 130. The same passage occurs at AN 3:36.

410 AN-a 3:36. For *vemānikapetas* see § 3:3,5.

411 The others are held by Sakka, Āḷavaka and Vessavaṇa.

412 For *kumbhaṇḍas* see § 3:4,5. It may be that here the word is used loosely in the sense of "demonic being" and refers to the nirayapālas but this is speculative.

3:3:12 SUFFERINGS OF *NIRAYA*

Niraya is a place of unceasing torment. Fire and burning feature prominently in descriptions of the pain endured by the beings there:

> With bodies burning constantly, inside and outside …
>
> Like an angry poisonous snake, the flames difficult to cross (Jāt 530)
>
> Tossed into a pit of blazing charcoal, the beings cry out with burning bodies … Jāt 541)
>
> Burning charcoal rains down, stones fall on the doers of cruel deeds,
>
> Hot winds hard to bear blow in *niraya*, there not the least happiness can be found … (Jāt 545, Eng. 544)

Sometimes this takes the form of boiling in a cauldron filled with molten metal.

> The destroyers of beings cook them like a piece of fish …
>
> He is boiled in an iron cauldron, he is cooked and his hide pierced with spears … (Jāt 530)
>
> Blazing, burning, afire, I see a very large iron cauldron,
>
> (Big as a mountain, filled with molten metal),
>
> Grabbing and twisting their necks, they pour boiling water over them.
>
> (They wrap a hot cord around their necks and throw them into the cauldron)
>
> (This is the kammic result of catching and killing birds and beasts)[413]

This form of torture is so prevalent that the verb *paccati* which means, "to be boiled, to be cooked", is sometimes used figuratively to refer to suffering in *niraya* generally.

Various and ingenious kinds of cutting, hacking and stabbing are also frequently mentioned:

> With sharp arrows and spears, struck and pierced, he is tortured (*paccamittā*) …
>
> He has killed, now he wanders in *niraya*, his belly and sides torn open,
>
> His body torn, flowing with blood.
>
> Spears, arrows, lances, various kinds of weapons rain down …
>
> He climbs a mountain covered in razors, horrible blazing and frightful,
>
> His body torn, flowing with blood … (Jāt 545, Eng. 544)

Often we hear of beings immersed in various kinds of filth, or even forced to eat or drink it:

> Disgusting, loathsome and putrid, a stinking mire of faeces,
>
> Resembling pus and blood, he stands immersed in that pool.

[413] Jāt 541. Commentarial additions in parentheses.

He has fallen to *niraya*, into a stinking pile of corpses, one hundred deep,

Their stench extends for one hundred *yojana*.

The smell blinds him, destroys his eyes …

Day and night they are struck on the head with an iron hammer,

There they are made to eat each other's foul vomit … (Jāt 530)

Sometimes, the *nirayapālas* are not needed to drive the suffering beings to consume foul things: their desperate hunger and thirst is sufficient:

niraya beings overcome by hunger are given blazing balls of excrement to eat.

There is a lake filled with urine and faeces, stinking, unclean and putrid smelling.

Hungry beings eat there; I behold this with fear …

There is a lake full of blood and pus, stinking, unclean and putrid smelling.

Overcome by heat, beings drink there … (Jāt 530)

Another way in which the hungry and thirsty are tormented is by the frustration of their desire:

There is seen abundant water in pools with pleasant banks.

Overpowered with the heat, beings drink there,

But drinking the water, it turns to chaff.

(The water turns to blazing chaff which burns right through their bodies, coming out below and causing unbearable pain).[414]

The suffering beings may also be attacked by various kinds of animals: fierce dogs with iron teeth, various kinds of birds such as crows, vultures and hawks and in the water of the caustic rivers or pools of filth there are needle-mouthed worms which bore into the flesh (Jāt 530 & 544). We can also add to the list of sufferings that the *niraya* realm is very crowded. There are far more beings in *niraya* than there are human beings on earth (SN 56:97, Eng. 56:102) and they are said to be packed in like mustard seeds (AN-a 1:48). It is often stated that in spite of being torn open, burned, devoured by animals or otherwise horribly damaged, the *niraya* beings are unable to die until their negative kamma is exhausted. Their bodies are continually restored to suffer again and again (MN 130).

414 Jāt 541. Commentarial addition in parentheses.

3:3:13 THE VARIOUS *NIRAYA* REALMS

The "geography" of *niraya* is complex, and the texts are problematic. With the *sagga* realms, the pleasant abodes of the devas, it is possible to construct a coherent and consistent scheme or "map" but this is not true of *niraya*. The Itivuttaka Commentary mentions eight *mahānirayas* ("great nirayas"), each with sixteen *ussada-nirayas* (*ussada* means a projection and implies that these secondary *nirayas* lie outside and adjacent to the principal ones) (It-a 3:5,4). The Saṃkicca Jātaka (Jāt 530) adds the detail that four of the *ussada nirayas* lie outside each of the four gates of the *mahānirayas*. All told, this amounts to a total of one hundred and thirty-six *nirayas*. The various listings of *nirayas* by name do not agree with each other.[415] Furthermore, there are numerous mentions of single *nirayas* in the texts which do not fit into any of the schemes. The next section will discuss the various *niraya* realms, bearing in mind that it is impossible to extract a consistent scheme from the texts.

[415] See Jāt 530, AN 10: 89 and MN 130 for three quite different lists.

3:3:14 THE MAHĀNIRAYA

There are only a few places in the canon, as distinct from the commentaries, where we find specific details about *niraya*.[416] The most systematic description is in two adjacent suttas of the Majjhima Nikāya, the Bālapaṇḍita and Devadūta Suttas (MN 129 & 130). We have already seen how a being destined for niraya is questioned by King Yama. At the conclusion of his inquiry, King Yama is silent and the unfortunate person is seized by the *nirayapālas*. These immediately subject him to various tortures:

> The *nirayapālas* torture him by driving a red-hot iron stake through each hand, each foot and through his belly. Next they throw him down and chop him with axes, turn him upside-down and chop him with adzes. Then they yoke him to a chariot and make him run over the blazing ground. They make him climb a mountain of burning coals, hot and blazing. Then they put him into a metal cauldron and cook him in a swirl of froth. As a result of these tortures, he suffers painful, racking and piercing feelings but he does not die so long as his negative kamma is not exhausted.[417]

After this initiation, the new *nerayikasatta* is thrown into Mahāniraya, "the Great *Niraya*". It is described in a stanza of verse:

> Square shaped, with a door in each wall,
>
> Walled in iron all around, and iron-roofed.
>
> There is an iron floor, of blazing fiery iron.
>
> Its flames extend one hundred *yojana* in every direction.

> Flames dash from each wall all the way to the far wall, and from the ceiling to the floor and from the floor to the ceiling. Every so often, after some long period of time, one of the doors opens. The *nerayikasatta* runs toward it, enduring great suffering from the flames which burns his skin and flesh and turns his bones to steam with every step, only to find the door slammed shut as he reaches it. After a very long interval he does manage to escape through the eastern door. (MN 130)

This is not however an end to his torment, as he then endures a forced tour through various secondary *nirayas*.

Immediately outside the eastern gate of Mahāniraya is **Gūthaniraya**, the "*Niraya* of Excrement." Here dwell the *sūcimukhas* "needle-mouths;" animals with sharp iron needle-like mouth parts who bore through the sufferer's skin, flesh and bones to feast on the marrow. They are as thick as an elephant's neck and as long as a ship. After making his way through the Gūthaniraya, the *nerayikasatta* enters the **Kukkulaniraya**, the "Niraya of Hot Coals." There, the being falls into a mass of hot coals as big as a gabled house. Very fine hot ashes rain down upon him and enter into the nine orifices of his body, causing great suffering.[418]

Next he enters the **Simbalivana**, the "Grove of Simbali Trees." These trees are one hundred *yojana* high and bear sixteen inch thorns on their bark. The thorns are described as being made of iron, very sharp and they drink men's blood. The *nerayikasatta* is forced to climb up and down the *simbali* trees.[419] This *niraya* is especially associated

---

416 See for instance Sn 3,10, Jāt 530.

417 MN 130, condensed and adapted from Bhikkhu Bodhi's translation, MLDB pp. 1032-33.

418 Additional details from Jāt 522.

419 Additional details from Jāt 530 and 536. This grove is not to be confused with the Simbalivana on the slopes of Mt Sineru, abode of the *supaṇṇas*. The tree called simbali in Pali is identified by the P.E.D. as the Indian Silk Cotton Tree, *bombax hep-*

with the act of adultery. The wrong-doers are forced to climb the painful thorny trees in order to reach their lover (or perhaps an illusory image of her) waiting at the top (Jāt 530).

Next to this is what appears to be a delightful mango grove. Moved by desire for the mangos, the being enters only to find himself in the **Asipattavana**, the Forest of Swords. Here, the trees bear sword-like leaves which move in the wind and cut off his hands and feet, his ears and nose. Once again, he endures great suffering.[420]

At last he comes to the **Khārodakā Nadī** the Caustic River.[421] There he is pulled about helplessly by the current, enduring great suffering until he is fished out with a hook by the *nirayapālas*. These ask him if he is hungry, then force open his mouths with iron tongs and feed him a red-hot iron ball. Then they ask if he is thirsty and they pour molten copper down his throat. These hot substances burn right through his body, coming out below and taking his intestines with them. Finally, having had their sport, the *nirayapālas* throw the hapless sufferer back into the Mahāniraya.[422]

---

taphyllum, which does indeed have a thorny bark.

420 Additional detail from Sn-a 3:10.

421 *Khāra* means "lye, potash or any alkaline substance" according to the PED. The Khārodakā River is identified by the commentary to this passage with the Vetaraṇī which we shall consider below.

422 All this mostly from MN 130, with additional details from the commentaries as noted.

3:3:15 AVĪCI

The description of Mahāniraya and its environs from the Majjhima Nikāya given above may well represent the original conception of *niraya*. This was greatly elaborated in the commentaries, and the number of different *nirayas* multiplied. We have noted above that there came to be eight *mahānirayas*. To distinguish the deepest, hottest, most horrible and greatest of these the name *Avīci* or sometimes *Avīcimahāniraya* came to be used. The name *Avīci* means "without respite." It is almost never met with in the *Sutta Piṭaka*. In two parallel passages describing conditions on earth in the cosmological past and future (AN 3: 56 & DN 26) the population is said to be *avīci mañño phuṭo bhavissati,* which Bhikkhu Bodhi translates straightforwardly as "one would think there was no space between people."[423] In this interpretation the word *avīci* is used as a simple adjective without reference to *niraya*. However, the commentary to these passages does make the connection, interpreting the passage to mean that the human population will be as dense as that of Avīci Niraya. The only unambiguous reference to Avīci the *niraya* in the Suttas is found in a verse passage of the Itivuttaka describing Avīci as "four-doored, terrible" (It 3:4,10). The commentary to the *Majjhima* passages cited above also identifies that Mahāniraya with Avīci.

Avīci is so named because it is without respite or interruption in four ways. The beings there suffer continuously from burning, without any relief. The flames shooting from wall to wall and from floor to ceiling fill the entire space without a gap. The beings there are packed in like grains of flour, filling the entire one hundred *yojana* space so that the beings cannot find room in any posture and are continually injuring one another. Finally, just as one drop of molten copper on the tongue renders six drops of honey negligible, so does one moment of intense pain cancel out six neutral moments, thus making the experience of pain here perceived as continuous (Jāt 530). The last point is no doubt intended to reconcile the description of Avīci with Abhidhamma theory which requires some neutral mind moments in the mental continuum.

The dimensions of Avīci are either ten thousand *yojana* square (Sn-a 3:7) or one hundred,[424] and it may be inferred from the story of Devadatta's torment that it is one hundred *yojana* from top to bottom (Dhp-a 1:12). If this doesn't simply represent two divergent traditions, the discrepancy may mean that Avīci proper is a one hundred *yojana* iron-walled cube and that all the surrounding subsidiary *nirayas* cover ten thousand *yojana*. It is often cited as the lowest point of the cosmos. When the entire world-system or universe is referred to the phrase "from Avīci below to Bhavagga above" is frequently used. (*Bhavagga* simply means "the highest becoming" or "the pinnacle of existence.")[425] Likewise, the limits of the *kāmabhūmi*, the sense-desire realm, are given as from Avīci to the world of the Paranimmitavasavatti devas, (SN-a 14:12) and the range of *rūpa*, form, as from Avīci to the Akaniṭṭhabrahmalokaṃ (SN-a 35:199). Although there does not seem to be any reference to the precise location of Avīci in the Pali sources, the *Abhidharmakośa* states that it is twenty thousand *yojana* below Jambudīpa.[426]

Avīci is chiefly known for its terrible fire. The flames fill the entire space enclosed by the iron walls and blaze forth outside them for another hundred *yojana*. Anyone standing at that distance from the wall would have the eyes burnt out of his sockets. The fire of Avīci is far more powerful than earthly fire and a solid rock the size of a house would be consumed in an instant were it placed within those walls (Dhp-a 1: 10). There is a story of an elder bhikkhu who wished to rouse the fear of Avīci in a slack disciple. Using his psychic power, he drew a spark of fire from Avīci, no larger than a firefly, and it consumed a huge mass of firewood in a single moment (SN-a 22:55). Nevertheless, the

---

423 Bhikkhu Bodhi, NDB, 253-54.

424 Jāt 530. Also, the verse passage in MN 130 quoted above can be taken to mean it is only one hundred yojanas across.

425 For example DN-a 1, MN-a 92, SN-a 6:2m among many others.

426 AK 3:5, p. 456. Malalasekera cites a tradition that Avīci is seven hundred miles directly beneath the Bodhi Seat. See entry for Avīci in DPPN.

beings suffering there are not burnt up because of the power of their kamma (Dhp-a 1:10 & Mil 2–3:4,6 Eng. v1 p. 91f.).

There is an idiomatic phrase in Pali equivalent to the English "when hell freezes over." When something is improbable to the point of impossibility it is said to be as likely as "Avīci being as cool as a water-lily grove."[427] Nevertheless, rare occasions are recorded when the fires of Avīci were indeed mitigated. The fires of Avīci going out is one of the wonders attending the birth of the Buddha-to-be (DN-a 14). Also, at one time Mahākassapa visited Avīci, created a circle of coolness and sat on a lotus preaching to the inhabitants (AN-a 1:191).

The image we have of Avīci from the texts is of an iron cube, relatively small on the cosmic scale, filled completely with vast numbers of suffering beings continuously burning in a terrible supernaturally ferocious fire generated by their own evil kamma. This node of intensely concentrated suffering lies at the very base of the entire *saṃsāric* cosmos. It may be said to be its foundation stone.

[427] For example MN-a 115, referring to the chance that a sotapanna would follow an heretical teacher.

3:3:16 THE VETARAṆI RIVER

The caustic river referred to in the *Majjhima* description of *niraya* is named by the commentary to that passage as the "Vetaraṇi Nadi", the Vetaraṇi River. Under that name, this river features prominently in subsequent descriptions of *niraya*.

In the Nimi Jātaka, (Jāt 541) the righteous human king Nimi was taken by Mātali, the charioteer of the devas, to Tāvatiṃsa. On the way, he was given a tour of the *niraya* realms. They began by flying over the Vetaraṇi River.

> Mātali showed the king the hard passage of the Vetaraṇi River,
>
> A boiling mass of caustic stuff, hot with crests of flame.

> Mātali turned the chariot towards *niraya* and showed King Nimi the Vetaraṇi River, arisen through the action of heat generated by kamma. There, the *nirayapālas*, bearing various kinds of blazing weapons, slash at and beat the *nerayikasattas*. Unable to bear the torment of those blows, they fall into the Vetaraṇi. The banks of that river are bounded with creepers bearing thorns like spears. There the beings suffer for many thousands of years. They are torn to pieces by the blazing razor-sharp thorns. From below, hot iron spikes the size of palm-trees stand up. After spending a long time falling upon the thorn creepers, the beings are impaled upon the stakes like so many fish, and there they are cooked for a long time. The stakes burn, and the beings impaled on them burn. Further downstream from the stakes are iron-leaved lotuses, sharp as razors. When the *nerayikasattas* drop off the stakes, they come into the iron lotuses, and suffer painful feelings there for a long time. There is a rain of caustic water, the waters burn and the beings burn and give off smoke. The bed of the river underneath is covered in razors. The beings, wondering what the water below is like, they sink down and are cut to pieces by the razors. They endure great suffering, impossible to bear and cry aloud with great terror as they wander about in the river. Sometimes they go downstream, sometimes they go upstream. If they go near the bank, one of the *nirayapālas* spears them out like fish. The beings utter great cries in their torment as the *nirayapālas* lay them out on the blazing ground, force open their mouths and push in red-hot iron balls (Jāt 541).

The other name of Vetaraṇi is, as we have seen, the Khārodakā River which means "Caustic Waters." The word *khāra* can refer to lye, potash or any highly alkaline substance.[428] Something which burns, like lye, seems appropriate as the waters are said to "bear a razor-like sharpness" *(tiṇhadhārakhuradhāra)* (Sn 3:10). In contrast to the Jātaka account above, where the *nirayapālas* drive the hapless beings into the river, another version states that they come to the river on their own accord, seeing it as "like the Ganges" and full of clear refreshing water. Under the spell of this illusion, they attempt to take a drink and fall into it (Sn-a 3:10).

The Vetaraṇi is cited as the place of rebirth for abortionists. There those who cut up fetuses endure being cut up by the razor-like lotuses (Jāt 530). The Vetaraṇi is sometimes used as a synecdoche standing for *niraya* as a whole, or even for any kind of unfortunate birth. For instance, it is said of one who has made much good kamma that he "has crossed Yama's Vetaraṇi River and arrived in the place of the devas" (SN 1:33).

---

[428] See definition in PED.

3:3:17 THE EIGHT MAHĀNIRAYAS

The Saṃkicca Jātaka (Jāt 530) contains an attempt at a systematic list of the eight *nirayas*. The **Sañjīva** ("living") **Niraya** is so-called because there the *nirayapālas* continually chop and slice the *nerayikasattas* into small pieces with various blazing weapons again and again, and yet they still live. In the **Kāḷasutta** ("measuring string") **Niraya** the *nirayapālas*, shouting and jumping about, strike the beings with their weapons, throw them down and stretch them out on the hot ground. There, they are marked with a measuring line and hacked with hatchets into eight or sixteen pieces. The **Saṅghāta** ("knocking together") **Niraya** is where beings are crushed between two huge blazing mountains. There are two **Roruva** ("roaring") **Nirayas**, counted separately to make the total come to eight. These Nirayas are so-called because the beings there utter great cries of distress. In the **Jālaroruva** ("roaring net") **Niraya** beings are caught in an entangling brass net and tortured with flames which enter the nine orifices of the body and burn it up. The **Dhūmaroruva** ("roaring smoke") **Niraya** is filled with a caustic smoke which enters the nine orifices of the *nerayikasattas* and causes their bodies to emit steam. Avīci, here called **Mahāvīci** ("the great unremitting") **Niraya** has already been discussed at length. In the **Tāpana** ("roasting") **Niraya** the sufferers are impaled on stakes the size of palm tree trunks. The ground burns, the stakes burn and the beings burn. The beings there endure their long torment in enforced immobility. On the contrary, in **Patāpana** ("onward roasting") **Niraya** they are always in motion. The *nerayikasattas* there are forced with blows to climb a fiery mountain. When they reach the summit, a wind created by the force of their kamma blows them down again, head over heels. The ground below is covered with sharp stakes, and when they land they are pierced through.

Essentially the same list occurs in the Sarvastivādin text, the *Abhidharmakośa*. There it is stated that these *nirayas* are stacked one above the other with Avīci at the bottom followed in order by Saṃjīva, Kālasūtra, Saṃghāta, Raurava, Mahāraurava, Tapana and Pratāpana.[429] In the Pali sources there does not seem to be any clear reference to the spatial arrangement of the various *nirayas*.

---

429 AK 3:5, p.457. The spellings here are Sanskrit.

3:3:18 THE NIRAYAS IN THE KOKĀLIKA SUTTA

We have already had occasion to mention the story of Kokālika, the evil-minded bhikkhu who insulted Sāriputta and Moggallāna and was reborn for an immensely long time in the Paduma Niraya as a result. The canonical passage (AN 10:89) names ten *nirayas* with increasingly long life-spans. The commentary to this passage, however, belies the plain reading of the text and says these are not separate *nirayas*, but refer only to time periods spent in Avīci. This appears to be an attempt by the commentators to force a coherent scheme onto the original texts which do not really support this.

The names of the ten *nirayas*, according to the *Kokālika Sutta*, with tentative translations of their names, where possible, are:

1. Abbuda Niraya—"The Tumour *niraya*" or "The Fetus *niraya*"
2. Nirabbuda Niraya —"Free of Tumours *niraya*"
3. Ababa Niraya
4. Aṭaṭa Niraya
5. Ahaha Niraya
6. Kumuda Niraya —"White Water Lily *niraya*"
7. Sogandhika Niraya —"The *niraya* of Sweet Fragrance"
8. Uppalako Niraya —"The Blue Lotus *niraya*"
9. Puṇḍarīka Niraya —"The White Lotus *niraya*"
10. Paduma Niraya —"The Red Lotus *niraya*"

Each of these *nirayas* has a life-span twenty times that of the preceding one. We have seen that the life of a being in the Paduma Niraya is an immensely long one, many orders of magnitude greater than the lifetime of a universe either by ancient or modern reckoning.

This list, with its strangely ironic nomenclature, took on another meaning altogether in other schools of Buddhism. The *Abhidharmakośa* lists sixteen *nirayas*, eight hot and eight cold. The list of hot *nirayas* has been given above; the eight cold *nirayas* are obviously a variation of the list given in the *Kokālika Sutta*.

The Eight Cold Nirayas according to the *Abhidharmakośa*:

1. Arbuda
2. Nirabuda
3. Aṭaṭa
4. Hahauva
5. Huhuva
6. Utpala
7. Padma
8. Mahāpadma (AK 3:5, p. 459)

The names are said to derive either from the noises beings there make subjected to the intense cold ("*aṭaṭaṭa* … "), or from the shapes the bodies of the beings assume, like a lotus. The concept of cold nirayas is not found in the suttas or the oldest Pali commentaries, i.e. those of Buddhaghosa, but is mentioned in Dhammapāla's commentary to the *Udāna* (Ud-a 2:8).

3:3:19 LOHAKUMBHĪ NIRAYA

The *Lohakumbhī* ("copper cauldron") *Niraya* is gigantic cauldron filled to the brim with molten copper into which beings are thrown: (Sn-a 3:10)

> During the time of the Buddha Kassapa, when the life-span of humans was twenty thousand years, there lived in Bārāṇasi four rich young men who made a sport of lavishing their wealth upon the wives of other men and thereby seducing them. For twenty thousand years they thus carried on, committing many acts of adultery.
>
> When they died all four were born into Avīci Niraya and there suffered for the whole interval between two Buddhas. When they passed away from Avīci, the results of their bad kamma were not completely exhausted and they were reborn into a copper cauldron (*lohakumbhī*) sixty *yojana* in size. There they were boiled, rolling about like grains of rice in a cook-pot. They sank down for thirty thousand years until they touched the bottom of the cauldron, then rose up for another thirty thousand years before they reached the surface again. When they broke through the surface, the each of the four wished to utter a stanza, but it was impossible for them to utter more than one single syllable before they rolled over and began sinking to the bottom again (Dhp-a 5:1).

On two occasions, the four syllables "Du, Sa, No, So" were heard as terrible sounds in the night by human kings. Very long ago they were heard by Brahmadatta of Bārāṇasi and in the Buddha's time they were heard by Pasenadi of Kosala (Jāt 314). In both incidents, the brahmin advisers of the king said this indicated great danger and suggested a big sacrifice of animals and human victims as a preventive measure. These holocausts were prevented by the intervention of the Bodhisatta or the Buddha who saved the king from making terrible kamma. In Pasenadi's case, upon hearing the full explanation of the sounds, he also abandoned an evil desire to have another man's wife (Dhp-a 5:1 & Jāt 314). Versions or fragments of this story occur several times, with some variations, in the sources.[430] The Jātaka version has the four adulterers each born into a separate cauldron. In the Saṃyutta Commentary the place of their torment is named as the Nandopananda Lohakumbhī.

One more famous sufferer in Lohakumbī is Ajātasattu, the king of Magadha, who conspired with Devadatta and killed his father King Bimbisāra. He will be released after only a single journey to the bottom of the cauldron and back, sixty thousand years in all. His time will be cut short because he took refuge in the Triple Gem before the end of his life (DN-a 2).

In general, there is very little consistency of detail in the descriptions of Lohakumbhī. Sometimes the word seems to refer not to a separate *niraya*, but only to a particular mode of torture in an unspecified *niraya*. We have already seen that one of the preliminary tortures before being thrown into Avīci is boiling in a copper cauldron (MN 130). There neither is agreement as to the size of Lohakumbhī. While the *Dhammapada Commentary* gives it as sixty *yojana*, the *Sutta Nipāta Commentary* tells us that Lohakumbhī extends under the whole earth (*pathavipariyantika*), and is four hundred and twenty *yojana* in depth (Sn-a 3:10). The substance in the cauldron is said to be molten copper (ibid.) or "corrosive copper heated to boiling" (*pakkuthita khāralohodaka)* (Jāt 314).

Three stanzas from the *Sutta Nipāta* add further variety to the picture:

> Then they enter cauldrons of copper ablaze with fire;
>
> There they suffer for a long time jumping around in the flames.

[430] Besides Dhp-a 5:1 and Jāt 314 already cited, see SN-a 3:9 and Pv 4:15.

Then the evil doers are cooked in a mixture of pus and blood.

Whichever way they turn, they are soiled by the touch of the foul substance.

The water is the abode of worms, where the evil ones are cooked.

There is no place of refuge, as the cooking pots (*kapallā*) are all around. (Sn 3: 10)

As a final curiosity we may mention the explanation for the hot springs of Lake Tapodā near Rājagaha. It is said that a vast *petaloka* (realm of ghosts) surrounded the city and that the springs are fed by an underground stream which passes between two *mahālohakumbhinirayānas*, "great copper cauldron *nirayas*" (MN-a 133 & SN-a 1:20). This is a good example of the blurred boundaries between the realms which are often less clearly defined when we closely examine the details than they appear from neat summary lists.

3:3:20 LOKANTARA *NIRAYA*

One exceptional *niraya* is the *Lokantara Niraya*, "the *Niraya* Between-the-Worlds." The *cakkavālas* ("world-systems") are round at the base, bounded by a ring of tall iron mountains. These *cakkavāḷas* are infinite in number and extend horizontally through space in all directions. They are tightly spaced, and the rows are staggered, so that wherever three of them come together "like three cart-wheels," (DN-a 14) the iron mountain rings touch and a roughly triangular space is left between. It is in these empty spaces between the worlds that the Lokantara Nirayas are found.

This in-between place is a void abyss. There is nothing above, no ground below, only the universal water on which the world-systems rest and everywhere a profound darkness because the orbits of the suns and moons of the surrounding *cakkavālas* are lower than the tops of the iron mountains (ibid.). The beings that are born there have bodies three *gavutas* in size.[431] They are blind because no eye-consciousness can arise there. They cling like bats to the outer walls of the iron mountains, hanging upside-down (DN-a 14). Their world is extremely cold (MN-a 2).

For the most part, each being in Lokantara Niraya is totally alone, unaware that other beings even exist. However, on the four great occasions of a Buddha's life, when he descends into the womb, when he is born for the last time, when he attains Buddhahood and when he turns the Wheel of the Dhamma, a great light illuminates even Lokantara Niraya. The beings there are filled with wonder and exclaim, "other beings are born here too!" (DN 14)

Otherwise, their only contact with each other is accidental and fatal. As they creep along the surface of the mountain wall, on rare occasions two brush against each other in the dark. Each imagines that he has found something to eat. They struggle together and end up losing their grip on the wall, falling to the world-supporting waters (*lokasandhārakaudake*) below. Because of that water's extremely caustic nature, they are dissolved "like lumps of flour" (DN-a 14).

Kammic deeds that lead to rebirth in Lokantara Niraya include grave offences against one's mother or father, or against righteous *samaṇas* and brahmins, or habitual killing of others by the sword (AN-a 4: 127). However, Lokantara Niraya is especially associated with tenaciously holding to wrong views; this darkness of the mind results in the profounder darkness of the *niraya* (Jāt 545, Eng. 544). One late source states that this is the special *niraya* of the asuras.[432]

[431] One *gāvuta* equals one fourth of a *yojana*.

[432] *Buddhavaṃsa Nidānakathā*.

3:3:21 OTHER MISCELLANEOUS NIRAYAS

At one time, the Buddha was approached by a famous entertainer, Talapuṭa, the leader of a troupe who travelled about performing shows which featured singing, dancing and acting. He asked the Buddha if it was true what was said by the teachers of old in the actor's lineage, that those entertainers who delighted large crowds of people with truth and lies (*saccālikena*) would be reborn among the laughing devas (*pahāsānā devā*). The Buddha refused to answer at first, until asked for the third time, it being a rule often seen in the suttas, that a *Tathāgata* always answers when asked three times. The Buddha then stated that actors who by their performances lead beings further into lust, anger and delusion will end up being reborn into the Pahāso Niraya ("the laughing *niraya*") (SN 42:2). There, the *nirayapālas* sing and dance dressed in the manner of stage performers as they torture the former actors (SN-a 42:2).

In a parallel passage the Buddha is asked by a mercenary captain whether it is true that a soldier who fights well and dies in battle is reborn among the Parajitānā Devas ("the slain-by-another devas"). Once again, he is told after asking three times that one that lives by battle with thoughts of destruction and killing in his mind actually ends up reborn in the Parajitānā Niraya (SN 42:3). There, the beings armed with the five weapons, and bearing shields, mount chariots and are tortured by making continual battle upon each other (SN-a 42:3).

The commentary to both of these adjacent suttas states that these are not separate *nirayas*, but sections within Avīci. This is probably another attempt by the commentators to constrain the multiplication of *nirayas* and preserve some kind of coherent scheme.

3:3:22 THE ILLUSORY NATURE OF *NIRAYA*

Consider the following story taken from the Catudvāra Jātaka:

> Mittavindaka went to sea as a merchant. Because he had committed the evil kamma of striking his mother, the ship was becalmed in mid-ocean and would go no further. The sailors cast lots, determined Mittavindaka as the cause of the evil influence and cast him adrift on a raft. As soon as he was gone, a fair wind sprang up and the ship carried on its way.
>
> As for Mittavindaka, floating on his raft he came upon an island. There he saw a crystal palace with four beautiful women. These were *vemānikapetīs* ("mansion ghosts") who enjoyed seven days of heavenly bliss followed by seven days of peta-like misery.[433] For one week he enjoyed deva-like bliss in their company, but when they turned into petas he returned to his raft.
>
> Floating along, he came upon one island after another. The next had a palace of silver and eight maidens. These also were *vemānikapetīs* and when after seven days they lost their beautiful forms, turning into wretched *petīs*, Mittavindaka again took to his raft. In the same way he visited a gem palace with sixteen women and a golden palace with thirty-two. All turned into *petīs* after seven days.
>
> Leaving the island of the golden palace, his raft floated towards a city surrounded by a wall with four gates. In truth, this was an *ussada niraya*, where many beings suffered the results of their kamma. But to Mittavindaka it appeared as a city adorned with decoration. He entered the city, determined to make himself its king. There he saw one of the *nerayikasattas* with a razor-wheel upon his head. But to Mittavindaka it appeared as a lotus-crown. The five-fold bondage across the being's chest appeared to Mittavindaka as a decorated breast-plate, the blood trickling from his head as an anointment of red sandalwood and the suffering being's groans of agony sounded like sweet singing.
>
> Mittavindaka addressed the being, "Good sir, you have worn that lotus long enough! Give it to me." The other replied, "It is no lotus, but a razor-wheel." "Ha! You say that because you do not wish to give it up. Give it here!" The *nerayikasatta* thought to himself, "It must be that my kamma has reached its end. This fellow, like me, must have struck down his mother. Let him have the wheel!" He took off the razor-wheel and placed it on Mittavindaka's head. At that instant, the wheel crushed Mittavindaka down and he knew what it was. He cried aloud, "Take back the wheel! Take back the wheel!" But the other had disappeared. (Jāt 439)

This story illustrates in a vivid way several themes that we have seen throughout our examination of *niraya.* It is often stated that the flames and other tortures of *niraya* are generated by the kamma of the beings suffering there. Some early interpretations held that even the *nirayapālas* were illusory creations of kamma, and not real separate beings. The role of illusion tricking beings into suffering has been seen before, with the Vetaraṇi for instance seeming to be a cool refreshing river until the being goes to drink and falls into the caustic water filled with razor-like iron lotuses. In a deeper sense, we could say that all of *saṃsāra* is a kamma-created realm of illusion, but here in *niraya* it is more obviously so.

The story of Mittavindaka the merchant, with its dream-like quality is more than a little reminiscent of the Tibetan concept of a post-mortem journey through the *bardo* realms. One way of reading this story is to assume that Mittavindaka in fact drowned as soon as he was tossed from the ship and was driven deeper and deeper into realms of suffering by his own lust.

---

433 See § 3:3,5 for a discussion of *vemānikapetas*.

3:3:23 ASURAS

The *asuras* are a separate class or race of beings who dwell at the foot of Mt Sineru and are perpetually at war with the devas. In English translation they are sometimes referred to as "titans" or as "anti-gods." The theme of a war in heaven, and the overthrow of an older race of gods by a new generation, is found in many Indo-European cosmologies. In Greek myth we have the Olympians led by Zeus battling the titans, and in the Norse version it is the gods of Asgard against the storm-giants. This would seem to indicate that the motif is a very ancient one, pre-dating the expansion of the Aryans out of their original homeland.

The name *asura* is found already in the Ṛg Veda. In the earliest times it was no more than a general term applied to the gods. This is mirrored in the Persian *ahura*, which refers to the good deities, whose chief is Ahura Mazda. In India, however, the asuras came to be identified as a separate class opposed to the devas, who were also called *sura* so that we have the conflict between the suras and the asuras, "gods" and "anti-gods." The devas or suras came to represent the forces of light and spiritual progress while the asuras were the partisans of darkness and the lower appetites.[434]

The Buddhist version of the asuras is close to this latter conception. They were a race of deities older than the devas, the original inhabitants of Tāvatiṃsa. They are definitely portrayed as of a lower spiritual nature than the devas. A passage in the *Aṅguttara Commentary* describes the devas as virtuous, beautiful and pleasing whereas the asuras are simply "vile" (*bībhaccha)* (AN-a 4: 91). The asuras are listed among the four unhappy states of rebirth together with the beings in *niraya*, animals and petas (MN-a 62). The asuras as portrayed in the Pali sources are rough, prone to anger, and not very bright or courageous.

The separation of the asuras and devas, and the origin of their conflict is part of the story of Magha and his companions who were reborn as Sakka and the rest of the Thirty-Three.[435] When Sakka and the rest appeared in Tāvatiṃsa, the asuras were already dwelling there. The story of what happened next is told several times in the commentaries, with some variations.

The Jātaka Commentary version is the simplest:

> At that time, the asuras were dwelling in Tāvatiṃsa. Sakka, king of the devas, said, "I will not share this kingship." He gave the asuras a divine drink (*dibbapāna*) which made them drunk and taking them by the feet threw them down Mt Sineru. (Jāt 31)

The story as told in the Dhammapada Commentary is a little different:

> The asuras then lived in Tāvatiṃsa. They said, "New devas have been born!" They prepared some divine drink (*dibbapāna*). Sakka made sure that his own company did not drink any. The asuras drank as much as they liked. Sakka said, "I will not share the kingship with such as these," and gave order to take the asuras by the feet and throw them head first down to the great ocean. (Dhp-a 2: 7)

The Majjhima Commentary adds more detail:

> At that time the asura folk (*asuragaṇā*) lived in the Tāvatiṃsa deva-realm. They were alike to the devas in appearance and in life-span. When they saw Sakka and his company they prepared a drinking festival (*mahāpāna*) to greet the newly arisen devas. Sakka instructed his companions: "We made our own merit, it was not done with these others. Do not drink the wine (*gaṇḍapāna*). It will make you intoxicated." So they did not. The foolish asuras drank it and fell into a drunken sleep. Sakka, the king of the devas, ordered his

434 See Alain Daniélou, *The Gods of India*, chap. 10.

435 See the story of Sakka in § 3:5,16.

followers to take them by the feet and throw them down head first to the foot of Mt Sineru. (MN-a 37)

In the version from the Saṃyutta Commentary we learn why they are termed asura:

> After their death, the thirty-three companions arose in the deva-realm. The previous devas (*sesadevatā*) saw the great splendour of the newcomers, surpassing theirs, and said, "New devas have arisen!" The resident devas prepared some fragrant beverage (*gandhapāna*). Sakka ordered his own company, "My dears, do not drink any of this. Drinking it will make you intoxicated." They obeyed. The resident devas brought out the drink in golden vessels and drank as much as they liked. Having drunk, they fell asleep on the golden earth. Sakka said, "Take them by the feet." Sakka's companions threw the resident devas to the foot of Mt Sineru. Half-way down the slope of Mt Sineru, they regained consciousness and cried out, "Good sirs! We won't drink liquor! We won't drink liquor!" (*na suraṃ pivimha*) and so they acquired the name of *asura* (*a-sura* = "no liquor.") (SN-a 11:1)

This is certainly a contrived derivation, a device common to the commentaries. In any case there doesn't seem to be any further reference to the later drinking habits of the asuras, so it is not possible to determine if such hung-over declarations have any more weight among asuras than they do among humans.

At the bottom of Mt Sineru a ten-thousand *yojana* realm arose for the asuras to live in, by the force of their kamma, the *asurabhavana* (SN-a 11:1). The principal feature of this realm is the *Cittapāṭali* ("trumpet-flower") Tree which grows there and lasts for an entire kappa (AN-a 1: 322). When this tree flowered, the asuras knew by the difference in its blossoms that this was not the deva's *Pāricchattaka* Tree and that they were no longer in Tāvatiṃsa (MN-a 37 & SN-a 11:1). This would indicate that otherwise the *asurabhavana* resembled the original appearance of Tāvatiṃsa. (It should be noted that many of the defining features of that realm such as the Nandana Grove, the Vejayanto Palace and the Sudhamma Hall arose after the expulsion of the asuras by the force of kamma generated by Magha-Sakka and his companions).[436] The *asurabhavana* is located at the very bottom of Mt Sineru, under the ocean, (Sn-a 3: 11) and the asuras had to cleave the waters of the sea in two in order to ascend Mt Sineru and attack the devas (SN-a 11:1). The asuras are also said to keep pavilions (*maṇḍapādi*) by the shore beside the place where Mt Sineru rises from the ocean which they use for enjoyment (Ud-a 5:5).

It should not be thought that the asuras are in any sense aquatic beings.[437] The waters of the ocean are for them only a gateway to their realm, as we saw in the case of the nāgas. It is not only that their realm resembles the deva's world, but the asuras themselves are said to be like the devas in life-span, appearance, essence (*rasa*, lit. "taste"), power and wealth (SN 11:1). Therefore, we might imagine the devas looking down from Tāvatiṃsa and seeing the asura realm as if it were their own distorted mirror image reflected in the surface of the great ocean. The devas embody the epitome of worldly sensuality, and the asuras represent the opposite defilements of hatred, jealously and anger, with the human realm mid-way between the two (Sn-a 3: 11).

Having woken up in the asura-realm, the asuras at first did not realize that they weren't in Tāvatiṃsa anymore, but when they did, immediately went to war in order to try and win back their old home.

> (Seeing the Cittapāṭali Tree and not recognizing the blossoms) the asuras said to one another, "This is not the deva-city! There are the coral-tree (*pāricchattaka*) flowers, here there are trumpet-flowers (*cittapāṭali*). The old Sakka[438] has deceived us, making us drink liquor. We will seize the deva-city, let us go there and make war!"

436 For details see § 3:3:23.
437 Although the commentary to the *Māhasamaya Sutta*, DN 20, does call the asuras "ocean-dwellers", *mahāsamuddavāsino*.
438 *Jarasakko*—"old Sakka", an odd phrase considering that Sakka and his companions represented a newer generation of devas.

Mounting elephants, horses and chariots, taking up shields of gold, silver and gems they made ready for battle. Sounding the asura-drum they cleaved the waters of the great ocean in two and rose up. They poured up the slope of Mt Sineru like ants up an ant-hill. (SN-a 11:1)

Sakka, having heard, "The asuras are rising up!" went forth to the surface of the ocean to do battle. There he was defeated and began to flee in the one *yojana* and a half long Chariot of Victory along the southern face of the sea. Then the chariot, rising from the ocean entered into the Simbali Grove (the dwelling place of the *supaṇṇas*). The progress of the chariot cut down the Simbali Grove like so many reeds and the trees tumbled into the ocean. The young of the *supaṇṇas* falling to their destruction in the ocean let out a great cry.

Sakka asked Mātali (the charioteer), "Dear Mātali, what sound is that, which rouses such great compassion?"

"Sire, the passage of your chariot is cutting and tossing down the Simbali Grove and the young *supaṇṇas* are making that cry in fear of death."

Sakka replied, "Dear Mātali, I will not be the cause of their misery. Let us not for the sake of dominion (*issariyaṃ nissāya*) cause the destruction of life. For their sake, we will give up even our lives, surrendering to the asuras. Turn the chariot around." Hearing these words, Mātali the charioteer turned around to seek another route back to the deva world.

The asuras, seeing the chariot of Sakka turn around, said, "Surely Sakkas from other world-systems (*aññehi cakkavālehi*) are coming. Having received reinforcement, they are making the chariot turn around!" In fear of death, they fled back to the asura-realm. (Jāt 31)

After the victory of the devas, the Vejayanta ("Victory") Palace arose in Tāvatiṃsa by the force of the devas' good kamma. At this time too, Sakka established the five lines of defence against the asuras. First were the nāgas, to guard the approach through the ocean, then the *supaṇṇas* on the lower slopes of Sineru followed by the *kumbhaṇḍas*, the yakkhas and finally, the Four Great Kings. Only if the asuras managed to fight through all of these would Sakka himself, or one of his sons, come forth to do battle (SN-a 11:1). As a final safe-guard, Sakka had placed around the deva-city statues of himself as Inda wielding the thunder-bolt weapon. These are sufficient to terrify the asuras into fleeing back to their own city (AN-a 9, 39).

The war of the asuras against the devas is a perpetual one, it breaks out into active hostilities whenever the Cittapāṭali Tree flowers and reminds the asuras of what they have lost (MN-a 37). It is, however, a hopeless struggle. The two cities of the devas and of the asuras are said to be impregnable. When the asuras are stronger, the devas flee into their city and close the gates and "even hundreds of thousands" of asuras cannot storm the walls, likewise when the devas are stronger they cannot force their way into the asura city (SN-a 11:1). Despite the ferocious appearance and angry nature of the asuras, these wars are very low in casualties.

However, these battles are not fought with the cutting of skin or hide, or the flowing of blood. They fight only like young forest rams do, seeking to raise fear and trembling in their foes (ibid.). They make war like cow-herd boys, beating one another with sticks. (AN-a 9:39)

In any case, according to the *Abhidharmakośa*, the devas are hard to kill. They can only be killed by cutting off their heads, or cutting them in half through the waist. If their arms or legs are cut off, they can regenerate. The same passage states that devas never kill one another.[439] It is not stated whether these rules apply to the asuras as well.

[439] AK 4:3 p.668. See also Poussin's note 405, p. 745.

The behaviour of humans can have an effect on the outcome of these wars. When human morality is generally good, more people take a higher rebirth and "swell the ranks of the deva host." However, during times when human behaviour is shameless and immoral more become reborn in the asura realm, increasing the size of their army (DN 18 & 19). At such times, the devas are disappointed because there are not enough of them to play a game of "constellation" (*nakkhatta*).[440]

On rare occasions, the asura-deva wars may impinge on the human realm.

> At one time a certain man was sitting on the bank of the Sumāgadhāya Lotus Pond, near Rājagaha. While he was sitting there, he saw a four-fold army (infantry, elephants, cavalry and chariots) enter into a lotus plant. "I must be mad! I must be insane! I have seen that which does not exist in the world!" (SN 56:41)

Speaking of this incident, the Buddha explained that the man was not mad, that what he saw was actually so. The devas had defeated the asuras in a battle and the asuras in their terror had fled back to the asura realm through the lotus plant, to the utter confusion of the devas (ibid.). Sometimes the impact of the asura wars on humans is more direct, and harmful. It is said that there are seers living by the shores of the great ocean, and that when the asuras are defeated in battle and fleeing back to their own realm they pass through the hermitages of these seers. The asuras believe that the seers are devotees of Sakka, and assist him with their advice. Being enraged, the asuras on their way through destroy the leaf-huts, walk-ways and fruit-trees of the seers (SN 11:10).

[440] AN-a 3:37. No details of this game are given, but it seems to require a large retinue of *accharas*, see the commentary to the *Suvīra Sutta*, SN-a 11:1.

3:3:24 ASURINDA—LORDS OF THE ASURA

Three asuras are particularly named in the texts and called *asurajeṭṭhaka* "elders of the asuras" and *asurinda*, "lords of the asuras." These are Vepacitti, Rāhu and Pahārāda (AN-a 8:19).

Vepacitti is said to be the most senior of all the asuras (*asurānaṃ sabbajeṭṭhako)* (SN-a 11:4). His name might be rendered as "broken mind."[441] Originally, his name was Sambara:

> Once, at a time when the asuras were making ready for war, some righteous seers living near the ocean approached Sambara lord of the asuras, to ask for a promise of safety (*abhayadakkhiṇaṃ*, lit. "a gift of no fear"). Sambara replied that he would not give safety to the seers, calling them wicked partisans of Sakka. He said he would give them only fear.
>
> The seers therefore cursed Sambara and left. After receiving their curse, Sambara was seized by terror three times during the night (SN 11:10). Each time, he sprung up screaming as if he were struck by a hundred spears. The commotion was heard all over the ten thousand *yojana* wide realm of the asuras, and they all wondered "what has happened?" Sambara told them that nothing had happened, and they comforted him, "Do not fear, great king," and stayed with him until dawn. From that night he suffered from the sickness of a broken mind (*cittaṃ vepati*) and therefore was given the name Vepacitti (SN-a, 11:10).

Vepacitti is possessed of a powerful magic spell, called the Sambari Spell (*sambarimāya*) . Exactly what this spell does is unclear, but the commentary says it was the Sambari Spell which was used when the asura army escaped through a lotus plant (SN-a 56:41). It is also associated with fraud and deceit (SN-a 11:23) so may be a powerful spell of transformation. Sakka once offered to cure Vepacitti of his madness if he would teach him the Sambari Spell. Vepacitti consulted the other asuras but they forbade him to do so, fearing that Sakka who was already causing them enough trouble, would become even more powerful (SN 11:23). One oddity of this encounter is that the relevant sutta ends with a stanza spoken by Vepacitti where he tells Sakka that sorcerers go to *niraya*, as Sambara did, for one hundred years (ibid.). Since, as we have seen, Sambara is a previous name of Vepacitti himself, this verse is hard to explain. Perhaps Vepacitti was speaking figuratively, and meant that his madness was like being in *niraya*.

Vepacitti and Sakka have an ambiguous relationship. While they are the monarchs of mutually antagonistic realms, often at war, they are also in-laws, Sakka having married Vepacitti's daughter Sujā. The commentary says that sometimes they are enemies, and sometimes they travel about together (SN-a 11:9). The texts recount several episodes featuring the interaction of these two.

> At one time, after the devas had defeated the asuras in battle and captured Vepacitti the asura king, they bound him hand and foot and neck and placed him in the Sudhamma Hall. Whenever Sakka, king of the devas, entered or left the hall Vepacitti abused and reviled him, "You are a thief! An idiot! A fool! A bandit! You are a camel! A cow! A donkey! You are going to hell, to an animal birth! There will be no good destiny for you; you are bound for a lower rebirth! Old Sakka, you will not be victorious forever. One day the asuras will win, and then you shall lie in misery by the door in the asura realm." (SN-a, 11:4)

The bonds which held Vepacitti were said to be only in his mind, (ibid.) and this is made clear in another similar episode.

441 Assuming a probable derivation of *vepa-* from *vipāṭeti*, "to tear asunder." However, the equivalent asura in the Vedas is called *Vipracitti*, "The Sagacious," see Daniélou, *Gods of India*, p. 315.

After the defeat of the asuras, Vepacitti was bound hand and foot and neck and placed in the Sudhamma Hall. Whenever Vepacitti thought, "The devas are righteous, the asuras are unrighteous" his bonds would be released and he would be furnished with the five sense pleasures. Whenever he thought "The asuras are righteous, the devas are unrighteous" he would once again find himself bound hand and foot (SN 35:201). The bonds of Vepacitti were subtle like lotus thread or spider web, they were not cut by Sakka's knife or ax, but by Vepacitti's own mind. By his mind was he bound, by his mind was he freed. (SN-a 35:201)

This story was told by the Buddha with the purpose of comparing Vepacitti's bondage with that of Māra, which he said is even more subtle. There is one other mention of the magical binding of Vepacitti:

At one time Sakka king of the devas had gone into seclusion and the thought arose in his mind, "I should not do harm even to my enemies." Vepacitti the king of the asuras knew the thought which had arisen in the deva's mind. Later, when Sakka saw Vepacitti approaching he cried out, "Stop Vepacitti, you are caught!" and the asuras was bound hand and foot and neck. Vepacitti said, "Dear sir, do not abandon the thought which previously arose in your mind." Sakka made Vepacitti promise not to do any harm and then released him.[442]

One instance of the two divine in-laws travelling together concerns their visit to some seers in the forest, and highlights the differences in their character:

Once in the past Sakka and Vepacitti went together to see some righteous seers in the forest. Vepacitti entered the hermitage through the main gate, wearing his sandals with a sword at his side and a parasol over his head, treating those seers with disrespect. Sakka took off his sandals, gave his sword to another and put down his parasol, entering the hermitage through a lesser door. He treated those seers with proper respect. (SN 11:9)

At another time, a war was averted when Vepacitti proposed, and Sakka agreed, to settle matters by a debate, "a victory by good speech" (*subhāsita jayo*). Each of the two leaders were to speak some stanzas, and the winner would be chosen by a panel (*pārisajja*) jointly chosen by the devas and the asuras. Sakka insisted that Vepacitti go first, as he was the elder of the two. The commentary says this was a clever ploy by Sakka, because the person who goes last has the advantage in a debate. Vepacitti's verses spoke about how fools must be punished to restrain them, whereas Sakka spoke in praise of patience saying that restraint in the face of angry abuse is true strength. He was judged the winner (SN 11:5).

Rāhu is a very important cosmological figure, the being that is responsible for eclipses. In the Vedic version, Rāhu was an asura who was caught drinking the gods' soma and Viṣṇu cut off his head which now periodically swallows the sun or moon in its impotent rage. Rāhu is recognized as the eighth planet in the Hindu astrological system.[443] Although this planet is invisible, its movements can be mathematically calculated to predict the occurrence of eclipses.[444]

The Buddhist Rāhu is a very large and powerful asura with his head still very much on his shoulders. He is called the largest of all beings (AN 4: 15). The Pali says he is first among the *attabhāvī*, lit. "those possessed of self-being." The commentary glosses with *attabhāvavanta*, which might be rendered as meaning that he has the greatest limit to his being, or simply, the greatest size. Rāhu is 8,400 *yojana* in height. His chest is 1200 *yojana* across, the palms of his hands and the soles of his feet are 300 *yojana* wide, his finger joints are each 50 *yojana* long, the space between his

442 SN 11:7. some details added from the commentary.

443 Strictly speaking, Rāhu is not a "planet" but is one of nine *grahā* in the Vedic astrological system; together with the classical seven planets, they included two eclipse nodes; Rāhu and Ketu, being the two halves of the primordial demon slain by Vishnu. See "Nine Planets: Nava Grahas?' *Devasthanam*, Accessed at http://sanskrit.org/nine-planets-nava-grahas on 15.3.2018..

444 Daniélou, p. 315-316. Cf. the similar conception in Sumerian-Babylonian astronomy, *Nibiru*.

eyebrows is 50 *yojana* across, his forehead is 300 *yojana* across and his head is 900 *yojana* long.[445] When Rāhu stands in the great ocean the water comes up only to his knees and he thinks, "They always say this ocean is very deep, but how can it be called deep? The water doesn't even cover my knees!" (DN-a 15) For a long time, Rāhu avoided going to see the Buddha, thinking that even if he bent down he would not be able to see such a small person. When at last Rāhu did go to visit the Buddha, the Blessed One was lying on a low bed in his perfumed chamber. Rāhu found that he had to bend his neck upward in order to see him, and he was so moved by this display of power that he immediately became one of the Buddha's followers (DN-a 4 & MN-a 95).

The following is a description of how Rāhu causes eclipses:

> Seeing the brilliance of the sun or the moon, Rāhu becomes jealous. Having descended into their path, he stands with his mouth open. For the three-hundred *yojana* big solar or lunar *vimāna*, it is as if they were plunged into *mahānaraka* ("the great hell").The devatas living in the *vimāna* are seized with the fear of death and all cry out at once. Sometimes he just covers the *vimāna* with his hand, or his jaw or touches it with his tongue. Sometimes he holds it in his mouth with his cheeks puffed out, as if to eat it. But Rāhu is not able to obstruct the forward motion of the sun or moon. If he were to try, either the *vimāna* would break his head into pieces or he would be cast down. So, Rāhu is forced to move along with the sun or moon. (SN-a 2:10)

It may be surmised that when Rāhu takes the whole sun or moon in his mouth, a total eclipse occurs and that the other means of covering refer to partial eclipses. The sub-commentary explains that the irresistible force of the sun and moon is because their motion is determined by the law of kamma.[446]

There are two short back-to-back suttas in the *Devaputtasaṃyutta* of the Saṃyutta Nikāya which describe a lunar and a solar eclipse. Rāhu seizes the moon or the sun and the deva calls on the Buddha for refuge. The Buddha speaks a verse, ordering Rāhu to release his captive. Rāhu does so, then flees in terror to Vepacitti,

(Vepacitti -) Why, Rāhu, did you come in a hurry?

Why did you release Candimā (or Suriya)?

Having come as if in shock,

Why do you stand there frightened?

(Rāhu -) My head would have split in seven parts,

While living I would have found no ease,

If, when chanted over by the Buddha's verse,

I had not let go of Candimā (or Suriya).[447]

Rāhu can also affect the weather. Specifically, he is listed among the causes of drought because at times he gathers the rain in his hand and casts it into the sea.[448]

There is much less to be said about the third *asurinda*, **Pahārāda**. The only incident which includes any detail about him states that after the Buddha's awakening Pahārāda formed an intention to go see him, but procrastinated for

---

445 AN-a 4: 15. There are similar descriptions in DN-a 4 and SN-a 2:10 with some differences in detail.
446 SN-ṭ 2:10. See Bhikkhu Bodhi, CDB, footnote 158, page 388.
447 SN 2:9 & 2:10. Bhikkhu Bodhi's translation. CDB, p. 145-146.
448 AN 5: 197. Malalasekera in the DPPN says Rāhu uses the water to cool his body.

twelve years, saying all the time "I will go today, I will go tomorrow." When at last he did go, the Buddha spoke the *Pahārādasutta* to him, which concerned the eight wonderful qualities of the ocean in which the asuras find delight, used as metaphors for the eight wonderful qualities of the Dhamma (AN-a 8:19).

The *Mahāsamaya Sutta* (DN 20) which contains a long list in verse of beings who came to visit the Buddha, names a few additional great asuras. Besides Vepacitti, Pahārāda and Rāhu there are named Sucitti, Bali and Veroca. However, the commentary says that Veroca is another name for Rāhu. These characters are nothing more than names; no additional details are given except that Bali was Veroca's nephew and that he had a hundred sons all named Veroca after their uncle.

3:3:25 LOWER ASURAS—THE KĀLAKAÑJIKA

The same verse of the *Mahāsamaya Sutta* cited above also mentions two special classes of asura, the *dānaveghasā* and the *kālakañjikā*.[449] The commentary to the *Mahāsamaya Sutta* (DN-a 20) tells us that the *dānaveghasas* are archers; they do not seem to be mentioned elsewhere in the texts.

The ***kālakañjikas*** are a lower race of asura. They are very horrible (*mahābhisma*) (ibid.) in appearance:

> They have little flesh and blood, just like a dried up leaf. Their eyes stick out from their head like a crab's. Their mouth is like the eye of a needle on the top of their head and they go about bent over to find their food. (DN-a 24)
>
> Their body is all skin and bones and they suffer greatly from the heat and the cold. (DN-a 22)

They are also said to suffer greatly from thirst. There is mention of some *kālakañjika* asuras trying to drink from the Ganges, but the water boiled away when they approached and in the end they had to beg some passing bhikkhus to sprinkle water into their mouths (SN-a 22:79).

There is a discrepancy in the sources regarding the size of *kālakañjika* asuras. In some places they are said to have bodies of sixty or eight *hattha*. (A *hattha* is the distance from elbow to fingertip, about one and a half feet or a cubit).[450] This would make them huge in human terms but much smaller than devas or the higher asuras. Elsewhere, they are said to have, like the devas, a three *gāvuta* body (there are four *gāvuta* to the *yojana*) (DN-a 24). However, since they are said to vary in appearance, (AN-a 7, 44) this may not be a contradiction.

There was a somewhat pedantic controversy in early Buddhism as to whether living beings should be classified into five or six *gati* (stations of rebirth). To the canonical five, *niraya*, petas, animals, humans and devas, some schools added the asuras as a sixth. This debate is taken up in the *Kathāvatthu* ("Book of Debates") where the Theravāda proponent argues for five based on such sutta references as MN 12, where the Buddha tells Sāriputta, "There are the five *gati*." The argument goes on to divide the asuras: the higher type, those of Vepacitti's company (*vepacittiparisā*) are to be grouped with the devas, while the *kālakañjika* asuras are too classified as petas. Among the arguments it is said that the higher asuras intermarry with the devas, while the *kālakañjikas* do so with the petas (Kv 8:1). Each type of asura resembles either devas or petas in appearance, enjoyment, nutriment and life-span, and the commentary goes on to detail this:

> To begin with the *kālakañjikas*, they resemble the petas in having an appearance which is horrible, deformed and ugly. They have the same kind of sex-life as the petas. Like the petas, their food consists of saliva, mucus, pus and blood. Their life-spans have the same limit. They give and receive each other's maidens in marriage.
>
> The higher asuras resemble the devas in having a body which is beautiful, pleasing and radiant. Like the devas, they are possessed of the five sense pleasures. They eat a similar pure food (*sudhābhojana*) as the devas. (Kv-a 8:1)

There are several other texts which say that the *kālakañjikas* are "like the petas" (AN-a 7:44, UDa 2:8). The *kālakañjikas* who begged the bhikkhus for water, mentioned above, identified themselves when asked as petas ("*petohamasmi, bhante.*") (SN-a 22:79) We have seen before that the various classifications of beings which seem so definite in summary lists are often full of overlapping and doubtful cases when we examine the details. Nevertheless,

---

449 There are several variant spellings of this word—*kālakañcā kālakañcikā kālakañjakā kālakañjikā* are all found.

450 DN-a 22. AN-a 7:44. SN-a 46:51.

it is rather difficult to see why the *kālakañjikas* are classed as asuras at all.

Another problem of classification arises with the beings called ***dānavas***. The pre-Buddhist Vedas identify them with a class of lower asura, degraded because of their cruel and lustful natures, and so called because their original mother was the asura Danu.[451] Modern Buddhist writers and translators often define *dānava* as simply another name for asura and usually add the derivation from Danu.[452] However, there does not seem to be any passage in the Pali canon or commentaries which identifies *dānavas* with asuras or with anyone called Danu, and it is to be doubted whether this identification was made at all by Buddhists in the centuries during which these texts were composed. The revival of the Vedic notion can probably be traced to the *Abhidhānappadīpikā,* a twelfth century work composed in Sri Lanka which was cited by Malalasekera in his influential reference work the *Dictionary of Pali Proper Names* and therefore picked up by other modern writers.

Only two Jātaka stories feature *dānavas*, Jātakas no. 436 and 519. In both of these the *dānava* is portrayed as an earth-bound demonic or ogre-like being that lusts after human women. In both cases the being is also called *dānava-rakkhasa,* a *rakkhasa* being another monster originating in Vedic lore but in the Pali stories almost synonymous with a yakkha. Both of these stories contain archaic features which may indicate a pre-Buddhist source.

Finally, one reference which would strongly indicate that *dānavas* were not seen by the early Buddhists as asuras is in the description of the five lines of defence set up by Sakka around Tāvatiṃsa as described above. The third line is composed of *kumbhaṇḍas* and in the Jātaka version (Jāt 31) the text defines them as *dānavarakkhasas*. It would seem unlikely that asuras of any sort would serve as defenders of Tāvatiṃsa.

---

451 Daniélou, *Gods of India*, p. 307-308.

452 See DPPN under *Danu* and *dānava*. See also Horner's translation of the *Milindapañha*, vol. 1, p. 215, note 3, and Rouse's translation of the Jātakas, Jāt 436, where "asura" is used several times in the English text but not found in the Pali which uses *dānava* or *dānavarakkhasa* throughout.

CHAPTER FOUR—MISCELLANEOUS BEINGS

3:4:1 MISCELLANEOUS BEINGS

The tidy scheme of the five destinations of rebirth (*niraya*, peta, animal, human, deva) (DN 33) fails to account for several classes of being. We have already looked at the asuras, which are recognized by the tradition as being hard to classify. We might also note that any organizational scheme fails in many individual cases, as we have seen examples of beings who are considered as minor devas or as petas or yakkhas interchangeably. The only way to make sense of it is to recognize that the cosmos is a very complicated and messy place and any summary can only serve as a partial explanation. We shall now consider a few more kinds of beings who fall between the classifications, beginning with the yakkhas.

3:4:2 YAKKHAS

The category of *yakkha* (Skt. *yakṣa*) is especially problematic in this regard. The word is sometimes used so loosely that it may be taken as simply meaning "a being."[453] The distinctions between yakkhas and the lower level of devas, and the better sort of petas are especially blurry. While this should be borne in mind when encountering the word *yakkha* in the literature, it is also true that there is a specific race of beings known by that name, and it is the yakkhas properly so-called that we will be discussing here. These are fierce and monstrous beings, often possessing great power. They are usually malevolent, but when tamed by the Buddha or one of the arahants, they can become protectors of the Dhamma. In this capacity, an army of yakkhas forms the fourth (of five) lines of defence of Tāvatiṃsa against the asuras. These yakkhas are said to be "intoxicated by battle" (*yuddhasoṇḍa)* (Jāt 31). The yakkhas are in general subject to King Vessavaṇa,[454] one of the Cātumahārājika devas and Great King of the North, but some are identified as "being of Māra's faction" (SN-a 10:2).

In the Jātaka stories and other literature of the commentarial period the yakkhas are almost always depicted as fierce, magically powerful beings who seek to capture and devour unwary travellers. The picture in the suttas is more complex. In the Āṭānāṭiya Sutta, Vessavaṇa, in his capacity as king of the yakkhas, tells the Buddha that although there are some yakkhas who have faith in the Buddha and his teaching, the majority do not, because they find the keeping of moral precepts "distasteful and unpleasant" (DN 32). Later in the same sutta, Vessavaṇa goes on to state that "some non-human beings ... are fierce, wild and terrible. They heed neither the Great Kings nor their officers, nor their attendants. Just as the bandit-chiefs ... so do they behave."[455] But, he goes on to say, if a bhikkhu dwelling in a remote place is attacked by one of these, he may call out for succour to "the great yakkhas, their commanders and commanders-in-chief saying 'This yakkha has seized me, has hurt me, has harmed me, injured me, and will not let me go!" (ibid.)

There then follows a list of forty names of those great yakkhas one may call upon in such circumstances. This list of righteous yakkha chiefs demonstrates the point made previously about the blurring of categories in the source material, and the vagaries inherent in the term *yakkha*. Most of the names occur only here, or here and in a similar list of beings in the *Mahāsamaya Sutta*, (DN 20) and we have in these cases no other information about them. A few are names known from other texts as important yakkhas, notably Āḷavaka and Puṇṇaka. At least six of the "yakkha chiefs", however, are clearly identified elsewhere as devas of Tāvatiṃsa: Inda, Soma, Varuṇa, Pajāpati, Mātali and Pajunna. There is also Mucalinda, a nāga lord, and Janesabha which is probably a variant form of Janavasabha, the name of the *gandhabba* who was the reborn King Bimbisāra. In the text of the *Mahāsamaya* itself one of these "yakkhas", Cittasena, is identified as a *gandhabba*.

The kind of trouble that unreformed yakkhas could cause is well illustrated by the following episode taken from the *Udāna*:

> On a moonlit night, the elder Sāriputta was sitting outdoors, deep in *samādhi*. Two yakkhas happened to be flying through the air overhead. One of the yakkhas, seeing the moonlight reflected on Sāriputta's freshly shaven head, said to his companion: "It occurs to me, friend, to strike a blow on that bhikkhu's head."
>
> The other was aghast: "Do not do so friend! That is a *samaṇa* of very great potency." But the first yakkha did not heed his companion's warning and descending upon Sāriputta he struck the bhikkhu a mighty blow that could have felled a bull elephant. Immediately that yakkha crying out "I am burning!" fell into Mahāniraya.

[453] For example, Sakka is referred to as "that yakkha" by Moggallāna in MN 37.
[454] We shall examine this complex character in the section on the Cātumahārājika devas in § 3:5,6.
[455] DN 32, Maurice Walshe's translation, LDB, p. 471

It happened that Moggallāna was coming along the road at just this moment and witnessed the entire episode with his divine eye (*dibbacakkhu*) and when Sāriputta emerged from his meditation he asked him how he felt. "I am well friend, but I do have a slight head-ache."

"Marvellous it is, friend Sāriputta, marvellous it is that a mighty yakkha can strike a blow upon your head which would fell a bull elephant and you have only a slight head-ache."

"Marvellous it is, friend Moggallāna, that with your divine eye you can see the yakkhas! As for myself, I cannot see even a *paṃsupisācaka*!"[456]

The invisibility of yakkhas may be something they can control. In one story, a *yakkhinī* is clearly seen by the palace guards as she snatched the royal prince with the intent of eating him. However, she developed affection for the baby when it began to suckle her breast and she raised him as a yakkha, living with him in the charnel ground and feeding on human corpses. The problem was that the boy, being actually human, was unable to conceal his form from sight like his adopted mother, the *yakkhinī*. She gave him this power by feeding him "a certain root" (*eka mūla*) (Jāt 513). The implication was that she herself could naturally become invisible without external assistance.

In the following story, we see an example of a yakkha being converted to the Dhamma and even attaining stream-entry.

At one time the Buddha was staying at Taṃkitmañca, which place was frequented by the yakkha Sūciloma. This yakkha had been a lay-follower at the time of the Buddha Kassapa, but because he on one occasion entered the Dhamma hall with his body soiled from field-work and lay down upon a costly rug he was reborn as a yakkha with ugly features and hair on his body as coarse as so many needles. (His name means "needle-hair.")

When Sūclioma's friend, the yakkha Khira, came to visit him he remarked about the Buddha, "That one is a true *samaṇa*." To which Sūciloma replied, "We shall see just how much of a *samaṇa* he is." And he approached the Buddha and rubbed up his body against him. When the Buddha drew away from him, Sūciloma said, "Are you then afraid of me, *samaṇa*?"

"I am not afraid, but your touch is evil (*pāpako*)."

"I shall ask you a question, *samaṇa*, and if you cannot answer then I shall either overthrow your mind, split your heart asunder or grab you by the feet and toss you over the Ganges."

"I do not see anyone in the world who could overthrow my mind, split my heart asunder or toss me over the Ganges, but go ahead and ask your question and I shall answer it." (SN 10:3 & Sn 2:5)

Sūciloma asked the Buddha a question on Dhamma, and the Buddha replied in verse. Unsurprisingly, the yakkha's question reveals the troubled nature of his mind; he wanted to know where lust and hatred come from, and why the thoughts toss the mind around like mischievous boys might toss a crow. The Buddha's answer was that these defilements arise right here, generated by oneself alone. The commentary goes on to say that at the end of the Buddha's discourse, the yakkha attained to the state of a *sotāpanna* and as result of this attainment the needles fell off of his body and he became arrayed in deva clothes and garlands, because "stream-enterers do not exist in monstrous bodies" (SN-a 10:3). Not all yakkhas, apparently, were as evil minded as Suciloma. The very next sutta in the *Saṃyutta* records

456 Ud 4: 4. A *paṃsupisācaka* is a small demonic being of the woodlands, translated by John Ireland as a"mud-sprite."

the Buddha's encounter with the yakkha Maṇibhadda who lived in a *cetiya* (stupa) and addressed his question to the Buddha respectfully.[457]

Perhaps the greatest of the yakkha chieftains is Āḷavaka. His name means "forest dweller" and the story of his conversion is told in the *Suttanipāta*, and expanded at some length in the commentary. This episode is listed as one of the critical events in the life of the Buddha,[458] and was therefore considered important to the tradition. For this reason, and because the story has many interesting features which shed light on the development of the broader mythological picture, it is worth considering at some length.

The core of the story, as found in the sutta[459] is very simple.

> The Buddha was dwelling in Āḷavi, where was the dwelling-place (*bhāvanā*) of the yakkha Āḷavaka. The yakkha went up to the Buddha and challenged him, saying "Go out!" The Buddha replied "Yes, friend" (*sādhāvuso*) and began to leave. The yakkha then told to Buddha to "Come in!" and the Buddha again complies. This is repeated twice more, three times in all the yakkha orders the Buddha to go out and come in (*nikkhama ... pavisa*). On the fourth time, however, the Buddha refuses to obey. "I shall not go out, friend, do whatever you like."
>
> The yakkha Āḷavaka then says that he will ask the Buddha a question, and threatens that should he be unable to answer he will either overthrow the Buddha's mind, split his heart asunder or grab him by the feet and toss him over the Ganges. To which the Buddha replies that he does not see anyone in the world "including the devas, Māra and Brahmā, *samaṇas* and brahmins, devas and men" who can do these things to him. "Nevertheless, ask what you wish." (This is all exactly as in the story of Sūciloma).

Thus far, the sutta has been in prose, the remainder, including the conclusion, is all in metered verse. This may represent two strata in the text. The verses begin with a series of questions, asked by the yakkha and answered by the Buddha. At the conclusion, the yakkha announces that "today I have come to know what is for my good in the next life (*altho samparāyiko*) and how a gift can yield great fruit (*mahapphala*). Henceforth, I shall wander from town to town, village to village praising the Buddha and the goodness of his Dhamma."

The question and answer format of the doctrinal part of this sutta is common in the *Suttanipāta*, with a heavy use of metaphor, for example: "How does one cross the flood? By faith one crosses the flood." The emphasis throughout this series is on the level of worldly Dhamma, i.e. how to live a good life and attain a favourable rebirth rather than on liberation from *saṃsāra*. The final admonition of the Buddha is that "a faithful house-holder will not come to grief upon his death if he has these four things: truth, righteousness, courage and generosity (*saccaṃ, dhammo, dhiti, cāgo*)" (ibid.).

The story as expanded in the commentary to this text is much more detailed. It begins some time before the arrival of the Buddha on the scene. Let us consider that part first:

> At one time the king of Āḷavi was out hunting in the wilderness, and he became separated from his entourage. He was returning alone with the carcass of a deer when he strayed under the banyan tree which was the abode of the yakkha Āḷavaka. The yakkha had been granted permission by the yakkha king (Vessavaṇa) to eat everyone who came under the shade of this tree, so he seized the king intending to make a meal of him.
>
> The king, however, struck a bargain with the yakkha. He offered, in return for his life, to send Āḷavaka a

---

457 SN 10:4. His name means "Lucky Jewel."

458 See for example the introduction to Jāt 469

459 Sn 1: 10. The Āḷavakasutta Sutta.

human being and a pot of rice every day. Āḷavaka agreed, but warned that the king's own life would be forfeit should he fail to fulfill his end of the bargain.

For a time, the king was able to supply the yakkha's meal with prisoners from the jail in his capital city. When this supply was exhausted, he ordered that every family must provide one child. This expedient did not work for long, as people began to flee his kingdom with their families.

The day came when there was no one to send except the king's own son. The king said that while his son, the prince, was dear to him, nothing is dearer to a person than his own life. The king ordered the boy to be arrayed in his costliest finery and decreed that he would be sent the next day to feed the yakkha. That night, the small child lay sleeping in his mother, the queen's, lap, as she wept bitterly along with her sixteen thousand hand-maidens. "Tomorrow, he will be a yakkha's meal!"

In the morning, the Buddha surveyed the world with his Buddha-Eye (*buddhacakkhu*) and the tragic situation aroused his Great Compassion (*mahākaruṇā*). The Buddha also saw that the yakkha was ripe for the fruit of stream-entry, and the prince, should he live, would attain in this life to the fruit of non-returning. He arranged his robes and without a companion travelled the thirty *yojana* to the abode of the yakkha Āḷavaka. (Sn-a 1: 10)

The story thus far, up to the intervention of the Buddha, exhibits several archetypal mythological motifs. The king out hunting and separated from his companions entering into an other-worldly situation is also found, for example, in the Welsh *Mabinogion*. The demonic bargain leading to the imminent sacrifice of the first-born son is also a common element in myths and fairy-tales. But there is something more to this sacrifice. Two odd details raise provocative questions. First, the King is identified as Āḷavaka Rājā. He bears the same name as the yakkha and that is why the text almost always identifies the latter with the full appellation Āḷavakayakkha (rendered in translation as "Āḷavaka the Yakkha.") Second, there is a contradictory element in the choice of the prince for sacrifice in that the text casually mentions the grief of the "sixteen thousand" hand-maidens. (They are actually called *dhātiya* which means wet-nurse, presumably of the prince, which makes the number even more absurd). Granted, there is the ancient Indian love of impossibly large numbers, but it does put the choice of the prince in a new light. A hand-maiden a day would have kept the yakkha fed for more than forty years! Taken together, is what we see here a mythological echo of some ancient rite of human sacrifice involving a sacred king, as in Frazer's "Golden Bough?"

Moving on, the story after the arrival of the Buddha takes on a new and more elevated tone. Āḷavaka is no longer portrayed as a simple tree-spirit but as a mighty, and rather nasty, deity.

When the Buddha arrived at Āḷavaka's residence, the yakkha was away attending a council of yakkhas in the Himavā. Āḷavaka's palace was of eight stories, surrounded by a wall with gates and watchtowers and covered from above with a bronze netting. The whole was like an incomparable casket, protected from all sides, three *yojana* high.

The gate-keeper, a yakkha by the name of Gadrabho, greeted the Buddha with courtesy and informed him of the absence of his master. The Buddha said he would like to wait within. Gadrabho advised the Buddha strongly against this. "This is not suitable, Bhante. The yakkha Āḷavaka is coarse and rough. He has no regard for mother or father, for *samaṇas* and brahmins, or for the Dhamma. He will overthrow your mind, rend your heart asunder and grab you by the feet and either throw you over the ocean, or out of the world-system altogether!"

Three times the Buddha announced his intention to wait for Āḷavaka's return inside and three times the gate-keeper gave the same warning. At last Gadrabho saw that the Buddha was unafraid and he said, "If I let you into my master's house without his permission, my own life will be forfeit. I shall go and inform him of your arrival."

The Buddha entered into Āḷavaka's palace and sat on his celestial gem-throne (*dibbaratanapallaṅka*), emitting a glorious radiance. The yakkha's women came out to pay him reverence and he sat discoursing to them on the Dhamma. "In former lives, you lived morally and gave generously, and that is why you are enjoying your present happiness. In this present life, do not let yourselves be overcome by jealousy and meanness towards one another."

At that time, two other yakkhas named Sātāgiri and Hemavata were journeying to the council in the Himavā. They were flying overhead with a great retinue in various vehicles. Now, yakkhas cannot travel through the air just anywhere, but must follow fixed paths. The path to the Himavā passed directly over Āḷavaka's palace. Due to the presence of the Buddha, they were unable to pass overhead. The two yakkha chiefs descended to earth to investigate and were filled with joy to see the Buddha. They paid him homage and said, "Of great fortune is Āḷavaka that the Bhagavā is within his dwelling!" The Buddha gave them leave and they departed for the Himavā.

Meanwhile, the gate-keeper Gadrabho arrived at the Himavā and informed his master that the Buddha was waiting for him at his palace. Āḷavaka felt that his pride was humbled before the assembly, and when Sātāgiri and Hemavata arrived shortly afterward and sang the praises of the Buddha, telling Āḷavaka how fortunate he was to have the Teacher at his home, Āḷavaka became enraged. He stood with his left foot on Mt Manosilātata and his right on Mt Kelāsa, sixty *yojana* apart, and gave a great shout that was heard over the whole of Jambudīpa: "I am Āḷavaka!"

The yakkha flew back to his palace near the city of Āḷavi in a ferocious whirlwind which uprooted whole trees and scattered the roof-tiles of the city. He thought the storm-wind would drive the trespassing *samaṇa* away, but the wind did not even disturb the folds of the Buddha's robes. Āḷavaka then tried to kill the Buddha by unleashing an enormous rain-storm. Although it flooded the forest with a great deluge, the Buddha's robes were not moistened by as much as a dew-drop. Then Āḷavaka caused the mountains to erupt in fire and smoke and cast huge rocks into the sky, hoping to crush the Buddha, but the boulders turned to celestial flowers as they fell at his feet.

Growing more enraged, Āḷavaka the Yakkha kept attacking the Buddha. He sent a deluge of swords and arrows down upon him, then a rain of hot ashes, then a ferocious sand-storm and a shower of thick mud. All of these things also turned to flowers and fell at the Buddha's feet. But Āḷavaka was not yet ready to admit defeat and he caused a great black pall of darkness to descend upon the Buddha. "This horrifying sight will surely terrify that *samaṇa* and make him flee in despair!" But the Buddha dispersed the darkness with radiance like that of the sun.

But the yakkha had still not unleashed his final and most terrible weapon; Āḷavaka had not yet cast the banner Dussāvudha at the Buddha. This was one of the Four Great Weapons of the world: a cloth banner of awful power. If it was cast into the sky, no rain would fall for twelve years. If cast upon the earth, all the trees and grass would wither and nothing would grow again for the same number of years. If cast into the sea, the ocean would boil away entirely. If cast upon a mountain, even one as great as Mt Sineru itself, that mountain would shatter into pieces. As Āḷavaka took Dussāvudha in his hands the devas of the whole ten-thousand-fold world-system gathered in the sky to watch. "Today there will be a great battle, and having defeated Āḷavaka, the Blessed One will teach him the Dhamma!"

Āḷavaka unleashed this terrible weapon, hurling it like a blazing thunderbolt at the Buddha, but it fell harmlessly to the ground before him, and changed into a foot washing rag. Now the great pride of Āḷavaka the Yakkha was broken and the Buddha was able to conquer him with loving-kindness (*mettā*). When three times the despairing yakkha ordered the Buddha to leave his abode, and three times ordered him to return, the Buddha complied with courtesy, saying "So be it, friend" (*sādhāvuso*) .

But on the fourth time being ordered to leave, the Buddha refused to comply. Āḷavaka made one last attempt at bluster, telling the Buddha that he would ask him some questions, and if he could not answer them: "I shall overthrow your mind, split your heart asunder and grabbing you by the feet toss you over the ocean or beyond the world-system altogether." The Buddha replied that there was no-one who could do these things to him, but gave the yakkha permission to ask his questions.

Now in Āḷavaka's storeroom there was an heirloom of his house, dating back to the time of the previous Buddha, Kassapa. This was a golden tablet on which was inscribed, in vermillion paint, a series of questions and answers that his mother and father had exchanged with Kassapa Buddha. Āḷavaka asked these questions to the Buddha and was astonished to see that his answers agreed syllable for syllable with what was recorded on the tablet! At the conclusion, Āḷavaka attained to the state of stream-entry.

It was now morning and the king's messenger arrived with the little prince, intended for the yakkha's meal. The king's man handed the child to Āḷavaka, who now ashamed of his previous conduct, meekly handed him over to the Buddha, who handed him back to the king's messenger. From being passed this way from hand-to-hand, the prince ever after was known by the name of Hatthaka Āḷavaka. ("By the Hand Āḷavaka") The prince grew up to become one of the greatest of the Buddha's lay disciples. (ibid.)

We can see that the presentation of Āḷavaka has changed considerably in the latter part of the story. He is now presented as a very powerful nature deity, with all the elemental forces at his command. His potency is emphasized by his possession of one of the Four Great Weapons, and the shout that he uttered while standing astride the mountain peaks is classed as one of the Four Great Shouts.[460] In the first part of the story Āḷavaka is described as living under (or perhaps in) a banyan tree like a simple tree deva; in the later section his abode has been changed into a fabulous fortified palace. But the detail which speaks most strongly to Āḷavaka's importance is the gathering of devas from the ten-thousand-fold world-system (*dasasahassilokadhātu*) to witness his final defeat at the hands of the Buddha. This means that his conversion was regarded as an event of cosmic significance.

The metamorphosis of Āḷavaka from a kind of ogre living in a banyan tree devouring hapless travellers, to a great and wrathful world-shaking divinity can be interpreted in at least two ways: textually or mythologically. Textually,

[460] For the other Great Weapons, see the section on Vessavaṇa in § 3:5,7. The other Great Shouts were; that uttered by Puṇṇaka the Yakkha when he defeated King Koravya at dice, "I have won!" (Jāt. 546, eng. 545), that of Vissakamma when he assumed the form of a monstrous dog to chastise the back-sliding bhikkhus at the time when Kassapa Buddha's dispensation was waning, "I shall devour all, monk or nun or layman or laywomen, who perform evil deeds or speak against the Dhamma!" (Jāt 469 has Mātali doing this) and the shout of King Kusa when he confronted the seven kings who had come to contest the hand of his beloved, the princess Pabhāvatī, "I am the Great Lion-Roaring King Kusa!" (Jāt.531). All these shouts were said to be heard over the whole of the continent of Jambudīpa. Sn-a 1: 10.

what we are seeing here are successive chronological strata in the texts. There are four layers, composed at different times:

1—The verse passages of the sutta

2– The prose passages of the sutta

3—The first part of the commentary, before the arrival of the Buddha on the scene

4—The remainder of the commentarial story, featuring the encounter of the Buddha with the yakkha Āḷavaka, now portrayed as a mighty nature deity.

However the complete story was composed, the final version with all its seeming contradictions became an accepted part of the mature tradition, and should be considered as a whole. The myth of Āḷavaka demonstrates something we see often in Buddhist cosmology: the fluid nature of reality. The entity Āḷavaka the Yakkha may be a tree-ogre and a cosmic storm-god at the same time, manifesting in different ways at different levels. To the king, who is a human being of low moral character (hunters are always considered such in the Pali sources) he is seen as a fierce ogre living in a tree. The Buddha, with his vision surpassing that of the devas, penetrates to another higher or more fundamental level of reality and sees a divine being dwelling in a three-*yojana* high palace. It may be asked which the "real" yakkha is, but that only raises deeper metaphysical issues about the nature of reality and perception. One possible way to think about it is to see Āḷavaka as a single force or being manifesting differently at different levels, according to the perception of the viewer. To add another layer, given the confusion of the names, Āḷavaka might also be seen as a dark shadow of the king's own psyche, without negating his reality as a separate entity at the other levels.

Beside King Vessavaṇa himself, the only other yakkha found in the source material of comparable power to Āḷavaka is **Puṇṇaka**, Vessavaṇa's nephew:

> Vidhura was at that time a very great sage (*paṇḍita*) and his wisdom was acclaimed throughout Jambudīpa. The nāga king Varuṇa encountered him during a trip to the human world and later sung his praises to his wife the nāga queen, Vimalā. On hearing about the wonderful heart of the sage, she developed a craving for it and took to her bed feigning illness. She told her husband the king that only Vidhura's heart could make her well. In despair, Varuṇa enlisted the help of his lovely daughter, the nāga princess Irandatī. He told her to use her charms to recruit a mighty champion who could secure the heart of the sage.
>
> Dressing in her most beautiful finery, the lovely nāga princess went to a mountain in the Himavā and there adorned with jewels and flowers she sang and danced in order to arouse the passion of some great hero. It so happened that the yakkha chief Puṇṇaka was travelling overhead, riding on his fabulous mind-made horse (*manomayasindava*). He immediately fell in love with the princess, and agreed to undertake the quest for Vidhura's heart.
>
> Vidhura was the servant of King Koravya of the Kurus, and the king had a weakness for gambling. Puṇṇaka knew this, and decided he could win possession of the sage by playing at dice against him. Now, Puṇṇaka knew that the king would not wager Vidhura against any mean stake, but he also knew where there was a marvellous gem which had belonged to a Wheel-Turning King. This jewel was such that if a person gazed into it, he could see the whole of the world-system (*cakkavāḷa*), all the cities and towns, the mountains and oceans, the earth and the heavens above.
>
> Having secured this fabulous gem-stone, Puṇṇaka flew on his horse to the capital of the Kuru country and

challenged the king to a game of dice. King Koravya asked him who he was and where he came from, "For your speech is not that of a man of the Kurus." Puṇṇaka thought that if he announced his true name, the king would despise him and refuse to play, since he was just a servant of Vessavaṇa and not a noble. So he gave his name from his previous human birth: "I am Kaccāyana, a brahmin from the Aṅga country, sire."

So he wagered his jewel and his horse and the king, desirous to win these marvellous prizes, said that he would bet against these all that he had, saving only his own person, his queen, and his white parasol (*setachatta*—emblem of his sovereignty). Now, the king always won at dice because he had a guardian deva (ārakkhadevatā) who had been his mother in a previous life. She would hover in the air and protect him from bad throws. When Puṇṇaka became aware of this, he gazed directly at her with eyes wide and full of wrath. The deva, recognizing him as a powerful yakkha, fled in terror all the way to the iron mountains at the edge of the world-system. So, with the king bereft of his supernatural aid, Puṇṇaka easily won the game and as the dice fell his way on the final throw he clapped his hands and cried aloud three times: "I have won! I have won! I have won!" and the sound of this great shout was heard all over Jambudīpa.

Puṇṇaka claimed as his prize nothing more but the sage Vidhura only. Puṇṇaka bade Vidhura to grasp the horse's tail, and to plant his feet firmly against the horse's legs and he flew off with him into sky as the whole of the populace wept aloud. He took him to the Himavā and put him down on Kāḷāgiri, the Black Mountain. "What use is this sage to me alive? I will kill him, take his heart and give it to the nāga king and thereby win the lovely Irandatī and go to the realm of the gods! (*devaloka*)."

Puṇṇaka thought to himself that it would be better if he did not kill Vidhura with his own hand, so he tried at first to terrify him so that he would die of fright. The yakkha assumed his most horrible yakkha shape (*bheravayakkarupa*) seized Vidhura in his jaws and shook him about, making as if to eat him. But the sage was unmoved, showing no sign of fright. Puṇṇaka changed into a huge bull elephant, a lion and a monstrous large snake, but none of these frightful forms had any effect on the imperturbable sage. Then Puṇṇaka tried by raising a mighty wind to blow Vidhura off the mountain, but not a hair on his head was stirred. The yakkha then assumed the form of a giant elephant and shook the entire mountain to and fro with his enormous trunk, but he could not dislodge Vidhura from the mountain top. Nor could he terrify the sage by entering into mountain and uttering a fearsome sound.

At last the yakkha decided there was no other recourse but to destroy Vidhura with his own hand, so he seized him and flung him round violently, but before he could throw him off the mountain and dash him to bits on the rocks, the sage spoke: "Before you kill me, you would be wise to give me a chance to speak. Seldom does a sage like me arise in the world, and you should not miss the chance to gain some words of wisdom. Afterward, you can do what you like with me."

So Puṇṇaka set the sage down and listened as Vidhura discoursed to him about the way of living according to Dhamma. In the end, the yakkha's heart was turned and he contritely offered to take the sage home, but Vidhura wanted first to be taken to the nāga kingdom, where he also converted the nāga king and queen. The nāga king agreed that the heart of a sage is his wisdom, so he deemed the quest completed and gave his daughter to Puṇṇaka, and Puṇṇaka gave Vidhura the magic jewel. The yakkha then flew Vidhura back to the Kuru Kingdom, where there was great rejoicing at his safe return, and Vidhura presented the jewel to King Koravya.[461]

[461] Jāt 546 (Eng. 545), the Vidhurapaṇḍita Jātaka.

Vidhura is identified as a previous birth of the Buddha, which emphasizes the parallelism between the stories of Āḷavaka and Puṇṇaka; both of these powerful yakkha chiefs were turned from their murderous ways by the Buddha or Bodhisatta and subsequently became guardians of the *Buddhasāsana* (the Buddhist religion), being among the righteous yakkha chiefs upon which a bhikkhu in distress from supernatural forces may call.[462] A point of interest in the latter story, which sheds light on ancient Indian society, is that the word translated above as "servant" is *dāsa*, which can also be rendered as "slave."[463] It seems there was little distinction between the two categories. Vidhura is described as living in luxury with numerous wives and concubines, but King Koravya still has the authority to gamble his person away. Puṇṇaka too, is described as the *dāsa* of Vessavaṇa, and he needed the latter's permission before undertaking his quest. Furthermore, the reason Puṇṇaka, the mighty yakkha chief, does not reveal his true identity to the king is that he is worried that the latter might be prickly about caste and refuse to play with a *dāsa*!

This also illustrates a curious ambivalence in the nature of yakkhas. Although they are always portrayed, at least before a spiritual conversion, as fierce and bloody-handed, they are also bound by the strict laws of their kind and are subservient to their king, Vessavaṇa. Although they might devour people, they normally do so only within very specific limits set by King Vessavaṇa; for example only those who took shade under his banyan tree were available for Āḷavaka's meal. Likewise, although the yakkhas can fly through the air, they do so only along fixed paths. Also ambivalent is the yakkhas' place in the cosmic hierarchy; like some others among the mythological inhabitants ofthe *cakkavāḷa*, they are not easily placed in the thirty-one abodes or the five realms of rebirth. Existence as a yakkha is generally considered *duggati* (an unfortunate or low birth) but we have seen the Buddha telling the yakkha wives of Āḷavaka that their present state is the result of having made good kamma in the past.

These stories also illustrate something of the familial relations among the yakkhas. Āḷavaka has an heirloom passed down from his mother and father, and Puṇṇaka is described as the nephew of Vessavaṇa. This implies that the yakkhas give birth in the same manner as humans, but in some other stories they seem to be arise spontaneously, like the devas.[464] So, in several respects, yakkhas are hard to classify. Are they best considered a kind of demon or as a lower class of deity? Perhaps it is better just to think of them *sui generis* as a broad category of non-human beings; often the word *amanussa*, "non-human," is used as a synonym for *yakkha*.

The familial relations of yakkhas is poignantly illustrated by two similar stories from the Saṃyutta Nikāya. In the first, a *yakkhinī* (female yakkha) in a wretched condition is out with her little yakkha son searching for food when she hears Anuruddha, one of the arahants, chanting verses of Dhamma. She hushes her child when he fusses and expresses the wish that by hearing the Dhamma and practising harmlessness and virtue, they might obtain release from the *pisācayoni* (SN 10:6). This last word means literally "birth as a *pisāca*", a type of low being we shall considerbelow. The commentary adds further details. It says that the food they were seeking was urine, faeces, saliva and other such filth, which would make their state of existence much like that of the petas. The sweet sound of Anuruddha's voice pierced the yakkhinī to the marrow of her bones, and inspired her to follow the precepts from that moment on (SN-a 10:6). The other story is similar, except the yakkha mother had two children, a boy and a girl. They overheard the Buddha giving a discourse and this yakkha-mother too, shushed her hungry young ones and gained stream-entry by overhearing the Dhamma. The commentary says that all three were also transformed into devas. Even though thegirl child was too young to understand the Dhamma, and did not become a *sotāpanna*, she did obtain a deva existence through the influence of her mother.[465] These stories once again demonstrate the blurry boundaries between yakkhas, *pisācas*, petas and devas.

462 DN 32, the Āṭānāṭiya Sutta.

463 *Dāsa* originally referred to the non-Aryan inhabitants of India. See PED.

464 For example, Jāt 432 has instances of both kinds of birth.

465 SN 10:7 and commentary.

When we turn our attention to the Jātaka literature, we see that the demonic side of the yakkhas is definitely emphasized. We also learn many interesting details about the nature of these beings; for instance that they sometimes live in towns of their own (*yakkhanagara*), and that even when assuming a human form they can be recognized by their red eyes and by the fact that they cast no shadow, (Jāt 1) and that they are afraid of iron and palm-leaves (Jāt 510). Yakkhas are often portrayed as living in lonely places: deserts, forests or mountains. Sometimes a mountain is named after a yakkha, and sometimes the yakkha is named after the mountain.[466]

Some yakkhas live in charnel grounds and feed off the human corpses, but it is too simple to categorize them as simple monsters. There is, once again, the matter of their paradoxically law-abiding nature:

> At one time, the righteous ruler of Bārāṇasī, King Sīlavakumāra, had been overthrown by his enemy, the evil King of Kosala. The good king, together with his ministers, was taken to the charnel ground, buried up to their necks and left to perish there.
>
> It happened that there were many yakkhas in that charnel ground, who lived by devouring the flesh of corpses. Two of them fell to quarrelling over possession of a body which lay on the border of their respective territories. Unable to settle the dispute themselves, they took the matter to King Sīlavakumāra. "We cannot make a division ourselves, but this King Sīlavakumāra is righteous (*dhammika*) and he can make the division for us. Let us go to him!"
>
> So the yakkhas, dragging the corpse by the foot, went to where King Sīlavakumāra was buried and sought his counsel. He agreed to settle the dispute, but said that first he needed to bathe, to eat and to drink. Using their magical power (ānubhāva) they took everything needful from the usurper's palace and allowed the king to bathe, eat and drink. When he was done, the yakkhas asked if there was any other service they might perform. "Yes there is. Fetch me the royal sword (*maṅgalakagga*) which lies by the usurper's pillow." This the yakkhas did, and the king used it to divide the corpse length-wise from the head downwards. (Jāt 51)

The yakkhas are often depicted as wielding great power, sometimes for their own ends and sometimes in the service of human masters.

> At that time, ten brothers, each one a mighty hero, were conquering all of Jambudīpa.[467] But the city of Dvāravatī they could not conquer, because it was under the protection of the yakkhas (*amanussapariggahita* lit. "possessed by non-humans"). A yakkha in the shape of a donkey would patrol the hills outside the town, and if he saw an enemy approaching, he would bray like a donkey and the whole city would rise into the air by the yakkhas' power (*yakkhānubhāvena*) and come to rest out in the ocean on an island.
>
> In despair of completing their conquests, the Ten Brothers sought the help of a famous sage and he told them that they must find the donkey, and obtain his help by humbling themselves at his feet. This they did, and taking hold of the donkey's feet they begged him not to bray when they approached the city. The donkey-yakkha was willing to help them, but he told them that he could not refrain from braying. "However," he said "if you fix iron stakes into the ground at the four gates of the city, and attach iron ploughs to these posts with iron chains, the city will not be able to rise."
>
> This they did, and thus completed the conquest of the whole of Jambudīpa. (Jāt 454)

466 SN-a 10:1 where this is said of the yakkha Indaka who lived on Mt Inda. There was also a Yugandhara listed among the great yakkhas of DN 32.

467 The southern island-continent, in the context of this story it may be taken as equivalent to India.

The preferred diet of yakkhas is human flesh, either taken from corpses or from the killing of unwary travellers. The female yakkhas (*yakkhī or yakkhinī*) are if anything even more ferocious in this regard. They are often depicted as stealing and eating human babies:[468]

> A yakkhinī having assumed a pleasant human form tricked a woman into letting her play with that woman's baby boy. Having the baby in her grasp she quickly ran off with him, intending to make the child her dinner. The mother gave chase and caught the *yakkhinī* by the arm. The two stood fiercely quarrelling in the high street, each claiming the child her own. A crowd of townsfolk gathered, and they took the two women to the sage (*paṇḍita*) Mahosadha to settle the question as to who was the real mother.
>
> The sage knew the *yakkhinī* at once for what she was, by the sign of her red and unblinking eyes, but he made a demonstration of the case for the sake of the onlookers. He drew a line in the sand and asked the two competing "mothers" to hold the baby by the hands and feet and to pull. "Whoever succeeds in dragging the infant across the line may keep him."
>
> Of course, the real mother unable to bear the cries of the infant being so cruelly handled, released her hold immediately and stood weeping. By this action, she was revealed to all as the true mother. Mahosodha admonished the *yakkhinī*: "You are a great fool; by doing evil karma in the past, you have been reborn as a *yakkhinī* and yet you seek to do yet more harm. Henceforth, do not commit any more evil deeds."[469]

The female yakkhas are also notorious for assuming a beautiful appearance with which to seduce unwary men, who thereby come to destruction:

> To reach the famous centre of learning at Takkasilā, the traveler had to pass through a terrible wilderness known as *Amanussakantāro* ("the desert of the non-humans") which was infested with yakkhas. The *yakkhinīs* would magically create pleasant pavilions by the road-side, covered by brilliantly coloured canopies and full of enticing food and drink. There, a *yakkhinī* would be reclining on a soft divan in the form of a young and beautiful woman. She would call out to passersby: "Traveller! You look weary, hungry and thirsty! Come rest awhile, eat and drink." Once inside and seated on the couch beside the *yakkhinī*, the heedless traveller would be inflamed with lust by the beauty of her limbs, and by the intoxicating scent of her perfume. Yielding to passion, they would have carnal relations and immediately after she would devour him alive ("with the blood still flowing"—*lohitena paggharantena*). (Jāt 96)
>
> But sometimes, even in these ferocious *yakkhinīs*, softer feelings would prevail:
>
> Once there lived a certain horse-faced (*assamukhī*) *yakkhinī*. She had been granted a territory of thirty *yojana* in extent by Vessavaṇa in which she had leave to capture and eat any travellers. And this she did for many years. However, while she was carrying one handsome brahmin youth to her cave, her lust was inflamed by contact with his body, and instead of eating him she decided to keep him as her husband. Thereafter, whenever she went out hunting for her victims, she would seal the mouth of the cave with a great rock, for fear that her husband would run away. Now when she killed anyone, besides taking the corpse for her own dinner, she would also take whatever food and other provisions they might have been carrying back to the cave for the use of the brahmin.

---

[468] See also Dhp-a 1:4, Dhp-a 21:2, Jāt 513.

[469] Jāt 542, (Eng. 546) the Mahāummagga Jātaka.

In course of time she conceived by the brahmin and gave birth to a son of normal human appearance, although he had the strength and speed of a yakkha. When he grew older he asked his father why his mother looked so different from them. "She is a yakkha, my son, and we are human beings." The boy conceived a wish to go live among human beings and he contrived to escape with his father. He was able to remove the rock, which was beyond the strength of the brahmin, and the two fled away.

The *yakkhinī* gave chase, but they had managed to reach the river which marked the limit of her domain, and she was unable to cross over. She pleaded with them to return, pitifully asking them what her offence was, and why they wanted to abandon her. The boy replied that she was a yakkha, and they humans, and that they wished to live among their own kind. Despairing of their return, she said to her son, "If you must go, you should know that making a living among men is not easy. I know a magic charm (*vijjaṃ*—lit. "knowledge") known as the Cintāmaṇi Charm, by which one can read foot-prints left behind even twelve years ago. I shall teach this to you and by its means, you shall make a living."

This she did, while the son and husband stood listening on the far bank of the river. Having finished, she said that her heart was broken and that she could not live without them. She smote herself on the chest and immediately fell down dead. When they were sure she was dead, the two crossed back and made a funeral pile for her body, and cremated her with all due honour and ceremony. (Jāt 432)

There were some other aspects to the relations between humans and yakkhas that deserve note. Human beings sometimes worshipped yakkhas, and made sacrifices to them, although as often as not the meat ended up being taken by jackals and crows (Jāt 113). One story tells of a regular sacrifice made "in the presence of" a yakkha named Cittarāja (Jāt 276). From the Buddhist perspective, these rites were abhorrent, involving as they did the slaughter of living beings.

At that time, men were devoted to the worship of the devas (*devamaṅgalikā*) and made great sacrifices (*balikamma*) involving the slaughter of many goats. A righteous king on coming to the throne, intended to make a stop to these rites and had proclaimed by beat of drum that all destruction of living beings was to cease.

This enraged the yakkhas, and they held an assembly in the Himavā and decided to kill the king. They sent a certain ferocious yakkha wielding a blazing iron hammer as big as a roof-top to make an end of the reformer. But Sakka, king of the devas, intervened and stood in the air above the yakkha wielding his thunderbolt and the yakkha withdrew in fear. (Jāt 347)

Yakkhas are also known on occasion to take possession (*gaṇhāti* or *paviṭṭha*) of human minds, driving them mad. Āḷavaka was said to have done this: if a wandering ascetic chanced upon his abode and they were unable to satisfactorily answer his questions, he would use his psychic power to create a subtle form (*sukhumattabhāva*) and cause their minds to become deranged (*khittacittā*) (Sn-a 1: 10). In the Mahāumagga Jātaka (Jāt 542, eng 546) there is mention of a yakkha named Naradeva who would would take possession of a certain man on the night of the new moon and make him bark like a dog. Possession by a yakkha is given as one of the eight kinds of madness.[470] There existed a kind of seer known as a *bhūtavejja* who specialized in the exorcism of yakkhas (Jāt 228). One tale of yakkha possession that is interesting not only for the details it gives about the phenomenon, but also for a certain moral

[470] Jāt 378—the eight kinds of madness are; the madness of sensuality, of anger, of wrong views, of ignorance, possession by petas, possession by yakkhas, the madness caused by drink and that caused by despair.

ambiguity, is the story of the *sāmaṇera* (novice) Sānu:

> There was a *sāmaṇera* named Sānu who was renowned for the beautiful way he would teach the Dhamma, "as if he were bringing the Milky Way (ākāsagaṅga lit. "Sky-Ganges") down to earth." He would always make a determination, "may the merit of my preaching go to my mother and father." Now, his human mother and father knew nothing of this but there was a certain *yakkhinī* (female yakkha) who had been his mother in a previous existence and who always came with the devas to listen to his preaching. She would say, "I thank the *sāmeṇera* for the merit he is giving me." The devas held the *sāmaṇera* in reverence just as if he were Mahābrahma himself. On account of the *sāmaṇera*, the devas also held the *yakkhinī* in great esteem. Whenever the yakkhas held an assembly, they would praise her as "mother of Sānu" and give her the best seat, the best food and the best drink. Even yakkhas of great power would step aside for her, or give her their seat.
>
> When the *sāmaṇera* Sānu grew to manhood, he began to become discontented with the life of a bhikkhu and he returned to the home of his parents and declared his intention to return to the lay life. His mother attempted to dissuade him from this course of action, but to no avail. In the end she relented and began preparing some rice gruel for him, all the while still hoping he would change his mind.
>
> Just then the *yakkhinī* was wondering, "How is the *sāmaṇera*? Is he getting almsfood or not?" Upon investigating she discovered that he had returned to his family home with the intention of disrobing. "The *sāmaṇera* will bring me to shame among the great and powerful devas (*mahesakkhā devatā*). I must go and make an obstacle to his disrobing." So she went there and took possession of his body (*sarīre adhimuccitvā*); with his neck twisted around and saliva dribbling he fell to the ground. When his human mother saw the state of her son, she ran to him in all haste, took him onto her lap and embraced him. All the people of the village came and brought offerings, but she only wept and cried aloud:
>
> > Those who keep the *uposatha* days,
> >
> > And follow a holy life;
> >
> > With these the yakkhas do not sport,
> >
> > Thus I have heard from the arahants.
> >
> > But today, the yakkhas play with Sānu.
>
> The *yakkhinī* repeated these verses back to her, and said they were true. Then she spoke a further stanza:
>
> > If you would have Sānu awaken,
> >
> > Heed the words of the yakkhas.
> >
> > Do no evil deeds, openly or in secret,
> >
> > For if you make evil kamma, now or in the future,
> >
> > You will not escape from suffering,

Nor will you avoid being tormented.[471]

So saying, the *yakkhinī* released Sānu who woke up confused as to why he was in such a state, lying down across his mother's lap. (Dhp-a 23:5)

In the conclusion, after further conversation with his earthly mother, Sānu saw the error of his ways and returned to the bhikkhu life. This story has a number of significant details. We see here the blurring of the categories of yakkha and deva; the boy's former mother is always identified as a yakkha, yet she consorts freely with the devas. Her dubious moral character is evidenced by her motive for not wanting Sānu to disrobe: she too much enjoys the privileged treatment she gets from the devas and yakkhas. Notice also that until she speaks, Sānu's human mother and the others are not aware of her presence and yet they assume that the boy's fit is due to the intervention of yakkhas. The use by the mother of the masculine plural (*yakkhā*) is evidence that she is not directly aware of the *yakkhinī*. It would seem that this kind of seizure was always assumed to be the result of possession by yakkhas.

When we consider all the evidence, the yakkhas appear to be a class of beings that stand somewhere between the coarse physicality of humanity and the subtler nature of the devas. There is a wide spectrum within the classification of yakkha. The coarsest sort, often called *amanussa* (non-humans) are ferocious and rough, living off human flesh, sometimes even abiding in charnel grounds. The highest sort are barely distinguishable from the devas. They mostly give birth in the ordinary human way, and have family relations like us, but sometimes are said to arise spontaneously like devas. In some stories, like the incident with Sāriputta and Moggallāna, they are invisible to the ordinary human senses, again like the devas. And yet, they are coarsely physical enough to subsist on the flesh of corpses, or even filth. A passage in the *Milindapañhā* illustrates this ambiguity nicely. King Milinda asks the bhikkhu Nagāsena if there are indeed such things as yakkhas in the world, and if they are born and die like us. When he is told that indeed there are, he further inquires why we do not see their corpses. The answer is that we do. Their corpses take the forms of worms, insects, birds and beasts after death (Mil. 5:2,7 eng. v2 p90–91).

471 The word used is *uppaccati* which implies burning in *niraya*.

3:4:3 PISĀCAS AND PAṂSUPISĀCAKAS

The *pisācas* are a particularly nasty breed of small yakkha. The word *pisāca* is etymologically a distant cousin of the English word *fiend,* (PED) and many translations render it as "goblin." There are said to be "many, many" kinds of *pisāca* (DN-a 2) but only two are named in the texts: the *pisācillikā*[472] who live in the hollows of trees and the *paṃsupisācaka*[473] who live in dung heaps and refuse piles. The *pisācas* are extraordinarily ugly and frightful in appearance and it is a common phrase to say of someone ugly that he or she is "like a *pisāca*." Thus, in a section of the Vinaya (monastic rules) devoted to personal hygiene it is said that one who does not trim his nose hairs looks "like a *pisācillika*" (Vin Mv 3). Elsewhere, it is said of an ugly woman that she has "a basket-head, drooping breasts, a fat belly and is as frightful as a *pisāca*" (MN-a 66). A boy born deformed, with his hands and feet, eyes, ears, nose and mouth not in their proper place is said to be "as malformed as a *paṃsupisācaka*" (Dhp-a 5:3). A low-caste person is described as being of a "bad colour" (*dubbaṇṇo*) resembling a charred stump, "like a *paṃsupisācaka*" (SN-a 3:21).

The *pisācas*, like their cousins the yakkhas, are sometimes said to feed on human flesh.[474] Sometimes, however, they are seen to be feeding on filth, especially the wretched *paṃsupisācakas*.[475] The *pisācas* are often cited as being among those things which cause fear in lonely places (Vin Pāc 55 & DN-a 2). The *pisācas*, like the yakkhas and petas, can sometimes breath a deadly poison (Jāt 510). It is said that wherever the Buddha dwells the force of his *mettā* ("loving-kindness") protects all the humans in the area from the depredations of *paṃsupisācakas* (DN-a 4). In spite of the danger and terror inherent in all *pisācas*, the *paṃsupisācakas* are often cited as a byword for an insignificant being. For example, when the great gulf between the Buddha's power and that of his greatest disciples is compared, the difference is said to be like comparing a *paṃsupisācaka* with Sakka, king of the devas (AN-a 3:81).

The *pisācas*, unlike the yakkhas, do not have any well developed characters in the texts. None are given names, and as individual actors they rarely feature in the stories. There is, however, one brief anecdote that has some interesting details:

> A *paṃsupisācaka* is a *pisāca* born into a place of filth. If he holds a certain root (*eka mūla*) his body becomes invisible. Here is a story: there was a certain *yakkhinī* who had two sons and she left them at the town gate to go and search for food. The boys saw an elder bhikkhu wandering for alms and said to him, "*Bhante*, our mother has gone into the town looking for food. Please tell her that if she finds anything good, she should hurry back, her boys are suffering from hunger and are unable to bear it." The bhikkhu asked, "How can I see her?" They replied, "Here, *bhante*, take this piece of root and you will see." The elder knew of many kinds of yakkha, so asked the boys to tell him by what signs he could recognize their mother. They told him that she was deformed and frightful (*virūpa bībhaccha*) and would be found on the street where she expected to find some afterbirth. (Upon going into the town) he saw the *paṃsupisācaka* and passed on the boys' message. She asked, "How can you see me?" Then she saw the root and she seized it from him. Having taken the root, she became invisible once again. (MN-a 79)

We have already encountered this "certain root" in the section on yakkhas, but in that story it works somewhat differently. In the Jātaka story, a human boy eats some of the root to become invisible like the yakkhas. In this story, the human bhikkhu by simply holding the root enters the perceptual world of the yakkhas and is able to see the otherwise invisible *paṃsupisācaka*. The subcommentary adds little additional information about this root. It only

[472] Vin Mv 3, Vin Cv 5 & Sn-a 2:13.

[473] MN-a 29, MN-a 79, Ud 4:4.

[474] Ud-a 1:7 lists *yakkhas, rakkhasas, pisācas*, lions and tigers among the beings who eat humans. See also AN-a 5:55.

[475] MN-a 79 where a female paṃsupisācaka is seen eating some after-birth.

informs us that the root is between four fingers and a span in size and that it comes from "trees, plants, creepers and so forth," which isn't all that helpful. It goes on to say that whoever holds it becomes "of another birth" (*aññajātikāna*). Presumably then, the elder by holding the root actually became transformed into a yakkha and that is how he entered their perceptual world. The explanation concludes by stating that an invisible body is a natural power of the yakkha birth (*jātisiddhā dhammatā*) (MN-ṭ 79).

3:4:4 RAKKHASA

There is an important class of demonic beings in the pre-Buddhist mythology of India known as the *rakṣas*.[476] They were incorporated into the Buddhist system under the Pali form of their name as *rakkhasas*. The *rakkhasas* do not figure as prominently in the Pali sources as yakkhas, and are in many cases simply synonymous with the latter.[477] Sometimes when a being is referred to as a *rakkhasa*, rather than a *yakkha*, it is a hint that the story incorporates very old pre-Buddhist material. This is, for instance, the case in the Sambulā Jātaka[478] where Sakka, acting very much like the Vedic Indra, saves a princess from a *rakkhasa*.

There is one milieu which the Pali sources reserves for *rakkhasas* in particular and that is the haunting of lonely forest pools. Several stories feature a *rakkhasa* living in such a pool who devours all who come to bathe in or drink from its waters.[479] The danger is sometimes apprehended by the wise hero when he discerns that there are foot-prints leading into the pool, but none emerging again. The image of a *rakkhasa* haunted pond is used proverbially to say that something is abandoned and unused, as for instance a a miser's wealth.[480] The character of the *rakkhasa* in the pool is seldom developed, but one place where we hear a little more is the Devadhamma Jātaka.[481] The story concerns three royal brothers, Mahisāsakumāra ("Buffalo Prince"), Sūriyakumāra ("Sun Prince") and Candakumāra ("Moon Prince") who were in exile in the Himavā. Mahisāsakumāra, who was the Bodhisatta, asked his brother Sūriyakumāra to go to a nearby pond and fetch some water:

> Now, this pond had been given to a certain *dakarakkhasa* ("water demon") by Vessavaṇa who had said "All those who go down into the pond, you may eat, except only those who know what is *devadhamma* ("divine teachings"). Those who do not go down into the pond, you may not have." The *rakkhasa* asked everyone who went down to the pond the meaning of *devadhamma*, and ate those who did not know. So when Sūriyakumāra went down to the pond, without investigating first, the rakkhasa seized him and demanded "What is *devadhamma*?" The prince replied, "The sun and the moon are what is called *devadhamma*." The *rakkhasa* said, "You do not know the *devadhamma*," and dragged the prince underwater and placed him in his own abode.
>
> When Sūriyakumāra did not come back quickly, the Bodhisatta sent Candakumāra to the pond. He was also seized by the *rakkhasa* and asked about *devadhamma*. He said that the four directions were *devadhamma* and the *rakkhasa* said to him also, "You do not know the *devadhamma*," and dragged him under the water to his abode.
>
> When Candakumāra also did not return, the Bodhisatta thought there must be some obstacle. When he approached the pond he say two sets of foot-prints going toward it, and none returning, and he knew, "This pond must be held by a *rakkhasa*." So he armed himself with sword and bow and stood waiting near the pond. Seeing that the prince did not descend into the pond, the *rakkhasa* assumed the form of a woodsman and approached Mahisāsakumāra saying, "Good sir, you must be weary from travelling. Why do you not go into this pond, bathe, drink, eat of the lotus bulbs and having decked yourself with flowers, go on your way refreshed?"

---

476 The earliest reference is probably Rig Veda 10:87.

477 See Jāt 347 where the commentator explains that a yakkha is to be "reckoned as" a rakkhasa.

478 Jāt 519, discussed in more detail in the chapter on Sakka in § 3:5,16.

479 Dhp-a 10:8, Jāt 20, Jāt 58.

480 Dhp-a 4:5, Jāt 78 and Jāt 147 where the simile is used to indicate something well guarded.

481 Jāt 6. The same story is told at Dhp-a 10:8.

But the Bodhisatta knew, "This is a yakkha!" and he challenged him, "Was it you who took my brothers?" "Yes, it was I." "For what reason did you take them?" "I take all who descend into my pond who do not know the *devadhamma*." The Bodhisatta said that he indeed knew the *devadhamma*, but that he would not speak of it while he remained unwashed. So the *rakkhasa* bathed him, gave him food and drink, decked him with flowers and anointed him with scents and then prepared a decorated couch for him to sit upon, placed within a pavilion beside the pond. Thus comfortably placed the Bodhisatta proclaimed in verse:

One with self-respect and fear of consequence (*hiri-ottappa*)

Possessed of pure ways;

They are the true men,

These may be called those with *devadhamma*.

This answer satisfied the *rakkhasa* and he freed the two brothers and acted as their protector in the forest thereafter. When the old king died and Mahisāsakumāra took his rightful place as king he appointed his two brothers to high office and had an abode (āyatana) made for the yakkha in a delightful place, where he received the finest of garlands and of food.[482]

We can see from this story that a *rakkhasa* is indeed a kind of yakkha. Not only are the two terms used interchangeably in the text but the *rakkhasa* from the outset shows some characteristics normal to yakkhas: he is subject to their king, Vessavaṇa and he follows a strict law in his taking of victims. It is noteworthy that he is no longer referred to as a *rakkhasa* after his conversion by the Bodhisatta.

[482] Jāt 6. Somewhat abridged.

3:4:5 KUMBHAṆḌAS

The *kumbhaṇḍas* are a class of very odd looking beings. The name means "pot-testicles" because their testicles (*aṇḍa* lit. "eggs") are as large as a water-pot (*kumbha).*[483] They are also said to have large bellies (ibid.). They are subject to King Virūḷhaka, the Great King of the south. He is said to enjoy their songs and dances (DN 32). An army of *kumbhaṇḍas* forms the third line of defence of Tāvatiṃsa (Jāt 31). The *kumbhaṇḍas* are difficult to fit into any broader category. One passage identifies them as *dānava-rakkhasā* which are two kinds of yakkha,[484] while another calls them *kumbhaṇḍa-devatā* (DN-a 19).

Existence as a *kumbhaṇḍa* cannot be called a fortunate rebirth. The *kumbhaṇḍas* occur in a passage listing various demonic beings whose power is no match for Sakka's, putting them in company with *pisācās*, *rakkhasas* and *paṃsupisācas*, all more or less demonic beings (Jāt 347). We are told of a corrupt magistrate who was reborn as a *kumbhaṇḍa*. His testicles were so large that when he walked, he had to throw them over his shoulders, and when he sat down, he used them as a seat (SN 19:10).

There are almost no stories specifically about *kumbhaṇḍas*; there were the *kumbhaṇḍa-rakkhasas* who guarded Vessavaṇa's magical mangoes,[485] and little else. We have no names of individual *kumbhaṇḍas*, unless we count King Virūlhaka[486] as such. They also seem to have some association with King Vessavaṇa. Besides the troupe who guarded his mango tree, he is also said to have killed many thousands of them with his glance, scattering them like chaff, although he refrained from this murderous behaviour after becoming a *sotāpanna* (Vin-a Pār 3).

The *kumbhaṇḍas* presumably reproduce sexually as there is a mention of female *kumbhaṇḍas* called *kumbhaṇḍī* and young ones called *kumbhaṇḍapotaka* (boys) and *kumbhaṇḍapotikā* (girls) (DN 32).

---

483 DN-a 32 "their secret parts are as large as water-pots, thus they are called *kumbhaṇḍa*".

484 Jāt 31. This particular passage is omitted from the English translation.

485 Jāt 281. This story will be discussed in the section on King Vessavaṇa in § 3:5,7.

486 The Great King of the South whose special retinue is composed of kumbhaṇḍas. It is more likely that he should be considered a deva. See the chapter on the Cātumahārājika Devas in § 3:5,6.

3:4:6 KINNARAS

We have seen that many of the strange beings inhabiting the Buddhist cosmos are hard to classify, but there is one race whose ambiguous status is embedded in their very name. These are the *kinnara*, (from *kiṃ* + *nara*, "is it a man?") (PED) also known, especially in verse passages, as *kimpurisa* ("is it human?" also spelled *kiṃpurisa*). These are small woodland beings who in many ways resemble the lower devas. The *kinnara* are mostly known for their beautiful singing and dancing[487] and for their deep romantic attachment to their mates. Translators have variously rendered *kinnara* as "fairy", "sylph" (Cowell) or "faun" (Bodhi). In later artistic renderings, the *kinnara* are always shown as bird-like: either with a human head on a bird's body or the upper torso of a human (usually a woman) on a pair of bird's legs.[488] There is almost no support for this image in the old Pali texts. The only hint of a connection to birds is in a list of kinds of *kinnara*: "deva *kinnaras*, moon *kinnaras*, dark *kinnaras* and bird-ears-and-mantle *kinnaras* and so forth."[489] There is no explanation for this strange phrase, which in any case seems to refer only to one kind of *kinnara*, not to all.

On the other hand, there are several stories which involve human men falling in love with *kinnarīs* (female *kinnaras*),[490] which seems less than likely if they have the lower bodies of birds. One such story illustrates the charming ways of the *kinnara*:

> At one time, when Brahmadatta was king at Bārāṇasi, the Bodhisatta took birth as a *kinnara* in the Himavā, by the name of Canda ("Moon"), and he had a wife by the name of Candā.[491] The two lived together on a silver mountain called Mount Canda.
>
> Now, the *kinnaras* of Mount Canda remain in the mountains during the rainy season, but they descend to the low country in the hot season. At one such time, the *kinnara* Canda and his mate were wandering about from place to place, anointing themselves with the scent of flowers, feeding on the pollen, dressing themselves in flowers and playing at swinging from vines and singing songs with voices as sweet as honey. They came upon a small stream and descended into the water where they sported a while, scattering their flowers. Afterward, they emerged from the water, dressed themselves again in robes of flowers and made a bed of bamboo upon the silver sands and lay themselves down. Then Canda took up a piece of bamboo and made sweet sounding music with it. His wife, Candā, got up and danced the dance called "tender hands" (*muduhattha*) while singing with a honeyed voice.
>
> At that time there was a king of men out hunting in the Himavā and hearing the sound of their sweet music, he approached the spot softly and stood watching the *kinnaras* from a hidden place. He was stricken with love for the *kinnarī* and determined to kill her husband and take her for himself. And so he shot an arrow into Canda, who lamented with his dying breath:
>
>> My heart sinks in suffering, the darkness consumes me.
>>
>> It is for you, my Candā, that I grieve, there is no other pain.
>
> Candā, being intoxicated with delight, at first did not know that her mate had been shot. But when she saw him lying there senseless, wondered "what is the matter with my dear husband?" Looking closer she saw the

487 Jāt 547 where the songs and dances of the kinnara are listed among the wonders of the Himavā.

488 For example the kinnari statues common in Thailand, which have the upper body of a woman and the lower body of a bird.

489 Jāt 536. The Pali for the last type is *sakuṇakaṇṇapāvuraṇ*ādibhedā kinnarā.

490 Jāt 234, 485 and 542 (eng. 546).

491 Candā = a feminine form of the noun *canda*, "the moon.".

wound with blood flowing from it and overcome with unbearable sorrow she lamented in a loud voice. At this, the king showed himself and she exclaimed, "Here is the brigand who has slain my dear husband!" She ran off to a hill top and stood there, cursing the king:

May this, my heart-ache, be known by your own wife,

This, my heart-ache, seeing the slain *kimpurisa.*

May your wife and your mother know the loss of their prince,

You who have slain this blameless *kimpurisa*, all for the lust of me.

The king told her to cease lamenting, he would take her to be his wife and she would live in a royal palace, but Candā said she would rather die than live with the slayer of her husband. Hearing this, the king lost his passion for her and left her there, saying:

So, timid one, if you desire to live, go back to the Himavā.

Feed on plants and herbs, enjoy yourself with the other animals.

Candā returned to her husband's body, cradling him in her arms, After weeping and lamenting for a while, Candā detected some faint signs of life and she "made a complaint" (*ujjhānakamma*) against the devas. "Are there no guardians of the world? Have they gone away or perhaps they are dead, why do they not save my husband?" At this, Sakka descended in the form of a brahmin and revived Canda by sprinkling him with a magical water pot and admonished the happy pair to return to Mount Canda and never again to descend into the lands of human beings. (Jāt 485)

Another story of a human man falling in love with a *kinnarī* is found in an anecdote from the Umaṅga Jātaka:

In times gone by there was a brahmin named Vaccha who seeing the disadvantage in sense pleasures left home to practice austerities in the Himavā. Nearby his hermitage, there was a cave where many *kinnaras* lived. At the entrance there dwelled a spider. The *kinnaras* were being caught in its web, whereupon the spider would break open their skulls and drink their blood. Now, *kinnaras* are weak and timid and the spider was very great. Being unable to do anything for themselves, the *kinnaras* approached the hermit and he received them kindly. They told him why they had come, "Deva,[492] a spider is slaying us. Besides yourself, we have no other refuge. Please kill it and save us!" But Vaccha replied, "Go away. Those like me do not kill living beings."

Now among the *kinnaras* there was a *kinnarī* named Raṭṭhavatī who was beautiful and charming and who had no husband. She adorned herself and went to see the hermit saying, "Deva, I will be your handmaiden if you slay our enemy." Seeing her, Vaccha became enamoured. After making love with her, he went to the door of the cave and when the spider left his den, the hermit killed it with a club. Thereafter the two, Vaccha and Raṭṭhavatī, lived together and had many children. They dwelled in harmony until they died. (Jāt 542, eng 546)

The beauty of *kinnara* females is proverbial. It is high praise to tell a human woman that she has "eyes like a

[492] Used as a deferential mode of address.

kinnarī" (Jāt 458) or that she is "as graceful as a *kinnarī*" (Jāt 527). Yet there must be something about their appearance that is not quite human as the following story illustrates:

> It so happened that a hunter wandering in the Himavā by means of his skill captured a pair of *kinnaras* and brought them to the king. The king had never seen *kinnaras* before and he asked the hunter "Hunter, of what kind are these things?" "Sire, they can sing sweetly and dance delightfully. No human being knows how to sing and dance like these." The king gave much wealth to the hunter and said to the *kinnaras*, "Sing! Dance!" But the *kinnaras* thought, "If we sing and we get a syllable wrong, then we will have make a bad song. They will reproach us and punish us. Also, those who speak much, must tell lies." So out of fear of wrong speech, although the king commanded them again and again they would neither sing nor dance. The king, growing angry, said, "Kill them and cook their flesh and bring it to me."
>
> These are not devas, nor *gandhabbas*.
>
> They are but beasts, brought to me for profit.
>
> When cooked, one can furnish my supper,
>
> The other my breakfast.
>
> Then the *kinnarī* thought, "Without a doubt, the king will kill us. Now is the time to speak!" And she spoke aloud:
>
> A hundred thousand ill-made songs,
>
> Are not worth a fraction of one well sung.
>
> It is from fear of the defilement of wrong speech,
>
> And not from folly that we *kinnaras* are silent.
>
> Satisfied with the *kinnarī*, the king ordered that she be sent back to her home in the Himavā but that the other would still serve as his breakfast. On hearing this, the male *kinnara* then spoke as well:
>
> Just as the cattle depend on the rain,
>
> And men upon the cattle,
>
> I, o king, depend on thee,
>
> And my wife depends on me.
>
> Know we are a pair,
>
> And set us free in the Himavā. (Jāt 481)

After some further conversation (in verse) the king decided that "these are wise *kinnaras*" and sent them in a golden cage to be released into the Himavā. We can see from this anecdote that the *kinnara* are not wholly human in appearance, or the king would not have decided they were wild animals suitable for his breakfast. It also hints at their small size, which the fact of their being prey to a spider in the previous story also implies.

The *kinnara* are mainly found in the commentaries and the later verses of the *Khuddaka Nikāya*. Their sole mention in the four principal *nikāyas* is found in the *Aṅguttara* and concerns their reluctance to speak:

> There are two reasons why *kiṃpurisas* do not utter human speech. That they may not speak a falsehood, and that they may not accuse another wrongly. (AN 2: 60, eng 61)

The commentary to this passage cites two ways in which *kinnaras* can be made to speak:

> A *kinnara* was presented to King Asoka and he ordered it to speak, but it did not wish to. One of the king's men said that he could make it talk, so he prepared a cooking pot and a skewer and showed them to the *kinnara*, who said "It is not right that one should impale another upon a skewer." On another occasion, two *kinnaras* were brought to the king and again they did not wish to speak. Another man said he could get them to talk and he carried them out of the palace and into the market. There they saw ripe mangoes and fish for sale. Among them were some sour mangoes and some rotten ones. One of the *kinnara* said, "What poison these humans eat! How do they not get sick from it?" And the other agreed, "Surely they will get the leprosy!" (AN-a 2:61)

One final story illustrates the deep affection *kinnaras* have for one another:

> Aking had gone hunting in the Himavā and seeking game had penetrated far into that wild country. Following a delightful river up the slope of Mt Gandhamādana he came across two *kinnaras*. They were fondly embracing and covering each other with kisses while weeping and lamenting all the while. Approaching them softly the king asked:
>
> "I ask you, with your human-seeming form (*mānusadehavaṇṇa*), how are you known in the world of men?"
>
> "The wild animals deem us of human kind, but the hunters know us as *kimpurisa* (lit. 'is it human?')"
>
> The king asked them why they wept so. Their reply was that one night seven hundred years ago they had been out gathering flowers when a mountain torrent had suddenly rushed through a little stream and separated them from one another for an entire night.
>
> There we stood, on either bank,
>
> Gazing at one another.
>
> At times weeping, at times laughing;
>
> That night was very painful for us.
>
> The morning came with rising sun,
>
> The stream was dry.
>
> So we embraced once more;
>
> At times weeping, at times laughing.
>
> It was seven hundred years less seven,

Since we were parted so.

The king was astonished and asked them what was the lifespan of their kind, to which they answered one thousand years.

A thousand years is our life, huntsman.

And in that span there is no evil or sickness.

Little is our suffering and great our bliss;

But we are not freed from passion while life lasts. (Jāt 504)

The Buddha told this tale to Mallikā, the beloved wife of King Pasenadi to mend a quarrel between them. The king and his queen had been those very *kinnaras* in a long ago life. Once again we see the appearance of the *kinnaras* raises questions. The king addresses them as "human-seeming" implying that they have something almost, but not quite, like a human form. The *kinnara* folk remain a delightful mystery of the Buddhist cosmos.

CHAPTER FIVE—DEVAS

3:5:1 DEVAS

Above the human world in the cosmic hierarchy are the various levels of *devas*. The *devas* are beings of the *kāmabhūmi*, (plane of sense-desire) considered to have a fortunate rebirth, longer lives and more pleasure than human beings. They surpass humans in five qualities in particular: life-span (āyu), beauty (*vaṇṇa*), happiness (*sukha*), fame (*yasa;* the implication is that they have large retinues)[493] and power (ādhipateyya) (AN 3: 18). Devas are anthropomorphic in appearance, and always very beautiful. As beings of the *kāmabhūmi*, like human beings and animals, they are gendered and enjoy sexual relations.[494] Likewise, they consume solid food,[495] although their food, called *sudhābhojana*, (Jāt 535) is much subtler than ours. Their bodies also are more refined then ours, and free of all gross impurities (Dhp-a 14:1). We have no clear indication as to the physical size of *bhumma* (earth-bound) devas, although it seems they were at most of human stature. The devas of the *saggas* (heavenly worlds) on the other hand are often described as having *tigāvuta* bodies, which would make them eight kilometres tall.[496] Nevertheless, should they choose to do so, up to sixty devas can stand together on the point of an awl and not feel crowded (AN 2: 36).

Devas are normally invisible to human beings, because our visual consciousness is not refined enough to perceive them (MN 90). In the same way brahmās, who are beings of the *rūpabhūmi* (plane of form), are normally invisible to devas (DN 18). In both cases, the higher-level being may be perceived by the lower as a brilliant light.[497] In one sutta the Buddha recounts how before his full awakening his knowledge of devas grew in stages: first he perceived only a light, then he became aware of forms, then he was able to converse with them and finally acquired various knowledges about them such as to which class of deva they belonged and whether he had ever lived among them (AN 8: 64).

The mode of birth for devas is *opapātika yoni*, spontaneous rebirth. The new deva simply appears fully grown, perhaps already equipped with a palace and a retinue, if its merit is sufficient (MN 12 & SN-a 1:46). There sometimes exists a kind of parent-child relationship among devas: the young ones are called *devaputta* and *devadhītā*, ("deva son" and "deva daughter"). In this case they are said to appear upon the lap of their parent, usually their father.[498] Although the life-span of devas is very long, reaching 2.3 billion years in the highest of the *saggas*, they are mortal like all other beings in the Buddhist cosmos. However, for them death is as painless as birth. There is no prolonged death-agony. A few days before his passing, the deva observes in himself the "five signs": his garments become soiled, his garlands fade, his armpits grow sweaty, his body loses its glowing complexion and he becomes restless on his seat (DN-a 14). At the end, he simply disappears from that place.

The Pali word *deva* (it is the same in Sanskrit) derives either from the root *div*, meaning to play or make sport, or from the old Indo-Aryan *dejā*, meaning "to shine"[499] It is related to both the Latin *deus*, god and to the old Iranian *daevo*, from which we get the English "devil."

---

493 See PED for *yasa*.

494 DN-a 33. This point will be discussed further in the section on Paranimmitavasavatti devas, § 3:5,32.

495 See AN 5: 166 where the devas of the kāmabhūmi are called *kabaḷīkārāhārabhakkha* devas to distinguish them from the brahmās who are called *manomaya* ("mind-made") devas. Also, SN 1:43, "Both humans and devas delight in food".

496 This is found in the commentaries only. See for example DN-a 19 and SN-a 1:11. A *gāvuta* is one fourth of a *yojana*.

497 In DN 21, when Sakka comes with his retinue to visit the Buddha, the villagers see only a brilliant light and are terrified.

498 SN-a 2:1. However, *devaputtā* and *devadhitā* are sometimes used simply to indicate the gender of the being, without a parental reference implied.

499 PED for *deva*.

The name *deva* or the alternate form *devatā*[500] is sometimes used in a general way to refer to all beings superior to humans,[501] but is more precisely used to refer to the beings of the plane of sense desire only. These devas exist in several levels: there are the *bhumma* devas who dwell on this earth, usually in the forest, the *valāhaka* devas who live in the sky and clouds and influence the weather, and there are the devas of the six *saggas* or heavenly abodes.

The human realm is usually considered to be the ideal state for realization of the Dhamma, because of the balance of pleasure and pain. When the Buddha teaches Dhamma to the devas, they mostly become afraid and cry out, "We thought we were everlasting, not subject to change, but it is not so!" (AN 4:33) Their long lives of constant pleasure lull them into heedlessness.

Nevertheless it is possible for some devas to hear the Dhamma and to attain to the fruits of the path. This is said to be a good reason to memorize passages of Dhamma while still in human form, so that one may recall them easily if reborn as a deva. Devas may recall the Dhamma in four ways: more fortunate devas may recite passages to them, some earthly bhikkhu with psychic power may preach to them, some devas are advanced enough to teach on their own account and some may recover old memories by speaking with other devas who were previously bhikkhus (AN 4: 191). There are many incidents of devas attaining to stream-entry recounted in the canon. It is specifically stated that there are some *sotāpanna* devas to be found in each of the *saggas* (AN 6: 34).

In translations the devas are sometimes referred to as "gods." This is a natural enough association and there is probably a deep historical link between the devas of Tāvatiṃsa (at least) and the pantheons of Greek and Norse mythology via the Aryan expansion of the second millennium B.C. Nevertheless, the devas of Buddhist India differ from the gods of the West in at least two important respects. First, as mentioned above, they are mortal beings subject to birth and death (AN 5: 48). A human being may be reborn as a deva and when a deva dies he may be reborn human or even into the lower realms; indeed this is the case more often than not.[502] Second, the devas are in no way the creators of the world; nor are they its governors in any but the most remote and notional sense. To these two important considerations, we might also add that the devas are in general much better behaved than the gods. In contrast to the well-known escapades of Zeus, when Sakka impregnated a human woman to fulfill her wish for sons, he did so by gently touching her navel with his thumb (Jāt 531).

Rebirth into the deva realms is accomplished principally by acts of generosity, particularly when the giver makes an aspiration toward such rebirth.[503] However the truly wise spiritual seeker does not desire any kind of rebirth, no matter how pleasant; existence as a deva is seen by the awakened as sensual bondage (SN 1:46 & SN 1:11).

---

500 A feminine noun which does not presuppose the gender of the being referred to.

501 Thus the brahmās are called *manomaya devas* at AN 5: 166.

502 SN 56:101 f. (eng. 56:108 f.). It is a general rule that it is easier to be born down rather than up.

503 AN 8:35 and see Vv-a passim.

3:5:2 DEVAS OF THE EARTH AND SKY

The lowest class of devas are those who do not dwell in any of the *saggas* (heaven realms), but are bound to the same terrestrial space as the humans and animals. There are many different levels of happiness and power among the earth-bounds devas. Some are poor things, not nearly as wretched as the petas perhaps, but approaching that state. Others are beings of great might and power. Like the higher devas of the *saggas*, they are normally invisible to humans, or appear only as a brilliant light. They may interact with humans from time to time, usually benevolently, but are more often content to simply enjoy their own existence. They prefer wild places, especially forests, to areas of human habitation, although there are also devas who dwell in towns, *nagaradevatā*. The wide spread and range of habitations of these devas approach an animistic or pantheistic view of the natural world and is an important component in the traditional Buddhist reverence for nature.

3:5:3 BHUMMA DEVAS

The devas of the forest, and of the earth generally, are collectively known as *bhumma devas*, the word *bhumma* referring to the earth or soil. This is considered the lowest form of deva, and a person who makes merit, but may have some deficiencies in his virtue, is reborn there:

> A young man lived a life of heedless pleasure, and having wasted his inheritance, he took to armed robbery. Captured by the king's men, he was being led to his execution when a young woman took pity on him and gave him some sweet-meats. The Venerable Moggallāna was nearby, and he knew this man would be reborn in *niraya* if he did not make some merit quickly. So, the elder appeared before the man who stood with the sweets in hand. He offered them to the venerable elder bhikkhu. By this act, he would have re-appeared in the deva-world except that as his head was being chopped off, he had a mind of lust toward the young woman. As a result, he took birth as an inferior kind of deva, a tree-spirit whose abode was a large banyan tree inthe jungle. (Pv-a 1:1)

There are many kinds of *bhumma* devas, living in many kinds of abode. There are sea-devas (*samuddadevatā,* (Jāt 146, 190, 296)) river-devas (*nadīdevatā,* (Jāt 288)) forest-devas (*aṭavidevatā,* (Dhp-a 8:9) *vanadevatā,* (MN 45, SN 41:10, Jāt 13)) park-devas (*uyyānadevatā,* (Jāt 539) *ārāmadevatā,* (MN 45)) plant-, bush- or foliage-devas (*palāsadevatā,* (Jāt 370), *rucādevatā,* (Jāt 121)) grass-devas (*kusanāḷidevatā,* (Jāt 121)) as well as town-devas (*nagaradevatā,* (Jāt 497)) and household-devas (*antodevatā,* (Dhp-a 4:8)).

Some of these devas enjoy a kind of symbiotic relationship with human kind. Human beings venerate them, make ritual offerings to them and in return they protect the health and wealth of their human benefactors. These are called *balipaṭiggāhikā* ("those who receive offerings") devas. The Buddha approved of this practice, provided it did not involve sacrifice of living beings. He listed making such offerings among the factors which tend to growth of a lay person's health and wealth, (AN 5:58) and said that if proper respect is not shown to the *balipaṭiggāhikā* devas, then they will not be happy and will fail to provide protection (AN 5: 228). The commentary identifies these devas with family ancestors who have been reborn in that state (AN-a 5:58).

These domestic devas are also known as ārakkhadevatā ("guardian devas"), and these guardians appear in other contexts as well. One king with a penchant for gambling had an ārakkhadevatā, who had been his mother in a previous existence, who magically interfered with the dice rolls so that he always won (Jāt 546, Eng. 545). In another story, an abandoned baby prince was saved by his ārakkhadevatā who transformed herself into a she-goat and suckled him until some shepherds came along and adopted him (Jāt 536). In one very curious story, a battle between two armies is mirrored by a fight between the ārakkhadevatās of the two opposing nations who take the forms of a white bull and a black bull. Sakka had predicted that the white bull would triumph and his nation would win the war, but the general of the black bull's army, learning of this, overturned the deva king's prophecy by having his men kill the white bull with one thousand spears (Jāt 301).

The most common kind of *bhummadeva*, to judge by their frequent appearance in the stories, is a *rukkhadeva* or tree-spirit. They are often called according to the type of tree which is their abode, as for example a "bodhi-tree deva" (*assatthadevatā*) or a "nimb-tree deva" (*nimbadevatā*) (Jāt 311). They are generally imagined as living in a small invisible abode among the foliage, but at times it seems almost as if they are identified with the tree itself:

> A certain bhikkhu was cutting branches from living trees in order to construct a dwelling. In doing so, he cut off the arm of the *rukkhadeva's* son. The *rukkhadeva* was enraged, and considered killing the bhikkhu but

instead reported the incident to the Buddha, who laid down the rule against cutting living plants.[504]

Another story illustrates this point even more clearly:

A king desired to build himself a remarkable palace. All of the other kings in India had palaces with many pillars, so he determined to have one built with but a single mighty pillar. At first his carpenters thought this could not be done, but then they found a great Sāl Tree in the royal forest which looked strong enough to serve.

It was a noble, straight tree which was worshipped by folk of the towns and cities and received oblations from the royal family. It was an auspicious (*maṅgala*) Sāl Tree. They went and told the king of it, and he ordered it to be cut down. So the carpenters returned to the park with garlands in their hands, anointed the tree with the five-fold anointing (*gandhapañcaṅgulikaṃ*), tied a thread around it bound with flower blossoms, lit a lamp and offered oblations. They announced to the tree, "Here in seven day's time we will come and cut down this tree. The king commands the felling. Any devas living in this tree must go to another place. We bear you no ill-will."

Hearing this, the deva of the tree thought, "Without a doubt those carpenters will fell this tree. My dwelling (*vimāna*) will be destroyed. The limit of my dwelling is the limit of my life.[505] All around there are young sāl trees under my protection, where many of my deva relations dwell. Their dwellings too will be destroyed; the limit of my dwelling is also the limit of their lives. The loss of my own life does not afflict me as much as the loss of life of my kin. It is fitting that I give them life. (I.e. save them)."

Thinking thus, at midnight he entered the royal bed-chamber, richly adorned in his deva finery and filling the whole chamber with light. There he stood in the air beside the bed, weeping. Seeing this, the king was frightened and said,

Who are you, dressed in pure garment,

Standing in the air?

Why do you weep?

And whence comes my fear?

Within your kingdom, sire,

I am known as the Lucky Tree.

For sixty thousand years,

I have stood and been worshipped.

They built cities and towns,

504 Vin. Pāc. 11. There is a slightly different version of this story at Dhp-a 17:2 where the deva is clearly not to be identified with the tree.

505 *vimānapariyantikameva kho pana mayhaṃ jīvitaṃ.*

My Lord, my enemy.

They built many palaces,

But did not harm me.

They worshipped me, and so should you.

The king replied,

Never have I seen so great a tree;

Great in height and in girth,

Beautiful in form.

I will make a palace,

With one delightful pillar.

This I give to you,

And there may you live a long time, yakkha.

Hearing this, the *devarājā* replied:

Since it is arisen in your mind to destroy my body,

Cut me up piece by piece;

Cut the top, and then the middle and last the root.

If you cut me thus, my death will not be suffering.

Astonished, thinking this must be a more torturous way of death than one clean cut, the king asks why and is told that in this way there will be no danger of destruction to the young sāl trees, the deva's kin, who grow round about. Impressed, the king grants the tree his protection and abandons the plan to cut it down. (Jāt 465)

There exists a kind of class system among the *bhummadevas*, with the most exalted living in great trees, and the most humble in lesser vegetation. The following excerpt is from a Jātaka the Buddha told as a teaching against class prejudice:

A powerful deva-king (*mahesakko devarājā*) was reborn as a *rukkhadeva*, dwelling in a huge, straight, beautiful blessing-tree (*rucamaṇgalarukkho*) in the king's garden. In the same garden dwelt a humble deva in a clump of *kusa* grass. One day, the king ordered the big tree cut down to make a new pillar for his palace. The royal carpenters made a sacrifice to the tree, and announced that they would be felling it the next day. The *rukkhadeva* was distraught and fearful for the loss of his home, not knowing where he would flee with his children. None of his friends among the other devas were able to help, except for the *kusa* grass deva, who hit upon a ruse. He took on the form of a chameleon and caused the appearance of holes in the trunk of the blessing-tree. When the carpenters came with their saws and axes the next day they saw a trunk full of

> holes with a little lizard peeking out of one. Deciding it was too rotten to use as a pillar, they moved on. The blessing-tree deva remarked how of all these powerful devas, only the humble *kusa* grass deva had the wit to save his home. Truly, a good friend should not be chosen by his rank. (Jāt 121)

For this last idea to be made a point of implies that the opposite was sadly often the case. We can also learn from this story that even the humblest of devas have magical powers of transformation, and can make themselves visible to humans in some form if they so choose. Further, we learn from these stories of the family relations among devas, who are very fond of their children. *Bhummadevas* generally are born by spontaneous arising, like the higher devas, but later sources say that some of them also give birth via the womb (Vism 17:154). At times, there may be sexual attraction between devas and humans, as in the Samiddhi Jātaka (Jāt 167) where a female deva, (*devadhitā*, "daughter of the devas") sees a hermit bathing and declares her love for him, attempting without success to seduce him away from his asceticism.

At this lowest level of the devas, there is sometimes very little distinction made between devas, petas and yakkhas:

> A certain poor tailor lived in the same city as a wealthy merchant. The merchant was widely known for his great generosity, and when beggars came looking for the merchant's abode, the tailor would stand outside his shop, pointing the way with a joyful heart. Because of this, when he died he was reborn as a tree-deva in a banyan tree in a desert oasis. When weary travelers stopped in the tree's shade, they would see a golden hand, dripping with honey, pointing with a finger. And where the hand pointed, there would appear food and water. (Pv-a 2:9)

In the course of the story from which the above is an excerpt, this same being is called a *deva*, a *peta* and *yakkha* indiscriminately. The appellation of yakkha is generally used to emphasize the being's powers. On the contrary, the word peta implies a being in a state of suffering. Whereas a rebirth as a *bhummadeva* is classed as a happy one, and is the result of making merit, their happiness is not on the same level as that of the higher devas. For one thing, the pleasures they enjoy are dependent on a material basis. As we have seen, *rukkhadevas* suffer greatly when the trees they dwell in are felled.

There is, nevertheless, one important way in which the *bhumma* devas have an advantage over the higher devas. If a higher deva should attain to *arahatta*, the state of full awakening, he or she must immediately perish because an arahant cannot exist in an entirely sensual world. Even in the case of humans, a lay arahant must either die or go forth as a bhikkhu or bhikkhunī within seven days. However, a *bhumma* deva who becomes an arahant can continue to live in that state indefinitely because they can seclude themselves in a remote place far away from sensual attractions (DN-a 29).

The relations between *bhummadevas* and humans are complex. Sometimes humans worship *bhummadevas*, as we have seen, making food offerings at their trees. There are accounts of this happening in ancient India, and the contemporary Thai custom of building "spirit houses" is another form of this custom. Sometimes they reward their worshippers, for example by revealing buried treasures to them (Jāt 307). Although the devas are generally benevolent towards humans, it seems that our coarse physical form and particularly our odour is offensive to them. (On the other hand, the scent of a moral person is "pleasing to the devas" and travels even against the wind) (AN 3:80, Eng. AN 3:79).

> A thousand families seeking a home sailed in a large ship to a pleasant island, filled with all manner of fruit trees and other good things in abundance. A lone castaway lived there before them, and he warned them that powerful devas lived there too. He said that they would not trouble the people so long as they kept their living places clean and always buried their bodily waste. The people enjoyed life on the island for a long time, but

one day they held a festival and got drunk on toddy made from sugar-cane. While intoxicated, they emptied their bowels and their bladders heedlessly about the island. This angered the devas who decided in council to wait until their powers were at a peak on the full moon and then to cleanse the island with a mighty flood. A kind-hearted deva took it upon himself to warn the people, and advised them to build a new ship and sail away. Knowing this, a cruel-minded deva also appeared to the people and told them not to worry, the first deva was only trying to trick them into leaving. Half the human families followed a wise leader and built themselves a boat straightaway. The others listened to the second deva and all perished when waves poured over the island. (Jāt 466)

From this we can see also that the devas vary in terms of their morality, and have power to effect human life for good or ill. Sometimes they act out of simple mischief. One example is the *devī* (female deva) who played a mean trick on a good bhikkhu. He had gone into the bushes to relieve himself and when he emerged, she followed close behind him in the form of a pretty young woman hastily adjusting her garments. This caused him to suffer an undeserved scandalous reputation among his fellow bhikkhus. The *devī* suffered terrible karmic results from this prank, being reborn in *niraya*. When she finally became reborn as a human male and took ordination, the residue of his kamma caused him to be followed everywhere by the illusory form of a woman, so that he too suffered disrepute (Dhp-a 10:4).

Devas vary in terms of wisdom. The foolish and greedy ones set up their abodes in solitary trees close to human villages, hoping for worship and offerings, whereas the wise ones choose to dwell in remote, dense forests where the interlocking branches protect the trees against storms (Jāt 74).

Rukkhadevas, those living in trees, have some governance over the tree and have their duties to perform, *rukkhadhamma* or tree-duty:

Long ago, the great king Koravya had a mighty banyan tree called Supatiṭṭha. It's branches spread over twelve *yojana*. The tree produced an abundance of huge fruits, as sweet and delicious as honey. One portion of the fruit was enjoyed by the king and his concubines, another by the army, another by the common people, another was for the brahmins and *samaṇas*, and one was reserved for the birds and beasts. It happened one day that a man rested in the shade of Supatiṭṭha, enjoyed some of its fruit and then heedlessly broke a branch before going on his way. This angered the deva who dwelt in the tree and he caused it to stop bearing the wonderful fruit. King Koravya told this to Sakka, the king of the gods, and he made a mighty tempest which overturned the banyan tree and tore its roots out of the ground. The deva stood by the tree weeping for the loss of his home. Sakka appeared before the deva and asked him if he had been keeping *rukkhadhamma* ("tree-duty"). "But what is that?" "A tree keeps *rukkhadhamma* if when someone grubs for the roots, picks the leaves, plucks the fruit or strips the bark, he does not make it a cause for complaint. If you keep to your *rukkhadhamma* in the future, I shall restore your home to its former place." The deva promised to do so, and Sakka magically restored the tree. (AN 6: 54)

The Buddha told this story to the bhikkhu Dhammika as a parable with the meaning that he should bear any insult without animosity.

Bhummadevas, and occasionally higher types, are sometimes depicted as admonishing forest dwelling bhikkhus who have gone astray in one way or the other. An entire chapter of the Saṃyutta Nikāya is devoted to these episodes.[506] In each case, a bhikkhu or a group of bhikkhus, are found negligent in some specific way: thinking sensual thoughts, falling asleep, or associating too much with lay people. Then the deva inhabiting that part of the forest will appear to the bhikkhu and admonish him in several stanzas of Pali verse, after which the bhikkhu "acquires a new sense of

[506] SN 9:1 f. – the *Vanasaṃyutta*.

urgency." Sometimes the deva's verses are sarcastic or teasing, as in the story of the "scent-thief."

> A certain bhikkhu was in the habit of wading into a pond to smell the lotuses which grew there. The deva who lived there appeared to him and admonished him in verse:
>
> When you sniff this lotus flower,
>
> An item that has not been given,
>
> This is one factor of theft:
>
> You, dear sir, are a thief of scent
>
> When the bhikkhu objects (also in verse) that he has not damaged the plants, and asks why the deva does not admonish those who tear them up by the roots, she replies:
>
> When a person is rough and fierce,
>
> Badly soiled like a nursing cloth,
>
> I have nothing to say to him:
>
> But it's to you that I ought to speak.
>
> For a person without blemish,
>
> Always in quest of purity,
>
> Even a mere hair's tip of evil
>
> Appears as big as a cloud.
>
> The bhikkhu thanks her, and asks her to admonish him again in the future whenever she sees him going astray. But to this the deva speaks one final verse:
>
> We don't live with your support,
>
> Nor are we your hired servant.
>
> You, bhikkhu, should know for yourself
>
> The way to a good destination.[507]

Such woodland devas are also seen lamenting when good bhikkhus move away from their habitat (SN 9:4). There is also this story, from the *Visuddhimagga*:

> A certain elder bhikkhu was dwelling at the Cittapabbata Vihara (in Sri Lanka) and was devoted to the practice of *mettā* ("loving-kindness") meditation. At the end of the rains retreat, he started thinking of moving somewhere else. A deva living in a *maṇila*-tree at the end of his walking path began to weep. The elder asked

[507] SN 9:14. Verses as translated by Bhikkhu Bodhi, CDB, p. 303-4.

after the sound, and the deva introduced herself as Maṇiliyā and said she was weeping because he was going away. "As long as you dwell here, the devas are in harmony. If you leave, they will fall into quarrels and loose talk." So he agreed to stay where he was. (Vism 9:69)

A story about a river-deva living in the Ganges illustrates something of their nature and their relations with human beings:

When Brahmadatta was king of Bārāṇasi there were two brothers who travelled up the Ganges on some business whereby they made a thousand *kahāpaṇa* (a unit of money). Before boarding the boat for the return journey they ate a meal by the river bank and the elder brother threw the left-overs into the river for the fishes, giving the merit of the gift to the *nadīdevatā* ("river deva.") The deva rejoiced in the gift and thereby experienced an increase in her[508] divine power (*dibba yasa*). Reflecting on this, she knew what action had made this happen.

Now, whereas the elder brother was good and honest, the younger brother had a somewhat thievish nature. He made up a parcel of gravel to look like the parcel of money, and when they were in the middle of the river he pretended to accidentally kick it overboard. "Brother, the money has gone overboard! What should we do?" "It has fallen into water, there is nothing to be done. Don't give it another thought." But the thievish brother had made a mistake and kicked over the real parcel of money, leaving him with just the gravel.

The *nadīdevatā* thought, "By this one has my divine power increased. I will safeguard his property." So, by her power she caused a great fish to swallow the parcel of money, thus holding it safe.

When the brothers got home, the younger was at first elated at the trick he had played on his brother but when he opened the parcel and saw the gravel, he fell to his bed, sick at heart. Meanwhile, some fishermen had caught the fish in their net. Afterward, they went into the city to sell their catch. When people asked how much they wanted for the big fish, they said "One thousand *kahāpaṇa* and seven *māsaka"* (a small coin of little worth) The people laughed, "Now we have seen a fish worth a thousand *kahāpaṇa*!" At last the fishermen came to the door of the elder brother and said "Buy our fish." "How much is it?" "You can have it for seven *māsaka*, but for others it is one thousand *kahāpana* more."

So he bought the fish and gave it to his wife to cook. When she cut it open, they found the parcel of money. (Jāt 288)

There are a couple of points worth noting in this story. First, the mechanism by which the river deva increases her power is identical to the way the sharing of merit works in the case of petas.[509] The elder brother did not give an offering directly to the deva; he gave some scraps of food to the fish and made the merit over to her. Furthermore, the increase in her power occurred only after she rejoiced (*anumodati*) in the act of generosity. This is in spite of the doctrine that sharing of merit only benefits those in the peta realm. Another point of interest is the way in which the deva exercises her power to help her benefactor. She did not act directly, but through the agency of other beings: the fish and the fishermen. Both of these are beings who live dependent on the Ganges and may be considered in some sense under her dominion.

Some *bhummadevas* live in towns and cities; these are given the appellation *nagaradevatā*. It seems that their

508 The Pali *devatā* is a feminine noun and is so modified and inflected, but we cannot be sure of the gender of the deva here as the word is also used to refer to male devas.

509 See § 3:3,3.

favourite dwelling place is over a gateway, such as were found in the walled compounds which were the homes of the wealthy in ancient India:

> Anāthapiṇḍika was a very wealthy merchant, and a devout follower of the Buddha. His home had seven gateways, and over the fourth gateway there dwelt a *devī* who had wrong views (*micchadiṭṭṭhikā-devatā*). Whenever the Buddha or one of his disciples came to see Anāthapiṇḍika, she was compelled to leave her place and flee to the first floor. This annoyed her, so she appeared to Anāthapiṇḍika hovering in the air and attempted to persuade him to stop making meal offerings to the Buddha and the *Saṅgha*. Anāthapiṇḍika responded by expelling her from his home. She left weeping with her children in tow and appealed to the chief deva of the city (*nagara-pariggāhaka-devaputta*). He had no sympathy, calling her wicked. She then went to the Four Great Kings, with the same result. Finally, she went to Sakka, King of the Devas in Tāvatiṃsa, who told her that Anāthapiṇḍika had almost exhausted his wealth, and advised her that she could make amends by finding him more. This she did in three ways: by using her deva powers to recover some treasure he had lost at sea, by finding him new wealth in the form of a buried treasure and by going with some fierce young yakkhas to dun his negligent debtors. Afterward, she again appeared before Anāthapiṇḍika and begged his forgiveness, which he gave her after taking her to the Buddha to take the triple gem as refuge. (Jāt 40)

Here we have a fascinating glimpse into the internal government of the devas, and an example of both their powers and their vulnerability. The episode near the end which has yakkhas acting as bill-collectors may be a droll image, but nevertheless somehow appropriate; one imagines it would at least be effective![510]

[510] In Jātaka 155 we see a tamed yakkha employed as a tax-collector.

3:5:4 VALĀHAKA-DEVAS

The *valāhakadevas*, cloud-devas, dwell in the clouds and have some control over the weather. They are divided into cold-cloud devas, warm-cloud devas, storm-cloud devas, wind devas and rain devas. Creating weather is, for these devas, an act of play (*kīḷā*) (DN-ṭ 27). When a storm-cloud deva, for instance, causes a storm it is due to his "revelling in his own kind of delight" (SN 32:7). During the hot season they do not like to stir from their *vimānas*, it being too hot to play, hence it does not rain, "even a single drop" (DN-a 27). These devas, however, are not the sole cause of the weather; the commentary lists seven: the power of nāgas, the power of *supaṇṇas*, the power of devas, the power of an assertion of truth, natural weather (*utusamuṭṭhāna*- lit. caused by temperature), the workings of Māra and supernormal power (SN-a 32:1). The sub-commentary explains that normal seasonal changes are simply the work of natural processes, but unusual weather is caused by action of these devas.[511]

It is also said that the morality of human beings has an indirect effect on the weather; by causing the sky devas to become either pleased or annoyed. When the state of human morality is good the devas are pleased and the rain falls regularly in due season; when human morality is bad, the devas are displeased and withhold the rains (AN 4: 70). However, it may also happen that the cloud-devas are simply distracted by play and become heedless (AN-a 5: 197) because they are, after all, beings of the plane of sense desire. As this is said to be among the causes of failure of the rains which the prognosticators (*nemitta*) do not know and cannot see, it may explain why weather forecasts are so often wrong!

[511] Bhikkhu Bodhi, CDB, p. 1102, footnote 293.

3:5:5 THE TERRESTRIAL *SAGGAS*

Above the *bhummadevas* in the celestial hierarchy are the devas who live in their own special realms, known as *saggas*. In translation, these are often called the "sensual heavens" but just as in the case of translating *niraya* as "hell," the English words carry unwarranted cultural baggage. A *sagga* differs from the heaven of theistic religions in at least two important respects: First, the principle that there is no immortality in the Buddhist cosmos applies. Devas living in the *saggas* have very long life-spans by human standards, but when their kamma runs out they decease from that place and are reborn elsewhere. A *sagga* is not a final destination, but just one among many possible stations of transient rebirth. Second, the *saggas* are not even the highest possible position among these stations of rebirth. Above them are the planes of form and the formless, to be discussed later. And all of these are part of conditioned existence, that is to say *saṃsāra*, subject to imperfection and impermanence.

There are six hierarchically arranged *saggas* altogether. All are considered part of the *kāmabhūmi*, the plane of sense desire. The two lowest of these still have some physical connection with the earth as they are located on Mt Sineru, the great mountain at the centre of the world: the *Cātumahārājika Sagga* ("Realm of the Four Great Kings") half-way up the slope, and *Tāvatiṃsa* ("Realm of the Thirty-Three") at its summit. These realms have more interaction with the human realm than do any of the higher heavens. They also have considerable connections with each other: the Four Great Kings are the vassals of the Thirty-Three and serve, among other functions, as the first line of defence against the war-like *asuras* who are perpetually at war with these gods. There is considerably more descriptive literature to be found about these realms, particularly Tāvatiṃsa, than about any others. Usually when the texts refer simply to *sagga* it is Tāvatiṃsa that is implied.

3:5:6 CĀTUMAHĀRĀJIKA REALM OF THE FOUR GREAT KINGS

The *Cātumahārājika* (lit. "Four Great Kings") Realm is presided over by four powerful devas who each preside over one of the four cardinal directions. These are known as the *cattāro mahārājā* ("Four Great Kings") and are the protectors of the world. Each one is also the ruler of one race of beings who serve as his army and his retinue. The Four Great Kings are:

Dhataraṭṭha of the East, lord of the *gandhabbas*,

Virūḷhaka of the South, lord of the *kumbhaṇdas*,

Virūpakkha of the West, lord of the nāgas,

Vessavaṇa of the North (also called Kuvera), lord of the yakkhas.[512]

The division of the material world into four is a powerful archetype. In Buddhism we have the four elements, the four continents and the Four Great Kings. The idea of four elements is found also in European thought, via the Greeks, together with the old medical idea of the four humours. There is of course what may be the primary form of the archetype, the four cardinal directions. The division into four also shows itself in ancient India culture in the four castes and the four-fold army. These latter are the infantry, cavalry, charioteers and elephants and are the original basis of the game of chess with its pawns, knights, bishops and rooks.[513] It is also very possible that the four kings of our modern playing cards were originally the Four Great Kings of Mt Sineru.[514]

The Four Great King's primary role is that of guardians of the world, a role which they perform in several different ways. They, together with their retinues, serve as the first line of defence against the asuras who are forever attempting to storm Tāvatiṃsa. They stand watch while the gods of the Thirty-Three are in assembly, (DN 18) and they take a special interest in protecting the Dhamma and the Buddha. The Four Kings are said to have watched over the Bodhisatta while he was still in his mother's womb, to have been present at his birth and to have presented the baby to his mother, saying "Rejoice!" (DN 14). They stood guard over the oven while the maiden Sujātā prepared the Bodhisatta's meal of milk-rice (and Sakka stoked the fire!).[515] When the Buddha received his first meal offering after his awakening from two travelling merchants, it was the Four Great Kings who supplied him with an alms-bowl (Vin Mv 1).

One of their chief duties is to perform regular inspections of the human world on behalf of the Gods of the Thirty-Three:

> Four times every month, on the quarters of the moon, the Thirty-Three Devas of Tāvatiṃsa, sitting in solemn conclave in the Sudhamma Hall order the Four Great Kings to report on conditions in the human world. On the half-moon days, the Four Kings send out their ministers, on the new moon they send out their sons, and on the *uposatha* day of the Full Moon, they go out themselves. Riding in their glorious chariots, they travel from their abodes on Mt Sineru, each in his own direction, to the lands where human beings dwell. They tour the villages, the towns and the great royal cities. There the Great Kings ask the local devas if the people in that place are honouring mother and father, *samaṇas* and brahmins; whether they respect the clan-elders,

512 See DN 32, the Āṭānāṭiya *Sutta*.

513 The English designation "bishop" is a simple mistranslation. The King and Queen were originally the *rājā* and the *purohita* vizier or first minister.

514 Playing cards derived from the Tarot, which was brought to Europe by the Gypsies, who are probably of Indian origin.

515 GGB, p. 302.

keep the *uposatha* precepts and vigil and whether they are making meritorious kamma. The *bhummadevas* pay homage to the Great King and inform him that so-and-so of such-and-such a clan is doing these good things and the Great King writes his name on a golden tablet.

Having completed their tours, the Four Great Kings travel to the Tāvatiṃsa Heaven and present the golden tablets to the devas sitting there in the Sudhamma Hall. If many are those among human beings who are keeping the *uposatha* and making merit, the gods rejoice. "Surely the hosts of the devas will swell and those of the asuras diminish!" If however, there are few names on the golden tablets, the devas are downcast and say, "Alas! Surely now our hosts will diminish, and those of the asuras swell beyond number."[516]

The lesser devas of the Cātumahārājika realm may also be called upon to serve the higher devas of Tāvatiṃsa from time to time. We hear of the *devī* Bhaddā, for example, going to the Sudhamma Hall in Tāvatiṃsa to dance for Sakka and the other devas (DN 21).

The realm of the Cātumahārājika devas is, as noted, located half-way up Mt Sineru, at a height of 40,000 *yojana* from sea-level. There are found many gold, silver and crystal palaces in which the devas live (Vism 13:41). The *Abhidharmakośa* locates this realm on the fourth of four terraces jutting out from the flanks of Sineru. It also says that many devas of this realm dwell in villages and towns located on the seven great ring mountains (AK 3:5, Eng. p. 462). Some devas of this level may also live on earth, in Jambudīpa. This was the case of Pāyāsi who had a *vimāna* in a dessert region that was stumbled upon by some travelling merchants (Vv-a 84). One Jātaka story includes a detail which indicates some ambiguity about the location of the Cātumahārājika realm. A marvellous archer demonstrates his supernormal power by shooting an arrow upward through a bunch of mangoes, and it travelled all the way up to the Cātumahārājika realm before descending and falling through the same hole in the mangoes.[517] This would indicate that the Cātumahārājika realm is located directly above Jambudīpa, which contradicts the geography indicated everywhere else.

The Great Kings have authority over their retinue of dependent beings (yakkhas etc.) wherever they live in the world-system and these beings also serve as lines of defence against the incursions of the asuras (§ 3:5,6). It is not always clear whether Vessavaṇa is for instance, a yakkha, or Virūpakkha a nāga, or whether they are strictly to be considered devas. These categories, which seem so hard and fast in theory, become blurry when we get down to individual cases. Furthermore, since most, or perhaps all, of these kinds of beings are shape-shifters, this makes the distinction even less relevant.

The names of these gods are really more like titles of an office, because when one of these passes away a new one takes his place. In the case of the Four Great Kings, they are appointed by Sakka, King of Tāvatiṃsa (Jāt 74). The life-span of devas at this level is five hundred celestial years; each celestial day being fifty human years and the celestial year having three-hundred and sixty days, this makes their life-span nine million years in human terms.[518] Like the higher sensual heavens, the principle cause for one to be reborn "in the company of the Four Great Kings" is said to be gift-giving. However, this being the lowest of the heavens, it becomes the destination of a person who gives with a self-seeking mind, thinking only of the reward to be enjoyed in the hereafter (AN 7:52). And yet the pleasure here is said to make sovereignty in the human world seem of no account (MN 129 & AN 8:42)!

Each of the Four Great Kings has ninety-one mighty sons, each of whom is named "Inda" (DN 32). It is suggestive

[516] AN 3: 37 text & commentary. Note: the *uposatha* is the holy day of Buddhism, which falls on the quarters of the moon. Devout Buddhists will then keep the eight precepts and do a meditation vigil through the night. For the wars of the devas and asuras see the chapter on Asuras in § 3:3,23.

[517] Jāt 181. A second arrow went all the way to Tāvatiṃsa and did not return, because there it was caught by a deva.

[518] AN 8: 42. The DPPN says 90,000 years, but this must be a miscalculation.

that the total of these Indas is 364, close to the number of days in a year. Inda is the Pali form of the Sanskrit *Indra* who was a powerful war-like storm god in the early Vedas. In the Pali sources, Inda is identified with Sakka. There is some curious symbolism here, with a higher level reflected and multiplied in a lower, and a hint of solar symbolism with 364 days organized into four seasons, but this is not expanded upon in either the canon or the commentary.

At least three of the Great Kings also had daughters.[519] A Jātaka tale speaks of Kāḷakaṇṇī, daughter of Virūpakkha and Sirī, daughter of Dhataraṭṭha, going together to bathe at Lake Anotatta and disputing over who had precedence and therefore the right to enter the water first. Kāḷakaṇṇī is said to be dark of hue and not pleasing to see. Her name means "dark misfortune" and she appears to be a sort of goddess of bad luck. She says of herself:

> I go to the slanderer, the spiteful, the angry,
>
> The envious, the miserly and the cheat.
>
> And I make all their gains vanish away.

Sirī, whose name means "good fortune", is the opposite. She is said to be of a divine complexion (*dibba vaṇṇa*) and to be of firm stance (*pathabyā supatiṭṭhitā*). Their fathers declined the role of judging between them and so did the other two Great Kings and Sakka, so the task in the end was left to a human seer, who chose Sirī (Jāt 382).

The characters of three of the Great Kings are not developed in the sources; the exception is Vessavaṇa, King of the North and Lord of Yakkhas.

519 See the next section for a story involving the five daughters of King Vessavaṇa.

3:5:7 VESSAVAṆA

Vessavaṇa is a multi-faceted and complex character. In the distant past, he was very ferocious, but is now a devout follower of the Buddha and his Dhamma, and a *sotāpanna*.[520] Vessavaṇa has at least three roles in the scheme of cosmic governance: he is the Great King of the North, the overlord of the yakkhas and the King of the continent of Uttarakuru, in which capacity he is usually known by the name of Kuvera. Besides all this, he seems by implication to have some seniority over his colleagues, the other Great Kings; for instance he acts as their spokesman when they go to see the Buddha[521] and he is intimate with Sakka (MN 37).

Vessavaṇa's importance is emphasized by his name being included in a short list which sometimes occurs in verse passages as poetic shorthand for "all the gods."

> They honour you, both the Nāradas and the Pabbatas,
>
> Inda, Brahmā, Pajāpati, Soma, Yama and Vessavaṇa.
>
> Tāvatiṃsa with Inda, all the Devas honour you.[522]

(We will meet with most of these gods later. The Nāradas and Pabbatas are not found outside of these formulaic verse passages and the commentary only says they are two groups of devas who are renowned for their wisdom. There are many of these obscure corners in the Buddhist cosmos).

As the Lord of the Yakkhas we mostly encounter Vessavaṇa either settling their disputes, usually over the possession of a *vimāna*,[523] or granting them special privileges in return for service.

Being chief justice not only of the yakkhas but of the lesser devas who inhabit the Cātumahārājika realm, cannot be easy and in one story we see Vessavaṇa being distracted by the press of business, and taken advantage of:

> Puṇṇaka was a powerful general of the yakkhas, and the nephew of Vessavaṇa. He wanted to undertake a quest to win the hand of the beautiful nāga princess Irandatī, but dared not go without his uncle's permission. When Puṇṇaka went to see Vessavaṇa, the latter was busy settling a dispute between two devas over the possession of a *vimāna*. Puṇṇaka tried to explain what he wanted, but it was obvious that his uncle was not listening at all. So the yakkha got his permission by a ruse. He went and stood near the disputant whom he rightly guessed would win the case and when Vessavaṇa told the deva to go and take possession of what was his, Puṇṇaka took aside some devas as witnesses and said to them, "Did you hear? My maternal uncle has given me permission to go forth on my quest." (Jāt 546, Eng. 545)

The special privileges which Vessavaṇa grants to yakkhas usually take the form of a limited right to capture and devour people. This may consist of a right to eat anyone who strays within a certain limited territory, (Jāt 432) who stands in the shade of a certain tree, (Jāt 398) who fails to answer a riddle (Jāt 6) or in one case, who neglects to say "Long life to you!" when someone sneezes (Jāt 155). These special limitations, which are found in many Jātaka tales, provide the perfect set-up for the clever hero, usually the Bodhisatta, to foil the evil yakkha:

> A yakkha named Makhādeva dwelling in a banyan tree had been given permission by Vessavaṇa to eat anyone who stood in the shade of that tree. The Bodhisatta at that time was a poor man named Sutana and he

---

520 AN-a 7:53. A *sotāpanna* is a "stream-enterer", first of the four stages ofawakening.

521 DN 32, Ātānātiya Sutta.

522 Jāt 547, Vessantara Jātaka.

523 *Vimāna*—a dwelling place of the devas, to be described later.

took on the task of taming the yakkha to win a reward from the king. He approached the tree wearing sandals and standing under a parasol; thus he was neither standing on the ground, nor using the shade of the tree and the yakkha could not harm him. He spoke with the yakkha, admonishing him for his evil ways and converted him to the path of peace. (Jāt 398)

The service these yakkhas render to Vessavaṇa is hard. The term varies, but twelve years seems to be the most common. Female yakkhas are often mentioned as being obliged to serve Vessavaṇa by fetching him water from Lake Anotatta for a period of "four or five months." At the expiration of this time, they are set free but can be "exhausted to the point of death" (Dhp-a 1:4). In some cases, they actually do die in his service, (Jāt 513) or are killed for stealing his water (Jāt 510).

Before Vessavaṇa became a *sotāpanna*, he was terrible in his wrath. He wielded a club called *Gadāvudha* and when he threw it, it would smash the heads of thousands of yakkhas and then return to his hand. Gadāvudha was one of the four chief weapons of the world. (The others were: Vajirāvudha, the thunderbolt of Sakka, Nayānavudha, Lord Yama's eye and Dussāvudha the drought-producing cloth of Āḷavaka) (Sn-a 1:10). It is said that even a wrathful glance from Vessavaṇa could scatter and destroy a thousand of his servants (Jāt 281).

Vessavaṇa in his previous birth was a wealthy Brahmin who owned seven sugar-cane mills and gave the produce of one to charity for twenty thousand years, and this merit earned him rebirth as one of the Four Great Kings.[524] We are not told when or how Vessavaṇa became a *sotāpanna*. At the time of Vipassī Buddha, Vessavaṇa was already a follower of the Dhamma, (ThA. 1:7,6) but since this was in a previous kappa (world-age) it was probably another Vessavaṇa. Vessavaṇa is shown as taking a personal interest in the Dhamma practice of human beings:

The lay-women Velukantakī made a practice of beginning her day by chanting the *Parāyana Paritta* before dawn. One day Vessavaṇa happened to be travelling through the sky overhead, going from the north to south. Hearing her beautiful chanting, he descended and appeared at her window. He praised her chanting and she asked who he might be. "Elder Sister, I am your Elder Brother, the Great King Vessavaṇa." He used this strange form of address because although he was her elder in years, by several millions, she was his elder in the Dhamma, because she was an *anāgāmī* ("once-returner", the third stage of enlightenment) while he was just a *sotāpanna*. Vessavaṇa informed Velukantakī that Sāriputta and Moggallāna would be passing through her town that morning and asked her to offer them the meal on his behalf. When she agreed, he magically filled her store-house with rice, and it remained full throughout her life-time. (AN-a 7:50)

Vessavaṇa could still show his terrible aspect towards those of immoral conduct:

Nandiya was a lay-man of Bārāṇasī, and he made much merit with charitable offerings to the poor and meal-offerings to the bhikkhus. Once, when he was obliged to travel on some business or other, he instructed his wife Revatī on how to continue the daily offerings. But she was an unbeliever, and resentful of the expense, so she stopped giving to the poor altogether and gave only coarse food to the bhikkhus. At the same time, she scattered bits of fish-bone and other rubbish in the street, and blamed the bhikkhus, attempting to turn the townsfolk against them.

When the time came for her to die, Vessavaṇa sent two yakkhas to Bārāṇasī to announce that in seven-days she would be cast into *niraya*. Revatī locked herself in her room and sat there in great fear. On the appointed day two yakkhas of ferocious appearance dragged her by the arms from her house and marched her through the streets for all to see. They then took her to the Tāvatiṃsa heaven to show her the wonderful palace where

[524] DN-a 32, the commentary to the Ātānātiya Sutta. This must have been during the period when human life-spans were longer.

> Nandiya had been reborn. She begged them to let her join him, but they said her wishes were no concern of theirs and they cast her into a terrible hell of filth, where she suffered for a very long time. (Vv-a 52)

Another frequently mentioned aspect of Vessavaṇa's character is his great wealth. The extent of his riches was proverbial; many times when some other person's wealth is emphasized, he is said to be "as rich as Vessavaṇa," or to be enjoying sense pleasures "like King Vessavaṇa."[525] In later Buddhism, especially in East Asia, Vessavaṇa became something like a patron deity of prosperity. His role as the archetype of an extremely wealthy monarch is mostly associated with his governance of the fabulous northern continent of Uttarakuru where he is known by his other name of Kuvera.

Among Vessavaṇa's fabled possessions, the most famous is his magical mango tree.

> At one time, the King of Bārāṇasī had a very clever pet parrot. It came to pass that the queen developed a craving for an "inner-mango" (*abhantarāmbha*) and took to her bed as if overcome by illness. Consulting his wise-men, the King was told that the inner-mango was a name for the magical mangoes which only grew on the tree belonging to King Vessavaṇa on the Golden Hill deep in the Himavā forest, and furthermore it was said that no human being could ever manage to pick one of these, because the tree was very well guarded.
>
> So, the King thinking on the matter decided to send his parrot on the quest. The loyal bird, after a long journey over the seven mountain ranges of the Himavā came at last to the Golden Hill. And there stood the mighty mango tree, laden with luscious fruit. But there was no easy way to get them. The tree was surrounded by seven nets of brass and guarded by a thousand demon-like *kumbhaṇḍas*. (*kumbhaṇḍarakkhasa*)
>
> The brave little parrot was undismayed, and attempted to climb the tree stealthily at night while the *kumbhaṇḍas* lay snoring. But he became entangled in the brass netting and the metallic clinking it made while he struggled awakened the guardians. They seized him roughly and began to argue amongst themselves about what to do with him. One wanted to eat him whole, another to crush him to bits and yet another to cook him slowly over the fire.
>
> The parrot was unafraid and addressed them boldly, asking who their master was. They answered, "We belong to King Vessavaṇa and this is his mango tree. On his orders, none may partake of its fruit without his leave."
>
> "I too serve a King," replied the parrot. "And I will do his bidding even at the cost of my life."
>
> On hearing this, the *kumbhaṇḍas* had a change of heart. "It is plain to see that you are no common thief, but a noble bird. We dare not give you a mango, and incur the wrath of our lord. One angry glance from King Vessavaṇa and a thousand of our kind are smashed to pieces and scattered like so much chaff. But there is a holy ascetic living in a hut near here who is a favourite of Vessavaṇa and the king sends him some mangoes from time to time as a food-offering. He may have some on hand, and perhaps he would give you one."
>
> And so it was. The ascetic gave the parrot one of the wonderful mangoes to eat, and sent him back to his country with one more tied around his neck as a present for the queen. (Jāt 281)

An unexplained detail of this story is that Vessavaṇa's mango tree is guarded by *kumbhaṇḍas*. These odd beings are supposed to be the servants of Virūḷhaka, King of the South, and we would expect King Vessavaṇa to employ

[525] See for instance Vv-a 84 & Jāt 546 (eng. 545).

yakkhas as guards. They are qualified as *kumbhaṇḍa-rakkhasa* in the text, a *rakkhasa* being a kind of yakkha. Here we have yet another example of the vagaries which arise when we attempt to impose rigid classifications on the fantastic beings of the *cakkavāḷa*.

King Vessavaṇa has five daughters: Latā, Sajjā, Pavarā, Accimatī and Sutā. A story is told about a dancing contest held between them:

> The five sisters were brought by King Sakka (of Tāvatiṃsa) to serve as dancers. Latā was the most pleasing, because of cleverness in singing and dancing.
>
> At one time when the five sisters were sitting comfortably together a dispute arose among them concerning the skill of music. They went to their father, King Vessavaṇa, and asked, "Daddy (*tāta*), which among us is most skilled at dancing and so on?" "Daughters, call an assembly of devas to the shore of Lake Anotatta and perform for them there. Then your skill will be determined." And so they did.
>
> When Latā was dancing, the *devaputtas*[526] could not control themselves. They were filled with mirth, snapping their fingers wildly,[527] constantly cheering and shouting their praise, waving clothes in the air and making such an uproar that the Himavā trembled. But when the other sisters danced, the *devaputtas* sat as silent as cuckoo birds in the cold season. Thus the assembly made apparent the distinction of Latā. (Vv-a 32)

Latā had acquired such marvellous skill on account of the merit made in her previous human birth as a devout and dutiful wife (ibid.).

[526] *Devaputta*, lit. "deva son", in this context implying young male devas.

[527] A form of applause.

3:5:8 OTHER DEVAS OF THE CĀTUMAHĀRĀJIKA REALM

Although the special retinues of the Four Great Kings (*cattāro mahārājāno*) are the nāgas, *supaṇṇas*, yakkhas, *kumbhaṇḍas* and *gandhabbas*, these are not for the most part resident in the Cātumahārājika Realm on the slopes of Mt Sineru. The actual population of that realm is, instead, largely composed of devas. It may be assumed that this is, indeed, the most populous of the deva worlds, following the general principle that it is by far easier to be reborn in a lower realm than a higher one (SN 56:97 f., eng. 56:102 f.).

In general, rebirth into the sensual heavens is achieved through morality and generosity. In one passage in the *Aṅguttāra Nikāya*, discussing the different motivations for giving, it is stated that giving a gift with the thought, "this will be of benefit to me in my future births," is considered the lowest kind of merit and leads to rebirth among the Cātumahārājika devas. Such a rebirth is not to be despised, however. It is still considered meritorious to give a gift with this motivation, and the happiness of even the lowest devas is said to make kingship among humans appear "miserable" (*kapaṇa*) by comparison (AN 8:42).

The devas of the Cātumahārājika Realm live for five hundred celestial years (*saṃvaccharāni dibbāni*) which is equivalent to nine million years in earthly terms (AN 8:42). We are told they are "long-lived, beautiful and have great happiness" (DN 33). There appears to be a great deal of variation among them, enjoying more or relatively less sense pleasure according to the merit they have made. While some have a retinue of attendants (*orodha*, literally a "harem"), (DN-a 1) others may be born into an "empty mansion" (*suñña vimāna*) like King Pāyāsi who, while he made many gifts, did so in a careless (*asakkaccaṃ*) manner (Vv-a 84).

Not all the Cātumahārājika devas manage to live up to their allotted span of five hundred celestial years. We hear of two kinds of deva who die prematurely: the *khiḍḍāpadosikā* devas, those "corrupted by play" and the *manopadosikā* devas, those "corrupted by mind."[528]

The *khiḍḍāpadosikā* devas pass away because they are caught up in sensual delights and forget to eat:

> These devas spend an excessive amount of time in laughter and play (DN 1). They become forgetful about their food. These devas, it is told, celebrating a festival in honour of their own great beauty and splendour, attained through their distinguished merit, become so absorbed in their great enjoyment that they do not even know whether they have eaten or not. But when they have passed up the time for even a single meal, though they eat and drink immediately afterwards, they pass away and cannot remain. Why? Because of the strength of their kamma-born heat element (*kammajateja*) and the delicacy of their material bodies (*karajakāya*). In the case of men, the kamma-born heat element is delicate, and the material body strong … But in the case of devas, the heat element is strong and the body delicate. If they pass up the time even for a single meal, they cannot endure. Just as a red or blue lotus placed on a heated rock at midday … would only perish, in the same way … these devas pass away and cannot remain. (DN-a 1)

Elsewhere it is said that these devas are "burnt up by delusion."[529] It should be noted that this form of deva-death is not limited to the Cātumahārājika realm, but may occur among the higher devas as well. In fact it may be even more common among them because, as we ascend through the sensual heavens, the pleasures become ever more enticing while the devas' bodies become even more subtle.[530]

---

[528] The main source for these devas is the commentary to the *Brahmajāla Sutta*, DN 1. It has been translated by Bhikkhu Bodhi under the title "The All-Embracing Net of Views," referred to in following notes as "Net." Quotes are from Bhikkhu Bodhi's translation unless indicated otherwise. Bodhi's use of the word "god" has been changed to "deva" throughout.

[529] *mohassa anudahanatāya*, DN-a 33.

[530] Bodhi, *Net* p. 160. Buddhaghosa says in DN-a 1 that "some say that only the Nimmānarati and Parnimmaitvassavatti devas

The *manopadosikā* devas, on the other hand, are found only in the Cātumahārājika realm (AENV p. 160). They are "burned up" not by play, but by envy and animosity.[531]

> There are, bhikkhus, certain devas called "corrupted by mind" (*manopadosikā*). These devas contemplate each other with excessive envy. As a consequence, their minds become corrupted by anger towards one another. When their minds are corrupted by anger, their bodies and minds become exhausted, and consequently they pass away from that plane.[532]
>
> One young deva among them, it is told, wishing to celebrate a festival, set out by chariot on the roadway along with his retinue. Another of those devas, going out for a walk, saw the first one riding ahead of him. He became angry and exclaimed: "That miserable wretch! There he is going along puffed up with rapture (*pītiyā uddhumāto*) to the bursting point, as if he had never seen a festival before." The first, turning around and realizing that the other was angry—angry people being easy to recognize—became angry in turn and retorted" "What have you got to do with me, you hot-headed fellow? My prosperity was gained entirely by my own meritorious works (*dānasīlādīnaṃ*). It has nothing to do with you.
>
> Now, if one of these devas gets angry, but the other remains unangered, the latter protects the former (from passing away). But if both get angry, the anger of one will become the condition for the anger of the other, and both will pass away with their harems weeping. This is a fixed law (*dhammatā).* (AENV p. 160)

Their mutually reinforcing anger reaches such intensity that it consumes the heart-base (*hadayavatthu*) and destroys their "extremely delicate material body."[533]

The devas of this and all higher realms arise by way of "spontaneous birth" (*opapātikayoni*) appearing fully formed, in many cases sitting in the lap of a "parent" deva (SN-a 2:1). Although they do not reproduce sexually, sexuality is definitely a part of life in the sensual heavens. While we do not find this matter elaborated in the Pali sources, the *Abhidharmakośa* tells us that the devas of the Cātumahārājika and Tāvatiṃsa realms couple with one another in the manner of humans, except that the male does not emit semen, only "wind." The force of desire is lessened as one moves up through the heavens, and the relations between the sexes increasingly refined. The Yāma devas do not engage in penetrative sex, but only embrace, the Tusita devas hold hands, the Nimmānarati smile at one another, and the Paranimmitavasavatti devas satisfy their desire merely by gazing upon one another.[534]

Two very important beings who are reckoned among the Cātumahārājika devas are **Sūriya** and **Candimā**, the devas of the sun and the moon. These celestial bodies were conceived to be the *vimānas* of those devas. (A *vimāna* is the magical dwelling place of a deva or other non-human being. It is usually translated as "mansion" but they are also mobile, able to travel through the air at the deva's will, so in some contexts "chariot" works as well). The sun is fifty *yojānas* in extent and the moon forty-nine. Sūriya dwells within the sun and guides its travels through the sky, as does Candimā within the moon. The sun is made of crystal (*phalika*, which might also mean quartz) and the moon of silver.[535] The names Candimā and Sūriya may refer either to the devas, or to the celestial bodies which are their homes, and when it is necessary to distinguish between the two the epithet *devaputto* is appended to the name of the deva:

---

are meant. "See also AN-a 4:171 which lists several places where these devas go for their sport. All of these elsewhere are identified as being located in Tāvatiṃsa.

531 *dosassa anudahanatāya*, DN-a 33.

532 DN 1, Bhikkhu Bodhi trans. *Net* p. 67-68.

533 Bodhi, *Net* p. 161, quoted from the sub-commentary.

534 AK 3:5, p. 465. This doctrine was known to the Pali commentators, but rejected see DN-a 33 and the section on the Paranimittavasavatti Devas § 3:5,32 for a discussion.

535 DN-a 27, commentary to the *Agañña Sutta.*

Sūriyadevaputto or Candimādevaputto. Like other important devas, Sūriya and Candimā do not dwell alone in their *vimānas*, but have a suite of attendant devas (*paricārakadevatā*) (SN-ṭ 2:10).

From time to time, either the sun or the moon is seized by the monstrous asura Rāhu, who is jealous of their brilliance, causing what we know as an eclipse. He may just cover them partially with his hand or tongue, or he might take them whole into his mouth, swelling out his cheeks. At such times, the devas dwelling in the celestial *vimānas* feel as if they suddenly had been plunged into a dark hell realm, and are seized with fear for their lives. Rāhu, however, is unable to obstruct their progress for long because the motion of these bodies is determined by the laws of kamma (*kammaniyāmasiddho*), which no being can overcome. If he did not release them, his head would burst open or he would be dragged along and flung down.[536]

It appears, however, that Sūriya and Candimā themselves can, on occasion, alter their natural course:

> Paṇḍita was a young *sāmaṇera* (novice-monk) and a student of Sāriputta. While on alms-round with his teacher, on the eighth day after his ordination, Paṇḍitasāmeṇera saw, as they progressed through the village, a number of workmen engaged in their tasks. Being wise beyond his years, the sight turned his young mind towards the Dhamma. "If farmers can channel water to go where they wish, if fletchers can shape stone into arrow-heads and wheel-wrights fashion wood into wagon-wheels, why cannot I shape the mind?"
>
> Earnestly, he sought permission from Sāriputta to return to his hut and continue with his meditation. Sāriputta gave his blessing and promised to bring the lad a little food.
>
> Paṇḍitasāmeṇera made rapid progress in his meditation, and before the morning was out had attained the first three fruits.[537] The Buddha knew this by his psychic power, and so did the devas who set up a guard on the monastery grounds so that the *sāmaṇera's* meditation would not be disturbed by so much as the sound of a falling leaf.
>
> When Sāriputta returned from alms-round with some food for the *sāmeṇera*, the Buddha engaged him in conversation to delay him and leave Paṇḍita undisturbed. The young *sāmeṇera* was able to complete his inner work and attained to arahantship.[538]
>
> However, it was now close to noon and the time for eating had nearly passed.[539] To save the lad from going hungry, Sūriya and Candimā stopped the progress of their *vimānas* through the sky, and did not allow noon to arrive until after Paṇḍita had finished his meal. (Dhp-a 6,:5)

We are also told that both Sūriya and Candimā are *sotāpannas* (stream-enterers), having attained that state upon hearing the preaching of the *Mahāsamaya Sutta* (SN-a 2:10).

Pajjuna is a Cātumahārājika deva who rules over the wind and rain. He is called the king of the *vassavalāhaka* devas, (SN-a 1:39) the sky-dwelling devas of the weather. He sends the rain-clouds out of compassion for those beings that live dependent on rainfall (Th 1:1,1). When he attended the great assembly of devas (*mahāsamaya*) who cameto see the Buddha it is said that he "came thundering."[540] He has a daughter named Kokanadā who once went to pay her respects to the Buddha (SN 1:39).

Maṇimekhalā (her name means "jewelled girdle") is Cātumahārājika *devī* of the sea. She was appointed by

---

536 SN 2:9 & SN 2:10 and commentary. See also Bhikkhu Bodhi, CDB, note 158 on p. 388.

537 There are four stages of awakening, often called *phalā* ("fruits").

538 The fourth and final stage of awakening.

539 Bhikkhus and sāmeṇeras must finish their meals before solar noon.

540 DN-a 20. "Came thundering" = *thanayanto āgato*.

the Four Great Kings to save righteous people who were shipwrecked from drowning. It appears, however, that she is somewhat negligent of her duties. She features in two Jātaka stories, and in both cases she was not immediately aware that such a person had been lost at sea, being distracted from her watch by the enjoyment of her deva pleasures (*dibbasampattiṃ anubhavantiyā*). In both stories, she only comes to the unfortunate sailor's rescue after seven days when they are close to death. In one case she creates a magical ship laden with treasures for the drowning man to sail home in (Jāt 442). In the other case, she cradles him in her bosom and carries him through the air back to Jambudīpa: "thrilled by the divine touch" (*dibbaphassena phuṭṭho*) he falls into a swoon and awakens back in his home country (Jāt 539).

3:5:9 TĀVATIṂSA REALM OF THE THIRTY-THREE

Tāvatiṃsa is the second of the sensual *saggas*, and the highest realm still in contact with the earth. It is located at the peak of Mt Sineru, 84,000 *yojana* above "sea-level" (Vism 7.42). The name *Tāvatiṃsa* is a variant form of the numeral "thirty-three"[541] and refers to the thirty-three chief devas of this realm, which form a kind of governing council of the world. The idea of there being thirty-three chief gods was a common Indo-Aryan heritage, and is also found in Vedic and Zoroastrian sources (PED) Loosely speaking, this is the realm that is the Indian equivalent to Olympus or Valhalla,

Nowhere can we find a definitive list of the Thirty-Three, although we are told that the first four seats in their council chamber were occupied by Sakka, Pajāpati, Varuna and Īsāna (SN-a 11:3). Other devas mentioned by name who are likely to be included in that number are Soma, Yasa, Venhu, Vissakamma and perhaps Sujā, the chief queen of Sakka and Mātali, the charioteer of the gods, if females and *gandhabbas* are allowed to be included.

However, it seems unlikely that any *devī* (female devas) are to be considered among the number of the Thirty-Three, given the Jātaka story which relates their origin:

> At one time the Bodhisatta came to birth as a boy in a great family in the village of Macala, in the kingdom of Magadha. He was given the name of Magha. There were thirty-three families in that village, and when Magha had grown to manhood, all the principal men became his fast friends and under his influence strictly kept the five precepts and performed meritorious deeds.
>
> They would go forth each day, every man carrying a tool, and repair the roads, dig wells and build rest-houses for travellers. After a while, the village headman grew uneasy as the moral influence of the thirty-three companions undermined his revenue from the sale of liquor and from the collection of fines from wrong-doers. He decided to make a false accusation of banditry against them.
>
> The king ordered that the companions were to be trampled to death by the royal elephants. But because of the force of their merit, the elephants refused to harm them. The king asked them what magic spell (*manta*) they had, and Magha told them their magic was the five precepts. The king was pleased with them, released them and gave them great wealth.
>
> The companions could now undertake even more magnificent acts of merit and decided to build a large hall (*sāla*) at the cross-roads. As the companions had by this time abandoned all desire for women (*mātugāmesu pana vigatacchandatāya*) they refused to let any woman share in their meritorious works. However, there were four women in Magha's house, Sudhammā, Cittā, Nandā and Sujā and of these, the first three wanted very much to share in the merit of the good works.
>
> To accomplish this, Sudhamma resorted to a ruse. She paid a carpenter to build a pinnacle (*kaṇṇikā*) and she put it away in the house. When the great hall was nearly complete, Magha was unable to obtain a pinnacle to complete the project and the carpenter told him there was no suitable wood to be had. Sudhamma brought her pinnacle forth, and offered it on condition that the women be allowed to share in the merit. Magha was reluctant at first, but at last relented.
>
> So the lady Sudhamma contributed the pinnacle, Cittā had a pleasure grove (*uyyāna*) planted and Nandā saw to the digging of a water-tank. Sujā did nothing at all.

---

541 PED. The regular form is *tettiṃsa*.

When in due time, all of these passed away, Magha was reborn as Sakka and together with his boon companions became the devas of the Thirty-Three (*Tāvatiṃsa*). The ladies Sudhammā, Cittā and Nandā were reborn as hand-maidens (*pādaparicārikā*) of Sakka but Sujā, who had given nothing at all, came to birth as a crane in a forest lake.[542]

The devas of the Tāvatiṃsa realm have a lifespan of one thousand celestial years (*dibbāni saṃvaccharāni*), and since one day in their realm is equal to one hundred human years in length, and the celestial year is reckoned at three hundred and sixty such days, this makes their life-span, in human terms, thirty-six million years (AN 3:71, Eng. AN 3:70). The natural size of their bodies is given as three *gāvutas*, i.e. probably about eight km, in height.[543]

542 Jāt 31—Kūlavaka Jātaka.

543 There is a stock phrase used to indicate someone being reborn in this realm, *tigāvutoattabhāvo nibbatti*, see the Devatāsaṃyuttaṃ of the *Saṃyutta Nikāya*, passim. There are four gāvutas in a *yojana*.

3:5:10 PHYSICAL DESCRIPTION OF TĀVATIṂSA

The devas of Tāvatiṃsa dwell in a beautiful city made of gold, jewels and other precious materials. This city was said to have arisen by the power of the kamma made by Magha and his companions building the great hall.[544]

This city is ten-thousand *yojana* from the eastern gate to the western gate, and the same from north to south. It has two thousand gates in all, and is adorned with many parks and ponds. In the center is the mighty Palace of Victory (*vejayanto nāma pāsādo*), seven hundred *yojana* high, made of the seven precious things.[545] It is adorned with a standard (*dhaja*) of three-hundred additional *yojana*.

> On golden staffs are standards of jewel; on jewel staffs are standards of gold. On staffs of coral are standards of pearl; on staffs of pearl are standards of coral. There are staffs made of the seven precious things bearing standards of the seven precious things, and in the middle of these is the three-hundred *yojana* high standard, made of the seven precious things. The whole palace thus is one-thousand *yojana* in height.
>
> In the city there is also a great tree, *koviḷāra pāricchattaka*,[546] three hundred *yojana* around. At the foot of the tree, there is a stone slab sixty *yojana* long, fifty *yojana* wide and fifteen *yojana* thick. This slab is the rose-coloured throne of Sakka, king of the devas, the *paṇḍukambalāsana*. When he sits upon it, he sinks to the depth of half his body, when he stands it returns to its previous shape. (Dhp-a 2:7)

Other texts mention decorated gateways in the encircling wall, which is made of the seven precious things andis sixty *yojana* thick, and a great high-street, sixty *yojana* wide and paved with gold (Jāt 544, Eng. 542). The chief gateway is called *Cittakūṭadvārakoṭṭhakā* (possible translation: the "Beautiful Mountain Guarded Door") and it is guarded by statues of Inda (Sakka in his war-like manifestation) who stand there "like tigers" (Jāt 541).

Prominent among the features of Tāvatiṃsa are the many pleasure parks and gardens. The chief of these is the **Nandanavana**, "The Grove of Delight." It is adorned with various lovely trees and ponds, and features a Nandana Lake (Jāt 220). The Nandanavana is always thronged with *devatās* and their retinues of *accharās*[547] who come to enjoy themselves. We hear of festival days (*ussavadivasa*) when the devas congregate here to make merry (Vv-a 1). A typical story, one among many in the *Vimānavatthu*, is of a woman who made an offering of flowers to the Buddha and afterwards was reborn as a female deva who would spend her time singing, dancing, gathering garlands of *Paricchattaka* blossoms and generally playing in the Nanadanavana, surrounded by a retinue of one thousand *accharās*. The verses describing her blissful existence speak of her dancing:

> While you are dancing with all your limbs in every way, deva-like sounds (*dibbā saddā*) stream forth, delightful to hear.
>
> While you are dancing with all your limbs in every way, deva-like scents (*dibbā gandhā*) are wafted around, sweet scents, delightful … .
>
> And the perfume of those sweet-scented, delightful garlands on your head blows in all directions, like the *mañjūsaka* tree.

---

544 *Sālāya nissandena* Dhp-a 2.7.

545 *Sattaratana*, i.e. gold, silver, pearls, rubies, lapis-lazuli, coral and diamond, ref. PED.

546 Identified by the PED with the Coral Tree, *Erythmia Indica*.

547 *acchāra*. Commonly translated as "celestial nymph", these are the wondrously beautiful dancing girls who entertain the devas, see § 3:5,11.

You breathe that sweet scent, you see unearthly beauty (*rūpaṃ amānusaṃ*—lit. non-human forms), *devatā*.[548]

As the most delightful place in the Tāvatiṃsa realm, itself the highest of the realms connected to the earth, Nandanavana is considered the epitome of sensual pleasure. When an earthly garden is given the highest praise, it is compared to Nandanavana.[549] In the Saṃyutta Nikāya we hear of a newly arisen deva, overwhelmed by the delightful experience of all five senses, exclaiming. "He does not know bliss who has not seen Nandanavana!" (For this, he is rebuked by a wiser deva who reminds him that all compounded things are subject to destruction and that the highest bliss is the stilling of formations) (SN 1:11).

So delightful is Nandanavana that it is here where devas choose to go at the end of their life-spans. Not only does the fear of death dissolve "like a snow-ball," (SN-a 1:11) under the spell of Nandanavana's divine beauty, but it is believed among them that a deva who dies here will take a fortunate rebirth.[550] Not only Tāvatiṃsa but every *sagga* has its own Nandanavana, and it is, for instance, from the Nandanavana in Tusita that the Bodhisatta passed away before taking his final human birth as Siddhattha Gotama, who became the Buddha (ibid .).

Three other gardens of Tāvatiṃsa are named in the texts. **Cittalatāvana** was made manifest by the kamma of Cittā, one of Magha's four wives. She had planted a lovely garden with many varieties of trees and flowering vines to adorn the great hall built by Magha and his companions. She herself was reborn as one of Sakka's hand-maidens (*pādaparicārikā)* (Jāt 31). The Cittalatāvana was best known for its great abundance of flowering vines ("vine" is *latā* in Pali). It is so beautiful that the radiance of the devas who visit it is dimmed by comparison (Vv-a 37). Here grows the āsāvatī creeper, which flowers only once in a thousand years. An intoxicating drink is made from the fruit which causes the drinker to lie in a pleasant stupor upon his divan for four months (Jāt 380). The **Phārusakavana** is named for the *phārusaka* berry which grows there. This is identified as the *Grewia Asiatica* plant,[551] and is used to make a more wholesome and refreshing drink (Vin Mv 6). The **Missikāvana** is not described in any detail, but the name means loosely either "Grove of Many Kinds." or "Grove of Bodily Union."[552]

A very important feature of Tāvatiṃsa is the **Sudhamma Hall**—the full name is *Sudhammādevasabhaṃ* (lit. "Good Dhamma Deva Hall")—where the Thirty-Three meet in assembly. Its dimensions are variously given as five-hundred (Jāt 31) or nine-hundred (Dhp-a 2:7) *yojana*. Perhaps one number refers to its height, and the other to its extent, although this is not made clear. The Sudhamma Hall is said to be the most delightful structure in the world, and it is a common saying "even nowadays" (*yāvajjatanā*) to say of any beautiful building that it is "like the Sudhamma Hall." There, under a *yojana* wide white parasol sits Sakka, lord of the devas (*devānamindo*) upon a golden couch, ruling over devas and humans (*devamanussānaṃ kattabbakiccāni karoti*) (Dhp-a 2:7).

There are four occasions for the meetings of the devas: the beginning and end of the *vassa*, (the "rains retreat" of the monastic order), for the teaching of Dhamma or for the blossom festival (*pāricchattakakīḷānubhavana*).[553] At the beginning of the *vassa*, the full moon of the month of Āsāḷha (roughly, July), the devas investigate where on earth various communities of bhikkhus will be staying for the rains, and organize their protection (DN-a 18).

In two related suttas of the Dīgha Nikāya (DN 18 & 19) we have a description of such an assembly taking place at the beginning of the *vassa*. There are said to be a great many assembled devas, including all of the Thirty-Three and the Four Great Kings together with their own attendant devas. King Dhataraṭṭha of the East sits in the east, facing west and likewise with the other three Great Kings, each in his own place which implies a circular arrangement for the

548 Vv, 38.I.B. Horner trans.

549 See for ex. Jāt 525 and 542 (eng. 546).

550 Jātaka Nidānakathā.

551 See "Book of the Discipline", Horner, note 6 on p. 339.

552 The latter is the definition given in the PED. Perhaps a place for romantic trysts?

553 Described in the section on the Great Trees in § 1:14.

whole. It is said that those devas, newly arrived in Tāvatiṃsa, who have lived the lived the holy life under the Buddha, have a greater splendour (*atirocanti vaṇṇena*) than the others. The devas of the Thirty-Three discussed the matters at hand (the protection of bhikkhus on earth, according to the commentary) and gave their instructions to the Four Great Kings, who for this purpose stood unmoving beside their seats. This procedure demonstrates the way of governance of the devas: the decision-making is done collectively by the Thirty-Three under the kingship of Sakka and the discussion is witnessed by a greater assembly of lesser devas. The implementation of the decision is then entrusted to the Four Great Kings, who work the will of the devas in the human realm.

Then there occurred a visitation by a *mahābrahmā*[554] named Sanankumarā. This episode has many interesting aspects which reveal details about relations between the various realms. At the outset all that is seen by the assembled devas is a "glorious radiance" (*uḷāro āloko*) coming from the north. The devas are unable to perceive the brahmā in his natural form, it is "beyond the range of their vision."[555] To be seen by the devas, Sanankumarā was obliged to assume a coarser form; on this occasion he transformed himself into the appearance of the *gandhabba* Pañcasikha,[556] and remained hovering in space seated in a cross-legged posture. He chose this form because Pañcasikha is "dear to all the devas" (*kira sabbadevatā attabhāvaṃ mamāyanti)* (DN-a 18). Sanankumarā performed one additional transformation and multiplied his body thirty-three times and sat down beside each of the great devas on their divans, causing each to think the brahmā was addressing him alone (DN 18).

It is a general rule that a being who wishes to manifest in a lower realm must assume a coarser form suitable to that realm to be visible to its inhabitants. This is implied in many instances of devas appearing in the human sphere. For instance, when the devas of Tāvatiṃsa come to visit the Buddha on one occasion, the villagers nearby perceive only a terrifying brilliant light and imagine that the mountaintop is aflame (DN 21). Likewise, in Sakka's many visitations to humans, he always takes on an earthly form, usually of a brahmin. This may be in part for purposes of disguise, as he seems to prefer to do his work incognito, but at least a couple of instances may be cited which indicate that such a form is necessary in order to be seen at all. In Jātaka 347 a yakkha attempts to smite the Bodhisatta, but is stopped by Sakka. The yakkha, but not Sakka, is seen by the Bodhisatta. In Jātaka 194 Sakka is said specifically to "assume a visible form" (*dissamānakasarīra*) in order to be seen. The exception to this rule is that the Buddha and others who have developed the "divine eye" faculty (*dibbacakkhu*) are able to perceive beings invisible to others.[557]

---

554 A being from a much higher realm, see § 3:6,7.

555 DN-a18—*so devānaṃ cakkhussa āpāthe sambhavanīyo pattabbo na hoti.*

556 See the section on Gandhabbas § 3:5,22.

557 Vism 13.72. See also the story previously cited from Udāna 4: 4, where Moggallāna is able to see a yakkha but Sāriputta cannot.

3:5:11 *ACCHARĀS* CELESTIAL NYMPHS

There are often references to devas in the sensual heavens being endowed with the "five cords of divine sense-pleasure" (*dibbā pañca kāmaguṇā*). Beautiful gardens full of flowers and blossoming trees, and an ambience full of music and dance, have already been referred too, but this makes up only a portion of the devas' pleasures. Firstly, we may mention that the devas themselves are often described as of "extremely pleasant appearance."[558] They are also said to be radiant, with a glorious brilliance which is compared to the morning star, (Vv-a 9) or even to the sun and moon (Vv-a 30). They wear the finest cloth and are gorgeously adorned with gold, jewelled ornaments, and especially flower-garlands.[559] Male devas always appear to be twenty years old, female ones to be sixteen (DN-a 14).

Especially beautiful are the ubiquitous ***accharās***, (Sanskrit *apsara*) usually translated as "nymphs." The *accharās* are a class of minor female devas whose erotic charms form one of the principal delights of Tāvatiṃsa. The loveliness of the *accharās* was proverbial, and it is common in the texts to hear the beauty of a human woman praised by saying that she was "just like a divine nymph."[560] Besides the natural beauty of their form, like the other devas they are often said to be radiant and sometimes compared to the star *Osadhi.*[561] The *accharās* are always adorned with finery and jewels, and are skilled in the arts of music and dance.

Very frequently *accharās* are described with the adjective *kakuṭapāda*, usually translated as "dove-footed." This has led to some representations in later Buddhist art of beautiful female forms with bird-like talons instead of feet. This does not seem to have been the original intention of the word, and would, it seems rather spoil their erotic charm![562] Kakuṭapāda probably referred to the colour or perhaps the softness of their feet. There is a passage in the commentary to the *Suttanipāta* which says that they were all disciples of Kassapa Buddha and had given him an offering of oil to anoint the feet, and hence were eventually reborn as "dove-footed" (Sn-a 1: 12). This seems a contrived explanation, given the vast numbers of *accharās* found in Tāvatiṃsa, (Sakka's retinue alone constitutes twenty-five millions) and it may be that the phrase seemed odd already at the time the commentaries were composed. The adjective itself is a rare one; according to the PED, the word *kakuta* occurs only in this compound, never independently.

In a Jātaka story there is a long verse passage in praise of the beauty of the *accharā* Alambusā:

> The ascetic Isiniṅga was so advanced in his practice of sense-restraint that Sakka became afraid that he would accumulate enough merit to replace him on the throne of Tāvatiṃsa, so the King of the Devas decided to send the *accharā* Alambusā to tempt him. Sakka remarks that while the Nandana Grove is full of lovely *accharās*, none has Alambusā's skill in knowing how to entice a man. When the hapless Isiniṅga saw her approaching his hermitage, he spoke aloud a long plaintive series of verses:
>
> > "Who is this, radiant like lightning or the healing star?
> >
> > Adorned with bracelets and earrings?
> >
> > With complexion like the sun, and scent of sandalwood.
> >
> > With her well-formed thighs of great enchantment, who is this woman lovely to behold?

---

558 *Abhikkantavaṇṇā*. This phrase is common for instance in the Devasaṃyutta of the SN. It is translated by Bhikkhu Bodhi as, "of stunning beauty ".

559 See Vv-a passim, ex. 1. 3. 2.

560 *Devaccharāpa ṭibhāgā* see for example Jāt 132, 152, 327, 387 among many others.

561 See for instance Jāt 523 quoted below. This star is likely Venus or possibly Sirius.

562 It is also possible that these images have simply been misidentified and were supposed to be *kinnara*.

Your waist tender and pure, your feet firmly planted,

Your gait is sensuous, you overthrow my mind!

Tapering are your thighs, like an elephant's trunk.

Smooth are your buttocks, like a dicing board.

Like the petals of a lotus, your navel is pleasantly shaped,

Adorned with dark markings, it is seen from afar.

Twin breasts, milky and firm, like pumpkin halves without stalks.

Long is your neck, with shell-like markings, like an antelope's.

Lovely are your lips and your tongue.

Your upper and your lower teeth are well-polished with tooth-stick,

Both gums are flawless, your teeth are pure.

Dark as liquorice berries are the marking around your big, wide beautiful eyes.

Not too long and neatly bound with golden pins,

Your hair has the fragrance of sandal-wood."

> With her feminine cunning (*itthimāyākusalatāya*) Alambusā knew that if she remained standing there the seer would never approach her, so she pretended to flee from him, and he chased and easily caught her. Isisiṅga lay enchanted in Alambusā's lovely arms for three years, the time passing as if it were but a single moment, until at last he awoke to the shock and the shame of having violated his vows.[563]

The detail of their embrace lasting three years, but seeming like a moment, is significant in that we have once more an indication of the strange and dream-like quality of these realms, and of the fluid nature of time. It must be noted, in Alambusā's defence, that she was very reluctant to take on this assignment, protesting to Sakka that to seduce a seer would be terrible kamma, and afterward she asked him for the boon of never being required to do the same again (Jāt 523).

Isisiṅga was not the only human to fall into woe through the charms of the *accharās*: after once getting a glimpse of them, the householder Sujātā, wasted away with such hopeless passion that he died of starvation (Jāt 537).

The most well-known episode involving the *accharās* may be the story of the bhikkhu Nanda, a half-brother of the Buddha. Among other interesting details, it emphasizes the beauty of the *accharās* by way of comparison. It occurs in several places in the texts.[564]

Before ordaining as a bhikkhu, the venerable Nanda had been engaged to the most beautiful girl in the Sakyan

[563] Jāt 523. The translation does not convey some of the complex word-play in the original which requires the aid of the commentary to decipher. For instance, the reference to her tongue is to "the place of the fourth consciousness" (*catutthamanasannibhā*). The commentary also helpfully informs us that besides being round, Alambusā's buttocks were vast (*visālā*)!

[564] The *Theragatha*, *Udāna*, *Dhammapāda*, and Jātakas all have versions of it.

land. The last time he saw his fiancée, she had been standing in the door-way combing her hair as she asked him to return to her soon. Nanda's decision to take the robe was a sudden one, made out of deference for the Buddha, and he began to regret it, as he could not get the image of his beloved standing in that doorway out of his mind.

The Buddha, knowing the trouble Nanda was having living the holy life, invited him to take his hand and by supernormal power, the Buddha together with Nanda flew through the air to Tāvatiṃsa on the top of Mount Sineru. On their way through the Himavā, they passed over a region devastated by forest-fire. There they saw a pitiful, half-scorched she-monkey clinging forlornly to a branch. The Buddha asked Nanda to take note of this.

Having arrived in due course at Sakka's throne in Tāvatiṃsa, the king of the devas came together with a retinue of five-hundred *accharās* to pay respects to the Buddha. The Buddha asked Nanda which was prettiest, his Sakyan fiancée or the dove-footed *accharās* of Tāvatiṃsa? Nanda replied without hesitation that compared to these nymphs, his former beloved was no different than the burnt monkey of the Himavā. The Buddha replied that should Nanda continue diligently with his practice, after death he would be reborn as a deva in Tāvatiṃsa and have five-hundred *accharās* of his own.

The bhikkhu Nanda began to practice with more diligence, but his fellow monks disparaged him. "This bhikkhu Nanda follows the holy life for the sake of desire for *accharās*! He follows the way of the hired servant, the way of the merchant (*bhatakavāda ca upakkitakavāda*)." Hearing this, Nanda became ashamed and at last undertook the holy life in real earnest. After some time he achieved the goal of the practice and became an arahant.

Nanda went to pay his respects to the Buddha and to release him from his promise of *accharās*. The Buddha replied that he was freed from his promise as soon as Nanda had freed his mind from grasping. (Ud 3:2 & Jāt 182)

This story illustrates nicely the increasing refinement of the pleasures in the higher realms. While looking down from the height of resplendent Tāvatiṃsa, one sees no difference between a burnt she-monkey and the most beautiful of the Sakyan maidens, a race renowned for its beautiful women. Furthermore, this story offers an important reminder that even the most refined pleasures of the devas are conditioned, impermanent, and ultimately empty. Indeed, while the she-monkey, the Sakyan maiden, and the nymph were once seen respectively as burnt, beautiful, and divinely resplendent, for one who has realized the unconditioned, there is no longer any difference between them!

Few are the human males who can resist the lure of the heavenly *accharās*. We do meet one such steadfast individual in the following story from the *Saṃyutta Commentary*:

Forgetting the middle path, a certain bhikkhu became overly zealous in his practice, neglecting to eat and sleep until it undermined his bodily health. Racked by severe pains, he continued to do his walking meditation until at last he fell over dead.

He was immediately reborn as a deva in the Tāvatiṃsa heaven, standing in the doorway of a gorgeously decorated *vimāna*. Inside were one thousand *accharās* playing musical instruments. They beckoned him to come inside and partake of heavenly enjoyment. The new deva, however, did not understand that he had died. He looked at the lovely nymphs with the perception of a *samaṇa* and felt ashamed. He hung his head and tried to pull the fine cloth of his deva garments over his shoulders, like a monk's rag-robe.

Seeing this gesture, the *accharās* understood his mind, and brought him a full-length mirror. "See! You are now a deva. The time for a bhikkhu's practice is finished, now is the time to enjoy heavenly delight." The deva, understanding at last, was appalled. "It is not for the sake of sense pleasure that I was practising Dhamma, but for the sake of the supreme release of *nibbāna*!"

Instead of entering into the *vimāna*, the deva descended to earth and approached the Buddha, followed by his retinue of *accharās*. He spoke this verse before the Buddha:

"Resounding with a host of nymphs, (*accharāgaṇa*)

Haunted by a host of demons! (*pisācagaṇa*)

This grove is to be called 'Deluding' (*mohana* instead of *nandana*)

How does one escape from it?"[565]

What is the condition of life for the *accharās* themselves? It is certainly considered a happy rebirth, if not a very elevated one, more or less the female equivalent of the *gandhabbas*. The term *accharā* may indicate more a social class among the devas rather than a separate race of being. The several distinct words used to refer to female inhabitants of the heavenly worlds, *devī*, *devadhītu* (lit. "daughter of the gods'), and *accharā* are used somewhat interchangeably, to which must be added the gender neutral word *devatā*. The *Saṃyutta Commentary* says explicitly that *accharā* is another name for *devadhītu*.[566] In one place, Sakka's own daughter, the *devī* Hirī, is referred to as an *accharā*.[567] The distinction between *devatā* and *accharā* is especially blurred in one story, the *Guttilavimāna*, (Vv-a 33) where a female being addressed as *devatā* is said to have been reborn as an attendant of Sakka, with her own retinue of *accharās*. At one point in the verses, she declares "A nymph am I, who can assume any form at will, the most glorious of a thousand nymphs. Behold the fruition of my merit."[568] Once again we find that the distinction between the various kinds of beings is not always clear-cut.

This said we most often hear of *accharās* constituting the retinues of more senior devas. It should be noted that not only male devas enjoy this privilege. There are several examples in the *Vimānavatthu* of female *devīs* possessed of their own *vimānas* and retinues, typically of one thousand *accharās*.[569] In one place we are told of a female *devatā* who was "served by many and various males and females" (*anekacittaṃ naranārisevitaṃ*).[570] The same chapter goes on to say that the chief *devatā* is surrounded by nymphs who "dance, sing and enjoy themselves." (*pamodayanti*) It would seem that if the *accharās* are indeed subservient to the higher devas, they are not unhappy with their lot, nor do they always take a passive role. At one time Sakka's *accharās* begged him to fetch a famous human musician from earth, and the king of the devas meekly complied with their request (Jāt 243).

There are a few references to *accharās* living independently. Jātaka 541 mentions five hundred *accharās* "clever in song and dance" living in their own mansion. Then there is this curious passage from the Majjhima Nikāya which does not fit very well into the context of the verses preceding or following it:

In the middle of the ocean

---

565 SN 1:46. The story is from the commentary, the verse is Bhikkhu Bodhi's translation of the Saṃyutta, CDB, p.122.

566 SN-a 1:11.Commentary to the *Nandana Sutta*.

567 Jāt 535. But this may be a poetic trope.

568 Horner's translation, *Minor Anthologies IV*, p. 67.

569 Vv-a passim. The first chapter in the collection is typical in this regard.

570 Vv-a 11—the commentary explains this means that she has *devadhītus* and *devaputtas* as servants.

There are mansions aeon-lasting,

Sapphire-shining, fiery-gleaming

With a clear translucent lustre,

Where iridescent sea-nymphs dance

In complex, intricate rhythms.[571]

There are also, especially in the later sources, mention of female devas who belong to grades lower than the *accharās* properly so-called. In some places, Sakka's retinue is said to consist of twenty-five millions (or two-and-a-half *koṭi*) of *accharās*,[572] but elsewhere this is said to consist of twenty-five millions of *paricārikā* (translated as "hand-maidens") and five-hundred *accharās*, implying a higher status for the latter (Jāt 182).

Among the various sense pleasures of Tāvatiṃsa, music and dance are frequently mentioned. One of the female devas in the *Vimānavatthu* describes how she is woken from her sleep in the morning by sixty thousand musical instruments. There follows a list of the names of some of the instruments composing this celestial orchestra, but we do not have any more information about them.[573]

For the *accharās* and other devas, dancing seems to be a favourite pastime. This is aided by one of the favourite drinks of the devas, *madhumadāva,* which is said to induce suppleness for the dance (Vv-a 50). Since the Pali word *madhu* means "honey" this may be a kind of mead. The food of the devas is *sudhābhojana*, often translated as "ambrosia." *Sudhābhojana* probably has a liquid or loose texture, because it is served in a cup. It is described as being white, pure and sweet-smelling and the consumption of it is said to conquer many defilements (Jāt 535).

571 MN 50, Bhikkhu Bodhi's translation, MLDB, p. 436.

572 See for one example Jāt 535.

573 Vv-a 18. It is even unclear whether the names are meant to represent musical instruments or musicians, although the commentary prefers the former explanation.

3:5:12 VIMĀNAS

A dwelling place of a deva is called a *vimāna*, commonly translated as "mansion."[574] The nature of a *vimāna* is most thoroughly developed in one small book of the *Khuddaka Nikāya*, the *Vimānavatthu*. The canonical book is, like the Jātakas and the Dhammapada, a collection in verse to which prose stories have been appended by the commentators. The verses and stories take the form of morality lessons and mostly follow a fixed pattern. First, the glory and happiness of a deva is described and this is followed by a description of the kamma done in his or her previous human existence which merited this divine reward. In the course of this text we have many descriptions of *vimānas* and can discern something of their form and nature.

Vimānas vary greatly in detail from one another, and these differences depend on the degree of merit made by the deva. They are usually described in extravagant fashion as being brilliantly luminous, made of precious substances; most often gold is mentioned, but gems and lapis-lazuli[575] are also commonly found, and they are often surrounded by parks, groves and lotus ponds. The interior may include multiple rooms and storeys, furnishings such as divans, many musicians and dancers (*gandhabbas* and *accharās*) and sometimes song-birds.[576]

The following example, one of the more detailed in the collection, is quite typical:

On a mound of gold sits a *vimāna* entirely radiant,

Covered by a golden net, full of tinkling bells,

Eight-sided pillars, very well made, all of lapis-lazuli.

The trim is adorned with the seven precious things:

Lapis-lazuli, gold, crystal and silver

Cat's eye jewels and rubies.

On the delightful mosaic floor no dust settles ever,

Yellow beams support the roof

Four stair-cases are there, one in each direction,

The many jewelled inner-chambers are brilliant as the sun.

Four railings are there, dividing the space in a measured way.

It shines forth brilliantly in all four directions. (Vv-a 78)

Sometimes the size of the *vimāna* is given, and although this varies somewhat, by far the most common is twelve *yojana*. While this may seem huge, it should be recalled that the devas themselves are said to be three *gavutas* (three-quarters of a *yojana*) in size. Reduced to a human scale, this would make the *vimāna* perhaps one hundred feet long. Still a large dwelling, deserving of the name "mansion", but far from excessively so, as the interior must accommodate not only the chief deva but many hundreds or even thousands of attendant minor devas. One thousand *accharās* is

574 The dwelling places of other beings such as yakkhas and even petas are also sometimes referred to as vimānas, but we are here concerned only with those of the devas of Tāvatiṃsa.

575 *Veḷuriya*, which might also mean beryl.

576 All these details are found in multiple places in the Vv-a.

a very common number, and to this must be added the musicians. In two extreme cases, we hear of *devīs* who are awakened from sleep each morning by an orchestra of sixty thousand pieces! (Vv-a 18 & Vv-a 50) This seeming discrepancy highlights once again the magical and dream-like quality of these realms. Although the outside dimension may be only twelve *yojana*, the interior filled with throngs of devas does not seem cramped.

Vimānas are not fixed to one spot but are able to travel through the air by the psychic power (*iddhi*) of the owner (Vv-a 44). They are said to travel as swiftly as thought (*manojavaṃ)* (Vv-a 2). The devas may travel in their *vimānas* to attend festivals, to visit Nandana or other groves or even, on rare occasions, to the human realm. There are several incidents in the *Vimānavatthu* of devas coming with their mansions and retinues to see the Buddha.[577]

Devas may nonetheless use other conveyances to travel, such as chariots (*ratha*). We have two descriptions of such marvellous chariots, (Vv-a 63 & 64) as brilliant as the sun, covered all over with gold, jewels and lapis-lazuli and pulled by one thousand horses. These steeds are described in extravagant terms as covered in jewels, tall, swift, powerful and obedient. Their trappings make a delightful musical sound as they course through the sky. The *rathavimāna* is seven *yojana* in size and of course comes fully equipped with a retinue of *accharās*. We also hear of flying elephants with spacious pavilions on their backs. On the enormous tusks of one such elephant, there are said to be lotus ponds and on the lotuses *accharās* whirling in dance while *gandhabbas* make music (Vv-a 41).

The *vimāna* arises as a direct result of the kamma made by someone in the earthly realm. When asked how his glorious *vimāna* had come to be, the Cātumahārājika deva Serīsaka replied: "I have received this pleasure not by chance arising, nor by ripening (*pariṇāmajaṃ*), nor did I build it, neither was it a gift of the devas. It came into being as the result of the good kamma I myself made" (Vv-a 84). Like the devas themselves, the *vimāna* simply arises fully formed, in a single moment. This may occur long before the death of the person on earth, the *vimāna* arising at the instant of some good kamma being made. There the *vimāna* stands awaiting its owner, who after his human death is greeted there joyously by his retinue of minor devas like relatives celebrating the return of a traveller (Dhp-a 16:9). The action taken to earn a *vimāna* in Tāvatiṃsa may be great or trifling. In the stories of the *Vimānavatthu*, sometimes it is good morality in general but most often a simple offering such as some water, a handful of rice or the like. Two factors accentuate the effect of the kamma: the quality of the recipient and the mind of the donor. Gifts given to arahants or to the Buddha are of very powerful effect, although gifts given to the *saṅgha* as a whole are best of all. In one story, two sisters made offerings: one gave to individual bhikkhus but the other gave to the *saṅgha*. The former was reborn into a *vimāna* in Tāvatiṃsa, and the latter came to birth among the *nimmānaratī* devas (A *sagga* much higher than Tāvatiṃsa) (Vv-a 34).

The mind-state of the donor is equally important for determining the efficacy of the gift. An aspiration made while making the offering may result in a specific result. An example may cited of a woman who made an offering to Sāriputta with the mental determination: "By the power of this meritorious offering, may there be for me a divine elephant with a splendid pavilion and seat on his back, may there be heavenly bliss and at all times, lotuses" (Vv-a 5). Naturally, upon her decease she found herself in Tāvatiṃsa mounted upon an elephant:

> A beautiful *devī*, mounted on an elephant, with a bejewelled harness;
>
> Pleasing, powerful, moving swiftly through the air.
>
> With lotus spots, with lotus eyes, resplendent with lotuses
>
> His limbs lotus powdered, his trunk golden wreathed
>
> On roads lotus strewn, adorned with lotuses

[577] See Vv-a 51, for a notable example.

The elephant treads smoothly, pleasantly, without a jolt.

As it steps forward, there is the peal of golden chimes,

Their pleasing sound like that of the five musical instruments.

Seated on her elephant, robed in pure cloth, adorned

Among her great *accharā* host, her beauty outshines them all. (Vv 5)

If the mind is composed, tranquil, unified and full of faith even a very trivial act may bear great fruit. One layman merely re-arranged some flowers at a stupa, but did so using the act as an occasion for meditation upon the qualities of the Buddha, and was therefore reborn in a twelve *yojana* large golden *vimāna* (Vv-a 85).

3:5:13 BIRTH AND DEATH

(NOTE: although we are here discussing the Tāvatiṃsa realm, most of what follows in this section holds for the devas of the other sensuous plane saggas as well).

When thinking about the devas of the Buddhist tradition, it should never be forgotten that they too are subject to birth and death; they are in no sense immortal like the gods of other pantheons. Existence as a deva is just one more possible station of rebirth in the endless wheel of *saṃsāra*, albeit one of much longer duration than the human. The Buddha declared that no *samaṇa* or brahmin, no deva or *māra* can find security against aging, disease, death or the results of kamma (AN 4: 182). The devas themselves, immersed in an exquisitely pleasant and seemingly endless dream-like existence, may not always be aware of the fact of their own mortality. "When the devas, long-lived, beautiful, extremely blissful, living in magnificent *vimānas*, hear the Dhamma taught by the Buddha, for the most part they fall into fear and tremble, 'We thought we were permanent, ever-lasting but it seems that is not so" (AN 4: 33).

The devas of the sensual plane, including of course, Tāvatiṃsa, are divided into two genders and presumably engage in sexual intercourse. The Pali canon and commentaries, despite all the florid passages describing the beauty of the *accharās*, are rather reticent on this point.[578] However, the *Abhidharmakośa* tells us that the devas of the two lowest heavens, the Cātumahārājika and Tāvatiṃsa devas, "... unite by coupling, like humans, but they appease the fire of their desire through the emission of wind, since they do not have any semen" (AK 3:5, Eng. p. 465).

The act must be entirely for pleasure, since the devas do not reproduce sexually. Birth into these realms is by way of *opapātikā yoni*, "spontaneous arising." The deva simply appears fully formed, often into a *vimāna* already present, there to be greeted by his or her retinue. This experience is likened to "waking from sleep," (*suttappabuddhā).* We have seen above how the bhikkhu who died suddenly and was reborn into Tāvatiṃsa was initially confused. It is said to be normal for newly arisen devas not to know where they are, or what has happened to them, when they suddenly arise in a *vimāna* to the sound of musical instruments, surrounded by heavenly dancers. They find out when they are "reminded" (*sāritā*) by one of their retinue (MN-a 123). On the other hand, it would seem from many incidents that the devas can recall at least their immediately preceding existence; we often hear of a deva reflecting on the meritorious deeds that earned him his magnificence. One story, where the transition was more striking than most, concerns a frog that was accidentally crushed after crawling out of his pond attracted by the sound of the Buddha's voice. He was immediately reborn as a deva in a twelve *yojana vimāna* surrounded by the usual throng of *accharās* and reflected upon the marvel that transferred him there from a watery pond (Vv-a 51). It may be the absence of any pain or trauma in the birth process that enables the devas to retain this continuity of memory, which humans generally lack.

Nevertheless, there are many references in the texts to deva-sons and -daughters, *devaputto* and *devadhītu.* In many cases, this seems to be no more than a linguistic convention to establish the gender of the deva in question, but it is also said, for example, that Sakka had four daughters (Jāt 535). The commentary to the Saṃyutta Nikāya informs us that the familial relationship is established when a newly arisen deva appears in the lap of his or her parent (SN-a 2:1). We hear much less about the details of the birth of the minor devas who constitute the retinues, but there is one story in the *Dhammapāda Commentary* which bears on the matter:

> A woman named Rohinī was inflicted with a severe skin disease, because in a previous existence she had done the evil deed of putting itching powder into the bedding of a rival. After listening to a discourse of the Buddha's, with her mind concentrated and full of faith, she attained to the state of a *sotāpanna*, and was

[578] DN-a 33 discusses variant doctrines about the sexuality of the devas and comes to the tentative conclusion that the devas of all the *saggas* do engage in sexual intercourse. This passage will be discussed more fully in the section on the Paranimmitavas-savatti devas.

instantly cured of her disease.

Upon her death, many years later, she was reborn in Tāvatiṃsa endowed with a gloriously beautiful form. She came into existence just at the corner between the territories of four devas. Each wanted her for his own, and they took their quarrel to Sakka, king of the devas. Sakka looked at Rohinī and then asked the four disputing devas to state the condition of his mind after looking at the beautiful new *devī*.

One said his mind was as tumultuous as a battlefield, the second said his mind was racing as swiftly as a mountain river, the third said he could not take his eyes off her, it was just as if they were seized in a crab's claw and the fourth replied that his mind would not keep still, it was whipping about like a flag in the wind.

Sakka declared: "Your minds are over-powered by this form. As for myself, I want to live; I do not want to die. And if I do not get Rohinī then I shall surely die." The four devas replied as one, "Oh Mahārāja, that you should die, must not be!" So Sakka took Rohinī as his own dear wife, and they went off to enjoy various amusements together (*asukakiḷa*). When Sakka has spoken, no one may gainsay him. (Dhp-a 17:1)

In another passage, the commentary states that while deva sons and daughters are born in the lap of the parental deva, minor devas of a more servile class have their own places of birth. Female servants (*pādaparicārikā itthiyo*) appear in the bed of their lord, those of a presumably higher grade called "ornamental and decorative" (*maṇḍanapasādhanakārikā devadhītā*) appear beside the bed and those who are to become serving people or work-men (*veyyāvaccakarā*) are born "within the bounds" (MN-a 37). The image of the *saggas* we have from the commentarial literature mirrors ancient Indian society, or an idealized version of it, and the joys of heaven in no way include an egalitarian ideal.

Even though the devas of Tāvatiṃsa live for 1000 celestial years, or 36,000,000 years of the earth, they do eventually come to the end of their life-span. Although these devas are not prone to sickness in the human sense, their life-span may be cut short in a few ways; we have discussed above while describing the Cātumahārājika devas the fate of the *khiḍḍāpadosikā* devas, those "corrupted by play" and this kind of death occurs in Tāvatiṃsa also. As well, the devas might meet death in their wars with the asuras, or they may pass away simply through the exhaustion of the merit that caused their rebirth there (Vism 8:3).

There is a kind of aging in Tāvatiṃsa, but it is much less painful than the human form. When a deva draws near to the end of his life, he is made aware of this fact by the arising of the "five signs." These are: the withering of his garlands, his clothes appearing soiled, sweat coming out of his armpits, his body growing ill-favoured (*kāye dubbaṇṇiyaṃ okkamati*) and his becoming restless on his seat (It 3:4,4). If the deva then grows afraid and laments his fate, he is admonished by Sakka, king of the devas, as to the impermanence of all formations. Sakka then takes him by the arm and leads him to Nandanavana, where as we have seen above, all his fear of death melts away like a snowball in the sun (SN-a 1:11).

One such death is briefly described near the beginning of the Vessantara Jātaka:

Phusatī was the chief queen of King Sakka. When her time in Tāvatiṃsa drew near to completion, and the five signs appeared, Sakka escorted her with great pomp to the Nandanavana. There she reclined in a gorgeously adorned divan while Sakka sat beside her. The king of the devas told her that he would grant her ten boons for her next earthly existence.

At first, Phusatī was merely frightened and asked what evil deed she had done to be sent away from this dear place. Sakka gently replied that she had committed no sin, that her merit was exhausted and her time to pass away had come. He again urged her to name her ten boons, while there was still time.

Phusatī at last accepted the reality of her situation, and named her boons. She asked that in her next life she would again be a chief queen, that she have dark eyes, that she would again bear the name Phusatī, that she would have a son, that she keep a slim figure always, even while pregnant, that her breasts would always remain firm, that she not grow grey-haired, that she would have soft skin and that she have the power to save anyone condemned by the king.

When she had finished naming her boons, Phusatī passed away from that world and was reborn into the womb of King Madda's queen. She would grow up to become the mother of Prince Vessantara, the last human birth of the Bodhisatta before his attainment of Buddhahood. Eventually, she would also take birth as Mahāmāyā, the mother of Siddhattha Gotama, the Buddha of this age. (Jāt 547)

It may seem that Phusatī's requests were for the most part motivated by vanity, but it was something more poignant. It was a deva's horror of the depredations of human aging, a process that must seem cruel and terrible to them. Human existence is seen from the perspective of most devas as repugnant. When one deva was asked by Sakka to take a human birth to benefit the world, he was at first reluctant: "O king, the world of men is hateful and loathsome (*paṭikūlo jeguccho*): they who dwell there do good and give alms longing for the world of the gods."[579] What is more, we smell bad to them, even from seven *yojana* away (DN 23). The exception is that the scent of the wise and good, such as the Buddha and the arahants, is delightful to them (Dhp-a 15:8). And the wisest of the devas long for human birth, for the increased opportunity to practice Dhamma.[580]

Another story illustrates birth and death in the deva worlds:

> At one time the deva Mālabhāri went, together with his entourage of *accharās*, to a pleasure-garden for amusement. Five hundred of the *devadhītus* were climbing among the branches of a great tree, gathering blossoms to make a garland to adorn the *devaputta*. One of the *devadhītus* suddenly died while among the branches, her body vanishing like the flame of a lamp.
>
> She was reborn into a family of Savātthi and given the name Patipūjikā. She retained the memory of her previous existence, and always yearned to rejoin her beloved husband (*sāmika*) Mālabhāri. She made an earnest aspiration to gain renewed rebirth in Tāvatiṃsa and spent much time making merit by helping with the care of the eating-hall for the bhikkhus. At sixteen years of age Patipūjikā was married off into another family, which she regarded as a great misfortune, and she never ceased longing for her return to Mālabhāri.
>
> In the course of a long life, during which she had four sons, she always continued to keep strict morality and perform meritorious deeds, and always with the strong aspiration to be reborn again in Tāvatiṃsa.
>
> At last, one day, after giving gifts, making *pūja*, listening to Dhamma and taking the precepts her time was finished and Patipūjikā died. She was immediately back in the pleasure garden in Tāvatiṃsa, and the other *accharās* were now adorning Mālabhāri with his flowery wreath. Seeing Patipūjikā, her husband asked her, "I have not seen you since early this morning. Where did you go?"
>
> "I died, my lord."
>
> "What is that you say?"

[579] Jāt 489, W.H.D. Rouse trans. p. 201

[580] As for example, did Sakka in DN 21

"Just so, my lord."

"Where were you reborn?"

"Into a family of Sāvatthi."

"How much time did you spend there?"

"For ten months, I lie in my mother's womb. For sixteen years I stayed with my family, then I was married into another family and there I had four sons. But I always gave gifts and made merit with the aspiration to be returned to you."

"How old were you in human years?"

"One hundred years."

"Only that?"

"Yes, my lord."

"Given such a short span of human life, is it then to spend as if asleep, heedlessly given over to desire, or to giving gifts and making merit?"

"What are you saying, my lord?"

"Having only a short and uncertain span of life, even so humans are as heedless as if they were immortal." The *devaputta* Mālabhāri was seized with a great emotion of awe and dread (*saṃvega*). "Having only a hundred years in a human birth, and yet they spend it as if asleep. How then can we be freed from suffering?" (Dhp-a 4:4)

This story illustrates the different time scales of the human and deva realms. While one hundred years of a busy life had gone by for Patipūjikā, for Mālabhārī it was still the evening of the same day in Tāvatiṃsa. It is to be noticed that the five signs are not mentioned here. Perhaps Patipūjikā was simply too heedless to notice them, but one commentarial passage does state that these only occur for devas of great powers (DN-a 14).

3:5:14 THE BUDDHA TEACHING IN TĀVATIṂSA

The seventh *vassa* (rains retreat) of the Buddha was spent in Tāvatiṃsa. This occurred immediately after the Buddha had performed the "Twin Miracle" (*yamakapāṭihāra*) before a great multitude. This refers to a supernormal feat where he emitted streams of fire and water simultaneously. This is a miraculous display that can only be performed by a Buddha.[581]

The Buddha reflected, "Where did the Buddhas of the past go to spend the *vassa* after performing this miracle?" Investigating this question he found that they went to the Tāvatiṃsa deva realm. So the Blessed One proceeded to Tāvatiṃsa by taking only two steps. He placed one foot on the top of the Yugandhara Mountains and with the next stepped onto the peak of Mt Sineru.

Sakka, the king of the devas, thinking that the Buddha would likely take his seat on the Paṇḍukambalasila throne (Sakka's stone seat) was concerned that the devas would not be able to sit conveniently near him and hear the teachings, because of the throne's great size relative to a human body. The throne is sixty *yojana* long, fifty *yojana* wide and fifteen *yojana* thick. Knowing the doubt in Sakka's mind, the Buddha draped his outer robe (*saṅghāṭi*) over the throne, covering it completely. Sakka remained doubtful, thinking that despite having draped it with his robe, when the Buddha sat in the middle of the throne his figure would seem small and insignificant. When the Buddha took his seat there, it was just like he was sitting comfortably on a small stool. Sakka was truly amazed and regretted his doubts.

The Buddha remained in Tāvatiṃsa for the three months of the *vassa* ("rains retreat"), preaching to a vast concourse of devas extending in all directions around his seat for many *yojana*. In a special place of honour on his right side sat his mother, who had been reborn as a male deva in Tusita and had descended to the Tāvatiṃsa realm for the occasion. The Buddha taught the *Abhidhamma* to the devas during that time. Every morning he would descend to earth and take his morning bath in Lake Anotatta after which he would meet with Sāriputta and give him a summary of what had been taught in Tāvatiṃsa the day before. Then he would proceed to the northern continent of Uttarakuru to walk for alms to make his daily meal.

At the end of the *vassa* when the Buddha was ready to return to the human realm, Sakka ordered Vessakamma[582] to make three stairways with the head in Tāvatiṃsa and the foot at Saṅkassa City where Sāriputta had made his residence. The stairway on the right was of gold and for the use of the devas. The stairway on the left was of silver and for the use of the *mahābrahmās*. The jeweled stairway in the middle was for the Buddha.

Standing at the head of the jeweled stairway, the Buddha looked up and saw all the way to the brahmā worlds. He looked down and saw all the way to the nethermost of the *nirayas*. Looking in any direction, he saw hundreds of thousands of world-systems. At that moment, the devas could see the humans and the humans could see the devas just as if they were face-to-face.

As the Buddha descended the stairway Pañcasikha on his right-side played his *vīṇa* (a stringed instrument), paying homage to the Blessed One with sweet *gandhabba* music. Mātali on the Buddha's left honoured him with heavenly flowers. Mahābrahmā held a royal parasol over the Buddha and Suyāma, king of the Yāma devas, carried a fly-whisk. Later a *cetiya* (stupa) was built at Saṅkassa to mark the spot where the Buddha's

581 Because it involves the impossibility of using the powers from two incompatible jhānas, the fire and water kasinas.

582 The architect of the devas, to be discussed below.

foot first touched the earth. (Dhp-a 14: 2)

The short summaries of the Buddha's teachings in Tāvatiṃsa as given to Sāriputta are considered to be the origins of the *Abhidhamma Pitaka*. Sāriputta expounded upon them each day to five hundred disciples who had a special merit; in the time of Kassapa Buddha they had all been bats living in a cave where bhikkhus were chanting the *Abhidhamma*. Although in animal form they were unable to understand the meaning, they did "grasp some sign from the sound" (*sare nimittaṃ aggahesuṃ*) (ibid.). The descent of the Buddha from Tāvatiṃsa is a favourite motif in Buddhist temple art.

3:5:15 THE GREAT DEVAS OF TĀVATIṂSA

It has been already noted in the context of the Four Great Kings that the names of the devas are really more like titles of an office; when a Sakka dies, another one is born, so that there is always a Sakka. However, the situation may be a bit more subtle than that. The names are used like names, not like titles; Sakka has a title, *devānamindo*, "lord of the gods." As well, the personality of the particular deva remains more or less constant throughout the stories, even though in many cases the individual rebirth is identified as being this or that person of the Buddha's time. It may be best to regard this flux within a continuity as just another aspect of the voidness of self, *anattā*, a central concept in Buddhist thought. The elements of a personality are empty and dependently arisen and it may be best to think of two different, but intertwined, continuities: that of the personality *Sakka Devānamindo*, and that of the being reborn as Sakka.

In the next section, we shall be examining several of the great devas of the Tāvatiṃsa realm. Many individual devas are named in the texts, but for the most part we know little or nothing about them other than their names. Further, there is nowhere a definitive list of just who constitutes the "Thirty-Three" (the English meaning of *Tāvatiṃsa).* The devas selected for consideration here are the most important; those few known to be in the Thirty-Three and all those who figure prominently in the stories. We begin, appropriately, with the King of the Devas Sakka, about who there is more written in the sources than all the rest combined.

3:5:16 SAKKA

The devas of Tāvatiṃsa are that group which is most clearly derived from the older Indo-Aryan pantheon found in the Vedas. Sakka is the Buddhist version of Indra, the heroic and war-like champion of the Vedas, the Pali form of whose name is *Inda*. This name is sometimes used in the Pali texts[583] and we are told explicitly in one passage that "Sakka is Inda."[584] Nevertheless, although he retains many traces of the original Indra the character of Sakka is quite distinct. By the time the canon and commentaries were written, Inda-Sakka has become thoroughly Buddhist. Although he still wields a thunderbolt, he mostly uses it to threaten rather than to slay. Furthermore, while the Vedic Indra had a definite role as a creator-god, separating earth and sky, releasing the waters of life and leading out the sun to shine in the beginning of things,[585] there is absolutely no trace of this in Sakka.

Sakka may be said to the Supreme Being but only in a very limited and specific sense. He is the one who sits on his throne at the very summit of Mt Sineru, the highest point of the terrestrial world-system and has rulership over the whole. However, there are realms and beings above the earth, and Sakka is well aware of this. Furthermore, he is seen often paying respects to the Buddha and the arahants. His rulership over the devas consists in large part in presiding over the assemblies in the Sudhamma Hall, as we have seen. He is also, so we are told, kept very busy judging disputes which arise between devas such as the one concerning the new *devī* Rohinī (MN-a37). Sakka is also overlord of the Four Great Kings of Cātumahārājika and, is responsible for appointing them in the first place[586] We have already spoken of his role as war-chief in the perennial battles with the asuras, (§ 3:3,23) a function in which he most displays his origins as Indra. Sakka's governorship of the human realm consists in his oversight of the fortnightly inspections made by the Cātumahārājika devas, and in occasional direct interventions to assist the righteous and correct wrong-doers. We shall describe some of these below, as well as some instances in which Sakka's interventions have a more selfish motivation.

We can perhaps gain some insight into the nature of Sakka and his relationship to Indra by a consideration of his epithets:

Devānaminda—This is Sakka's most commonly used title, and it means "lord of the gods." The word *inda* here is a common noun meaning "lord" or "master" but the resonance with the proper name Inda is hard to ignore.

Sahasakkha—"The Thousand-Eyed." This was also an epithet of Indra's. It is not to be interpreted literally; Sakka is always depicted with just the ordinary two. The text explains that it means he can attend to a thousand thoughts at once.

Purindada—The original Sanskrit form *purbhīd* meant "destroyer of cities" but is explained by the commentator as a Pali compound meaning "previous giver" for his generosity in his former human existence. A clearer example of the Buddhification of the old Vedic war-god could not be asked for![587]

Vatrabhū—The commentator gives two possible derivations. The first, which seems rather strained, is that it means "rulership through conduct" (*vattena aññe abhibhavati*). The second is that it refers to the defeat of the asura Vatra. This is a clear reference to Indra's epic battle with the demonic Vṛta.[588]

---

583 It is the preferred form in the *Suttanipāta*, for instance.

584 Jāt 521—"*sakkoti indo*," perhaps more literally, "Inda is called Sakka".

585 Nicolás, Meditations Through the Ṛg Veda, p. 119f.

586 We are told this specifically about Vessavaṇa and can safely assume it applies to the other three as well.

587 Nicolás p. 143 and see DPPN under Inda.

588 See Nicolás p. 120-121

Other epithets of Sakka are not apparently derived from Indra, but reflect his own nature:

Maghavā—This epithet is given because his name as a human was Magha (Jāt 31). However, this involves a narrative contradiction because the Jātaka identifies that Sakka as a previous birth of the Bodhisatta and yet the title is used of the Sakka of the Buddha's time, who is obviously a different individual. That this contradiction does not appear to have bothered the commentators may be either just an oversight, or another indication of the empty nature of personal identity in the context of Buddhist thought.

Vāsava—This derives from Magha's gift of a rest-house (āvasatha).

Sujampati—This refers to Sakka as the husband of the asura maiden Sujā.

Kosiya—very frequently used by others addressing Sakka familiarly, much like a given name.[589]

Sakka is a frequent character in the Jātaka stories, appearing in about one eighth of the total collection. In at least nineteen of the stories, it is the Bodhisatta who is born as Sakka. We are told in the *Aṅguttara Nikāya* that the Buddha had been Sakka thirty-six times (AN 7:62). In eight Jātakas, Sakka is identified with Anuruddha. Moggallāna and Kāḷudāyi were also Sakka in one story each[590] If there is any significant difference in the personalities of these various Sakkas, it is not easy to find. As a rule, Sakka is identified as the Bodhisatta in those stories in which he is a central figure in the narrative, unless some other important figure is the Bodhisatta, in which case Sakka is identified as a previous birth of Anuruddha. In most of Sakka's appearances he is not identified as a previous birth of anyone in particular and often plays a very minor role in the story. For instance, in several stories Sakka's only role is to order Vissakamma, the divine architect, to fashion a pleasant hermitage for some great ascetic, usually the Bodhisatta. His appearances in the *Dhammapāda* stories are very similar. There is also an entire chapter of the Saṃyutta Nikāya devoted to Sakka, as well as important incidents told in the Dīgha and Majjhima Nikāyas.

The picture that emerges of Sakka from these stories is a complex one, his is the most well-developed and nuanced character in the mythology. Despite his great powers and his awesome role as *devānamindo*, Sakka emerges as endearingly human. He is mostly a force for good, and is devoted to the Buddha, whom he venerates. And yet, Sakka remains subject to very ordinary defilements, especially sensuality but he can also act quite selfishly in defence of his interests and position.

Sakka's interventions in human affairs are usually triggered by a sign which warns him of trouble; either his throne manifests heat (āsanaṃ *uṇhākāraṃ dassesi*) or his dwelling trembles (*bhavanaṃ kampi*). This is said to happen when his life-span is coming to an end, when his merit is near exhaustion, by the force of righteousness (*dhammika*) exhibited by a brahmin or *samaṇa* of great supernormal power (*mahiddika*) or when some person of great power (*mahānubhāvasatta*) is seeking to take his place (Jāt 440). At other times, these signs occur when some righteous person on earth is in distress and in need of divine aid.

In the Sambula Jātaka, Sakka rescues a princess:

> Sotthisena was a prince of Bārāṇasi and his wife was the fair and virtuous Sambulā. It came to pass that the prince was afflicted with leprosy and in his despair determined to leave human company and live alone in the forest. Despite his protests, the noble Sambulā insisted on accompanying him and serving as his nurse and help-mate.

[589] For these epithets, see SN 11:12 and *Bodhi*, CDB, p. 386, note 146.

[590] Jāt 78 and 488 respectively. These three were all arahant bhikkhus in the Buddha's time.

One day, when she was out gathering fruits in the forest she stopped to bathe in a mountain pool. There she was spied by a cruel *dānava*[591] who was inflamed with lust for her. After she had risen from the pool and dressed he emerged from concealment and announced himself, proposing that she come away with him as his bride.

"What use to you is your sickly prince? If you come with me, I shall make you the chief of all my four hundred wives and fulfill your every whim."

But the good princess would hear none of it, and only wished to return to her rightful husband as quickly as possible. Enraged by her refusal, the *dānava* seized her by the arm and said, "If you will not be my wife, you shall serve just as well as breakfast!"

Sambulā cried out, "Are there no devas, no protectors of the world, to prevent such lawlessness?"

At that moment, by the force of her goodness, Sakka's dwelling trembled and his throne grew hot. Investigating the cause, he quickly determined that the righteous princess was in grave danger. Swiftly, the king of the devas went to that spot, and stood in the air poised above the *dānava* with his thunderbolt-weapon Vajira in his hand. "This is a noble woman, her virtue as bright as a flame! If you do not release her, you *rakkhassa* ("demon") I shall split your head into seven pieces!"

In fear for his life, the *dānava* released Sambulā at once. Sakka, thinking that he would try the same again, bound him with a divine fetter (*devasaṅkhalika*) and carried him far away, over three mountain ranges, before releasing him. He then admonished Sambulā against negligence and returned to his own abode. (Jāt 519)

In this story, Sakka appears very much like Indra, and the tale as a whole has an archaic feel. That the monster in the tale is identified as a *dānava* may be significant. In most Jātaka stories this type of role would be filled by a yakkha and it is uncommon to encounter *dānavas*. Late Pali sources identify them as a class of asuras, the descendants of Danu,[592] which in turn followed the description in the pre-Buddhist Vedas.[593] Also, here we have Sakka wielding his thunderbolt, the *Vajirāvudha*, which is one of the four great weapons. If Sakka were to throw it at the peak of Mt Sineru it would pierce through all one-hundred and sixty-eight *yojana* of rock to the root of the mountain far below the ocean (Sn-a 1:10). Despite the threat of splitting his head into seven pieces, Sakka does not in the end slay the *dānava*, he merely transports him far away where he cannot threaten the princess anymore; Indra would have just blasted the demon and been done with it. This story appears to be a reworking of an older, pre-Buddhist legend, with the deva-hero now exercising the Buddhist virtue of non-harming.

Another episode in which Sakka comes to the rescue of a royal lady in distress occurs in the Mahājanaka Jātaka:

There was civil war in Mithilā with two royal brothers vying for the throne. When the reigning king's army was defeated, he himself killed and his capital city occupied, his pregnant wife fled the royal city disguised as a common market woman, with the royal jewels concealed in an old basket. No one recognized her and she made it safely out of a postern gate in the city wall. But there she sat by the road-side in utter distress. The queen had led a sheltered and pampered life, with no practical knowledge of the outside world. She had only heard of a fair city, Kālacampā, beyond the frontier of the kingdom and conceived an idea that she and her unborn child would be safe there. But she had no idea of where it was, or even which direction was north or

591 A demonic being, either a yakkha or an asura.

592 See DPPN which cites the *Abhidhānappadīpikā* written in Sri Lanka in the twelfth century A.D.

593 Daniélou, p. 307.

south. So she sat beside the road calling out in a pitiful voice: "Is anyone going to Kālacampā?"

Now, it was no ordinary baby in the queen's womb, but the Bodhisatta himself. Sakka's dwelling trembled and he investigated the cause. "There has arisen a great being in that womb; it behooves me to go there!" He created a cart with a bed in the back and assuming the form of an old man he drove past the city-gate where the queen sat forlorn. Sakka cried out, "I am going to Kālacampā! Does anyone wish a ride?"

"Alas, father, I am heavy with child and could never climb into your cart. Perhaps you could find room for my basket and allow me to walk along behind?"

"What are you saying? I am a master cart-driver; there is no one like me. Have no fear, climb in!"

So saying, Sakka caused the earth behind the cart to rise up like a goat-skin bellows filled with air and the queen easily stepped into the cart and lay down on the soft bed. In a few hours, she peeked out of the covering of the cart and saw the watch-towers of a great city coming into view.

"What city would that be, father?"

"Kāḷacampā City, my dear."

"But how could that be! It is more than sixty *yojana* from Mithilā!"

Sakka replied, "I know a short-cut." (Jāt 539)

We see here a very common theme of Sakka appearing among humans in the guise of an old man, although it is not stated in this case, this is usually a brahmin. We also see the great deva's use of supernormal power, and have a glimpse into his sense of humour. I have taken a small liberty in using a colloquialism for Sakka's last reply; a literal translation would be "I know a straight road," (*ahaṃ ujumaggaṃ jānāmi*) but it seems Sakka's intention to have a little fun is clear. He uses the same phrase in another story (Dhp-a 1:1) when he leads a blind arahant to Savatthi in an impossibly short time.

Sakka's encounters with holy men, seers or ascetics, is somewhat ambivalent.[594] In very many of the Jātakas, when Sakka makes a cameo appearance it is to order Vissakamma, the architect of the devas, to create a pleasant hermitage for some person, usually the Bodhisatta, who is making a great renunciation and abandoning the world of affairs for a quiet life in the forest.[595] Sometimes Sakka appears to an ascetic in order to teach him, as in Jātaka 372 where he admonishes one who was displaying excessive grief over the death of a pet deer.

However, more often Sakka is seen testing an ascetic's virtue. Sometimes the motivation for this may be quite selfish: Sakka's throne grows hot because of some holy man's virtue and the king of the devas grows apprehensive that someone may be about to take his place. In these cases, Sakka can behave quite badly:

At one time there was a great ascetic (*tāpaso*) named Lomasakassapa, and by the force of his severe austerities (*ghoratapo*) he caused the dwelling place of Sakka to tremble. "By the force of his virtue, he will cause me to fall from my place! I will have a talk with the king of Bārāṇasi, and then we shall break his asceticism."

594 The Jātakas, the main source for such stories, refer to incidents occurring before the arising of the Buddha so there were no bhikkhus as such. The seekers who lived an ascetic life-style in the forest are called *isi*, from the Sanskrit *ṛṣi*, usually anglicized as "rishi".

595 Very many Jātakas, see for example nos. 70, 509, 547.

So Sakka went to the city of Bārāṇasi and appeared in the king's bed-chamber, filling the entire room with the glorious light of his form.

"Arise, o king!"

"But who are you?"

"I am Sakka."

"Why do you come here?"

"King, do you wish to be the ruler of all Jambudīpa? Do you want to be like Sakka, free of birth and death? Do you wish these things, or do you not?"

"I do so wish!"

"Then you must bring the sage Lomakassapa here and have him perform a great sacrifice, slaughtering living animals, and then these things shall be yours."

So the king sent a messenger to Lomakassapa, offering him as much land as he desired, but the wise hermit scorned the offer. Sakka again appeared before the king and told him that he should send his beautiful daughter the princess Candavatī to tempt him with an offer of marriage. When the hermit saw her all adorned and as lovely as an *accharā*, he lost all moral sense and agreed to perform the sacrifice. (Jāt 433)

As it happened, at the critical moment on hearing the pitiful cries of the animals led to slaughter, Lomakassapa came back to his senses and was unable to wield the knife. But the point to note here is the length to which Sakka was willing to go to lead the good man into a morally depraved act. The claim that Sakka is free from birth and death is of course false, and Sakka must have known it to be so, as he was motivated by the fear of his own death. He seems to have been shamelessly playing upon the superstitions of the king. Also, neither of these royal gentlemen, deva or human, hesitated in the idea of using Candavatī as bait.

Nor was this the only time Sakka resorted to such low tricks:

At one time a deer in the forest ate some grass where a hermit had urinated. Some of his semen was mixed up in it, and as a result the deer became pregnant and gave birth to a human child. Finding the baby, the old hermit adopted him and gave him the name Isisiṅga ("the fawn seer"). Isisiṅga grew up in the forest having only the old hermit for company, and became a great ascetic in his own right. So much so, that the dwelling place of Sakka was shaken and the king of the devas grew apprehensive that someone had arisen in the world who would take his place.

So Sakka caused the rains to stop falling on the lands of the King of Kāsi for three years. A terrible drought brought famine and hardship upon the land. When all seemed lost, Sakka appeared in a glorious radiant form in the bed-chamber of the king. Sakka told him that the rains had stopped because of Isisiṅga. "In the Himavā, there is a great ascetic named Isisiṅga, and whenever it looks like it is going to rain, he glares up angrily at the sky and the rains stop."

"What can we do?"

"If his virtue were to be broken, then he could not stop the rain."

"But who could do that?"

"Your daughter, Niḷinikā." (Jāt 526)

The subsequent encounter of Niḷinikā and Isisiṅga involves a bit of ribald comedy. Naliṇkā was dressed in the crude bark garment of an ascetic, and when she sat down the garment fell open. Because he had never seen a woman before and was quite ignorant even of the concept, Isisiṅga upon seeing her thus exposed asked what had become of her member. She replied that she had been wounded there by a bear. Asked if it was painful, she said it was itchy, (*kaṇḍu*—a word sometimes used metaphorically for lust) and that no magic charm or medicine could stop it itching, but she could teach him how to scratch it![596]

Sometimes, when Sakka discovers that the ascetic is not striving to become a new Sakka, he is delighted and respectfully offers his aid:

The Bodhisatta was in that existence an ascetic living on an island and subsisting of the leaves of a single tree which fell upon the ground. Sakka's throne grew hot beneath him and Sakka wondered, "Who would make me fall from my place?" Investigating the cause, he discovered it was the ascetic. "I will test him. He lives off nothing but a handful of wet leaves. If he seeks the state of a Sakka, he will give them to me, if he doesn't he won't"

So Sakka appeared before the Bodhisatta in the form of a brahmin beggar and the ascetic gave him all the leaves he had collected, joyful in having this opportunity to make merit. Sakka came again the next day, and the day after. The same thing happened each time. The ascetic was now quite weak from hunger.

Sakka then appeared before him in a glorious form, radiant as the rising sun. "Tell me, ascetic, why do you sit here on this island in the blazing sun, living on leaves? Do you aspire for the state of Sakka or of Mahābrahma? Do you strive for human or celestial success?"

The Bodhisatta answered, "I want none of those things. I seek only omniscience (*sabbaññuta*—implying Buddhahood). A new birth, followed by the breaking up of the body, all that is confusion and suffering, O Sakka Vāsāva!"

Delighted with the ascetic's words, Sakka granted him a series of boons. The holy seer asked not for wealth or power, but to be freed from all desire, to not be associated with fools, to know only wise men and to have opportunities to give. Finally, for his last boon he asks the king of the devas:

"O Sakka, Lord of All Beings, grant me the boon that you will not come to see me ever again!"

"But many men, and women too, follow religious duties with the fond wish of seeing me!"

"Such is your divine appearance, wonderful, delightful to all the senses (*sabbakāmasamiddhinaṃ*), that seeing you I may become intoxicated and this is why I fear the sight." (Jāt 480)

Of the many stories where Sakka tests the resolution of some righteous being, perhaps the best known and loved is the one found in the Sasapaṇḍita Jātaka:

At that time, the Bodhisatta had come to birth as a hare living in the forest. This hare was very wise, and

596 ibid. H.T. Francis omitted this section from the PTS translation, the hiatus is marked by asterisks in the text, Cowell 1995, Vol. 5, p. 102. For a translation and analysis of this Jātaka see Ānandajoti 2010.

together with three friends, a monkey, a jackal and an otter, he made a vow that on the *uposatha* day they would never refuse to give some of their food if asked for by a beggar.

On the *uposatha*, the other three animals had some food they had found that would be suitable to give, but the poor hare had nothing but grass, which cannot be eaten by humans. Thinking on this, the hare made a resolution that if asked for food by any beggar, he would give the flesh of his body.

Upon the little hare making this resolution, Sakka's throne grew hot. Investigating the reason, he decided to test the hare. Assuming the form of a brahmin beggar, he appeared on earth and begged food from each of the animals in turn. When he approached the hare, the little animal experienced great joy of mind and said:

"Brahmin, it is good that you have approached me seeking food. Today I shall make a gift never before given. And you shall not break the precept against taking life. Go now and gather firewood, make a fire and call for me when there is a blazing mass of hot coals. Then I shall come and throw myself into the fire. Then when my flesh is well-cooked, you may eat and do the duties of an ascetic (*samaṇadhamma*)."

Sakka caused a fire to spring up with his magic power (ānubhāvena) and called for the hare. The little hare rose from his bed of grass. Thinking, "If there are any insects in my fur, they shall be destroyed," he shook his whole body three times to cast them off. Then, with a heart full of joy he leapt into the flames like a royal swan alighting in a lotus pond. But the fire failed to heat even the pores of his skin; it was as if he had landed in a pile of snow.

"Brahmin! This fire of yours is quite cool! What is the meaning of this?"

"I am no Brahmin, wise hare, I am Sakka come here to test you."

Then the hare uttered a lion's roar: "If not only you, but all the inhabitants of the world-system came to test me, they would never find me unwilling to give!"

Sakka announced, "Wise hare! Your virtue shall be remembered for an entire kappa!" Sakka then extracted some of the essence of a mountain and used it to mark the face of the moon with the image of a hare, so that the generosity of the Bodhisatta would be remembered for the rest of the age. (Jāt 316)

Another animal tested by Sakka was a wolf who, being unable to find food decided to make a virtue out of necessity and thought he may as well make an *uposatha* fast. The wolf did not do as well as the hare. When Sakka appeared in the form of a goat, the wolf immediately forgot his vow and began to chase him (Jāt 300). In another story, Sakka tested the virtue of a courtesan:

In those days, the Kuru people were renowned as the most virtuous in Jambudīpa, making it a point of honour never to break the precepts even in trivial matters. Sakka decided to test the virtue of a courtesan (*vaṇṇadāsī*) in the Kuru city. Appearing in the guise of a youth, he gave her a thousand pieces of money and said he would be coming for her shortly, and then returned to Tāvatiṃsa. For three years she refused to accept even so much as a chew of betel from any other man, for the sake of not breaking her contract.

At last she was reduced to an extreme of poverty and went before the Chief Magistrate to plead her case, "I do not know even if the youth is alive or dead." The magistrate released her from her contract. After that, Sakka appeared before her again and offered her another thousand. She drew back her hand and said, "I cannot take this. You are the man who has already paid me." Sakka then revealed himself as the king of the devas and praising her virtue, filled her house with a great quantity of the seven precious things. He admonished her to remain vigilant and returned to Tāvatiṃsa. (Jāt 276)

In these, and many similar stories, Sakka acts like a trickster figure. On some occasions he is actually rebuked by the victims of his testing. In order to test the famous wise man Osadha, Sakka assumed human form and stole a chariot. Sakka and the rightful owner were brought before the sage, to see if he could solve the case. Osadha knew right away that it was Sakka, because of his unblinking eyes. He told the king of the devas never to do the like again (Jāt 542, eng. 546). On another occasion Sakka, fearful of losing his throne, tried to stop a merchant from his generous giving by making all his wealth disappear. At the end of the story, the merchant reproaches Sakka for doing a base thing. He who had attained his high station by generosity, was now trying to stop others (Jāt 340). Likewise Sakka was rebuked by Suppabuddha the leper when he tested him:

> "You are a poor, wretched fellow. I will give you great wealth if you declare: "There is no Buddha, no Dhamma, no *Saṅgha*. Enough of Buddha, Dhamma, *Saṅgha* for me!"
>
> "Who are you?"
>
> "I am Sakka."
>
> "You are a great fool (*andhabāla*). You are without shame (*ahirika*). I am already a wealthy man; I have the riches of virtue, self-respect and fear of wrong-doing (*sīla, hiri, ottappa*). I have learning, generosity and wisdom (*suta, cāgo, paññā*) . My life is neither wretched nor worthless" (Dhp-a 5:7)

When Suppabuddha is eventually reborn as a deva in Tāvatiṃsa some of the other devas snobbishly complain how someone who had been so low class in the human realm could now be so glorious, but Sakka came to his defence and praised him as a good Dhamma follower (SN-a 11:14).

At other times we see Sakka performing small acts of kindness. He used a magic water-pot to revive a dying *kinnara* in answer to to heart-felt plea of his mate (Jāt 485). One time, full of joy at winning a battle over the asuras, Sakka looked around to see if there were any being whose wish he could fulfill. He saw a crane standing on a hill-top and saw its thought; the crane found the hill delightful and only wished it could stay there all day without having to go and get food and water. Sakka caused a nearby stream to flood all the way up to the hill-top so the crane could catch fish and drink without moving from its place (Jāt 380). One of Sakka's most spectacular interventions was when he helped the musician Guttila win a music contest. The old musician had been challenged by his upstart pupil and fled to the woods in shame. This is when Sakka appeared before him:

> "Fear not, I am Sakka. I shall be your support. When you play against your opponent, break one string of your vīṇā[597] and your music shall be just as good as before. Your opponent will not be able to match that. Carry on breaking the strings of your vīṇā until you are playing just with the body, and the beautiful sound of your playing will fill all of Bārāṇasī for the space of twelve *yojana*.
>
> "Furthermore, take these three dice. Every time you cast one into the air, three hundred *accharas* will descend from Tāvatiṃsa and dance in the arena to sound of your music." (Jāt 243)

There are definite limitations to Sakka's power. He is not always able to foresee the results of his actions. In a few

[597] A seven-stringed instrument, similar to a lute.

stories, a newly born Sakka returned to earth to assist the relatives he has left behind. In one such incident, Sakka had been one of a band of four brothers, all ascetics. He gave a magical item to each of the remaining three; an axe that could chop wood all by itself, a double-sided drum that when beaten on one side frightened away the owner's enemies, and on the other caused them to become his firm friends. The last brother got a magical bowl that always filled itself with curds. Alas, these wonderful items did the brothers little good. A rogue swindled the first brother out of his ax and used it to kill all of them and gain possession of the magical items (Jāt 186). In another story, Sakka predicts the outcome of a battle, but the king on the side supposed to lose heard tell of it and changed his plans, winning the day (Jāt 301). (This story is also of interest because it features a single combat between the guardian devas of the two nations in the form of a white and a black bull). Some specific limitations to Sakka's powers are mentioned; he is unable to free a body from disease, or to purify a person's morality (Jāt 440). In one of his numerous tests of human virtue, Sakka asked a king to give him his eyes. Later, he restored the man's sight but the text makes it clear that it was not by his own power, but by the power of the king's own meritorious kamma (Jāt 499). It is clear from all these episodes that Sakka, although in the exalted position of *devānamindo*, "lord of the gods," is far from being omnipotent or omniscient and is even capable of serious moral lapses. In the last analysis, Sakka is just one more wanderer in *sāṃsara*. The Buddha declared specifically of Sakka that he was not free of passion, anger or delusion (*rāga, dosa, moha*) nor of birth, old-age, death and suffering (AN 3: 37).

He has had his fair share of family problems too. Recall from a previous chapter the tale of how Magha became Sakka, and of Magha's four wives. Three of them contributed to his building project (over his initial objection to the involvement of women) and were subsequently reborn as his attendants in Tāvatiṃsa. But the one he really loved, Sujā did nothing at all and took a lower rebirth as a crane:

> After his other wives had been reborn in Tāvatiṃsa, and received wonderful dwellings as a result of their deeds, Sakka began to wonder why Sujā had not appeared. He investigated the matter and saw that she was now a crane living in the forest. Sakka took the bird to Tāvatiṃsa to let it see the pleasant state that was the result of merit. "Henceforth, keep the five precepts!" he admonished the crane and instructed it on what those entail.
>
> A little later, to check up on the crane, Sakka assumed the form of a fish and lay without moving in the pond. The crane thought, "this one must be dead!" and took it up in its beak. When the fish began to wriggle its tail, she immediately let it go. "It is alive after all!" Sakka said, "Sadhu! it is good that you are protecting your precepts!" and returned to his abode.
>
> Sujā was then born into a family of potters in Bārāṇasi. There too she kept the precepts. Sakka came to her district in the form of an old peddler with a hand-cart full of golden cucumbers. "Take my cucumbers! Take my cucumbers!" When the people offered to buy them, he said they were not for sale for any price, but free for one who keeps the precepts. "We don't know anything about any precepts, who is this cucumber man anyway?" said the people as they left that place. Sujā heard tell of these strange cucumbers and thought, "I keep the precepts, these must be for me!" Sakka asked her, "Do you guard your precepts, my dear?" "Yes father, I do." "Then these are yours," and he pushed the cart to her door and left.
>
> At the end of that life-time, Sujā was reborn as the daughter of Vepacitti, king of the asuras. Because of her previous virtue, she was endowed with a very beautiful form. When she came of age to marry, Vepacitti announced that his daughter would choose her husband according to her own wishes, and he ordered all the asuras to come to an assembly. Sakka appeared at the assembly in the guise of an old asura. Sujā was led out, beautifully adorned, and bidden to choose her husband by placing a garland around his neck. When her

eyes lit on Sakka because of their past-life affection her heart was flooded with a great love for him, washing through her like a wave, and she declared "This one is my husband!"

The host of young, powerful asuras were abashed. "That one is old enough to be her grand-father!" Taking Sujā by the hand, Sakka revealed his deva form and roared aloud, "I am Sakka!" The asuras were enraged, "We have been deceived by old Sakka!" (*jarasakka*) They tried to seize him, but just at that moment, Mātali the charioteer arrived in Sakka's great Chariot of Victory (*vejayantaratha*) pulled by one thousand Sindh horses and the happy couple made their escape, hotly pursued by the host of angry asuras.

As the chariot sped up the slopes of Mt Sineru towards the city of the devas, it entered the Sippalivana, a forest inhabited by many *supaṇṇas*. There was a great sound of heart-rending cries coming from below. "What is that sound, Mātali?" "My lord, it is the young of the *supaṇṇas*, many of them are being destroyed by the passage of our chariot." Sakka was appalled, and ordered Mātali to stop the chariot at once. The asuras, coming up behind, saw that Sakka had stopped. They thought the reason must be that he was expecting reinforcements, and in fear of a great deva army they returned to the asura city and hung their heads in shame.

On their arrival in Tāvatiṃsa, Sakka installed Sujā as the chief of his twenty-five million[598] *accharas*. She said to him, "Great king (*mahārāja*) here in the deva world, I have no mother or father, no brother or sister. I would ask of you a boon. Wherever you go, there I would go too." Sakka made this promise, saying "Sadhu!" (Jāt 31, Dhp 2,7)

An archetypal story: the hero gets the girl and the cavalry rides in for a rescue in the nick of time! Not only did Sakka acquire Sujā as his chief wife, he also acquired a father-in-law in Vepacitti, and we will already had occasion to comment on the touchy relations between these two.[599] It is a detail typical of Sakka's "human" side that of all his women, the one he truly loves is the bad girl. It should also be stated that Sakka did not seem to keep his promise very well. We seldom hear of Sujā accompanying her husband in his various travels into the human realm. The royal couple went to earth once in the form of a pair of swans (Dhp-a 2.9) and on another occasion posed as poor weavers to give alms to Mahākassapa (Dhp-a 4: 10). One notable example, although hardly a romantic outing, is found in the Kharaputta Jātaka where the two of them take the form of goats and copulate in the street to attract the attention of King Senaka's horses, allowing them to teach the king by way of a conversation between horse and goat, which Senaka was able to understand:

> The king's horse: "Indeed it must be true, as the *paṇḍit* says, that goats are foolish. This fool is not aware that what he openly does in the street should be done only in secret."
>
> The he-goat: "Son of a donkey, it is you who are the perfect fool. You should know this, you with a twisted cord through your mouth, and your head hanging down. You are such a surpassing great fool that when you are untied, you do not run away. But that Senaka you carry is an even greater fool than you." (Jāt 386)

The back-story here is that the king had been given a magic spell by a nāga allowing him to understand the speech of animals, but the spell came with a warning that if he gave it away he would immediately die by fire. His wife had been nagging him for some time, wanting to learn the spell herself, and heedless of the consequences. King Senaka being "under the power of women" (*mātugāmavasiko*) was about to succumb when Sakka and Sujā came down to

598 two and a half *koṭi*.

599 See the section on asuras in § 3:3,23.

stop him.

Sakka has two sons and four daughters that we know of. All of them caused him some trouble. The two sons were named Suvira and Susīma and an identical story is told about both:[600]

It may happen that, from time to time, the asuras become powerful and break through all five lines of defence and threaten the city of the devas itself. On these occasions, the Four Great Kings inform Sakka and he mounts the Chariot of VIctory and takes the field himself, or it may be that he sends one of his sons.

On this occasion, he ordered Suvira to go into battle, but Suvira was negligent and of a lustful nature (*pesetukāmo*). Three times he was given the order, "Suvira my son, the asuras are attacking the devas. Go out and meet them in battle." And three times he replied, "Yes, my lord," but from negligence failed to do so. Instead, he wandered down the golden highway into Nandanavana and played at "Constellation" (*nakkhatta*) with his retinue of *accharas*. (SN-a 11:1)

Sakka's subsequent conversation with his son is recorded in verse, and displays an exasperated parent's sarcasm:

Suvīra: "That a lazy man who does not toil

Nor attend to his duties

Might still have all his desires fulfilled

Grant me that, Sakka, as a boon."

Sakka: "Where a lazy man who does not toil

Might achieve unending bliss:

Go there, Suvira,

And take me along with you."[601]

Sakka also had four daughters, named Āsā, Saddhā, Sirī and Hirī whose names may be rendered into English as Hope, Faith, Luck and Honour:[602]

The four *devadhītas* were fond of bathing and sporting in the waters of Lake Anotatta in the Himavā. There, one day, they encountered the brahmin sage Nārada. This brahmin had developed his powers to such a degree that he was able to travel to Tāvatiṃsa and back. He was in the habit of taking his day's rest in Nandanavana or Cittalatāvana, before returning to his abode in the Himavā. When he appeared before the divine ladies, he was carrying a fresh blossom from the Päricchattaka Tree, a lovely flower found only in Tāvatiṃsa.

The daughters of Sakka begged him for the blossom: "This pure, sweet-scented flower is honoured by the devas, no human nor asura is worthy of it." Nārada replied that he had no need of it, and would happily bestow it upon whichever among them was considered supreme (*jeṭṭha*). Thus the sage by his words stirred

600 These are found in a *Suvira Sutta* and a *Susīma Sutta*, no. 1 and 2 of the *Sakkasaṃyutta*. The texts are identical except for the name given for the devaputta. They are not identified as Sakka's sons in the canon, only in the commentary.

601 ibid. Bodhi trans. CDB, p. 317-318.

602 Francis translates Sirī as "Glory" which is one definition given by the PED, but the relevant verses seem to apply more to "Luck." Hirī is often translated as "shame".

a quarrel among the divine sisters. They asked him to judge among them, but he said they should take their quarrel before "the Lord of Beings," meaning their father, Sakka.

So, inflamed by the quarrel, intoxicated by the pride of their own beauty, the four went back to Tāvatiṃsa and begged Sakka to settle the dispute as to which was to be judged best. Sakka also refused to judge between them, knowing that if he picked one, the others would become angry. So he sent them with a cup of *sudhābhojana*, the food of the devas, back to earth to see another sage, Kosiya by name. He instructed them to give the heavenly food to Kosiya, explaining that this sage had made a vow never to eat without sharing. He would offer some of the ambrosial food to whichever of the four he judged the best. (Jāt 535)

There follows a long series of verses in which each daughter speaks in favour of her eponymous virtue, and the sage counters with criticism of how the qualities of Hope, Faith and Luck can also lead beings astray. Only Honour does he find without fault, so awards the title of the foremost among them to Hirī. Reading between the lines in the story, it seems that the original cause of the dispute, possession of the divine blossom, was forgotten in the daughter's mutual jealousy and that it may have been a clever ploy of Nārada's to get rid of them and keep it for himself! Sakka here appears in the role of the hapless parent caught between the squabbles of his children.

Before leaving the topic of Sakka's familial relationships, mention must be made of an incident where Sakka bestowed the boon of sons on a queen by supernormal means:

At that time, in the Malla Kingdom there ruled a righteous king named Okkāka. All was well in his kingdom except that none of his 16,000 wives had produced an heir to the throne. The people grew upset about this and assembled in the royal courtyard. Addressing them from the balcony, the king asked what was wrong, and they told him that they were afraid for the future of the kingdom if he had no heir to follow him. "But what am I to do?" asked Okkāka.

They told him that he must perform the royal duty to seek a son. He should send forth into the street one hundred dancing girls of low rank to perform the sacred dance (*dhammanāṭakaṃ katvā*) and if within a week, one of them conceived, well and good. If not, them he must send forth one hundred ladies of middling rank, and if that too failed, the following week he should send forth one hundred of the highest rank.

This was done, the royal women were sent forth and indulged in pleasure (*yathāsukhaṃ abhiramitvā*) among the townsfolk. Yet none of them conceived. The people saying that it must be that all these women were of bad morals, with insufficient merit, demanded that the king send forth his chief queen, the virtuous Sīlavatī. The king assented, and it was announced that in one week the queen would be sent forth, and that all the men should assemble at the palace.

On the seventh day, Queen Sīlavatī, beautifully adorned descended from the palace fervently wishing for a son. By the power of her virtue, Sakka's abode grew hot and investigating the cause, he decided to grant Sīlavatī the boon of sons. He commanded two devas to make ready for rebirth into the human realm. Thinking, "I must not let the virtue of the queen be broken!" he descended to earth and approached the palace yard in the form of an aged brahmin.

A great crowd of men were assembled there, each one bathed and adorned and all saying "I shall get the queen! I shall get the queen!" When they saw Sakka in the form of an aged brahmin they laughed at him, "What are you doing here?" He replied, "You can't blame me. Even if my body is aged, my passion has not diminished, and I will take Sīlavatī away with me if I can get her." Then, Sakka by his supernormal power went to the front of the crowd, and none were able to stop him. When the queen descended, beautifully arrayed in all her glory, Sakka took her by the hand and led her away. The men muttered to each other, "Do you see, friend? The old brahmin has taken away the queen, the most beautiful one. He does not know his place!" The queen thought, "An old brahmin is taking me," but she felt neither irritated nor ashamed. The king, however, looking out the window, was very displeased.

Sakka led her out of the town gate. Just outside the city walls, he created a house in which a straw bed could be seen through the open door. "Is this where you live?" she asked. "Yes. Up until now, I was alone. Now there are two of us. You go inside and lie down on the bed while I go and beg for alms, so we can have some rice to eat." Saying this, he gently caressed her with his hand. The divine touch (*dibbasamphassa*) suffused her being and robbed her of her senses, making her fall asleep.

By his power, Sakka transported her to Tāvatiṃsa where she lay upon a gorgeously decorated divine couch. After seven days, she awoke to splendour, and she knew this was no human brahmin, but Sakka. There she saw Sakka sitting under the Pāricchattaka Tree, surrounded by a host of heavenly dancers. She rose from her bed and paid her respects to the king of the devas. He said, "I would give you a boon, queen. What would you have?" "Please, deva, I would have a son." "Never mind one son, I shall give you two. One shall be wise but not handsome, the other shall be handsome but not wise, which would you have first?" "The wise one, deva." "Very good." Sakka then gave her five gifts: a piece of *kusa* grass, a piece of heavenly cloth, a stick of heavenly sandal-wood, a flower from the Pāricchattaka Tree and the *kokananda vīṇā*.

Then Sakka transported her back to the royal palace and laid her down beside the sleeping king. He then touched her navel with his thumb, and in that instant she conceived the first of her sons. In the morning, the king was suspicious about her story. "I saw you going off with that old brahmin. Are you trying to deceive me?" She showed him the *kusa* grass, but he was not impressed. "*Kusa* grass can be found anyplace." But when she showed him the heavenly cloth, he believed her. (Jāt 531)

This curious story may contain some old pre-Buddhist elements. The sending of the royal women out into the streets is reminiscent of the sacred prostitution practiced in Mesopotamia, and the idea that a child conceived during orgiastic rites is the child of a god has echoes in pre-Christian Europe. Certainly, the idea that an heir to the king could be produced in such a manner involves magical rather than logical thinking. In the continuation of the story, the boy born to Sīlavatī after her adventure was named Kusa after the grass. He was the Bodhisatta. He grew up to be a mischievous and misshapen dwarf who after many rather comical adventures wins the heart of a lovely princess. The *vīṇā* plays a minor role in this courtship, but of the rest of Sakka's gifts, there is no other mention. The incident of Kusa's conception by the touching of Sakka's thumb to the queen's navel is similar to an incident in Jātaka 497 where a very powerful ascetic with Brahma-like powers fathers a son in the same way.

For all of Sakka's majesty and power, he could sometimes display surprising humility. On one occasion, he appears on earth in the guise of an old weaver to give alms to Mahākassapa, one of the Buddha's arahant disciples. Mahākassapa, easily recognizing the king of the devas, admonished him, asking why Sakka was trying to deprive some poor person of the opportunity of making merit. Sakka replies that he himself is poor:

"What? You have power and sovereignty over the devas, how can you be poor?"

"*Bhante*, it is like this. The time I came into being was not a Buddha-period. I had no opportunity in my past to make merit by giving to a Buddha or to the arahants. There have arisen in my neighbourhood three devas, Cūḷarathadevaputto Mahārathadevaputto and Anekavaṇṇadevaputto ("little chariot deva-son, great chariot deva-son and deva-son of many colours.") These three had the opportunity to give to the Buddha and his arahants. They are more splendid and glorious than me. When they come down the street, playing at "Constellation" with their attendants, I have to flee and escape into my house." (Dhp-a 4: 10)

It seems that even the king of the devas finds it hard to keep up with the Joneses! Another story in which Sakka displays humility is also one where the tables are turned for once, and the tester becomes the tested:

At one time a certain brahmā[603] decided to test Sakka's power of patience. He manifested as an ugly hunch-backed yakkha and sat on Sakka's throne. The devas of Tāvatiṃsa grumbled, grew angry and complained. "It is amazing, this ugly hunch-backed yakkha is sitting on Sakka's throne!" But the more the devas complained and found fault, the more the yakkha grew handsome and pleasing in appearance. They told this to Sakka, and he said, "This must be an anger-eating yakkha."

So, Sakka approached the yakkha seated on his throne, and paid him reverential salutation. With his robe thrown over one shoulder and his hands joined in añjali,[604] he declared, "I, sir, am Sakka Devānamindo! I, sir, am Sakka Devānamindo!" The more Sakka declared his name in a respectful manner, the more the yakkha grew uglier again until in the end he vanished completely.[605]

During the lifetime of the Buddha Gotama (the "historical" Buddha of the current age) Sakka was his devout follower, and always treated him and his great disciples with the utmost respect. Some of the books of the later Pali tradition attribute many marvels to the great events of the Buddha's life, many of which involve Sakka. For instance, at the Buddha's birth, we are told by the *Jinālāṅkāra*[606] that at the moment of the Buddha's birth the ten thousand Sakkas of ten thousand world-systems stood and blew their conches.[607] When the Prince Siddhattha Gotama renounced the world and cut off the long hair of his top-knot, he tossed it into the air where it was caught by Sakka who raised a *yojana* high stupa, the Cūḷāmaṇi Cetiya, in Tāvatiṃsa to enshrine it.[608]

Sakka often visited the Buddha, to seek teachings from him (eg.SN 11:15 & SN 11:16) or simply to venerate him. At one time he went to the Buddha's dwelling together with the brahmā Sahampati and the two great beings stood on either side of the door-way praising the Buddha in verses. On this occasion, the brahmā criticized Sakka's verse as not the proper way to venerate a *Tathāgata* (SN 11:17). On another occasion, Sakka emerged from his palace and raised his joined hands in a reverential salutation. Mātali the charioteer asked, "Devas and humans worship you, Sakka Vāsava, who is it that you worship?" Sakka replied it was the Buddha and the *Saṅgha* (SN 11:19). In the next sutta, the same happens but Mātali's question is phrased differently, he asks Sakka:

"It is these that should worship you -

The humans stuck in a putrid body,

Those submerged in a corpse,

603 A class of being higher than the devas, see § 3:6.
604 A salutation with joined palms.
605 SN 11:22—the detail that the yakkha was actually a brahmā is added by the commentary.
606 A devotional poem of 250 stanzas composed most likely in Burma, see Malalaseekera, *Pali Literature of Ceylon*, p. 109.
607 Quoted from GGB, v. 1, p. 225
608 Jātaka Nidānakātha.

Afflicted with hunger and thirst."[609]

Sakka replied that he envied the bhikkhus, who moved about freely without attachment and lived without conflict.

A very important sutta for the relationship between the Buddha and Sakka is the *Sakkapañha Sutta* (DN 21). In this discourse, Sakka visits the Buddha in the Indasāla cave. The commentary tells us that he had an urgent reason for this visit; Sakka had seen the five signs which warn a deva of his imminent death (DN-a 22). Sakka arrived with the entire company of the Thirty-Three and many other devas. When the devas arrived at the cave-mouth, a brilliant light was seen by the villagers who grew afraid and thought the mountain was on fire. Sakka found the Buddha rapt in meditation, and he sent in Pañcasikha the *gandhabba* to attract his attention, which he did by singing a highly inappropriate love-song.

With the Buddha now emerged from meditation, Sakka instructed Pañcasikha to announce the arrival of the devas by saying, "Sakka Devānamindo together with his ministers and his attendants pay homage to the Blessed One with their heads to his feet." In reply, the Buddha said, "May Sakka Devānamindo and his ministers and attendants be happy. For all beings seek happiness: devas, humans, asuras, nāgas, *gandhabbas* and whatever other kinds of beings there may be." When the devas entered the cave, by their power the rough places became smooth, the narrow places became wide and the darkness was dispelled by a brilliant light.

Sakka has come to ask the Buddha some questions on Dhamma, but like two old friends, they first engage in some pleasant conversation. The Buddha says that it is wonderful that Sakka, with so many things to do, can find time to visit him. Sakka replies that he has long sought the opportunity, and recalls an earlier occasion when he also found the Buddha in meditation but did not disturb him. The Buddha replied that he recalls that time, the sound of Sakka's chariot wheels roused him. Sakka then remarks that since the Buddha has been teaching, many new devas are being born to swell the ranks of Tāvatiṃsa, and tells a long story in verse about some of them. At the end of this section of the sutta, the Buddha thinks, "For a long time this yakkha has been pure. Whatever he asks will be connected with meaning, (*atthasañhitaṃ*) not otherwise. Whatever explanations I give him, he will be quick to understand." And he gave Sakka permission to ask whatever he wanted.

Sakka and the Buddha then engaged in a Dhamma discussion, with Sakka asking a series of questions about the overcoming of defilements and the Buddha answering. At the conclusion, Sakka tells the Buddha that in the past he has asked the same questions of various other *samaṇa*s and brahmins, but never got a satisfactory answer. They always reacted in the same way, being delighted to have seen the king of the devas and wishing to become his followers. "In the end, they became my disciples, instead of my teachers."

Sakka recalled the happiness he had felt after defeating the asuras, "Whatever was the nutriment (*ojā*) of the devas, and the nutriment of the asuras, henceforth we shall enjoy both!" but said that such happiness, which is based on sticks and swords, is not conducive to detachment, dispassion and cessation (*nibbida virāga nirodha*), and is not to be compared to the happiness that comes from hearing Dhamma. The Buddha asks him what other things, which when recalled to mind, give Sakka similar happiness. Sakka answers in six stanzas, declaring his six joys in verse. These amount to a series of predictions about his future rebirths.

Being mindful of the continuation of my existence as a deva

I shall obtain another existence, know this sir.

When I have died from this divine form, with the destruction of my non-human life,

Unconfused I will enter into a womb, that delights my mind.

---

609 SN 11:20. Bodhi trans., CDB, p. 336.

(The commentary to this passage says Sakka will be born into a *khattiya* clan in the human realm. Entering into womb "unconfused" (*amūḷho*) means with recollection of the previous life-time).

I with unconfused wisdom, dwell in the teaching delighted.

Rightly I shall abide, with clear comprehension and mindful.

Having fared rightly, if I become awakened (*sambodhi*)

I shall dwell having known, this will be the end.

(The commentary to this passage says *sambodhi* refers to the attainment of *sakadāgāmi*, "once-return", the second stage of awakening which will be, for Sakka, the end or goal (*anto*) of his human existence).

When I have died from human form, the human life destroyed

I shall again become a deva, the highest in the deva realm.

(The commentary says this refers to another rebirth as Sakka Devānamindo)

You most excellent devas, the glorious *akaniṭṭhas* (highest brahmā world)

This shall be my final existence, this shall be my abode.

(The commentary to this passage say that after obtaining *anāgāmi*, "non-return, the third stage of awakening, as Sakka. he will "go upstream" being born in the Aviha world then passing from there to the Akaniṭṭha realm).[610]

At the conclusion, it is stated that Sakka attained stream-entry (*sotāpatta*) during the discourse, together with eighty-thousand devas. In addition, the commentary states that at the conclusion Sakka died but was instantaneously reborn as a new Sakka.[611]

There are some difficulties of interpretation in the details of Sakka's predictions. I take the first stanza to be a reference to Sakka's immediate rebirth which differs from Maurice Walshe[612] who translates it in such a way as to imply a human birth. My reading of Sakka's future career may be summarized as (1) renewed existence as Sakka, (2) a human birth as a *khattiya*, where he will attain the second stage of awakening, (3) one more life-time as Sakka, during which he will attain third stage, (4) a life-time in the Aviha Pure Abode world and (5) a life-time in the Akiniṭṭha Pure Abode, where he will attain arahantship making an end to renewed existence. There may be other ways to interpret the text, but only in matter of details.

Even after his attainment of stream-entry, Sakka could still be negligent at times as we see in another text, the *Cūḷataṇhāsankhaya Sutta*:

> At one time Sakka came to see the Buddha at Sāvatthī and the Buddha taught him the way to liberation through non-clinging. Sakka rejoiced in the Buddha's words and then vanished from that place. Mahā Moggallāna (the Buddha's chief disciple skilled in psychic powers) was standing nearby and it occurred to him to wonder, "Did this yakkha understand the Buddha's words when he rejoiced, or did he not? Suppose I were to find out."
>
> So, just as a strong man might bend or stretch his arm, Moggallāna vanished from that place and reappeared

610 For a discussion of these realms, see § 3:6,17.

611 The commentary to the next sutta, DN-a 22 adds this detail. DPPN states that this was evident only to the Buddha and to Sakka himself. I have not been able to find a reference to verify that. See also Dhp-a 15:8.

612 See Walshe, LDB, p. 318. Rhys Davids translation is closer to my reading.

in Tāvatiṃsa. There Sakka was enjoying himself listening to five hundred heavenly musicians in the Ekapuṇḍarīka ("Single-Lotus") Pleasure Park. Sakka greeted the arahant warmly and invited him to take his ease on a prepared seat. Upon taking his seat, Moggallāna asked, "Kosiya, (a name of Sakka) could you repeat in brief the discourse the Buddha gave you on the complete destruction of craving? It would be good to hear it."

"Sir Moggallāna, I am busy and have much to do! I have not only my own business to attend to, but the business of the Thirty-Three. That which was heard well and attended to well, does not vanish so easily. Sir Moggallāna, in the past there was a great war between the devas and the asuras. When the war was concluded with our victory over the asuras, I had the Vejayanta Palace ("the Palace of Victory") built. Sir Moggallāna, this Palace has one hundred towers. Each tower has seven hundred upper chambers. Within each chamber are seven *accharas*, each with seven hand-maidens (*paricārika*). Would you like, Sir Moggallāna, to see this delightful palace?" The venerable Moggallāna consented in silence.

So Sakka together with his favourite vassal, Vessavaṇa, approached the Vejayanta Palace, letting Moggallāna take the place of honour in front. When the hand-maidens in the palace saw Moggallāna approaching they became shy and embarrassed and hid in their inner rooms. The devas led Moggallāna on a tour of the palace, showing him the various pillars of gold, silver, coral, pearl and other precious stones each capped in gold and decorated with figures of snakes. "See how delightful is the Vejayanta Palace!"

Moggallāna remarked, "It is your glory, Kosiya, that you have made such merit in the past. Among men, when something is very delightful they say it is just like in Tāvatiṃsa." Then the arahant reflected, "This yakkha is living with too much negligence. What if I were to rouse a sense of urgency in him?" Using his accumulation of psychic power (*iddhābhisaṅkhāraṃ*) Moggallāna struck the base of the palace with his big toe, causing the whole structure to shake and tremble and wobble. Sakka and Vessavaṇa were amazed, "It is wonderful, it is marvellous that this *samaṇa* of great power and majesty can cause this place of the devas to shake and tremble and wobble with his toe!"

Then Moggallāna, seeing that Sakka was awe-struck with his hair standing on end, repeated his question, "What was the teaching the Buddha gave to you?" and this time the king of the devas answered in full. When Moggallāna was satisfied, he departed back to the human realm. Some of the devas standing nearby asked Sakka, "Sir, was that your teacher, the Buddha?" "No indeed, that was Mahā Moggallāna one of my fellows in the holy life (*sabrahmacārī*).[613]

The fact that Sakka refers to Moggallāna at the end as one of his *sabrahmacārī* may be significant. Usually *brahmacāri* refers to a celibate spiritual seeker, which Sakka was certainly not. Most likely, it refers to the fellowship of those who have attained to one of the stages of liberation, which would indicate that this sutta occurs after Sakka became a *sotāpanna.* Note also that Moggallāna is hardly in awe of Sakka, referring to him more than once as "this yakkha." Once again this story reveals a very recognizable "human" side of Sakka Devānamindo. After listening to a Dhamma talk, on the elimination of craving no less, he is next seen taking his ease surrounded by musicians and dancing-girls and when asked about the discourse replies to the effect that "I'm a busy man. I'll get around to it."

One of the final meetings of the Buddha and Sakka is found in a *Dhammapāda* story:

About ten months before his *parinibbāna* (death) the Buddha was at Veluvagāma. There, he was stricken with

613 MN 37, some details added from the commentary.

bloody diarrhoea. Sakka became aware of this and thought: "My teacher is ill, and in need of service. It would be good for me to help him." Giving up his three *gāvuta* body, Sakka approached the Buddha's body in the form of a human and massaged his hands and feet.

"Who is there?" asked the Buddha.

"Bhante, it is I, Sakka."

"Why have you come here?"

"To serve you in your illness, *Bhante*."

"Sakka, to the devas the smell of humans from even one hundred *yojana* away is like having a putrid corpse tied to their necks. You should go away. There are many bhikkhus to act as my nurses."

"*Bhante*, even standing eighty-four thousand *yojana* away[614] the scent of your virtue can be smelled. I will nurse you."

So Sakka cleaned the bodily discharges of the Buddha with his own hand, nor did he turn away his head or make an unpleasant face as if disgusted. After serving the Buddha's bodily needs for a suitable time, he went back to his own place.

The bhikkhus were amazed that the king of the devas had served the Buddha in this fashion, and remarked at the great affection he must have for his teacher. The Buddha said that indeed he does have great affection. The Buddha recounted for the bhikkhus the time when Sakka, in fear of his imminent death, had come to see him in the Indasāla cave and as a result of hearing the teachings, he attained to stream-entry and was instantly reborn as a young Sakka. (Dhp-a 15: 8)

When the Buddha passed into his final *nibbāna*, Sakka was there together with a great host of other devas. After the Buddha passed, Sakka spoke a simple and beautiful stanza that has ever since been an integral part of Buddhist funeral chanting:

Aniccā vata saṅkhārā, uppādavayadhammino.

Uppajjitvā nirujjhanti, tesaṃ vūpasamo sukho.

Impermanent, alas, are compounded things. it is the nature of things to arise and pass away.

Having come into existence they cease. Their appeasement is the highest bliss. (DN 16)

614 The height of Tāvatiṃsa above the earth.

3:5:17 OTHER GREAT DEVAS OF TĀVATIṂSA

Sakka is the only deva of Tāvatiṃsa for whom we have such rich source material and for whom we can sketch a multi-faceted character. The rest are for the most part little more than names in various lists.

The *Dhajagga Sutta* (SN 11:3) says that when the devas are in battle with the asuras, should fear arise they are instructed to look up at the crest of Sakka's standard to give them courage. Should they be unable to see the crest of Sakka's standard, they should look to the crest of Pajāpati's standard, failing that, the crest of Varuṇa's standard, then Īsāna's. The commentary to this passage says that these three, Pajāpati, Varuṇa and Īsāna occupy the second, third and fourth places in the council of the devas. They are called "*devarājas*" and Pājapati is said to be similar to Sakka in appearance and age. This is the only passage in which we can with any confidence name any of the Thirty-Three ruling devas besides Sakka himself.

These three are all derived from important deities of the Vedic period. Pajāpati (Sanskrit *Prājapati*) was a figure identified as involved in the creation of the world. Already in the pre-Buddhist period an ambiguous figure, Prajapāti in some versions of his story was the primeval sacrificial victim from whose dismembered body the world was made (Barnett 1923: 48 f.). Varuṇa was the supreme law-giver, and in very early times may have been the supreme god (Wallis 1887: 97). Īsāna is in the Vedas an epithet of Rudra, who is an early form of Shiva. In one myth he is the slayer of Prajāpati (Barnett 1923: 57 f.)

However important and powerful these deities were in the pre-Buddhist conception, the versions of them found in the Pali sources are thoroughly domesticated. There is no trace of their roles as creators or law-givers or dispensers of justice, Pajāpati and the others now take their seats below Sakka in the Sudhamma Hall and we never hear their individual voices. Some remnant of their association with brahminical religion is sometimes found when they are cited in various lists. For instance, in the *Tevijja Sutta* (DN 13) the Buddha is critiquing brahminical practice and cites in one place the gods to whom they pray:

> "We invoke Inda, Soma, Varuṇa, Īsāna, Pajāpati, Brahmā, Mahiddhi, Yama."

In the Jayadissa Jātaka (Jāt 513) a king and queen afraid that their beloved son is about to be eaten by a yakkha utter a prayer for his salvation, calling on various deities:

> "Soma and King (*rājā*) Varuṇa and King Pajāpatī and Candimā and Sūriya."

In the Bhūridatta Jātaka (Jāt 543) a brahmin explaining his religion says that various deities attained to that state through having performed sacrifice in the past, he names:

> "Dhātā, Vidhātā, Varuṇa, Kuvera, Soma, Yama, Candimā and Sūriya"

As a final example, in the Vessantara Jātaka (Jāt 547) various deities are named as rejoicing in King Vessantara's great acts of giving:

> "They rejoiced, Inda and Brahmā, Pajāpati, Soma, Yama and Vessavaṇa. All the devas of Tāvatiṃsa rejoiced, together with Inda."

Note that whenever he is mentioned in these lists, Sakka is always called "Inda" which reinforces the Vedic origin of this whole pantheon.

The name **Pajāpati** means either "lord of beings" or "rich in progeny" (PED). In a couple of places, both in the Majjhima Nikāya, Pajāpati is named in a context which implies the name may simply be a reference to a generic powerful deity. Both of these texts are associated with criticism of wrong views. The Mūlapariyāya Sutta (MN 1) is a difficult philosophic sutta where the Buddha explains how ordinary beings perceive (*sañjānāti*) and then conceive (*maññati*) various categories of objects ultimately leading to false views concerning a self. The same formula is repeated for the perception of earth, water, fire and air, then beings (*bhūtā*), devas, Pajāpati, Brahmā, then various classes of brahmā gods, then various conceptual categories beginning with the immaterial bases and the six senses. The commentary to this passage asserts that *Pajāpati* here refers to Māra because he might be considered the overlord of all the devas. This seems somewhat unlikely, but it does indicate that the concept of *Pajāpati* is a vague and elusive one.

The other reference is from the Brahmanimantanika Sutta, (MN 49) the story of Baka the Brahmā which we will treat more fully below (§ 3:6,11). In this context, we are only concerned with the episode where Baka, possessed of a false view of his own cosmic importance, is trying to convince the Buddha that he should worship him:

> (One of Baka's subordinate brahmās, possessed by Māra, was speaking to the Buddha), "Before you, bhikkhu, there were *samaṇas* and brahmins who found fault with and criticized earth, water, fire, air, beings, devas, Pajāpati and Brahmā and after death they all took a lower rebirth. There were those who praised and delighted in earth, water, fire, air, beings, devas, Pajāpati and Brahmā and after death they all took a higher rebirth."

This is an abbreviated form of the list from the *Mūlapariyāya Sutta*: once again Pajāpati is included along with Brahmā somewhat in the sense of a generic deva.

Varuṇa is a very common name in the sources. The DPPN has listings for eighteen beings named Varuṇa, including the deva. Two of the other Varuṇas are of interest here, in that there may be some remote connection to the deva. The two chief disciples of Revata Buddha were named Varuṇa and Brahmadeva.[615] The names linking two powerful deities are at least interesting, and may or may not have any original connection with the gods.

The other reference is from the Ghaṭa Jātaka, (Jāt 454) which is a curious tale that certainly has very old pre-Buddhist origins. A princess named Devagabbhā ("Womb of the Devas") gives birth to ten sons by a father named Upasāgara ("Upon the Sea"). Most of these sons have names associated with deities; they are, in order of birth, Vāsudeva, Baladeva, Candādeva, Suriyadeva, Aggideva, Varuṇadeva, Ajjuna, Pajjuna, Ghaṭapaṇḍita and Aṅkuro. Vāsudeva is sometimes addressed as Kaṇha, the Pali form of Krishna. Bala and Ajjuna (Sanskrit Arjuna) are also characters from the Krishna stories. Aggi is the god of fire. These ten brothers were raised in secret by a servant so became known as the Ten Slave Brothers and were powerful heroes of the type seen in the early heroic age mythologies of many countries. In other words, they were not of a high moral character, following a career of robbery and conquest until they ruled all India, with various magical encounters along the way. The brothers came to a bad end, dying by violence mostly at each others hands. The whole story is not very Buddhist in tone and has more of the feel of an adventure tale from the early days of the Aryan conquest.[616]

There is one ambiguous reference that may indicate that Varuṇa sometimes possessed people, perhaps in the capacity of a shamanic seer. In the Vessantara Jātaka (Jāt 547) when Queen Maddi is distraught over the loss of her children it is said that she trembled like a *vāruṇī* which the commentary explains is a sorceress (*ikkhaṇikā*) possessed by the yakkha. This is very little to base any conclusions on, but there is a resemblance here to the Delphic Oracle of Greece who was possessed by the god Apollo, who resembles the Vedic Varuṇa in that they are both rational and lawful gods in pantheons otherwise full of warrior types.

Other than what has already been discussed, there seems to be no other references to Īsāna in the sources. Despite the later importance of Shiva in India, in the Buddhist sources the fourth deva of Tāvatiṃsa is a figure even sketchier than Pajāpati or Varuṇa.

---

615 Jātaka Nidānakatha. Revata was a Buddha of a previous kappa.

616 See the footnote on page 51 of Cowell's translation and the entry for Andhakaveṇhudāsaputtā in the DPPN.

3:5:18 VISSAKAMMA

Vissakamma is the architect or builder of the devas.[617] Vissakamma derives from the Vedic deity *Viśvakarman*, the "All-Maker", and his function remains similar, but more limited. We meet Vissakamma in very many episodes, but see little of his character. He plays a purely functional and subordinate role, almost always he is seen creating something, a hermitage or palace, for the use of the Bodhisatta in one of his births and doing so under instruction from Sakka.

In at least eight Jātaka stories[618] an almost identical sequence occurs. The Bodhisatta leaves home, intent on living the recluse life and proceeds to the Himavā, sometimes with a large train of followers. Sakka's throne grows hot and investigating the cause, he sees that a great being has made a renunciation. Sakka than commissions Vissakamma to make a suitable hermitage for the use of the Bodhisatta and his followers. When Vissakamma makes anything the verb used is *mapeti* which means "to create" rather than "to build" implying that his work is done by purely magical means.

As should be expected of anything made by the architect (*vaḍḍhakī*) of the devas, the hermitages made by Vissakamma are very beautiful:

> Sakka commanded Vissakamma, "Go and make a hermitage (*assama*) thirty-six by fifty *yojana* in size. And when you have made that, supply it with everything necessary for those who have left the home life (*pabbajitaparikkhāra*)." Vissakamma assented by saying "Sadhu!" and on a clear piece of land beside a pleasant river he created the hermitage. The huts he equipped with beds strewn with leaves and everything the hermits would need. Each hut had a door, a path for walking-meditation and a plank for hanging the robe. The whole was plastered with lime. Here and there were flowering plants and shrubs. At the end of each walking path was a well for drawing water and a fruit tree, each single tree bearing all kinds of fruits. This he did with his deva-powers (*devatānubhāvena*). Vissakamma made a sign in vermillion writing, "Whosever has abandoned the pleasures of the senses, may take these requisites" and posted it on the outer wall. Finally, he banished all noisy animals and birds and monstrous non-human beings (*duddasika amanussa*) from the area and returned to his own place. (Jāt 509)

Vissakamma created other things as well. In previous ages of the world, he built at least three entire cities: Kāsika, Vebhāra and Sobhana.[619] He has also created several palaces for righteous kings, always decorated with a great exuberance of gold and jewels:

> Sakka ordered Vissakamma, "Build King Mahāsudassana a dwelling, a palace to be named Dhamma." "Very good, sire." So Vissakamma left the place of the Thirty-Three and swiftly appeared before King Mahāsudassana. "I have come to build you a dwelling, a palace named Dhamma." And the king consented in silence.
>
> The Dhamma Palace was a *yojana* in length and a half a *yojana* in width. The outside of the palace was covered with tiles of four colours; the tiles were made of gold, silver, lapis-lazuli and crystal and extended to three times the height of a man.
>
> The Dhamma Palace had eighty-four thousand pillars, a fourth of these were made of gold, and another fourth each of silver, lapis-lazuli and crystal. The flooring was of planks made of the same four precious substances.

---

617 The Pali is *vaḍḍhakī* which may be used for a builder in wood or in stone. It is equivalent to the Greek τέκω□ = *techne*. See footnote in Cowell, "Jataka 4". p. 203.

618 Jāt 70, 505, 509, 510, 522, 525, 538, 540, 547.

619 Ap 45-10, 48-3 & 49-5.

> There were twenty-four staircases, also made of the same four things. The stairs of gold had newels and knobs of silver, the stairways of silver had newels and knobs of gold, those of lapis-lazuli had newels of crystal, those of crystal had newels of lapis-lazuli.
>
> The palace had eighty-four thousand chambers, (*kūṭāgāra*) some of gold, some of silver, some of lapis-lazuli and some of crystal. The gold chambers were furnished with silver divans, the gold rooms with silver divans, those of lapis-lazuli with ivory divans and the rooms of crystal had hard-wood divans. The golden chambers had silver doors, decorated with a figure of a silver palm-tree, its leaves and fruit were made of gold. The silver chambers had golden doors with silver palm-trees and golden fruit and leaves. The lapis-lazuli rooms had crystal doors with crystal palm-trees figured on the door, with its leaves and fruit of lapis-lazuli. The crystal rooms had lapis-lazuli doors with lapis-lazuli palm-trees bearing crystal fruit and leaves. (DN 17)

As an architect, Vissakamma definitely decorates with a theme in mind. The small note of practicality where the pairing of substances is broken is interesting. Couches made of crystal or lapis-lazuli might be too easily broken, so ivory and hard-wood was used instead.

We usually don't get to see Vissakamma at work, but in one episode we do a get a glimpse of his methods:

> At that moment Sakka's throne became hot, and knowing the cause he addressed Vissakamma. "Go sir, and make for Prince Mahāpanāda a jewel palace nine *yojana* long, eight *yojana* wide and twenty-five *yojana* high." So Vissakamma taking the form of a mason (*vaḍḍhakī*) appeared among Prince Mahāpanāda's workmen and said, "You can go and take your breakfast now." Being alone on the work-site, Vissakamma struck the ground with his staff and in that instant the twenty-five *yojana* high palace appeared on that site. (Jāt 489)

Vissakamma created other magical items. On two occasions, when the Buddha and a *saṅgha* of almost five hundred bhikkhus wanted to make a journey Vissakamma created five hundred pavilions (*kūṭāgāra*) during the night, so that they were in place on the monastery grounds in the morning. The Buddha and the *saṅgha* entered these and they flew through the air with great rapidity to their destination.[620] On one of these occasions, we are informed of the detail that the pavilion used by the Buddha had four doors, those used by the two Chief Disciples had two, and those for the rest of the bhikkhus had but one (MN-a 145).

After the Buddha's *parinibbāna*, King Ajātasattu built a stupa over his share of the relics. Vissakamma created some kind of mechanical device to protect them, the Pali for this device is *vāḷasaṅghāṭayantaṃ* and the most likely interpretation is that it was a revolving sword-wheel.[621] Several centuries later King Asoka wanted to collect all the relics of the Buddha and divide them up to put in eighty-four thousand stupas around his empire. When he approached the *vāḷasaṅghāṭayantaṃ* Vissakamma appeared in the guise of a village youth and shot an arrow into the heart of the mechanism to stop it and allow King Asoka entry. When the mechanism stopped turning, a jewelled sign appeared saying, "Enter wretched king." Asoka was offended, wondering how such a one as he could be called "wretched" (DN-a 16). No explanation is given for the sign, perhaps it simply means Vissakamma has a sense ofhumour.

Vissakamma was involved in the Buddha's life at other times, even before his awakening:

> When prince Siddhattha was seven or eight years old, his father the king asked his privy councillors, "What is it that children of tender years like the best for play and sport?" "They like playing in the water, sire." So the king assembled his workmen and began to dig an artificial pond. Sakka the king of the devas observed what was happening and said, "It is not proper that a great being (*mahāsatta*) should have human pleasures,

[620] SN-a 35:71, Dhp-a 21: 8, & MN-a 145.

[621] See DPPN under Vissakamma.

he should enjoy heavenly pleasures." And he commanded Vissakamma, "Go and make the Bodhisatta a water park for playing in." Vissakamma asked, "Of what kind, sire?"

Sakka instructed him that it was to be free of mud and slime, to be strewn all over with jewels and coral, surrounded by a wall made of the seven precious things and capped with coral, and there should be a set of stairs going down into the water, to be made with silver steps and the handrails decorated with gems. There should be a golden boat with a silver seat, a silver boat with a golden seat, a jewel boat with a coral seat and a coral boat with a jewel seat. There should be fountains of gold, silver, jewels and coral. And the water should be well covered with lotuses of five colours.

Vissakamma assented saying "*Sādhu*!", descended to the royal grounds and created a pleasure pond exactly according to these instructions during the night when everyone was asleep. (AN-a 3:39)

Many years later, on the day before he left the home life forever, Prince Siddhattha was sitting beside his divine water pond. Sakka feeling his throne grow hot, spoke to Vissakamma, "Tomorrow at mid-night the Bodhisatta will make his great renunciation. You should go and adorn him in heavenly finery, this will be the last time he will wear adornments."

Vissakamma, as quickly as a strong man might bend his arm, disappeared from Tāvatiṃsa and appeared before the Bodhisatta in the guise of a barber (*kappaka*). He began to wrap the prince's head with cloth to fashion a turban. On feeling the touch of Vissakamma's hand, Siddhattha knew, "This is not a human being, this is a deva." He wrapped the cloth around his head ten thousand times. How could the prince's head be strong enough to bear ten thousand folds of cloth? You should not think that! The cloth was like the petals of flowers.[622]

We can draw a few conclusions about the nature of Vissakamma from these episodes. Vissakamma is the only deva who retains even a trace of the creative function that was so important for the gods of the pre-Buddhist period. Even so, his acts of creation are of a very specific nature. It is to be noted that his works are always in the human sphere: the *vimānas* and palaces of the devas themselves are generated by their acts of merit and never fabricated by Vissakamma. Nor does he have any role in the broader creation of the world itself. Buddhist thought has always been opposed to the idea of creation by a god as an act of arbitrary will which violates the dependent origination (DN 1).

Vissakamma is a builder (*vaḍḍhakī*) rather than a creator, even if he works by magical means. His works are of an architectural nature: hermitages, palaces, pleasure parks. Even when he makes vehicles to move the Buddha and his bhikkhus a great distance, they are not fashioned as chariots but as pavilions or sheds (*kūṭāgāra*) which nonetheless fly in the manner of the devas' own *vimānas*. The pre-Buddhist Viśvakarman was said to have once created a divinely beautiful apsara to tempt a demon,[623] but it is unthinkable that Vissakamma could create a living, sentient being. (True, he does make fruit-trees and lotuses as part of the "landscaping" for his larger projects, but this is incidental to his primary function and in any case, plants are not considered sentient in Buddhist theory).

Vissakamma's actions are always on the behest of Sakka and for the benefit of great beings like Bodhisattas, Buddhas and arahants. They are not part of the natural order of things, but rare and exceptional infusions from a higher realm.

---

[622] Jātaka Nidānakathā and also see GGB p. 267.

[623] Hopkins, *Hindu Gods and Heroes*, p. 162.

3:5:19 MĀTALI

Mātali is a *gandhabba* and the charioteer (*saṅgāhaka*) of Sakka. We see a little bit more of Mātali's character in the texts than we do of Vissakamma. He is loyal to his lord, but sometimes a bit familiar and even capable of taking the opposite side in a debate. When Sakka showed patience and mercy to his enemy Vepacitta, Mātali asked:

> When face to face with Vepacitti
>
> Is it, Maghavā, from fear or weakness
>
> That you endure him so patiently,
>
> Listening to his harsh words?

Sakka and Mātali argue the issue back and forth for several stanzas; Sakka's position is that patience is the higher virtue and that it is folly to argue with a fool. Mātali makes the case for a tough approach:

> Fools would vent their anger even more
>
> If no one would keep them in check.
>
> Hence with drastic punishment
>
> The wise man should restrain the fool.[624]

In a series of short suttas in the Saṃyutta Nikāya (SN 11:18–20) Sakka is seen making an act of reverence with folded hands before mounting his chariot. Mātali asks incredulously who it can be that Sakka worships, when he himself is worshipped by devas and humans. Sakka replies in verses praising the Buddha and the *Saṅgha*. At the end, Mātali says that he too shall worship whom Sakka worships. In one of these exchanges, Mātali expresses some disgust with the idea of worshipping humans:

> It is these that should worship you -
>
> The humans stuck in a putrid body,
>
> Those submerged inside a corpse.
>
> Afflicted with hunger and thirst.[625]

Mātali acts as Sakka's driver on many occasions; we have already seen how Mātali enabled Sakka's escape with his bride on his wedding day. He also drives the chariot when Sakka goes to war with the asuras, or when he goes on a pleasure jaunt to one of the heavenly parks "to view the pleasant grounds" (*subhūmiṃ dassanāyā*) (SN 11:18). On three occasions, Sakka sent Mātali in the chariot to fetch a righteous human and bring him for a visit to Tāvatiṃsa. The trip of King Nimi was especially noteworthy because of the long tour Mātali gave him of the various *nirayas* (hell-realms) and heavenly *vimānas*.[626]

The chariot of Sakka, driven by Mātali, is called the *Vejayantaratha*, "the Chariot of Victory." It is one-hundred and fifty *yojana* long (DN-a 16) and is pulled by one thousand Sindh horses (Jāt 541). In numerous stories it is seen

[624] SN 11:4. Bodhi trans., CDB, p. 321-22.

[625] SN 11:20. Bodhi trans., CDB, p. 336.

[626] *Nimi Jātaka* no. 541, for the others see Jāt 243 & 494.

to fly through the air, so presumably these are flying horses, which would not be inappropriate for the livestock of Tāvatiṃsa. A verse passage describes the Vejayanta Chariot:

(In obedience to Sakka's command, Mātali mounted the Vejayantaratha)

Smoothly gliding, it ascended; shining, resplendent with glorious fittings.

Like well-worked *jambu* gold, it is decorated with golden images.

As beautiful as the setting moon, there are figures of elephants, cows, jays, tigers, panthers.

Antelope, deer and various birds and animals figured in lapis-lazuli as if arrayed for battle one with the other.

One thousand tawny royal horses, unconquerable, as strong as young elephants.

Adorned with golden chain-mail on the head and breast, they go on a word of command, no need for a goad.

When Mātali ascended in this excellent vehicle, a great roar could be heard in all directions.

The sky, the earth, the rocks, the trees and the great ocean all trembled at the sound. (Jāt 535)

When Mātali descended to earth in the chariot to fetch the musician Guttila to Tāvatiṃsa, the awestruck people thought that a second moon had appeared in the sky (Jāt 243).

Mātali sometimes accompanies Sakka on his missions to the human realm, very often with Pañcasikha as well. In two similar tales, these three together with Candā and Suriya, transform into brahmins to teach a miser a lesson (Jāt 450 & 535). In one story, Sakka, Mātali and Pañcasikha transform into animals: a jackal, a fish and a bird respectively (Jāt 374). Probably the most important of these transformations is that found in the Mahākaṇha Jātaka: (Jāt 469)

Many years after the Buddha Kassapa had passed away, his teachings were falling into decline. Bhikkhus and bhikkhunis were following house-holder's ways and having sons and daughters together. In general, people were falling into the ways of wrong conduct and when they died, taking lower rebirth for the most part.

Sakka became concerned that no new devas were appearing in Tāvatiṃsa and looking over the earthly realm, he saw the reason why. "What can be done?" he wondered. Pondering the question he decided, "I have the means. I shall manifest a terrifying form to the humans and afterward teach them the Dhamma and in that way I shall stop the decline of the teachings and make the *sāsana* (religion) last another thousand years."

For this purpose, Sakka transformed Mātali into a huge and horrible black dog, with four canine teeth as big as bananas and a belly as fat as a pregnant woman's. Sakka himself took on the form of a woodsman, armed with a huge bow and a javelin of iron and led the dog by a cord around its neck. They descended to earth at a spot one *yojana* from the city of Bārāṇasi. Sakka cried out in a loud voice, "This world will be no more!" (*nassati loko*), terrifying the populace. Sakka and Mātali approached the entrance to the city and he repeated the cry.

The king ordered the city gates shut, but Sakka together with his dog leapt over the wall, eighteen *hattha* (cubits) high and stood within the city. Trembling with fear, the people fled to hide in their houses. The big black dog chased them through the streets and many fled into the palace grounds. The king together with his wives fled into the upper storey of the palace.

The big black dog reared up with his front paws on the window ledge and uttered a tremendous bark. This bark was heard from the lowest *niraya* to the highest *devaloka*. The whole world-system was filled with the one sound of Mātali's bark. This was one of the four great shouts heard throughout the whole world.[627]

The people were too terrified to say a word, but the king raised his courage and addressed Sakka, "Dear huntsman, why does your dog bark?" "He is hungry, great king." So the king ordered all the food in his house-hold to be given to the dog, who gulped the whole down in one great bite and roared again. Sakka said he was still hungry. So the king had all the food of the horses and elephants brought to the dog, and again he swallowed the lot in one bite. He did the same again when all the food of the entire city was brought to him. The king thought, "This is no ordinary dog. This is without a doubt a yakkha. I must determine why they have come here."

When asked, Sakka replied, "This dog has not come to hunt game, great king, but to bring misfortune to men." Alarmed, the king asked, "Will this dog eat the flesh of all men, or your enemies only?" "Just my enemies, great king. Those fond of misconduct and behaving in wrong ways" (*adhammābhiratā visamacārino*). (Jāt 469)

There follows in the text a long set of verses describing the various types of misconduct by bhikkhus and lay people with the refrain, "on these I will release the dog." At the end of the Jātaka the Buddha reveals that he was Sakka at that time, and that Mātali was Ānanda.

627 The other three are found in Jāt 531, Sn-a 1: 10 & Jāt 546 (eng. 545).

3:5:20 ERĀVAṆA

In a previous chapter we recounted in brief the story of how Magha and his companions became Sakka and the other Thirty-Three great devas (§ 3:5,16). Near the beginning of Magha's career of good works, the village head-man made a false accusation against Magha and the others and the king ordered them to be put to death by trampling, but the royal elephants refused to harm them. When Magha's good name had been restored, the king gave him much wealth including the chief of the royal elephants. This animal served Magha in his good works, and when he died he was reborn as a deva in Tāvatiṃsa who could assume the form of a magnificent magical elephant. This was Erāvaṇa, Sakka's great royal elephant.

> The elephant was reborn as a *devaputta* named Erāvaṇa. There are no animal births in the deva realm. When it is time to depart for the pleasure gardens, he abandons his own form and becomes a one hundred and fifty *yojana* long elephant named Erāvaṇa. For the use of the Thirty-Three he creates thirty-three heads measuring two or three *gavutas*, in the middle of all is the thirty *yojana* head named Sudassana for the use of Sakka. On top of Sudassana is a twelve *yojana* jewelled howdah, and from time to time he raises a *yojana* high standard made of the seven precious things. Around the howdah is a net of tinkling bells; these are moved by a gentle wind and produce a sound like a five-piece musical ensemble playing divine music. In the middle of the howdah is a one *yojana* jewel seat, and there sits Sakka. The rest of the Thirty-Three sits each on his own head on a jewel seat.
>
> On each of the thirty-three heads, Erāvaṇa has created seven tusks, each fifty *yojana* long. On each tusk are seven ponds, in each pond are seven lotus plants, on each plant are seven flowers, on each flower are seven petals and on each petal seven *devadhītas* dance. Thus everywhere on the fifty-*yojana* tusk is a dancing show. This is the great magnificence in which Sakka the *devarājā* travels.[628]

[628] Dhp-a 2: 7. The thirty-three "heads" are called *kumbha* in Pali which the Pali English Dictionary lists as "the frontal globes of an elephant" but traditionally Erāvaṇa is always depicted with multiple heads. My interpretation agrees with Malalasekera in his DPPN entry for Erāvaṇa.

3:5:21 NOTE ON ANIMALS IN TĀVATIṂSA

In the descriptions of the *vimānas* in the Vimānavatthu we come across multiple references to song-birds, (Vv-a 11: 35 & 36) elephants,[629] horses[630] and even to fish in lotus pools (Vv-a 44 & 81) as among the marvellous adornments of a deva existence. We have seen that Sakka has a chariot pulled by one thousand horses and a marvellous elephant named Erāvaṇa. Nevertheless, the commentarial tradition is quite insistent that there are no animals in Tāvatiṃsa. It is carefully explained in the above passage that Erāvaṇa is a normal three *gāvuta* high anthropomorphic deva who transforms into the shape of an elephant when Sakka wishes to ride. In other texts it is said that Erāvaṇa is only called an elephant by convention, (DN-a 20) and that he takes the form of an elephant "for fun" (*kīḷanakāle hatthirūpena*) (Vv-a 1). As for Sakka's thousand *Sindh* horses, it is stated that they are *manomaya*, "mind-made" (Jāt 494). This would imply that they are apparitional, not real beings with their own minds and kamma. Presumably, the same concept would apply to the various animals mentioned in the *Vimānavatthu*.[631]

The presence of real animals in Tāvatiṃsa was one of the early controversies among Buddhist schools. The Katthāvatthu is a late addition to the Abhidhamma that consists of summaries of controversies between the schools on various points. It probably served as a Theravāda debating manual. It includes a discussion on this point. The Theravāda position is given that "there are no animals in the deva realm" which is countered by an Andhaka opponent by citing the examples of Erāvaṇa and Sakka's horses. The Theravāda reply is a *reductio ad absurdum*: "are there then elephant stables and barns full of fodder there? Are there moths and scorpions too?" (Kv 20: 4)

It would seem from this that the objection to actual animal life in Tāvatiṃsa is the intrusion of the grossly biological into an otherwise subtle and refined existence. The idea of the animals being either temporary transformations of ordinary devas or purely apparitional is not inconsistent with the generally protean and dream-like nature of existence in these realms. It is slightly odd that the Theravāda and the Andhaka debaters take the opposite position in a parallel controversy concerning the reality of the punishing demons in *niraya*. In this case, the Andhakas insist the "hell-wardens" are strictly apparitional, generated by the evil-doer's own kamma, while the Theravāda spokesman counters with textual references to prove that they are actual beings (Kv 20: 3).

While it is held to be impossible to be born as an animal in Tāvatiṃsa, it is possible for an animal to be reborn as a deva. Erāvaṇa is one example: Kanthaka, the horse who carried Siddhattha away from the palace for his great renunciation is another. His rebirth as a deva is recounted in the Vimānavatthu (Vv-a 81). There also was the curious case of a frog that was drawn from his pond by attraction to the sound of the Buddha's voice and was accidentally trod upon by one of the audience. He too was reborn in a heavenly *vimāna* surrounded by *accharas* (Vv-a 51).

---

629 Vv-a 5: 41, 60, 61 & 62.

630 Vv-a 16, 47 & 64.

631 Although I cannot find this explicitly stated.

3:5:22 GANDHABBAS

Gandhabbas are primarily known as a class of minor devas in the *saggas* who serve as celestial musicians. The word *gandhabba* (Skt. *gandharva*) is also used in three other senses, which partially overlap in meaning. It may refer to a special class of earth-bound devas and is sometimes used to refer to human musicians. Finally, it is used to refer to the "entity seeking rebirth", one of the three factors needed for conception. The concept of *gandharvas* as a race of minor devas, or as beings intermediate between humans and devas, was known to the *Vedas* and *Brahmanas* but they were defined vaguely in the pre-Buddhist literature, only acquiring their role as musicians very late, in the *Mahābharata.*[632]

Leaving aside for the moment the last, and most problematic, use of the term as referring to an agent in the rebirth process and the use of *gandhabba* to refer to human musicians,[633] a usage parallel to that of *deva* as an honorific term for human kings, we are left with two somewhat divergent concepts of *gandhabba* as minor deva. There are those living in the *saggas* and serving the higher devas, mostly but not exclusively, as entertainers and there are those who live on the earthly level as minor entities of the forest. These two conceptions of a *gandhabba*'s nature could be seen as entirely separate, or as a single race of beings existing on a spectrum and performing different roles.

Considering the terrestrial kind first, there is a short chapter devoted to *gandhabbas* in the Saṃyutta Nikāya,[634] where they are described as dwelling in fragrant roots, fragrant flowers, fragrant sap and so forth (*gandha* is the Pali word for "scent"). They are long-lived, beautiful and abounding in happiness. It is considered a meritorious rebirth and some humans desire rebirth in that realm, which may be had by making merit with body, speech and mind, and making an aspiration for such rebirth, or particularly by making gifts of fragrant roots, flowers and so on. In another place we are told that they go through the air; the word used is *vihaṅgamo,* (AN 4:36) which is elsewhere a poetic synonym for bird. Two other references to *gandhabba* depart somewhat from this gentle, sylvan image. The Ātānātiya Sutta of the Dīgha Nikāya includes the *gandhabbas* among those beings who may "with hostile intent" disturb solitary bhikkhus in their meditation, some of them being "wild, fierce and terrible" (DN 32). In another place they are listed among those great beings (*mahā bhūta*) that live in the ocean, together with the sea-monsters, asuras and nāgas (AN 8:19). In several places, where races of beings are listed, *gandhabbas* are distinguished from devas; for example when the brahmin Doṇa asks the Buddha, "are you a human? Are you a deva? A *gandhabba*? A yakkha?" (AN 4:36) Likewise, when it is said that many kinds of beings revere and follow the Buddha the *gandhabbas* are included along with devas, humans, asuras and nāgas (DN 30). The Cātumahārājika deva Dhataraṭṭha, the Great King of the East, is the lord of the *gandhabbas*, and he "enjoys their songs and dances" (DN 20 & 32).

Turning to the *gandhabbas* born into the *sagga* realms, principally Tāvatiṃsa: they are definitely considered to be the lowest class of devas residing there. A devout human woman, who was reborn as a male deva of Tāvatiṃsa, spoke disparagingly about three bhikkhus who had been reborn as *gandhabbas*: "Three bhikkhus following the holy life under the Buddha were reborn into the inferior (*hīna*) bodies of *gandhabbas*. They were devoted to the pleasures of the five senses and they served us and attended upon us." The commentary to this passage says this was by making music for the devas. After being rebuked by the deva, "It is a sorry sight to see followers of the Buddha reborn into the lowly state of *gandhabbas*," two of them renounced sense pleasure and were reborn as brahmās, but one proved incorrigible.[635] In another place it is said that virtuous beings are reborn into one of the various classes of devas, or "at the least," among the *gandhabbas* (DN 18). The music of the *gandhabbas* can serve as the accompaniment to the

[632] Jayarava 2015.

[633] This use occurs several times in the Jātakas. See especially Jāt-a 243. In Jāt 524 nāga musicians are referred to as *gandhabba*.

[634] The Gandhabbasaṃyutta, SN 31:1 f.

[635] DN 21. The commentary says that these bhikkhus had kept their precepts but had previously made the wish to be reborn as *gandhabbas*.

dancing shows of the *accharas* (Vv-a 64). We hear of the *gandhabbas* performing as an orchestra of five instruments in the Citralatāvana, one of the wonderful pleasure parks of Tāvatiṃsa (Vv-a 64). The *gandhabbas* may also serve as messengers for the higher devas, as when the *gandhabba* Pañcasikha is sent to report to the Buddha about the proceedings in a council of the devas (DN 19).

The role of *gandhabbas* in the rebirth process is very problematic, and discussion of this point has been lively.[636] My purpose here will not be to attempt a resolution, but merely to lay out the problem from the relevant sources. To begin with, there are two passages in the Majjhima Nikāya which describe the start of a new life at conception. Both are essentially identical:

> Conception (*gabbhassāvakkanti* lit. "appearance of the embryo") occurs with three (factors): union of mother and father, the mother is in her season, and a *gandhabba* is present (*paccupaṭṭhit.*).[637]

> The commentary to this passage says:

> *Gandhabba* is a being arriving at that place (*tatrūpagasatto*). It does not stand nearby watching the union of the mother and father. It is a being which, through the mechanism of kamma (*kammayantayantito*), takes the opportunity to be reborn. (MN-a 38)

The sub-commentary says that the being is attending to a sign (*nimitta*) of a suitable rebirth (*uppajjanagatiyā*) and that this sign is called a "scent" (*gandha*) (MN-ṭ 38). Hence, the being taking rebirth is called *gandhabba* because it figuratively "smells" the place of rebirth.

This last definition seems contrived, and it probably was. The orthodox Theravāda doctrine, as codified in the *Abhidhamma* and the commentaries, does not allow for any kind of "intermediate state" (*antarābhava*). "Immediately after the death-consciousness has ceased, a rebirth-linking consciousness is established in the subsequent existence."[638] In other words, as soon as a person dies, he or she is immediately reborn into a new womb. This is in stark contrast to many other schools of Buddhism. The *Kathavatthu* contains a debate on this question where the Theravāda interlocutor is forced to defend his position against a Buddhist of another school.[639] The doctrine of an "intermediate state" between death and rebirth reaches its most elaborate formulation in the Tibetan teachings about the *Bardo*.

Thus, the idea of a dead person becoming some kind of disembodied spirit and physically travelling to the point of conception, whether we call this entity a *gandhabba* or not, is anathema to the orthodox Theravāda interpretation. Obviously, this makes the formulation in the *Majjhima* problematic, hence the attempt of the sub-commentator to explain it away as a figure of speech. It certainly makes the *gandhabba* of the rebirth process completely distinct from the other kinds of *gandhabba*.

Leaving aside the Theravāda for the moment, when we look at the *Abhidharmakośa* we find an interpretation that synthesizes some of the divergent ideas about *gandhabbas*. This text definitely classifies the *gandharva* (the Sanskrit form is used here) as an intermediate being. It is "mind-made" (*manomaya*), travels through the air and feeds on odours. It is to be considered as belonging to the continuity of the new life, thus is already a human-to-be or a deva-to-be etc. Lower *gandharvas* feed on foul odours, higher ones on sweet odours. It is invisible to ordinary vision and its travels are not impeded by any material object; the *gandharva* can pass even through diamond. Vasubandhu cites

636 For the problem of the "intermediate state in Theravāda" and the role of the *gandhabba* therein see for instance Peter Harvey, 1995: 89-105, Bhikkhu Anālayo 2014, and Jayarava, 2015.

637 MN 38 & MN 93. The latter text goes on to critizise the idea of caste being innate by asking whether the *gandhabba* can be said to be of any particular caste.

638 CMA. 5:37. See also Vism 14.124 and Kv 8:2.

639 Kv 8:2. The debate hinges on another controverted passage, discussing the different kinds of *anāgāmī*, some of whom attain arahantship "in the interval." See AN 3:87 (eng. 3:86) and SN 46:3.

controversy about the length of time a being spends as a *gandharva*; some say seven days, others seven weeks and yet others say it is indeterminate. When the *gandharva* is to become a human being, it eventually finds the copulating couple who are to be its parents. If it is to become a male, the *gandharva* develops sensual attraction to the woman (its future mother) and animosity as a rival towards the man (its future father). These gender roles are reversed if the *gandharva* is to be reborn female.

> When the mind is troubled by these two erroneous thoughts, it attaches itself through the desire for sex to the place where the organs are joined together, imagining that it is he with whom they unite. Then the impurities of blood and semen is found in the womb; the intermediate being, enjoying its pleasures, installs itself there. Then the *skandhas* ("aggregates", Pali *khandha*) harden; the intermediate being perishes; and birth arises that is called "reincarnation" (*pratisaṃdhi*).[640]

No doubt Buddhaghosa was aware of this doctrine and rejected it when he was composing the commentary to the Majjhima passage cited above. That is why he felt the need to explicitly state that the *gandhabba* is not "a being standing nearby watching the union of the mother and father."

[640] AK 3:5. p. 465. Pruden's translation. All the details cited above are from AK3.

3:5:23 PAÑCASIKHA

One individual *gandhabba* whom the sources frequently mention is Pañcasikha. He is depicted as playful, sensuous and of a youthful and pleasing appearance; when the brahmā Sanankumāra assumed a coarse form in order to be visible to the devas of Tāvatiṃsa, it is the form of Pañcasikha that he chose because "the form of Pañcasikha is dear to all the devas."[641] He plays a *vīṇā*, a string-instrument to akin to a lute (DN 21). But this is no ordinary *vīṇā*, it is the *beluvapaṇḍuvīṇā*, a magical *vīṇā* made of *beluva* wood (from the bael or stone-apple tree, *Aegle marmelos* (PED). Ordinarily, the base would be fashioned from a gourd). When a string is plucked, the beautiful tone reverberates for four months (Sn-a 3:2). Its various fittings are fashioned from gold, sapphire and coral (DN-a 21).

The *beluvapaṇḍuvīṇā* had originally belonged to Māra:

> For seven years Māra had sought to find some weakness in the Buddha by which he could tempt or frighten him. He had been like a crow circling a stone, thinking it was a piece of meat, and had reaped only weariness and frustration. At last, Māra acknowledged his defeat and in despair disappeared from the Blessed One's presence. As he did so with a great weariness overcoming his limbs, the magical *vīṇā* slipped from under his arm and was immediately picked up by Sakka, king of the devas. This he gave to the Pañcasikha. (Sn-a 3:2)

In his previous human existence Pañcasikha had been a boy who wore his hair in five top-knots. He made much merit building pavilions for travellers at cross-roads and digging wells, but died young. He was reborn as the *gandhabba* Pañcasikha but retained his youthful appearance.[642] His body is of a golden colour. He wears a thousand cart-loads of ornaments and nine jarfuls of scent.[643] His celestial garments are brightly coloured and he still wears his golden hair in five top-knots (ibid .).

Some modern writers have seen the *gandhabbas* as "the male counterpart to the *accharas*,"[644] but another detail of Pañcasikha's story demonstrates that this is too simplistic. There are female *gandhabbas*. We know this because Pañcasikha was in love with Bhaddā Suriyavaccasā, a *gandhabba* maiden and the daughter of Timbaru, a chieftain of the *gandhabbas*. He had a rival for her affections in Sikhadi, the son of Mātali the charioteer of the devas. When Sakka and the other devas of the Thirty-Three went to visit the Buddha at the Indasāla Cave, they found him rapt in meditation. In order to attract the Blessed One's attention, they sent in Pañcasikha, who sang the song he had composed for Bhaddā Suriyavaccasā. The text describes this as a song about "the Buddha, the Dhamma, the arahants and love (*kāma*)" (DN 21), but really it is mostly about the latter:

Greetings to your noble father Timbaru, sunny one,[645]

He who sired the fair one who is the source of my joy,

Like a breeze to one who sweats, or a drink to one who thirsts,

You of radiant limbs, you are as dear to me as Dhamma is to the arahants.

Like medicine to the sick, like food to the starving,

---

641 DN-a 18—*sabbadevatā attabhāvaṃ mamāyanti.*

642 DN-a 19. The text here says he was reborn as a cātumahārājika deva, although everywhere else he is identified as a *gandhabba.*

643 These measurements seem a little less excessive if we recall that he as a body three *gavutas* in size.

644 E.g. Malalasekera in the DPPN entry "*gandhabba*".

645 *Sūriyavacchase* lit. "sun calf". The commentary says she was called this because her entire body emitted rays like the sun, from her feet to the top of her head.

Quench (*parinibbāpaya*) me dear one, be water for my flame.

Into a cool pond, fragrant with blossoms and pollen,

The elephant tortured by heat plunges.

So would I plunge between your breasts.

Like a wild elephant subdued by goad and spear,

I know not what I do, intoxicated by the shape of your thighs.

The desire[646] for you makes my mind spin around.

I cannot escape, like a fish that has swallowed the hook.

Embrace me, dear, with your lovely thighs.

Hold me in your dreamy eyes.

To be embraced by you, lovely one, is always my wish.

Small was my desire, curly-headed one,

But it grew little by little, like the gifts of the arahants.

Whatever merit I have made serving the arahants,

May it bear the fruit of being with you, beautiful in every limb.

Whatever merit I have made in the circle of the world (*pathavimaṇḍale*)

May it bear the fruit of being with you, beautiful in every limb.

Just as the Sakyan's son,[647] by meditating, clever and mindful,

Seeks the deathless, so do I seek you, my sunny one.

Just as the sage would delight in attaining *sambodhi* (Buddhahood),

So it would be my delight, lovely one, to couple with you.

If Sakka, the lord of Tāvatiṃsa, would grant me a boon,

It is you, dear, that I would ask for, so great is my passion.

Your father, so wise, like a *Sāl* tree in full blossom,

Him I venerate on account of his pure offspring. (DN 21)

646 *Gedhitacitta*—this might also mean "jealousy".

647 I.e. a Buddhist bhikkhu.

The Buddha's response to this inappropriate interruption was to courteously compliment Pañcasikha on the technical quality of his music: "Pañcasikha, your lute-playing harmonizes very well with your singing, neither overpowers the other." It seems that the Buddha was well aware of the short-comings of Pañcasikha. In another sutta, Pañcasikha asks the Buddha why it is that some beings attain *nibbāna* in this very life, while others do not. The Buddha replies that if one seeks out sense pleasures, takes delight in them, and remains attached to them, then because of that clinging, he cannot find release from them.[648] It is relevant to note that unlike Sakka, Vessavaṇa and some others among the non-human beings, we never hear of Pañcasikha attaining to the state of a *sotāpanna*.

After Sakka's audience with the Buddha he rewarded Pañcasikha by giving him Bhaddā Suriyavaccasā to wed, as well as making him king of the *gandhabbas* (DN 21).

We see another aspect of Pañcasikha in the Sudhābhojana Jātaka where along with Sakka and several other devas, Pañcasikha travels to the human world and assumes the form of a brahmin to teach a miser a lesson:

> Maccharikosiya was a very great miser. Although he owned eighty crores of gold, he would not share so much as a spoonful of porridge if he could avoid it. Nor would he spend money on himself, but lived dressed in rags and eating coarse unhusked rice. One day he had a craving for some sweet porridge made with ghee and honey, so he had a pot prepared and stole away to eat it in solitude in the forest, for fear that someone would ask him for a bite.
>
> Sakka, Mātali, Suriya, Canda and Pañcasikha approached him one by one in the guise of earthly brahmins and each begged for some food. The miser with great reluctance consented to give them a small portion each. As they were all eating, Pañcasikha took the form of a dog and began to urinate. The brahmins covered their bowls with leaves, but one drop splashed on Maccharikosiya's hand. When he went to fetch water for washing, the dog filled his pot of porridge to the brim with his urine. Enraged, the miser came at the dog with a stick but Pañcasikha changed form again and became a noble horse and began to chase after Maccharikosiya, all the while changing form: now he was dark, now white, now golden-coloured. He became spotted, he grew large, and he grew small. The miser fled in terror for his life and when he had been driven around back to where the brahmins sat, they had cast off their disguises and stood in the air to admonish him. (Jāt 535)

We are told at the end of this Jātaka that at that time Pañcasikha was a previous birth of Anuruddha. In another similar story, Pañcasikha was a birth of Ānanda. This would indicate that like many other deity-names, *Pañcasikha* is more the title of an office than a proper name. There is always a Pañcasikha and when one dies, another is born to take his place.

Mātali, the charioteer of the Tāvatiṃsa devas, is also probably to be identified as a *gandhabba*. His son, Sikhadi, was Pañcasikha's rival for the affections of the *gandhabba* maiden Bhaddā Suriyavaccasā which implies that they were all *gandhabbas*. In one place at least, he is explicitly identified as such,[649] although this is contradicted by another text which lists Mātali as one of the great yakkha chiefs.[650] We have already seen that once we get down to individual cases these classifications are often fuzzier than a neat summary would imply. It may be that *gandhabba*, at least when referring to those dwelling in the *saggas*, implies more a kind of class status, as a semi-servile deity, rather than a clear distinction of race. In any case, Mātali does not seem to share the general *gandhabba* characteristic of being a musician, but rather serves his master, Sakka, as a charioteer.

---

648 SN 35:102 (eng. 35:119). In the immediately preceding sutta, the Buddha gives the same teaching to Sakka.

649 The Mahāsamaya Sutta, DN 20.

650 The Aṭānāṭiya Sutta, DN 32.

3:5:24 THE HIGHER SENSUAL HEAVENS

The Tāvatiṃsa realm is the highest *sagga* which is still in physical contact with the earth, being situated on the summit of Mt Sineru. There are four additional *saggas* which are located in the space above in "aerial abodes."[651] These are, in order from the lowest to the highest: the realms of Yāma, Tusita, Nimmānaratī and Paranimmitavasavattī. There is much less to be found about them in the Pali sources by way of detailed description, compared to the abundant information about Tāvatiṃsa. We are told that each *sagga* has its own Nandana Grove.[652] From this we may infer that the higher *saggas* are in some respects translations or reflections of Tāvatiṃsa on a higher plane. The Pali sources are silent about the actual distances of the various *saggas* above Sineru, but there is a scheme outlined in the *Abhidharmakośa* in which each succeeding *sagga* is twice as high above "sea-level" as the preceding one. Thus, as Mt Sineru is 80,000 *yojana* high, the *sagga* of the Yāma devas is 80,000 *yojana* above the mountain's summit, or 160,000 above sea-level. Going upward, Tusita is 320,000 *yojana* high, Nimmānarati 640,000 and the Paranimmitavasavatti *sagga* is 1,280,000 *yojana* above sea-level (AK 3:5, Eng. p. 467).

---

651 AK 3:5, p. 465. Pruden's translation.

652 *Jātaka Nidānakathā*. For Nandana Grove, see the section on Tāvatiṃsa.

3:5:25 YĀMA

The realm of the Yāma devas is the lowest of the celestial *saggas*. These beings, and those above them, are beyond the troubles of the earthly plane and take no part in the wars against the asuras. They are said to "have arrived at divine bliss" (*dibbaṃ sukhaṃ*) (Vibh-a 18:6,1). One day in the Yāma world equals 200 human years, there are 360 days in a celestial year, and the life-span of Yāma devas is 2000 such years (AN 8: 42). This is the equivalent of 144,000,000 human years. The king of the Yāma world is named Suyāma, (DN 11) and he is mentioned as attending the Buddha with a yak tail fan at the time of his descent from Tāvatiṃsa after teaching there (Dhp-a 14: 2). This short summary constitutes just about everything we can learn about the Yāma realm from the Pali sources.

We can infer a little more. The Mahāsamaya Sutta (DN 20) contains a long list in verse of various beings that come to pay their respects to the Buddha. Much of this material is cryptic and no doubt includes many archaic elements. The stanza which mentions Yāmas includes a long list of names:

> The Khemiyas ("peaceful ones") Tusitas and Yāmas. The Kaṭṭhakas[653] endowed with fame (*yasassino*).
>
> The Lambītakas and Lāmaseṭṭhas, Jotināmas and Āsavas.
>
> The Nimmānaratas came, and then (*atha*) also the Paranimmitas.

These ten hosts came, in their manifold forms.

The commentary states that the Khemiya and Kaṭṭhaka devas live in the realms of the Yāmas and Tusitas. It is only in the Yāma realm and higher that there is freedom from strife, as manifested in the realms below by the Asura wars.[654] Of the ten classes of deva listed here, the second, the third and the last two are the names of the four celestial sensual heavens. The other six are mysterious, being found nowhere else. The commentary is of little help. It only says that the Jotināma devas are "luminous and splendid like a mass of flame" and the Āsavas are "full of desire" (DN-a 20). Lambītaka probably means "excellent ones" and Lāmaseṭṭha "foremost in sensual enjoyment".[655] It is possible that all these six classes of devas are groups within the Yāma world, given their placement in the series and the odd detail that the Yāmas are listed after the Tusitas.

The commentary to the Mahāpadāna Sutta (DN-a 14) talks about the effect on the cosmos when a king is unrighteous (*adhammika*). The unrighteousness spreads to his ministers, to the city and to the whole country. From there, the devas of the earth and sky become corrupted causing the winds and rain to become unseasonable, and even the sun and moon to go off course. Through their friendship (*mitta*) with those devas, the Cātumahārājika devas become unrighteous, followed by the Tāvatiṃsa devas. Mentioned last in the chain of unrighteousness are the Yāma devas, which indicates that there is still some connection there to the world below. But too much should not be made of this, because the text goes on to say that every assembly of devas and brahmas (*devabrahmaparisa*), even to the highest point of existence (*evaṃ yāva bhavaggā*) becomes unrighteous, saving only those who have attained some degree of liberation, the Noble Ones (*ariyasāvaka*).

The only story in which the Yāma devas figure even marginally is that of Sirimā the courtesan.

Sirimā was a famous courtesan of Rājagaha. She was so highly sought after that she could command the price of

---

[653] "The meaning of *kaṭṭhakā* is unclear…The Sarvāstivādin who translated a Prakrit version into Sanskrit interpreted it as "black/dark blue" or "wicked, bad", *kṛṣṇa* = Pali *kaṇha*. Perhaps *kaṭṭhakā* can be interpreted as "naughty ones" since they indulge in sexual pleasures, just like the naughty god Kṛṣṇa." Nyanatusita, private correspondence.

[654] The commentary has *khemiyā devā tusitapuravāsino ca yāmādevalokavāsino ca*. It might also be possible to interpret *khemiyā* as an adjective and the phrase translated as "Peaceful are the devas who live in the Tusita city and the world of the Yāmas", but then there would be the problem of making the number of deva hosts equal to ten.

[655] Suggestions by Nyanatusita.

a thousand *kahāpaṇas* (a unit of money) a day. She had a retinue of five hundred women in her employ:

> Uttarā was a pious lay woman married to a wealthy unbeliever. He would not let her go to attend on the Buddha during the rainy season retreat, as she wished. Her father was also a very wealthy man and on her behalf he hired Sirimā to serve as a substitute wife for two weeks so that Uttarā could cook for and serve the bhikkhus. Sirimā came to enjoy the luxury of her temporary home and in her vanity grew jealous of the real wife. One day she threw a ladleful of hot ghee at her. But Uttarā focussed her mind on *mettā* ("loving-kindness") and was not burnt. Seeing this, Sirimā had a sudden change of heart and became a lay disciple herself.
>
> In time, Sirimā became a *sotāpanna* ("stream-enterer", first stage of awakening) and gave up her life as a courtesan. She was still very beautiful. One day she was making a food offering when a young bhikkhu fell into love-sickness at the sight of her. After that he could neither eat nor sleep nor meditate.
>
> It wasn't long after this that Sirimā died of a sudden sickness and was reborn as a *devī* in the Yāma realm, chief queen (*devī*) of King Suyāma. She had a retinue of five hundred deva maidens (*devakaññā*). In Rājagaha, the Buddha asked that her body not be cremated immediately, but be left to decay a while first. The king complied and put a guard around her corpse to keep the vultures and jackals away. After a while, the king, at the request of the Buddha, had her corpse displayed in the street. A proclamation was made, "Who will have this body for a thousand *kāhapaṇa*? For five hundred? For two hundred?" No one would take it even for a *kākaṇikā* ("farthing") when previously men had vied with one another to spend a thousand *kāhapaṇa* on her. This lesson cured the young bhikkhu of his lust.
>
> During the cremation, the devī Sirimā herself, together with her five hundred deva maidens riding in chariots came to witness, surrounding the cremation ground. She there became an *anāgāmī* ("non-returner" third stage of awakening) as she listened to the Buddha discourse on the impure nature of the body.[656]

Even this single episode is doubtful. In the *Vimānavatthu* version of this story there is no mention of Suyāma and Sirimā is said to be reborn in the Nimmānaratī realm.

To learn a few more details about the Yāma world and its inhabitants, we must leave the Pali sources behind and turn to the *Abhidharmakośa*. That text tells us that the overall dimensions of the Yāma realm are identical to those of Tāvatiṃsa, reinforcing the image of the higher realms as more sublime translations of the lower.[657] The height of the individual Yāma devas is cited as three-quarters of a *krośa* in size. This is a unit of measurement not found in the Pali, but according to the *Abhidharmakośa* itself, a *krośa* is one eighth of a *yojana*.[658] This measurement is not compatible with the Theravāda system. The Pali sources often state the height of the Tāvatiṃsa devas as being three-quarters of a *yojana*, and it would not be likely given the general assumptions of the cosmology, to have a higher class of beings smaller than a lower class.

The passage of time in the higher *saggas* is not measured by the sun, which does not rise above the height of the Yugandhara Mountains[659] but by the singing of birds, the opening of flowers and the natural sleep cycle of the devas.

The Yāma world is still on the plane of sense desire, the beings are divided into genders and they make love with

---

656 Sn-a 1:11, Vv-a 15, Dhp-a 11:2 & 17:3.

657 AK 3:5, p. 468. in the text Vasubandhu implies some doubt about this by prefacing it with the remark "according to one opinion"

658 . See AK 3:6, p.474, for units of measure.

659 40,000 yojanas above sea-level.

one another. However, as we ascend through the levels the sensuality becomes more refined and sublime. While the devas of the two "terrestrial" *saggas* copulate much like human beings, except that the males emit no semen, the Yāma devas make love simply by embracing.[660]

[660] All these details from AK 3:5.

3:5:26 TUSITA

The fourth *devaloka* is called *Tusita*, often it is given as *Tusitapura*, "the City of Tusita." One day and night in Tusita is the equivalent of 400 human years. The life-span of the beings there is 4000 celestial years, each of three hundred and sixty celestial days. This works out to 576,000,000 human years. The name derives from the verb *santussati* which means "to be contented, pleased or happy" (PED). The devas there are said to be "satisfied and delighted" (*tuṭṭhā pahaṭṭha*) (Vibh-a 18:6). Tusita is said to be the most delightful (*ramaṇīyo*) of the *saggas* (AN-a 3:34). The king of Tusita is named Santusita and he gained this distinction by exceeding the other devas in morality and generosity(AN 8: 36). In Tusita, the experience of sensuality is more refined and subtle than in the lower *saggas*. There, the devas make love simply by holding hands.[661]

661 At least according to the *Abhidharmakośa*. See AK 3:5, p. 465.

3:5:27 THE BODHISATTA IN TUSITA

The reason that Tusita is called "the most delightful" is because of its special place in the cosmos; Bodhisattas always take their penultimate birth there, prior to their final existence as human beings during which they attain Buddhahood. The career of all Bodhisattas follows an archetypical pattern. After initially making the aspiration for Buddhahood in the presence of a living Buddha, who makes a prophecy validating the aspirant, the Bodhisatta spends countless lifetimes over the course of many kappas arduously perfecting the ten *pāramis*, qualities of spiritual perfection.[662] The last to be completed is always the *dānapārami*, the perfection of generosity. The Buddha Gotama, the Buddha of our historical period, accomplished this in the *Vessantara* birth (Jāt 547) when, as King Vessantara, he made a resolution to never refuse a request for a gift and gave away his wealth, lost his kingdom and in the climax of the story, even gave away his wife and children. With the ten *pāramis* now complete, the Bodhisatta has attained the prerequisite spiritual qualities to become a Buddha. Before that happens he, however, experiences one last blissful existence as a deva of Tusita, as kammic consequence of his many meritorious deeds (Dhp-a 1: 13).

The commentary to the *Mahāpadāna Sutta* (DN-a 14) describes this process in the case of Vipassī Buddha, who lived ninety-one kappas ago.

> All the Bodhisattas experience an existence like Vessantara, and perform a great giving (*mahādānāni datvā*), upon which the earth quakes seven times. Upon death, the Bodhisatta arises in the next mind moment in Tusita. Vipassī lived there for the full span of fifty-seven *koṭi* of years plus sixty times one hundred thousand more.[663]
>
> At last the five signs (*pubbanimittā*) appeared, heralds of his imminent death. (1) From the moment of his rebirth there, he had been adorned with flower garlands, and for five hundred and seventy-six million years these had remained fresh. But now they withered. (2) Likewise, his richly decorated garments now became wrinkled and soiled. (3) Devas never experience heat or cold, but now for the first time sweat fell drop by drop from his arm-pits. (4) The bodies of devas never experience the ravages of old age, brokenness of teeth and greyness of hair. For their entire existence male devas have bodies like twenty year old youths, and female *devīs* those of sixteen year old girls. Even now he did not decay like an aged human, but his body grew weary. (5) During their long lives devas do not know even the name of dissatisfaction, but now at the end the Bodhisatta sighed with restlessness and could not get comfortable on his seat.
>
> Thus, the devas know they have but seven days left by human reckoning (*manussānaṃ gaṇanāvasena*).[664]
>
> Just as in this world, portents such as earthquakes and meteors herald the deaths of kings but not of commoners, so too the five signs do not manifest for all devas, but only those of great power. And just as among humans, only learned astrologers can interpret the signs, so too only the wise among the devas understand the five signs. Likewise, at the moment of their rebirth, devas of little merit ask "Who know where I have arisen?" and feel afraid until the dancers and musicians tell him where he is.[665] But a wise one knows "I have given

[662] The ten *pāramis* are *dāna* (generosity), *sīla* (morality), *nekkhama* (renunciation), *paññā* (wisdom), *viriya* (energy), *khanti* (patience), *sacca* (truthfulness), *adhiṭṭhāna* (resolution), *metta* (loving-kindness) and *uppekkhā* (equanimity). For a very detailed description of the Bodhisatta path see GGB.

[663] The literal translation of the Pali numbers. A *koṭi* is ten million. The total is 576 million.

[664] This is a problematic phrase. If we convert seven human days to deva time it amounts to less than four minutes, certainly far too little for all that is to transpire.

[665] This detail is from MN-a 123.

gifts, guarded my morality and practiced meditation. I have come to the *devaloka* to experience happiness."

Vipassī Bodhisatta recognized the five signs and he knew, "Now in my next existence I will become a Buddha" and he was not afraid. The devas of the ten thousand fold world-system (*dasasahassacakkavāḷa*) assembled and entreated him, "Dear sir, you have completed the ten *pāramīs* not for the not for the sake of enjoying existence as Sakka, nor as Māra, nor as Brahmā, nor as a *cakkavatti* (a universal monarch) but for the sake of transcending the world and attaining Buddhahood. Now is the time for Buddhahood."

The Great Being (*mahāsatta*) did not immediately give his consent. He said, "It may be time, it may not be time," because first it was necessary to perform the five-fold investigation (*pañcamahāvilokana*). The Bodhisatta inquired as to time, continent, clan, nation and mother. (1) During periods when the human life-span exceeds one hundred thousand years, the time for a Buddha is not suitable because beings do not know aging and death and cannot see the three characteristics of suffering, impermanence and not-self. During periods when the human life-span is less than one hundred years the time is also not suitable because beings then are full of defilement and cannot be admonished. Trying to teach them is like "striking blows with a stick on water." In Vipassī's time the life-span was eighty thousand years, so suitable for a Buddha to arise. (2) There are four continents (*dīpa* lit. "islands") together with their retinue of lesser islands. On three continents Buddhas are never born, they are always born on Jambudīpa. (3) Of all the countries in Jambudīpa, Buddhas are always born in the "Middle Country" (*majjhimadesa*—roughly, the Ganges valley and adjacent lands). Here also are born all paccekabuddhas, chief disciples, great disciples and *cakkavattis* as well as other powerful *khattiyas*, brahmins and house-holders. Vipassī was to be born into the city of Bandhumatī in the Middle-Country. (4) Buddhas are always born into a clan (*kula*) belonging to whichever caste is most highly esteemed at the time. At that time, the *khattiyas* ("warrior-nobles") were the most esteemed. Vipassī was to be born as the son of King Bandhumā. (5) A Buddha's mother cannot be a loose woman (*lolā*) or a drunkard. She will have perfected her *pāramīs* for a hundred thousand kappas and keep unbroken morality. Bandhumatī was a queen such as this, and she was to become Vipassī's mother.

Having made the five investigations, Vipassī Bodhisatta announced "Now is the time, dear sirs, for me to become a Buddha," and he dismissed the assembled devas saying, "Go thou"(*gacchatha, tumhe*). Those devas having departed, he entered Nandana Grove surrounded by the Tusita devas. Every *devaloka* has a Nandana Grove and there the devas go to die. They wander about remembering their past meritorious deeds. So too did Vipassī, and while wandering there he died.

The Bodhisatta Vipassī descended from Tusita and entered into his mother's womb, with mindfulness and full awareness (*sato sampajāno*). Thus is the natural law (*dhammatā*).

It is a natural law that when a Bodhisatta enters his mother's womb a brilliant light exceeding that of the devas appears, and the entire ten thousand fold world-system trembles and shakes.

It is a natural law that after seven days, the mother of the Bodhisatta dies and is reborn in Tusita. She dies not die because of the birth, nor from the effects of aging. The Bodhisatta had stayed in her womb as if dwelling in a magnificent *cetiya* (stupa). It is not possible for another to dwell there afterward. The mother of the Bodhisatta being still in the prime of life, when the passions of beings are strong, it would not be possible for her to guard her womb. So she dies, this is the natural law. (DN-a 14)

The Buddhavaṃsa (v. 67) gives another, more poetic, version of the deva's appeal to the Bodhisatta:

kālo deva mahāvīra, uppajja mātukucchiyaṃ.

sadevakaṃ tārayanto, bujjhassu amataṃ padaṃ

"It is time, great hero god. Arise in the mother's womb!

[For] helping [the world] with its gods to cross over [saṃsāra], awake to the deathless state!"[666]

The Majjhima Commentary gives some details about Gotama Buddha's prior existence as a Tusita deva, in the context of discussing his recollection of past lives according to name, clan, appearance, nutriment, pleasure and pain and life-span. In Tusita, his name was Setaketu. Among devas, there is only one clan (*ekagotto*). His appearance was golden coloured (*suvaṇṇavaṇṇa*). His nutriment was divine ambrosia (*dibbasudhāhāra*). His pleasure was the experience of divine happiness (*dibbasukhapaṭisaṃvedī*) and his suffering was merely the suffering of conditioned existence itself (*dukkhaṃ pana saṅkhāradukkhamattameva*). His span of life was the full 576,000,000 years (MN-a 4).

When the Buddha went up to Tāvatiṃsa to teach the Abhidhamma to the assembled devas, his mother descended from Tusita to listen, and was seated in the place of honour to the right of the Buddha (Dhp-a 14:2). There might be a trace of confusion in the tradition between Tāvatiṃsa and Tusita. A verse in the commentary has Sāriputta remarking, at the time of the Buddha's descent from Tāvatiṃsa, "Never have I seen, nor has anyone heard, such lovely teachings, from the one descended from Tusita with his retinue" (ibid.). The same verse occurs without context in the Suttanipāta and the commentary explains that this refers to the Buddha's initial descent at the time of his conception. That text, however, does not account for the mention of a "retinue" (*gaṇi*) very well, taking it as referring to his retinue of devas while still in Tusita, and his retinue of arahants on earth (Sn-a 4: 16).

The being, who will become the next Buddha, Metteyya, is now dwelling as a deva in Tusita. His name there is Nātha and he is said to be continuously teaching Abhidhamma to the assembled devas.[667]

[666] Translation by Bhante Nyantusita.

[667] See DPPN under "Metteyya" which cites only "tradition. This is from the local Sri Lankan tradition where Nātha is a popular deity. In medieval Sri Lanka the bodhisattva Avalokiteśvara transformed into the god Nātha, who then was identified with coming Buddha Metteyya. This process is decribed in detail by Holt in the book *Buddha in the Crown: Avalokiteśvara in the Buddhist Tradition of Sri Lanka.* Thanks to Bhikkhu Nyanatusita for pointing out this reference.

3:5:28 OTHER PERSONS REBORN IN TUSITA

Several other persons are mentioned in the texts as having been reborn into Tusita. These were always persons with a strong devotion to the Dhamma, and in those cases where we are told their level of attainment, often *sakadāgāmī*.[668] This was the case of the brothers Purāṇa and Isidatta, (AN 6:44) as well as Anāthapiṇḍika's daughter, Sumanā. Despite being a *sakadāgāmī* she pined to death for want of a husband. On her death bed she addressed her father as "little brother" and he thought she was delirious until the Buddha explained that she was referring to the fact that she was the elder in the spiritual sense, as Anāthapiṇḍika was only a *sotāpanna* (first stage of awakening) (Dhp-a 1: 13).

When Anāthapiṇḍika himself died, he also was reborn in Tusita with a three *gāvuta* body, shining like a mass of gold and enjoying a *vimāna* and a pleasure garden. Reflecting on how he had come to this happy condition, he felt gratitude to his teachers and appeared in his deva form on earth to pay his respects to the Buddha and Sāriputta, illuminating the whole of the Jetavana monastery (MN-a 143).

The Dhammapada Commentary tells the story of a lay disciple who was given the choice of *devalokas*:

> A certain righteous lay disciple together with his entire family was much given to the distribution of alms. At last he grew ill and lay on his death-bed. He requested that eight or sixteen bhikkhus come to recite for him.[669]
>
> As the bhikkhus were chanting the *Satipaṭṭhāna Sutta*, at that very moment six chariots arrived from the six deva worlds, each a *yojana* and a half long, richly adorned and drawn by a thousand Sindh horses. The devas all cried out, "Let us take you to our *devaloka*! Look, your vessel of clay is broken; take up a vessel of gold! Arise into our *devaloka* to experience bliss!"
>
> The lay disciple, not wanting to interrupt the Dhamma recitation, cried out "Wait! Wait!" The bhikkhus thought they were being addressed by him, and thinking, "We are not wanted here," (lit. *idāni anokāso* "here there is no space") got up from their seats and left. His daughters asked him why he had told the bhikkhus to stop their recitation. "I was not speaking to them, but to the devas. Six deva chariots are poised in the air above and calling to me, each to his own world." But his daughters were not able to see the chariots.
>
> The lay disciple asked, "My dear, which is the most delightful (*ramaṇīyo*) deva world?" "Dear father, the Tusita world is the most delightful. All the Bodhisattas, and the Buddha's mother and father, dwell in Tusita." Their father then told her, "Take a flower garland and throw it into the air, saying 'Let this garland adhere to the chariot from Tusita.'" She did so. The wreath hung from the pole of the Tusita deva's chariot, but the people there saw only a wreath suspended in the air. The lay disciple told them it was hanging on the chariot pole and said, "If you think of me, and wish to be reborn near me, please do acts of merit like I did." So saying, he died and mounted into the chariot.
>
> Immediately, he arose in the form of a deva three *gavutas* in height, decorated with sixty cart-loads of adornments, attended by a thousand *accharās* in a golden *vimāna* twenty-five *yojana* in size which appeared for him. (Dhp-a 1:11)

We have already seen how Queen Mallikā arose in Tusita after spending seven days in *niraya*.[670] Another person

[668] *sakadāgami*—the second stage of awakening, the "once-returner" who after existence as a deva will be reborn human only once more, there to attain full awakening as an arahant.

[669] To this day in Theravāda countries, even numbers of bhikkhus are sent for funeral chanting, odd numbers for happy occasions.

[670] See section on lfe-spans in *niraya* at § 3:3,9.

who spent one week in a lower form before taking birth as a Tusita deva was the bhikkhu Tissa:

> The bhikkhu Tissa was given some fine robe cloth by his sister. Before he had a chance to make it up into a robe, he died suddenly from indigestion and was reborn as a louse living in that same robe-cloth. After the cremation ceremony, the bhikkhus decided to divide the cloth among themselves. The louse heard this and grew agitated, running this way and that through the cloth crying "They are going to steal my property!"
>
> In his perfumed inner chamber, the Buddha heard this sound with his divine ear element (*dibba sotadhātu*). He thereupon instructed Ānanda to have the robe-cloth set aside for seven days, and to allow its division only on the eighth day.
>
> Later, when asked by the bhikkhus to explain this command, the Buddha told them that the bhikkhu Tissa had been reborn as a louse and if they had divided his property at that time he would have developed ill-will against them and on that account been reborn in *niraya*. But now he had died as a louse and arisen in Tusita *devaloka* (Dhp-a 18:3).

SUMMARY

Tusita has a special place in the cosmology because of its connection with the Dhamma. Pious Buddhists, like the dying layman in the story cited above, may have an aspiration to be reborn there, and thus into the presence of a Bodhisatta. Many beings with the first or second stages of awakening are reborn there. This is why it is called "the most delightful" of the *saggas*, even though on a scale based on purely worldly considerations, the happiness of the two higher *saggas* surpasses it (MN 97). Tusita nevertheless is a world within the plane of sense-desire, and the beings there are still "subject to the bondage of sensuality, under Māra's dominion" (SN 5:7). Despite being a special place of contentment and wisdom, Tusita is still a part of *saṃsāra*. At best, we may consider it a way station on the path to *nibbāna*.

3:5:29 THE NIMMĀNARATI DEVAS

The fifth sensual *sagga* is the realm of the *Nimmānarati* devas. These are the devas "who delight in creating." The name derives from the Pali verb *nimmināti*, "to build, fashion or make, to make or create by miracle," and the noun *rati*, "fondness, pleasure" (PED) Their peculiar characteristic is the power to create any object they desire. "Whatever the Nimmānarati devas will for themselves as a sense object, that they create and enjoy, play and make sport with" (Vv-a 16). "Whatever natural or artificial object (*pakatipaṭiyattārammaṇato*) they desire, that they instantly create and greatly enjoy any pleasure they wish" (Vibh 18:6). Their king (*devarājā*) is named Sunimmita (DN 11). Like the *devarājās* of the other realms, he surpasses his subjects in ten respects: in divine span of life, in divine beauty, in divine happiness, in divine glory (*dibba yasa*—possibly means a greater retinue), in divine power (*dibba ādhipateyya*—or "divine dominion"), and in divine forms, sounds, scents, taste and tactile objects (AN 8: 36). When the lay woman Visākhā, called "chief among the supporters of the *Saṅgha*", died she was reborn as Sunimmita's chief consort (Vv-a 44). A day in the Nimmānarati *devaloka* is equivalent to 800 years in the human realm, and their life-span is 8000 such years, or 2,304,000,000 years in human terms (AN 3:71, eng. 3:70). When the beings there make love, they do so merely by smiling upon on another (AK 3: 5, eng. p. 465).

3:5:30 MANĀPAKĀYIKA DEVAS

The *manāpakāyika* devas are a special class of female Nimmānarati devas (AN-a 5: 33). The name means "of pleasing form" (*manāpa* + *kāya*). An encounter of some of these with bhikkhu Anuruddha is recorded. (Anuruddha was the foremost of the Buddha's disciples in the development of the divine-eye (*dibbacakkhu*) attainment, which allows powers of vision beyond the ordinary, such as the ability to see otherwise invisible beings).

> At one time a large number of *manāpakāyika* devas approached the elder bhikkhu Anuruddha. After bowing to him, they stood to one side and said, "We, *Bhante* Anuruddha, are the devas called '*manāpakāyika*'. We can exercise mastery and control over three things. We can assume whatever colour we wish for. We can acquire any pleasure we wish for. We can obtain any sound we wish for." (The commentary explains the latter as "the sound of a voice, the sound of music, and ornamental sounds.")
>
> Then the elder Anuruddha thought, "May these devas become blue, of blue colour with blue clothes and blue ornaments." Then those devas, knowing the thought of the bhikkhu, became blue in colour, with blue clothes and ornaments.
>
> Then the elder Anuruddha thought, "May these devas become yellow, of yellow colour with yellow clothes and yellow ornaments." Then those devas, knowing the thought of the bhikkhu, became yellow in colour, with yellow clothes and ornaments.
>
> And the same thing occurred when Anuruddha wished for them to become red and then white.
>
> Then one of those devas sang, another danced, and another made music by snapping her fingers. Just as when a highly skilled five piece musical ensemble performs, the sound is pleasurable, enticing, beautiful, lovely and intoxicating, so too was the ornamental sound (*alaṅkārānaṃ saddo*) of those devas. Thereupon the elder Anuruddha restrained his sense-faculties (*indriyāni okkhipi*).
>
> Then those devas (seeing that Anuruddha had closed his eyes) said, "The venerable one is not enjoying this" and disappeared from that place.[671]

Rebirth among the *manāpakāyika* devas is said to be the special reward of women who fulfill the duties of a wife well. This is given in a list of eight qualities:

1. Going to whatever husband her parents have arranged for her, she undertakes whatever duties need to be done and is pleasant in her conduct and speech
2. She honours those whom her husband honours.
3. She attends with skill and diligence to her domestic chores.
4. She manages the household servants and slaves well.
5. She protects the family wealth.
6. She is a faithful lay follower and takes refuge in the Buddha, Dhamma and *Saṅgha*.
7. She keeps the five precepts.
8. She is generous, delighting in giving.[672]

[671] AN 8:46. The phrase in the last paragraph in parentheses is taken from the commentary.
[672] AN 8:46. See also AN 5: 33 and Jāt 269.

3:5:31 NIMMĀNARATI AND THE NATURE OF SENSE-DESIRE

With the Nimmānarati we have reached the second highest level of the *kāmabhūmi*, the plane of sense desire. It includes all the various beings at the different levels we have considered so far, from the lowest *niraya* through the worlds of humans and devas. Beings in this sphere of existence relate to the world primarily through the senses, and are most strongly motivated by the desire for pleasant sense objects and the escape from unpleasant ones. As we ascend through the worlds of the devas, the experience of sensuality becomes more refined, subtle and exquisite. At the level of the Nimmānarati devas, there is a fundamental difference from the levels below. Those in the lower realms, including humans and the devas of the first four levels, can only enjoy those sense-objects which are presented to them, whereas the devas of the Nimmānarati level can create whatever they desire (DN 33).

According to the *Abhidhamma*, all sense experience is the result of past kamma.[673] This causal link is more immediate and obvious in the deva worlds than it is among humans. We have seen how the *vimānas*, pleasure-groves and other delights of the sensual *saggas* appear, as it were miraculously, fully formed by the force of the *kusala kamma* ("skilful deeds") of the beings reborn there. Among the Nimmānarati devas the process is more immediate still. The power of their meritorious kamma is so great that they can manifest any desired object at will.

The very first line of the Dhammapada states:

> All things originate with the mind, the mind is the chief, all things are mind-made.

At the level of the Nimmānarati devas, this fundamental law of saṃsāric reality is clearly manifested.

---

673 See Abhidh-s, CMA Ch 4 and Vism Ch 14.

3:5:32 PARANIMMITAVASAVATTI DEVAS

The *Paranimmitavasavatti Devas* constitute the highest level of the sensual desire plane, which is bounded by Avīci *niraya* below and this realm above (DN-a 15). The name means "those who wield power over the creations of others" (*para* = "other" *nimmita* = "created object" *vasa* = "power or authority" and *vatti* means "to wield or exercise"). One day in the Paranimmitavasavatti world equal 1600 years in human terms, and their life-span is 16,000 deva years, each of 360 such days (AN 3:71, Eng. AN 3:70). This works out to being 9,216,000,000 human years. Their king (*devarāja*) is named Vasavatti and he is reckoned supreme among those who enjoy sense pleasures (Vibh-a 17:5).

These devas do not create their own sense pleasures, but wield a certain power over the devas below them who manifest the desired objects. "Whatever occurs to their mind, the others over whom they wield power, know this and create that object" (Vibh-a 18:6). These others must be the Nimmānarati Devas, who are the only ones with the power to create desired objects at will.

> The Paranimmitavasavatti Devas enjoy the creations of others. The others, having known their mind, create whatever objects of enjoyment they desire. They wield power there. How do the others know their mind? It is in the nature of their service (*pakatisevanavasena*). Just as a skilful cook knows what the king wants to eat, and so makes lots of it, just so, they know what the Paranimmitavasavatti Devas want. Thus, naturally (*pakatiyā*) having known what sense objects give pleasure, just these they create. (DN-a 33)

As the Paranimmitavasavatti Devas occupy the highest position in the *kāmabhūmi* ("plane of sense desire") their sense pleasures are the most exquisite and refined. Thus, of all beings who take physical nutriment, their food is the most subtle (MN-a 9). The *Abhidharmakośa* informs us that they make love simply by gazing into one another's eyes (AK 3: 5, Eng. p. 465). We have seen how this text describes the refinement of sexuality as we move up through the *devalokas*. It should be noted, however, that this is a Sarvāstivādin source.[674] The Theravāda commentaries were aware of this doctrine but rejected it. The passage quoted just above goes on to say:

> Those over whom they wield power serve them with sexual intercourse (*methunaṃ sevanti*). But some elders say: "by the mere holding of hands, by a mere look, by mere smiling they complete the act of pleasure." In the commentary (*aṭṭhakathā*, meaning the old Sinhala commentary on which Buddhaghosa's work was based) this is rejected: "But this is not so Since it is not possible to accomplish the act of sex without bodily touching. Since sensual pleasure is natural in the sense-desire realm too". (DN-a 33)

We can only speculate why the Theravāda commentators rejected this description of the increasing refinement of sexuality in the deva worlds, a concept that is intuitively appealing and consistent with what we otherwise know about those realms. It may be based on the *Abhidhamma* teaching that the tactile sense base is the only one which can produce pleasurable feeling directly.[675] If the Pali commentarial view is correct, it raises another interesting speculation: are the Nimmānarati Devas mostly female, and the Paranimmitavasavatti Devas entirely or mostly male? There is little enough to go on here, but other than their king, Sunimmita, the only Nimmānarati devas mentioned in the sources are female, and we have seen that this is the rebirth destination of dutiful wives.[676] When considering these sorts of issues raised by the texts, it should not be forgotten that the ancient Indians who produced them were the products of a patriarchal culture and that their assumptions about appropriate gender roles were very different from ours.

---

674 The Sarvāstivāda was an important early school of Buddhism in India, doctrinally close to the Theravāda in most matters.

675 See Bodhi, CMA pp. 117–18.

676 See AN 5:33 & AN 8:46.

CONCLUSION

We have now reached the summit of the plane of sense-desire. In the realm below this one, the beings are able to create any desired object by a simple act of will. This might seem to be the furthest limit to which the fulfillment of sense-desire can be taken, but there is something still better. The Paranimmitavasavatti Devas do not even have to be bothered with performing an act of will to satisfy their sensuality. There is an odd paradox here. From one perspective, we can visualize them as all-powerful overlords bending others to their will, as their name implies. However, they can just as easily be seen as completely passive consumers of sense objects: "having known what they want, just these objects which give pleasure they (the servant devas) create." In the whole of the sense-desire realm, beings strive and suffer to attain their desired objects. Here we see that the final goal, the peak experience of sensuality, is an utterly futile existence of supine luxury.

3:5:33 MĀRA

There is one inhabitant of the Paranimmitavasavatti realm who has a very special significance in the cosmology. This is Māra: the tempter, tormentor and adversary of those who are following the path of liberation. Although the Paranimmitavasavatti realm is ruled by the devarāja Vasavatti, Māra does not submit to his authority, but together with his own retinue rules one region of this realm "like a rebel prince in a frontier province" (MN-a 1). Māra is a very powerful deity; he is called "foremost of sovereigns" (ādhipateyya, lit. "over-lord") (AN 4:15) and his power extends over the whole sensual-desire plane.

Sense perceptions and sense pleasures are said to be "Māra's domain, Māra's sphere, Māra's bait and Māra's pasture" (MN 106). He makes it his mission to prevent any being escaping from this realm which he sees as his. The name *Māra* derives from *maraṇa*, "death."[677] "Those beings who desire to transcend his domain, he kills (*māreti*) if he can, if he cannot then he wishes them dead (*maraṇaṃ*), hence he is called *Māra*" (Sn-a 1:2). A slightly different explanation of his name is given elsewhere: "he incites beings to their harm and so causes their death" (Ud-a 6:1). The importance of Māra in the cosmological scheme is shown by a passage in the Milindapañha which lists eight things which are "mighty and unique" (*mahanto, so eko yeva*) in the world; Māra is included in the exalted company of the Buddha, the earth, the sea, Mt Sineru, space, Sakka and Mahābrahma.[678] Māra's power extends to some degree even beyond his special domain of the sense-desire realm. It is said that the five aggregates (*khandha*) are subject to him, (SN 23:1) and even that his domain extends to the whole of *saṃsāra* (AN-a 8:29). Either of these formulations would be the equivalent of all conditioned existence, including also those realms beyond the plane of sense-desire. Indeed, we shall see below incidents of Māra's sway extending into the world of the brahmās who exist in a higher plane than the sensual devas including Māra himself.

Māra is sometimes used as a metaphor or synedoche, and the *Dīgha Commentary* distinguishes between four "Māras": Māra as the aggregates of body-mind (*khandhamāra*), Māra as death (*maccumāra*), Māra as the defilements (*kilesamāra*) and Māra the deva (*devaputtamār.*).[679] This last is the unique entity, the powerful deva named Māra. It is this being who is the subject of this chapter.

Something of Māra's character can be gleaned by looking at his various epithets:

Pāpimā—"The Evil One" because he is "exceedingly wicked."

Kaṇha—"The Black One" because he is "endowed with dark kamma."

Antaka—"The End-Maker" because he seeks to "make an end of those endowed with the virtues beginning with dispassion."

Namuci—"No Release" because "without spiritual practice beings are not set free" from his power.

Pamattabandhū—"Kinsman of the Negligent" so-called either because "the heedless bind (*bandhati*) themselves in his snares, or because they are reckoned as his kinfolk (*bandhū*)."[680]

As with Sakka and other important individuals in these realms, the designation *Māra* should be considered as an office rather than a personal name. Māra is, like all other beings, mortal and when he dies a new Māra arises to take his place.[681]

---

677 See PED. The word Māra is sometimes used as a personification of "death," see for example SN 23:1 and SN-a35:48.

678 Mil 5:1,1 eng. v2 pp. 43–44. "Unique" in this context means that only one of these entities can exist in a world-system at a time.

679 DN-a 1. The *Visuddhimagga* adds one more, Māra as kamma-formation, ābhisaṅkhāramāra. Vism 7.59.

680 DN-a16, explanations from the sub-commentary

681 See the story in the Māratajjanīya Sutta, MN 50, considered below at § 3:5,40

3:5:34 MĀEA AND THE BUDDHA I—BEFORE FULL AWAKENING

The biggest threat to Māra's dominion is the arising of a Buddha in the world. Not only is a Buddha fully released from Māra's power, but he teaches countless others the path to liberation. Māra therefore did everything in his power to prevent Siddhattha Gotama from attaining Buddhahood, and when he failed in that, to obstruct the progress of his teaching. The Pali texts recount many episodes of Māra confronting the Buddha. The first in chronological order occurred when the Prince Siddhattha had made the decision to renounce the worldly life and was leaving through the city-gate mounted on his loyal horse Kanthaka:

> At that moment, Māra thought, "I will turn the Bodhisatta back." He came to that place and standing in the air said, "Dear sir, do not depart. Seven days from now the Wheel-Treasure will manifest for you. You will make an empire over the four great continents and their retinue of two thousand islands. Remain here, dear sir."
>
> "Who are you?"
>
> "I am Vasavatti."
>
> "Māra, I already know that the Wheel-Treasure will manifest for me. Empire is not my purpose. I will become a Buddha and make the ten thousand fold world-system resound."
>
> Māra thought, "From this day onward, whenever he has a mind moment of lust or ill-will or cruelty, I will know it." Waiting for a chance, like a shadow he followed the Bodhisatta without turning aside.
>
> But the Bodhisatta, having cast aside the possession of a Wheel-Turner's empire like a piece of spittle left the city with great dignity. (Jāt-nid 2)

The status of a Wheel-Turning Monarch (*cakkavatti*) is the supreme worldly achievement and the rejection of this signifies the Bodhisatta's renunciation of the whole of *saṃsāra*.[682] Therefore, the threat to Māra's dominion was very great and he made the determination to keep his eye on this one. One detail of interest here is that Māra falsely identifies himself as Vasavatti, but this does not fool Prince Siddhattha. We shall see other examples below of Māra appearing in false guise.[683]

We next hear of Māra when the Bodhisatta was sitting by the banks of the Nerañjara River. Because of this location, we can infer that it was near the end of the six year period of the Bodhisatta's practice of austerities, shortly before the final effort under the Bodhi Tree. Due to his extreme fasting, the Bodhisatta was at this time very emaciated. Verses in the Padhāna Sutta tell us how Māra attempted once again to divert the Bodhisatta from his path:

> I was striving by the Nerañjara River
>
> Endeavouring with meditation, to attain the release from bonds.
>
> Namuci speaking in a compassionate voice approached me:
>
> "You are emaciated, of bad colour. You are near death.

---

[682] For the *cakkavatti* see § 3:1,10

[683] Malalasekera, in his article on Māra in the DPPN, advances the theory that Māra and Vasavatti were originally one entity only distinguished later, partly on the strength of this passage. I do not find it convincing, and think it is a more straightforward explanation that Māra was simply lying to conceal his identity.

There are in you one thousand parts of death to a single one of life.
Life is better, sir. Live and make merit.
Walk the holy life, perform the fire sacrifice!
Much merit will be heaped up, why perform this striving?
Hard is the road of striving, hard to perform, hard to achieve."

These verses were spoken by Māra, standing near the Buddha.

When Māra had spoken thus, the Blessed One said:

"Pamattabandhu, Pāpima, with a purpose you have come here.
I have not the slightest need for merit.
To those who have the goal of merit, to them Māra is worthy to speak.
There is faith, energy and wisdom found in me.
Indeed I am resolute, why do you ask about life?
The streams and rivers, this wind dries up.
Why should not my blood dry up when I am striving?
The blood dries up, the phlegm and bile wither away.
In the wasting of the flesh, the mind is betterpurified.
More mindfulness and wisdom and samādhi are established.
This mind is not seeking sense pleasure, behold a purified being.
Sensuality is your first army, the second is discontent I say.
The third is hunger and thirst, the fourth is called desire.
The fifth is sloth-and-torpor, the sixth is called cowardice.
The seventh is doubt, the eighth is hypocrisy and callousness.
Gain, fame and honour, and glory wrongly obtained,
Having high regard for oneself, disparaging others
These are your armies Namuci, the striking force of Kaṇha,
Which no coward can defeat. To conquer them is to find bliss.

I hold my life of as little account as this blade of muñja grass.

It is better to die in battle than to live defeated.

Some samaṇas and brahmins are submerged, they do not see.

That path they do not know, by which the good go.

I see the army all around, and Māra and his mount.

I go forth to battle, I will not be moved from my place.

That army which the world with its devas cannot overcome,

That by wisdom I shall break, like an unfired bowl with a stone.

Having mastered thought, with mindfulness well established,

I shall wander from country to country, training many disciples.

These sent forth, diligent followers of my teaching,

Free of desire they shall go, and wherever gone they shall not sorrow." (Sn 3:2)

This simple text became the kernel of much embellishment in later literature as the story of the Buddha's encounter with Māra by the Nerañjara was fleshed out with many additional details.[684] The most elaborate version found in the Pali commentaries is from the introduction to the Jātaka tales. It is worth translating this passage in full. After the brief sutta quoted above, this Jātaka version is the next retelling of an episode which became central to the stories of both Māra and the Buddha. It is also of significance because it is from an early source considered authoritative by the Theravāda tradition:

The Bodhisatta, putting his back to the Bodhi Tree and his face to the east, made the firm resolve:

"Let skin and sinews and bones waste away,

Let the flesh and blood of the body dry up without remainder.

Until I have reached total awakening I will be bound to this seat."

He sat down in the unconquerable posture, not to be moved by a hundred thunderbolts.

At that time the devaputta Māra thought, "Prince Siddhattha wants to go beyond my power, I will not let him go now." He went to the Māra-host (*mārabala*) and informed them of this matter. Shouting the praise of Māra, the Māra-host went forth. The Māra-army (*mārasena*) of Māra stretched twelve *yojana* before him, to left and right twelve *yojana*.

Behind him it reached to the cakkavāla wall (i.e to the edge of the world-system), above him nine *yojana*. The sound of their shouting like the earth beginning to split open was heard for a thousand *yojana*. Then Māra

[684] One of the best known early versions can be found in the *Buddhacarita*. In modern times everyone from Joseph Campbell to Thich Nhat Hanh has retold the story.

mounted on his elephant Girimekhala, one hundred and fifty *yojana* high, created one thousand arms and took up various weapons. As for the rest of Māra's company, no two persons took up the same weapon. Assuming various colours and various faces, they came to overpower the Great Being.

At that time, the devas of the ten-thousand-fold world-system stood speaking the praise of the Great Being. Devarājā Sakka stood blowing his conch Vijayuttara. Now this conch is one hundred and twenty *hattha*(i.e. cubits) long. Once this conch is blown, the sound lasts for four months until it becomes silent. The nāgarājā Mahākāla stood speaking praise of the Bodhisatta in more than one hundred stanzas. Mahābrahmā stood bearing the white parasol. But as the Māra-host approached the Bodhimaṇḍa ("the site of awakening") not one of these could hold his place. Coming face to face they fled away. The black Nāga king dived into the earth and went to his five-hundred *yojana* nāga realm Mañjerika, and sat there with both hands covering his face. Sakka putting the Vijayuttara conch on his back went and stood at the edge of the world-system. Mahābrahmā having placed the white parasol at the summit of the world-system fled to the Brahmaloka. Not one deva was able to remain; the Great Being sat all alone.

Māra said to his company, "There is no other person like this Siddhattha son of Suddhodana. We cannot give battle from the front, we shall attack from the rear." The Great Being looked around on three sides and saw that all the devas had fled leaving the place empty. And furthermore he saw the Māra-army spread over the northern side. "I am one person alone and against me alone this great effort of power is being made. In this place there is no mother or father or brother or any other relative. But the ten *pāramis* (qualities of spiritual perfection developed through many life-times) have for a long time been like my paid retainers. The *pāramis* shall be my sword and my shield, with which I shall defeat this host ." So he sat, contemplating the *pāramis*.

Then said Māra, "I shall make even Siddhattha run away," and raised a whirlwind. in an instant, a wind rose up from the four directions. Having split mountain-tops of half a *yojana*, one *yojana*, two *yojana*, three *yojana* in size, having uprooted forests of plants and trees, all around villages and towns were smashed to bits. But by the merit of the Great Man, its power was destroyed. Having reached the Bodhisatta, it was unable to flutter so much as the hem of his robe. Then said Māra, "By submerging him with water I will slay him." And he produced a great deluge of rain. By his power, having caused hundreds and thousands of clouds to come together like a roof, they poured forth rain. By the power of the rain the earth was split and the waters reached to the tops of the trees. But it was not able to moisten the robe of the Great Being by so much as the measure of a dew-drop. Then he raised a rain of stones. Very great mountain tops smoking and blazing fell from the sky. But upon reaching the Bodhisatta they became garlands of deva-flowers. Then he produced a rain of weapons. One-edged and two-edged swords and arrows smoking and blazing fell from the sky. These too, falling upon the Bodhisatta became deva-flowers Then he raised a rain of charcoal. Charcoal embers the colour of *kiṃsuka* flowers (i.e. bright red) fell from the sky. At the feet of the Bodhisatta they became a sprinkling of deva-flowers. Then he raised a rain of hot ash. Very hot, the colour of fire the ash fell from the sky. There fell at the Bodhisatta's feet deva-sandalwood powder. Then he raised a rain of sand. Exceedingly fine sand smoking and blazing fell from the sky. At the Bodhisatta's feet fell deva-flowers. Then he raised a rain of mud. Mud smoking and blazing fell from the sky. At the Bodhisatta's feet fell deva-ointment (*dibbavilepana*). Then thinking, "By terror I will make Siddhattha flee" he raised a darkness. As if endowed with four limbs was the great darkness Having reached the Bodhisatta the darkness was dispelled as if by the brightness of the sun.

Thus Māra by these nine assaults, the whirlwind etc. was unable to make the Bodhisatta run away. Māra cried out to his troops, "Why do you stand there, lackeys![685] Seize this prince Siddhattha, kill him, make him run away!" Having addressed his company, seated on the back of his elephant Girimekhala, he took up his wheel-weapon, the Cakkāvudha, and approached the Bodhisatta. "Siddhattha rise up from that seat. You have not won it (*pāpuṇāti*), it is won by me." he said. The Great Being heard this and said the following. "Māra, by you the ten pāramis were not perfected, neither the lesser pāramis, nor the higher pāramis. Not given up by you were the five great renunciations. Neither did you strive for the sake of knowledge, nor for the sake of the world. Not perfected by you was the way of awakening. By me all these were completed, thus not by you but by me is this seat won."

Māra was angry, and unable to endure his rage, he released his wheel-weapon at the Great Person. By the Buddha's contemplation of the ten *pāramis* the wheel-weapon turned into a canopy of flowers above him. Now at any other time when with anger Māra throws the razor-bearing wheel-weapon, it can cleave a solid stone pillar like a bamboo shoot. But now it rested there as a flower canopy. The rest of Māra's company said, "Now he shall rise from his seat and flee!" and threw gigantic stone hammers at him. But the Great Person contemplated the ten *pāramis* and the hammers fell to the ground as clusters of flowers. The devas standing at the edge of the world-system stretched forth their necks and raised their heads. "Lost, alas, is Prince Siddhattha's attempt to reach the summit of becoming. What indeed can he do?"

Then said the Great Person "Having completed the *pāramis*, the bodhistta's seat on the awakening day (*bodhisattānaṃ abhisambujjhanadivase pattapallaṅko*) is won by me." And he said to Māra—"Māra who has witnessed the giving of gifts by you?" Māra stretched out his hand in the face of the Māra-army and said, "These each have witnessed." In an instant the Māra-company cried "I have seen it! I have seen it!", making a sound like the earth splitting open. Then Māra said to the Great Person, "Siddhattha, who witnessed your giving of gifts?" The Great Person said "You have conscious (*sacetana*) witnesses to your gift-giving, but I have in this place no one conscious to be a witness. Leave aside the gift-giving by me in the remainder of my births, standing only on the Vessantara becoming—the seven-hundred-fold great gift-giving existence; this unconscious (*acetana*) great solid mass of earth (*ghanamahāpathavī*) is my witness." From beneath his robe, he stretched out his right-hand as he declared, "In my Vessantara becoming were you witness or were you not witness of my seven-hundred great gift-givings?" He stretched out his hand to the surface of the great earth and the great earth said, "I witnessed you at that time," as if with hundreds of shouts, thousands of shouts, hundreds of thousands of shouts. Thus the army of Māra was over powered.

Then Grimekhala the elephant said to the Great Person, "Given by you Siddhattha was the great gift, the supreme gift." Contemplating the giving of Vessantara the one hundred and fifty *yojana* high elephant Girimekhala bend his knee to the ground. Māra's company ran away in all directions, no two going the same way. Casting off their head gear and garments, they fled away, running straight ahead in whatever direction they faced. Then the assembly of devas seeing the flight of Māra's army declared, "This is the birth of Māra's defeat! Prince Siddhattha is victorious, let us make a victory pūja!" The nāgas cried out to the nāgas, the *supaṇṇas* to the *supaṇṇas*, the devas to the devas and the brahmās to the brahmās. With flower garlands in hand they came to the bodhi seat of the Great Person. The rest of the devas of the ten-thousand fold world system paid reverence with flowers in hand and stood praising him in various words. The sun had not yet set when the Great Person dispersed the host of Māra. The bodhi tree paid reverence by sprinkling his robes with blossoms. (Jāt-nid 2)

685 *Bhaṇe*, a term used to address inferiors

When we compare this version with the earlier one found in the Padhāna Sutta, the most evident difference is in the nature of Māra's army. The ten armies of Māra in the Padhāna Sutta are treated as metaphors for various defilements: sensuality, discontent and so forth. In the Jātaka version, the defilements are not mentioned and the armies are fully personified as demonic beings intent on the Bodhisatta's physical harm. Nevertheless, we should not push the metaphorical interpretation of the Padhāna account too far, for instance by interpreting Māra himself as a metaphor. There is no ground in the text for assuming that Māra himself represents simply a psychological state of the Bodhisatta—he is definitely meant to be a real entity.[686] Note also a concealed parallelism with the canonical original in which the list of Māra's "armies" comprise ten defilements; in this commentarial passage Māra makes ten assaults on the Bodhisatta with various weapons, and the Bodhisatta opposes them with the ten *pāramis*. The ten assaults of Māra in which he unleashed violent storms of various kinds ending with the use of a personal magic weapon are identical with those unleashed by the yakkha Āḷavaka in the story of his encounter with the Buddha.[687] Most of the first seven attacks represent elemental forces of nature: earth, air, fire and water. The fourth attack, with a rain of weapons, which are technological artifacts, might represent either the defilement of anger or more fundamentally, the element of consciousness. The eighth, mud, represents a deluge of filth, a quality often associated with the lower realms as is also the ninth, darkness. It is impossible to know if one of these stories was cribbed from the other, or if this list common to both was significant *a priori* as representing the total forces of the conditioned world under the command of both these powerful entities.

The flight of the devas in the face of Māra's army should not be seen as simple cowardice; Sakka, for example, has the attribute of a warrior-deity habitually at war with the asuras. This retreat of the devas tells us something about the nature of *saṃsāra*. With the notable exception of Brahmā, all of these devas and nāgas, no matter how potent, remain part of the plane of sense-desire and their entire existence is centred around satisfying their sense-desires. They are completely unable to oppose Māra not through any lack of martial prowess, but because he personifies that which is central to their own being. These devas, with their golden vimānas and their flocks of lovely dancing girls were powerless to resist the being who stands at the summit and as the personification of sensuality. The case of Mahābrahmā is somewhat different as the brahmās are in a realm beyond sense-desire. But Māra's influence extends even into the *rūpabhūmi*, the plane of form where the brahmās reside. Here, his weapons are not sensuality but pride, wrong-view and the desire-to-be (*bhavataṇhā*).[688] It is noteworthy that Mahābrahma's flight was not completely headlong, in that he took time to plant the white parasol, an ancient Indian emblem of sovereignty, on the summit of the world (presumably Mt Sineru). Thus he at least contested Māra's supremacy, albeit from a safe distance.

The climax of the episode is the Bodhisatta touching the earth and calling it to witness, which instantly disperses Māra's host in a panic flight. The image of the Buddha in the "earth-touching" *mudra*, with one hand extended down so the finger-tips touch the ground, later became a favourite motif of Buddhist art and the story has been retold with variations throughout the generations. It is worth therefore closely examining the Jātaka version, which is the oldest one extant.

Māra challenged the Bodhisatta's right to sit on that spot, a place charged with cosmic significance. This was the *Bodhimaṇḍa,* the "place of awakening". The word *maṇḍa* is short for *maṇḍala* meaning a circle.[689] This particular point on the earth was chosen by all previous Buddhas and is the only place where the attainment of Buddhahood is possible (MN-a 26; Jāt-nid 2). Māra challenges the Bodhisatta by saying he "has not won" the right to sit on that place. The verb used in Pali is *pāpuṇāti* defined by the PED as "to reach, attain, arrive at, obtain, get to, learn" and the sense

686 The conclusion of this sutta, quoted below, makes this clear.

687 A point noted by Sn-a 1:2 For the story of Āḷavaka see the section on yakkhas in § 3:4,2.

688 We shall return to this theme in considering the case of Baka the Brahmā at § 3:6,11

689 See PED

here is that the right to sit in the Bodhimaṇḍa must be earned. This Prince Siddhattha has indeed done, by perfecting the *pāramis* over hundreds of life-times, and he throws the challenge back at Māra by focussing on the single *pārami* of *dāna*, "generosity or giving." This was the last pārami perfected by the Bodhisatta. This was accomplished in his previous human birth as King Vessantara (Jāt 547). Māra, too, claims to have made great gift-giving and he calls his host as witnesses. Of course they noisily assent, "we have seen it! we have seen it!" This may be simple falsehood on their part as we certainly have no reason to assume that anyone in Māra's thrall would tell the truth. Nevertheless, there may have been some truth to Māra's claim. Whatever else Māra may be, he remains a deva of the highest order, the Paranimmitavasavatti realm. We have seen that generosity is a prime requisite for rebirth into the deva realms,[690] and it can be inferred that to be born as Māra, a being must have made significant merit. Nowhere is it implied that birth as Māra is an unfortunate one. When the Bodhisatta was living as a deva in Tusita, and the time came for him to take human birth for the last time, the other devas implored him by saying "Dear sir, you have completed the ten pāramīs not for the not for the sake of enjoying existence as Sakka, nor as Māra, nor as Brahmā, nor as a *Cakkavatti* but for the sake of transcending the world and attaining Buddhahood" (DN-a 14). This implies that rebirth as Māra is as desirable as that of Sakka or Brahmā or a *Cakkavatti*.

The Bodhisatta declares that he has no living witness. Specifically, he says that he has no witness who is *sacetana* "conscious" or more literally, "with intentional thought." This is because he has spent 576,000,000 years as a deva in Tusita since his death as Vessantara. Instead he calls on the "great earth," *mahāpathavī* to be his "unconscious," *acetana* witness. When his finger-tips touch the earth the "unconscious" earth responds with speech, declaring aloud, "I have witnessed you at that time." (Those familiar with later literary versions may be surprised that there is no mention here of the earth quaking). This was an event of great significance. The insensate material cosmos itself, there at the very "navel of the world,"[691] affirmed the right of the Bodhisatta to the supreme seat in the world-system. Māra was left without recourse, his own elephant bent its knee to the Bodhisatta and the rest of his army fled away helter-skelter. Māra may be the supreme over-lord of the conditioned realm, but the Bodhisatta sat immoveable on the verge of the unconditioned, and was utterly beyond Māra's power.

690 See Vv passim
691 *Buddhacarita* 13:68

3:5:35 MĀRA AND THE BUDDHA II—AFTER FULL AWAKENING

Māra did not give up after Siddhattha Gotama attained to Buddhahood. On the contrary, Māra continued to watch him closely for another full year, looking for any mental defilement upon which he could seize and get the Buddha back under his power, or at the very least to prevent him from teaching others the way to escape from his realm.

One week after attaining Buddhahood, the Buddha was sitting under the Goat Herder's Banyan Tree (*ajapālanigrodha*) reflecting on how good it was to be free from the ascetic practices which he now saw as useless and productive of suffering. Māra, knowing with his own mind the thoughts in the Buddha's mind, addressed him in verse:

> Abandoning those ascetic practices which purify men
>
> Being impure you think yourself pure, but you have left the path of purity.

But the Buddha knew, "This is Māra Pāpimā," and responded with verses of his own, declaring the futility of asceticism. Māra understood: "The Bhagavā, knows me! The Sugata knows me!" (These are epithets of the Buddha). Grieving and sorrowful, he disappeared (SN 4:1). This denouement becomes a repeated theme. Māra works most often by stealth and when he is known for what he is, he is defeated. This episode also illustrates the variety of Māra's tricks in that he appeals here not to sensuality but to a perceived guilt at having abandoned asceticism.

Sometime during the first five weeks, Māra appeared before the Buddha in the form of a huge bull elephant, with the intention of causing terror in him. The elephant's head was like a great block of stone, his tusks like pure silver and his trunk like a gigantic plough pole. The Buddha was not in the least frightened, nor fooled as to the identity of his visitor:

> You've wandered a long time in *saṃsāra*, making beautiful and ugly forms.
>
> Enough Pāpima! You are defeated, Antakā.

Māra realized that "the Blessed One knows me!" and disappeared (SN 4:2). Later in the Buddha's career, Māra attempted these shape-shifting tactics again. At one time he appeared as a huge serpent (SN 4:6), and at another he assumed "various shining forms, both beautiful and ugly" (SN 4:3). In both instances the Buddha knew who it was, and Māra, "sad and unhappy, disappeared from that place."

Eight weeks after the awakening, Māra again approached the Buddha and said, "Blessed One, you have perfected the pāramis and realized omniscience. You have achieved your goal. Why do you now concern yourself with the world? Now is the time to enter *parinibbāna*, Blessed One." (DN 16). *Parinibbāna* is the final *nibbāna* of an awakened one; the cessation of the aggregates or physical death. The Buddha of course rejected this advice

When the Buddha began his teaching career in earnest, Māra turned his attention to thwarting the spread of the Dhamma. After the first rains retreat at Isipatana the Buddha decided to send the first sixty bhikkhus, all of them arahants, out into the world to spread the teaching. Māra thought, "This samaṇa Gotama is, as it were, conducting a great war. Not one or two is sent forth, the Dhamma will be taught by a crowd of sixty. Even if only one person were to teach, this would displease my mind, let alone all these! I must stop them." Māra appeared and accused the Buddha in a verse of still being bound by snares both human and divine, i.e. still subject to sense-desires. The Buddha denied this and declared, "You are defeated (*nihato* lit. "humiliated"), Antaka!" (SN-a 4:5) A nearly identical exchange occurred shortly after when the Buddha addressed the new bhikkhus sent back by the sixty teachers (SN 4:4).

3:5:36 MĀRA AND THE BUDDHA III—MĀRA'S DAUGHTERS

After dogging the Buddha's foot-steps for seven years, six before the awakening and one after, Māra finally realized that he would never find a moment of defilement on which he could seize and get the Buddha back under his power.[692]

Māra's last attempt to find some fault with the Buddha has the air of desperation about it:

> Are you sunk in sorrow, that you meditate here in the forest?
>
> Have you lost wealth, or do you desire it?
>
> Perhaps you've committed a crime in the village.
>
> Why is it that you don't make friends?
>
> You aren't sociable with anyone!

The Buddha declares his freedom from sorrow, for the desire even for existence and from any sense of "me or mine." He tells Māra, "This you should know, Pāpima. My path you cannot see." Māra then admits that the Buddha has found the path to the deathless (*amata*) but asks him what point there might be in teaching it to others. To this, the Buddha replies that when people ask him about what lies beyond this realm of birth and death, he tells them. Māra finally admits the hopelessness of his task and compares himself to a crab taken from its pond and tortured by village boys. Every time the crab extends one of its claws, the boys would cut it off or smash it. "Even so, sir, you have broken up and cut off all my manoeuvres, tricks and schemes. Now, sir, I am unable to find any opportunity of approach to the Blessed One" (SN 4:24).

The conclusion of the Padhāna Sutta tells us what happened in Māra's own words:

> "For seven years I have followed the Blessed One's footsteps.
>
> I have not found any opportunity, he is fully awake and mindful.
>
> A crow circled around a stone which had the colour of flesh;
>
> 'This may be something tender, this may be something delicious.'
>
> Not obtaining anything edible, the crow departed from there.
>
> Like the crow striking the stone, I have been disappointed in Gotama."
>
> Overcome with grief, the *vīṇa* dropped from his armpit,
>
> And that sad yakkha disappeared from there. (Sn 3:2)

The *vīṇa* was Māra's musical instrument, and it was this same one which was taken up by the gandhabba Pañcasikha, and which he used to play a rather inappropriate love-song in the presence of the Buddha (Sn-a 3:2 & DN 21).

> Then the devaputta Māra, having fallen into despair sat by the highway scratching marks in the dirt with a stick and contemplating the various qualities of the Buddha.

[692] Sn-a 3:2 and SN-a 4:24 define the seven year period. The chronology here is problematic, see the discussion at the end of this section.

"I have not perfected the ten parāmis, so I have not become like him. I have not attained to omniscience, nor reached the great compassion, so have not become like him."

At that time the three daughters of Māra, Taṇhā, Arati and Ragā ("Desire", "Discontent" and "Passion") were looking for him. "Our father is not seen at present, where could be be?" They found him there, sitting by the highway scratching in the ground with a stick. They went up to him and asked, "Why, daddy (*tāta*), are you so sad and unhappy?"

"My dears, the great samaṇa has passed beyond my power. For a long time I have looked for a chance, but I have not been able to see one, that is why I am sad and unhappy."

"If that is so, think not of it. We ourselves will use our power, and having taken him, will bring him here."

"It is not possible, my dears, to use your power on this one. He is unshakeable: established in confidence is this man."

"Daddy, we are women. We will ensnare him with lust and having captured him, bring him here. Do not think about it."

So the three daughters of Māra approached the Blessed One and said, "We will serve at your feet, samaṇa." But the Buddha paid no mind to their speech and did not even open his eyes to look at them.

The daughters of Māra said to one another, "The preferences of men are various. Some have affection for young virgin girls, some for young women, and some for women in middle-age. What if we seduce him in these various forms?" So one by one they each created one hundred forms. They manifested virgin girls, young women who had not yet given birth, those who had given birth once or twice, middle-aged women and older women. Six times these approached the Blessed One and said, "We will serve at your feet, samaṇa." But the Buddha paid no attention to them, for he was sitting in the unsurpassed liberation that is the destruction of the basis of becoming (*anuttare upadhisaṅkhaye vimutto*).[693]

Then the daughters of Māra went off to one side and said to one another, "Our father spoke truth: there is an arahant, a well-farer (*sugato*) in the world. This one is not easily taken by desire. He has escaped Māra's domain. Thus, he sorrows so. If we had attacked any samaṇa not beyond passion with these tactics, either his heart would have burst, or he would have vomited hot blood or he would have lost his mind or he would have dried up, withered and faded away like an old reed." (SN 4:25)

In the Saṃyutta account, each of Māra's daughters in turn then addresses the Buddha with a stanza to which the Buddha replies. Taṇhā's verse repeats that of Māra given above at the beginning of this section starting with "Are you sunk in sorrow, that you meditate here in the forest?" The Buddha replies that he "has conquered the army of the dear and the pleasant and meditates alone, having found bliss." Arati asks more pertinently: how does he meditate that sensual perceptions do not seize him? The gist of the Buddha's answer is that he dwells "without constructing, mindful, without attachment (*asaṅkharāno satimā anoko*)." Ragā's verse is not a question, but a statement. She declares that he will lead many out of the reach of the King of Death (*maccurāja*), presumably meaning her father.

They then returned to their father who berated them for their folly:

You fools! You sought to break a rock with a lotus stalk.

---

693 Jāt-nid. 3. see also SN 4:25 and Dhp 14:1

You tried to cleave a mountain with your nails,

To chew iron with your teeth.

With a great rock on your head, you stepped into the abyss.

It was like knocking your breasts into a post.

You depart from Gotama disappointed. (SN 4:25)

The Jātaka account adds a curious variation, which it qualifies by saying that "although some teachers say this, it should not be believed." In this version, when the daughters appear in the forms of old women "with broken teeth and grey hair" the Buddha says, "and so you shall remain." Although the reason for rejecting this version is not stated, it is presumably because such a command would not be compassionate on the part of the Buddha. We can also assume this never happened because desire, discontent and passion are still very much with us and don't seem to have lost any of their power since the Buddha's day (Jāt-nid 3).

Regarding the beauty of Māra's daughters, it should be remembered that they are Paranimmitavasavatti devīs, representing the very summit of sensuality. Later, when the Buddha rejected the suggestion of marriage to the beauty Māgaṇḍiyā, he recounted how he had not been tempted even by the daughters of Māra, devīs who had "golden bodies free from phlegm and other such impurities." So why would he desire a merely human female, whose body was "like a decorated vessel filled with dung" (Dhp-a 14:1).

A note on the problem of chronology. Fitting these incidents into the chronology of the Buddha's career is problematic. On the one hand, they are clearly meant to occur in close sequence at the end of the seven year period of Māra's close pursuit, but on the other hand, they are located at the Goat Herder's Banyan Tree where the Buddha stayed for the five weeks after his awakening. The three principal sources, the *Dhammapada*, the Māra Saṃyutta and the Jātaka Nidana versions all contain this contradiction to some degree. Various solutions, none of them wholly satisfactory, present themselves. Perhaps the Buddha made a return visit to that locale one year afterwards, although this is nowhere recorded as happening. Perhaps Māra was watching the Bodhisatta for some months before the renunciation. This would contradict the text of the Suttanipāta and Saṃyutta commentaries which explicitly define the period of Māra's close pursuit as comprising the six years of austerities plus the first year after awakening (Sn-a 3:2 & SN-a 4:24). The *Dhammapada* account also marks the beginning of this period at the Bodhisatta's home-leaving (Dhp-a 14:1). It would, however, receive some oblique support from a passage in the *Milindapañha* which says that a "certain deva of Māra's group" tried to tempt the Bodhisatta with world dominion before the home-leaving (Mil 5:3,2 eng. v2 p111). Most likely, the discrepancy may simply be a confusion in the texts between two separate traditions. In the end, the question must be settled arbitrarily, and I have chosen here to place these incidents one year after the awakening.[694]

[694] Bhikkhu Bodhi briefly discusses this issue in the footnotes to his translation of the Saṃyutta Nikāya, CDB, see notes 316 and 322 on pages 421-22

3:5:37 MĀRA AND THE BUDDHA IV—OTHER ENCOUNTERS

Although Māra abandoned his close pursuit of the Buddha, he did not cease altogether from harassing him and attempting to thwart the spread of the Dhamma. Māra returned to his abode in the Paranimmitavasavatti deva realm and from there he checked from time to time on what the Buddha was doing back in the human world (MN-a 49). Several subsequent encounters of Māra and the Buddha are recorded.

Although he clearly should have known by then the futility of the task, Māra occasionally tried to arouse defiled states of mind in the Buddha. Once, when the Buddha was walking on the Gijjhakūṭa Mountain ("Vulture's Peak") Māra shattered some nearby boulders, attempting without success to arouse fear in the Buddha (SN 4:11). On another occasion, Māra tried once more to corrupt the Buddha with the temptation of worldly power:

> In those days, people were oppressed by kings. When the Buddha contemplated the unrighteous actions of kings who would punish and oppress the people, he was moved to compassion and he thought, "Is it possible to exercise rulership without killing or being killed, without conquering or being conquered, without sorrow or causing sorrow? Is it possible to rule righteously?"
>
> Māra knew the thoughts of the Buddha. "The samaṇa Gotama is considering now whether it is possible to exercise sovereignty. It must be that he desires rulership. Now, rulership is a cause of heedlessness. Now I have an opportunity to go to him and make an effort."
>
> Māra went to the Buddha and said, "Blessed One, you have well developed the four *iddhipāda*.[695] If the Blessed One were to wish, 'may the Himavā, king of mountains, become gold', it would become gold. Then with that wealth you could do that which wealth allows, and could rule righteously."
>
> The Buddha replied with a stanza declaring his transcendence of all sense desire and ended by saying to Māra, "I admonish you, Pāpima. Know this, my nature is not the same as your nature. Thus I admonish you." (Dhp-a 23: 8 & SN 4:20)

On two recorded occasions Māra insulted the Buddha as he lay down to sleep. In the first episode, the Buddha lied down mindfully on his right side after doing walking meditation most of the night:

Māra: "Why do you sleep? Why do you sleep?

> What is this? You sleep like a wretch (dubbhago).
>
> (Like a corpse, like one unconscious)
>
> There is an empty hut, so you sleep.
>
> What is this? The sun has risen, and you sleep."[696]

The Buddha replied that if one who is free from attachment desires sleeps, "what is it to you, Māra?" The word *dubbhago* translated here, and by Bhikkhu Bodhi, as "wretch" literally means a person with bad luck. It is the etymological opposite of *bhagavā*, "the blessed one", and may be a deliberate play on words. The commentary adds an additional riposte by the Buddha, "you are like a fly buzzing around hot porridge and, unable to land, only gets

[695] "Bases of power", spiritual qualities that allow for success in any endeavour. The implication here is that these qualities allow for the performance of supernormal feats.

[696] SN 4:7. the line in parentheses is added from the commentary

more irritated" (SN-a 4:7).

The second episode occurred after Devadatta had tried to kill the Buddha by rolling a boulder down the slope of Gijjhakūṭa Mountain, leaving him wounded by a stone splinter in the foot. The Buddha was experiencing severe painful feelings but "he mindfully endured them without mental suffering." When he folded his outer robe to make a mat and lie down on his right side, Māra approached him:

Māra: "Do you sleep out of laziness? (*mandiyā*) Or are you intoxicated by poetry?

(Like a poet who thinks up poems, until he is drunk with them)

You must not have much to do!

Alone on your solitary bed,

Sleepy-faced, why do you doze?"[697]

The Buddha replied in three stanzas, the gist of his reply being, "My mind is at peace, so why shouldn't I sleep?" Māra then disappeared.

Unable to find a flaw in the Buddha, Māra focussed his efforts on attempting to obstruct his teaching. At one time the Buddha was discoursing on the Dhamma before a large assembly. Māra thought, "I shall make them blind (*vicakkhukammāya*)." The commentary explains that this means to destroy the "wisdom eye" (*paññācakkhu*) of the assembly, in other words to confuse them with a terrifying sound or vision. Māra then addressed the Buddha:

Māra: "Why do you roar like a lion, so confident before the assembly?

There is indeed a rival wrestler (*paṭimallo*), so why do you think you are the victor?"

Buddha: "The great heroes (*mahāvīrā*) are confident before the assemblies,

The Tathāgatas of great power, having overcome desire for the three worlds." (SN 4:12)

The Buddha's confidence before the assemblies recalls the Parisā Sutta of the *Aṅguttara Nikāya*. There, the Buddha is said to appear incognito in various assemblies both human and non-human, to speak on the dhamma. One of these assemblies is that of Māra's company (AN 8: 69). We are not told how Māra reacted to the dhamma being preached in his own inner sanctum, but we can well imagine that he was not pleased. This counter-tactic of the Buddha's, together with the allusion to "rival wrestlers" illustrates that the relationship between these two had something of the nature of a struggle about it. It was a conflict for the minds of beings, with Māra always attempting to keep them "bound in his snares" of desire and fear, and the Buddha attempting to set them free.

On another occasion, Māra again attempted to "blind" the wisdom-eye of the assembly and accused the Buddha of getting caught up in the attachment and aversion of teaching, in other words the vanity of praise and blame. The Buddha replied that he taught only out of compassion for others, and Māra being disappointed once more, disappeared (SN 4:14). Māra would also attempt to create distractions when the Buddha was instructing his disciples. At one time while the Buddha was teaching the bhikkhus, Māra took the form of an ox and threatened to blunder into the row of alms bowls which the bhikkhus had left outside to dry in the sun (SN 4:16). On another similar occasion, a sudden earth-splitting noise at first frightened the bhikkhus until the Buddha told them that the earth was not splitting open, it was only Māra (SN 4:17).

[697] SN 4:13 the line in parentheses is added from the commentary. The word *mandiyā* translated here at "laziness" might also mean "stupidity" or "dullness." Bhikkhu Bodhi translates it as "in a daze."

One such episode turned out a little differently. Māra attempted to disrupt one of the Buddha's discourses by appearing as a roughly dressed farmer asking about his missing oxen. The Buddha as usual recognized him: "What do you have to do with oxen, Pāpima?" But this time, instead of disappearing as soon as he was recognized, Māra attempted to challenge the Buddha in front of the assembled bhikkhus.

"The eye is mine, samāṇa, visible forms are mine, eye-consciousness is mine, eye-contact is mine. The ear is mine, sounds are mine, ear-consciousness is mine, ear-contact is mine. The nose is mine, odours are mine, nose-consciousness is mine, nose-contact is mine. The tongue is mine, flavours are mine, tongue-consciousness is mine, tongue-contact is mine. The body is mine, tactile sensations are mine, body-consciousness is mine, body contact is mine. The mind is mine, mind-objects are mine, mind-consciousness is mine, mind-contact is mine. Where can you go, samāṇa, to escape me?"

The Buddha acknowledges that all six senses are within Māra's domain and belong to him. But he goes on to say:

"Pāpima, where there is no eye, no ear, no nose, no tongue, no body, no mind, no visible forms, no sound, no odours, no flavours, no tactile sensations, no mind-objects, no eye-consciousness etc., no eye-contact etc., there you cannot go."

Māra: "That which is called 'mine' and those who say 'it is mine'. If your mind is like this, you won't escape me, samāṇa."

Buddha: "I am not one who speaks of 'me' and 'mine',

Know this Pāpima, you cannot see my path."

Then Māra Pāpima disappeared from that place. (SN 4:19)

Māra was capable of taking possession of other beings and using them for his purposes. The verb rendered "to possess" is *anvāvisati* in Pali, and might also be translated as "to enter into."

At one time the Buddha went into the brahmin village of Pañcasālā for alms, but Māra possessed the villagers and planted the thought in their minds, "don't let the samāṇa Gotama get any alms." So after walking for alms, the Buddha left the village with his bowl as clean as when he had entered it.

Then Māra approached the Blessed One, "Did you get any alms, samāṇa?" "Was it you, Pāpima, that made it so that I didn't receive any alms?" "Well then, sir, go into the village a second time and I will make sure you do get some alms."

(But Māra lied when he said this; he intended for the Buddha to be mocked by the village boys).

The Buddha replied to Māra:

"You make demerit Māra, when you insult the Tathāgata.

Do you think, Pāpima, that your evil deed (*pāpa*) has no result?

We live in bliss (*sukha*), who have nothing at all.

We shall feed on rapture (*pīti*) like the Abhāssara Devas"[698]

The Buddha's reply is to remind Māra that despite his high station within *saṃsāra*, he is himself still trapped within it, and so subject to the results of his own deeds. (We shall see this idea developed further when we consider Māra's encounter with Moggallāna). The Abhāssara Devas are beings in the brahmā world who are beyond sensuality and physical food. Their level of consciousness is equivalent to second jhāna, of which *pīti* and *sukha* are both factors (see § 3:6,8).

Some of Māra's encounters with the Buddha took the form of simple dialogues or debates. Māra once appeared before the Buddha and declared that, "He who has sons, delights in them. He who has cattle, delights in them." The Buddha replies that, "He who has sons, sorrows over sons. He who has cattle, sorrows over cattle" (SN 4:8). In another encounter, Māra declares that "Human life is long, death has not yet come, the wise man lives like a suckling baby." Māra, as a deva living more than nine billion years, obviously cannot believe this himself. The Buddha replies that "Human life is short, the wise man lives as if his turban is on fire" (SN 4:9). One of these exchanges is a little different: Māra is not seen challenging the Buddha but seems to be genuinely curious. He appeared before the Buddha disguised in the form of "a certain man" (*aññataro puriso*) and asked, "Sir, what is meant by 'crossing over to the far shore'? (*pāraṃ pāranti*)." The Buddha knew immediately that it was Māra and replied, "Pāpima, what have you to do with 'crossing over'? Only those who are free from desire can cross over" (Dhp-a 26:3).

[698] SN 4:18. Sentence in parentheses taken from the commentary.

3:5:38 MĀRA AND THE BUDDHA V—PARINIBBĀNA

Māra's final encounter with the Buddha occurred three months before his passing into *parinibbāna*.[699] The following is a summary account of the essential details:

> The Buddha was dwelling in Vesāli. He asked Ānanda to accompany him for the day's abiding to the Cāpāla Cetiya.

Ānanda was the Buddha's attendant. A cetiya is a kind of shrine or memorial, later often called a *stupa*. The Cāpāla Cetiya was a pre-Buddhist sacred site which had been turned into a *vihāra*, i.e a dwelling place for bhikkhus. The commentary tells us that it had previously been the residence of a yakkha named Cāpāla.

> Having reached the Cāpāla Cetiya, the Buddha sat down on a prepared seat. He addressed Ānanda in these words:
>
> "Delightful, Ānanda, is Vesāli. Delightful is the Udena Cetiya, the Gotamaka Cetiiya, the Sattamba Cetiya, the Bahuputta Cetiya, the Sārandada Cetiya. Delightful is the Cāpāla Cetiya.
>
> "Whoever, Ānanda, has thoroughly mastered the four *iddhipādā* ("bases of power", spiritual qualities that give success to any endeavour, including the psychic powers) may, if he wishes, live for a kappa or the remainder of a kappa (*kappāvasesa*)."

This passage has been the source of some controversy, hinging on the meaning here of "a kappa or the remainder of a kappa." The word *kappa* usually refers to a very long period of time, the life-cycle of an entire world-system. Thus, the straightforward reading would be that the Buddha is here claiming that he could prolong his life to the end of the world. However, the commentary explains that the kappa referred to here is an āyukappa, or full life-span. A full human life-span varies with the various periods of the cosmic cycle, at the time of the Buddha, it was defined as one hundred years. The commentary goes on to define *kappāvasesa* as meaning "a century, or a little more." This seems a strained interpretation of *vasesa*, which means "remainder or residue," almost the opposite of "a little more than." But the commentary goes on to make a couple of cogent arguments in defence of this interpretation. The Buddha was gravely ill, and had been so for ten months already. He was only suppressing the disease through constant efforts in meditation. The Buddha had reached four fifths of the full span of human life and his body was broken and deteriorating; he was only remaining alive for the sake of his disciples and *parinibbāna* now seemed dear (*piya*) to him. More cogently, the commentary calls this present kappa a *bhaddakappa*, ("a fortunate kappa"), which means that this world-system during its total life will see the arising of five Buddhas. The implications are not spelled out here, but it follows that if Gotama Buddha (who was the fourth) were to remain alive until the end of the kappa, he would be for some time co-existent with Metteya Buddha (who will be the fifth). This would mean that two Buddhas would exist at once in the same world-system, which is stated elsewhere to be an impossibility (MN 115 & DN 19).

> But even though the Buddha had given such a clear sign, Ānanda did not implore the Buddha to remain "for the welfare and happiness of the world," because his mind was pervaded (*pariyuṭṭhitacitto*) by Māra. The Buddha made his statement a second and third time, but still Ānanda did not comprehend the clear sign, because his mind was pervaded by Māra.

---

699 I.e. the end of life, cessation of the bodily and mental formations. The Buddhist tradition does not speak of the "death" of a fully awakened being because the ordinary process of death followed by subsequent rebirth has ceased.

The commentary explains that Māra is able to pervade anyone's mind with the *vipallāsā* ("distortions" or "hallucinations") who has not gone beyond them. Ānanda was a sotāpanna, ("stream-enterer," a person at the first level of awakening) so he had gone beyond the vipallāsa of views, but not of those of the mind or of perceptions. So Māra pervaded his mind with a frightful vision so that even though the Buddha's clear sign was "right in his face" (*mukhena hatthaṃ*) he was unable to comprehend its meaning.

> Then the Buddha said to Ānanda, "You may go now, and do as you wish." And Ānanda, taking his leave, went and sat under another nearby tree.
>
> And soon after Ānanda had left, Māra approached the Buddha. Standing to one side he addressed the Blessed One:
>
> "Enter *parinibbāna* now, venerable sir, Blessed One (*parinibbātu dāni, bhante, bhagavā*). Enter *parinibbāna* now, Well-Farer (*sugato*). Now is the time for *parinibbāna*, venerable sir. It was said previously by the Blessed One, 'I will not enter *parinibbāna* until my bhikkhus and male lay disciples, my bhikkhunis and female lay disciples, become well-trained, learned, confident, knowing the Dhamma by heart and practicing the Dhamma well, and until they can teach the Dhamma, explaining and analyzing it and refuting the doctrines held by others, until they can manifest the wonder of teaching (*sappāṭihāriyaṃ dhammaṃ desessantī* or "teach with the manifestation of wonders"). But now your disciples have accomplished all of these things. Enter *parinibbāna* now, venerable sir, Blessed One. Enter *parinibbāna* now, Well-Farer. Now is the time for *parinibbāna*, venerable sir, Blessed One!"

Māra's speech here is much abbreviated from the original which has many repetitions. It is to be noted that Māra speaks to the Buddha in a very respectful way, using his epithets *bhagavā* and *sugato* and addressing him as *bhante*. This may be mere pretence on Māra's part, but the possibility that Māra has at the end has come to have some genuine respect for the Buddha is an appealing one that cannot be ruled out. After all, he has closely watched this man for more than a half century and in all that time not found a single weakness which he could exploit. Be this as it may, Māra still has an agenda and wants very much to see the Buddha leave the world. No doubt the possibility that the Buddha could remain in existence for the rest of the kappa must have appalled Māra.

On a linguistic note, which has some doctrinal significance, the first time that Māra asks the Buddha to end his life, he uses an imperative verb, *parinibbātu,* which could be rendered literally as "extinguish" or "blow out" as with a candle.[700]

Then the Buddha replied to Māra: "Be at ease, Pāpima. It won't be long now until the Tathāgata enters *parinibbāna* (*parinibbānaṃ bhavissati* lit. "will become extinguished"). In three months from now, the Tathāgata will enter *parinibbāna*."

> There, at the Cāpāla Cetiya, the Blessed One mindfully and with clear comprehension (*sato sampajāno*) relinquished the life-principle (āyusaṅkhāra). When the Blessed One relinquished the life-principle, there was a great earthquake and thundering, dreadful and terrifying.[701]

This was to be the last time Māra approached the Buddha. The commentary emphasizes that the Buddha did not make his decision based on Māra's pleading, nor on that of Ānanda's, but only according to his own wishes and the

700 See PED for *nibbāna* and *nibbāpeti*

701 DN 16, SN 51:10, Ud 6,1. The three accounts are almost identical. The references to the commentaries mostly refer to the Udāna Aṭṭhakatha

well-being of his teaching and his disciples (Ud-a 6:1).

It is to be noted that although he was sitting nearby, Ānanda was unaware of the presence of Māra and of his exchange with the Buddha. That Māra was invisible to Ānanda is not unusual, but it seems that the conversation must have been silent as well, carried on directly mind to mind. A little later, the Buddha informs Ānanda of Māra's visit and then Ānanda begs the Buddha to remain for the duration of a kappa. But too late![702]

702 DN 16. Ānanda would later be criticized for this by the elders at the First Council, see Vin. Cv 11

3:5:39 MĀRA'S ENCOUNTERS WITH OTHERS I —THE BHIKKHUNĪS OF ANDHAVANA

Māra did not confine his attention to the Buddha, but also attempted to divert his disciples from the path. There is, for instance, a short collection recounting Māra's attempts to tempt bhikkhunīs practicing in solitude. These stories are found in the Bhikkhunīsaṃyutta of the Saṃyutta Nikāya, (SN 5:1 f.) and they follow a fixed formula. The sutta begins with the bhikkhunī having gone for alms, resorting to the woods of the Andhavana ("Blind Grove" or "Dark Grove") for alms. This must have been a forbidding place – it certainly had a grim history. Back in the time of Kassapa Buddha five hundred thieves waylaid, blinded and robbed a lay disciple there. Because he was a sotāpanna, the thieves' kamma was immediate and they all went blind. They lived there in that forest for the remainder of their lives, and so it gotits name (SN-a 5:1).

In that grim place she was approached by Māra, who desired to arouse "fear, stupefaction and terror" (*bhayaṃ chambhitattaṃ lomahaṃsaṃ*) in her and so to make her fail in her practice. Māra would recite a stanza of verse, playing upon some possible human weakness. The bhikkhunī, hearing this, would ask herself, "Who is reciting this verse? Is it a human being or a non-human being? It is Māra Pāpima!" and she would then utter a reply. Māra would realize that "she knows me!" and "sad and unhappy, he would disappear from that place."[703]

Māra's attacks on the bhikkhunis illustrate a wide gamut of his tricks. Of course, he tried using his most obvious weapon, sensual desire:

(to Āḷavikā)

> There is no escaping this world, what use is seclusion?
>
> Enjoy sensual delights, or you will regret it later. (SN 5:1)

(to Vijayā)

> You are a young woman, with a beautiful body. I am a young man.
>
> Come, lady, let us enjoy the music of a five-piece ensemble. (SN 5:4)

Māra is not above using grief as a possible point of weakness. Kisāgotamī had lost a child:

(to Kisāgotamī)

> Your son is dead, why do you sit alone with a sorrowful face?
>
> Alone in the middle of a forest, do you seek for a man?[704]

Sensual pleasure is not limited to the earthly kind, and nor are Māra's snares:

(to Upacālā)

> There are Tāvatiṃsa, Yāma, Tusita, Nimmānarati and Vasavatti devas.
>
> Direct your mind there, and you shall experience their delights. (SN 5:7)

---

703 these elements common to all suttas in SN 5:1 f.

704 SN 5:3. The story of how Kisāgotamī had transcended her grief is told at Dhp-a 8:13.

Māra's two principal weapons are sensuality and fear, and his approach to Uppalavaṇṇā blended the two:

(to Uppalavaṇṇā)

Bhikkhuni, having come here you stand at the root of the flowering sāl tree.

Your beauty is second to none.

You fool, are you not afraid of wicked men? (SN 5:5)

Another form of desire is the desire for being, (*bhavtaṇhā*) and Māra uses that as well:

(to Cālā)

Why don't you like birth? Once born, a being can enjoy sensual pleasure.

Who told you, bhikkhuni, not to like birth? (SN 5:6)

Māra can also prey upon a person's insecurities, and he made this attempt also with one of the bhikkhunis:

(to Somā)

That state which is hard to attain, is attained by the seers.

It is not to be had by women, with their two-fingered wisdom (*dvaṅgulapañña*). (SN 5:2)

In the patriarchal society of ancient India many women must have laboured under a sense of inferiority, but Somā was well beyond this. She replied that "womanhood doesn't matter to the well trained mind … one who thinks, 'I am a man' or 'I am a woman' or 'I am anything else', that one should Māra address" (ibid.). *Dvaṅgulapañña* might also be rendered as "two-inches of wisdom." Māra's statement is clearly meant to imply that women don't have enough wisdom to develop higher states of consciousness. The commentary explains this phrase as meaning that women have limited wisdom, just enough to hold a thread with two fingers while sewing (SN-a 5:2).

Māra can also attempt to corrupt beings at a higher level, by suggesting wrong views:

(to Selā)

By whom was this puppet (*bimba*, i.e. the body) made?

Who is the maker of this puppet?

From where did this puppet originate?

Where will this puppet vanish to? (SN 5:9)

(to Vajirā)

By whom was this being (satta) made?

Who is the maker of this being?

From where did this being originate?

Where will this being vanish to? (SN 5:10)

Māra's attempts to corrupt the bhikkhunīs of the Andhavana were without result, as they were all awakened beings. They knew him right away for who he was and made suitable replies. Ālavikā stated that "sense desires are like swords" (SN 5:1). Upacālā that "all realms of rebirth are under Māra's bondage, all are on fire," (SN 5:7) and Vijayā, whom Māra tried to seduce in the form of a handsome youth, spoke about the foulness of the body (SN 5:4). Uppalavaṇṇā's reply was a little different. She was the bhikkhunī who was foremost in mastery of the psychic powers, (AN 1:237) the female counterpart of Moggallāna:

Should a hundred thousand wicked men like you come here.

My hair will not be raised, I will not be afraid.

Though I am alone, I do not fear you Māra.

I can disappear, or enter into your belly.

I can stand among your eyelashes, and you wouldn't see me there.

I have mastered my mind, and the bases of power (*iddhipādā*).

I am freed from all bonds, so I don't fear you friend (āvuso). (SN 5:5)

3:5:40 MĀRA'S ENCOUNTERS WITH OTHERS II—MOGGALLĀNA

A text in the Majjhima Nikāya[705] is of particular interest for the light it sheds on Māra's nature and history. It involves an attempt by Māra to bother Moggallāna, who was one of the Buddha's two chief disciples, renowned for his mastery of the psychic powers:

> Mahāmoggallāna was outside his hut, doing walking meditation. Māra went into his belly and penetrated into his stomach. Moggallāna wondered, "Why is my stomach so heavy? It feels like it is full of wet beans!" So Moggallāna left his walking path, entered into his dwelling and sat down on the prepared seat. Having sat down, he carefully investigated the matter, and he saw that Māra had entered into his stomach. He said, "Depart, Pāpima! Do not plague the Tathāgata or the Tathāgata's disciples, or it will cause unhappiness and suffering for you, for a long time."
>
> Māra thought, "This samaṇa does not know me, he does not see me. Even his teacher would not know me so quickly, so how can his disciple know me?" But Moggallāna said, "I do indeed know you, Pāpima. I know you are thinking that I do not know you or see you, that even my teacher would not know you so quickly, so how could his disciple? Depart Pāpima! Do not make long suffering and unhappiness for yourself!"
>
> Māra then thought, "This samāṇa does indeed know me", and he left through Moggallāna's mouth and stood in the doorway. Moggallāna said to him, "I see you there, Pāpima. Do not think, "he does not see me". You are standing in the doorway, Pāpima."
>
> Moggallāna goes on to tell Māra a story about a past life, when he himself had been Māra:
>
> "In a previous existence, Pāpima, I was Māra. My name was Dūsi, I had a sister named Kāḷī and you were her son. So you were my nephew."
>
> The commentary explains Moggallāna's reason for telling this story to Māra:
>
> The elder thought, "The celestial devas find the smell of humans repulsive even a hundred *yojana* away. And yet Māra, an urbane (*nāgariko*), immaculate (*paricokkho*), very powerful and majestic devarāja entered into my belly, cooking there in that foul place. And he sat in that loathsome space with the intention of doing an evil deed. Another would be ashamed to treat his relative thus. I shall reply to the hostility of my kinsman with kind words." (MN-a 50)

The commentary also explains that although this Māra was Māra Dūsi's nephew, we should not assume that the position of Māra, or of any *devarāja* (king of devas) is hereditary. When one Māra dies, someone else who has made the appropriate kamma is born into that role (ibid.).

Although it is intriguing to speculate on the identity of Dūsi's sister Kāḷī, and her possible connection to the Hindu goddess of that name, the commentary tells us nothing more about her, and she appears nowhere else in the texts. *Kāḷī* means "dark" or "black" and was a fairly common name; the DPPN lists nine women of that name.[706] Being named "The Dark One" did not necessarily have any sinister or demonic connotations, and in most cases referred only to a dark complexion. Two of the Kāḷīs found in the texts did have something of a "dark" aspect in the other sense of the word. One was a yakkhī who ate children, (Dhp-a 1:4) and the other was an attendant at a burning ground, responsible

---

705 MN 50, the Māratajjanīya Sutta

706 A derivation from *kāla* "time" is unlikely because that word is never spelled with a retroflex ḷ, see PED s.v. *kāla*.

for performing cremations. She is described as a "huge woman with a crow-like body." This Kāḷī was nevertheless a devout person. She provided fresh bodies for bhikkhus intent on corpse meditation, and at one time made a milk-bowl out of a human skull and gave it to the elder Mahākāḷa.[707] This does sound rather tantric, and suggests a possible precursor to the Hindu Kālī, a goddess who makes her first appearance in the literature some centuries later.[708]

Returning to Moggallāna's story:

> At that time, the Buddha Kakusandha had appeared in the world. His two chief disciples were named Vidhura and Sañjīva. The Māra Dūsi thought, "I do not know the comings and goings (āgatiṃ vā gatiṃ) of these good bhikkhus. What if I were to possess (*anvāvisati*) these brahmin house-holders and tell them to abuse, scold, revile and harass those good bhikkhus? Perhaps if they are so abused, it will bring a change to their minds so that I can find an opportunity."

The commentary explains that Māra not knowing the bhikkhus "coming and going" means that when one died, Māra was unable to determine where he had been reborn (MN-a 50). This implies the bhikkhu was an arahant and had entered *nibbāna* which is beyond Māra's ken.

> So the brahmin householders, possessed by Māra Dūsi, abused the bhikkhus. "These so-called samaṇas (*samaṇakā*), dark, menial off-spring of the kinsman's feet (*bandhupādāpaccā*), they say 'We meditate! We meditate!' With drooping shoulders and downcast faces, weak and stiff they meditate (*jhāyanti*), they pine (*pajjhāyanti*), they fret (*nijjhāyanti*), they ponder (*apajhāyanti*). They meditate, they pine, they fret, they ponder like an owl in a tree waiting for a rat to come along … like a jackal by the river-bank waiting for a fish to come along … like a cat by a rubbish pile waiting for a mouse to come along … like a donkey with his burden taken off … they meditate, they pine, they fret, they ponder."

The brahmins were displaying a nasty caste prejudice by calling the bhikkhus "dark and menial." The bhikkhus, of course, were drawn from all castes and this was a scandal to the haughty brahmins. The phrase *bandhupādāpaccā* "offspring of the kinsman's feet" is a common one in similar contexts, (eg. DN 3 & DN 27) and refers to the brahminical origin myth whereby the different castes sprang from different parts of Brahma's body; the brahmins from his mouth and the *suddas* (the menial caste), from his feet. The series of verbs used to describe the bhikkhus' meditation involves a play on the word *jhāyati*, "to meditate" or more literally, "to do jhāna."

The sutta goes on to state that most of these brahmins after death were reborn in *niraya*. This implies that Māra's possession of a being is not complete control but rather a malign influence. If the brahmin's actions were not volitional, there would be no kammic result.

For his part, the Buddha Kakusandha urged his bhikkhus to practice the meditation of the four *brahmavihāras* ("divine abidings", in English usually given as loving-kindness, compassion, sympathetic joy and equanimity). In this way, they did not allow the brahmins' abuse to arouse thoughts of ill-will, and they did not give any opening to Māra Dūsi. Being frustrated in his endeavour, Māra Dūsi tried a different tack:

> So Māra Dūsi thought to himself, "Despite my actions, I still do not know the comings and goings of these good bhikkhus. What if I were to possess the brahmins and tell them to honour, respect, revere and venerate the bhikkhus? Perhaps if they are so honoured, it will bring a change to their minds so that I can find an opportunity."

707 Tha 8: 6. See also Dhp 1: 6

708 Around 600 A.D. See *Britannica Library*, s.v. "Kali," accessed January 4, 2017, http://library.eb.com/levels/referencecenter/article/44396

The brahmins who followed his advice this time went on to rebirth in the deva realms. The Buddha Kakusandha urged his bhikkhus to practice meditations which counter mind-states of greed and sensuality: the foulness of the body, the repulsiveness of nutriment, disenchantment with the world and impermanence. In this way, the bhikkhus did not entertain mind-states of greed and so once again, Māra Dūsi found no opening. But he did not give up. Moggallāna continues the tale of his former existence:

> Then the Buddha Kakusandha went into the village for alms, followed by the elder Vidhura. The Māra Dūsi possessed a certain boy and caused him to throw a rock at Vidhura's head. Vidhura continued to walk behind the Buddha with his scalp split open and blood trickling down. The Buddha Kakusandha turned and looked with his elephant's look (*nāgāpalokita*). "This Māra Dūsi does not know any limit." As the Buddha looked at him, Māra Dūsi died from that place and was reborn in Mahāniraya.

The "elephant look" of a Buddha refers to the characteristic of all Buddhas that when they turn to look behind them, they do not turn just their neck, but their whole body, like an elephant does. According to the commentary, the bones of a Buddha's neck are not flexible like those of ordinary people, but are fixed in place. Also from the commentary:

> Māra Dūsi did not die there, but returned to the Vasavatti deva realm and died from that place to be reborn in *niraya*. The Buddha's look did not cause his death. He died because he had struck a Noble Disciple and that caused the cutting short of his life-span.

> Moggallāna goes on to describe his sufferings in Mahāniraya:

> My body had a human form, but I had there the head of a fish. The nirayapālas impaled me with stakes. They told me "Friend (*mārisa*), when one stake meets another in your heart, you will know a thousand years have gone by." I suffered in that *niraya* for many years, many hundreds of years, many thousands of years.

The sutta concludes with Moggallāna admonishing Māra in a long series of verses, declaring his own power and warning Māra that by attacking such a bhikkhu, he will incur much suffering. The concluding stanzas are a final warning:

> There has never been found a fire
>
> Which intends, 'Let me burn the fool.'
>
> But a fool who assaults a fire
>
> Burns himself by his own doing.
>
> So it is with you, O Māra.
>
> By assaulting the Tathāgata,
>
> You generate much demerit.
>
> Evil One (*pāpima*), do you imagine that your evil (*pāpa*) will not ripen?
>
> Doing thus, you store up evil
>
> Which will last long, O End-Maker!

Māra, shun the Enlightened One,

Play no more your tricks on bhikkhus!"

So the bhikkhu chastened Māra

In the Bhesakaḷa thicket

Whereupon the sombre spirit (*yakkha*)

Disappeared right then and there.[709]

The story of Māra Dūsi illustrates an important concept: in Buddhism there is no irredeemable or absolute evil. This Māra was, if anything, more hurtful and wicked than the Māra of the Buddha Gotama's time. As a result of his actions he suffered immediate result of his kamma and was reborn in a terrible *niraya* world, but in spite of all this he went on to eventually become a fully awakened and liberated being as the Buddha's disciple Moggallāna.

[709] MN 50. The final verses are Bhikkhu Bodhi's translation, MLDB, p. 438.

3:5:41 MĀRA'S ENCOUNTERS WITH OTHERS III —DEVAS AND BRAHMĀS

Māra's power extends over the entire *kāmabhūmi* ("plane of sense-desire") and to some degree, even beyond that. In one recorded instance, he possessed the mind of a deva and caused him to utter a stanza in praise of seeking rebirth in the deva realm (SN 2:30). We have seen how the devas fled before Māra's host at the time of the Buddha's awakening. The *Mahāsamaya Sutta* (DN 20) records another occasion when a great host of devas assembled to pay respects to the Buddha, and this time the Buddha's power thwarted Māra's attack. After a very long list of all the various devas and other beings, the sutta concludes:

All the devas had come, with Inda and with Brahmā.

Māra's army also came, now see Kaṅha's("the Black One's") folly.

"Come! Seize them! Capture them! Bind them with passion!

Surround them! Let no one escape!"

Thus did the great general exhort his dark army.!

Striking the ground with his hand, he made a frightful noise.

Like a storm in the rainy season, with thunder and lightning.

But then withdrew, enraged and powerless.

The All-Knowing One (i.e. the Buddha) saw and understood.

Then the Teacher warned his disciples:

"Know this bhikkhus, Māra's army has come."

Having heard, the disciples remained vigilant.

Those without passion cannot be moved by desire or by fear.

Winning every battle, glorious, beyond fear.

All beings rejoice at the victory of his disciples. (DN 20)

The commentary explains that the Buddha thwarted Māra's assault by using his power so that the assembled devas neither saw nor heard Māra's frightful manifestations (MN-a 20).

Māra's primary dominion is the *kāmabhūmi* ("plane of sense-desire") which includes the realms of humans and devas, but to some degree he also has power within the lower reaches of the *rūpabhūmi* ("plane of form"), the realm of the brahmā deities. We have already seen how Mahābrahmā fled together with the other devas in the face of Māra's host (Jāt-nid 2). The Brahmanimantanika Sutta (MN 49) recounts a visit of the Buddha to the brahmāloka and Māra's attempts to interfere with his teaching there. We shall postpone a more detailed consideration of this sutta until the chapter on the brahmā worlds, and at this time shall only look at what it tells us about Māra and the upper limits of his authority.

The brahmās are deities on a higher plane than the devas, and they are beyond sensual desire. This means that one of Māra's principal inducements is useless there. Instead, he uses the defilements of false view (*micchādiṭṭhi*) and desire of being (*bhavataṇhā*) against them. The brahmās are divided into various levels which correspond to the levels of jhāna (meditative absorption), as we shall see in more detail later. Although it is said in one place that Māra's domain is the whole of *saṃsāra*, (AN-a 8:29) the Brahmanimantanika Sutta gives good reason to suppose that he has no effective power beyond the brahmā worlds of the first jhāna level. The commentary states explicitly that Māra can possess the minds of *brahmapārisajja* brahmās but not that of higher level brahmās. The *brahmapārisajja* brahmās ("brahmā's assembly") are the lowest of three classes of first jhāna brahmās. However, Māra does seem to have an indirect influence on Baka the Mahābrahmā who is the principal protagonist of this sutta. The reason the Buddha decided to intervene is that Baka had fallen under the delusion that he is the supreme being, a delusion that is supported by lesser brahmās who are possessed by Māra directly. Māra is described as being angry that the Buddha is teaching there, and that thousands of brahmās are in danger of escaping his sway; they are said to be "in his hands." Māra had followed the Buddha in invisible form (MN-a 49) and spoke only through the medium of brahmās under his possession, but of course this did not fool the Buddha, who called him to account.

The consciousness of brahmās is equivalent to that experienced in the four jhānas, states of deep meditative absorption. The various levels of the brahmā worlds are ranked according to their corresponding jhānas, and the jhānas are defined by the presence or absence of certain mental factors. It would be too long a digression to explain this fully here,[710] but suffice it to say that *vitakka-vicāra*, usually translated as "applied and sustained thought" are present in first jhāna but absent in the higher jhānas. Baka lives in the brahmā world which corresponds to first jhāna,[711] and so Māra is able to use discursive thought and argument to influence him, but not sensuality. We do not hear of Māra ever working his mischief in any higher brahmā realm. Those beings are beyond ordinary thought as well, so Māra has no useful weapon left to wield against them. Jhāna is said to "blindfold Māra," (MN 25) by suppression of the hindrances one becomes temporarily removed from his power. This corresponds to the condition of the higher brahmās. They are beyond his immediate reach, but have not escaped his dominion absolutely because they are still subject to rebirth and falling into a lower state of being.[712]

[710] See § 3:6,8 for a fuller discussion.

[711] The DPPN identifies him as an Abhassara level brahmā but this is an error.

[712] Except for those anāgāmīs born into the Suddhāvāsa Realms, see § 3:6,17.

3:5:42 OTHER EPISODES CONCERNING MĀRA

Māra sometimes assumes various disguises in his attempts to divert seekers from the path. In one instance he approached some young bhikkhus in the form of an elderly brahmin ascetic, "with his hair matted in a top-knot, wearing a cloak of cheetah hide, old, bent and wheezing, leaning on a staff." He advised them to enjoy sensual pleasures while they were still young, but the bhikkhus resisted his blandishments and he departed "shaking his head, wagging his tongue and with a furrowed brow." When told of the encounter, the Buddha pronounced that "this was no brahmin but Māra Pāpima come to make you blind" (*vicakkhummāya* i.e. "to confuse you.") (SN 4:21)

Sūrambaṭṭha was the lay disciple called "foremost in unshakeable confidence" (AN 1: 255). Upon hearing the Buddha discourse on the Dhamma he attained to the state of a sotāpanna (first stage of awakening). Māra then paid him a clandestine visit:

> Then Māra thought, "This one called Sūrambaṭṭha belongs to me, but today the Teacher got a hold of him. One who hears the Teacher has the path manifest for him. I must know whether he has escaped from my sphere or not." So Māra assumed the form of the Buddha, together with the thirty-two marks, and bearing robe and bowl appeared at Sūrambaṭṭha's door. Sūrambaṭṭha thought, "The Buddha has come back. Buddhas do not come for no reason, I wonder why he has returned?" He greeted the Buddha respectfully and asked him for the reason for his return visit. In the guise of the Buddha, Māra said, "Sūrambaṭṭha, in giving you a talk on Dhamma, I neglected one point. I had said that the five aggregates (*khandā*—constituents of body and mind) are all impermanent, suffering and without a self. But they are not all like that. There is one that is permanent, stable and eternal."
>
> But Sūrambaṭṭha thought, "This statement is very grave. Buddhas are never careless in their teaching. This is indeed Māra, the enemy of the Buddha," and he said, "You are Māra!" The words of the noble disciple were like a hatchet blow, which Māra could not withstand. "Yes, I am Māra." Sūrambaṭṭha declared, "Should a hundred thousand Māras come here, my faith in the Buddha would not be shaken." He snapped his fingers at Māra and ordered, "Begone from my doorway." Māra could not remain there, but disappeared straight away. (AN-a 1: 255)

Māra often feigns an interest in the well-being of his intended victims, as in the following episode:

The bhikkhu Godhika six times attained to *sāmāyika cetovimutti* ("temporary liberation of mind") and six times fell away from that state because of an illness affecting his wind, bile and phlegm. Upon reaching the temporary liberation of mind a seventh time, he thought "Six times have I fallen away from this state. What if I were now to wield the knife?" (i.e. commit suicide).

> Māra knew the mind of the bhikkhu and he thought, "This bhikkhu intends to wield the knife. One who wields the knife is indifferent to life. Having established insight (*vipassana*) they can attain arahantship. I must prevent him from doing so. He will not heed my words, so I shall have the Teacher stop him."
>
> Māra approached the Blessed One in disguise and spoke the following verses:
>
> > Great Hero, Great Wise One, glorious and powerful
> >
> > You who have transcended all fear and enmity,
> >
> > I bow down at your feet, Possessor of Vision.

Conqueror of death,

A disciple of the Great Hero wishes for death.

Forbid him, O Resplendent One!

How, O Blessed One, can a disciple devoted to your teaching,

A student who has not reached the goal, do this thing, O Famous One!

At that very moment, Godhika used the knife. The Buddha, knowing it was Māra who addressed him, spoke the following stanza:

So the wise do, who do not yearn for life.

Having torn up the root of craving, Godhika has attained final *nibbāna.*

Then the Buddha went with a company of bhikkhus to the place where Godhika lay dead. At that same moment, Māra was thinking, "Where has this elder's rebirth consciousness established itself?" The Buddha pointed out to the monks a smoky dark shape searching about in all directions. "This, bhikkhus, is Māra Pāpima, seeking the consciousness of the clansman Godhika. But the consciousness of Godhika is not established anywhere, he has attained final *nibbāna.*"[713]

This sutta raises a number of important doctrinal issues. What, for instance, is meant by *sāmāyika cetovimutti,* "temporary liberation of mind"? The *Saṃyutta Commentary* defines it as "with momentarily repeated application (*appitappitakkhaṇe*) he is freed from obstructive states, and is intent on the object of a mundane attainment" (SN-a 4:23). The corresponding passage in the *Dhammapada* version (Dhp-a 4:11) specifically identifies it with jhāna. Whatever its exact nature, sāmāyika cetovimutti is clearly not *arahatta* (full awakening). This has a bearing on the problem of the bhikkhu's suicide and the Buddha's apparent approval of the act. It would take us too far from the theme of this book to consider this question in the depth it deserves, but suffice it to say that suicide is generally condemned in Theravāda Buddhism (Vin Pār 3). There are three similar cases of bhikkhus who "wielded the knife" mentioned in the suttas, Godhika, Vakkali (for whom Māra also searched in a dark and smoky form) (SN 22:87) and Channa (MN 144). None of the three was an arahant at the moment of "wielding the knife" but all three attained to arahatta in the moments before their demise. Since an arahant is not subject to rebirth, the negative kamma of self destruction is rendered null and void. The words of a modern Thai master of the forest tradition, Ajahn Maha Boowa, may be worth quoting here: "The story of Ven. Godhika should serve as quite some food for thought. Ven. Godhika went to practice meditation, made progress step by step, but then regressed. They say this happened six times. After the seventh time, he took a razor to slash his throat—he was so depressed—but then came to his senses, contemplated the Dhamma, and became an arahant at the last minute. That's the story in brief. When he died, Māra's hordes searched for his spirit. To put it simply, they stirred up a storm, but couldn't tell where he had been reborn."[714]

For our purposes, the most salient details come at the end of the story. Māra is unable to find, or seemingly to comprehend, what has become of one who has transcended his sphere of power completely. Māra is used to beings moving from realm to realm, still fettered by desire and delusion. When someone manages to break free of birth and death altogether he is completely baffled. It is also noteworthy that the bhikkhus perceive him only as a vague form described as "dark and smoky' thrashing about in all directions. Compare this perception with the more usual one of

[713] SN 4:23 and Dhp-a 4:11. Some details are from the commentaries, including Māra's inner reflections.

[714] Maha Boowa, *Straight from the Heart.*

devas manifesting in this realm; when they are seen at all by ordinary humans it is as a brilliant light (eg. DN 21).

On occasion, Māra delegates the making of mischief to lesser devas of his entourage:

> Some women who were the companions of the pious Visakhā had taken to drinking liquor. On one occasion, they accompanied her to the vihāra to listen to the Buddha and sat themselves in the assembly hall after having drunk liquor. Then a deva of Māra's company (*mārakāyikā devatā*) thought, "I will possess the bodies of these women and cause them to misbehave in front of the samaṇa Gotama." Thereupon, some of the women clapped their hands and laughed in front of the Buddha, while others got up and began to dance. The Buddha knew what was going on and he thought, "I shall not allow the devas of Māra to get an opportunity here." To frighten the women, the Buddha caused a ray to issue forth from his eyebrows which caused a great darkness. The women were overcome with a fear of death and the liquor in their bellies dried up. The Buddha then ascended to the top of Mount Sineru and caused a ray brighter than the sun or moon to issue forth. He then admonished the women for their heedlessness which allowed one of Māra's devas to possess them. (Dhp-a 11:1)

The Kathavatthu records a dispute over whether it were possible for arahants to have an involuntary discharge of semen. The Theravāda denied this was possible, but two other early schools held that it was. Their position was that while the arahant is free of lust, a discharge may still occur because devas of Māra's company convey the semen to them. The Theravāda reply was to ask where the semen comes from, because arahants produce none and devas have none (Kv 2:1).

Māra is mentioned twice in the Jātakas. In Jātaka 40 he attempts to starve a *Paccekabuddha* to death by creating a pit of hot coals between him and his donor. Since this story, like all the Jātakas, occurred in the remote past it is not clear whether this is the same Māra as in the time of the Buddha Gotama. In Jātaka 389 we are told of a previous birth of the Māra known from the suttas. In this story he is born as a serpent who attempts to kill the Bodhisatta.

It is beyond the scope of this book to consider the many variations of the Māra character encountered in later schools of Buddhism.[715] However, it is hard to resist including an episode from the Sarvāstivāda text the *Aśokavadāna* ("Legend of King Aśoka"):

> Upagupta was an elder bhikkhu living at the time of King Aśoka. He was said to be "a Buddha without the marks." Māra was not pleased that Upagupta's teaching was leading many beings to the path that leads out of his domain. Three times he disrupted Upagupta's sermons. The first time, he caused a shower of pearls to fall upon the audience, who lost all interest in the teaching and scrambled for the precious pearls. The word of this spread, and many more people came for Upagupta's next sermon, and this time Māra caused a shower of gold coins.
>
> The third time, a very great crowd arrived for Upagupta's talk and Māra caused a heavenly display of music together with dancing by celestial *apsāras* (Pali—*accharās*, "nymphs"). The formerly dispassionate men in the crowd turned away from Upagupta, fascinated by the divine sounds and forms.
>
> Māra was very pleased with himself, and went up to Upagupta and put a garland of flowers around his neck. Upagupta knew it was Māra. The elder took the carcass of a man, a dog and a snake and transformed them into flower garlands. Māra was delighted and thought he had won over Upagupta as well and allowed the garlands to be hung around his neck. These transformed back to their natural forms and Māra, a being devoted to sensuality, was appalled. He found that he had no power to remove them.

715 Although this is a fascinating topic. Interested readers are referred to Michael David Nichols, *Malleable Māra.*

Māra went to seek help from Mahendra, from Rudra, from Upendra, from the Lord of Riches, from Yama, Varuṇa, Kubera and Vasāva and to many other devas. All of these, and even Brahmā could not remove the carcasses from his neck. Brahmā advised him to return to earth and go for refuge to Upagupta.

He pleaded with Upagupta, appealing to his compassion. In the discussion between these two, Upagupta brought Māra to appreciate the great compassion of the Buddha, and the wickedness of his own ways. Māra was repentant and prostrated before the elder, his mind filled with faith for the Blessed One and he begged to be released from the foul carcasses.

Upagupta agreed on two conditions: Māra must never harass the bhikkhus again and as a personal favour to Upagupta he should manifest the bodily form of the Buddha. "Although I have seen his dharma-body (*dharmakāya*) I was born too late to see his physical body (*rūpakāya*)."

Māra readily agreed but stipulated that Upagupta should not bow to the form of the Buddha, "because if one like you venerates one like me, I shall burst into flame." So, just as he had previously done to mislead Sūrambaṭṭha, Māra manifested the form of the Buddha, together with the thirty-two marks. He appeared in this form accompanied by the forms of the chief disciples and many other renowned arahants of that time. Upagupta was unable to restrain himself at the sight and bowed. But Māra was unhurt, and the elder explained that he was bowing out of reverence for the Buddha, and not to Māra's person.

Māra went into the city of Mathurā and personally rang the town bell, proclaiming aloud that, "Whoever desires the bliss of heaven and release, should listen to the Dharma of Upagupta. And those who have never gazed upon the Tathāgata, let them look at the elder Upagupta!"[716]

We are not told what became of Māra after his conversion. But, as desire and fear continue to torment living beings we may safely assume that some new Māra has taken his place. Perhaps the Māra of our Buddha's time came to a happier ending than Māra Dūsi and retired to enjoy the pleasures of Paranimmitavasavatti for the remainder of his long life-span.

[716] Condensed from John S. Strong, trans. *The Legend of King Aśoka*, . p. 185-198.

3:5:43 MĀRA- CONCLUSION

It is inevitable that the western student of Buddhism will want to compare Māra with Satan. There are some similarities between these two figures. Just as Māra tempted the Buddha, Satan tempted Christ in the desert. Māra is frequently called by the epithet Pāpima, "the Evil One", which has a Satanic ring to it. Both Māra and Satan are the great adversaries of the good in their respective cosmologies.

Nevertheless, the two figures are quite distinct and are almost certainly independently derived.[717] Although Māra is described as ruling his quarter of the Paranimmitavasavatti realm "like a rebel prince" (*dāmarikarājaputto*) (MN-a 1), this is a local rebellion only, in that Māra does not accept the authority of Vasavatti Devārāja. It is not, like Satan's, a rebellion against the fundamental order of things. For one thing, in Buddhism there is no Supreme God to rebel against. Furthermore, Māra himself is the representative and chief defender of the established order of *saṃsāra*. In a sense, it is the Buddha who is the rebel.

Māra is not strictly speaking a demonic being, he is a very high level deva. His power extends from *niraya* to the celestial saggas, and even to some extent beyond as we saw in the case of the brahmā Baka. Moggallāna was appalled that such a refined being would demean himself so far as to squat in the elder's filthy bowels (MN-a 50). Māra's existence is not one of torment, except in so far as he inflicts it upon himself in his endlessly frustrated attempts to subvert the arahants.

There is also the possibility of interpreting Māra in purely psychological terms, as a literary personification of purely internal states like lust and fear. There is some justification for this found in the canon itself. The Buddha says that the five *khandha* ("aggregates," constituents of the body-mind system) are Māra (SN 23:1) and elsewhere that the six senses are Māra (SN 35:48, eng. 35:65). But it would be a mistake to think that this precludes the external existence of Māra as a distinct entity. The commentaries make an explicit distinction between Māra as metaphor and Māra as deva (DN-a 1). In the introduction to his translation of the Mārasaṃyutta, Bhikkhu Bodhi makes a salient point:

> But it is evident that the thought world of the suttas does not conceive of Māra only as a personification of humankind's moral frailty, but sees him as a real evil deity out to frustrate the efforts of those intent on winning the ultimate goal. The proof of this lies in his pursuit of the Buddha and the arahants after their enlightenment, which would not be credible if he were conceived of merely as a psychological projection.[718]

To understand Māra, and indeed Buddhist cosmology generally, we need to avoid the pitfalls inherent in seeing him through modern, western glasses. He is neither Satan nor a psychological projection. If we make the attempt to understand Māra in his own ancient, Indian and Buddhist context, what picture emerges?

Māra is first and foremost a very high level deva. His position was attained through the making of kamma which must have been predominantly *kusala* ("skillful"). However, he remains himself a prisoner of the saṃsāric defilements of pride, desire and ill-will and his current activities are storing up a great deal of *akusala* ("unskillful") kamma. Although he fancies himself the lord and master of *saṃsāra*, he is himself very much subject to its impersonal and implacable laws. We have seen how one previous Māra ended up being tormented in *niraya* (MN 50). Thus he went from the very summit of the sense-desire realm to its ultimate nadir in a single moment.

Māra's goal is not primarily to make beings suffer. Although it is said that those in his bonds swell the ranks of the *niraya*, peta and asura realms, (It 3:5,4) he is content to see them born into the deva or even brahmā worlds, just so long as they do not escape the cycle of birth, death and rebirth. Some of the villagers possessed by the Māra Dūsi were reborn in *niraya* as a result of their actions, but others went to on to deva rebirth (MN-a 50).

---

[717] Unless there is some ancient link via Zoroastrianism's Ahriman, but this seems unlikely.

[718] Bhikkhu Bodhi, CDB, p. 79.

Māra's weapons are deceit, illusion, fear and desire, the very fabric of continued existence in the round of *saṃsāra*. Māra together with his host of attendant devas can appear so terrible and awesome that he makes even the devas, nāgas and brahmās flee away in hapless terror (Jāt-nid 2). And yet after his repeated defeats by the Buddha we see him as a small wretched figure squatting by the road side scratching in the ground with a stick (SN 4:25). His power is great, but it is based on illusion. "I know you, Māra," is enough to disarm him utterly.

If Māra is to be seen as a personification at all, it is not something as small as personal defilement that he personifies but the whole vast and impersonal process of birth, death and rebirth that is *saṃsāra*. Māra is an entity that represents and embodies *saṃsāra* in the same way that a monarch personifies and represents his kingdom. But he himself is trapped within its bounds and is unable to comprehend what may lay outside its borders. We have seen Māra in the form of "dark smoke" searching in frustration for the rebirth consciousness of a deceased arahant (SN 4:23). Although he appears terrible, he is in the end, when known for what he truly is, a pathetic and deluded figure.

CHAPTER SIX—BRAHMĀS

3:6:1 RŪPABHŪMI—THE PLANE OF FORM

Everything we have considered so far, from the beings writhing in the agony of *niraya* up to those enjoying the sublime pleasures of the celestial deva realms, is included within the *kāmabhūmi*, "the plane of sense desire." This is a realm of bewildering complexity, but all of the diverse beings who inhabit the various levels of the *kāmabhūmi* share an underlying psychological structure. They all relate to the world primarily through the five physical senses, and unless they have developed enough spiritual maturity to transcend their native sphere, they are all primarily driven by the desire to experience pleasant sense objects and to avoid painful ones. For a being caught in this level of existence, the processes of sensation, desire, gain and loss, pleasure and pain seem all-encompassing. It is nearly impossible for such a being to even imagine a form of existence not dominated by the senses and their tyrannical desires.

In the Buddhist cosmology, however, there are two higher levels of existence which, although still conditioned and part of *saṃsāra*, have left subjugation by the senses behind. These are the *rūpabhūmi* and the *arūpabhūmi*: the planes of Form and the Formless. The *rūpabhūmi* is the realm of the brahmās, beings considered to be of a higher spiritual state than even the devas. Devas are, in the most essential aspects, closer to human beings than to the brahmās. Like us, the devas are sensual beings, a state of suffering that the brahmās have transcended. (It should be noted, however, that such transcendence is only temporary as a brahmā can eventually be reborn back into the plane of sense-desire).

The brahmās dwell in celestial realms far above the sensual plane, in nested hierarchies of *brahmalokas* ("brahmā worlds") representing successively more refined levels of spiritual development, sixteen levels in all. The word *brahmā* is derived from the Sanskrit root *bṛh*, "to increase, to be great". It also occurs in compounds in the form *brahma*. In this form it means "sacred" or "divine". Words derived from *brahmā* and *brahma* include *brāhmaṇa* ("brahmin", a member of the priestly caste), *brahmacariya* ("the holy life", "celibacy") and *brahmavihāra* ("divine abiding", meditation on loving-kindness etc.).[719]

A note on terminology: There is some variation in the use of the words *deva* and *brahmā*. *Deva* can be used either specifically or generally. When used specifically, it refers to deities of the plane of sense desire: the earth-bound or *bhumma* devas and the devas of the six *saggas* ("heavens"). In this usage, it is sometimes specifically contrasted to the brahmās as in *Suttanipāta* 3:6 which speaks of three "fields" (*khetta*): the human, the deva and the brahmā. When used generally, it refers to all beings beyond the human level. The word *brahmā* also shows some variations in use. It is most often used in a highly specific way to refer only to those beings of the first three levels of the *rūpabhūmi* corresponding to first jhāna which may be called the *brahmaloka* proper. The beings in the higher *rūpabhūmi* levels are then called by the specific name of their class followed by the word deva, as in AN 5: 170, which speaks of ābhassarā devas and *subhakiṇṇa devas*. To add to the confusion, at least one passage of the *Abhidhamma Commentary* (Vibh-a 18:6) classes the first nine levels of the *rūpabhūmi* as the *brahmāloka*. Most modern writers use the word brahmā to refer to all *rūpabhūmi* beings.[720] These variations in terminology need not cause confusion if we pay attention to the specific entities being described; the problem is strictly a semantic one.

---

[719] See PED entry for *brahmā* for more examples.

[720] See for instance the entry in DPPN for *brahmaloka*.

3:6:2 THE STATE OF BEING IN THE RŪPABHŪMI

The word *rūpa* means "form" and can be used in at least two senses. It can refer to physical form, i.e. matter or the body, as in the list of the five *khandha*, the "aggregates" which constitute the totality of a being, body (*rūpa*), consciousness, feeling, perception and mental formations. Or it can mean "visible form" or the object of eye-consciousness. When used to refer to this particular realm of beings, either or both of these connotations apply. The beings here belong to a state of being called variously *rūpadhātu* ("form element"), *rūpabhava* ("form becoming"), *rūpāvacara* ("form sphere"), *rūpaloka* ("form world") or *rūpabhūmi* ("plane of form") and the *rūpa* element is meant to contrast this realm not with the *kāmabhūmi* but with the *arūpabhūmi*, because in the latter there is no form in either sense of the word.

The words *rūpaloka, rūpāvacara, rūpadhātu* or *rūpabhūmi* are sometimes rendered into English as "fine-material realm." This is a loose translation meant to convey the idea that the material basis of this world is of a subtler nature than the matter (*rūpa*) known here on earth. Their bodies are said to be *manomaya*, "mind made" (MN 60). They do not eat physical food, not even the subtle food of the devas, but subsist on the bliss of jhāna.[721]

The association of brahmā level beings with jhāna is central to the definition of their status. *Jhāna* refers to the state of meditative absorption attained through the development of *samādhi*, the "non-wavering" attention to an object.[722] Development of meditation to the level of jhāna is a prerequisite for rebirth into the brahmā worlds (AN 4:124 & Vism 11:123). Furthermore, the various levels within the rūpabhūmi are mainly defined by the level of jhāna to which they correspond.

The inhabitants of the *rūpabhūmi* are possessed of two physical senses only: those of sight and hearing (Kv 8:7 & Vism 7.13). There are no unpleasant sights or sounds in the brahmā worlds, although they may encounter them if they turn their attention to the sense-desire realm (Vism 17:180). The brahmā beings are genderless, "the male and female organs are not found there" (AN-a 1: 283). They are said, however, to have the appearance of males (*purisasaṇṭhāna*) (ibid.). Birth is similar to that found in the deva realms; it is apparitional and the new brahmā simply appears "as if awakening from sleep" (AN-a 11: 15).

By definition, the beings of the *rūpabhūmi* are possessed of form. Their appearance is nowhere described in comprehensive detail, but there is good reason to conclude that it is more or less anthropomorphic. It is said, for example, that even though they lack the senses of smell and taste, they are possessed of noses and tongues (Kv-a 8:7). Their bodies are said to be radiant (*pabhā*) and decorated with ornaments (SN-a 6:5). The natural form of their bodies is too subtle to interact with beings on lower planes, so they must assume a gross body (oḷārika attabhāva) if they wish to manifest to humans or devas (AN 3:128, eng. 3:127 & DN 18).

Like the devas, they dwell in *vimānas* of surpassing beauty (E.g. Vism 3: 98). The brahmaloka itself is a level ground covered in jewels. It, and the *vimāna*, has no maker or creator but arises through the forces of kamma and natural processes (*kammapaccayautusamuṭṭhāna*) (DN-a 1). One passage gives five characteristics of a brahmā: they are unencumbered with wife or wealth (*apariggaha*), without hatred (*averacitto*), benevolent (*abyāpajjacitta*), pure (*asaṃkiliṭṭhacitta*) and powerful (*vasavattī*).[723]

---

721 SN-a 6:3. *sappītikajjhānena yāpenti* and DN 1, DN 27: *pītibhakkhā.*

722 It would take us too far afield to go deeply into the theory of jhāna here. Interested readers can find the classic description in Ñāṇamoli, tr. *the Path of Purification*, Vism Ch 4 and see § 3:6,8 below.

723 DN 13.These characteristics are given as part of a critique of the brahmin priests, who are said to be the opposite in every respect.

3:6:3 PRE-BUDDHIST CONCEPTIONS OF BRAHMĀ

In later Hinduism Brahmā is one of the trinity of supreme deities along with Śiva and Viṣṇu. It would, however, be anachronistic to assume that the Indians of the Buddha's time conceived of Brahmā with anything like the attributes and qualities later assigned to him. The idea of Brahmā as the Supreme Being and the creator god was one which developed gradually in Indian thought. Brahmā as a deity does not appear at all in the Ṛg Veda. In the earliest versions of the creation myth, it is Prajapati who fills this role, and later texts retroactively identify him as Brahmā under another name.[724] In the Upanishads, a distinction is made between *Brahmā* (masculine) and *Brahman* (neuter). The former is a personified deity, and the latter an impersonal supreme cosmic principle. This distinction is not, however, consistently maintained and the Upanishads represent a range of philosophical views.[725] For instance, the *Talavakāra Upaniṣad* has Brahman (neuter) acting as a very powerful personified entity:

1. Brahman obtained the victory for the Devas. The Devas became elated by the victory of Brahman, and they thought, this victory is ours only, this greatness is ours only.
2. Brahman perceived this and appeared to them. But they did not know it, and said: "What sprite (*yaksha* or *yakshya*) is this?"
3. They said to Agni (fire): "O Gâtavedas, find out what sprite this is." "Yes," he said.
4. He ran toward it, and Brahman said to him: "Who are you?" He replied: "I am Agni, I am Gâtavedas."
5. Brahman said: "What power is in you?" Agni replied: "I could burn all whatever there is on earth."
6. Brahman put a straw before him, saying: "Burn this." He went towards it with all his might, but he could not burn it. Then he returned thence and said: "I could not find out what sprite this is."[726]

There is always a problem of chronology when dealing with Indian history, and it is not possible to definitively decide which texts were extant at the time of the Buddha, whose own dates are a matter of some controversy. Furthermore, all the evidence, both external and internal to the Buddhist canon, indicates that there were a great many schools of thought competing in the India of the day, and this also makes it impossible to describe a clear-cut pre-Buddhist or contemporary non-Buddhist view of Brahmā to compare with the Buddhist ideas about the brahmā beings.

That the Buddhist conception of brahmā functions, at least in part, as a sustained mythological critique of the non-Buddhist view is nevertheless beyond doubt. Our best guide to understanding exactly what the Buddha was critizising is, by default, the description of non-Buddhist arguments presented in the canon itself.

We find a good description of the pre-Buddhist Brahmā in the *Brahmajāla Sutta* (DN 1). This sutta is a sustained polemic, refuting various wrong-views and the section dealing with the theistic view describes the deluded self-image of a brahmā who imagines himself as the one and only creator god and lists his own epithets: "I am Brahmā, Mahābrahmā, the Overlord (*abhibhū*), the Unconquered (*anabhibhūta*), the Omniscient One (*aññadatthudasa* lit. "one who sees all"), Wielder of Power (*vasavattī*), the Lord (*issara*), the Maker (*kattar*), the Creator (*nimmātar*), the Excellent One (*seṭṭha*), the Designator (*sañjitar* i.e., he assigns each to his proper caste), the Master (*vasī*), the Father of All Beings (*pitā bhūtabhabyānaṃ*)." He is (falsely) conceived of as the first of all beings, and as eternal.[727]

In the Buddhist texts, the brahmin priests are depicted as the especial devotees of the god Brahmā. Thus, Sāriputta says "these brahmins are intent upon the *brahmāloka*", and teaches a dying brahmin the meditation on the *brahmavihāras* ("divine abidings": loving-kindness, compassion, sympathetic joy and equanimity), thus neatly

---

724 W.J. Wilkins, *Hindu Mythology, Vedic and Puranic* passim. See especially p. 96 f.

725 The Pali form *brahmā* (masc.) carries over some of this ambiguity. The root-form of the word is *brahman*, and it has an irregular declension that has an accusative more like a neuter noun.

726 *Talavakāra Upaniṣad* 3, translated by Max Müller(1879:149–150).

727 Ibid. and see also SN 6:5.

merging the pre-Buddhist and the Buddhist conceptions.[728]

Brahmins are depicted performing ceremonies of worship to Brahmā:

> (A certain brahmin lady) would every day make ritual offerings (to Brahmā). The whole house was sprinkled with herbs and parched corn, banners were raised around the yard, fragrant torches were lit and everywhere around was filled with the scented smoke. This brahmin lady would get up very early and rinse herself all over sixteen times with scented water. Keeping her mind pure, she would ladle out some rice gruel and say, "Mahābrahmā, eat!" She would put it in a golden bowl together with honey and ghee, and bring it to a small spirit chair set up at the back of the house. She would walk around to each corner of the house and sprinkle some of the food offering, until the ghee was running down her arm to the elbow. She would go down on bended knee and chant, "Eat, blessed Mahābrahmā, taste, blessed Mahābrahmā, enjoy, blessed Mahābrahmā!" Thus saying, she would feed Mahābrahmā. (SN-a 6:3)

We can detect more than a hint of satire in this description. In the sutta an actual Buddhist brahmā manifests to tell her that "The *brahmāloka* is far away and Brahmā does not eat such food."[729] The Buddhist conception of brahmās as very elevated, but still mortal and conditioned, beings is clearly juxtaposed to the brahminical idea of Brahmā as a supreme deity. Buddhists did not worship brahmās and the implied criticism is that such worship is misplaced and useless. It is to be noted that the supreme deity of the Vedas, Indra, becomes Sakka or "Inda", in the Buddhist Tāvatiṃsa and the supreme deity of the *Upanishads*, Brahmā, becomes a class of beings in yet another, and higher, Buddhist realm. Thus, the Buddhist cosmology incorporated and superseded the various older versions.

728 MN 97. But the Buddha criticized him for this, saying that he stopped short and should have taught the brahmin about nibbāna.

729 SN 6:3. The brahmā in the story is Sahampati.

3:6:4 BRAHMAKĀYIKA—BRAHMĀS OF THE FIRST JHĀNA LEVEL

The first three levels of the *rūpabhūmi* correspond to the first meditation jhāna. This means that the natural state of consciousness of these beings is equivalent to that of a human meditator in the first jhāna, and that attainment of that jhāna is the prerequisite for rebirth there.[730] This is the level of *rūpadhātu* that can be considered the *brahmaloka* proper, and the beings dwelling here are the ones who are called brahmās in the most specific use of that term. There are three classes or levels of these brahmās, from the lowest to the highest they are: *brahmāpārisajja* ("Brahmā's assembly"), *brahmāpurohita* ("Brahmā's ministers") and *mahābrahmā* ("the Great Brahmā"). While late sources such as the *Abhidharmakośa* place these levels in three specific locations, each successively further away in space from the earth, the depiction in the suttas is of three separate classes inhabiting one cosmological space,[731] just as animals, ghosts and humans share the earth. *Brahmakāyika* (meaning either "those of Brahmā's company" or "those with a brahmā's body") is a generic word for all three classes.

We have seen that the *rūpabhūmi* levels are located at a very great elevation above not only the earth, but the sensual *devalokas* as well.[732] The immense physical distance reflects the great spiritual elevation of these worlds from those which lie below (SN-a 6:3). The physical arrangement of these worlds is in complex nested hierarchies. There may be between a thousand and a hundred thousand entire world-systems beneath a single *brahmāloka*. The brahmās are said to be able to review the thousands of world below them just as a man might examine some gall-nuts held in the palm of his hand (MN 120).

A note on life-spans: The life-spans of the beings from this level and beyond are measured in kappas. This is a term of cosmological time corresponding to the entire cycle of a world-system. It should be pointed out there that for first jhāna level brahmās, the kappa referred to is not a full kappa but an *asaṅkheyyakappa* ("intermediate kappa") or roughly one fourth of a full kappa.[733] This distinction is necessary to fit the life history of the brahmās into the bigger cosmological scheme. The life-spans of beings above the first jhāna level are measured in full kappas.

---

730 We will go into this a little deeper in the section on "The Mind of Brahmā" at § 3:6,8.

731 See for example SN 6:14.

732 See Part One, section on Multiple World-Systems.

733 AN-ṭ 7:44. See Bhikkhu Bodhi's comments on Abhidh-s 5:14, CMA, p. 198.

3:6:5 BRAHMAPĀRISAJJA—BRAHMĀ'S ASSEMBLY

Each *brahmaloka* is ruled over by a *mahābrahmā* ("great brahmā") who is served by a population of lesser brahmās. The rank-and-file of the brahmā worlds are the *brahmapārisajja* ("Brahmā's assembly"). A person is born into this class if he or she has developed the first jhāna but only to a minor degree (AN-a 7:44). Both pronouns are used advisedly, because the commentary tells us that a woman who develops jhāna can be reborn here, or as a *brahmapurohita*, but not as a *mahābrahmā*. In the new brahmā existence, she will nevertheless have a male appearance, even though brahmās are basically genderless (AN-a 1:281). Like many of the other beings we have encountered, brahmās are capable of bodily transformation. When a great host of brahmās came to listen to the Buddha, he said they were so closely spaced that sixty could fit on the head of an awl; this was due to the power of their "peaceful minds" (AN-a 2:37).

A *brahmapārisajja* being has a life-span of one-third of a kappa. The radiance of their bodies is less than that of the higher classes of brahmās (AN-a 7:44). The Buddha would sometimes appear among them incognito to teach Dhamma, as he did with other kinds of assemblies (MN 12). The Buddha would also teach openly in the brahmā world from time to time. The brahmapārisajja beings were not always dutiful students, however. When the Buddha Sikhī went there with his disciple Abhibhū he asked the latter to speak, and the *brahmapārisajja* beings grumbled, "Why does the disciple teach in the presence of the teacher?" The Buddha had Abhibhū perform various supernormal feats which overawed the brahmās and won them over (SN 6:14). Likewise, when the Buddha Gotama went to see the brahmā Baka for the purpose of correcting the latter's false views, Māra possessed one of the *brahmapārisajja* beings and caused him to criticize the Buddha (MN 49). This last incident is significant because it clearly places these lowest tier brahmās as being within the range of Māra's power, even though they are, by definition, outside the plane of sense-desire. The commentary makes clear that in the *rūpabhūmi* it is only the *brahmapārisajja* beings that can be possessed by Māra, and not any of those of the higher levels (MN-a 49). These are beings that have just barely transcended the range of sensuality.

The *brahmapārisajja* beings that arise in an established *brahmaloka* do so after the prior appearance of a *mahābrahmā*. It can often happen that both ruler and ruled fall into a mutually reinforcing delusion about their true natures, and the *brahmapārisajja* beings worship the *mahābrahmā* as the Supreme Being and their creator:

> In their imagination, they come to think "We have been created by him." Thinking thus, they bow before his feet, bending over like crooked fish-hooks. (DN-a 1)

This delusion eventually finds its way to the human realm and becomes the basis for theistic religion. (We shall return to this idea in more detail when we consider *mahābrahmās*). Being beyond sense desire, and having no need to eat, it would seem that the needs of a brahmā for any kind of service would be minimal. We do have at least one incidence of a *brahmapārisajja* being serving as a messenger for his *mahābrahmā*, taking a Dhamma question to Moggallāna on earth (SN 6:5).

3:6:6 BRAHMAPUROHITA

The brahmās of middling rank, the *brahmapurohita* beings, attain that state of rebirth by developing first jhāna to a moderate degree. Their life-span is half a kappa, and the radiance of their bodies is greater than that of the *brahmapārisajja* beings (AN-a 7:44). In English translation, they are usually called "Brahmā's ministers."

In Sanskrit usage, a *purohit* is a brahmin priest who presides at sacrificial ceremonies.[734] In the Pali texts, a *purohita* is a high-ranking brahmin who serves the king in both ritual and political capacities. "The king's head-priest (brahmanic), or domestic chaplain, serving at the same time as a kind of prime minister" (PED). It seems that the Indian states of the Buddha's time were governed by a kind of dyarchy of the two noble (*ariyan*) castes, with the *rājā* at the top representing the chief *khattiya* (warrior-caste) seconded by a *purohita* who was always a brahmin and who often assumed day-to-day executive functions.[735]

It is impossible to say just how far the analogy from human *purohitas* applies to the *brahmaloka* variety. As a class, they are not very well defined and seldom mentioned in the texts. We cannot say in what capacity they serve their *mahābrahmā*. One difference is that while a human king had only one *purohita*, a *mahābrahmā* is served by a large retinue of *brahmapurohitas*.

No individual *brahmapurohita* is named anywhere in the sources, nor do we ever hear their voices. They are not actors in any stories. We are told of two *gandhabbas* (a lowly class of devas) who by establishing themselves in first jhāna attained to rebirth as *brahmapurohitas*. At the very moment of achieving jhāna, the gandhabbas, now unable to bear such a lowly sense-desire existence, died and were immediately reborn in the *brahmaloka*. Sakka and the other devas were amazed that these "of lower rank" had so far surpassed them.[736] But this is a story about devas, and after their death and rebirth, we lose sight of the former *gandhabbas*.

There is also a brief mention in verse:

> A great host of devas, powerful and glorious,
>
> Ten thousand in all, everyone a *brahmapurohita*,
>
> Came to honour Moggallāna, and stood there with joined hands. (Th 20)

Most of the attention of the sources is paid to the highest class of brahmās, the *mahābrahmās*, and it appears that the function of the two lower grades is mostly to enhance the lustre of their lord as a glorious retinue.

---

734 See *Britannica Library*, s.v. "Brahman," accessed January 4, 2017, http://library.eb.com/levels/referencecenter/article/16155.

735 For examples see DN 5, DN 19 and MN 51.

736 DN 21. The details about their mode of death are from the commentary.

3:6:7 MAHĀBRAHMĀ

The only really independent actors in the first jhāna level of the *rūpabhūmi* are the beings called *mahābrahmā*, "great brahmā", one of whom rules in solitary splendour over each brahmaloka. Each *mahābrahmā* also presides over a thousand or more world-systems (*cakkavāḷa*) each with its central mountain, four continents and associated *saggas* (heavenly worlds). This structure is not fully worked out into a coherent and consistent system in the early sources,[737] but the important point to bear in mind here is that for our world, and for many neighbouring worlds unseen by us, there exists only one *mahābrahmā*. It is not difficult to see how he could be taken to be a supreme being, as in the Brahmā of the *Upanishads* for instance. In fact, many *mahābrahmās* make this mistake themselves. The *Brahmajāla Sutta* (DN 1) describes what happens at the beginning of a new world-cycle:

> There comes a time when the world-system is unfolding (*vivaṭṭati* or "expanding"). In the expanding world, an empty brahmā *vimāna* manifests. Then a certain being of the Ābhassara world (second jhāna level) dies because of the exhaustion of his life-span, or the exhaustion of his merit, and is reborn in that empty *vimāna*. There he dwells, mind-made (*manomaya*), feeding on rapture (*pītibhakkha*), self-luminous (*sayaṃpabha*), moving through space (*antalikkhacara,* i.e. flying), glorious (*subhaṭṭhāyī*). And he abides like that for a very long time.
>
> Then, on account of having dwelled so long in solitude, longing and discontent arise in him. "Oh, that other beings would come here!" Then other beings dying from the Ābhassara world are reborn here as his companions. They too are mind-made, self-luminous, move through space and are glorious. And they too abide there for a very long time.
>
> Then the being who arose in that world first thinks, "I am Brahmā, Mahābrahmā, Overlord (*abhibhū*), the Unconquered (*anabhibhūto*), Omniscient (*aññadatthudaso*), Wielder of Power (*vasavattī*), Lord (*issaro*), the Maker (*kattā*), the Creator (*nimmātā*), the Eldest (*seṭṭho*), the Ordainer (*sajitā*), the Master (*vasī*), the Father of All Beings (*pitā bhūtabhabyānaṃ*). These other beings were created by me. How so? Previously I thought, 'May other beings come here', and by the power of my mental determination (*manopaṇidhi*) they have come to this place."
>
> The other beings also think, "He must be Brahmā, Mahābrahmā, Overlord, the Unconquered, Omniscient, Wielder of Power, Lord, the Maker, the Creator, the Eldest, the Ordainer, the Master, the Father of All Beings. And we were created by this blessed (*bhavanta*) Brahmā. How so? We can see that he arose here first, and we arose after him.
>
> The being that arises there first has a longer life, more beautiful appearance and greater power than the beings that arise afterwards, who are shorter lived, not as beautiful and less powerful than him. (DN 1)

The commentary expands upon the epithets the *mahābrahmā* awards to himself:

abhibhū—having conquered, I stand immovable, I am supreme.

anabhibhūto—no other has vanquished me.

aññadatthudaso—by the power of vision, I see all things.

---

737 See the discussion in the section on Multiple World-Systems at § 1:17.

vasavattī—I wield power over all persons.

issaro kattā nimmātā—In the world, I am Lord. I made and created the world. The earth, the Himavā Mountains, Mt Sineru, the *cakkavāḷa*, the great ocean, the sun and the moon were all created by me.

seṭṭho sajitā—In the world, I am supreme. I am the Ordainer. "You be a *khattiya* ("warrior"), you a brahmin ("priest"), you a *vesso* ("merchant"), a *sudda* ("labourer"; these are all caste distinctions), a householder, a renunciate. Likewise, I ordain that one be a cow, another be a camel."

vasī—I am the master of all skills (*ciṇṇavasitāya vasī*).

pitā bhūtabhabyānaṃ -All beings, no matter whether they are spontaneously born, womb-born, egg-born or moisture-born, are my children (DN-a 1).

The sub-commentary explains why the new brahmās do not recall their past lives:

> Is it not the case that devas can recall their immediate past life? It is true, but only if in that past life they were firmly established in an understanding of the workings of kamma. These beings were believers in the creative power of a supreme being in their previous life also. (DN-ṭ 1)

When one of the lesser brahmās eventually dies, and is reborn in the human realm, it may happen that he becomes an ascetic and through the practice of meditation acquires some memory of his life in the *mahābrahmā's* retinue including the idea that that *Mahābrahmā* is the supreme creator god. He might then proclaim this teaching as a religious truth revealed by a vision (DN 1). In this way, the Buddhist texts describe the origin of theistic religion, which is called *Ekaccasassatavāda* or "One-way Eternalism", meaning that the world and the beings in it were created at some moment in the past and then continue on forever. The Buddhist picture of Mahābrahmā and his retinue thus incorporates, transcends, explains and refutes the Vedic-Upanishadic religion, all at the same time.

As to their physical form, *mahābrahmās* are glorious, radiant and beautiful to behold. The form of a mahābrahmā is called "the best of all sights," (AN 5:170) and "incomparable" (MN-a 95). The devas never grow tired of beholding them (Vv-a 17). They have the form of a male person (*purisasaṇṭhāna*), but without sexual organs (AN-a 1:281 & MN-a 115). Their limbs are said to be straights "like the pillars in a deva city" without protruding knees or hips.[738] The only reference to their size appears to be a curious statement to the effect that a *mahābrahmā* has a "great body, two or three times the size of a farm field in Magadha" (DN-a 20). This is odd not only in its phrasing, but because this would make a mahābrahmā smaller than a deva. The speech of a mahābrahmā has eight characteristics: it is well enunciated (*vissaṭṭho),* easily understood (*viññeyyo*), sweetly pleasant (*mañju*), good to hear (*savanīyo*), distinct (*bindu*), not rambling (*avisārī*), profound (*avisārī*), and melodious (*ninnādī*).[739] The voice is said to be pure because it is not obstructed by bile and phlegm (MN-a 91). Having transcended the sensual plane, the brahmās are not burdened with all the messiness and nastiness that comes with animal and human biology. The purity and subtlety of their being is far beyond even that of the devas. When a newly reborn brahmā came to see the Buddha in his natural form, he could not remain upright but sank into the earth like hot ghee into sand. The Buddha was obliged to instruct him to "create a gross body" (*oḷārika attabhāva*) (AN 3:128, eng.3:127).

A frequently remarked upon attribute of *mahābrahmās* is their luminosity. They are listed along with such objects as the sun and the moon among things which shine brilliantly.[740] A Mahābrahmā is able to illuminate an entire

738 MN-a 91. A characteristic they share with the Buddha.
739 DN 18 & MN-a 91. The translation of some of these terms is somewhat conjectural.
740 MN-a 53. But not as brilliant as the Buddha's halo of radiance.

cakkavāḷa ("world-system") with a single finger, and ten *cakkavāḷas* with ten fingers (Dhp-a 5:11). The light which emanates from the body of a *mahābrahmā* surpasses that of lesser first jhāna brahmās, and is given as the primary feature distinguishing them from *brahmapārisajja* and *brahmapurohita* beings (AN-a 7:44). When a *mahābrahmā* manifests himself to beings of the plane of sense-desire, he first appears to them as a brilliant light, before he assumes a gross body which they can perceive (DN 11, 18 & 19).

An important, if not defining, feature of a *mahābrahmā* is the possession of a large retinue of lesser brahmās, who serve and praise him. These are numbered in many thousands (MN-a 27). Mahābrahmā is included in the list of *devarājās*, together with Sakka, Suyama and the rest (MN-a 62). However, there are a few mentions of a class of brahmās called *paccekabrahmā*, "solitary brahmā".[741] They are nowhere defined in the text or commentary, and the sub-commentary only states that they are brahmās who go about alone, without a retinue (SN-ṭ 6:6). We can infer from the few times individual *paccekabrahmās* are mentioned that they are more spiritually advanced than most first jhāna level brahmās; all the individuals named are *anagāmis* (one who has reached the third of the four stages of awakening). It may be that in their clear wisdom they find the adoration of lesser beings unwanted.

[741] See SN 6:6 and the few following suttas for examples.

3:6:8 THE MIND OF BRAHMĀ

The brahmās of this level enjoy a mental state that is the equivalent of first jhāna.[742] Attaining jhāna is compared to "entering into a *brahmāvimāna*" (MN-a 24). To understand the state of existence of a brahmā we need to pursue a brief digression into the theory of the jhānas.

The jhānas (Sanskrit *dhyāna*) are states achieved by meditation, primarily marked by a deep stability of mind. There are four jhānas of the *rūpabhūmi* (plane of form) and four of the *arūpābhūmi* (plane of the formless).[743] These represent increasingly refined states of consciousness. The first jhāna is defined by the absence of the five hindrances (*nivāraṇa*) and the presence of five factors. The five hindrances are sensual desire (*kāmacchanda*), ill-will (*vyāpāda*), sloth-and-torpor (*thinamiddha*), anxiety and restlessness (*uddhaccakukkucca*) and sceptical doubt (*vicikicchā*). These do not arise in the mind-stream of a person in first jhāna, or in that of a brahmā. The five defining factors which do arise are:

1. *Vitakka*—the factor which directs the mind onto an object, often translated as "initial application of mind".
2. *Vicāra*—the factor which steadily holds the object in mind, often translated as "sustained application of mind."
3. *Pīti*—the factor which takes delight in an object, variously translated as "happiness", "zest" or "rapture."
4. *Sukha*—the factor of a general highly pleasant mental feeling. Usually translated as "bliss".
5. *Ekaggatā*—The mental factor of unification of mind upon a single object. It is commonly translated as "one-pointedness" but a more literal rendering might be "gone to oneness". It should not be thought that the mind in jhāna is narrowed to a point, instead it is wide and expansive, but completely stable, "non-wavering."[744]

It is important to remember that although jhāna is a refined state, it is not the goal of the Buddhist path, which is *nibbāna*, the unconditioned. Jhāna and the *rūpabhūmi* remain within the bounds of *saṃsāra*; the hindrances are not eradicated by it, merely rendered quiescent. Similarly, a *mahābrahmā* has not eradicated the root of ill-will, he has only suppressed it with *mettā* ("loving-kindness") (MN-a 55).

Mettā is one of the four states called the *brahmavihāras* (lit. "dwellings of Brahmā"). The other three are *karuṇā* "compassion", *muditā* "sympathetic joy" and *upekkhā* "equanimity." Whereas meditation on any object culminating in jhāna leads to rebirth in the *brahmaloka*, the development of these four as objects of meditation are especially associated with brahmā level rebirth,[745] and of these four, meditation on *mettā* in particular leads to a rebirth at the *brahmakāyika* level.[746] We can say that *mettā* is the normal emotional state of brahmās.

Because of the parallelism between jhāna and the mind of a brahmā, both of which are classed as *rūpabhūmi* states, we can use knowledge of either one to gain a deeper understanding of the other. To take a clear practical example, because *samādhi* is often rendered as "concentration" and *ekaggatā* as "one-pointedness" beginning meditators often assume they need to narrow or "concentrate" their minds to a point. But when we recall that a *mahābrahmā* can observe up to a hundred thousand world-systems "like a man holding a pile of gall-nuts in his hand" (MN 120) we can see how mistaken this approach is. The mind in jhāna, like the mind of a brahmā, is vast and expansive.

---

742 Bodhi, CMA, 1, 18-21.

743 This is complicated by a different system elaborated in the abhidhamma which counts five form sphere jhānas. We need not concern ourselves with this distinction here.

744 The abhidhamma definiton of *samādhi*, a closely related factor. See Vism 14.139. Although the jhānas are quintessentially simple states of mind, the study of them is quite involved, and we are only scratching the surface here. Interested readers are referred to the *Visuddhimagga*, chapter 4 for a classical treatment. A good modern study is Henepola Gunaratana, *The Path of Serenity and Insight.*

745 See DN 13, MN 83, AN 8:1.

746 AN 4: 125. The other three lead to rebirth in higher levels of the *rūpabhūmi*.

Some *mahābrahmās* are subject to pride and false views, as we have seen. But others are disciples of the Buddha and may even have attained to one or another of the stages of awakening.[747] It is clear, however, that even the wisest and most highly attained *mahābrahmās* are beneath the Buddha in the spiritual hierarchy. It is said that even a sixteen thousand kappa old mahābrahmā whose defilements are extinguished (implying that he is an arahant) praises the Buddha as "highest, eldest and best in the world, without a superior" (AN-a 8:11). Likewise, a *mahābrahmā* wielding power over ten thousand world-systems can serve the Buddha or the arahants like a monastery attendant (*kappiyakārako)* (AN-a 1:174). There are several examples of this. A *mahābrahmā* carried the Buddha's robes and bowl at the time of the first alms-round after his awakening (AN-a 1: 188), and a *mahābrahmā* was among the deities who came to serve Sāriputta during his final illness (SN-a 47:13). (But these were all dismissed by him). It is possible for brahmās to attain to one or more of the stages of awakening; at the time of the Buddha's first sermon, when the ascetic Kondañña gained *sotāpatti* ("stream-entry") so did eighteen *koṭi* (I.e. 180,000,000) of *mahābrahmās* (AN-a 1: 170).

[747] This is denied by the *Abhidharmakośa* which states that "An Aryan is never reborn among the Mahābrahmas, because this heaven is a place of heresy." tr. Poussin. AK 6:4, p.968.

3:6:9 SAHAMPATI

Individual brahmās feature in several incidents in the text. Several are named. In other cases the word *Mahābrahmā* is used like a proper name and presumably refers to the *mahābrahmā* of this local group of world-systems. Most of these examples concern the relations of Mahābrahmā to the Buddha. For instance, we are told that when the Buddha descended from Tāvatiṃsa after teaching there for a rainy season, Mahābrahmā held a parasol over him, (MN-a 26) an act of symbolic significance in that the parasol was an important insignia of sovereignty in ancient India. It is noteworthy that when individual brahmās are named, or featured in stories, they are always either *mahābrahmās* of the first jhāna level or beings inhabiting the Suddhāvāsa level, the realms reserved for *anāgāmīs*. In the second, third and fourth jhānas the factors of *vitakka* and *vicāra* are absent. These mental qualities also associated with cognitive thought and speech; therefore their absence would disqualify brahmās of those levels from active participation in the affairs of the world. It is also not always clear whether we are dealing with a *mahābrahmā per se* or a being from the Suddhāvāsa. In at least one place, a Suddhāvāsa brahmā is also called a *mahābrahmā*.[748]

The most important *mahābrahmā* to feature in the stories is certainly the Brahmā Sahampati who was intimately involved in the Buddha's career. At the time of the Buddha Kassapa, he had been a human bhikkhu named Sahaka. In that life, he developed his meditation to the level of first jhāna and after death was reborn in the *brahmaloka*, where he was known as Sahampati.[749] One text says that his name there was originally Sahakapati (based on his human name) but that it was misheard and the mistake stuck (Bv-a 1). Another says that the bhikkhu Sahaka eliminated sensual desire through the development of the five *indryas* ("faculties"), which would imply that he was an *anāgāmī*, (SN 48:57) which in turn would imply that Sahampati is a Suddhāvāsa Brahmā.[750] Other considerations work against this supposition, as we shall see.

The most significant encounter of the Brahmā Sahampati and the Buddha occurred in the eighth week after the Buddha's awakening while he was sitting under the goat-herd's banyan tree at Nerañjarā.

> This reflection arose in the mind of the Blessed One: "This Dhamma obtained by me is profound, hard to see, hard to understand. It is peaceful and most excellent. Not to be found by reasoning, it is subtle and can only be experienced by the wise. But this generation delights in attachment, takes pleasure in attachment, is devoted to attachment … if I were to teach this Dhamma, they would not understand it and it would only bring weariness and vexation to me."
>
> Because of these reflections, the Blessed One was inclined to inaction, to not teaching the Dhamma.
>
> Then the Brahmā Sahampati knew the mind of the Blessed One with his own mind and thought, "The world will be lost, the world will perish because the mind of the *Tathāgata*, this perfectly awakened Buddha, is inclined to inaction, to not teaching the Dhamma." Then just as a strong mind might bend forth his arm or draw it back again, so did the Brahmā Sahampati disappear from the *brahmaloka* and appear before the Blessed One. Then Brahmā Sahampati arranged his robe over one shoulder, bent his right knee to the earth, put his palms together and spoke to the Blessed One, "Teach, *Bhante*, the blessed Dhamma! Teach the good Dhamma! There are beings with but little dust in their eyes who perish through not hearing the Dhamma. There are those who will understand the Dhamma." Then he spoke these verses:

[748] AN-a 1: 216. In another place, a brahmā from the second jhāna level is also referred to as mahābrahmā. Dhp-a 15: 2.

[749] SN 48:57, SN-a 6:1 & MN-a 26

[750] The sources are divided on the status of Sahampati. MN-a 26 places him specifically in the first jhāna brahmā world, whereas Sn-a 3:10 just as definitively identifies him as a Suddhāvāsa brahmā.

In former times, in Magadha

There arose impure teachings,

thought up by those still stained.

Open the door to the deathless!

Let them hear the Dhamma of the stainless Buddha!

Just as from a rock on a mountain peak,

  one might survey the people standing below.

Just so, wise one, mount the Palace of Dhamma,

  you of the all-seeing eye;

Being yourself free of sorrow,

Behold the sorrowing people, suffering in birth and death.

Rise up, hero, victor of the battle!

Leader of the caravan, free of all debt, wander through the world!

Teach the Dhamma! There are those who will understand!

Having heard the brahmā's request, out of compassion the Blessed One surveyed the world with the eye of a Buddha (*buddhacakkhu*) and saw some with much dust in their eyes and others with but little … and having seen, he answered the Brahmā Sahampati:

Opened is the door to the deathless.

Let the faithful listen and become free.

Foreseeing difficulties, I did notspeak

this subtle Dhamma among humans, O Brahmā!

Brahmā Sahampati thought, "The Blessed One has given his consent to my request and will teach the Dhamma." Paying his respects and keeping his right side to the Buddha, the Brahmā Sahampati disappeared there and then.[751]

This was a moment of crucial importance in the establishment of the Buddhist teaching. It is significant both that such an exalted being chose to intervene, and that he did so on bended knee before the Buddha. To this day it is traditional for one of the lay people present at a Dhamma talk to make a formal request of the teaching bhikkhu by reciting a passage from this sutta in Pali. It should be noted that the commentary seems reluctant to fully accept the Buddha's initial reluctance to teach. It explains that he wanted Sahampati to make his request because the people hold Brahmā in great respect, and that will incline them to listen to his teaching (SN-a 6:1).

[751] SN 6:1. See also MN 26. The Buddha's speeches have been abridged.

Brahmā Sahampati had several other conversations with the Buddha. Shortly after his decision to teach, the Buddha made a further resolution. He had realized that a person dwells in suffering who does not have reverence and devotion, but could see no living being worthy of his deference so decided to devote his life to serving the Dhamma. Sahampati again knew the thought in the Buddha's mind and appeared before him to praise this resolution and to state that all the Buddhas of the past had made the same determination, as will all the Buddhas of the future (SN 6:2). After the Buddha had begun to teach, while he was dwelling among the matted hair ascetics at Uruvelā, Brahmā Sahampati was among the divine beings who came one after another to hear the Buddha teach Dhamma. The first night, the Four Great Kings had come, on the second it was Sakka and on the third Sahamapati. Each in turn lit up the entire grove with a brilliant light which astounded the matted hair ascetics, but Sahampati's radiance was the most "excellent and glorious" (Vin Mv 1).

In several texts we see Sahampati acting as the Buddha's advisor. On one occasion, the Buddha had dismissed some noisy bhikkhus from his presence saying they could not live with him anymore. First a delegation of local *khattiya* laymen and then Sahampati appeared to entreat the Buddha to forgive them, using as arguments the similes of a seedling which comes to harm through lack of water and a young calf which comes to harm when separated from its mother. The Buddha consented to Sahampati's request and again received the noisy bhikkhus into his presence (MN 67). In a similar incident, after dismissing some quarrelsome and greedy bhikkhus from his presence (they had been disputing the disposition of some requisites offered to the *saṅgha*) the Buddha had already decided in his own mind to take them back when Sahampati, having perceived the thought in the Buddha's mind, appeared to affirm and praise this decision.[752] It was Sahampati who informed the Buddha that the evil minded bhikkhu Kokālika had died and been reborn in *niraya* (SN 6:10 & AN 10:89). Likewise, after Devadatta had caused a schism by breaking with the *saṅgha*, Sahampati appeared before the Buddha to utter a verse:

Just as the fruit kills the plaintain tree

And an embryo slays a mule

So does honour destroy an unworthy person. (SN 6:12)

At other times, Brahmā Sahampati manifests before the Buddha simply to praise him or to affirm some point of Dhamma. Thus, while the Buddha was still dwelling under the Goat-Herder's Banyan tree, shortly after the incident of Sahamapati's request to teach, the Buddha was reflecting upon the four foundations of mindfulness (*satipaṭṭhāna*) when the brahmā appeared again to speak in praise of this idea. He spoke, as usual, in verse and called the Four Foundations a "one-way path" (*ekāyana*) leading to *nibbāna*.[753] On a subsequent occasion, Sahamapti appeared before the Buddha to speak a series of verses praising seclusion and to state that it was personally known by him that many thousands had attained to awakening in this very life (SN 6:13). Once, Sahampati came together with Sakka to the Buddha's dwelling and the two deities stood each by one of the doorposts and uttered a verse in praise of the Buddha. Sakka said:

Arise, victorious hero!

Wander the world without a burden, free of debt.

Your mind is well liberated,

Like the full moon.

[752] SN 22:80. the details about the bhikkhus' fault is from the commentary.

[753] SN 47:18. The Four Foundations are mindfulness directed towards the body, the feelings, the mind and the mental contents.

But Sahampati reproved him: "It is not thus, king of devas, that *Tathāgatas* are to be praised," and spoke his own verse:

Arise, victorious hero!

Wander the world, leader of the caravan, free of debt.

Teach the Dhamma, Blessed One!

There are those who will understand. (SN 11:17)

As Bhikkhu Bodhi notes in his translation to the Saṃyutta Nikāya, the commentary gives no explanation as to why Sahampati's version is to be preferred, and he goes on to suggest that it is because Sakka's verse praises only those qualities which the Buddha shares with all arahants, while Sahampati focuses on the quality of the Buddha as teacher.[754] In any case, we see here that Sakka stands in relation to Sahampati as a junior.

Sahampati was the first to utter a verse at the time of the Buddha's passing into final *nibbāna*:

All beings in the world will lay down the body,

Even so the Teacher, peerless in the world,

The Tathāgata, possessed of power, fully awakened,

Has come to final *nibbāna.*[755]

Sahampati almost never appears in stories which do not involve the Buddha. He is included in a list of deities paying respects to a bhikkhu who has just attained arahantship, (DN-a 2) and he is the Brahmā who appeared to the old woman to chastise her for the foolish practice of "feeding" Brahmā, whom we met previously,[756] and that is about all.

Who is Brahmā Sahampati? The first thing to note is that he is a being of great cosmic power and significance. His intervention with the Buddha after the great awakening was a critical incident for the whole future history of the world. The exalted cosmic nature of Sahampati is emphasized in a few other references. He is said to have paid homage to the Buddha by presenting him with a jewelled garland the size of Mt Sineru (Vism 7.23 & Sn-a 2:1). At the time of the Bodhisatta's great sit under the Bodhi Tree, after the defeat of Māra, Brahmā Sahampati held a three *yojana* wide white parasol over the Bodhisatta, like a "second full moon" (Bv-a 27). Again, at the time of the Buddha's descent from Tāvatiṃsa after teaching the devas, it was Brahmā Sahampati who held the parasol over him.[757]

The last two incidents, involving the parasol (*setacchatta*), give us additional insight into Sahamapati's nature and importance. They tell us that Sahampati can be identified as the *mahābrahmā* who is the direct overlord of this particular *cakkavāḷa* (and by inference, many thousand adjacent *cakkavāḷas*). The parasol in ancient India was an important symbol of sovereignty, serving roughly the same symbolic space as the sceptre for European royalty. Here we see Sahampati wielding the parasol in this world and what is more, holding it over the Buddha as an act of deference. It should also be noted in this regard that in other versions of these incidents, the deity wielding the parasol is identified only as "Mahābrahmā", implying the *mahābrahmā* of this world-system.[758] However, there remains the detail of Sahampati's past life as a bhikkhu under Kassapa Buddha, earlier in this kappa. It is hard to reconcile this

754 Bodhi, CDB, vol 1, note 649 p. 498.

755 DN 16 & SN 6:15. The others to utter stanzas were, in order, Sakka, Ānanda and Anuruddha.

756 SN 6:3. See § 3:6,3.

757 Jāt 483, story of the present.

758 See the Dhp-a 14: 2 version of the descent from Tāvatiṃsa and the *Jātaka* Nidanakatha story of the encounter with Māra discussed in the section on Māra in § 3:5,34.

biography with the career of a supreme *mahābrahmā* who, as we have seen, is the first to arise in his world at the beginning of the kappa.

If we focus on Sahampati's relationship with the Buddha, we can think of him in yet another way: as the positive equivalent of Māra. Both of these deities have several encounters with the Buddha, often at critical points in his career. But whereas Māra's role is to oppose and hinder the Blessed One, Brahmā Sahampati's is to assist, honour and encourage him.

3:6:10 SANAṄKUMĀRA

Another *mahābrahmā* who features prominently in the texts is Sanaṅkumāra. A very long time ago, in a previous human birth, while still a youth (*kumāra* = "young man") he developed first jhāna and dying young was reborn in the *brahmaloka*. His youthful human appearance, as a lad wearing his hair in "five top knots" (*pañcacūḷaka*) was pleasing to him, so he retained it as a brahmā. His form is described as "exceedingly beautiful" (*abhikkantavaṇṇa*) (SN 6:11). By the time of the Buddha, he was already very ancient (*sanantana* = "ancient, primeval") so he was known as Sanaṅkumāra, "The Ancient Youth" (SN-a 6:11 & MN-a 53).

The most important activity of Sanaṅkumāra is preaching Dhamma to the devas of Tāvatiṃsa. Twice a week the devas gather in the Sudhamma Hall to listen to Dhamma, and then either Sanaṅkumāra, Sakka, some other *devaputta* qualified to teach or a human bhikkhu with supernormal power gives a teaching (DN-a 19). No other brahmā is mentioned as performing this duty.

One such manifestation of Sanaṅkumāra is described in the *Javasabha Sutta*. A great conclave of devas was assembled in the Sudhamma Hall of Tāvatiṃsa discussing the welcome increase in the number of new devas:

> Many devas were assembled in the Sudhamma Hall considering and discussing some matter of importance when a glorious light was seen in the northern direction, exceeding in its brilliance the radiance of the devas. Then Sakka, king of the devas, addressed the Thirty-Three: "Dear sirs, when such a sign is seen, when a glorious light shines forth, when such brilliance appears, it means that Brahmā will manifest. Such a brilliant light is a portent of Brahmā's manifestation."
>
> When such signs are seen, then Brahmā will appear.
>
> This is the sign of Brahmā: a light vast and great.
>
> The Tāvatiṃsa devas sat each in his own place and thought: "Let us come to know this light, and what its result is. And having found out, let us go toward it." The Four Great Kings did likewise, and all the devas were of one mind awaiting what would come of the great light.
>
> Whenever Brahmā Sanaṅkumāra appears to the Tāvatiṃsa devas he creates (*abhinimmināti*) a gross form (*oḷārika attabhāva*) with which to manifest before them, because the Tāvatiṃsa devas lack the ability to see his natural form which is beyond their range of vision.[759] He surpasses these other devas in beauty and in majesty, just as a figure made of gold surpasses a human figure. When Brahmā Sanaṅkumāra manifest to the Tāvatiṃsa devas, not one of the company prostrates, nor rises from his place, nor offers the brahmā a seat. Instead, they sit cross-legged in silence with palms joined together thinking, "Now upon whichever deva's divan[760] he wishes, there the Brahmā Sanaṅkumāra will sit." Whichever deva receives this honour is as awe-struck and delighted as a newly anointed warrior-king.
>
> Then Brahmā Sanaṅkumāra having created a gross form with the appearance of a youth, manifested in the guise of Pañcasikha.[761] Rising upwards, he sat cross-legged in the air, just as a strong man might sit on a well-appointed divan, or on the ground. Seated thus, observing the delight of the Tāvatiṃsa devas, Sanaṅkumāra

---

759 The commentary to this passage expands this into a general rule: devas of a lower plane cannot perceive devas of a higher plane unless the latter assume a gross form. DN-a18.

760 *Pallaṅka*, a kind of long seat or couch designed for cross-legged seating.

761 A *gandhabba*, see § 3:5,23.

uttered the following stanzas:

The devas of Tāvatiṃsa together with Inda rejoice.

They praise the Tathāgata, and the teaching of the Good Dhamma.

Newly arisen devas they see, beautiful and glorious.

Those who have well lived the holy life and now fare here.

They outshine the others in beauty and glory.

The students of he with supreme wisdom, the wise ones have come here.

Seeing this, they rejoice, the devas of Tāvatiṃsa together with Inda

They praise the *Tathāgata*, and the teaching of the Good Dhamma.

Thus did Brahmā Sanaṅkumāra speak. The speech of Brahmā Sanaṅkumāra is endowed with eight qualities. It is well enunciated, easily understood, charming, pleasant to hear, distinct, succinct, profound and melodious. One whose speech has these eight qualities is said to be "brahmā-sounding" (*brahmassaro*).

Then Brahmā Sanaṅkumāra created thirty-three forms and sat down beside all of the Thirty-Three each on his separate divan. He then spoke these words: "What do you think of it, honoured devas of Tāvatiṃsa? The Blessed One has acted for the welfare of the multitude, for the happiness of the many, out of compassion for the world, for devas and for humans. Of those who have gone for refuge to the Buddha, Dhamma and *Saṅgha* and who keep the precepts of morality some, after death and the break-up of the body, some have gone on to rebirth among the Paranimmitavasavattī devas, some among the Nimmānaratī devas, some among the Tusitā devas or the Yāma devas or the Tāvatiṃsa devas or the devas of the Cātumahārājika realm. Even the very least among them have arisen among the *gandhabbas*."

Thus did Brahmā Sanaṅkumāra speak. And each deva thought, "He is sitting on my divan, he is speaking to me alone!"

With one voice, all the apparitions (*nimmita*) spoke.

With one silence, all the apparitions became quiet.

Every deva, including Inda, thought:

"He sits on my divan, he speaks to me alone."

Then Brahmā Sanaṅkumāra collected the forms into one and sat next to Sakka upon his divan (DN 18).

(There follows a long series of teachings by Sanaṅkumāra upon various topics of Dhamma).

When Sanaṅkumāra assumed the form of the *gandhabba* Pañcasikha, the commentary tells us that it was because this form was beloved by the devas (DN-a18). It was also a form not so very different from his own: a youthful figure with five tufts of hair. In fact, since *Pañcasikha* means "five tufted" the commentary may be making an unwarranted assumption that the *gandhabba* of that name was intended. The Pali could just as correctly be read as "he manifested in the form of a five-tufted youth." In another passage describing Sanaṅkumāra the word *pañcasikha* is clearly used in this adjectival sense (SN-a 6:11). On another level of interpretation we could say that Sanaṅkumāra is Pañcasikha translated to a higher plane; both have the form of good-looking youths and are known for their beautiful voices. Just as the *gandhabba* Pañcasikha acted as a messenger to the Buddha (DN 21) so was Sanaṅkumāra identified by the Buddha as a "brahmā-messenger" (*brahmā pesa)* (AN 11:10).

In the sutta immediately following the one quoted above, another manifestation of Sanaṅkumāra is related in identical words. The different content here is in his teaching to the devas. In this sutta he relates a past life of the Buddha as Mahāgovinda, a royal minister. Sanaṅkumāra himself was instrumental in this lifetime of the Bodhisatta, manifesting before him at a critical moment:

> (Mahāgovinda had entered into retreat in the forest for the four months of the rainy season, practising the meditation on compassion). At the end of the four months Mahāgovinda found only discontent and weariness. "I have heard it said by venerable brahmins and teachers of long-standing that if one enters into the meditation on compassion for the four months of the rains, then one can see Brahmā and have conversation and discussion with him. But I have neither seen nor conversed with Brahmā."
>
> Then Brahmā Sanaṅkumāra knew with his own mind the thoughts in the mind of Mahāgovinda and as quickly as a strong man might bend forth or withdraw his arm, he disappeared from the *brahmaloka* and appeared before the face of the brahmin Mahāgovinda. And the brahmin Mahāgovinda felt fearful and stupefied and his hair stood on end before this sight never seen before. Thus, fearful, awestruck, with hairs standing on end he addressed Sanaṅkumāra in verse, and the brahmā replied in kind:
>
> Mahāgovinda: Beautiful, majestic[762] and glorious one, who are you sir?
>
> Not knowing, I ask, how may we know you?
>
> Sanaṅkumāra: I am known as "the youth" (*kumāra*) and "the ancient one" (*sanantana*) in the brahmā world,
>
> All the devas know me thus. Know this Govinda.
>
> Mahāgovinda: A seat, water, oil for the feet, sweet cakes—are for Brahmā.
>
> Ask for what offerings you will, those we will give.
>
> Sanaṅkumāra: I accept your offerings. Now you, Govinda, may ask
>
> For a boon here-and-now or for the good of your future existence.
>
> This is your opportunity to ask, what is it you wish?
>
> (Mahāgovinda chose to ask about something which would benefit his future lives and the verse dialogue continued:)
>
> Mahāgovinda: I ask you, Brahmā Sanaṅkumāra,
>
> The doubter asks the one free from doubt among the views of others,
>
> Where to stand and what training to follow,
>
> Whereby a mortal man might reach the deathless brahmā world?
>
> Sanaṅkumāra: Having destroyed all thought of "mine", one becomes a Brahmā among men.

[762] *Vaṇṇavā yasavā,* lit. colourful and famous.

Being solitary, resolved on compassion.

Pure of scent, he abstains from sexual intercourse.

Here is the stand-point, here the training to follow.

For the mortal man to reach the brahmā world. (DN 19)

In the sequel, Mahāgovinda says he understands most of this instruction but asks for clarification of "pure of scent" (*nirāmagandho*). Sanaṅkumāra explains in a further stanza of verse that this means being free of the stench of the defilements (ibid .).

It is to be noted that Mahāgovinda exhibits a brahminical rather than a Buddhist concept of Brahmā. He offers the brahmā cakes and he calls the *brahmaloka* "deathless" (*amata*). Nor does Sanaṅkumāra attempt to correct these views. There are two possible explanations for this seeming lapse. Perhaps Sanaṅkumāra was, at that time, still subject to wrong view himself (although he could hardly have believed that brahmās want sweet cakes!) We have seen already that some brahmās imagine themselves to be immortal. On the other hand, Sanaṅkumāra might simply have judged that Mahāgovinda was not yet spiritually advanced enough to grasp the concept of impermanence.

Whatever the spiritual state of Sanaṅkumāra might have been at the time of Mahāgovinda, in the distant past, by the time of the Buddha Gotama he had attained to the stage of *sakadāgāmi* ("once-returner", the second stage of awakening). In the *Mahāsamaya Sutta* he is included among those brahmās identified as "Buddha's sons", which the commentary defines as meaning "*ariyabrahmās*" (DN-a 20) The word *ariya*, commonly translated as "noble" has a technical meaning in the suttas and is reserved for those who have attained to one or another of the stages of awakening. More specifically, the conclusion of the *Janavasabha Sutta* (which describes a manifestation of Sanaṅkumāra to the Tāvatiṃsa devas and is extensively quoted above) he speaks about the great numbers of *sotāpannas* and *sakadāgāmis* (first and second stages of awakening) that have arisen among the Magadhans since the Buddha began teaching. But he then goes on to say:

In regard to those other beings, who have gained more merit,

My mind is incapable of reckoning them. I would be ashamed to speak a falsehood. (DN 18)

In other words, Sanaṅkumāra is unable to comprehend the minds of those who have attained stages beyond his own.

At one time Brahmā Sanaṅkumāra appeared before the Buddha, his radiance illuminating the entire bank of the Sappinī River. He paid homage to the Buddha then uttered this verse:

The *khattiya* is senior for those who take caste as their standard.

The one perfected in knowledge and conduct (*vijjācaraṇasampanna*), is senior among devas and humans.

The Buddha approved his saying, which pleased Sanaṅkumāra. Keeping the Buddha to his right side as a mark of respect, he then disappeared (SN 6:11). This brief encounter takes on added significance in that the Buddha quoted the verse at least four times on subsequent occasions. Sometimes he meant to put the haughty brahmins in their place and the emphasis was on the first line (DN 3). At other times, he used it in the higher sense, emphasizing the second line which implies that awakening trumps caste (MN 53 & AN 11:10). At the conclusion of the *Aggañña Sutta*, both senses are conveyed at once (DN 27). The Buddha said that this verse was well-spoken by Sanaṅkumāra, it was meaningful (*atthasaṃhita*) and that he approved of it (MN 53).

3:6:11 BAKA

As we have seen, not all the *mahābrahmās* are as spiritually advanced as Sahampati and Sanaṅkumāra; some of them are subject to wrong views and delusions of grandeur. One important brahmā of this type is Baka whom we have encountered before in the chapter on Māra (§ 3:5,41).

Another thing that makes Baka interesting is that we have an account of his career through several lifetimes. Many kappas ago, he spent several successive lives living as a hermit, developing meditation and psychic powers which he used to help people in distress.

At one time, Baka had been a hermit practising austerites (*tāpa*) in a desert waste. One day a merchant caravan of five hundred carts lost their way while crossing the desert. Unable to determine the direction, they wandered for seven days without food or water, perishing in the heat. "Now our life is over," so saying they released their bullocks and lay down to sleep under their carts. Seeing this the hermit thought, "They shall not perish in my sight." By the exercise of his supernormal power (*iddhānubhāvena*) he diverted the course of the Gaṅgā River (the Ganges) toward the caravan and created a jungle thicket nearby. The men drank from the stream, watered their cattle and gathered grass and wood for the onward journey in the jungle thicket. They determined the direction and were now in good health to carry on.

At a subsequent time (i.e. in another life) Baka was again practising austerities, this time supported by a village in the border region. He lived in a jungle thicket by the bank of a river. One day, bandits descended from the hills and attacked the village, taking many people to sell as slaves. They took them up into the hills and having tied them up securely, settled down to eat a meal. The hermit heard many cries of distress from cows and buffaloes, from girls and boys. "They shall not perish in my sight." By his supernormal power, he cast off his own form (*attabhāva*) and appeared as a warrior-king surrounded by a four-fold army (i.e. infantry, cavalry, chariots and elephants). With war drums beating, he advanced upon that place. The approach of the royal army was reported to the bandits by their scouts and saying, "We do not fight with kings," they cut the bonds of their prisoners and abandoning their meal they fled away. The hermit led the people back to their own village.

In yet another lifetime Baka was once more a hermit, this time living by the banks of the Gaṅgā. It happened one day that some people passed by on a raft with a gaily decorated pavilion amidships. They were on their way to visit their kinfolk and were making merry, eating and drinking. As they floated downstream, they threw the dregs of their drinks and bits of broken meat into the Gaṅgā. This enraged the king of the Gaṅgā nāgas,[763] "They are throwing their rubbish down upon me! I will seize all these people and drown them in the river!" Creating a form as large as a big ship he broke the surface of the water spreading his serpent's hood. The people were seized with the fear of death and all together let out a great cry. This was heard by the hermit who said "They shall not perish in my sight." Thinking quickly he created by his supernormal power the form of a *supaṇṇa*[764] and flew there. Seeing his approach, the *nāgarājā* became afraid for his life and dived under the water. The people were then able to carry on their journey in safety (Jāt 405 & SN-a 6:4).

In yet another existence, Baka was again a hermit named Kesava and the Bodhisatta was his favourite disciple Kappa. The old hermit was so attached to his student that when the two were separated he grew ill and only recovered when they were reunited (Jāt 346). So the Buddha and Baka had at least one previous connection, and we can conclude that there were others. When the Buddha visited Baka he briefly recounted these exploits in verse and ended each stanza with the refrain:

> That ancient observance (*vatasīlavatta*) of yours,

---

[763] Nāgas are powerful shape-shifting serpents who dwell under bodies of water. See (§ 3:2,4).

[764] *Supaṇṇas* are gigantic birds and the natural enemy of the nāgas, upon whom they prey. See (§ 3:2,5).

I remember like one awakening from a dream. (SN 6:4)

This implies that he was there. Since there is no mention of the hermit having disciples in the three stories where he uses his powers to save innocent lives, it is likely that the Bodhisatta was at that time one of the people saved. Since these lives occurred in the very ancient past, in a previous kappa,[765] it could have been before the being who eventually became Gotama Buddha began his Bodhisatta career.

Baka's subsequent lives in various brahmā worlds is also described:

> In a time when no Buddha had arisen in the world, Baka had gone forth as an *isi* and developed meditation on a *kasiṇa*.[766] In this way he developed the fourth jhāna and had not fallen away from that attainment at the time of his death. He was reborn in the Vehapphala *brahmaloka* and had a life-span there of five hundred kappas. During that lifetime he developed the lesser attainment of the third jhāna and upon passing away from that realm was reborn in the Subhakiṇha *brahmaloka* and there had a life-span of sixty-four kappas. In that lifetime he developed the second jhāna and was reborn among the Ābhassara brahmās where he had a life-span of eight kappas and practised the first jhāna. Upon his decease from that realm he was reborn as a first jhāna brahmā with a life-span of one kappa. (MN-a 49)

It was in this form that he was visited by the Buddha. It is clear from his dialogue with the Buddha that he had forgotten his previous lifetimes, and this ignorance was an important factor in his falling into false views. This downward trajectory meant that his previous states of existence were unknown and unknowable to him because they were "beyond his range" (āpātha). There is no explanation of why Baka while enjoying the experiences of a higher attainment would choose to practise a lower one. We can only conclude it was the all too "human" failing of desire for coarse experience. For instance, while experiencing the sublime *upekkhā* ("equanimity") of the fourth jhāna realm, his mind must have conceived a longing for the relatively coarser *sukha* ("bliss") of the third jhāna.

The wrong views to which Baka subscribed were a direct result of this forgetfulness. As the first being to arise in his world at the beginning of a cycle, he came to believe that he was the one and only supreme creator.[767] In the dialogue of the Buddha with Baka and his minions, Baka welcomes the Buddha with the following words:

> "Come, dear sir, welcome! It is long since you have come this way! This, dear sir, is permanent. It is constant. It is eternal. This is not subject to death. Here there is no birth, no ageing, no dying or passing away or being reborn. From here, there is no greater state and there is no escape beyond this." (MN 49)

The initial greeting, "it is long since you have come this way," is just a polite form; there is no indication that the Buddha ever visited Baka in his realm before.[768] There follows a long dialogue in the course of which one of Baka's attendants, possessed by Māra, attempts to get the Buddha to acknowledge Baka's supremacy. Baka himself repeats much of the argument, the gist of which is that the Buddha should "bind" himself (*ajjhosati*) to a long list of conditioned phenomena beginning with the four elements and ending with Pajāpati and Brahmā. This is, obviously, directly contrary to the Buddhist goal of detachment from *saṃsāric* becoming: bound to the conditioned, one cannot realize the unconditioned. Baka says this will ensure a better rebirth and that "this will bring you close to me, into my

---

765 This is explicitly stated in the commentary.

766 An *isi*, or "rishi" is a term for pre-Buddhist ascetics. A *kasiṇa* is a physical object like a coloured wooden disk used as a focus for meditation.

767 See DN 1 for a detailed description of this process.

768 See AN-a 6,34 where another use of this greeting is specifically called, "a polite form of speech" that does not imply a previous visit.

domain, for me to do with as I like and to punish."[769] This hardly seems persuasive. The commentary explains that the first clause is meant as an inducement, the latter as a threat, and that the "punishment' consists of being given a deformed or dwarfish form (MN-a 49).

The Buddha, who is in any case beyond rebirth, is naturally having none of it. Instead he puts Baka in his place by revealing to him the true context and limitations of his existence:

> As far as moon and sun revolve, protecting and illuminating in each direction.
>
> Over a thousand such worlds do you wield power.
>
> And there you know the various beings; those who are subject to passion, and those free from passion.
>
> You know the various states of beings and their comings and goings. (MN 49)

The commentary goes on to explain that although Baka is sovereign over one thousand worlds, there are other brahmās above him who wield authority over two thousand, three thousand, four thousand, five thousand, ten thousand or even one hundred thousand world-systems (MN-a 49). So, although Baka's power and knowledge are vast in human terms, they are limited and are far from being supreme in the cosmos. Furthermore, as the Buddha next pointed out:

> "There are, brahmā, other bodies (*kāya*) that you do not know and that you do not see, but I know them and see them. There is the body called Ābhassarā (the second jhāna level brahmā world) that you passed away from before coming here. You have dwelt here so long that you have forgotten, therefore you do not know it or see it, but I know it and see it. So my knowledge is not a level with yours, but surpasses it."

The Buddha then informs Baka of the existence of the third and fourth jhāna level brahmā worlds in similar terms.

The dialogue between the Buddha and Baka at last comes to an impasse when Baka is unable to come up with a cogent reply, so he instead proposes a contest or "game" (*laḷitaka)* (MN-a 49). Each in turn will demonstrate his power by attempting to vanish from the sight of the other. This episode is only briefly mentioned in the sutta, but the commentary adds more detail and ends with a comic touch:

> Baka attempted to disappear by reverting to his natural form (*mūlapaṭisandhi*, lit. "root becoming"). The natural form of a brahmā is subtle, it is beyond the range of others; to be seen they must assume a constructed form (*abhisaṅkhatakāya*). However, the Buddha prevented him from going into his natural form. Failing in this attempt, Baka then attempted to conceal his form by covering it with darkness but the Buddha dispelled the darkness. Unable to disappear, Baka fled from his *vimāna* to the root of a tree and hid there, squatting on the ground. Seeing this his attendants said, "So this, Brahmā, is how you vanish!" and he was downcast by their mockery. (MN-a 49)

The Buddha then easily vanishes from the sight of Baka and his assembly, but they can hear his voice as he utters some verse proclaiming that he has overcome both being and non-being. This overawes the brahmās and they recognize the supremacy of the Buddha and accept his teaching. Thus, by saving him from wrong view, the former student repaid his debt of gratitude to his former teacher of so long ago.

Before leaving the topic of Baka, we should briefly note one small detail. In this case we have a rare instance of being able to number his *brahmapurohitas*. There is a reference in verse by Baka to "we seventy-two" (SN 6:4) which is not explained there or in the commentary. It can only mean himself and seventy-one attending *brahmapurohitas*.

---

[769] MN 49 the word "punish" is Bhikkhu Bodhi's translation for the obscure verb *bāhiteyya*.

3:6:12 BRAHMĀS AT THE MAHĀNIRAYA

The *Mahāsamaya Sutta* (DN 20) is a text mostly in verse which recounts in a long series of stanzas a "great assembly" (the meaning of *mahāsamaya*) of various devas and other beings who have come to honour the Buddha. One stanza lists the brahmās who were in attendance:

> Subrahmā and Paramatta, sons of the potent one,
>
> Together with Saṅankumāra and Tissa,
>
> Came to the meeting in the forest.
>
> A thousand *mahābrahmās* from a thousand *brahmalokas* ("brahmā worlds") came.
>
> Reborn brilliantly, of great power, with awe-inspiring forms (*bhismākāyo*, or "terrible bodies")
>
> Here ten lords (*issara*) have come, each individually wielding power.
>
> And there in their midst is Hārita with his retinue.[770]

Interpreting the text with the help of the commentary we learn that "the potent one" (*iddhimant*) is the Buddha, and the identification of these brahmās as his "sons" implies that they are *ariyabrahmā*, "noble brahmās", meaning that they have some degree of awakening.

Turning to the individually named brahmās: **Paramatta** is just a name to us, he occurs here and nowhere else, and **Saṅankumāra** we have already met. **Tissa** had been a bhikkhu under the Buddha and recently died and been reborn as a brahmā. In the brahmā world, he was known as Brahmā Tissa, of great power and glory (*mahiddhiko mahānubhāvo*). On two separate occasions Moggallāna used his psychic power to visit Tissa in his brahmā world in order to ask him about the degree of spiritual attainment among the devas. On the first occasion, Tissa tells Moggāllana that some, but not all, devas in each of the sensual *saggas* are indeed *sotāpannas* (AN 6:34). On the second visit, he speaks about the brahmā worlds and says that those brahmās who are content with a brahmā's life-span, beauty, happiness, glory[771] and power and who do not know of an escape higher than that do not have knowledge of who among humans is liberated. But those who are not contented with those attributes of a brahmā, and who do conceive of a higher state, are able to know who is liberated (AN 7:56).

Of the "ten lords", the commentary says only that although each of the thousand brahmās wields his own power, ten are lords. This indicates that there is a defined hierarchy among the brahmās. **Hārita**, who walks in their midst and is probably meant to be one of the ten, is mentioned several times in the texts as an example of one enjoying a large or glorious retinue.[772] The commentary to the *Mahāsamaya Sutta* says he is "foremost" (*jeṭṭhaka*) among the brahmās, just as Sakka is among the devas and that his retinue is one hundred thousand strong (DN-a 20). Nothing more is known about him.

Subrahmā is identified as a *paccekabrahmā*. The word *pacceka* is defined as "single, by oneself, separate"(PED). A *paccekabrahmā* is a brahmā who "goes about alone, without a retinue."[773] Despite being so defined, in the three

[770] DN 20. This stanza poses some problems of interpretation. I have departed from the translations of both Rhys Davids and Maurice Walshe in reading the Pali as meaning one thousand mahābrahmās rather than a single mahābrahmā ruling over a thousand worlds. The text can be interpreted either way, but the commentary supports my reading.

[771] *Yasa*—or perhaps meaning "retinue".

[772] See DN-a 1, DN 33, MN-a 53, SN-a 35:196.

[773] SN-ṭ 6:6 Similarly, a *paccekabuddha* is a fully awakened person who lives between Buddha periods. He differs from a full

suttas (other than the *Mahāsamaya*) in which he appears Subrahmā is always accompanied by another *paccekabrahmā* named Suddhāvāsa.[774] In all three suttas, which occur sequentially in the Saṃyutta Nikāya, the two *paccekabrahmās* go to see the Buddha and stand by the door-posts of his meditation hut. Two of these incidents are very brief and have parallel wording. One of the two utters a brief verse lamenting the foolishness of some errant bhikkhu who has "attempted to measure the immeasurable." Subrahmā says this of Kokālika (SN 6:7) and in the next sutta Suddhāvāsa uses almost identical language about Katamorakatissaka, a follower of Devadatta (SN 6:8).

The first sutta in this series has a more involved story. When the two come to see the Buddha they find him deep in meditation and do not wish to disturb him. So Subrahmā says to Suddhāvāsa:

> "There is a certain brahmā world that is luxurious and opulent. The brahmā there dwells in negligence. Come, dear sir, let us go there and inspire him to diligence."

They travel together to that brahmā world and attempt to encourage the brahmā there to go and see the Buddha for his own edification.

But the brahmā failed to heed their words. He manifested his own form multiplied one thousand times and said, "Do you see, dear sir, my power (*iddhi*) and majesty (*anubhāva*)?"

> "I see, dear sir, that such is your power and majesty."

> "When such is my power, and such is my majesty, why then should I go to see any *samaṇa* or brahmin?"

> Then the *paccekabrahmā* Subrahmā manifested his own form multiplied two thousand times. "Do you see, dear sir, my power and majesty? The power and majesty of the Buddha is greater than either yours or mine. You, dear sir, should go and pay your respects to the Buddha."

> There follows an exchange of verses:
>
> (The brahmā of that world)—Three hundred *supaṇṇas*, four hundred geese,
>
> And five hundred tiger-birds; (created by) meditation (*jhāyino*).
>
> This *vimāna* shines, illuminating the northern direction.
>
> (Subrahmā)—However much your *vimāna* shines, illuminating the northern direction,
>
> Having seen the fault of form (*rūpa*), how it ever trembles,
>
> The wise person takes no delight in form.

The brahmā has fallen into pride because of his ability to manifest various forms but Subrahmā declares the unreliable and insubstantial nature of these phenomena. *Rūpa* ("form") is a complex word with different nuances depending on context. It can refer to the object of visual consciousness, i.e. a "visible form" or to the aggregate of matter or body in general. The level of the cosmos inhabited by these brahmā beings is called the *rūpaloka*, "the world of form." It seems that Subrahmā is playing with various levels of meaning here, chiefly to free the errant brahmā from being lost in the illusion of his own "forms." The sutta concludes with the statement that the brahmā did go to see the Buddha "at a later time.

Buddha in that he establishes no teaching which survives beyond his own time.

[774] SN 6:6, SN 6:7 & SN 6:8.

3:6:13 SECOND JHĀNA LEVEL—THE ĀBHASSARA BRAHMĀS

Although the *mahābrahmās* and their human worshippers may imagine that they represent the summit of the cosmos, this is not so. As the Buddha explained to Baka, there are realms higher and more subtle yet. The realm of the Ābhassara deities corresponds to the second jhāna. The ordinary consciousness of the beings there is the equivalent to that experienced by a human meditator who has entered second jhāna, and if he does not "fall away" (*aparihīnajjhāna*) from that state upon his death he will be reborn there.[775] The meditation on *karuṇā* ("compassion") is also given as a way to rebirth among the Ābhassara brahmās. Just as brahmins seek rebirth in the brahmaloka as their goal, the Ābhassara realm is said to be the goal of "great ascetics" (*mahātāpasa)* (MN-a 11).

We have seen that the first jhāna is characterized by five factors: *vitakka* ("initial application of mind"), *vicāra* ("sustained application of mind"), *pīti* ("rapture"), *sukha* ("bliss") and *ekaggatā* ("gone to oneness"). The progression through the jhānas is always toward greater simplicity and subtlety and at each successive stage, factors are dropped. The second jhāna is marked by the presence of either three or four factors: *vitakka* falls away and eventually *vicāra* as well, leaving *pīti* as the dominant factor of this mental state.[776]

The beings in the Ābhassara realm dwell "feeding on rapture" (*pītibhakkha*) . Although this adjective is also applied to the brahmās of the first jhāna level, (e.g. DN 1) applied to the Ābhassara beings it becomes almost proverbial. After Māra invaded the mind of some villagers to deny the Buddha alms food, the Buddha says he will instead "feed on rapture like the Ābhassara devas" (SN 4:18). The best sound in the entire cosmos is said to be the sound of the Ābhassara beings continually exclaiming, "Oh! The bliss! Oh! The bliss!" (*aho sukhaṃ*) (AN 5: 170). They are said to be "overflowing with happiness, drenched with happiness, completely filled with happiness, immersed in happiness."[777] The physical realm inhabited by the Ābhassara brahmās is described as a "most excellent jewel covered level plain."[778]

The name Ābhassara can be interpreted as "shining body" (ābhā + *sarīra*),[779] and the description of these beings emphasizes their radiance. Their bodies are like the flickering flame of a torch (DN-a 15 & MN-a 1). This association with fire is also found in their cosmological role as the lowest level which survives when all the lower realms are destroyed by fire at the end of a kappa. Their realm is said to be the limit (*sīma*) of the fire element, and when an illustration of fire going a long distance is sought, it is said to be able to go "as far as the Ābhassara realm" (SN-a 6:13 & SN-a 44:9). At the end of a cycle which is destroyed by fire, beings are mostly reborn here and from here populate the new worlds at the beginning of the next cycle.[780] The Bodhisatta long ago spent seven kappas being reborn as an Ābhassara brahmā and then at the onset of the next kappa, being reborn as a *mahābrahmā* in an empty *vimāna* (It 1:3,2).

The name Ābhassara may be used as a generic term to refer to all brahmās of the second jhāna level, but it more precisely signifies only the highest grade of these, those who have mastered second jhāna to a superior degree. They

---

775 See AN-a 1:188 & MN-a 4. For the equivalence of jhāna and brahmā consciousness, see CMA Ch. 5.

776 This is a slight simplification. The abhidhamma uses a different system which lists five rather than four jhānas by dividing the second into two depending on the presence or absence of *vicāra*. See Vism Ch 3 & 4. A good discussion of jhāna and jhāna factors can be found in CMA 54–59.

777 DN 33. *sukhena abhisannā parisannā paripūrā paripphu ṭā.*

778 Abhidh-s 2:5. The Pali is *paṇītaratanapabhāvabhāsitekatalavāsino* and the same description is given for the other higher brahmā worlds.

779 But see PED which says that the etymology of the word is uncertain and offers two possibilities for its derivation: ā + *bha + *sar = "from whose bodies are emitted rays of light" or ābhā + *svar* = "to shine or to be bright." Suwanda Sugunasiri offers yet another possibility: "hither-come-shining-arrow", *Dhamma Aboard Evolution,* p. 48. The important point is that all of these derivations in one way or another are based on the radiant quality of these beings.

780 AN 10. 29—The cosmological role of the Ābhassara beings at the end of a cycle is very important. See § 2:3-5.

have a life-span of eight kappas. Those who have mastered the jhāna only to a middling degree have a life-span of four kappas and are known as *Appamāṇābha* ("immeasurable radiance") brahmās. Those who have only an inferior mastery of jhāna become *Parittabha* ("limited radiance") brahmās. They have a life-span of two kappas.[781] All three grades are said to dwell on the same level.[782] Despite this nomenclature, the second jhāna level brahmās are classed as beings that are "alike in body, but different in perception." The difference is said to be that some of them possess the factor of *vitakka* and some do not (AN-a 7:44). In one text there is an alternate way of classifying these beings: they are divided into four grades instead of three. These are called, from the highest to the lowest, *Parisuddhābha* ("pure radiance"), *Appamāṇābha, Parittabha,* and *Saṃkiliṭṭhābha* ("defiled radiance"). The difference is said to be in the degree of development of the meditation object (MN 127).

The Ābhassara are beings even more subtle and refined than the *mahābrahmās*. Their lives are extremely joyful ones, and very long by human standards as they outlive entire world-systems which come and go beneath them. It is significant that we have no stories about individual Ābhassara beings to compare with those of the devas and first jhāna brahmās. None is known to us by name. Because their psychological make-up lacks the factor of *vitakka* and sometimes *vicāra* as well, which are associated with speech and thought, they exist in blissful inactivity. To put it simply, they are too "blissed out" to have any concern for or involvement with the worlds below them. And yet these beings too, are part of *saṃsāra* and when their long lives at last come to an end they are, unless they have attained to some degree of awakening, subject to rebirth in the lower realms.[783]

---

[781] DN-a 15, MN-a 1, AN-a 4: 123.

[782] MN-a 1. This is contradicted by later systems such as that of the *Abhidharmakośa* which allocates a separate plane for each class.

[783] AN 4: 123. It may be objected that the Aggañña Sutta has a story about Ābhassara beings fulfilling their cosmic role at the beginning of a cycle. However, this concerns beings in the process of falling away from the Ābhassara state and not Ābhassara beings in their native realm. We have covered this topic in the section on cosmological time. See § 2:5.

3:6:14 THIRD JHĀNA LEVEL—THE SUBHAKIṆHA BRAHMĀS

The third jhāna is characterized by two factors only, *sukha* and *ekaggāta*, the factor of *pīti* having dropped away. Mastery of this jhāna by a human meditator leads to rebirth in the *Subhakiṇha* realm. The practice of *muditā* ("sympathetic joy") meditation is also said to lead to this realm.[784] The name *subhakiṇha* means "strewn with beauty."[785] The two characteristics that are always mentioned in descriptions of the Subhakiṇha beings are their radiant beauty and their great happiness. Their bodies are called "one great mass of beauty" (*subhena sarīrappabhāvaṇṇena ekagghanāti*), and their radiance is compared favourably to that of the Ābhassara beings in that it is steady and does not "flicker" (DN-a 15). This is the difference between the jhāna factors of *pīti* and *sukha*. *Pīti*, which predominates on the second jhāna level, is a thrilling kind of happiness, commonly translated as "rapture", whereas *sukha* (at least in the context of jhāna) is a deeper, more refined and "oceanic" kind of happiness, often translated as bliss. The happiness of these brahmās is externally manifested as a steady brilliant glow, all the flashy fireworks having been left behind. Whereas the radiance of the Ābhassara brahmās is compared to a torch, that of the Subhakiṇha brahmās is like the lustre of pure gold (MN-a 1).

The bliss of the Subhakiṇha brahmās is described in superlative terms. Like the Ābhassara beings, they are said to be "filled with happiness, overflowing with happiness, drenched in happiness," but that of the Subhakiṇha brahmās is also said to be *santusitā*, "contented" (DN 33). They are "extraordinarily blissful" (*ekantasukhaṃ)* (MN 57). Although the factor of *sukha* is present in the lower brahmā realms, here it is pure, existing without the admixture of *pīti* (AN-a 3:23). Indeed, it is the best kind of happiness to be found anywhere in the cosmos (AN 5: 170).

The third jhāna level brahmās are also divided according to their degree of attainment. Those who had developed third jhāna only to a lesser degree are classed as *Parittasubha* beings. Those who had mastered it to a middling degree are called *Appamānasubha* beings. Those who have fully mastered the jhāna are reborn as *Subhakiṇha* beings properly so called, although the designation can be used generically for all the third jhāna level brahmās, who all dwell on the same plane (MN-a 1).

We have seen that the Ābhassara world is said to be the supreme goal of the "great ascetics." Likewise, the Subhakiṇha level is the goal of the "wanderers" (*paribbajaka)* (MN-a 11). These were spiritual seekers often mentioned in the suttas. They lived a homeless life similar to that of the Buddhist bhikkhus, but were depicted as prone to false views and to disputing about those views. One encounter of the Buddha with the *paribbajakas* highlights for us the difference between jhāna as an attainment and a brahmā world as a state of existence. One of the *paribbajakas*, named Udayin, declares that the goal of his path is an "extraordinarily pleasant world" (*ekantasukho loko*), and that the way to it is the keeping of moral precepts and the practice of asceticism. The Buddha replies that development of the third jhāna is the way to "an extraordinarily pleasant world." But, Udayin objects, surely that state of jhāna is itself such a world and the goal has been reached. The Buddha continues that the third jhāna is only the way to the extraordinarily pleasant world, not that world itself. At this the assembly of *paribbajakas* become dismayed and cry out, "We are lost! We are lost among the doctrines of our teachers!" The commentary explains that these wanderers had lost the way to attain jhāna and regarded that state as the goal toward which they strived, not realizing that it was merely the prerequisite for rebirth in the Subhakiṇha world. Of course, even that "extraordinarily pleasant world" is not the goal of the Buddhist path, and the Buddha makes that clear in the following dialogue.[786] This sutta stands as a clear

---

784 AN 4: 125. A statement which leads to a contradiction with the developed theory of jhāna. See Bhikkhu Bodhi, NDB, note 817.

785 See ASa 5. The commentator says that the name should properly be spelled *subhakiṇṇa* and many modern reference books offer this as the primary spelling, but it does not seem to appear elsewhere in the texts.

786 MN 79 & commentary.

indication that the brahmā worlds are not to be understood as poetic metaphors for their equivalent jhāna states, but as real destinations of rebirth.

At the end of a kappa in which the cosmos is destroyed by water, everything below the Subhakiṇha realm is submerged and destroyed. This occurs less often than the destruction by fire.[787]

There is some contradiction in the texts regarding the life-span of the Subhakiṇha brahmās. The developed theory found in the Abhidhamma texts has the life-span doubling at each successive level so that the Parittasubha beings live for sixteen kappas, the Appamānasubha beings for thirty-two kappas and the Subhakiṇha brahmās for sixty-four kappas.[788] However, in the sole mention of this in the suttas, which must be regarded as the oldest source, it is simply stated that the Subhakiṇha beings have a life-span of four kappas (AN 4:123). The commentary does not resolve the discrepancy.

Just as in the case of the Ābhassara brahmās, there are no stories about the Subhakiṇha brahmās and we are not told any of their names, if indeed they have any.

[787] SN-a 16:13, AN-a 4: 156, Ita 3:5,10. This topic has been explained in § 2:8.

[788] See Vibh 18:6 and also Abhidh-s 5.

3:6:15 FOURTH JHĀNA LEVEL—THE VEHAPPHALA BRAHMĀS

The fourth jhāna transcends even the bliss of *sukha* and replaces it with *upekkhā* ("equanimity"), which is a neutral feeling (i.e neither pleasure nor pain) characterized by a deep peacefulness (Vism 14.128). Beings in the fourth jhāna level are not divided into grades like all the brahmās below them,[789] but are all classed together being "alike in form and in perception" (DN-a 15 & AN-a 7:44). Their life-span is given as being five hundred kappas (AN 4: 123). Rebirth into this realm is acquired by the attainment of the fourth jhāna or, logically enough, by mastering the meditation on *upekkhā*, which is the fourth *brahmavihāra*.[790] Their plane is not destroyed at the end of a kappa; the highest level of destruction is reached when the world-system is destroyed by wind which reaches as high as the Subhakiṇha level only (SN-a 16:13). The name *Vehapphala* means "Great Fruit".

The Vehapphala level is considered somewhat separate and above all the other brahmā worlds. In a couple of passages the brahmā worlds are listed as being "nine plus Vehapphala" (MN-a 26 & MN-a 41). This agrees with the role of *upekkhā* in meditative development. The fourth jhāna and the fourth *brahmavihāra* both transcend the emotive tone of the other states in their respective groups. The fourth jhāna is the only one which is not blissful, and the *brahmavihāra* of *upekkhā* is the only which does not include an aspiration ("may all beings be happy") but just accepts beings as they are. We can also add that the state of "Equanimity about Formations" (*saṅkhārupekkhā*) is a critical phase in the development of insight (*vipassanā*) and is the prerequisite for full awakening.[791]

789 At least in the Theravāda system. The *Abhidharmakośa* divides the fourth jhāna level into three grades, maintaining the pattern established in the first three levels. See AK 3:5, p. 366.

790 AN 4: 125. The other three brahmavihāras are *mettā, karuṇā* and *muditā*, "loving-kindness", "compassion" and "sympathetic joy".

791 See Mahasi Sayadaw, *Progress of Insight.* The treatment of *upekkhā* in this paragraph is somewhat simplified and ignores the distinction between *upekkhā* as a mental formation and *upekkhā* as a feeling.

3:6:16 ASAÑÑASATTA—THE UNCONSCIOUS BEINGS

Although the fourth jhāna plane is not divided into grades like the other three, there is a special class of brahmā beings that dwell in one region of the Vehapphala world. These are the Asaññasatta, the "Unconscious Beings."[792] They have a maximum life-span of five hundred kappas during which time they exist as immobile physical bodies only, without any trace of consciousness or the other mental factors. As soon as a single moment of perception arises in them, they fall away from that realm and are reborn elsewhere.[793] The length of their life-span is not fixed but is determined by the force of kamma of the original jhāna, "like the force imparted to an arrow by the bow-string" (DN-ṭ 1).

This curious state of unconscious existence is considered to be an inopportune plane (*akkhaṇabhūmi*) in which there is no prospect of further spiritual development (ibid.). Rebirth among the Asaññasatta brahmās occurs when a human meditator, always qualified as being an "outsider" (*bāhiraka*), i.e. a non-Buddhist, after emerging from fourth jhāna reflects upon the disadvantage of thought and perception, as being causes of suffering, and resolves to eliminate the mental process altogether.[794]

There is no detailed description of the Asaññasatta beings or their abode in the ancient Pali texts, but we can cite a vivid passage from a medieval Thai work, *The Three Worlds According to King Ruang*:

> The brahmas who live in this level are 96.000 *wa* tall[795] and do not have the slightest residue of mind. The faces and bodies of these brahmas are like golden images that have been newly polished by an artisan, and they look very beautiful indeed. Anyone who dies in a sitting posture while he is thinking about being born in this level of the brahma world will be born there in a sitting posture until the end of his life-span. Among those in the brahma world there are also those who die while they are standing and are born as brahma standing in this brahma world. These brahmas remain without any quivering and without making the slightest movement in any part of their bodies; not even the eyes of these brahma blink or look during their entire lifetimes—and they do not know anything at all.
>
> The interior of the gem castles of these brahma are very spacious indeed. There are flowers, perfumes and spices, and other fragrant things that, through the entire lives of these brahma, are always superb and very excellent; these flowers never wither, never die and never fall off, and the fragrances of the perfumes, spices and other fragrant things never fade or disappear. The flowers appear as if they had been neatly arranged. They are neat, in good order and very beautiful indeed, and they surround these brahmas in every direction.[796]

It would seem, according to this text, that they are surrounded by a great deal of entirely pointless splendour. It should also be noted that the scented flowers and perfume would not be noticed in any brahmā world, as everyone in the *rūpaloka* is devoid of the sense of smell.

Returning to our original sources, the case of the bhikkhu Sobhita may be cited. He once declared that he could remember five hundred kappas, which would be a claim of supernormal attainment and thus a disciplinary offence; if falsely made it would have been a *pārājika*, an offence of disrobing. However, as the Buddha explained, Sobhita was

---

[792] Sometimes translated more literally as "non-percipient beings," as for example by Bhikkhu Bodhi. For their sharing the same level as the Vehapphala, see MN-a 1 and AK 2:4, p. 222, which situates their dwelling in a "raised place" within the fourth jhāna plane.

[793] DN 1 together with commentary and sub-commentary. AK says their next birth is necessarily in the sphere of sense desire, AK 2:4, p.222.

[794] DN-a 1. This meditation is especially associated with the use of the wind *kasiṇa*.

[795] A *wa* is 6 and 2/3 feet, so they are 639,360 feet high according to King Ruang. Definition of a *wa* is from TW p. 67.

[796] Reynolds, trans., *Three Worlds According to King Ruang*, p. 249-50.

only claiming to recall a single existence as an Asaññasatta being. Because of the difficulty of recollecting such an existence, where one is only conscious at all at the moments of initial rebirth-linking and at death, Sobhita was named by the Buddha as the disciple foremost in the recollection of past-lives. Sobhita's own description of the experience was "I recall five hundred kappas like a single night."[797]

There is a debate in the *Kathāvatthu* about whether the Asaññasatta beings are indeed conscious at the moments of birth and death (Kv 3:11). Strangely, the Theravāda position is that they are not, although this seems to contradict the passages from the canon and commentary cited above. If they are not conscious at least at those initial and terminal moments how indeed could Sobhita have recalled that existence at all?

The nature of this strange realm raises interesting questions about the nature of the mind and of time. In the commentary this is given in the form of a question: "How, after the elapse of many hundreds of aeons, can consciousness arise again from a consciousness that has ceased so long ago?" The answer is that the elapse of time has no bearing, the last consciousness in the series, even if it ceased five hundred kappas ago, can still act as the proximity condition (*anantarapaccayā*) for the newly arising consciousness.[798] According to Abhidhamma theory, each mind-moment immediately conditions the next; this mode of causation is called "proximity condition" because the first moment is followed immediately by the second, and acts as one of its causes. Ordinarily, conscious mind-moments follow one another in a close sequence, like falling dominoes. Here, however, there is a gap, an exceedingly long gap, between mind-moments, but the sequence remains unbroken even though the rest of the cosmos went through five hundred cycles of expansion and contraction in the interval. The cosmos and the mind each have their own independent and unbroken series.

In modern times we have a close analogue of the Asaññasatta "experience" (if we may call it that!) in the form of being put under general anaesthetic for surgery. The anaesthetist places the breathing mask on the patient's face and asks him to count backwards from ten. He begins to count and after reaching seven or six, he immediately opens his eyes in the recovery room. This is quite unlike sleep, during which, no matter how deep it may be, upon awakening there is always a sense of time having passed. In anaesthesia, the sequence of mind-moments remains subjectively unbroken although many hours may have passed in the rest of the world. Thus, Bhikkhu Sobhita recalls five hundred kappas "like a single night."

797 Vin Pār 4 and commentary, AN 1: 227 and Thg 2:3,3.

798 DN-a 1. Quoted text is Bhikkhu Bodhi's translation from "The All-Embracing Net of Views" p. 174.

3:6:17 SUDDHĀVĀSA—THE PURE ABODES

A person who attains the third of the four stages of awakening is called an *anāgāmī*, ("non-returner"). Since one of the characteristics of the third stage is the total eradication of sensual desire, such a person can never be reborn again into the sphere of sense desire. There is no motive force present compelling consciousness to arise again in that sphere. However, the *anāgāmī* has not yet overcome the defilement of desire-for-becoming, *bhavataṇhā*, which manifests as the desire for existence in the form plane, *rūparāga*, or in the formless plane, *arūparāga*. Therefore, while there still remains in the anāgāmī the motive force for further rebirth, it can only be into those realms which have left sensuality behind, the *rūpabhūmi* or the *arūpabhūmi*. At the very summit of the *rūpabhūmi* there are five special planes of existence known collectively as the *Suddhāvāsa*, ("Pure Abodes") into which only *anāgāmīs* can be reborn.[799]

[799] For an excellent short summary of the four stages and the fetter overcome at each, see Bhikkhu Bodhi's introduction to his translation of the *Majjhima Nikāya*, MLDB, p. 41 f.

3:6:18 REBIRTH INTO THE SUDDHĀVĀSA

A meditator who has developed fourth jhāna and reached the third stage of awakening is, after death, reborn into the Suddhāvāsa (MN-a 52 & AN-a 4: 124). He arises there seated at the root of a tree in a pleasant park and exclaims, "Oh! The happiness!" (MN-a 114). Once arisen in a Suddhāvāsa, the new brahmā will never again take rebirth in a lower realm, hence the appellation of "non-returner" (AN-a 2:37). He will eventually attain to the fourth stage of enlightenment of arahants and upon his subsequent passing will never be reborn again, having exited *saṃsāra* altogether. A Suddhāvāsa brahmā who has attained to the stage of arahant but has not yet passed away is called a *khīṇāsavā suddhāvāsabrahmā,* "a Pure Abode brahmā with the defilements extinguished" (DN-a 14).

The Suddhāvasa, therefore, is a very special place. As it is inhabited only by *anāgāmīs* and arahants who are on their way out of the cycle of rebirth, it is not considered part of the "round" (*vaṭṭa*) but the "end of the round" (*vivaṭṭa)* (MN-a 1). We may consider it as a kind of antechamber to the exit door of *saṃsāra*. The Suddhāvāsa is called the "campground of the Buddha." The Pali word, *khandhavāra*, particularly refers to a resting place for caravans and the image evoked is that of a pleasant last oasis before reaching one's final destination.[800]

The Suddhāvāsa deities are said to be superior to those devas who subsist on food, (AN-a 5: 166) i.e. the sensual devas, and to have bodies created by jhāna (AN-a 5: 44). A deva of the sensual sphere who attains to the stage of *anāgāmī* is unable to continue in his former state of existence but immediately dies and is reborn into the Suddhāvāsa. This is because the *saggas* ("heavens") of the sensual sphere are filled with "playful folk" (*laḷitajana*) who are given to finery and ornaments and who spend all day in singing, dancing and coquetry (MN-a 71 & MN-ṭ 71). A being who has utterly transcended sensuality has no place in a realm essentially generated by such desires; he can no longer maintain existence in a level with which he has no connection.

[800] DN-a 15. For definition of *khandhavāra*, see PED under "khandha".

3:6:19 DIVISIONS OF THE SUDDHĀVĀSA

Within the category of Suddhāvāsa there are five separate realms, each successively higher and more refined than the last. In order from the lowest to highest we have:

Aviha—The name is said to mean that for one who has arrived here there is no more diminishing or falling back. The Aviha beings have a life-span of one thousand kappas.

Atappa—"Those who do not endure suffering", the Atappa beings have a life-span of two thousand kappas.

Sudassa—"Those endowed with a pleasant form", the Sudhassa beings live for four thousand kappas.

Sudassi—These beings are so called because they both see beautiful forms and experience joy. The Sudassi devas live for eight thousand kappas.

Akaniṭṭha—The name is literally "not a junior" and is given to these beings because they are at the very summit of embodied existence, and are therefore the most "senior" of the inhabitants of *saṃsāra.* They have a life-span of sixteen thousand kappas.[801]

The Abhidhamma classifies all of these realms as part of the fourth jhāna sphere, together with the Vehapphala and the Asaññasatta realms. The determination as to which realm someone who has mastered fourth jhāna will be reborn into is said to depend on the diversity among their objects of consciousness (ārammaṇana), objects of thought (*manasikāra),*[802] desire (*chanda*), aspiration (*paṇidhi*), resolve (*adhimokkha*), aspiration (*abhinīhāra*) and wisdom (*paññā*). Oddly enough, this passage makes no mention of the attainment of the state of *anāgāmī* as a prerequisite for birth in the Suddhāvāsa worlds, although the commentary does explain that the "diversity of wisdom" refers to the difference between those with mundane (*lokiya*) and supramundane (*lokuttara*, lit. "beyond the world") levels of understanding; the latter implies having attained one of the stages of awakening (Vibh 18:6,2). Once born into one of the Suddhavāsa worlds, a being can only progress to a higher one, he can never again regress to any lower station of rebirth (AN-a 2:37). The Suddhavāsa realms are sometimes empty, because *anāgāmīs* only arise during the dispensation of a Buddha and there are sometimes an incalculable number of dark kappas in succession during which no Buddha arises (MN-a 1).

A different scheme is found in the *Abhidharmakośa* which states that the particular Suddhāvāsa level an *anāgāmī* is reborn into depends upon his or her strongest spiritual faculty (*indriya*). An anāgāmī endowed with faith (*saddhā*) is reborn into the Aviha realm. One whose strongest faculty is energy (*viriya*) will become an Atappa deity. The faculty of mindfulness (*sati*) leads to rebirth among the Sudassa brahmās, stability of mind (*samādhi*) leads to the Sudassi realm and wisdom (*paññā*) to the Akaniṭṭha level.[803]

---

[801] The derivation of the names is according to the commentary found at DN-a 14. Like most commentarial derivations these may not be etymologically sound, being more like punning or playing with word forms. The life-spans are found at VibhVibh 18:6.

[802] The commentary says this refers to the meditation object.

[803] AK 6:4, p.977. This classification by predominant faculty is cited by Bhikkhu Bodhi in CMA p. 128, and by Dr. Sunthorn Na-Rangsi in *Four Planes of Existence in Theravāda Buddhism*, p. 28. These were following Ledi Sayadaw's new subcommentary on the *Abhidhammatthasaṅgaha*, called *Paramatthadīpanī*, p. 246. The ultimate source is probably the 12th century, "new" subcommentary on the *Abhidhammāvatāra*, the *Abhidhammāvatāra-abhinavaṭīkā* by Sumaṅgala, who might have based himself on a Sanskrit Sarvāstivāda source. Thanks to Nyanatusita Bhikkhu for pointing out these references.

3:6:20 THE BUDDHA AND THE SUDDHĀVĀSA

One of the powers of the Buddha is the recollection of all his past lives (MN 12). During the Bodhisatta's long wandering in *saṃsāra*, the one realm into which he was never born was the Suddhāvāsa (MN 12). This is for the obvious reason that, if he had on some occasion attained to the state of an *anāgāmī* and been reborn as a Suddhāvāsa deva, his Bodhisatta career would have come to an end; he would have attained *arahatta* there and never returned to a human birth in order to become the Buddha. Nevertheless, as an abode of *anāgāmīs* and arahants, the Suddhāvāsa has a special connection with the Buddha. On many occasions, beings from that realm manifested themselves on earth to interact with the Buddha, and one sutta tells of a tour the Buddha himself made of the various Suddhāvāsa realms:

> At one time the Buddha was dwelling in seclusion at Ukkatthā, sitting by the root of a royal *sāl* tree. There, the thought arose in his mind: "It is not possible to find an abode of beings in which I have not previously dwelt, during my long wandering, except the abode of the Suddhāvāsa devas.[804] What if I were to go there now?" Just as if a strong man had stretched out or drawn in his arm, the Buddha disappeared from the root of the royal *sāl* tree and manifested in the realm of the Aviha devas.
>
> There, many thousands, many hundreds of thousands of Aviha devas approached the Buddha. Having saluted the Buddha, they stood with one shoulder bared[805] and addressed the Buddha in these words, "It has been ninety-one kappas, dear sir (*mārisā*), since we were visited by the Blessed Buddha Vipassī." (The devas then recount a brief biography of the Buddha Vipassī concluding with) " ... and we, dear sir, who practised the holy life under the Buddha Vipassī and have destroyed sensual desire, arose here."
>
> (Other groups of many hundreds of thousands of Suddhāvāsa beings approach the Buddha. These were, in turn, former disciples of the Buddhas Sikhī, Veasbhū, Kakusandha, Konāgamma and Kassapa. Finally ...) many thousands, many hundreds of thousands of Aviha devas approached the Buddha. Having saluted him, they stood with one shoulder bared and addressed him in these words, "Dear sir, in this auspicious kappa (*bhaddakappa*)[806] the present Buddha, arahant and fully awakened, has arisen in the world. The Blessed One was born into a *khattiya* clan, of the *khattiya* caste,[807] the clan of Gotama. In the Blessed One's time, the life of men is short and passes quickly. Few indeed reach the age of one hundred. (The devas recount the principal biographical details of the Buddha's life and conclude ...) and we, dear sir, who practised the holy life under the Blessed One and have destroyed sensual desire, arose here."
>
> Then the Buddha, together with the Aviha devas, went to the Atappa realm. There, he was approached and saluted by many thousands, many hundreds of thousands of Atappa devas, who addressed the Blessed One in these words. : "It has been ninety-one kappas, dear sir (*mārisā*), since we were visited by the Blessed Buddha Vipassī." (They similarly recount the biographies and claim discipleship of the last seven Buddhas, beginning with Vipassī and ending with the present Buddha Gotama). Then the Buddha went, together with the Aviha and the Atappa devas to the Sudassa realm, then with all of these to the Sudassī realm and then with all of the Suddhāvāsa devas to the realm of the Akaniṭṭha devas. (At each stage, the scene of many hundreds of thousands of devas reciting the biographies of the Buddhas is repeated). "And we, dear sir, who practised the

[804] Maurice Walshe mistranslates this line in LDB, p. 219.

[805] A traditional gesture of respect, perhaps originating in pre-buddhist times as a way of demonstrating that one was not carrying a weapon.

[806] A kappa in which five Buddhas are born.

[807] I.e., a warrior-noble.

holy life under the Blessed One and have destroyed sensual desire, arose here."[808]

As the Suddhāvāsa devas have life-spans measured in the thousands of kappas, they watch entire world-systems come and go but they take an active interest only in the rare instance of a Buddha arising. After the destruction of an old world-system, the first sign of a new one arising is a great deluge of rain which first floods the ruins of the old system as deep as the first jhāna level of the brahmā worlds. When the waters subside, the various earthly and heavenly realms emerge ready for habitation. The first sign of new life is the appearance of a lotus plant in the muddy ground of Jambudīpa at the site of the *mahābodhipallaṅka*, the "great awakening seat", the exact spot on earth at which each and every Buddha comes to full awakening:

> The Suddhāvāsa brahmās say to one another, "Let us go forth and view the portents." They approach the *mahābodhipallaṅka*. If no Buddha is to arise in the new kappa, then there will be no blossoms on the lotus plant. Seeing this, the Suddhāvāsa brahmās say, "Alas! There will be darkness. Beings will perish and the lower realms will become full. The six realms of the devas and the nine realms of the brahmās shall be empty," and they become displeased. If, however, at this time of flowering they behold a blossom on the plant they say, "An all-knowing Bodhisatta will descend into his mother's womb, shall go forth and, having become fully awakened, will turn the wheel of the Dhamma … the four lower realms will dwindle, the six realms of the devas and the nine realms of the brahmās shall become full." Their joyful utterance is heard as far away as the brahmā worlds. (DN-a 14)

There may be anywhere between zero and five lotuses on the plant, and this determines the number of Buddhas to arise in the new kappa. (The current kappa will have five altogether, Gotama was the fourth so there remains one more to come). The Suddhāvāsa brahmās take the lotus flower, if there is one, and open it. Inside the unfolded petals they find the eight essential requisites of a bhikkhu: three robes, a belt, a needle and thread, a water-strainer, a razor and the alms-bowl. These they carry away and preserve them in their own realm until the distant time when the Bodhisatta comes to make his great renunciation and leave the home-life. Then one of them descends and presents these requisites to the Bodhisatta to begin his career as a *samaṇa*, which will culminate in the attainment of perfect Buddhahood.[809]

To prepare the way for the Buddha, Suddhāvāsa devas come to earth in the guise of brahmin priests and insert the teaching of the "thirty-two marks" into the Vedas. These are physical attributes by which a Buddha may be known. In this way, men of influence (*mahesakkha*) will be able to recognize him. These verses, called *buddhamanta*, are not to be found in the Vedas as they are known today (or in the time of Buddhaghosa for that matter) because after the passing of the Buddha, they gradually disappear and are lost.[810]

When the Bodhisatta is born, the infant emerging from the womb as effortlessly as flowing water, he is first received in a golden net by *khīṇāsavā* (lit. "destroyed defilements" i.e. arahant) Suddhāvāsa brahmās, who pass him on to the Four Great Kings, before he is laid down upon a white cloth before the awaiting humans. When the Bodhisatta has grown to manhood, and goes out for a pleasure jaunt with his charioteer, *khīṇāsavā* Suddhāvāsa brahmās keep watch over him. They say to each other, "The Bodhisatta is stuck in the pleasures of the senses like an elephant mired in muck. Let us arouse mindfulness in him." To this end, they manifest as the four divine messengers: an old man, a sick man, a dead man and a *samaṇa*. These are visible only to the Bodhisatta and his charioteer, but not to the rest of the entourage.[811]

---

808 DN 14. The passages in brackets are condensed. I have changed the original from a first person account by the Buddha to a third person narrative.

809 Ap-a 1:1. See also GCB p. 278. For the eight requisites, see DN-a 2.

810 DN-a3 and Sn-a 3:7. For the thirty-two marks see MN 91 & § 3:1,9.

811 DN 14 and commentary. These biographical details are told of the former Buddha Vipassi, but they also became associated

On three specific occasions, the Suddhāvāsa brahmās make prophetic announcements which cause a "great uproar" (*kolāhala*)[812] amongst the human population. One thousand years before the appearance of a Buddha, they don the ornaments and head-gear of brahmās and go about among humans joyfully extolling the virtues of a Buddha. Later, there comes a time when there is a "great uproar" among both humans and devas vociferously debating what constitutes the "auspicious" (*maṅgala).*[813] At this juncture, the Suddhāvāsa brahmās announce that in twelve years the Buddha will settle the question by preaching the *Maṅgala Sutta*. Likewise, seven years before the Buddha gives the teaching of the three purities, the *Moneyya Sutta*, they cause an uproar by going about predicting this.[814]

It can be seen by these examples that the Suddhāvāsa brahmās, although they are classified as belonging to the fourth jhāna level, cannot abide in a continual state of jhāna. They are far too active for that. We do not have any parallel examples from the texts concerning the second, third and ordinary fourth jhāna level brahmās, as they abide in a state of jhānic absorption. Furthermore, we know some of the individual Suddhāvāsa brahmās by name but none of these others.

Ghatīkāra[815] was a potter at the time of Kassapa Buddha. He was a devout lay follower of the Buddha and a good friend to Jotīpāla, a brahmin student who was a previous birth of Gotama Buddha. Ghatīkāra did not ordain as a bhikkhu because his blind and aged parents depended upon him for their support. However, he lived as much like a bhikkhu as is possible for a layman. Ghatīkāra remained celibate and did not dig for the clay needed for his pottery, taking instead only that which had been dug up by animals or other people. Furthermore, he did not engage in trade involving gold and silver coins but practised instead a kind of gift economy. He laid out the finished pots outside his dwelling and made it known that anyone who wished could take one, and that anyone who wished could leave rice and other provisions for him and his parents.

Ghatīkāra was also a generous supporter of Kassapa Buddha and the *Saṅgha*. He made it known that they could take whatever they needed from his stores. It came to pass that one rainy season Kassapa Buddha's hut began to leak. The bhikkhus took thatch from the roof of Ghatīkāra's hut and left it "open to the sky." However, by the power of Ghatīkāra's merit, no rain fell upon his dwelling every again. Indeed, no rain will ever fall upon that spot for the duration of the kappa. Because of his exemplary life, Ghatīkāra attained to the state of an *anāgāmī* and when he died was reborn in the Avihā realm.[816]

It was the Suddhāvāsa brahmā Ghatīkāra who presented the Bodhisatta Siddhattha with the bhikkhu's requisites at his going forth from the home life, the same eight requisites which had appeared in the lotus at the beginning of the kappa (Jāt-nid 2), this honour falling to him because of his ancient friendship with the Bodhisatta. One subsequent conversation between the Buddha and the Suddhāvāsa brahmā Ghatīkāra is recorded. He informed the Buddha that seven of his bhikkhus had now been reborn in Avihā (SN 1:50). One of these was Upaka, who in his previous human state had been the Ājīvaka ascetic whom the Buddha encountered on the road shortly after his awakening. At that time, Upaka had been doubtful of the Buddha's attainment, saying merely, "May it be so, friend," (*hupeyyapāvuso*) wagging his head in the Indian fashion and going off by a side-road. Much later, after a period as a married householder he ordained as a bhikkhu and became an *anāgāmī* (Vin Mv 1 & Dhp-a 24:9). Another was Pukkusāti. He had

with the life of Gotama Buddha. Indeed, they are archetypal and apply to all Buddhas.

812 *Kolāhala*—"shouting, uproar, excitement, tumult, foreboding, warning about something, hailing." PED.

813 *Maṅgala*—"auspicious, prosperous, lucky, festive". PED.

814 For the "great uproars" see KdpA 5, for the *Maṅgala Sutta*, see Khp 5 and Sn 2:4. For the *Moneyya Sutta* see AN 3: 123. It is not clear why among all the Buddha's teachings these two are singled out for a prophecy. There are five *kolāhalas* altogether, the other two involve predictions made by sense-sphere devas; they announce the coming of a wheel-turning monarch and the end of a world-system.

815 Also spelled Ghatikāra.

816 MN 81 has the fullest account of Ghatīkāra's life. For the miracle of the open hut see Jāt 20 which lists the four miracles which will last for an entire kappa.

been the king of Takkasilā, but renounced his throne to seek out the Buddha and ask for the going forth. On his journey, he shared a chance lodging the Buddha without at first recognizing him. Hearing the teachings from the Buddha, Pukkusāti attained to the state of an *anāgāmī* then and there but was shortly afterward killed by a mad cow and reborn in Avihā (MN 140). The identities of the other five are more doubtful, and even the spelling of some of their names differs between recensions of the canon.[817]

Another story concerns a group of seven bhikkhus during the dispensation of Kassapa Buddha:

> At the time when the religion of Kassapa Buddha was in decline, seven bhikkhus seeing the alteration in the novices and so on, decided that while the religion had not yet disappeared, they should make their own refuge secure. So they paid homage to the golden *cetiya* (the stupa enshrining the relics of Kassapa Buddha) and entered the forest. Seeing a certain mountain they said, "Let those who are attached to life turn back. Let those seeking release ascend the mountain." Seeing a flight of steps, they all together climbed the mountain and there performed the duties of *samaṇa*s.
>
> The eldest among them attained to *arahatta* in a single night and in the morning went to Lake Anotatta where he rinsed his mouth and cleaned his teeth with a tooth-stick. Then he went for alms to Uttarakuru (the northern continent, on the far side of Mt Sineru). When he returned, he said to the others, "I have gone for alms in Uttarakuru. Did we not agree that the first to obtain arahantship would go for alms so that the others may eat?" They replied, "It is not so, friend (*no hetaṃ, āvuso*). When we have produced an attainment like yours, then we shall eat." On the second day the next bhikkhu became an *anāgāmī* and he also went for alms and offered to share with the others, but they again refused. Of these, the first bhikkhu eventually entered *parinibbāna* (i.e. died as an arahant without further rebirth) and the *anāgāmī* was reborn in the *brahmaloka*. The other five were unable to attain *nibbāna* and wasted away after seven days and were reborn in the *devaloka*. At the time of Gotama Buddha they all passed away from there and were reborn into human families. (MN-a 23)

That the arahant bhikkhu went for his morning rounds to such impossibly distant places indicates the use of psychic power. Perhaps he intended to demonstrate his attainment by the presentation to the others of the exquisite food of Uttarakuru. In any case, it does not seem to have worked. The reply of the others implies that they did not believe him; they addressed him with the familiar āvuso and not the respectful *bhante*. The *brahmaloka* to which the anāgāmī went was of course one of the Suddhāvāsa worlds.

All of the five unsuccessful ones became bhikkhus again under Gotama Buddha and all eventually attained *arahantship*. The Suddhāvāsa being who had been their companion continued to watch over them and he came to the assistance of two of them. He appeared before the young bhikkhu Kumāra Kassapa in a radiant form and set him a series of riddles which the Buddha later solved. By contemplating the Buddha's answers, insight arose in Kumāra Kassapa and he attained *arahantship* (MN-a 23). Bāhiya Dārucīriya (the second element of the name means "bark clad") was a well-known and revered ascetic who had arrived at the false view that he was an arahant. The same Suddhāvāsa being appeared before him and disabused him of that conceit and advised him to seek out the Buddha,[818] in none of these texts is the deity himself named.

One of the Buddha's foremost lay disciples was Hatthaka of Āḷavi.[819] After he died as an anāgāmī he was reborn in Aviha. Shortly after that he came back to earth to see the Buddha:

---

[817] These were Palagaṇda, Bhaddiya, Khaṇḍadeva (or Bhaddadeva), Bāhuraggi (or Bāhudanti) and Piṅgiya (or Siṅgiya).

[818] Ud-a 1:10. The other three companions became Pukkusāti, Sabhiya and Dabbamallaputta.

[819] This is the same Hatthaka who, when an infant, was saved by the Buddha from being eaten by the yakkha Āḷavaka, see § 3:4,2.

> At one time the Blessed One was dwelling in Savatthī … during the night the *devaputta* Hatthaka approached, brilliantly illuminating almost the entire grove. Thinking, "I will stand before the Blessed One," but he sank down and became submerged (into the earth) and was unable to remain standing. It was as if oil or ghee had been sprinkled onto sand …
>
> The Blessed One addressed him, "Hatthaka, create a gross body" (*oḷārikaṃ attabhāvaṃ abhinimmināhi*). The devaputta Hatthaka obeyed; he created a gross body, saluted the Blessed One and stood to one side.[820]

As a brand new Suddhāvāsa brahmā, Hatthaka had not yet learned the knack of manifesting himself in lower planes. This passage is a neat illustration of the relative subtlety of matter in the higher brahmā worlds.

On the occasion of the Great Assembly recorded in the *Mahāsamaya Sutta*,[821] when a great concourse of devas and other powerful beings assembled in the presence of the Buddha and a *saṅgha* of five hundred arahant bhikkhus, it was four Suddhāvāsa beings who opened the proceedings by uttering verses in praise of the *Saṅgha*. The commentary says they had been in meditation when the other deities began assembling and were at first curious as to why the brahmā worlds all seemed empty. Realizing that they were late, they decided they had better not arrive empty handed and agreed to each bring a verse of praise.[822]

820 AN 3: 127. He is identified as coming from Aviha in the concluding verse.

821 DN 20, see also SN 1:37.

822 SN-a 1:37. "empty-handed" is a literal translation, the Pali idiom is the same—*tucchahattha*.

CHAPTER SEVEN—THE ARŪPA PLANE

3:7:1 ARŪPABHUMI—THE FORMLESS REALMS

Beyond the plane of sense-desire and the plane of form there exists the "formless plane", *arūpabhūmi*. This is a realm inhabited by beings that are made up of mental factors only, without any trace of physical form. They are mind-only and have no bodies. This makes them very difficult for us to imagine and impossible to visualize. Within the *arūpabhūmi* there are four planes of existence:

ākāsānañcāyatana—the sphere of boundless space

viññāṇañcāyatana—the sphere of boundless consciousness

ākiñcaññāyatana—the sphere of nothingness

nevasaññānāsaññāyatana—the sphere of neither-perception-nor-nonperception.

Each of these corresponds to a meditative state which may be experienced here in the human realm. Collectively, these are called the *arūpa jhānas*. They may be considered refinements of the fourth jhāna as they have the same two factors: *ekaggatā* ("unity of mind" or "one-pointedness") and *upekkhā* ("equanimity"). They differ from fourth jhāna, however, in each having a specific and successively refined immaterial object.[823] One who has mastery of the formless attainments here on earth may be reborn into one of the formless realms after death (AN 4: 171).

[823] See Dhs 1:1,3 and Bodhi, CMA, p. 61f.

3:7:2 IMMATERIAL NATURE

In all other forms of existence, mind occurs only in association with a physical base. This makes it difficult for us to conceptualize the mode of existence of beings dwelling in the *arūpabhūmi*. It should not be imagined that these beings have some kind of ghostly or immaterial form, they do not. No physical form means just that. This has some intriguing implications. For one thing, the existence of this realm serves as an illustration of the principle that, in Buddhist theory, mind is not derivative of matter but an independent factor. For another, the non-physical nature of these beings implies that they have no physical attributes which would include extension and location. They cannot be properly said to be anywhere at all, except perhaps for the lowest realm of boundless space which can be understood as existing everywhere at once.[824]

Perhaps because of these startling implications, not all early Buddhist schools were in agreement on the immaterial nature of the *arūpa* realms, although both the Theravāda and the Sarvāstivāda were. The *Kathāvatthu* records a controversy with the Andhaka School ("among others") who argued that the non-existence of matter would violate the dependent origination which states that "because of consciousness there comes to be body and mind." These theorists postulated a subtle matter still present in the *arūpa* realms, an idea firmly repudiated by the Theravāda interlocutor.[825] The *Abhidharmakośa* of the Sarvāstivāda also supports the view that "no matter" means "no matter" and also reports that there were other views extant. The text specifically mentions three alternate interpretations: that there exists "subtle matter", or "tiny matter" (i.e. that the beings are infinitesimally small) or "transparent matter" (AK 8:1, p.1221f.).

The difficulty of comprehending such an alien form of existence is no reason to reject the clear intention of the texts. If the *arūpa* plane possessed some kind of subtle matter there would be no reason to set it up as a category separate from the *rūpa* plane of which subtle matter is already posited. Further, just as the plane of form is said to be the escape from sense-desire, so the plane of the formless is said to be the escape from form (*rūpa)* (DN-a 33). This would not be so if form still existed on that plane. The only way to think about these realms is in terms of pure mind.

824 AK 3:1, p 366 is explicit about this.

825 Kv 8:8 and commentary.

3:7:3 EXISTENCE IN THE ARŪPABHŪMI

Beings that exist in the *arūpa* state are at the very summit of *saṃsāric* existence, not of course in a spatial sense, but in the sense of being the most refined and subtle form of existence. Evil, unskillful states (*pāpakā akusalā dhammā*) arise only in association with form, not without form (AN 2:83, eng. 2:82). The happiness of the formless exceeds the happiness based on form.[826]

> Among the five destinations (of rebirth) those of the devas[827] are the best (*seṭṭha*). Among these, those of the formless beings are the most glorious (*ukkaṭṭha*). They are very far removed from defilement (*kilesa*) and suffering (*dukkha*). Their abidings (*vihāra*, lit. "dwelling") are endowed with tranquillity, excellence (*paṇīta*), imperturbability (ānañja). Their life-spans are exceedingly long.[828]

Thedurationoftheselifespansisgivenas 20,000 kappas for theā*kāsānañcāyatana,* 40,000 for the *viññāṇañcāyatana,* 60,000 for the ākiñcaññāyatana and 84,000 for the *nevasaññānāsaññāyatana.*[829] The *Dhātuvibhanga Sutta* (MN 140) tells us that if a meditator directs his mind with purified equanimity to the base of boundless space, with his mind dependent (*taṃnissita*) on that, it can remain there for a very long time, which the commentary specifies as 20,000 kappas. The word ānañja meaning "steadfast, immoveable, imperturbable" is sometimes used as a synonym for the formless sphere.[830]

Whereas the brahmās of the *rūpabhūmi* are said to be "mind-made" (*manomaya*) the beings of the *arūpabhūmi* are "perception-made" (*saññāmaya*) . "Use of sticks and swords, quarrels, abuse, slander and false speech occur on account of form (*rūpa*). But none of these exist in the immaterial (*arūpa*) sphere" (MN 60). The *arūpa* beings, having no bodies, do not possess physical senses, but experience only the mind-sense (Vibh 18). This implies that these beings are self-contained, living entirely within a self-generated world of mind objects. The outer universe is no concern of theirs. On those occasions in which all the devas assemble, even from thousands of world-systems, specific exceptions are made for the *arūpa* devas and the *asaññasatta* (unconscious beings) (DN-a 20 & It-a 3:4,3). No individual in these realms is named for us in the texts, nor are there any stories about them.

Existence here is considered to be a spiritually advanced state, but it is not complete liberation. The *rūpa* plane is called a "fleshy" or "carnal" liberation (*vimokkho sāmiso*), whereas the arūpa plane is a "spiritual" or "non-carnal" liberation (*nirāmiso vimokkho*). However, *arahantship* is "more spiritual than the spiritual" (*nirāmisā nirāmisataro vimokkho)* (SN 36:31). Although these beings exist on a very refined plane, they are still subject to some degree of defilement. Although the root defilement of ill-will (*dosa*) cannot arise in their minds, the other two roots of desire (*lobha*) and delusion (*moha*) can (Vibh 18:3,2). Desire here takes the form of the craving for immaterial existence (Vibh 17:3). The defilement of delusion occurs among them in the form of not understanding the Third Noble Truth, that of cessation (*nirodha)* (SN-a 5:6).

So refined are these states, whether accessed in meditation or as a post-mortem destination, that many ascetics of the Buddha's time mistook them for full liberation. This is the case for the two teachers of the Bodhisatta during his years of seeking: Āḷāra Kālāma who taught the way to the ākiñcaññāyatana and Uddaka Rāmaputta who taught the *nevasaññānāsaññāyatana* (MN 26). Among the false views listed by the Buddha, we find the teaching that the self

826 AN 2: 77. This seems contradictory in that the feeling tone of the formless abidings is *upekkhā* ("equanimity") but *sukha* ("happiness") may here be used in a more figurative sense, meaning something like "well-being."

827 The term "deva" is here used in the most generic sense, to include all beings above the human level.

828 DN-ṭ 2.See another translation of this passage by Bhikkhu Bodhi, *The Discourse on the Fruits of Recluseship*, p. 90.

829 VibhVibh 18:6. The *Abhidharmakośa* gives them as 20, 50, 60 and 80 thousand respectively. AK 3:5, p.471.

830 AN 4:190. Definition is from the commentary.

is immaterial and survives death (DN1 & MN 102). and this may be explicitly identified with one or the other of the *arūpa* states. For instance, some "*samaṇas* and brahmins" hold that:

> Perception is a disease, a boil, perception is a dart. But non-perception is idiocy (*sammoha*). This then is the excellent condition: *nevasaññānāsaññaṃ* (neither perception nor nonperception). (MN 102)

The difference between the four planes within the *arūpabhūmi* may be understood as an increasing refinement of perception. Within each successive level perception (*saññā*) takes an increasingly subtle object and because of that becomes increasingly subtle itself.

The ākāsānañcāyatana, the base of boundless space, as a meditative state is achieved by "surmounting the perception of diversity" (MN 66). The multiplicity of objects in the world are no longer apparent, perception is focussed on the boundless emptiness of space in which these objects are situated.

We must make a short digression here and clarify what the ancient Buddhists understood by space, which is a little different from the modern concept. Some schools, among them the Sarvāstivāda, held space to be unconditioned (*asaṅkhata*),,[831] but for the Theravadins, *nibbāna* is the only unconditioned element. Space (ākasa) exists in three modes: as delimited (*paricchedākāsa*), as abstracted from the object (*kasiṇugghāṭimākāsa*) and as openness or emptiness (*ajaṭākāso*) (Kv-a 6:6). The first refers to such examples as the space defined by the walls of a room or the opening of a well. The second refers specifically to the procedure in meditation when the yogi removes the *kasiṇa* object (e.g. the mental image of a coloured disk) to meditate upon the space left behind. The third is close to what we mean by space today: an emptiness that can be filled with objects whose distance from one another may be defined as taking up some unit of space which may be measured in kilometres or *yojana*. Of these, only the first, space as delimited, refers to something real and it is obviously conditioned in that we can dig or fill in a well and thereby condition the space within. The other two are, to the Theravadins, mere concepts without ontological substance.[832] The boundless space which is the domain of the ākāsānañcāyatana beings is thus doubly empty: it is the merest shadow of a ghost of the material universe. Beings in this state of existence are said to experience the supreme perception (AN 5: 170).

But even this concept, vacuous as it may be, is abandoned in the *viññāṇañcāyatana*, the sphere of boundless consciousness. Here concepts of space no longer apply and perception is solely focussed on the boundless nature of consciousness when space, the last ephemeral referent to the external world, is removed. In the next sphere, that of ākiñcaññāyatana, the sphere of nothingness (lit. "no-thing-ness") perception removes itself even from the fact of being conscious and rests on nothing at all. However, even this remains a kind of concept and the final sphere, *nevasaññānāsaññāyatana,* neither perception nor nonperception, abandons the idea of nothingness as well. These beings are said to have the supreme form of existence.[833]

The *Visuddhimagga* explains the name of this sphere thus:

> The perception here is neither perception, since it is incapable of performing the decisive function of perception, not yet non-perception, since it is present in a subtle state as a residual formation.[834]

The text goes on to illustrate this with a couple of similes. An iron bowl may be smeared with oil to prevent rust.

831 AK 1:1, p.59. Because space neither hinders matter nor is hindered by it.

832 Kv 6:6. Einstein would agree with the Theravāda that space is conditioned but for entirely different reasons.

833 AN 5: 170: *idaṃ bhavānaṃ aggaṃ*. The contraction of this phrase would be *bhavāgga*, and in the Sanskrit form *bhavāgra* is used frequently in the *Abhidharmakośa* as an epithet of the sphere of neither perception nor nonperception. The Pali *bhavāgga* seems to be strictly reserved as an epithet of arahants.

834 Vism 10.50-51. Ñāṇamoli trans. *Path of Purification*, p. 332.

If someone wants to use it to eat from, he may be told "Sir, there is oil in the bowl." But if he then asks to fill his oil tube from it, he may be told "Sir, there is no oil." Similarly, a novice and an elder are walking for alms when the novice sees water on the path and says, "Sir, there is water. Remove your sandals." But if the elder asks for his bathing cloth he may be told, "Sir, there is no water." Furthermore, it is not only perception that exists in this subtle residual state but all the mental factors; there is there neither consciousness nor non-consciousness, neither feeling nor non-feeling and so on (Vism 10.50f).

3:7:4 UNDERSTANDING THE ARŪPA REALMS

It is truly difficult to imagine formless existence. This is both because of its extreme subtlety and because of the vast difference from our own experience. For the realms of the sensual devas, and even of the brahmās, there is at least some image we can call to mind. Not so here.

The best way to acquire some idea of the formless is not through examination of the texts and rational thought. Rather, it is to attempt to touch these states directly via meditation. As a practical exercise, we may describe a meditation loosely based on the *Cūḷasuññata Sutta* (MN 121). The meditator begins with what is called "contemplation of village", that is simple awareness of the ordinary space around one, filled as it is with objects and people. Then, in each successive stage, the meditator removes by non-attention one aspect of the field of reality and pays attention to what remains. Contemplation of village is followed by contemplation of forest, which means removing human constructs such as buildings and roads from awareness and focussing on what remains: the natural world of earth, water and vegetation. Following this, the living world is removed and one focuses only on the underlying earth element: the rocks and soil, hills and valleys and ultimately the mass of the planet itself. When this is removed one becomes aware of the underlying space occupied by the earth. Since there are no boundaries in empty space, this easily becomes boundless. Now there is only the meditator's consciousness filling boundless space. When attention is withdrawn from space, only boundless consciousness remains. When the meditator ceases to pay attention to this, he focuses his awareness on the underlying nothingness. Finally, attention is withdrawn even from the concept of nothingness and the mind rests in the subtle state of neither perception nor nonperception.[835]

CONCLUSION

As we progress upward through the spheres of existence, from the *kāmabhūmi* (plane of sense-desire) through the *rūpabhūmi* (plane of form) to the *arūpabhūmi* we are moving from complexity and diversity towards subtlety and pristine simplicity.[836] The *arūpa* realms, and the *nevasaññānāsaññāyatana* in particular, can be called the minimal state of *saṃsāra*. This is still an existence subject to kamma, craving, *dukkha* (suffering) and the rest of the package which is manifest existence. But just barely so.

However, it still remains a quantum step to emerge from the conditioned existence of *saṃsāra* into the unconditioned state of *nibbāna*. It is stated in the *Abhidharmakośa* that no one existing in the formless realms can achieve *nibbāna* unless they had already attained to one of the states of awakening before arising there (AK 6:6, p 1015). This is because the suffering and impermanence inherent in *saṃsāra* is so attenuated that no impulse for spiritual progress is present.

For one who is an arahant or an *anāgāmī*, the meditative progression explained above contains one additional step. By withdrawing the mind from the most subtle object, that of neither perception nor nonperception, the awakened meditator can enter the state called *nirodhasamāpatti* ("attainment of cessation") which is defined as "the non-occurrence of consciousness and its concomitants owing to their progressive cessation," and of which it is said, "the peace it gives is reckoned as *nibbāna* here and now."[837]

It is admittedly difficult to understand the *arūpa* condition, but it is worth the effort to make the attempt. Contemplating what these realms may be like gives us insight into at least two important subjects. They can help us to understand the manifest reality that is *saṃsāra* by stripping it down to its barest essentials. This is manifest

[835] MN 121. Somewhat more detailed instructions by the author may be found at www.arrowriver.ca/dhamma/formless.html. Accessed Oct 16, 2017. It should be noted that the actual sutta and commentary refer to contemplation of earth *kasiṇa* rather then earth element as given here.

[836] See MN 66, which characterizes the entry into the formless as transcending the perception of diversity.

[837] Vism 23.16 f. The quotations are from Ñāṇamoli's translation.

existence at its absolute bare minimum, without the layers of confusion found in those realms "below." As well, the contemplation of a realm which is mind-only can give us powerful insights into the nature of mind in the abstract. What would it be like without the encumbrance of a body and physical senses?

PART FOUR – AFTERWORD

"Cosmologists are often in error, but never in doubt."
Leonard Susskind, *The Black Hole War*, p.21.

4:1 THREE COSMOLOGIES

Every human culture has wondered about the greater world in which we find ourselves, and asked questions about space and time and the beings that exist in the universe. People in every time and place have attempted to answer these questions by developing cosmological models, conceptual worlds in which to live. An interesting topic for contemplation is how living in each of these universes affects the lives and thoughts of the inhabitants. It could be argued that it wouldn't have made much difference. People in all cultures go about their business of making love, war and money without much concern about cosmological questions; but this is to take a very superficial view. The higher life of philosophy and spiritual development is inevitably shaped by the background of the culture's worldview. The cosmological background must affect any thought beyond the immediate concerns of daily living and have subtle and not so subtle influences on art, literature, religion, philosophy and ethics. To take one obvious example: whereas the Western sense of time and history has always been linear, India has seen it as cyclical. One implication is that, to the Indian mind, history didn't really matter. It is very difficult for modern scholars to determine a chronology for ancient India because the ancient Indians were never very much interested in keeping the kind of dated annals which serve as the raw material of history in the West. Our first precise date in Indian history is the invasion of Alexander in 327 B.C., which we have from Greek sources.

It would take a book much larger than this one to adequately explore this theme across a representative span of cultures. Here I propose something much more modest – to present a few preliminary considerations about just three cosmologies: the ancient Indian one, the Buddhist articulation of which has been the theme of this book, the pre-modern European model and the modern scientific one. These three are likely those of most interest to the readers of this book, and they provide some suggestive points of comparison.

4:2 MEDIEVAL EUROPE

In premodern Europe, the accepted model of the universe was the geocentric one inherited from the Greek and Hellenistic periods, often called the Ptolemaic model after the second century A.D. astronomer Claudius Ptolemaeus, usually called just *Ptolemy*. The earth in this system is by far the largest solid object in the universe and is located at the centre. Arrayed around it are successive crystalline spheres in which the sun, moon and planets travel and the whole is bounded by a sphere of the "fixed stars." This model was developed as an attempt to account for the observed movements of the heavenly bodies. However, beginning with Plato, one assumption was made for entirely philosophical reasons: the objects beyond the orbit of the moon being in the celestial realm must be perfect and therefore must move in perfect circles.

This assumption made it difficult to reconcile the model with increasingly accurate observation, so various additions were concocted to "save the appearances." The planets do not move directly on the surface of their spheres but on smaller spheres called *epicycles* which move on the main spheres. This explained retrograde motion, when a planet as viewed from earth appears for a time to change direction. However, to make the model work while maintaining the principle of uniform circular motion required additional complications. The spheres were centred not at the centre of the earth but at a hypothetical point some distance away called the *eccentric*. Additionally, a more complicated mathematical kludge called the *equant* was added which was yet another point, different for each planet, from which uniform circular motion could be observed, even if it was not uniform when viewed from the earth. The whole system became so complicated that King Alfonso X of Castile, after studying Ptolemy, was reputed to have said, "Had I been present at the Creation, I would have given some useful hints for the better ordering of the universe."[838]

The complexities of this model can seem absurd to the modern reader, but it did fit the available data quite well. The heliocentric system proposed by Copernicus was slow to catch on, not just because of religious obscurantism, but because as a newly developed model it did not always fit the data as well as the thoroughly worked out geocentric one. The really big conceptual breakthrough came with Kepler, who was the first thinker in two thousand years to abandon the fixed idea of uniform circular motion and correctly see the planets' orbits as ellipses.

Two features of this cosmology are important for our purposes. First, it placed humanity at the very centre of things on the immobile earth around which the whole clockwork revolved. Second, the whole structure was very limited in size and definitely bounded. Roger Bacon calculated the distance to the outermost sphere, that of the fixed stars, at 65,357,700 miles,[839] which would fit the entire universe within the orbit of Venus according to modern scientific reckoning. Furthermore, this *was* the entire universe. There was no conception in European thought of any physical worlds beyond this one.[840] There seem to have been various opinions about the locations of heaven and hell (the Christian equivalents of the *devalokas* and *niraya*) but if we can take Dante as a source, the heavens were located within the spheres and associated with the various planets and hell was under the earth,[841] thus again limiting the cosmos to one fixed structure.

This structure was limited in time as well. Although the geocentric system was first developed by the Greeks in

[838] On *Quotes,* http://www.quotes.net/quote/19198. Accessed Oct 16, 2017. This statement may be apocryphal. For details of this cosmology see "*What is the Geocentric Model of the Universe?* ", *Universe Today,* http://www.universetoday.com/32607/geocentric-model. Accessed Oct 16, 2017.

[839] Albert Van Helden, *Measuring the Universe*, p.36.

[840] But some Islamic scholars did postulate multiple worlds. See . *The Free Library*. S.v. Fakhr al-Din al-Razi on physics and the nature of the physical world: a preliminary survey. " Retrieved Jan 09 2017 from https://www.thefreelibrary.com/Fakhr+al-Din+al-Razi+on+physics+and+the+nature+of+the+physical+world%3a...-a0128606463.

[841] "Christianity, Heaven and Hell", *Facts and Details*, https://web.archive.org/web/20171022133130/http://factsanddetails.com/world/cat55/sub353/item1402.html. Galileo used Dante's description to calculate the depth of Hell at 405 1/2 miles below the surface of the earth.

pre-Christian times, it became a fixed part of Christian belief in the Middle Ages and the eschatological view of time having a definite first and last point, creation and final destruction, became another pillar of the premodern European worldview. The time scale involved was as limited as the spatial one. Archbishop Ussher famously calculated the very day on which God finished his act of creation: October 22, 4004 B.C. Furthermore, it was widely believed the world would end sometime around 2000 A.D. (The idea was that six millennia of existence corresponded to the six active days of creation). The history of the universe was conceived as a cosmic drama with a beginning a middle and an end, and the concept of time was not only limited but linear. History mattered because it was part of a cosmic drama leading to a final resolution. Some Christians held the doctrine of predestination, that God had pre-ordained every detail of the history of the world at the moment of creation.[842]

[842] This is especially associated with Calvinism but was held by some Christians from Patristic times onward. See *Britannica Library*, s.v. "Predestination," accessed January 9, 2017, http://library.eb.com/levels/referencecenter/article/61239.

4:3 MODERN SCIENCE

The tiny clockwork geocentric universe in which western man lived for more than a thousand years became subject to serious doubt before the end of the sixteenth century with the heliocentric speculations of Copernicus. It did not go away all at once, or easily. The new model was fiercely resisted by the established power of the Catholic Church; Galileo was put under house arrest and Giordano Bruno was burnt at the stake. For a while the genius of Tycho Brahe gave the geocentric model new life in a modified form: the sun and moon orbited the earth and the remaining planets orbited the sun. But in the long run the simplicity and clarity of the heliocentric system won out, especially after Kepler removed the last mathematical objections by postulating elliptical orbits for the planets and Isaac Newton explained the mechanics of their movements with his theory of gravitation.

In the nineteenth century stellar parallax was measured for the first time,[843] proving that the "fixed stars" were very much further away than previously thought possible and discoveries in the field of geology opened up the time dimension expanding the age of the earth from a few thousand years to hundreds of millions (now thought to be 13.8 billion). In the early twentieth century Einstein's theory of relativity undermined the idea of absolute time, and the discovery of the red shift indicated an expanding universe with its origins in a Big Bang and what were previously thought to be nearby gaseous nebulae were shown to be very distant galaxies,[844] each composed of many millions of stars. The opening years of the twenty-first century have shown that these stars are commonly surrounded by a retinue of planets.

In short, the universe has become very much bigger, very much older and a lot stranger than anyone had previously imagined. Scientific cosmology is still full of unanswered questions about the origin, shape and final fate of the universe. These questions may very well never be definitively answered, as indeed the Buddha intimated.

---

843 *Stellar Parallax*, s.v. http://www.universetoday.com/47182/stellar-parallax/. Accessed Oct 16, 2017.

844 *Britannica Library*, s.v. "Galaxy," accessed January 5, 2017, http://library.eb.com/levels/referencecenter/article/110642#68104.toc

4:4 THE BUDDHIST COSMOS

The ancient Indian cosmology, including the Buddhist version of it, and the modern scientific model resemble each other far more than either one resembles the premodern European cosmology. Both the Buddhist and the scientific models place the abode of human beings in a peripheral and minor locale within a greater whole. Both of them postulate a vast, possibly infinite, number of worlds. Both of them see the universe as existing within a very vast span of time. In the Buddhist model this is infinite in both directions having no beginning and no ending. Some modern theories suggest a cyclic nature for the universe on very long time scales: if the amount of matter in the universe is sufficient, gravity will eventually slow down and reverse the expansion causing in the end a Big Crunch when everything is annihilated in a singularity, possibly followed by another Big Bang.

Of course, we must not push the analogy too far. The *cakkavāḷas* are not solar systems. The ten-thousand fold world-system is not a galaxy. The multiple worlds of ancient India are never associated with the stars. The resemblance is more in the nature of underlying spirit than in any catalogue of details. It would be anachronistic to force one model upon another. We should try and appreciate the Buddhist system on its own terms.

Nevertheless, it is hard to resist the idea that living in an insignificant corner of an open ended, vast universe places us moderns more in sympathy with ancient Indian modes of thought than it does with medieval Europeans who lived at the centre of a small, short-lived cosmos. The essentials of Buddhist philosophy work very well in either the cosmos of countless *cakkavāḷas* or that of countless galaxies. It does not fit so well into the clockwork of crystalline spheres. It may not be entirely coincidental that Buddhism began to be seriously studied and practiced in the West around the same time as the discoveries of relativity and quantum mechanics.

All this being said, there are nonetheless important differences between the modern and the ancient world-systems. These stem from their entirely different motivations. In the West, beginning with the classical Greeks, the purpose of the cosmology was to explain the observed phenomena. The geocentric model developed by Plato, Aristotle and Ptolemy was a reasoned attempt to account for what could actually be seen in the sky. It was not their intention that during a long age it became enshrined as religious dogma. The system was dismantled the same way it was created, by looking at the sky, taking measurements and carefully thinking it through. This process continues today, technologically enhanced, but essentially the same. The emphasis is on what is "out there" without regard to human concerns or consciousness.

We have already seen that the Sineru-centric Indian-Buddhist system does not account for the observed motions of the heavenly bodies at all well. Although surprising to anyone more familiar with the history of science in the West, it would be a mistake to assume that this is simply due to a primitive level of scientific understanding. India was not behind the Greeks in the development of math and science, including astronomy; in some respects they were well ahead, as in the invention of the zero.[845] Neither does the Sineru-centric model represent merely a very early stage of thought, it continued to be elaborated down to the time of Buddhaghosa and Vasubandhu, by which time Indian science had advanced considerably not least because it was now in contact with the science of the Greek world. Moreover, the Sineru cosmology was adhered to in Buddhist countries well into modern times.

The model of the *cakkavāḷa* was not developed to explain the movements of the heavens at all; at best these were a very minor afterthought. It was developed to explain something very different: the workings of *saṃsāra*. This hinges on a key difference between those two great and precocious civilizations: the Greeks were primarily extroverts and the Indians introverts. From well before the Buddha's time the greatest minds in India were devoted to unravelling

[845] The word zero is the French or Italian translation of Medieval Latin *zephirum* from Arabic *sifr* "cipher," which is the translation of Sanskrit śūnya "empty, naught". Ṣee "Zero", *Online Etymology Dictionary*, https://www.etymonline.com/word/zero. Accessed 27.1.2018.

the mysteries of the mind, of existence and of finding the means to liberate oneself. The Greeks wanted to understand how the world worked, the Indians wanted to learn how to transcend it. The Indian-Buddhist cosmological model may not account for the movements of the sun and the planets but it does account very well for the multiple levels of consciousness known to exist by the inward going explorers who ventured into the forest from time immemorial.

The Buddha's radical breakthrough was to see through all the fantastic panoply of the cosmos, the vertical hierarchy of *devalokas* and brahmā realms and the horizontal expanse of multiple ten-thousand fold world-systems; to see through all of it and know that in all its fascination and all its terror it is ultimately transient, conditioned, futile and empty. In the *Vimānavatthu* the laywoman Uttarā says, "The circle of the world is too narrow, the realm of Brahmā is too low," and this statement is approved by the Buddha (Vv-a 15). Her words are only profound and powerful if we understand just how immensely high the world of Brahmā is, and how very wide the circle of the world. It is not just our immediate, petty human condition which must be abandoned, but all of it. In Tibetan Buddhism there is something called a "mandala offering": the practitioner folds her hands into a complex mudra representing Mt Meru and the Four Continents and then offers the whole for the liberation of sentient beings. It is a beautiful and powerful image for the relinquishment of conditioned existence which is all the more evocative when we understand just what, and how much, is being offered.

4:5 VIEWS

There is another way to look at the difference between the three cosmologies: that is according to the view (*diṭṭhi*) that they represent. The Buddha analyzed the possible views, or philosophical positions in great detail in the *Brahmajāla Sutta* (DN 1) and listed sixty-two wrong views which represented schools of thought in India at the time. These views fall into two broad categories: the eternalist view (*sassatavāda*) and the annihilationist view (*ucchedavāda*). The eternalist view holds that beings are possessed of an eternal essence, a soul, *atman* or *jīva*, which survives death in some form or other. This view is usually associated with a belief in a Creator God. The annihilationist view holds that beings are cut off and utterly annihilated at death; it is essentially what in modern terms we would call philosophical materialism. The Buddha took a middle position between these two, which he called the *paṭiccasamuppāda* ("dependent arising"). Put simply, this is a strong assertion of causality. No thing anywhere, of any kind, exists as an independent entity. Everything that exists is dependent on multiple causes in an interdependent net. There is no inherent substantial self-existent entity anywhere. In Indian philosophical language, there is no *svabhāva* ("own-essence"). Applied to living beings, this implies the doctrine of not-self (*anattā*). There is rebirth in a beginningless and endless chain of cause and effect, but there is no thing, no self or *atta* which transmigrates from body to body.

It seems like a paradox to many that Buddhism teaches no abiding self but does include rebirth in its system. This only seems like a conflict if you implicitly assume a self which continues from moment to moment within this life. Rebirth is nothing more than a continuation of the chain of cause and effect. Not only is it not a contradiction, but it is also a logical requirement of the idea of causation. Each new conscious moment arises with a previous consciousness moment as a proximate cause. This means that the first conscious moment in a new life must have had a predecessor or it would have been a kind of creation *ex nihilo*. After death, the next consciousness moment will arise in a form, human or otherwise, determined by the kamma of the expiring being.

The small geocentric model of the universe formulated by the Greeks and adopted by the medieval Christians represents a model of the cosmos compatible with the eternalist view. God created this little clockwork universe for the beings he also created. It, and they, have a definite moment of beginning. The realms above the earth are eternal in the forward time direction, as are the beings. Their brief span on earth has significance in that their deeds determine their eternal fate. Likewise, the events on that earth are significant in that history leads up to a pre-ordained final apocalypse. Time is linear, one-way and the events within it have importance.

The vast multi-world cosmos of the modern scientific cosmology is entirely based on observation and is not dependent on any pre-conceived view. However, the tendency is for scientific thinkers to adopt, implicitly or explicitly, the annihilationist view. Philosophical materialism is not made logically necessary by the findings of science, but it does provide a useful practical basis for those whose primary interest is understanding the outer world. Largely this is an historical legacy. The scientific view in its infancy had to fight against the dogmas of the eternalists. It became imperative to explain things without reference to God. Unfortunately, this intellectual tendency went too far and the role of mind as an independent agency was ignored as well.

When applied to human beings, the materialist paradigm holds that mind is a derivative function of matter: neurons firing in the brain. Matter comes first, mind is nothing but matter in motion and human beings are just complex machines made out of meat. To the Buddhist, this is quite literally putting the cart before the horse (or the ox):

> Mind is the forerunner of all things
>
> Mind is their chief
>
> They are made by mind

If with a corrupted mind,

One acts with body or speech

Then suffering follows

Like the wheel follows the foot of the ox. (Dhp 1:1)

Consciousness will never be explained solely by reference to the workings of the brain. If it were possible to do so, then consciousness would have to be explicable by an algorithm, at least in theory. This is not possible, not because consciousness is too complex, but because it is so intrinsically simple. It just *knows*, in the sense of having experience. Many mental processes can be reduced to algorithms. For example, because of the mechanics of vision and pattern recognition, facial recognition software is possible. However, there is an unbridgeable chasm between what happens when a computer programme recognizes a face, and when you or I do it. The algorithmic portion of the process may be analogous, but at the end of the line when a human does it, there is something else: an experience or a subjectivity. The computer just outputs bits of data but the operator at the terminal reading the display *knows*.

Future generations may regard the contemporary adherence to materialism as a quaint and slightly comic folly, as we do the decants and eccentrics of Ptolemy. Oddly perhaps, it is not the life sciences which are leading the way beyond materialism, but physics. Quantum mechanics makes it impossible to explain the outer world without reference to an observer; until an observation is made reality, only exists as a mathematical abstraction, a field of probabilities. If mind were given its proper place as a causal factor in its own right, then many mysteries might be easier to solve: everything from the way a protein folds in a cell to why the initial symmetry was broken after the Big Bang.

The Big Bang itself presents a problem for a philosophic explanation of the universe. What caused it to happen? What, if anything, can we say about the universe (if that word makes sense in the context) before the Big Bang? The state of things immediately prior to the Big Bang is generally said to be a *singularity*,[846] where the ordinary laws of physics do not apply. Science begins an infinitesimal moment after the Big Bang. It can say nothing about the ultimate origin of things, and the thinking here becomes quasi-theological: the Big Bang is the causeless cause. Western thought has always, or at least since Aristotle, insisted that there must have been a First Cause. With the adoption of Christianity, this of course became identified with God.

Such an explanation is totally unsatisfactory from the point of view of Buddhist philosophy. Causality admits no exceptions. If the Big Bang model is a true expression of reality, which the evidence seems to indicate, then there must have been something prior which caused it to happen. In the ancient Buddhist model, when a new world-system comes into being it is caused by the kamma of the beings who perished in the destruction of the old system. Once again, mind is prior to and takes precedent over form. There is no God acting as creator. There is only kamma (which originates in the mind) acting as a natural law. Beings that die without being fully awakened die with desire and kamma outstanding and by the laws of cause and effect, this means that the next consciousness moment which arises must arise somewhere else. When the entire world-system is destroyed, the force of kamma generates a new world for the beings to be reborn into.

[846] *Big Bang Theory: Evolution of Our Universe*, http://www.universetoday.com/54756/what-is-the-big-bang-theory/ Accessed Oct 16, 2017.

4:6 MODERN SCIENCE AND ANCIENT WISDOM

We have seen that the Buddhist universe goes through cycles of destruction and re-arising by fire, water and air, each destroying a wider range of world-systems. If the reader will indulge a speculative flight of the imagination, it may be possible to transpose this onto the modern scientific cosmology, if we take "fire," "air," and "water" metaphorically. The smallest destruction, that by fire, is the destruction of a single solar system when its star reaches the end of its hydrogen fuel supply and turns into a red giant or explodes in a supernova. In the latter case the stellar material is recycled and becomes the seed for new worlds. An entire galaxy may be destroyed when all the material in it flows, like water down a drain, into the central black hole. The interior of a black hole, like the universe before the Big Bang, is a singularity about which nothing meaningful can be said. It has been speculated that the material is not destroyed but is transposed elsewhere, appearing again through a "white hole". Finally, if the amount of matter in the universe as a whole is sufficient, it will eventually collapse in on itself into another great singularity, the stars and planets drawn inward or to speak metaphorically, blown by the winds of gravity. Another Big Bang can follow and the whole catastrophe of existence begins anew.

There may be other imaginative ways to reconcile the traditional cosmology with modern scientific understanding. For example, a large portion of the matter and energy comprising the universe is "dark" and unaccounted for. One might imagine that this somehow composes the other realms, even Mount Sineru. Or perhaps these things exist in a higher spatial dimension; if we could perceive the solar system in the fourth or fifth spatial dimension it might include a central mountain which does not impinge on our third dimensional space.[847] Modern physics leaves a lot of room for such speculation, in ways that the physics of the nineteenth century did not. In my opinion though, this is not the most fruitful approach since it confines our thinking to the strictly material, and this level was never the prime interest of the ancient Buddhists.

The modern scientific cosmology, if detached from the materialist view, is compatible with Buddhist teachings in a way that the old geocentric model of concentric spheres is not. This was not immediately apparent and the impact of western science on the Buddhist world did cause some intellectual problems.[848] But it was fairly quickly resolved and never reached the level of the crisis of faith which occurred in the west when Christianity was confronted with science. For example, in Japan Sato Kaiseki wrote a carefully researched book attempting the impossible task of reconciling the observable facts of astronomy with a Sineru centred cosmological system. His Zen teacher, Ekido took a brief look at it and threw it back at him saying, "How Stupid! Don't you realize that the basic aim of Buddhism is to shatter the triple world …? Why stick to such worthless things and treasure Mount Sumeru? Blockhead!"[849] The precise configuration of the universe is not essential to the Four Noble Truths.

The classical Buddhist model of Mount Sineru and the multiple ten thousand fold world-systems was, as has been said, not developed in order to explain astronomical observations. This was never a primary concern. Instead, the Buddha and his followers, like Buddhaghosa, were much more concerned with understanding the mind and accounting for the various levels of consciousness. Even here, the concern in the end is a practical one. How can a living being enmeshed in the manifold world transcend it all and achieve total liberation?

---

847 "And the room provided by large extra space dimensions might allow for something even more remarkable: other nearby worlds—not nearby in ordinary space, but nearby in the extra dimensions—of which we've been so far completely unaware." Greene, *Fabric of the Cosmos*, 2004. The author is referring to the extra spatial dimensions required by string theory.

848 See Lopez 2010 chapter 1

849 See Lusthaus 2001: 101. .

4:7 THE PSYCHOLOGICAL INTERPRETATION

While a strictly literalist interpretation of the texts about cosmology is no longer tenable, we should avoid falling into the opposite extreme, so tempting to the modern mind, of reading it all as simply psychological metaphor. For this to be so, one of two possibilities must apply: Either the compilers of the texts were deliberately and consciously speaking in metaphor, or they were working from some more primitive level of psychological understanding and were externalizing mental states. We can dismiss the latter case rather easily. A tradition that was capable of the profound psychological subtleties of the *Abhidhamma* could not possibly have fallen into such a primitive error. But when they spoke of the sufferings of *niraya* or the bliss of the *rūpaloka* were the Buddha and his later followers deliberately using metaphors to express psychological truths? I do not think so. To begin with there is the statement of the Buddha, made in a context that is quite unequivocal, that "yes, devas do exist."[850] Further, consider that the commentaries were well aware of the possibilities of metaphor. For example, they precisely defined when the concept of *Māra* referred to an inner state, and when it referred to an actual entity, *Māra Devaputta*. I think we have to conclude that the texts meant what they said.

The so-called psychological interpretation does a disservice to the tradition. It is rather demeaning to our spiritual ancestors, and one cannot help wondering what the devas themselves make of it. "Do they really imagine we are just their mental states? Silly, arrogant humans."[851] Besides, it doesn't work very well. There are indeed important parallelisms between the internal and the external, most significantly between the *jhānas* and the *brahmalokas*. But there is much more to the worlds of the brahmās than that. Furthermore, much of the cosmological material makes no sense at all when interpreted in psychological terms. The massive central mountain Sineru is a keystone of the whole structure and has no obvious psychological counterpart, nor does the nested system of multiple worlds. The real problem is that the psychological interpretation not only trivializes the whole system but actually obscures the more important lessons we can learn from it. If there are parallels, it is far more illuminating to see our small human psyche as a limited reflection of the greater whole than vice-versa.

Bhikkhu Bodhi has written to this point with his usual lucidity:

> … The external universe, according to the *Abhidhamma*, is an outer refection of the internal cosmos of mind, registering in concrete manifest form the subtle gradation in states of consciousness. This does not mean that the *Abhidhamma* reduces the outer world to a dimension of mind in the manner of philosophical idealism. The outer world is quite real and possesses objective existence. However, the outer world is always a world apprehended by consciousness, and the type of consciousness determines the nature of the world that appears. Consciousness and the world are mutually dependent and inextricably connected to such an extent that the hierarchical structure of the realms of existence exactly reproduces and corresponds to the hierarchical structure of consciousness.
>
> Because of this correspondence, each of the two—the objective hierarchy of existence and the inner gradation of consciousness—provides the key to understanding the other. The reason why a living being is reborn into a particular realm is because he has generated, in a previous life, the kamma or volitional force of consciousness that leads to rebirth into that realm, and thus in the final analysis all the realms of existence are formed, fashioned, and sustained by the mental activity of living beings. At the same time these realms provide the stage for consciousness to continue its evolution in a new personality and under a fresh set of

---

850 MN 100: *ṭhānaso metaṃ…viditaṃ yadidaṃ -- atthi devā.* The word *ṭhānaso* ("with cause or reason") implies the certainty of personal experience.

851 "Smelly too". See Dhp-a 15:8.

circumstances.[852]

In terms of practice also there is a huge problem with the psychological interpretation of the cosmology. The goal of the Buddhist path is the realization of the unconditioned and this requires a transcendence of the self. If the whole cosmos is reduced to a representation of our own internal mental space this only reinforces the image of a self. Meditation becomes psychoanalysis and nothing more. It is essential that the meditator comes to understand that her problems are not uniquely hers but are part of the warp and woof of the great *saṃsāra*. To realize liberation, it must all be relinquished. A sense of vastness puts it all into the proper perspective. It is not all about you.

When we examine the teachings about the cosmos given by the Buddha, as distinguished from his commentators, we find that they are always given to teach some specific point bearing on the spiritual project of liberation. The *Sattasuriya Sutta* (AN 7:66) about the end of the world-system was taught to make a strong point about impermanence. To the ancient Indian nothing could be imagined that seemed more solid and unchanging than Mt Sineru, and yet this too will one day be reduced to ash. One purpose of the *Aggañña Sutta* (DN 27) about origins is to ridicule and refute the brahminical doctrine of the divine origin of caste; another is to illustrate mythologically how subtle consciousness becomes trapped in coarse materiality through the agency of desire. The stories and teachings about the brahmā worlds, such as the Buddha's visit to Baka, (MN 49) speak important truths about the subtler levels of mind, both its potential and its limitations. Likewise, Moggallāna's visit to Sakka in Tāvatiṃsa (MN 37) teaches us about the unsatisfactory and illusory nature of even the most refined sensual existence.

There are many other important spiritual lessons we can learn from a deep contemplation of the manifold levels of existence. We can, for instance, gain a deeper understanding of this sensual realm we live in when we consider it from other positions than just the familiar human one. Because the Buddha warned again and again about the dangers inherent in sensual desire, students can sometimes take an extreme position. Either they become rigidly puritanical justifying the outsider's criticism that Buddhism is anti-life, or they cannot take on the teaching at all and revert to hedonistic indulgence. The correct way of understanding this teaching is not to see sensuality as immoral *per se* but as limiting. Sensual desire and indulgence confine us within the bounds of the plane of sense-desire and our consciousness cannot experience the higher levels or liberation. When we look at the worlds of the devas we see that it is not a matter of absolutes. Sensuality becomes more and more refined as we ascend the levels until in the highest deva realms it is just barely what we would consider sensual: the Paranimmitavasavatti devas make love just by looking into one another's eyes. From there, it is not such an unimaginable step to the realms beyond sensuality altogether.

In the Buddhist cosmology, all the complexity and drama occurs in the *kāmabhūmi*, the plane of sense desire. This realm is vast and vastly differentiated, from the torments of *niraya* and the miseries of the petas to the colourful world of animals and humans, through the six levels of sensual heaven. The world of the senses encompasses all of it: pain, pleasure, compassion, and conflict. It is so vivid and overwhelming within that realm that it is hard to imagine any other mode of being. If, however, we were situated in the lowest level of the brahmā worlds, all this would seem very far away. From the perspective of the brahmās, a panorama of one thousand world systems lies at a vast distance below. As one ascends through the brahmā levels, the view becomes ever more expansive, encompassing at last one trillion world systems. How subtle, simple and purified is their existence! They cannot even imagine wanting to enter into the turmoil and suffering below them. It is the same for the jhānic mind in regard to the experience of the senses.

Buddhist cosmology, viewed as an analogue to our mental states, can help us understand the development of deep meditation. For example, there is, in my opinion, a problem with the translation of *samādhi* as "concentration." Meditators think they need to narrow the mind onto the object, and this is exactly the wrong way to go. The mind with strong *samādhi* is an expansive one. The mind of a brahmā encompasses a trillion worlds! *Samādhi* is explained in

[852] Bhikkhu Bodhi, CMA, p. 188.

the old texts as "non-wandering,"[853] which has a different feel altogether. The world of the brahmā beings is calm and peaceful but it is certainly not constricted. Instead of "placing awareness on the object," we should think in terms of opening the mind to the object: non-wavering in a great vastness.

There are other ways that the study of the brahmā realms can help us understand the nuances of the teachings about jhāna. For example, it might help clarify the distinction between *pīti* ("rapture") and *sukha* ("bliss") to contemplate part of a list in the *Aṅguttara* (AN 5: 170) that describes "the best of" in various categories. The best sound in the universe is the cry of the Ābhassara brahmās, those of the second tier, the level of jhāna where *pīti* predominates. These gods continually cry out, *Aho sukho*! "Oh, the happiness!" However, the best joy in the universe is experienced by the Subhakiṇha brahmas of the third tier, corresponding to the jhāna marked by *sukha*. These gods "rejoice in silence."

Then there is the Ārupa realm, those beings who are pure mind without any trace of physicality. The inclusion of this realm certainly demonstrates that Buddhist thought is non-materialist; it allows that beings can exist with a mind but without any kind of physical substrate. It is very useful to think about and attempt to imagine what the existence of these beings might be like. Discerning the difference between mind and matter is a vital question and one that is not so easy for us who are bound up in a physical body.

853 Vism 14.139. The Pali is *avisārala.*

4:8 PERCEPTION

Once we transcend naive realism and materialism and allow the mental factors back into the equation, we can think about these issues in an entirely new way. This from the thirteenth century Zen Master Dōgen:

> All beings do not see mountains and water in the same way. Some beings see water as a jeweled ornament, but they do not regard jeweled ornaments as water. What in the human realm corresponds to their water? We only see their jeweled ornaments as water.
>
> Some beings see water as wondrous blossoms, but they do not use blossoms as water. Hungry ghosts see water as raging fire or pus and blood. Dragons see water as a palace or a pavilion. Some beings see water as a forest or a wall. Some see it as the dharma nature of pure liberation, the true human body, or as the form of body and the essence of mind. Human beings see water as water. Water is seen as dead or alive depending on causes and conditions.
>
> Thus the views of all beings are not the same. You should question this matter now. Are there many ways to see one thing, or is it a mistake to see many forms for one thing? You should pursue this beyond the limit of pursuit. Accordingly, endeavours in practice-realization of the way are not limited to one or two kinds. The ultimate realm has one thousand kinds and ten thousand ways.
>
> For this reason, it is difficult to say who is creating this land and palace right now or how such things are being created. To say that the world is resting on the wheel of space or on the wheel of wind is not the truth of the self or the truth of others. Such a statement is based only on a small view. People speak this way because they think that it must be impossible to exist without having a place on which to rest.[854]

Dōgen is speaking about the way perception shapes the actual experiential world. Consider the world experienced by a bat, which is blind, or nearly so, and constructs its model of reality by echo location, a sensory world we can barely imagine. Or try and imagine the world inhabited by an earthworm, a fish or a mosquito. Perhaps the best way to think of the cosmology of the texts is to think of it as the way you would perceive the world if you were a deva.

I would like to suggest one even more speculative idea. Perhaps the Mount Sineru cosmology was actually "real" to our ancestors, in the sense that their perception was closer to the level of devas than ours. There does seem to have been a major shift in human consciousness at some point in early modern times. When we became more cognizant of the material world, allowing the scientific revolution of the seventeenth century for example, did we lose some other subtle level of perception as a trade off?

The Christian writer Robert D. Romanyshyn has suggested something like this in regard to why the vision of angels does not come so easily to moderns:

> The invention of this way of seeing (the "linear perspective vision in fifteenth century Italian art"), as if you were staring one-eyed through a window at a world receding toward a vanishing point, or as if you have a camera eye on the world, has become a cultural convention, a habit of mind, a disposition of the soul. Through its development and under its influence we have become spectators of a world, which has become primarily a spectacle, a matter of light, inhabiting a body which has become primarily a specimen. Of the many values which this vision has inscribed upon the soul of modernity not the least of which is the hegemony of vision or the rule of the "despotic eye," the one which surprisingly and unexpectedly touched upon the angel was

---

[854] Dōgen, Mountains and Water Sutra, Kotler and Tanahashi trans.

the transformation of depth which this vision achieved.

He goes on to explain the principles of perspective in painting. The key point is that the vision of the world is reduced to a linear grid where horizontal distance replaces the older idea of vertical levels.

> The world explained, the world within which all levels of existence are reduced to the same plane, is inhospitable to beings who belong to other levels … The window through which the detached spectator observes the world … which was actually a grid, projects an objective landscape of evenly paced grid coordinates, and from that space beings like angels are destined to be banished and to become mere mental phenomena, mere subjective realities.[855]

It is impossible to speak meaningfully about the reality (or otherwise) of any part of the Buddhist cosmology without at least attempting a discussion of what "reality" means. The Buddha, in his teaching, refrained from purely metaphysical definitions. There was, at that time, a sort of standard questionnaire which was put to philosophers and mystics:

Is the world eternal? (*sassato loko*)

Is the world not eternal?

Is the world infinite? (*anantavā loko*)

Is the world finite?

Is the soul (*jīva*) the same as the body?

Is the soul one thing and the body another?

Does the *Tathāgata* exist after death?

Does the *Tathāgata* not exist after death?

Does the *Tathāgata* both exist and not exist after death?

Does the *Tathāgata* neither exist nor not exist after death?[856]

The Buddha categorically refused to answer such questions, saying instead that his teaching was about suffering and the end of suffering only. Someone who demands an answer to such questions is like a man pierced by an arrow who refuses to have the doctors remove it and treat his wound until he learns the answers to such questions as: of what wood is the shaft made? Of what kind of bird was the feather taken? Was the man who shot me tall or short, fair or dark? He would die from his wounds before he learnt all this (MN 63).

The Buddha's teaching is always first and foremost a practical one. The emphasis is not on metaphysical determinations about ultimate reality, but about how we can liberate ourselves from the suffering of the conditioned world. This means that the subjective side of the question must take priority. Ultimate reality may be an undecidable issue but we can ask, what is real for the observer?

It is useful, indeed necessary, to consider the creative role of perception (*sañña*) in constructing reality; if not

---

855 Robert D. Romanyshyn, "On Once Encountering an Angel" in *The Angels* ed. Robert Sardello.

856 DN 9, SN 33:1, MN 63.

some unknowable ultimate metaphysical reality, but at least the immediate practical reality in which we actually live. Without exception, everything we know about the outer world is mediated through the five physical senses. Even when these are enhanced technologically, it is still a human eye that peers through the microscope and human eye-consciousness which sees the forms and human perception which determines them to be a bacterium or a crystal fragment. We never can experience the outer world directly. Instead, what we experience is a simulation or model of that world generated by the mind based on signals received by the senses. Any such perception must be incomplete due to limitations in the sense organs. Dogs can hear sounds which we cannot, just as we can see colours they cannot.

It can be said that we dream the world into being. However, the difference between waking consciousness and dreaming during sleep is that in waking life the dream-world we create for ourselves is tightly constrained by the signals coming in from the outer world in the form of light waves, sound waves etc. When we are asleep, our perception is not so tightly bound and is free to create images and sounds from fragments of thought and memory. The world we dream when we are awake is a mostly reliable model of whatever is actually out there; it can never be perfect but it is close enough for us to live in and manipulate the world. When we are asleep, the world we live in is an entirely mind created one: a world of *nimittas*.

As an aside, we may note with interest that this way of understanding things is not so far off the quantum mechanical one of modern physics.[857] The world out there is nothing more than a mathematical field of probabilities which can be expressed as a "wave function." This function collapses into a definite reality only when the observer takes a reading of it. An electron has an equal chance of being at point A or point B and in "reality" exists only as a fuzzy field of possibility spread out between the two until the physicist takes a measurement after which it is definitely located at one or the other. Schrödinger's poor little kitty only becomes alive or dead when we open the box.

Returning to our consideration of perception and its role in creating our actual experienced reality: we have looked at the difference between waking and dreaming and seen that it is a matter of more or less constraint by the incoming signals. What if the realms of the devas are somewhere between the two? Their world, like ours, is generated for them by the faculty of perception based on incoming signals from some hypothetical outer world but the creative constraint is less than that of our waking consciousness and more than that of a sleeping dreamer. We have had occasion to note the often dreamlike quality of the various realms. We have seen, for example, how, for an evil person brought to the nāga realm, the wonderful crystal palace was perceived as a dark prison and the lovely nāga maidens as horrible *yakkhinīs*.

As we move upward through the deva realms, we find subtler and more sublime realities. The signal constraint is becoming less and less and the dreaming more fluid. In the realm of the Nimmānarati devas, those "who delight in creation" who can create any desired reality at will, the experience must be like a many million yearslong lucid dream. *Niraya*, at the other extreme, is a terrible nightmare from which one cannot awake.

This parallel with the dream state applies only to the sense-desire realm. In the realms of form and the formless it is quite otherwise. There, the human level analogue is not dreaming, but the meditative absorption of jhāna. This is a level of consciousness unlike either ordinary waking consciousness or the dream state, both of which are within the plane of sense-desire. In these higher planes, signals from the senses become increasingly irrelevant as we ascend. We are told that the bodies of the brahmā beings are "mind-made" (*manomaya*). In the formless realm the physical senses, and indeed the physical sense organs, are entirely absent. The physical laws as we understand them simply do not apply at these levels.

So, are the other realms "real?" We may not be able to assert that with absolute certainty, at least without the possession of the *dibbacakkhu* ("divine eye"). But neither can we answer the question with a definite negative without taking on a naive realist position about this experienced human realm. All we can know with complete certainty is our

---

[857] At least this is so in the Copenhagen interpretation.

own conscious mind; and we know that consciousness occurs in different levels. The untrained person experiences at least three: waking, dreaming and deep sleep. With the development of meditation one can experience the jhānas of form and the formless as well. There is no good reason to doubt that these levels can also occur as states of existence.

Beyond all these states of attainment and of existence there remains the ineffable state of the unconditioned, *nibbāna*. All the panoply of *saṃsāra* with all its wonderful and terrifying manifestations is, when all is said and done, nothing more than a shadow play, "a tale told by an idiot, full of sound and fury, signifying nothing,"[858] when contrasted with *nibbāna*. When contemplating the cosmos, it is essential to remember that the purpose of understanding it is to transcend it.

858 Shakespeare, *Macbeth*, 5:5.

PART FIVE – APPENDICES

5:1 UNITS OF MEASURE

YOJANA – a measure of distance, approximately 12 km.

The *yojana* is a very important unit of length, often used in this book. There is considerable uncertainty about its exact length but it is definitely several kilometres. Thanissaro Bhikkhu gives it as 16 km,[859] the *Pali-English Dictionary* defines it as "a distance of about 7 miles" (11.3 km)[860] Monier-Williams gives various possibilities, ranging from 2 ½ miles to 9 miles (4 km- 11.5 km).[861] The word *yojana* also means a yoke for oxen and the unit of length originally derived from the distance an ox-cart could travel in a day.[862] Since that would obviously vary greatly with terrain, it may account for the vagaries inherent in the measurement at least in the earliest period under consideration. It is, however, highly likely that by the time the commentaries were written the value of the *yojana* had been standardized.

T. W. Rhys Davids did a careful enquiry into the length of a *yojana*, tabulating all references in the literature where distances are given between known points and came to this conclusion: "We have no data as yet for determining the sense in which the word *yojana* is used in the Three *Piṭakas* … (but) in the fifth-century Pali literature (i.e. the commentarial period) it means between seven and eight miles."[863] This seems to be the best estimate available and this book has used the estimate of 7.5 miles or 12 km throughout.

Other Units of Length

gāvuta = ¼ of a *yojana*.
hattha = a "cubit", the length between the finger-tips and the elbow, about 46 cm.
aṅgula = an "inch", the length of one finger joint, about 2.5 cm.

KAHĀPAṆA—a unit of coinage representing approximately US $50–$100 in modern money.

It is notoriously difficult to ascertain equivalent values for ancient money in modern terms. There are essentially two methods to arrive at an approximation. Either estimate the value by finding examples of prices for various commodities or determine the value by finding the weight of a coin in gold or other precious metals. Both of these methods are problematic. Comparing prices for commodities is often misleading because intrinsic values of things change. In ancient India, for example, goods made of cotton were much rarer and more valuable than they are today. Using the precious metal weight has its own problems. It assumes that the value of gold is a fixed standard, which the historical data doesn't support. Furthermore, coins are often given a fiat value higher than the metal weight would warrant.

For the kahāpaṇa we have the additional problem of limited data to work with, so any conclusion should be

859 Thanissaro, *Buddhist Monastic Code,* vol. 1, glossary.
860 PED for "*yojana*".
861 Monier-Williams, *Sanskrit-English Dictionary.*
862 Both PED and Monier-Williams cite this derivation.
863 T. W. Rhys Davids, *On the Ancient Coins and Measures of Ceylon*, p. 17.

regarded as tentative. There are not nearly enough examples of prices given to even attempt any conclusions using that method. Fixing the value by the weight of gold has only a little more chance of success. One late source fixes the value of a *māsaka* (1/20 of a *kahāpaṇa*) at the weight in gold of four rice grains.[864] This raises the further issue of how much a grain of rice weighs, which is highly variable. Taking a value of 29 milligrams[865] for the weight of a rice grain, we arrive at a value for the *kahāpaṇa* of about 1/10 of a troy ounce of gold. The market price of gold as of the middle of 2016 is about $1200 per troy ounce, which would make the *kahāpaṇa* worth about $120. We should adjust this downward because gold in 2016 was at an historic high.

Some oblique support for this general range of value can be had by comparing the *kahāpaṇa* to the Greek *drachma*, which served a comparable purpose in a society of about the same cultural and technical level. Greek sources say that one *drachma* was the usual daily wage for a skilled workman. This would make a dollar value of about one hundred not unreasonable.[866]

Other units of money:
māsaka = 1/20 kahāpaṇa.
pāda = 5 māsaka or ¼ kahāpaṇa.

KOṬI—A number representing ten million.

Although the Pali English Dictionary defines *koṭi* as "(a) number, the 'end' of the scale, i.e. extremely high, as a numeral representing approximately 100,000," this does not agree with other authorities. Nor does it seem likely on the face of it since *satasahassa* is "plain Pali" for 100,000 making a special numeral word superfluous.

The Vedic numeral system counted one koṭi as 10,000,000[867] Childers and Monier-Williams agree with this definition.[868] The modern Indian name for "ten million" is one *crore*, which word derives from *koṭi*. The basic meaning of *koṭi* in Pali is "an end or an extreme point." As a number it represents the highest numeral in common use: 100 x 100,000.

Granted, some uses of this number result in absurdly high figures such as King Mahāsudassana possessing among his legendary wealth 84,000 *koṭi* of garments, (DN 17) but we should never discount the ancient Indian fondness for big numbers.

UNITS OF COSMIC TIME

Confusion can arise when speaking about the divisions of a kappa because the terminology used in the *Visuddhimagga* and the *Abhidharmakośa* do not agree. The following is an attempt to sort out the various usages.

In the Pali texts an *asaṅkheyya* ("incalculable") *kappa* is one of the four principal divisions of a *mahākappa*. In the *Abhidharmakośa* an *asaṃkheyya kalpa* (the Sanskrit equivalent) refers instead to a very much longer period consisting of one quadrillion (10^15) *mahākalpas*[869] The *Abhidharmakośa* does not seem to have a generic word for

---

864 *The Vimativinodanī*, a 12th century work composed in Sri Lanka. Cited by Thanissaro Bhikkhu in *The Buddhist Monastic Code*, vol. 1, p. 61.

865 This figure is ".029 grams" s.v. *http://www.bluebulbprojects.com/measureofthings/faq.php#q10*, accessed Feb 27, 2018. If we were to use the standard unit of a grain as a unit of measurement we should about double the value. However, a grain (7000 to a troy oz.) is a European measurement based originally on a grain of weight. There is no reason to consider it applicableto ancient India.

866 *Coin Week*: http://www.coinweek.com/education/worth-purchasing-power-ancient-coins/. Accessed Oct 16, 2017.

867 OMICS International, http://researChomicsgroup.org/index.php/Indian_numbering_system#Vedic_numbering_systems.

868 See obo.genaud.net/backmatter/appendixes/weights_and_measures/weights_and_measures.htm and Monier-Williams *Sanskrit-English Dictionary*.

869 AK 3:6. p. 480. The text goes on to state that a bodhisattva requires three of these "incalculables" to attain Buddhahood!

the four divisions of a *mahākappa*.

The *Abhidharmakośa* uses *antarakappa* ("intermediate aeon") to refer to another lesser division, twenty of which make up one of the four great divisions. In the Pali canon and commentaries, however, the term *antarakappa* is rarely used. When it is, it has a generic meaning as a period of some indeterminate length.[870] Two examples are the seven day "sword interval" mentioned in the *Cakkavatti-Sīhanāda* Sutta (DN 26) and in the description of the false views of other teachers such as Makkhali Gosāla where "sixty-two *antarakappa*" is part of a long nonsensical list(DN 2). Unless specified otherwise, this book follows the Pali usage. The following table summarizes the terminology:

TABLE SEVEN—EXPLANATION OF TEMPORAL TERMS

Pali (*Visuddhimagga*)		**Sanskrit (*Abhidharmakośa*)**	
name	**usage**	**name**	**usage**
antarakappa	an indeterminate period; length varies with context	antarakalpa	a fixed sub-division equal to 1/20 of a mahākalpa
asaṅkheyya	generic term for each of the four phases of a mahākappa	asaṃkheyya kalpa	a very long period of time; 10^15 or one quadrillion mahākalpas

870 Although late Pali sources do occasionally use it in the same sense as in the *Abhidharmakośa*, as 1/20 of one of the four phases of a *mahākappa*.

5:2 BIBLIOGRAPHY

PRIMARY SOURCES

Pali texts referred to from the Burmese Sixth Council edition as digitized by the Vipassana Research Institute (http://www.tipitaka.org). These were accessed using the Digital Pali Reader: http://Pali.sirimangalo.org/

TRANSLATIONS

Ānandajoti, Bhikkhu, "Naḷinikājātakavaṇṇanā (Jātaka 526)", *Ancient Buddhist Texts,* 2010. Accessed on http://www.ancient-buddhist-texts.net/Texts-and-Translations/Jatakas/526-Nalinikajataka.htm at Oct 16, 2017.

Barua, Dwijendralal. *Buddhakhetta and Buddhāpadāna,* Poona: Bhandarkar Oriental Research Institute, 1946. Retrieved from http://www.ancient-buddhist-texts.net.

Bodhi, Bhikkhu. *The Connected Discourses of the Buddha* / Saṃyutta Nikāya, Boston: Wisdom Publications, 2000.

Bodhi, Bhikkhu. *The Numerical Discourses of the Buddha / Aṅguttara Nikāya,* Boston: Wisdom Publications, 2012.

Bodhi, Bhikkhu. *A Comprehensive Manual of Abhidhamma / Abhidhammasangaha*, Kandy: Buddhist Publication Society, 1999.

Bodhi, Bhikkhu. *The All-Embracing Net of Views / Brahmajāla Commentary*, Kandy: Buddhist Publication Society, 1978.

Cowell, E.B. ed. *The Jātaka*, Oxford: Pali Text Society, 1995.

Griffith, Ralph T.H. *Hymns of the Rig Veda*, Benares: E.J. Lazarus and Co., 1889.

Horner, I.B. *Milinda's Questions / Milindapañha*, Oxford: Pali Text Society, 1963.

Horner I.B. and Gehman H.S. *Minor Anthologies IV / Vimānavatthu* and *Petavatthu*, Oxford: Pali Text Society, 1974.

Ireland, John D. *The Udāna*, Kandy: Buddhist Publication Society, 1990.

Müller, Max. *The Upanishads*, Part I, Oxford 1879.

—. *The Upanishads*, Part II, Oxford 1884.

Ñāṇamoli, Bhikkhu. *The Path of Purification / Visuddhimagga*, Seattle: BPS Pariyatti, 1999.

de la Valleé Poussin, Louis and Pruden, Leo M. *Abhidharmakośabhāṣyam of Vasubandhu*, Berkeley: Asian Humanities Press, 1988–1990.

Rhys Davids, T.W. *Dialogues of the Buddha* /Dīgha Nikāya, Oxford: Pali Text Society, 1899–1921.

Walshe, Maurice. *The Long Discourses of the Buddha* /Dīgha Nikāya, Boston: Wisdom Publications, 1995.

SECONDARY SOURCES

Amaro, Ajahn & Pasanno, Ajahn. *The Island*, Abhayagiri Monastic Foundation, 2009.

Anālayo, Bhikkhu. "*Rebirth and the Gandhabba*", *Mahachulalongkornrajavidyalaya University Journal of Buddhist Studies*, 2008, vol. 1 pp. 91–105.

Barnett, Lionel D. *Hindu Gods and Heroes*, London: Murray, 1923.

Bischoff, Roger. *Buddhism in Myanamar, Wheel 399–401*, Kandy: Buddhist Publication Society, 1995.

Daniélou, Alain. *The Gods of India*, Rochester: Inner Traditions, 1985.

Dhammika, S. "A Naughty Jataka", *Dhamma Musings,* 12.9.2008. http://sdhammika.blogspot.ca/2008/09/naughty-jataka.html. Accessed 16.10.2017.

—. "The Strangest Sutra of Them All", *Dhamma Musings*, 12.8.2010. http://sdhammika.blogspot.ca/2010/08/

strangest-sutra-of-them-all.html. Accessed 16.10.2017.

—. *Nature and Environment in Early Buddhism,* Kandy: Buddhist Publication Society, 2018.

Eraly, Abraham. *Gem in the Lotus*, London: Weidenfeld & Nicolson, 2004.

Gethin, Rupert. *Cosmology and Meditation*, University of Chicago journal "History of Religions" vol 36 no. 3, 1997.

Gombrich, Richard F. *Theravāda Buddhism: A Social History from Ancient Benares to Modern Colombo*, Oxon: Routledge. 2006.

Gunaratana, Henepola. *The Path of Serenity and Insight*, Dehli: Motilal Banarsidass, 2009.

Harvey, Peter. *The Selfless Mind*, New York: Routledge Curzon, 1995.

Hopkins, E. Washburn. *Epic Mythology*, Strassburg: Verlag Von Karl J. Trübner, 1915.

Jayarava, *Gandharva and the Buddhist Afterlife*, *Jayarava's Raves,* 2 January 2015. Accessed 16.10.2017 on http://jayarava.blogspot.ca/2015/01/gandharva-and-buddhist-afterlife-part-i.html.

Jayatilleke, K. N. *Facets of Buddhist Thought: Collected Essays,* Kandy: Buddhist Publication Society, 2009..

Karunadasa, *The Theravāda Abhidhamma*, Kandy : Buddhist Publication Society, 2015.

Karunaratne, T. B. *The Buddhist Wheel Symbol,* BPS Wheel 137–138, Kandy : Buddhist Publication Society, 1969.

Kieschnick, John and Shahar, Meir eds., *India in the Chinese Imagination*, Philadelphia: University of Pennsylvania Press, 2013.

Kloetzli, W. Randolph. *Buddhist Cosmology*, Delhi: Motilal Banarsidass, 1983.

Kloppenborg, Ria. *The Paccekabuddha / Wheel 305–7*, Kandy: Buddhist Publication Society, 1983.

Law, Bimala Churn. *Geography of Early Buddhism*, London: K. Paul, Trench, Trubner & co.,1932.

Lopez, Donald S. *Buddhism and Science*, Chicago: University of Chicago Press, 2010.

Lusthaus, Dan. *Buddhist Phenomenology: A Philosophical Investigation of Yogacara Buddhism and the Ch'eng Wei-shih Lun*, London: Routledge, 2002.

Maha Boowa, Ajahn, *Straight from the Heart*, 1994.

Mahasi Sayadaw, *Progress of Insight*, Kandy: Buddhist Publication Society, 1998.

Malalasekera, G.P. *Dictionary of Pāli Proper Names*, Oxford: Pali Text Society.

Malalasekera, G.P. *The Pali Literature of Ceylon*, Kandy: Buddhist Publication Society, 1994.

Mingun Sayadaw, *The Great Chronicles of Buddhas*, Singapore: 2008.

Müller, Max. *The Upanishads*, Oxford 1879.

De Nicolás, Antonio T. *Meditations through the Ṛg Veda*, Boulder: Shambala, 1978.

Nichols, Michael David. *Malleable Māra*, unpublished thesis, 2004.

Payutto, P.A. trans. Bruce Evans, *Good, Evil and Beyond*, Bangkok: Buddhadhamma Foundation, 1996.

Punnadhammo, Ajahn, *Voidness Meditation*, http://arrowriver.ca/dhamma/formless.html

Reynolds, Frank E. and Reynolds, Mani B. trans. *Three Worlds According to King Ruang*, Berkeley: Asian Humanities Press, 1982.

Rhys Davids, T.W. *Buddhist India*, New York: G. P. Putnam's Sons, 1903.

Rhys Davids, T.W. & Stede, William. ed., *Pali-English Dictionary*, Oxford: Pali Text Society, 1995.

Sendel, Tania ed. "Anatomy, Physiology and Reproduction in the Stallion", *Ontario Ministry of Agriculture, Food and Rural Affairs*. Accessed 16.10.2017 on http://www.omafra.gov.on.ca/english/livestock/horses/facts/11-003.htm.

Shah, Bipin. *Sacred Numerology and Axial Thoughts of Ancient India*, undated. Accessed 16.10.2017 on www.academia.edu.

Strong, John S. *The Legends of King Aśoka*, Princeton: Princeton University Press, 2014.

Sugunasiri, Suwanda H.J. *Dhamma Aboard Evolution*, Toronto: Nalanda Publishing Canada, 2014.

Na-Rangsi, Sunthorn. *Four Planes of Existence in Theravāda Buddhism*, BPS Wheel 462, Kandy: Buddhist Publication Society, 2006.

Tambiah, S.J. *World Conqueror and World Renouncer*, Princeton: Cambridge University Press, 1977.

Ṭhānissaro Bhikkhu *Buddhist Monastic Code*, Mettā Forest Monastery, 2007.

Universe Today, website., *http://www.universetoday.com*

Van Helden, Albert. *Measuring the Universe*, Chicago: University of Chicago Press, 1985.

Wallis H. W. *Cosmology of the Rig Veda*, London: Williams and Norgate, 1887.

Wujastyk, Dominic. "Jambudvīpa, Apples or Plums?" in Studies in T*he History of the Exact Sciences*, ed. Charles Burnett et. al., Leiden-Boston: Brill, 2004.

5:3 GLOSSARY

(These are not meant as full definitions, but as reminders to terms introduced in the text.)

Ābhassara—second level brahmā world.

abhidhamma—the collection of scriptures dealing with psychology and metaphysics.

Abhidharmakośa—a Sarvastivadin text composed by Vasabandhu. accharā—"celestial nymph"; a female deva who serves as a dancing girl.

Ājīvaka—a prominent school of non-Buddhist ascetics.

ākāsagaṅga—the Milky Way, lit. "the Sky-Ganges"

ākāsānañcāyatana—realm of boundless space; first arūpa level

ākiñcaññāyatana—realm of nothingness; third arūpa level

Akaniṭṭha—fifth level of Suddhavāsa and the highest point in the physical cosmos.

āṇākkhetta—"field of authority"; a grouping of one trillion world-systems

anāgāmī—"non-returner", third stage of awakening.

Ānanda—the Buddha's attendant.

Anotatta, Lake—a wonderful lake in the Himavā with magical properties.

antarakappa—a subdivision of a kappa

Aparagoyāna—the eastern continent.

ariyan—lit. "noble"; technically, someone who has attained to one of the stages of awakening.

arūpabhūmi, (arūpaloka, arūpāvācara, arūpadhātu, arūpabhava)—the plane of the formless; realm of the mind only beings.

asaṅkheyyā kappa—"an incalculable" period of time; in standard usage, one of the four divisions of a mahākappa.

Assakaṇṇa—seventh of seven circular mountain ranges around Sineru

asaññasatta—the unconscious beings; a special class of brahmās.

asura—demi-gods, titans; they live at the base of Mt Sineru and perpetually make war upon the devas.

Atappa—second level of the Suddhavāsa

Āvici—the lowest and worst of the hell-realms.

Aviha—first level of the Suddhavāsa.

Baka—a brahmā who held wrong views who had an encounter with the Buddha.

bhaddakappa—an aeon like the present in which five Buddhas arise.

Bhagavā—"The Blessed One"; an epithet of the Buddha.

Bārāṇasī—modern Varānasi (formerly Benares)

bhikkhu—a Buddhist monk.

bhikkhunī—a Buddhist nun.

Bodhimaṇḍa—lit. "Circle of Awakening"; the location in Northern India upon which all the Buddhas achieve Buddhahood.

Bodhisatta—a being on the path to Buddhahood. "The Bodhisatta" refers to Siddhattha Gotama before his awakening.

brahmā—a divine being of the realm of form; having transcended sensuality they are higher than devas.

brahmakāyika—generic term for first jhāna level brahmā beings.

brahmaloka—realm of the brahmā beings, usually refers to the first level of these.

brahmāpārisajja—one of "brahmā's assembly"; lowest level of brahmā being

brahmāpurohita—one of "brahmā's ministers"; second level of brahmā being brāhmana—a brahmin.

bhumma deva—earth-bound deva; the lowest class of devas.

buddhakhetta—a "Buddha-field"; a grouping of multiple world-systems.

cakkaratana—"Wheel Treasure"; another name for the dhammacakka, "Dhamma Wheel", one of the seven treasures of a *cakkavatti.*

cakkavāḷa—a world-system consisting of Mt Sineru, the surrounding mountains and oceans and the island-continents.

cakkavatti—a wheel-turning monarch; ruler of the entire world.

Candimā—the moon

Cātumahārājika—the Four Great Kings or their realm and its inhabitants. Lowest of the sensual heavens.

cetiya—a stupa; memorial monument

Chaddanta—the noblest tribe of elephants; possessed of great strength and the ability to fly.

Cittapāṭali—the great tree of the asuras.

dānava—a monstrous being; a kind of yakkha or asura.

deva—a divine being within the sensual realm.

Devadatta—the Buddha's evil cousin. devadhītu—

"daughter of a deva"; a female deva. Devānaminda—

"Lord of the Devas"; a title of Sakka. devaputta—

"son of a deva"; a male deva.

devī—a female deva.

dhammacakka—"Dhamma Wheel"; the magical wheel that appears in the sky to herald the appearance of a *cakkavatti*

Dhataraṭṭha—Great King of the East.

dibbacakkhu—the divine eye; a psychic power of enhanced vision allowing one to see, for instance, invisible beings.

gandhabba—a lesser deva; a heavenly musician. gati—

"destination"; one of the five possible realms of rebirth.

gāvuta—a unit of measure, one fourth of a *yojana* or about 3 km.

hattha—a unit of measure; a cubit or about eighteen inches.

Himavā—mountains to the north of Jambudīpa; roughly speaking the Himalayas.

Īsadhara—second of seven circular mountain ranges around Sineru.

Jambudīpa—the southern continent upon which we live.

Jātaka—a story of the Buddha's previous lives.

jātikhetta—"field of birth"; a group of ten thousand world-systems in which there may only ever be a single Buddha at a time.

jhāna—a state of meditative absorption equivalent to the consciousness of a brahmā god.

kahāpaṇa—a unit of money.

kālakañjika—a wretched kind of asura which resembles a peta.

kāmabhūmi, (kāmaloka, kāmāvācara, kāmadhātu, kāmabhava)—the plane of sense desire. Includes devas, humans and the lower realms.

kamma—volitional action which bears consequences in the future; the sanskrit is "karma".

kapi—a monkey, the "good" kind

kappa—an aeon; usually a mahākappa is implied, i.e. a period of time equal to the life of a world-system.

kappa saṃvaṭṭati—the era during which the universe folds back or contracts.
kappa vivaṭṭati—the era during which the universe unfolds or expands.
Karavīka—third of seven circular mountain ranges around Sineru.
khattiya—the warrior-noble caste.
khīṇāsavā—synonym of "arahant"; lit. "destroyed defilements"
kiṃpurisa—a small wood-land being. The name means "is it human?"
kinnara—another name for kiṃpurisa.
kolāhala—a great uproar made by devas at moments of cosmic significance.
koṭi—a number representing 10,000,000
kumbhaṇḍa—an odd being like a little man with enormous testicles.
loka—world, a sphere of existence.
lokadhātu—lit. "world-element". A world or a grouping of worlds.
lokantara *niraya*—the dark hell located in the empty space between world-systems.
mahābrahmā—chief brahmā of the first jhāna level brahmās
mahādīpa—an island-continent of which there are four.
mahākappa—a very long time period defined as from the beginning to the end of a world-system.
Mahāniraya—"The Great Hell"; another name for Āvici.
mahāpathavī—"The Great Earth"; the terrestrial zone or ground level of the cosmos.
mahāpurisa—a great man; bears 32 marks and will become a Buddha or a *cakkavatti.*
Mahāsammata—"The Great Elect"; the first human king.
Mahāsamudda—the great ocean
majjhimadesa—"The Middle Country"; the Ganges Valley, area of the civilized world.
makara—a sea monster; a gigantic fish.
makkaṭa—a monkey, the "naughty" kind.
manussa—human.
manussaloka—the human realm.
Māra—the tempter; a deva of the Paranimmitavasavatti realm.
Mātali—charioteer of Sakka.
Metteyya—the coming Buddha, last of this kappa.
Moggallāna—one of the Buddha's two chief disciples, renowned for his mastery of the psychic powers.
nāga—a powerful serpent being.
Nandanavana—chief pleasure garden of Tāvatiṃsa.
Nemindhara—fifth of seven circular mountain ranges around Sineru.
nerayikasatta—a suffering being in *niraya.*
nevasaññānāsaññāyatana—realm of neither perception nor non-perception; fourth arūpa level
nibbāna—the unconditioned, the end of suffering, the goal. Sanskrit = nirvana.
nikāya—in general, a collection; specifically, one of five collections of suttas.
Nimmānarati—the realm of "those who delight in creation." Fifth sensual heaven.
niraya—a hell realm.
nirayapāla—one of the wardens of *niraya*; a torturing demon.
opapātikā—"spontaneous birth"; as in the case of devas who appear into their world fully formed.
paccantimā janapadā—"The Border Countries"; the rest of Jambudīpa outside the majjhimadesa.
paccekabuddha—a fully awakened person who does not teach others; "a silent Buddha."

Pajjuna—king of the vassavalāhaka devas; god of wind and rain.
paṃsupisācaka—a type of pisāca that lives in filth.
Pañcasikha—a *gandhabba*; minstrel of Sakka. Pajāpati—
one of the supreme devas of Tāvatiṃsa. paṇḍaka—a
being of indeterminate gender.
Paṇḍukambalāsana—the throne of Sakka.
Paranimmitavasavatti—the realm of "those who wield power over the creations of others." Sixth sensual heaven.
Pāricchattaka—the great tree of Tāvatiṃsa.
peta—a hungry ghost.
petī—a female peta.
pisāca—frightful demonic being of the forests.
Pubbavideha—the western continent.
Rāhu—the powerful asura who causes eclipses by swallowing the sun or moon.
rakkhasa—a demonic being; an ogre. More or less synonymous with "yakkha."
rukkha deva—a tree deva.
rūpabhūmi,(rūpaloka, rūpāvācara, rūpadhātu, rūpabhava)—the plane of form; realm of the brahmā beings.
sagga—a world where the devas dwell; a heaven-realm.
Sahampati—the brahma who begged the Buddha to teaCh
sakadāgāmī—one who has attained the second stage of awakening.
Sakka—king of the devas of Tāvatiṃsa.
samādhi—meditative quality of mind characterized by stillness.
samaṇa—a holy wanderer; an ascetic.
sāmaṇera—a novice bhikkhu.
saṃsāra—the conditioned world; the round of rebirth.
sammasambuddha—a fully awakened Buddha, highest possible state of being.
saṅgha—the community of bhikkhus.
Sāriputta—one of the Buddha's two chief disciples; most renowned for wisdom.
Sarvāstivāda—an ancient school of Buddhism; the school of the *Abhidharmakośa*.
sīdantara—the circular seas which surround Mt Sineru in alternate bands with the mountain rings.
Siddhattha Gotama—the given and clan name of the Buddha.
Sineru, Mt—the great mountain at the centre of the world-system; 80,000 *yojana* high.
sotāpanna—"stream-enterer"; the first stage of awakening.
sotāpatti—the state of being a sotāpanna.
Sudhamma Hall—assembly hall of the devas in Tāvatiṃsa.
sudda—the labouring caste.
Sudassa—third level of the Suddhavāsa.
Sudassana—fourth of seven circular mountain ranges around Sineru.
Sudassi—fourth level of the Suddhavāsa.
Sudhamma—the assembly hall of the Tāvatiṃsa devas.
Suddhāvāsa—The Pure Abodes; realm of rebirth for anāgāmīs.
suññakappa—an empty aeon in which no Buddha arises.
supaṇṇa—a gigantic bird, enemy of the nāgas; also called a garuda.
Suriya—the sun.

Tathāgata—"the thus gone (or thus come) one". An important epithet of the Buddha, almost always used when he is referring to himself.

Tāvatiṃsa—the second sensual heaven, located at the summit of Mt Sineru.

Theravāda—"school of the elders"; the school of Buddhism prevalent in Sri Lanka and SE Asia.

tiracchāna—an animal; "one who goes horizontally."

Tusita—the heavenly realm where all the bodhisattas reside prior to their final human birth. Fourth sensual heaven.

Uposatha—the holy days of Buddhism marked by the phases of the moon. Also, the name of a tribe of magical flying elephants.

Uttarakuru—the northern continent, an earthly paradise.

valāhaka deva—a deva who lives in the sky and controls the weather.

Vehapphala—fourth jhāna level brahmā realm.

Vepacitti—king of the asuras.

vassavalāhaka devas—devas who live in the sky and make the weather.

Vasavatti—chief deva of the Paranimmitavasavatti realm.

vessa—the merchant and farmer caste.

Vessavaṇa—the Great King of the North.

vihāra—in general, a dwelling place; more specifically, a communal abode ofbhikkhus.

vimāna—abode of a deva; a flying mansion.

vimānapeta—a being who suffers as a peta for part of the month and enjoys deva pleasures for theremainder.

vīṇa—a stringed instrument similar to a lute.

Vinataka—sixth of seven circular mountain ranges around Sineru.

viññāṇañcāyatana—the realm of boundless consciousness; second arūpa level

Virūḷhaka—Great King of the South.

Virūpakkha—Great King of the West.

visayakhetta—"field of scope (of the Buddha's knowledge)"; largest buddhakhetta, a grouping of infinite world-systems which is coterminous with the whole universe.

Vissakamma—the architect (builder) of the devas.

yakkha—a non-human being, usually malevolent. Similar to an ogre.

Yama—doorkeeper and chief warden of *niraya*.

Yāma—the third sensual heaven.

yojana—a unit of measure, probably between 7 and 8 miles.

Yugandhara Mts.—range of mountains surrounding Mt Sineru; 40,000 *yojana* high.

Made in United States
Orlando, FL
25 June 2023

34507682R00254